DAT...

FIVE DAYS AT MEMORIAL

SHERI FINK

FIVE DAYS AT MEMORIAL

LIFE AND DEATH IN A
STORM-RAVAGED HOSPITAL

Crown Publishers
New York

Published in the United States by Crown Publishers, an imprint of the Crown Publishing
Group, a division of Random House, Inc., New York.
www.crownpublishing.com

CROWN and the Crown colophon are registered trademarks of Random House, Inc.

"The Deadly Choices at Memorial," by Sheri Fink. Copyright © 2009 by Pro Publica,
Inc. All rights reserved. Portions reprinted by kind permission of Pro Publica, Inc. First
published in the *New York Times Magazine*.

"Flu Nightmare: In Severe Pandemic, Officials Ponder Disconnecting Ventilators From
Some Patients," by Sheri Fink. Copyright © 2009 by Pro Publica, Inc. All rights reserved.
Portions reprinted by kind permission of Pro Publica, Inc.

"Rationing Medical Care: Health Officials Struggle With Setting Standards," by Sheri
Fink. Copyright © 2009 by Pro Publica, Inc. All rights reserved. Portions reprinted by
kind permission of Pro Publica, Inc. First published on MinnPost.com.

"Preparing for a Pandemic, State Health Departments Struggle with Rationing
Decisions," by Sheri Fink. Copyright © 2009 by Pro Publica, Inc. All rights reserved.
Portions reprinted by kind permission of Pro Publica, Inc. First published in the *New York
Times*.

"Doctors Face Ethical Decisions in Haiti" and "Rationing Health in Disasters," by Sheri
Fink. Copyright © 2010 by Sheri Fink. All rights reserved. First broadcast on *PRI's The
World*.

"In Hurricane's Wake, Decisions Not to Evacuate Hospitals Raise Questions," by Sheri
Fink. Copyright © 2012 by Sheri Fink. All rights reserved. First published on ProPublica
.org.

"Beyond Hurricane Heroics: What Sandy Has to Teach Us All About Preparedness,"
by Sheri Fink. Copyright © 2013 by Sheri Fink. All rights reserved. First published in
Stanford Medicine Magazine.

Endpapers: Memorial Medical Center complex, viewed from the south side, on Thursday
September 1, 2005. Brad Loper /*Dallas Morning News*

Library of Congress Cataloging-in-Publication Data is available upon request.

ISBN 978-0-307-71896-9
eISBN 978-0-307-71898-3

PRINTED IN THE UNITED STATES OF AMERICA

Maps by Jeffrey L. Ward
Jacket design by Chris Brand

10 9 8 7 6 5 4 3 2

First Edition

For Mary Fink,
every living moment

CONTENTS

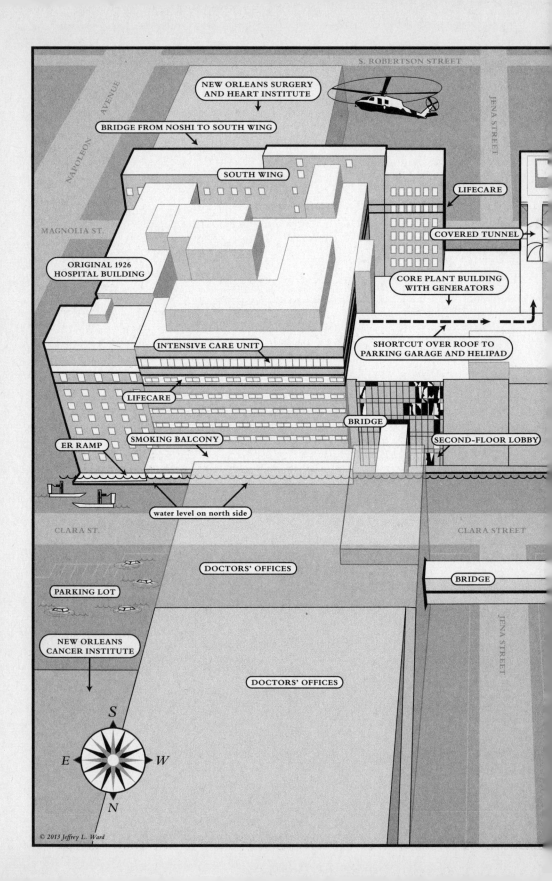

S. ROBERTSON STREET

NEW ORLEANS SURGERY
AND HEART INSTITUTE

BRIDGE FROM NOSHI TO SOUTH WING

SOUTH WING

LIFECARE

COVERED TUNNEL

MAGNOLIA ST.

ORIGINAL 1926
HOSPITAL BUILDING

CORE PLANT BUILDING
WITH GENERATORS

INTENSIVE CARE UNIT

SHORTCUT OVER ROOF TO
PARKING GARAGE AND HELIPAD

LIFECARE

SMOKING BALCONY

BRIDGE

SECOND-FLOOR LOBBY

ER RAMP

water level on north side

CLARA ST.

CLARA STREET

DOCTORS' OFFICES

BRIDGE

PARKING LOT

NEW ORLEANS
CANCER INSTITUTE

DOCTORS' OFFICES

NAPOLEON AVENUE

JENA STREET

JENA STREET

S
E — W
N

© 2013 Jeffrey L. Ward

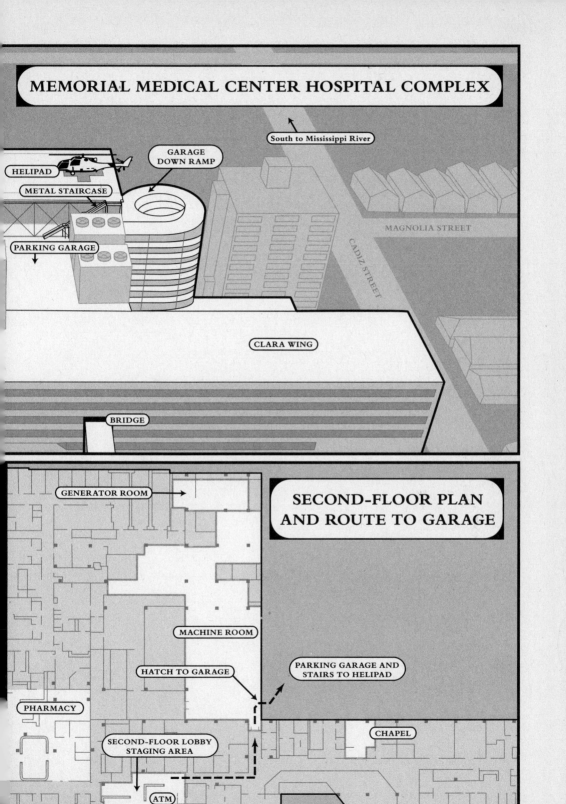

SELECTED INDIVIDUALS

Affiliations listed as at the time of the events in the book.
Relatives listed only if they appear in the book.

Doctors (many on staff at both Memorial and LifeCare)

Dr. Bill Armington—Neuroradiologist

Dr. Horace Baltz—Internal medicine specialist, one of the longest-serving medical staff members present for storm

Dr. Reuben Chrestman—Medical staff president; on vacation

Dr. Ewing Cook—Chief medical officer, retired pulmonologist experienced in critical care medicine

Minnie Cook, wife, former surgical intensive care unit nurse

Stephanie Meibaum, daughter, current surgical intensive care unit nurse

Dr. Roy Culotta—Pulmonologist and critical care specialist; grandmother sheltering at LifeCare

Dr. Richard E. Deichmann—Chairman, Department of Medical Services

Dr. Kathleen Fournier—Internal medicine specialist

Dr. Juan Jorge Gershanik—Neonatologist

Dr. Bryant King—Internal medicine specialist

Dr. John Kokemor—Internal medicine specialist; former coroner assistant under Dr. Frank Minyard

Dr. Anna Maria Pou—Otolaryngologist; head and neck surgeon, specialist in cancer surgery

Vincent Panepinto, husband

Peggy Perino, sister

Dr. Frederick Pou, father
Frederick Pou Jr., brother
Jeanette Pou, mother
Jeannie Pou, sister
Michael Pou, brother
Dr. Paul Primeaux—Anesthesiologist
Dr. John Skinner—Pathologist
Dr. John Thiele—Pulmonologist experienced in critical care medicine
Dr. John J. Walsh Jr.—Chairman, Department of Surgical Services

Memorial Medical Center
Nurses
Lori Budo—Surgical intensive care unit nurse
Cathy Green—Surgical intensive care unit nurse
Thao Lam—Medical intensive care unit nurse
Cheri Landry—Surgical intensive care unit nurse

Patients and Their Family Members (ages and locations as of time of storm)
Helen Breckenridge—77, intensive care unit, eighth floor
Jannie Burgess—79, intensive care unit, eighth floor
    Linette Burgess Guidi, daughter
    Johnny Clark, brother
    Gladys Clark Smith, sister
    Bertha Mitchell, niece
Essie Cavalier—79, fourth-floor medical ward
Donna Cotham—41, fourth-floor medical ward
Tesfalidet Ewale—66, intensive care unit, eighth floor
Merle Lagasse—76, fourth-floor medical ward
    Karen Lagasse, daughter
Rodney Scott—63, intensive care unit, eighth floor

Hospital Administrators, Managers, and Nonclinical Staff
Fran Butler—Nurse manager of fourth-floor west and south medical and
    surgical units
Sandra Cordray—Community relations manager; designated
    communication leader for Hurricane Katrina
Mary Jo D'Amico—Operating-room nurse manager
Curtis Dosch—Chief financial officer
Sean Fowler—Chief operating officer

L. René Goux—Chief executive officer

David Heikamp—Laboratory director

Father John Marse—Chaplain

Susan Mulderick—Nursing director, head of emergency preparedness committee, designated incident commander for Hurricane Katrina

Karen Wynn—Nurse manager of the intensive care units; head of hospital ethics committee

Eric Yancovich—Plant operations director and part of emergency leadership team

Tenet Corporate Officials

Michael Arvin—Business development director for Texas–Gulf Coast region

Trevor Fetter—President and chief executive officer

Bob Smith—Senior vice president for operations in the Texas–Gulf Coast region

LifeCare
Seventh Floor

Patients and Their Family Members

Hollis Alford—66

Wilmer Cooley—82

Emmett Everett—61

    Carrie Everett, wife

Carrie (Ma'Dear) Hall—78

George Huard—91

Alice Hutzler—90

Elvira LeBlanc— 82

    Mark and Sandra LeBlanc, son and daughter-in-law

Wilda McManus—70

    Angela McManus, daughter

Elaine Nelson—90

    Craig Nelson, son

    Kathryn Nelson, daughter

John Russell—80

Rose Savoie—90

    Doug Savoie, grandson

    Lou Anne Savoie Jacob, daughter

Ireatha Watson—89

LifeCare Nurses and Therapists
Cindy Chatelain—Registered nurse
Andre Gremillion—Registered nurse
Terence Stahelin—Respiratory therapist

Hospital Administrators, Directors, and Nonclinical Staff
Tim Burke—Administrator for LifeCare Hospitals of New Orleans; not
    present at hospital for the storm
Steven Harris—Pharmacist
Gina Isbell—Nursing director, LifeCare Chalmette campus, relocated to
    Baptist (Memorial) before the storm
Kristy Johnson—Physical medicine director
Therese Mendez—Nurse executive
Diane Robichaux—Assistant administrator, incident commander
Dr. John Wise—Medical director; absent for the storm

LifeCare Corporate Officials
Robbye Dubois—Corporate senior vice president for clinical services; in
    Shreveport, LA

People Involved in the Investigation
Louisiana Attorney General's Office
Attorney General Charles Foti
Julie Cullen—Assistant attorney general, head of criminal division
Virginia Rider—Special agent, Medicaid Fraud Control Unit; lead
    investigator, Memorial case
Arthur "Butch" Schafer—Assistant attorney general, Medicaid Fraud
    Control Unit; lead prosecutor, Memorial case
Kris Wartelle—Public information director

US Department of Health and Human Services, Office of the Inspector General
Artie Delaneuville—Special agent

Orleans Parish District Attorney's Office
Eddie J. Jordan Jr.—District attorney
Michael Morales—Assistant district attorney; lead prosecutor, Memorial case
Craig Famularo—Assistant district attorney, senior to Morales

Orleans Parish Coroner's Office
Dr. Frank Minyard—Coroner

Forensic Consultants
Dr. Michael Baden—Forensic pathologist, New York City
Dr. Frank Brescia—Oncologist, palliative care specialist, Medical
    University of South Carolina
Arthur Caplan—Bioethicist; chairman, Department of Medical Ethics, and
    director of the Center for Bioethics at the University of Pennsylvania
    (until 2012; now at New York University)
Dr. Steven B. Karch—Cardiac pathologist; former assistant medical
    examiner, San Francisco, CA
Dr. Robert Middleberg—Laboratory director, National Medical Services,
    Inc.
Dr. Cyril Wecht—Forensic pathologist; coroner, Allegheny County, PA
    (until 2006)
Dr. James Young—Special advisor to the Government of Canada on
    emergency management; president, American Academy of Forensic
    Sciences (2006–2007); former chief coroner of Ontario, Canada

Others
Government Officials
Louisiana governor Kathleen Babineaux Blanco (2004–2008)
US senator Mary Landrieu (since 1997)
Mayor Ray C. Nagin, City of New Orleans (2002–2010)

Emergency Responders and Experts
Knox Andress—Health resources services administration district regional
    coordinator for part of northwest Louisiana, based in Shreveport;
    registered nurse at CHRISTUS Schumpert Health System;
    communicated with LifeCare corporate officials during the disaster
LTJG Shelley Decker, US Coast Guard (now LT); at emergency command
    center, Alexandria, Louisiana
Cynthia Matherne—Health resources services administration district
    regional coordinator for part of southeast Louisiana, including New
    Orleans; based at the emergency operations center in New Orleans City
    Hall; communicated with Tenet Healthcare officials during the disaster
Michael Richard, US Coast Guard Auxiliary; at emergency command
    center, Alexandria, Louisiana

Dr. Robert Wise—Vice president, division of standards and survey
    methods, Joint Commission on Accreditation of Healthcare
    Organizations, JCAHO (now medical advisor, division of healthcare
    quality evaluation at the organization, renamed the Joint Commission)

Colleagues and Patients of Dr. Anna Pou
Dr. Daniel Nuss—Chairman, Department of Otolaryngology; head and
    neck surgery, Louisiana State University Health Science Center
James O'Bryant—53, patient of Dr. Anna Pou
    Brenda O'Bryant, wife
    James Lawrence O'Bryant, son
    Tabatha O'Bryant, daughter

Defense Attorneys
Eddie Castaing—Attorney for Lori Budo
Richard T. Simmons Jr.—Attorney for Dr. Anna Pou

NOTE TO THE READER

THIS BOOK RECOUNTS what happened at Memorial Medical Center during and after Hurricane Katrina in August 2005 and follows events through the aftermath of the crisis, when medical professionals were arrested and accused of having hastened the deaths of their patients. Many people held a piece of this story, and I conducted more than five hundred interviews with hundreds of them: doctors, nurses, staff members, hospital executives, patients, family members, government officials, ethicists, attorneys, researchers, and others. I was not at the hospital to witness the events. I began researching them in February 2007 and wrote an account of them in 2009, copublished on the investigative news site ProPublica and in the *New York Times Magazine*: "The Deadly Choices at Memorial."

Because memories often fade and change, source materials dating from the time of the disaster and its immediate aftermath were particularly valuable, including photographs, videotapes, e-mails, notes, diaries, Internet postings, articles, and the transcripts of interviews by other reporters or investigators. The narrative was also informed by weather reports, architectural floor plans, electrical diagrams, and reports prepared by plaintiff and defense experts in the course of civil litigation; and I visited the hospital and other sites depicted in the book.

Dialogue rendered in quotation marks is reproduced exactly as it was recalled in interviews, or is taken directly from transcripts and other primary sources. If one person recounted an important conversation, I generally attempted to contact all participants, but some declined to speak, and at times memories were at odds. The main text and Notes highlight areas of significant dispute and indicate the sources of quotes when they do not derive from interviews with me. Typographical mistakes are preserved in quoted e-mails to give the reader a sense of the urgency involved in their production.

This book relates the thoughts, impressions, and opinions of the people in it, perhaps the most fraught aspect of narrative journalism. Attributed thoughts or feelings reflect those that a person shared in an interview, wrote down in notes, a diary, or a manuscript, or, less commonly, expressed to others whom I interviewed. As any book reflects the interwoven interpretations and insights of its author, I have tried to make these distinct. All errors are mine.

PART I

DEADLY CHOICES

Blindness was spreading, not like a sudden tide flooding everything and carrying all before it, but like an insidious infiltration of a thousand and one turbulent rivulets which, having slowly drenched the earth, suddenly submerge it completely.

—José Saramago, *Blindness*

AT LAST THROUGH the broken windows, the pulse of helicopter rotors and airboat propellers set the summer morning air throbbing with the promise of rescue. Floodwaters unleashed by Hurricane Katrina had marooned hundreds of people at the hospital, where they had now spent four days. Doctors and nurses milled in the foul-smelling second-floor lobby. Since the storm, they had barely slept, surviving on catnaps, bottled water, and rumors. Before them lay a dozen or so mostly elderly patients on soiled, sweat-soaked stretchers.

In preparation for evacuation, these men and women had been lifted by their hospital sheets, carried down flights of stairs from their rooms, and placed in a corner near an ATM and a planter with wilting greenery. Now staff and volunteers—mostly children and spouses of medical workers who had sought shelter at the hospital—hunched over the infirm, dispensing sips of water and fanning the miasma with bits of cardboard.

Supply cartons, used gloves, and empty packaging littered the floor. The languishing patients were receiving little medical care, and their skin felt hot to the touch. Some had the rapid, thready pulse of dehydration.

Others had blood pressures so low their pulses weren't palpable, their breathing the only evidence of life. Hand-scrawled evacuation priority tags were taped to their gowns or cots. The tags indicated that doctors had decided that these sickest individuals in the hospital were to be evacuated last.

Among them was a divorced mother of four with a failing liver who was engaged to be remarried; a retired church janitor and father of six who had absorbed the impact of a car; a WYES public television volunteer with mesothelioma, whose name had recently disappeared from screen credits; a World War II "Rosie Riveter" who had trouble speaking because of a stroke; and an ailing matriarch with long, braided hair, "Ma'Dear," renowned for her cooking and the strict but loving way she raised twelve children, multiple grandchildren, and the nonrelatives she took into her home.

In the early afternoon a doctor, John Thiele, stood regarding them. Thiele had taken responsibility for a unit of twenty-four patients after Katrina struck on Monday, but by this day, Thursday, the last of them were gone, presumably on their way to safety. Two had died before they were rescued, and their bodies lay a few steps down the hallway in the hospital chapel, now a makeshift morgue.

Thiele specialized in critical care and diseases of the lungs. A stocky man with a round face and belly, and skinny legs revealed beneath his shorts, he answered often to "Dr. T" or, among friends, "Johnny," and when he smiled, his eyes crinkled nearly shut. He was a native New Orleanian, married at twenty, with three children. He was a golfer and a Saints football fan. He liked to smoke a good cigar while listening to Elvis.

Like many of the hospital staff around him, his professional association with what was now Memorial Medical Center stretched back decades, in his case to 1977, when he had rotated at the hospital as a Louisiana State University medical student. A classmate would later say that Johnny Thiele had turned into the sort of doctor they all wished to be: kind, gentle, and understanding, perhaps all the more so for having struggled over the years with alcohol and his moods. When Dr. T passed a female nurse, he would greet her by name with a pat on the back and sometimes call her "kiddo."

Thiele had undergone part of his training at big, public Charity Hospital, one of the busiest trauma centers in the nation, where he learned, when several paramedics burst into the emergency room in close succession, to attend to the most critical patients first. It was strange to see the sickest here at Memorial prioritized last for rescue. At a meeting Thiele had not attended, a small group of doctors had made this decision without consulting patients or their families, hoping to ensure that those with a greater chance of long-term survival were saved. The doctors at Memorial had drilled for disasters, but for scenarios like a sarin gas attack, where multiple pretend patients arrived at the hospital at once. Not in all his years of practice had Thiele drilled for the loss of backup power, running water, and transportation. Life was about learning to solve problems by experience. If he had a flat tire, he knew how to fix it. If somebody had a pulmonary embolism, he knew how to treat it. There was little in his personal history or education that had prepared him for what he was seeing and doing now. He had no repertoire for this.

He had arrived here on Sunday. He brought along a friend who was recovering from pneumonia and was too weak to comply with the mayor's mandatory evacuation order for the city, which had exempted hospitals. Early Monday, Thiele awoke to shouts and felt his fourth-story corner office swaying. Its floor-to-ceiling windows, thick as a thumb, moved in and out with the wind gusts, admitting the near-horizontal rain. He and his colleagues lifted computers away and sopped up water with sheets and gowns from patient exam rooms, wringing out the cloth over garbage cans.

The hurricane cut off city power. The hospital's backup generators did not support air-conditioning, and the temperature climbed. The well-insulated hospital turned dank and humid; Thiele noticed water dripping down its walls. On Tuesday, the floodwaters rose.

Early Wednesday morning, Memorial's generators failed, throwing the hospital into darkness and cutting off power to the machines that supported patients' lives. Volunteers helped heft patients to staging areas for rescue, but helicopters arrived irregularly. That afternoon, Thiele sat on the emergency room ramp for a cigar break with an internist, Dr. John Kokemor, who told him doctors were being requested to leave last. When Thiele asked why, his friend brought an index finger to the crook of his opposite elbow and pantomimed giving an injection. Thiele caught his drift.

"Man, I hope we don't come to that," Thiele said. Kokemor would later say he never made the gesture, that he had spent nearly all his time outside the building loading hundreds of mostly able-bodied evacuees onto boats, which floated them over a dozen blocks of flooded streets to where they could wade to dry ground. He said he was no longer caring for patients and too busy to worry about what was going on inside the hospital.

Wednesday night, Thiele heard gunshots outside the hospital. He was sure people were trying to kill each other. "The enemy" lurked as near as a credit union building across the street. Thiele thought the hospital would be overtaken, that those inside it had no good way to defend themselves. He lost his footing in an inky stairwell and nearly pitched down the concrete steps before catching himself. Panicked and convinced he would die, he reached his family by cell phone to say good-bye.

Thiele felt abandoned. You pay your taxes, he thought, and you assume the government will take care of you in a disaster. He also wondered why Tenet, the giant Texas-based hospital chain that owned Memorial, had not yet sent any means of rescue.

Finally, on Thursday morning, the company dispatched leased helicopters, while other aircraft from the Coast Guard, Air Force, and Navy hovered overhead awaiting a turn to perch on Memorial's helipad. Airboats came and went with the earsplitting drone of airplane engines.

The pilots would not allow pets on board the aircraft and watercraft, creating a predicament for the staff members who had brought them to the hospital for the storm. A young internist held a Siamese cat as Thiele felt for its breastbone and ribs and conjured up the anatomy he had learned in a college dissection class. He aimed the syringe full of potassium chloride at the cat's heart. The animal wriggled free of the doctor's hands and swiped and tore Thiele's sweat-soaked scrub shirt. Its whitish fur stuck to him. They caught the animal and tried again to euthanize it, working in a hallway perhaps twenty feet away from the patients in the second-floor lobby. It was craziness.

A tearful doctor came to Thiele with news she had been offered a spot on a boat with her beautiful twenty-pound sheltie. She had quickly trained it to lie in a duffel bag. Several of the doctor's human companions were insisting they would not leave without her. Since the floodwaters had surrounded them, the doctor had been sick to her stomach and continuously afraid. She wanted to go while she had this chance, but she felt guilty about abandoning her colleagues and the remaining patients. "Don't cry, just go," Thiele said. "An animal's like a child." He reassured her: "We gonna get by without you. I promise you."

Thiele walked back and forth through the second-floor lobby multiple times as he journeyed between the hospital and his medical office. As the hours passed, the volunteers fanning the patients on their stretchers were shooed downstairs to join an evacuation line snaking through the emergency room.

Thiele knew nothing about the dozen or so patients who remained, but they made an impression on him. Before the storm, the poor souls would have had a chance. Now, with the compounding effects of days in the inferno with little to no medications or fluids, they had deteriorated.

The airboats outside made it too loud for Thiele to use a stethoscope. He didn't see any medical records, he didn't feel he needed them to tell him that these patients were moribund. He watched a doctor he didn't know direct their care, a short woman with auburn hair. He would later learn her name: Dr. Anna Pou, a head and neck surgeon.

Pou was among the few doctors still caring for patients inside the stifling hospital. Some physicians had departed; those who hadn't were, for the most part, no longer practicing medicine—they had assumed the roles of patient transporters or were overseeing the evacuations outside where it was somewhat cooler. But Pou looked to Thiele like a female Lone Ranger. After enduring four stressful days and four nights of little sleep, she retained the strength and determination to tend to the worst-off. Later, he would remember her saying that the patients before them would not be moved from the hospital. He did not know if she had decided that, or if she had been told that by an administrator.

Hospital CEO L. René Goux had told Thiele that everyone had to be out by nightfall. A nursing director, Susan Mulderick, the designated disaster manager, had given Thiele the same message. The two leaders later said they had meant to focus their exhausted colleagues on the evacuation, but the comments left Thiele wondering what would become of these patients when everyone else left.

He also wondered about the remaining pets, which he'd heard would be released from their kennels to fend for themselves. They were hungry. And Thiele was sure that another kind of "animal" was poised to rampage through the hospital looking for drugs. He later recalled wondering at the time: "What would they do, these crazy black people who think they've been oppressed for all these years by white people . . . God knows what these crazy people outside are going to do to these poor patients who are dying. They can dismember them, they can rape them, they can torture them."

What would a family member of a patient want Thiele to do? There was no one left to ask; they had all been made to leave, told their loved ones were on their way to rescue.

The first thing, he thought, was the Golden Rule, do unto others as you would have them do unto to you. Thiele was Catholic and had been influenced by a Jesuit priest, Father Harry Tompson, a mentor who had taught him how to live and treat people. Thiele had also adopted a motto he had learned in medical school: "Heal Frequently, Cure Sometimes, Comfort Always." It seemed obvious what he had to do, robbed of almost any control of the situation except the ability to offer comfort.

This would be no ordinary comfort, not the palliative care he had learned about in a week-long course that certified him to teach the practice of relieving symptoms in patients who had decided to prioritize this goal of treatment above all others.

There were syringes and morphine and nurses in this makeshift unit on the second-floor lobby. An intensive care nurse he had known for years, Cheri Landry, the "Queen of the Night Shift"—a short, broad-faced woman of Cajun extraction who had been born at the hospital—had, he believed, brought medications down from the ICU. Thiele knew why these medications were here. He agreed with what was happening. Others didn't. The young internist who had helped him euthanize the cat refused to take part. He told her not to worry. He and others would take care of it.

In the days since the storm, New Orleans had become an irrational and uncivil environment. It seemed to Thiele the laws of man and the normal standards of medicine no longer applied. He had no time to provide what he considered appropriate end-of-life care. He accepted the premise that the patients could not be moved and the staff had to go. He could not justify hanging a morphine drip and praying it didn't run out after everyone left and before the patient died, following an interval of acute suffering. He could rationalize what he was about to do as merely abbreviating a normal process of comfort care—cutting corners—but he knew that it was technically a crime. It didn't occur to him then to stay with the patients until they died naturally. That would have meant, he later said he believed, risking his life.

He offered his assistance to Dr. Pou, but at first she refused him. She tried repeatedly to convince him to leave the area. "I want to be here," he insisted, and stayed.

With some of the doctors and nurses who remained, Thiele discussed what the doses should be. To his mind, they needed to inject enough medicine to ensure the patients died before everyone else left the hospital. He would push 10 mg of morphine and 5 mg of the fast-acting sedative drug Versed and go up from there as needed. Versed carried a "black box" warning from the FDA, the most serious type, stating that the drug could cause breathing to cease and should only be given in settings where patients were monitored and their doctors were prepared to resuscitate them. That was not the case here. Most of these patients had Do Not Resuscitate orders.

It took time to mix the drugs, start IVs, and prepare the syringes. He looked at the patients. They seemed lifeless apart from their breathing—some hyperventilating, some gasping irregularly. Not one spoke. One was moaning, delirious, but when someone asked what was wrong, she was unable to respond.

He took charge of four patients lined up on the side of the lobby closest to the windows: three elderly white women and a heavyset African American man.

It had come to this. Dr. T's mind began to form a question, perhaps in the faint awareness that there might be alternatives they had not considered when they set this course. Perhaps he realized at the moment of action that what seemed right didn't feel quite right; that a gulf existed between ending a life in theory and in practice.

He turned to the person beside him, the nurse manager of the ICUs who also served as the head of the hospital's bioethics committee. Karen Wynn was versed in adjudicating the most difficult questions of treatment at the end of life. She, too, had worked at the hospital for decades. There was no better human being than Karen. At this most desperate moment, he trusted her with his question.

"Can we do this?" he would later remember asking her. "Do we really have to do this?"

CHAPTER I

FOR CERTAIN NEW ORLEANIANS, Memorial Medical Center
was the place you went to ride out each hurricane that the loop current
of the Gulf of Mexico launched like a pinball at the city. But chances are
you wouldn't call it Memorial Medical Center. You'd call it "Baptist,"
its nickname since it had existed as Southern Baptist Hospital. Working
a hurricane at 317-bed Baptist meant bringing along kids, parents and
grandparents, dogs, cats and rabbits, and coolers and grocery bags packed
with party chips, cheese dip, and muffulettas. You'd probably show up
even if you weren't on duty. If you were a doctor and had outpatients
who were unwell, you might check them in too, believing Baptist a safer
refuge than their homes. Then you'd settle down on a cot or an air mattress, and the hurricane, which always seemed to hit at night, would rage
against the hospital and leave. The next day, the sun would rise and you
would help clean up the debris and go home.

For nearly eighty years the steel and concrete hospital, armored in
reddish-brown tapestry brick blazoned with gray stone and towering
over the neighborhood near Claiborne and Napoleon Avenues, had defended those inside it against every capricious punch the Gulf's weather
systems had thrown. In 1965, it "took the century's worst storm in
stride," weathering Hurricane Betsy "like a sturdy ship" and protecting

more than one thousand people who sheltered inside, its administrator bragged in the hospital newsletter. A year before Katrina, when "[Hurricane] Ivan knocked, Memorial stood ready." As Cathy Green, a nurse in the surgical intensive care unit, told her worried adult daughter when Katrina threatened: "If I'm in trouble at Baptist Hospital, if Baptist Hospital fails, it means the entire city would be destroyed."

Utter faith in the hospital traced back to its founding: "I have an optimism that is almost explosive," the president of the Southern Baptist Hospital Commission board of directors wrote in a letter to the hospital's superintendent in February 1926, less than a month before a simple luncheon in the basement cafeteria and a dedication in the chapel marked the hospital's opening. "In my humble opinion we have begun at New Orleans what is destined to be the greatest hospital in all the Southland."

The property of the $2 million hospital stretched for two city blocks. Breathless news of its opening, with accompanying ads, occupied nearly three full pages of the Sunday, March 14, 1926, *New Orleans Item-Tribune*. The newspaper profiled the superintendent of the "magnificent" hospital, fifty-year-old Dr. Louis J. Bristow, and filled several column inches with a list of more than fifty of the items Bristow had carefully selected for it, from electrocardiographs to potato peelers. The hospital, its potential patrons learned, had the appearance of a modern hotel or private home, providing a "general atmosphere of cheerfulness" found wanting in New Orleans's older hospitals. Nearly an entire page was given over to a tour that described such minute details as the lighting system that produced "ample illumination without glare," the steam-heated blanket warmers on each floor, and the "dainty electric reading lamp" perched on each bedside table gracing the hospital's private bedrooms. "Ice is frozen in cubes on each floor in sufficient quantities to supply all patients," one article trilled. The stories, which read more like press releases or ad copy than news, may well have been penned by superintendent Bristow himself, or perhaps his daughter, Gwen, a writer. "The new institution stands unsurpassed among the hospitals of the south in point of modern conveniences."

The age of electrical invention afforded a comfortable convalescence as doctors applied new technologies to their increasingly science-based practices. Suppliers of newfangled appliances filled the *Item-Tribune* with advertisements celebrating their affiliation with Southern Baptist. The Acme X-Ray Sales Co. had equipped the hospital with a Precision Type Coronaless Roentgen Apparatus, "internationally recognized as the foremost X-Ray machine." Barnes Electric Construction Co., Ltd., of Gravier Street, which had laid the hospital's electrical and phone wiring, had also installed a call system incorporating musical gongs and silent luminescent indicators. All operating rooms had been equipped with compressed air and vacuum attachments. The hospital's design included "ventilation methods productive of coolness in the summer" to shield patients from the Southern heat.

New Orleans Public Service Inc., NOPSI, a newly consolidated utility company, purchased a nearly full-page advertisement announcing it had installed Frigidaire electric refrigerators on every floor of Baptist. "If the hospital MUST have the protection of FRIGIDAIRE, surely the home, the store and the restaurant SHOULD have it." To a city where many homes still had iceboxes, the refrigerators' low, even temperatures were described as a form of health insurance, preventing food spoilage and "the incipient development of germ life."

Baptist had its own power plant. A smokestack rose seven stories above it. Workers prepared to feed the hospital's furnaces 20,000 gallons of oil per week.

Seven years earlier, city missionary Clementine Morgan Kelly had stood before congregants at a church meeting and announced the conclusion she had reached after years of "prayerful study, deep thinking, hard labor," and visits to medical charity wards. "The crying need of the hour is a Baptist hospital for New Orleans," she said. "We shall never convince

New Orleans of the seriousness of our purpose to give this city Christ's pure gospel, until we do missionary work through a Baptist hospital." Baptists could open people's hearts to Christ by engaging, as Christ did, in healing.

The Southern Baptist press spread Kelly's idea to a receptive church already engaged in a hospital-building movement. New Orleanians of other religions supported the idea too. Almost eight hundred city dwellers donated money to purchase land for the new hospital.

The Saturday afternoon of the hospital's dedication, superintendent Bristow, the champion who had brought Clementine Morgan Kelly's dream to fruition, rose to speak. "The purpose of the Southern Baptist Hospital, in a single phrase, is to glorify God," he said. Poor charity patients would have their own rooms like the wealthy instead of being placed in the ghettos of separate wards. "We do not wish to capitalize the sufferings of human beings, but to relieve them." The hospital opened its doors to serve its stated, three-pronged mission: the alleviation of pain, the prolongation of life, and the relief of suffering.

The operation was not boundlessly munificent. To receive charity care, a poor family had to supply a letter from a church that testified to the family's need and promised the hospital a donation. "We cannot undertake to help those whose own church declines aid," Bristow wrote. The definition of charity cases was narrow at first, limited mainly to widows, orphans, and the elderly. A poor man whose wife required treatment would be given credit and a lecture about how charity would steal his dignity. Bristow often used the stories of charity patients, especially children, to fill pamphlets soliciting donations for Southern Baptist. He highlighted the important missionary work Southern Baptist Hospital was performing as it won converts and raised the profile of "white Baptists" in New Orleans, who were a minority in the city's twenty-eight Baptist churches and whose Convention had a history of support for slavery, Jim Crow laws, and racial segregation.

The new hospital sat in one of the lowest parts of a city that dipped below sea level like a basement below the water table. Runoff had to be caught, channeled, and pumped skyward to expel it into surrounding lakes.

Around the turn of the twentieth century, $15.3 million had been spent on drains, canals, and pumps to help transform the soggy, typhoid- and malaria-ridden basin between the Mississippi River and Lake Pont- chartrain into a modern city. Since then, rapid development had paved over ground that had once absorbed rainfall, but when the hospital opened, the city hadn't increased its pumping capacity in a decade.

The 11,700 densely populated acres in the uptown drainage section of the city that encircled Baptist were served by a single pumping sta- tion that lifted the water into a relief canal that channeled it to another pumping station, which raised the water high enough to flow into Lake Pontchartrain. An upgrade in the area's pumping and canaling capacity had been envisioned to go along with the development, but while build- ings went up, the work below ground lay undone. With no storms of great magnitude, the improvements had not been prioritized.

SUNDAY, MAY 2, 1926

THE UNSEASONABLY HOT weather was subsiding, and that pleasant afternoon some families set out for Heinemann Park to cheer for the New Orleans Pelicans batters as they took on Little Rock. Oth- ers laid out the suits, dresses, and hats they planned to wear to a show at one of the downtown theaters along Canal Street. Many thousands were expected to ride the streetcar to New Orleans's giant public play- ground, City Park, for its annual opening fete. Sport exhibitions, musi- cal performances, vaudeville acts, and movies packed the schedule. In the evening, festivalgoers would be invited within the Ionic columns of an open-air peristylium and dance for hours to the beat of the Hotsy Totsy Jazz Band. Above them, a grand exhibition of fireworks would paint the heavens with Chinese Spiders, Silver Comets, Turkish Crosses, Caskets of Jewels, Revolving Wheels, Large Waterfalls, and a bouquet of a hundred skyrockets.

Storm clouds began assailing the city just after three p.m. Uptown, where Southern Baptist Hospital had been open less than two months, raindrops knocked against the steep sides of tarred roofs and slapped onto newly laid pavement, gathering in rivulets that quickly joined streams. Thunder rattled windows. The temperature dropped nearly twenty degrees. During the first four hours of the storm, a gauge recorded a rainfall of nearly six inches, a record-setting pace. Debris-clogged catch basins blocked water from entering drainage canals. Streams in the streets grew to torrents. "It looked," Realtor Harry Latter observed as he tried to get home, "as if the river had broken in New Orleans."

A train crashed into a car in the blinding rain, killing two people. Thousands of creosoted wooden paving blocks swelled, buckled roadways, broke free, and floated away. Cars stalled as water seeped under their radiators and drenched wires. Lifeless autos blocked streetcar tracks. Work crews braved the storm to encircle them with cables and tow them. Streetcar lines shut down, leaving people stranded beneath the clattering rooftops of homes, churches, and public places.

At City Park, the sudden deluge brought baseball, tennis, and golf games to a halt and drove crowds of people into a bandstand for shelter. A musician took the stage to entertain them, but the storm only grew more intense and the festival had to be postponed.

Lightning danced across the darkening sky above the peristylium in place of May fete fireworks. At around eight p.m., a bolt struck near the Telephone Exchange Building, throwing around 1,300 lines out of commission. Water backed up into the tubes that surrounded intercity telegraph wires as they ran through flooded manholes.

On the grounds of Southern Baptist Hospital, thigh-level water smothered the new gardens. Even high-riding cars parked nearby on

Napoleon and Magnolia Streets were bathed to within several inches of their seats.

Inside, water poured into the basement, quickly rising to a height suitable for baptismal immersion. Medical records, groceries, drugs, instruments, linen, and the hospital's main stove and dining room tables were submerged. Louis Bristow and other doctors waded into water filled with floating chairs. They reached for airtight containers and handed them up to be sorted by nurses.

The lights stayed on, but the elevators stopped working. About a hundred visitors and nonstaff nurses were also stranded at Baptist for the night. They picked up phone receivers and tried to dial loved ones but couldn't make a connection.

Firemen were called to tap the hospital's basement with their pumping engines. At five thirty the next morning, they were finally able to draw floodwater into the storm sewers faster than the basement was refilling. Employees and student nurses gathered in the small diet kitchens on each floor and filled patient trays with improvised meals, presumably from the Frigidaires. NOPSI, which also operated the city's stalled streetcar lines, came quickly to Baptist to replace its gas-powered kitchen.

Hundreds of unprotected cases of drugs and supplies had been destroyed. Of all the city's businesses, the new hospital was thought to have sustained the greatest losses, with initial estimates ranging from $40,000 to $60,000 in damage (between $525,000 and $800,000 in 2013 dollars).

Superintendent Louis Bristow sought to reassure the public. He told the *New Orleans Item* that each floor of the hospital had enough drugs and supplies to run normally for several weeks or until replacement supplies could be bought. "We are operating as usual," he said. "There was no suffering to any of the patients. Our staff met the emergency in splendid fashion."

More than nine inches of rain fell between midafternoon Sunday and midafternoon Monday. The storm had produced the greatest one-hour rainfall totals in the Weather Bureau's fifty-five years of record keeping in New Orleans—nearly three inches—and depending on where in the city the rainfall was measured, the heaviest or second heaviest twenty-four-hour rainfall. The city's drainage system had extruded more than six billion gallons of water into Lakes Pontchartrain and Borgne, the grandest performance in its history. Yet it had failed to keep pace with the storm, and recriminations followed. Thousands of flood-affected residents phoned complaints to authorities. An association representing the worst-hit district demanded an investigation of all responsible officials, contractors, and employees, down to the crews at the drainage pumping stations.

After the storm, the Sewerage and Water Board of New Orleans—which built, maintained, and operated the drainage system—took a drubbing from New Orleans's new mayor, Arthur O'Keefe, for failing to keep its drains and catch basins free of debris. Board officials fought back, blaming the city for failing to keep the streets swept, the public for "carelessly throwing trash in the streets," and Mother Nature for launching lightning bolts at power lines that supplied some of its pumps.

The board's longtime general superintendent, George G. Earl, had warned for a decade that the system simply wasn't capable of handling that much rain. Without funding to complete a planned expansion, flooding in the lower parts of the city was inevitable, yet residents professed shock when this occurred. "It is only when service fails that any thought is given to the provision of means for improving it," Earl lamented. The neighborhood along Napoleon Avenue near Southern Baptist Hospital was his main exhibit. Like any good politician, he seized the moment to reiterate his call for more funds.

Bonds would be needed to finance drainage system improvements, but increasing the city's bonded debt ceiling would require, by law, additional taxes and approval from the state legislature. The city's *Item* and *Morning Tribune* newspapers urged authorities to allow the city to borrow the funds. "An old and a finished city may well stand still, pay off its debts, stop borrowing and rock along. New Orleans, in the midst of vast private development projects, attracting the attention of the nation and of the world, must provide herself with needed funds and go ahead."

An article summarized the sentiments of prominent city business-men: "Something must be done, and durned quick." Charles Roth, president of the New Orleans Real Estate Agents' Association, was willing to see the city bonded for any amount, even $50 million if that's what it took to get New Orleans "out of the water and mud," he said. "The damage caused by these deluges to our homes and streets, to our business enterprises and our utilities, costs us many times more than the corrective measures would come to."

Realtor Harry Latter agreed. "All this has a very harmful influence upon real estate values, and that is the basis of all wealth."

Superintendent Earl presented several options to ensure against flooding. With around half a million dollars, the Sewerage and Water Board could improve pumping. Three million dollars could widen canals. "How much does the public wish to invest?" he asked. "That is the real question to be decided." The work would be done quickly "in the order in which it will do the greatest amount of good to the greatest number of people."

Earl aimed to improve the city's ability to handle moderate storms. He argued it would be "physically and financially impracticable" to prevent flooding in the worst deluges, "for barely in the city's history have such storms developed." Another expert estimated that to handle a storm as intense as that Sunday's would require eight times the current pumping equipment and eight times the outflow canal capacity. "There probably is not a taxpayer in New Orleans who would favor" the idea, he told a reporter.

Enthusiasm for the drainage work quickly waned. By the end of the year, taxpayers had not yet approved even the less ambitious options Earl had presented. No bond was issued. The Sewerage and Water Board's construction expenditures in 1926 were nearly identical to what they had been in 1925. Earl vented his frustration in his end-of-year report. "The general situation remains unchanged," he wrote, not "in any degree modified by the fact that recent events have happened."

The following spring, storms in the upper Midwest sent a great surge of water down the Mississippi toward the Gulf and New Orleans. The floodwater wiped out cities and towns as it went. In advance of its arrival, authorities attempted to reassure New Orleanians that the city's defenses were strong enough to save them from a looming catastrophe. Panic would be bad for business.

A storm hit on Easter weekend, days before the river's predicted rise. In less than twenty-four hours, 14.01 inches of rain fell. It was the greatest total twenty-four-hour rainfall in more than half a century of record keeping—nearly a quarter of the rainfall for a typical year. Only once in the eight decades that followed would daily rainfall surpass April 16, 1927, in New Orleans.

Streets again filled with water, and the city's drainage pumping stations struggled to keep pace. As the storm intensified around midnight, a lightning strike knocked down a 13,000-volt high-tension power line belonging to NOPSI where it crossed the main feeder wires for the Sewerage and Water Board's system. The resulting spark caused a short circuit that crippled the switching system of the drainage plant, damaged a submarine cable distributing electricity, and burned out one of the two 6,000 kW generators powering the city's entire drainage and sewage systems as well as the high-lift water pumps that provided reserves to the fire department. The wires were quickly repaired, but the generator coils would take weeks to replace. That left a patched-up power line and one-half of the normal power supply to dispatch the most intense rainfall ever recorded in New Orleans.

The next morning, the mayor and city authorities set out for the site of the power-line accident to demand that NOPSI supply additional power to the drainage system's plant. But the two power systems operated on different frequencies—one at 25 Hz and one at 60 Hz—and, due to the lack of an appropriate transformer, no transfer was possible. The engine of the mayor's car failed in the rising water as he tried to leave. Marooned, he had to await assistance.

Across the city, hundreds of cars were similarly trapped, and nearly all streetcar lines had halted operations. While floodwaters gradually receded in some areas, in others they rose again as Lake Pontchartrain overtopped levees and spilled out of drainage canals that cut through the city.

Water flowed up to the stages of the city's theaters, covered cemeteries, inundated stores, and stalled fire engines racing to respond to emergencies. City dwellers called police for help when water awakened them in their beds. Alarmed residents of one neighborhood fired gunshots into the air to attract attention. An armed band of robbers hit a series of abandoned homes by boat. Calls from "anxious mothers" poured into the *Times-Picayune* newspaper with "harrowing tales of suffering from lack of food and milk for children." The mayor sent police reserves to commandeer boats and deliver aid, but they were overtaxed by the number of people in need of assistance. The newspaper declared "virtually a complete failure of city authorities to provide relief," a charge the new mayor called "so manifestly untrue and unfair as to hardly need official notice." He cast the blame, as he had the previous year, on the Sewerage and Water Board, whose chief engineer declared that the flooded streets were due "principally to an act of God."

City leaders refused relief offered by the Red Cross and National Guard, arguing it was unnecessary and that accepting it would give the city "a black eye before the nation." Impromptu ferry captains shuttled people around town in flat-bottomed pirogues. Mothers pinned up their girls' dresses and rolled their boys' trousers and let them wade. On Sunday, a matriarch hiked up her skirt and led her family on an Easter stroll through shin-high water as a newspaper photographer snapped a picture of them. A six-foot-long alligator swimming down a street was captured and sent to the Audubon Park Zoo.

Again came calls for action. The homeowners' association of the hard-hit Lakeview District demanded that the levees be raised and the drainage system strengthened so that "the 'hand of God' will not be blamed as often for what the hand of man has neglected to do." It called on city authorities to use their charter rights to issue emergency bonds for the work rather than await approval of a larger refinancing plan. A *Times-Picayune* editorial backed the plan: "We believe the people of New Orleans stand ready to pay whatever sum may be needed for reasonably adequate and efficient protection against these temporary but costly flood nuisances."

Superintendent Earl agreed. He called for an increase in the city's debt limit from 4 percent to 5 percent of its assessed value (a negligible change when compared with the 35 percent limit in effect at the time of Katrina). Earl also called for higher and stronger levees. His board had no responsibility for the city's levee system, but levee failures affected his ability to drain the city. He also foresaw the rapid growth of New Orleans, as transportation companies increasingly used America's interior waterways. He feared that as the city expanded and land that accepted Lake Pontchartrain's occasional overflow was walled off with levees, the water level in the lake would rise.

Municipal employees spent days after the storm cleaning up debris, digging drainage ditches, picking up animal carcasses, and spraying pools of standing water with disinfectant. In much of the city, the flooding was shallow and short-lived, as the half-powered pumps gained traction.

In the area around Baptist Hospital, as well as Lakeview in the north and Gentilly in the east, the water rose for a longer time and reached a higher point than anywhere else in the city. Along Napoleon Avenue, the water rose to six feet and flooded the first floors of homes. The basement of Baptist filled with eight feet of water. For the second time in the hospital's short history, its operations were disrupted by flooding.

The swell of water from the upper Mississippi reached Louisiana two weeks after the Good Friday storm. On orders from the State of Louisiana, workers dynamited a levee below New Orleans to relieve pressure on the levees protecting the city, sacrificing the Parishes of St. Bernard and Plaquemines to save New Orleans at the behest of the city's business elite, who then failed to deliver promised restitution. This launched a grudge that would persist into the next century. The Mississippi River floods of 1927 led to one of the most expensive peacetime legislative initiatives of its time, the 1928 Flood Control Act. It tasked the Army Corps of Engineers with improving the levee and flood-control systems of the lower Mississippi River, giving the federal government full responsibility for the river, and granting the Corps immunity from liability for damage that might result from its work. Decades later, the Corps became more involved in flood protection projects for the city of New Orleans itself, including the drainage canals leading to Lake Pontchartrain.

Over the years and decades following the 1927 storm, the Sewerage and Water Board obtained funds to improve the New Orleans drainage system. One of its engineers designed the world's largest pump, and fourteen of them were custom-made for the city. Drainage capacity had nearly quadrupled by the end of the twentieth century to more than 45,000 cubic feet per second.

Still, the area around Baptist Hospital in the Freret neighborhood remained the site of some of the worst flooding. The city failed to get a handle on it. Staff had to develop their own coping mechanisms. In the first years of the twenty-first century, workers knew a moderate storm could fill the streets around Memorial Medical Center with enough water that they would have to park their cars a block or so away on "neutral ground"—the high berms between lanes. Hospital maintenance men would put on waders and pull colleagues to work in a battered metal fishing boat kept suspended from the ceiling in the parking garage basement. Equipment, supplies, food, records, and linens were again stored in the basement. Many Memorial employees had long ago stopped seeing water as a significant threat.

CHAPTER 2

BEFORE THE STORM
SATURDAY, AUGUST 27, 2005

GINA ISBELL PULLED a white scrub shirt and navy-blue pants over her ample frame. The forty-year-old registered nurse had received a worrisome call at home from her boss that morning. Hurricane Katrina, revving in the Gulf of Mexico, had strengthened overnight and now had a good chance of steering into southeast Louisiana. A hurricane watch covered a wide swath of coastline. Katrina's strength was rated Category Three on the Saffir-Simpson Hurricane Wind Scale, projected to grow to a fearsome Four or even a catastrophic Five. Meteorologists predicted landfall on Monday, with hurricane conditions possible by Sunday night.

Isbell's home, her family, and her hospital were in St. Bernard Parish. LifeCare, the specialized hospital where Isbell served as nursing director, occupied a single-story building there in Chalmette on Virtue Street. The question was whether to move the patients somewhere safer, just in case. The risks of transporting very sick patients for a false alarm had to be weighed against the risk that floodwaters could rise over the rooftop if the forecasts were accurate.

St. Bernard had been slowly rebuilt after its surrender to spare New

Orleans from the 1927 floods, but a series of subsequent calamities kept residents uneasy whenever weather disasters threatened. Many remembered the levee breaks, devastating flooding, and pumping-system failure that followed the Category Three Hurricane Betsy in 1965. St. Bernard residents had little faith that their officials or their levees would protect them.

It seemed wise to move the patients. Waiting for more certainty in the forecast would leave less time for action and make it harder to secure ambulances.

LifeCare had two other campuses in the area, including a leased space on a high floor of Memorial Medical Center that offered heady views of the city. This "hospital within a hospital" provided long-term treatment to very sick, often elderly and debilitated patients. Many of them were dependent on mechanical ventilators and underwent rehabilitation at LifeCare with the goal of breathing on their own and returning home or to nursing facilities; LifeCare was not a hospice. It had its own administrators, nurses, pharmacists, and supply chain. The staff still called the location "LifeCare Baptist" even though Tenet Healthcare Corporation had bought Baptist Hospital and changed its name to Memorial ten years earlier. Most of the St. Bernard patients, LifeCare's leaders decided, would be moved there, and the remaining few to another nearby hospital.

Isbell called up the nurses she'd assigned to the "A" team at the start of hurricane season. They would join her at LifeCare Baptist during the storm and the "B" team would come to replace them after the storm had passed. The "A"s Isbell chose were strong nurses, team players, the ones she would want by her side at a stressful time. They had volunteered for the assignment. Working at an unfamiliar hospital would only add to the challenge.

Isbell had a passion for taking care of those whose long lists of medical problems put off some other health professionals. It took until nightfall to transfer nineteen of them to the Baptist campus. A twentieth died en route.

The patients traveled in clusters, up to four to an ambulance, because ambulances were already in short supply. They went with their own medicines, which the pharmacist prepared for them. Paraplegic patient Emmett Everett, who weighed 380 pounds, went from, and was resettled on, his own "Big Boy" bed.

The elevator doors opened on the seventh floor to face a wall adorned with the LifeCare philosophy.

LifeCare
Hospital
restoring hope
instilling desire
rebuilding confidence

LifeCare occupied three long hallways on the seventh floor of Memorial Medical Center—north, west, and south. The corridor to the east was devoted to Memorial's marketing department. Isbell wove back and forth between patient rooms and nursing stations, ensuring her charges were registered and properly situated. When she exerted herself like this her round cheeks flushed a pretty pink. A phone call came in for her, but she was too busy to take it. Instead she passed a message to the caller, the daughter of one of her favorites, ninety-year-old Alice Hutzler. Hutzler had been wheeled into Room 7305, a spacious room on the west-side hallway with two televisions, a clock, and three roommates, including Rose Savoie, another elderly lady. Isbell knew Hutzler from repeated stays and fondly called her "Miss Alice." To Isbell, Miss Alice looked perky, even with the stress of the move. "Perky" was relative. Hutzler suffered from heart disease, diabetes, dementia, and a stroke that had left her partially paralyzed. Now she was recovering from pneumonia and bedsores contracted at a nursing home. The fact that she would likely survive to make it back there meant, Isbell knew, a great deal to her attentive, loving family. Isbell passed a reassuring message to Hutzler's daughter: "Tell her she's here, and I'm going to take very good care of her."

That night, LifeCare appeared to have made the right bet by moving patients out of the single-story hospital in St. Bernard Parish. The National Weather Service upgraded its hurricane watch for New Orleans to a warning delivered in an eerie all-caps bulletin, a format designed for the archaic Teletype: "THE BOTTOM LINE IS THAT KATRINA IS EXPECTED TO BE AN INTENSE AND DANGEROUS HURRICANE HEADING TOWARD THE NORTH CENTRAL GULF COAST . . . AND THIS HAS TO BE TAKEN VERY SERIOUSLY." Heavy rains were expected to begin in twenty-four hours.

CHAPTER 3

DAY ONE
SUNDAY, AUGUST 28, 2005

ON SUNDAY MORNING, Katrina's huge, Technicolor swirl filled the Gulf of Mexico on television screens throughout Memorial Medical Center. The Category Five storm packed the greatest intensity on the Saffir-Simpson scale. Dire forecasts shocked even the most seasoned hands. "MOST OF THE AREA WILL BE UNINHABITABLE FOR WEEKS . . . PERHAPS LONGER," the National Weather Service's New Orleans office warned. Katrina was "A MOST POWERFUL HURRICANE WITH UNPREC-EDENTED STRENGTH," certain to strike within twelve to twenty-four hours. "AT LEAST ONE HALF OF WELL CONSTRUCTED HOMES WILL HAVE ROOF AND WALL FAILURE. ALL GABLED ROOFS WILL FAIL . . . LEAVING THOSE HOMES SEVERELY DAMAGED OR DESTROYED. [. . .] POWER OUT-AGES WILL LAST FOR WEEKS . . . AS MOST POWER POLES WILL BE DOWN AND TRANSFORMERS DESTROYED. WATER SHORTAGES WILL MAKE HUMAN SUFFERING INCREDIBLE BY MODERN STANDARDS."

Local leaders appeared on-screen to tell residents they needed to leave and leave now. The grim-faced president of a parish near New Orleans warned those who intended to stay to buy an ax, pick, or hammer so they could hack their way to their rooftops and not die in their attics like many Hurricane Betsy unfortunates had. He told them to "remember the old ways" and fill their upstairs bathtubs with water; after the storm that would be the only source for drinking, bathing, and flushing toilets.

The mayor of New Orleans, Ray Nagin, didn't give his residents advice about the old ways. He ordered them to leave. At around ten a.m., he signed a mandatory, immediate evacuation order for the city. The order had been delayed by many precious hours, he would later admit, as his staff attempted to resolve logistical and legal questions, including whether he had the legal authority to issue it; as far as he knew, no previous New Orleans mayor had mandated an evacuation, although state law allowed the governor, parish presidents, and, by extension, him to do so.

Nagin read his order aloud to the public at a press conference with Louisiana governor Kathleen Babineaux Blanco. He stood in a white polo shirt before the inscrutable New Orleans city seal, on which a wriggling green form prowled beneath a figure that suggested the Roman sea god Neptune. An amphora under the crook of his arm was tipped, its contents gushing. "The storm surge most likely will topple our levee system," Nagin warned. "We are facing a storm that most of us have feared." Flooding, Blanco added, could reach fifteen to twenty feet.

While the mayor commanded everyone to leave, many didn't have cars or other means to do so, and officials knew that the city's plans to help transport them had significant holes, including a lack of sufficient drivers. Residents who could go on their own were already stuck in traffic on the interstate leading out of town. The Superdome, the giant stadium that hosted the New Orleans Saints football team, was designated as a "shelter of last resort." New Orleanians who had no way to get out of the city could take a shuttle bus there. Mayor Nagin appealed to one population in particular. "If you have a medical condition, if you're on dialysis or some other condition, we want you to expeditiously move to the Superdome," he said. He didn't mention what kind of help people could expect there.

Many tourists whose flights had been canceled had no ability to flee on their own either, and so Nagin's evacuation order exempted essential hotel workers to serve them. It also exempted essential criminal sheriff's office workers, who were needed to keep their eyes on prisoners at the parish jail. They, too, were not being moved.

A questioner at the press conference asked for a clarification: "People should stay put in the hospitals . . . or what?" The mayor said he had exempted hospitals and their workers. People might get hurt in the hurricane. If hospitals closed and turned them away, that would, he said, create "a very dangerous situation."

The possibility that a very dangerous situation could develop inside the hospitals if they stayed open had occurred to other officials who were, at that very moment, on a conference call discussing the matter. Louisiana had received more than $17 million from a federal grant program to help prepare its hospitals for bioterrorism and other emergencies after the September 11, 2001, attacks and subsequent anthrax mailings. A FEMA representative on the call wanted to know which hospitals in flood-prone regions of the state had located both their generators and electrical switching gear above ground-floor level. In and around New Orleans, only two out of about a dozen and a half hospitals had. Memorial was not one of them.

An emergency response leader from the US Centers for Disease Control and Prevention alerted several colleagues to the problem in an e-mail hours later. "It is assumed that many of the hospital generators will lose power given the expected height of the water." He reported that around 2,500 hospital patients remained in New Orleans as Katrina advanced on the city. That should not have been a surprise. Planning sessions had gone on, after lengthy delays, for more than a year for a model "Hurricane Pam." FEMA had sponsored an emergency exercise in New Orleans earlier that very week. The scenario assumed the presence of more than 2,000 hospital patients in New Orleans during a catastrophic hurricane. No one had yet figured out how so many patients might be evacuated in a flood, and federal health officials had not participated in the latest planning sessions.

Dispatchers for the region's largest ambulance company, Acadian, were swamped with calls to transport patients from threatened hospitals, nursing homes, and houses. Many of the roughly two dozen ambulances the company made available were frozen on the jammed interstate. To save time, some ambulances began delivering patients to the Superdome instead of taking them out of town.

The main hospital in St. Bernard Parish, Chalmette Medical Center, managed to begin evacuating, but after the first round of critically ill patients left, ambulances never returned. Administrators from one New Orleans hospital wanted to move nine of their sickest patients to western Louisiana. But unless they could arrange an urgent, costly airlift, it seemed to be too late. The roadways were now so clogged with evacuees, the vulnerable patients could be trapped for up to a day in an ambulance before arriving. One nursing home had, before hurricane season, retained a New Orleans tour company at a cost of $1,400 to drive its residents to Mississippi in seven large buses in case of emergency. The dispatcher had reported on Saturday night that he only had two buses and no driver and would not fulfill the contract.

———

AROUND MIDDAY, Linette Burgess Guidi burst into the intensive care unit at Memorial Medical Center, located her mother, and flew to her bedside. She planted kisses on her mother's face. Jannie Burgess opened her large, almond-shaped eyes, raised her head from the pillow, and looked pleased. "Linette?"

"Yes, Mother, it's me. I'm here. I wouldn't be anywhere else." Burgess Guidi had arrived the previous evening from her home in the Netherlands after learning her mother's uterine cancer had spread and was inoperable. She looked down at her mother's hands in mock horror. "Your nails look terrible, Mother. You need a manicure."

Jannie Burgess had always been a lady who knew her lipstick, powder, and paint. She was seventy-nine years old now and obese, but in her youthful prime she had been tall with an hourglass figure and unlimited access to the beauty parlor owned by her older sister Gladys. She had fled an abusive husband as a young mother and lost her only son in Vietnam, but she knew joy, too, loved putting on the perfume and grabbing her daughter, Linette. "Let's dance, let's dance!"

The elderly woman drifting in and out of consciousness had a history, and Burgess's theatrical daughter couldn't resist describing it to the young, dark-haired nurse who had been assigned to care for her mother that day. The nurse was worried and distracted. Her husband had come into the unit holding their toddler son. He pled with her to leave town with them for safety, but the nurse stayed on duty.

Linette Burgess Guidi took to regaling her with stories. Was she aware that Jannie Burgess was a licensed practical nurse who had worked thirty-five years in New Orleans's hospitals and nursing homes? "Oh, really?" the nurse replied. "I didn't know that."

Burgess had taken up nursing to support her children after working jobs as various as taxi dispatcher and secretary to a mortician. But practicing nursing in mid-twentieth-century New Orleans had presented an unsettling paradox for a woman like Burgess with light-brown skin; she could care for patients at many of the private hospitals, but could not receive care at them. Though Jannie Burgess was born just a few months after Memorial opened in 1926 as Southern Baptist Hospital, it would be more than four decades before she could be a patient there.

In fact, Baptist was one of the last Southern hospitals to submit to integration. Medicare and other federal hospital programs were introduced in the mid-1960s, and hospitals were ineligible for reimbursements if they discriminated against or racially segregated patients. Baptist refused to join the programs. "It is our conviction," a 1966 hospital statement said, "that we can serve all of the people better if we remain free of governmental entanglements that would dictate the terms and conditions under which this hospital shall be operated."

New Orleanians sent supportive letters to the hospital's administrator. "It's heartening to realize that there are still some who do not succumb to the dictates of socialism," one person wrote. "Congratulations," wrote another, "on retaining the integrity of the hospital in the face of the ever growing pressure of the Federal government to take away the rights of the business and professional men of this nation."

The hospital began quietly accepting African American patients in 1968, in line with newly adopted nondiscrimination statements made by the Southern Baptist Convention. The denomination's history was entwined with segregation, but its actions were now changing under pressure. The following year, in November, the hospital set aside its opposition to Medicare and began participating in the health insurance program for seniors, "to ease the financial burden for these elderly patients," its administrator explained in a hospital newsletter. In 1969, the federal government declared Southern Baptist Hospital in compliance with the Civil Rights Act of 1964. The decision to accept Medicare was good for business. The number of patients over sixty-five years old at Southern Baptist nearly tripled over the first two weeks.

Tensions persisted. A decade later, between the years 1979 and 1980, at least six employees filed charges of race discrimination against the hospital with the Equal Employment Opportunity Commission, the agency responsible for enforcing key parts of the Civil Rights Act of 1964 (in at least two of the cases, the agency found no cause to believe the allegations were true). One of the six employees, African American engineer Issac E. Frezel, sued Southern Baptist Hospitals, Inc., in federal district court. He alleged that it had violated his rights under the Civil Rights Acts of 1964 and 1866 by engaging in illegal racial discrimination when it placed him on probation for "unauthorized shift changes," passed him over for promotion, and, ultimately, fired him. In his suit, he contended that a white coworker involved in the same offense was not disciplined. The hospital's lawyers argued that nothing illegal had occurred. The suit settled out of court for an unreported sum.

When Jannie Burgess had received poor treatment from patients as a nurse at various New Orleans hospitals, she did what she felt she had to do: gritted her teeth and smiled and kept going. She had a long career, and after retirement moved into senior housing at Flint-Goodridge Apartments, the pre–Civil Rights era site of Flint-Goodridge Hospital, once the only private hospital in New Orleans where "Negro" patients could receive care and their doctors could pursue residency training. Burgess cared for an ailing brother at home and grew softer and rounder with age.

Surgery and chemotherapy had stalled her uterine cancer. She recovered and lived well for two years. In early August 2005, her legs wouldn't carry her properly. She was admitted to Memorial to investigate the cause of her severe weakness. She had a bowel blockage. A surgeon opened her abdomen and found cancer in her liver. The tumor couldn't be removed. "I don't want to live on machines," she said, and so her doctor gave her a Do Not Resuscitate order. She developed an infection, possibly as a result of the surgery, and her kidneys began to fail, possibly as a complication of the antibiotics used to treat the infection. To stay alive if her kidneys stopped working she'd need dialysis to clean her blood. Under no circumstances, she said, did she want that. The doctor discussed these preferences with Burgess, her sister, and a doting niece, then shifted the goal of her care from treating her medical problems to ensuring her comfort. She was scheduled to move out of intensive care and onto a regular medical floor as soon as a bed became available. Small doses of morphine had been ordered as needed to control any pain.

Burgess's daughter, Linette, had lived overseas for more than two decades with her Italian husband. Mother and daughter talked frequently, but visits were rare and often did not go well. While Jannie Burgess had helped integrate New Orleans hospitals, Linette had done the same for the New Orleans Playboy Club, becoming its first African American Bunny in 1973. This distinction had brought shame to the observant Catholic mother she referred to as a Holy Roller. Years of tension over various issues followed. Today's visit was something of a reconciliation.

With the mayor demanding that New Orleanians evacuate the city, the relatives who had driven Linette Burgess Guidi to the hospital were anxious to begin their exodus west. It was time to leave. She told her mother she loved her and thanked her for all she had done to raise her and make her the woman she was. "Release, let it go," Burgess Guidi said to her mother. She told her she'd be back to see her on Wednesday.

———

ALL STAFF MEMBERS assigned to work the hurricane at Memorial were to sign in by noon to pick up wristbands and room assignments. They parked their cars in multistory garages above the flood-prone streets. They emptied car trunks full of hurricane provisions onto borrowed carts and pushed them down the hospital corridors. Those with pets carried kennels and a requisite three-day supply of food to the medical records department on the ground floor, checking the animals into rooms that filled with the sounds of frenzied barking. They wrote the pets' names on tracking forms and promised to keep them out of patient areas.

Unlike many others, Dr. Anna Maria Pou didn't bring much with her to Memorial when she arrived early Sunday afternoon: no family members, no pets, no coolers packed with snacks and junk food. It was the surgeon's first hurricane at the hospital, and when she arrived the activity struck her as highly disorganized. She sought the company of the experienced operating-room and recovery-room nurses and offered to help them move equipment. The main hospital, an amalgamation of the 1926 building and subsequently built wings, was separated from Memorial's new surgical suites by a bridge that administrators feared could collapse in the storm. Pou lugged supplies and equipment from the new building to an old set of operating theaters in the main hospital. She organized the rooms so that she and any other surgeon could operate in them during the storm if necessary.

Other doctors retreated to private offices to sleep, but Pou had decided for the moment not to do that. She was there to work. "I'll just sleep on a little stretcher with y'all," she said to the nurses. They carried stretchers to an empty endoscopy procedure suite to create an ad hoc bedroom. Staff members set up a table and unloaded abundant, picniclike provisions, having been told to bring food for three days, the amount of time local hospitals and their employees were expected to be self-sufficient in emergencies. They watched as Pou unpacked only a six-pack of bottled water, crackers, tuna fish, and something that flashed in her hand. "What's that?" a nurse asked Pou. "That's a can opener," Pou replied. Was that all she thought she needed? The nurses howled.

Water, tuna, and crackers were all Pou had been able to scrounge up at home. She didn't cook. Although she was beautiful, funny, and sociable by nature, at age forty-nine her life revolved around her surgical career.

She hadn't always known she would be a doctor, but even her elementary-school classmates had predicted that the caring girl with the good grades would follow in her father's footsteps. Dr. Frederick Pou was a Dominican Republic–born, New Orleans–raised internist, well known in the community but often absent from the family's large, two-story white colonial on Fontainebleau Drive. His wife, Jeanette, was the daughter of Sicilian immigrants. She gave birth to eleven children, and he worked tirelessly to provide for them. He treated patients in a corner house in the Bywater, a working-class neighborhood on the opposite side of town. He sometimes scheduled office appointments until ten p.m. and returned home for dinner after midnight.

Frederick Pou made weekend house calls, and his wife sent Anna Maria and her siblings along with him on alternating weekends so they could spend more time with him. In this way, Pou learned early what a doctor's job was.

The children helped raise one another. Anna was the seventh, and her older siblings doted on her when she was little. One liked to dress her up in doll clothing and lead her across their lawn and the broad, tree-shaded street to show her off at St. Rita Catholic School. Later, as a grade-school student there, Pou listened closely to the nuns who taught her. They talked about purgatory and the importance of being good. A nun held up a picture of a snowman. That was the soul, pure and white. She drew an ugly black mark on it. That was what sin did.

Pou went to a Catholic all-girls high school, Mercy Academy, where the mascot was a high-stepping poodle. Pou and her siblings were popular, attractive kids, petite in stature like their father, the smallest in his family. Most of the siblings strongly resembled one another with brown hair, prominent eyelids, and full brows that contrasted with peach-hued skin. Anna had the wide, dimpled smile of a prom queen. She frequented the Valencia Social Club, mingling with other local teens who stopped by after school for a snack at the diner and partied to the beat of live bands in the evenings.

As Pou grew older, it became her turn to help mother the younger ones, driving them to after-school activities and helping prepare meals. Taking care of others was a family value, taught and modeled by her parents, a way of doing good. When friends of Pou's younger brothers came over to play, she treated them sweetly. Some of the boys developed crushes on her.

At Louisiana State University, Pou had started out pre-med, but then changed her major against her father's advice. Instead of a doctor she became a medical technologist in a hospital laboratory, running tests for infections. This switch in her professional direction disappointed her father. He told her she wouldn't be satisfied.

One warm day in the late 1970s, Pou attended a party that spilled across the grounds of a restored plantation house a half hour's drive across Lake Pontchartrain from the city. The attendees were college-age kids and twentysomethings—the "uptown group" as they referred to themselves—private-school and Catholic-school graduates who had been raised, like Pou, in the graceful homes on the city's western curve along the Mississippi.

The cool waters of a long swimming pool beckoned. One young man challenged another. Who could swim the farthest without coming up for air? They took sips of their gin and dove in.

The two thrashed out one long lap. In the middle of the return lap, the challenger surfaced. His competitor trounced him, swimming to the end of the lane, then rubbing it in by floating in place without lifting his head.

A friend jumped in and playfully shoved the macho victor underwater. He stayed down. It took a while before everyone realized he was no longer holding his breath. He wasn't playing a game. He was unconscious, drowning in the shallow water.

Someone hauled him out of the pool. His skin looked grayish. There was no doctor at the party. They were all just kids, most of them drunk and some of them stoned. There was a veterinary student, but it was someone else who reacted.

Anna Pou rushed to the young man's side, rolled him over, and bent to his lips. She blew breaths into his mouth and quickly revived him. Pou suggested he go to a hospital. He considered her advice, grabbed another gin, and went to play volleyball.

Friends remarked on how quickly Pou had taken control of the situation. A few years later, she realized her father had been right. Being a laboratory technologist didn't fulfill her. She applied and was accepted to medical school at Louisiana State University, where her father and uncle had also trained. She was thirty years old.

One night during medical school, Pou attended an outdoor pig roast hosted by medical residents. She met one of their friends, a tall, handsome pharmacist who flew his own single-engine Cessna propeller plane. They made a beautiful couple, with personalities as different as their heights. Pou was outgoing, dramatic, and testy at times. She worked and played with gusto. Vince Panepinto was smart and engaging but more reserved. It took a few drinks before he felt ready to join her on the dance floor.

Over the next few years of their relationship, Pou's career took precedence. Panepinto followed her around the country as she did a surgery internship in Memphis and then studied otolaryngology, the "ear, nose, and throat" specialty, at a tough, exacting residency program in Pittsburgh. During her last year there, one of her brothers, five years her senior, died of lung cancer. He was only forty-three. The way the cancer attacked him was horrific. Pou said she was haunted by the way he "lingered."

While he was sick, Pou applied to yet another training program so she could subspecialize in surgery for head and neck cancers. She was accepted at a hospital in Indiana. This meant another relocation, and this time her husband Panepinto didn't join her. He moved back to New Orleans to await the end of her training.

If Pou was on a quest to do good in the world, she was taking it to an extreme. Many otolaryngologists had satisfying careers treating routine earaches and sinus infections. The field had a reputation among doctors as being one of the few surgical specialties to offer a reasonable work-life balance. What Pou trained to do in Indiana was at the most arduous end of the specialty spectrum. Microvascular reconstructive surgery was a mix of plastic surgery and cancer surgery. It was physically grueling and technically demanding. Some operations lasted an entire day and through the night.

The goal was often to restore the ability to speak, swallow, and breathe in patients with tumors or injuries of the tongue, throat, larynx, and other parts of the head and neck. Pou learned to repair disfiguring defects by repurposing other tissues from the body. A rarely used thigh muscle could do the work of a tongue. A flap of skin from the forearm filled in for missing facial skin. A bit of leg or hipbone served to rebuild a jaw. Under a microscope, she sewed tiny blood vessels and nerves together to keep the tissues alive and restore function.

In the academic medical world Pou had entered, fully trained surgeons—the "attendings"—ruled the operating theaters. The younger resident doctors, medical students, and nurses ranked below them and were expected to follow orders. Coming from a big family, Pou knew how to get along with people, but her respect for hierarchy had its limits. She turned on the Southern charm, manners, and deference with attendings who were good to their patients. Some of these doctors became beloved mentors. Others, whom she judged to care more about their careers than their patients, earned her distrust and irreverence.

When Pou finally finished her training in 1997, she was forty-one. She had not had children along the way. There had been many factors to consider, from her demanding career path to the fact that she had many nieces and nephews to dote on. She had also seen how hard her mother had worked to raise her own children. These included a banker, a nurse, and a real-estate broker. They had, on many occasions, made Jeanette Pou proud and happy. Three of the Pou girls had paired up with men whose names bespoke Italian heritage—a Panepinto, a Perino, and a Pappalardo—no doubt delighting their Sicilian-American mother. But Anna Maria had also seen how children can break a mother's heart. Three of her siblings had died, one was diagnosed with a serious illness, and her oldest living brother was a federal fugitive indicted for drug trafficking who had gone on the lam in Mexico. A dedicated, loving mother, Jeanette Pou had steered her family through these crises. Anna Pou directed a great deal of her own dedication and love toward her patients. Both women brought a toughness and tenacity to their callings. Others in the family referred to them as "the steel magnolias."

Pou finished her training, and she and Panepinto selected Galveston as their new home. Pou had received a job offer there from the University of Texas Medical Branch. She worked at the only large hospital on the island of Galveston. The hospital had existed for more than a century, and about a quarter of all Texas-trained doctors had studied there. As with many teaching hospitals, something of a trade was involved. The patients, often poor, received care regardless of their ability to pay. In exchange, budding doctors learned their craft by practicing on them. The hospital served a prison population as well. It seemed like a good fit for Pou, who enjoyed teaching and had a passion for treating the poor, as her father had done.

The year after Pou was hired, the hospital began to ration care for people who couldn't afford to pay for it. UTMB faced an $80 million budget deficit and declining state support. Just over a quarter of its patients were uninsured, and many others had inadequate coverage. Now each one was financially screened and charged an entry fee before being allowed to see a doctor. Those who couldn't pay, or who already owed the hospital money, could be turned away. Exceptions were made for children and patients in emergencies, as required by law. Nearly everyone else was at the mercy of a committee of doctors and administrators tasked with choosing who would and who wouldn't get care. Committee members were allotted $25,000 each month and had to decide which impecunious patients would receive drugs, surgeries, or other treatments, much as Louis Bristow, decades earlier at Southern Baptist Hospital, had decided which of his supplicants would receive charity care.

The complex cancer surgeries Pou had spent years learning to perform were expensive. Each patient's recovery relied on far more than her own skills and efforts. A team of professionals from more than a half dozen other medical disciplines, from radiation therapy to rehabilitation, often needed to be involved. Finding the resources to care for these patients when they lacked health insurance was difficult. Pou vented about her predicament in phone calls with friends. "This is the worst!" she'd begin, pouring her frustration into entertaining tales of woe. "I've never had a day like this!" Friends could never be sure which was the truly worst day of Pou's life. Those less fond of her found her overdramatic and hyperbolic—too quick to blame others when something went wrong with a patient, as in Dr. So-and-So didn't care enough or didn't do a good enough job. Small problems turned into bigger problems. Pou was not always willing to step back and allow other specialists to do their work, and some of them viewed her as controlling.

That drive to be the one on the team always doing her best, however, made her into a strong patient advocate. She was soon promoted to director of the Division of Head and Neck Surgery in her department. She made great friendships in Galveston, but her work came first. Almost two years after she moved into her house, Pou invited colleagues for a visit. She switched on the oven. The house filled with smoke. The packing materials were still inside.

Another time, when a surgeon's wife asked Pou to help out with Junior League, Pou accepted, despite her packed schedule. The surgeon's wife asked her to print off labels for a large event mailing. "My grandmother would roll over in her grave," Pou said. Invitations were hand lettered in New Orleans. The surgeon's wife reminded her she was in Texas now. It didn't matter. Pou used her spare free time at night to address the envelopes one by one.

Pou was a lady. She might spend her days in surgical scrubs, but she made it a point to find a favorite Texas hairdresser. Raoul coaxed her straight cinnamon locks into a proper hairdo. On the occasions she had to dress up, Pou tempered New Orleans exuberance with a classic uptown finish, pairing pearls with plunging necklines that flattered her figure.

During those years in Texas, Pou's father died, leaving her mother a widow in New Orleans. The beloved chairman of Pou's department stepped down. He had been an innovator in the field and had mentored Pou and taken great interest in her career. A new chairman was promoted from within the department. He was four years younger than Pou and had a PhD in addition to his medical degree. The two weren't close.

The program seemed headed in a different direction, with more emphasis on research. Pou's passion was for taking care of patients. She decided to leave, weighing offers from as far away as San Diego.

Over the years, at various national meetings of her specialty, Pou had developed a friendly relationship with the head of otolaryngology at Louisiana State University, Dr. Daniel W. Nuss, whose private practice was located at Memorial Medical Center. Nuss, too, treated head and neck cancers and had built a program focused on tumors and reconstruction—Pou's type of work. His program also served patients at the Medical Center of Louisiana at New Orleans, better known as Charity Hospital, including prisoners and many people who lacked health insurance. They had both trained in Pittsburgh and grown up in New Orleans; one of Nuss's brothers had briefly dated one of Pou's sisters. Nuss had asked Pou several times if she would ever consider moving back to New Orleans. Now Pou was ready to say yes.

"Dr. Pou, we regard this as an exciting opportunity, and it is indeed with pleasure that we invite you to join our faculty," Nuss and the dean of LSU's medical school wrote in her official employment offer. Pou inked her acceptance in April 2004.

While the state university employed Pou and provided her with liability insurance, Memorial Medical Center made an important contribution to her move, advancing the university more than $350,000 to pay her first year's salary and expenses against her future earnings as a surgeon. In exchange, Pou would join Memorial's medical staff and also see patients in its emergency room when she was on call, without additional pay. It was a no-lose situation for profit-conscious Tenet Healthcare, Memorial's owner. The university had to pay back the guarantee payments, and with university physicians on staff, Memorial qualified as a teaching hospital and was eligible for additional funds from Medicare.

On September 1, 2004, Pou took up her position as an associate professor at LSU in New Orleans. She began seeing patients in October.

The move was meant to be a permanent one. In November, Panepinto purchased a $349,000 house near the hospital, taking out a loan for 80 percent of its price. In early 2005, the couple sold their home in Galveston.

Pou was given a tour of Memorial and introduced to the operating-room nurses. "Dr. Poo?" one asked. "No, Pou," she said, pronouncing it her family's way, "Poe," as if it rhymed with "toe." "Sorry," the nurse said. She sized up Pou, a tiny lady rolling a tiny piece of Samsonite luggage behind her. This was the much-heralded new surgeon? "You gotta see this!" the nurse whispered to a colleague. Judging her on looks alone, the nurses didn't believe that the diminutive Pou was capable of performing tedious, draining, backbreaking all-day operations. She didn't appear to have that kind of stamina.

Pou would have to prove herself. She did not win over everybody she met.

DR. HORACE BALTZ WAS, at seventy-one when Katrina approached, one of the hospital's longest-serving doctors and a former president of its medical staff. He had treated patients at Memorial and Baptist for more than four decades and still performed basic blood tests by hand rather than sending them to a lab like just about every other doctor did. In his office, he kept a large black-and-white photo of a nurse in a white cap holding a cup of water to the lips of an elderly man lying on a cot. He and the nurse had worked together in 1965 caring for displaced residents after Hurricane Betsy.

Baltz was the son of a motion-picture projectionist, the youngest of five children, and the first in his family to attend college. He could remember, from his days as a high school delivery boy for the neighborhood drugstore, filling prescriptions for Dr. Frederick Pou, Anna's father.

Proud, boisterous, and principled, Baltz liked to reminisce about the days when the community's "medical giants" strode the halls of Southern Baptist Hospital. In the course of his career, he had witnessed two significant changes in the practice of medicine. One was the advent of high-technology life support for patients with critical illnesses. Southern Baptist was believed to have been the first hospital in the Southeast to purchase a "crash cart"—a piece of equipment wheeled in during a Code Blue to resuscitate patients who had stopped breathing or whose hearts had stopped beating. The cart contained drugs, a respirator to fill the lungs with oxygen, an aspirator to clear the airway, a cardiac monitor to keep tabs on the heart's electrical rhythm, a pacemaker to stimulate the heartbeat, and a defibrillator to shock a dying heart back into a functional rhythm. It was a momentous purchase, trumpeted by an article in the local newspaper in 1967. At the same time, Baptist expanded its physical plant and added piped-in oxygen and an intensive care unit for heart patients, complete with alarm systems to alert staff to irregular heartbeats and other emergencies. "In the event of a failure in City electrical power, each unit will be on our auxiliary power, so that no interruption can ensue," Baptist's administrator wrote in a June 1967 newsletter.

Intensive care grew to become a major specialty at Memorial and across the country. With it came new ethical challenges and a changing definition of what constituted "extraordinary measures" in medicine. When should life support be instituted? Critical care, transplant surgery, and other new practices were expensive. On the heels of their invention came the second big change: cost consciousness and the rise of for-profit medicine. By the early 1980s, health care was a medical marketplace. "Many of us have trouble accepting the business motive in medicine rather than the professional ethic," Baltz told a Baptist Hospital newsletter writer in the mid-1980s. Baptist was still nonprofit and faith-based, but it had to compete in an increasingly commercialized environment. Its doctors, and many across the country, feared being told by accountants and other nonclinicians what tests and treatments they could give to which patients.

As doctors began to rely more on machines and focus more on business, Baltz worked to remind his Baptist Hospital colleagues of the ethical tenets of their profession. As medical staff president, he urged them to stay compassionate and be selective about adopting new technologies. Baltz encouraged the establishment of an ethics group at the hospital and participated in a discussion of groundbreaking cases, including that of fifty-eight-year-old Clarence Herbert, a comatose patient whose doctors were tried for murder in Los Angeles after they withdrew his life support and IV fluids. The investigation followed from a nurse's complaints, an indication that difficult end-of-life decisions could create fissures between doctors and nurses. Family members also alleged that doctors had misrepresented Herbert's chances of recovery so they would agree to withdraw life support. The charges against the doctors were ultimately dismissed. "The ways and means of dying must be carefully considered," Baltz commented in the newsletter.

Over the years, Baltz continued the dialogue with colleagues. Life-Care leased the seventh floor of the main building in 1997, establishing the long-term acute care hospital within the main hospital. A Medicare payment change created incentives for these types of business arrangements, and they proliferated at hospitals around the country. Baltz engaged in spirited debates over coffee with colleagues who believed excessive resources were being poured into LifeCare's typically elderly, infirm patient population. "We spend too much on these turkeys," one of them said. "We ought to let them go."

"You have no right to decide who lives and who dies," Baltz would answer. Through these conversations, he learned that some of his fellow doctors adhered to what Baltz thought of as the "Governor Lamm philosophy." In 1984, at a time of growing budget deficits and ballooning medical costs, Colorado governor Richard Lamm criticized the use of expensive, high-tech medicine to keep some patients alive almost indefinitely, regardless of their age or prognosis. At a meeting of the Colorado Health Lawyers Association, Lamm bolstered his argument by citing a recent critique of antiaging research penned by the prominent University of Chicago bioethicist Dr. Leon R. Kass. "We've got a duty to die," Lamm said, "and get out of the way with all of our machines and artificial hearts and everything else like that and let the other society, our kids, build a reasonable life."

Lamm's words were picked up by an attentive *Denver Post* reporter and caused a nationwide furor. With the appearance of crash carts and the expansion of intensive care medicine in the 1960s and '70s, hospitals had become adept at keeping sick people alive longer. Medicare covered the new technologies regardless of cost, and by the 1980s some policymakers worried about the projected growth in medical spending. Lamm's comments awakened the public to the problem and demonstrated the tension between the "business motive" and medicine's burgeoning end-of-life dilemmas.

Lamm's rationing directive rankled for many reasons. To limit life-saving care would be to deny the human impulse to rescue individuals in extremis. To handicap the race for new treatments that might prolong life would be to call off the eternal search for the elixir of immortality.

Plus it would be bad for capitalism. At the time, the US-Soviet war urge was sublimated into battles for technological innovation. We were going to the moon. Why not also cure cancer or raise the dead?

Also the relatively recent eugenic and Nazi subversions of science and medicine—their conceptions of "lives not worth living" and the sick logic of ridding society of certain of its members to enhance the perceived health of the larger body—had ingrained in Americans an aversion to assigning lower values to certain lives.

On the other side, with drug and device developers figuring out how each organ that threatened to quit could be repaired or replaced, the practice of life support surged ahead of the practice of relieving pain, both physical and existential. Patients weren't given much of a say in how much of this new medicine they really wanted if they became critically ill and unable to speak for themselves.

And there were deeper, more unsettling questions. How now to define death? When was it permissible, even right, to withhold or, more wrenchingly, withdraw life-sustaining care? For a few weeks after a reporter cast Lamm's remarks before them, regular Americans looked these questions in the eye.

They quickly looked away.

———

BALTZ LEARNED of Anna Pou soon after her arrival at Memorial in the fall of 2004. One of his patients had developed a pouch in the esophagus that trapped food and caused problems eating and swallowing. It was Pou's turn to do ear, nose, and throat consultations, and Baltz asked some of the nurses about her. Who was she? What was she like? They raised their eyebrows. From what little they volunteered, Baltz guessed that they considered Pou a loose cannon, someone to avoid.

When Pou came to see Baltz's patient, she didn't merely offer her opinions. From Baltz's perspective, she took over like a commander and failed to discuss important aspects of his patient's care with him. Baltz judged her competent, but lacking in finesse. After the incident, he took it upon himself to give her some constructive criticism. He made it a practice to improve the work of those around him, especially younger, newer doctors. Pou seemed to listen to him.

After having spent seven years in Galveston, it would have been a challenge adjusting to the culture, etiquette, tools, and systems of any new hospital. When Pou was passionate about something, whether or not she was right, she stated her beliefs as unequivocally as a partisan talk-show host. Projecting surety was a defensive skill some doctors developed during their training, when attendings "pimped" them, barraging them with tough questions before their peers during rounds. Often, too, patients and families wanted clear answers when there weren't clear answers to give.

One day, Pou cornered the nurse in charge of her postsurgical patients at Memorial. "We can't have this!" she said. The previous night, one of her patients had become confused after surgery. Nurses caught him trying to get out of bed and pulling at the breathing tube in his neck. A nurse had paged the medical resident on duty to order a set of soft, loose cuffs with long straps. The nurses tied the straps to the bed and placed the soft cuffs on the man's wrists. This would limit his movements and keep him safe until he was less agitated. When Pou arrived the next morning and saw her patient restrained, she was unhappy. She told the head nurse to ask a hospital risk manager for workers who would sit at the patient's bedside twenty-four hours a day and watch him to make sure he was safe without the restraints. It was an unusual request. It earned Pou respect from the nurse in charge. To her, it meant that Pou had compassion for her patients.

Unlike many surgeons who manifest their authority by getting ugly or impatient in the operating theater, Pou was methodical and explained things carefully to residents and nurses. She had a way of speaking like a schoolteacher, enunciating her words to draw out each syllable and nodding her head for emphasis.

Perhaps more than anything it was the type of patients Pou cared for that impressed those around her. These patients were dealing not only with cancer, but also the way it deformed their faces. Some coughed and sputtered and had a hard time speaking. Pou split her time between several hospitals. At Charity, she created a clinic for low-income patients with head and neck cancers to receive advanced treatments and reconstructive surgery. She convinced an array of doctors and therapists to provide these services without receiving additional pay.

On January 15, 2005, Pou attended an annual banquet at the Ritz-Carlton in New Orleans to celebrate the installation of Memorial Medical Center's elected medical staff leaders. The festivities took place under crystal chandeliers. The Blackened Blues Band belted out rock, blues, and soul music. Giant trays of oysters and shrimp balanced on the banquet table beside bouquets bursting with lilies, birds-of-paradise, and irises. Dessert tables adorned with Mardi Gras beads, masks, and candles held trays laden with tarts.

Pou wore a short-sleeved pantsuit with a double strand of pearls and pearl drop earrings and a sleek, chin-length hairstyle. She spent the evening socializing with other members of the medical staff and their spouses, flashing her broad, toothy smile for the event photographer.

The doctors' lavish party contrasted with the troubled state of Memorial's parent company, Tenet Healthcare, which owed hundreds of millions of dollars in fees and settlements for allegations of fraud and unnecessary surgeries at other hospitals. Tenet faced falling stock prices, multibillion-dollar operating losses, a federal lawsuit for overbilling Medicare to inflate revenues, and a class-action lawsuit by shareholders for allegedly having misled investors. As part of an aggressive shift away from this troubled history, Tenet had moved its corporate headquarters from California to the Gulf South in Dallas, and was in the process of selling twenty-seven hospitals that weren't meeting financial goals.

The doctors affiliated with Memorial followed the news, but they still had much to celebrate. Only three years after the hospital's new surgery center opened, executives had recently cut the ribbon on a new, $18 million cancer institute across the street from the main hospital. They had also completed a $5 million renovation of the labor and delivery center. Memorial had passed a midterm hospital accreditation survey, and it boasted some of the highest employee satisfaction rankings of any of Tenet's dozens of hospitals in several states. For the staff at Memorial, the year 2005 looked bright.

———

POU HAPPENED TO BE on duty for her department when Katrina threatened, meaning she was expected to stay for the hurricane. Dr. Dan Nuss, the department chairman, called her, concerned. "I think this is the real thing," he said. None of their postsurgical patients, spread over several area hospitals, were terribly sick. Nuss urged Pou to sign out the patients' care to other doctors. Pou's husband agreed. Two resident physicians were on call with Pou that weekend. She dismissed them so they could be with their families. "Leave town," she advised them. At four p.m. on Sunday, the National Hurricane Center warned for the first time that battering waves and a mountain of water forced up by Katrina's winds—towering as high as twenty-eight feet above normal tide level— could overtop some levees protecting the city. Pou felt obligated to stay in case anyone trapped in the city needed the kind of specialized care she and few others could provide. Pou's department did most of its roughly 1,000 surgeries a year at Memorial, and she decided to base herself there.

As the surgical staff hunkered down that Sunday evening, the endoscopy suite they had claimed for quarters took on the atmosphere of a slumber party. Many of the nurses and Pou were coevals. They had grown up in New Orleans, attended private and Catholic schools, and now, with time to talk, they found they had friends in common. The nurses knew Pou's first serious boyfriend from his work as an anesthetist at Memorial. "If you saw him now!" they teased her. He was a sturdy man with playful eyes, apple cheeks, and a lopsided smile who now had a wife, three daughters, and a graying, receding hairline. Pou took out her lipstick and began applying it. "What are you doing?" a nurse asked her. "It's midnight! What are you doing?"

Pou said she wanted to look her best in case she saw him. The nurses laughed and reassured her. He had recently left his job.

It was hot outside, but cold in the hospital; the plant operations team had lowered the thermostat to make the buildings extra cool while there was still city power. If the hurricane knocked out utilities, air-conditioning would be lost because the hospital's backup power system wasn't designed to run it. The nurses knew from previous experience it would heat up quickly. Pou made a few phone calls to friends and family. If anything bad happened, they could find her at the hospital, she said lightly. "What are you doing there?" a friend in Houston asked after watching the ominous weather forecasts. "Get out!" But Pou wasn't changing her mind. "I'm going to stay," she said.

As the storm approached, there were about 183 patients at Memorial—a little more than usual due to last-minute storm admittances—and nearly as many staff members' pets. LifeCare-Baptist had an additional 55 patients, including the ones nursing director Gina Isbell had helped move from the St. Bernard campus. Around 600 staff members had arrived to provide care, along with hundreds of family members and companions. Memorial served a diverse clientele, a short drive to the genteel mansions of Uptown and a half-mile from a public housing project. Some community members had also come for shelter. Administrators tallied the census of humans in the medical center buildings at between 1,800 and 2,000.

Lightning flashed in the dark night. Rain rippled onto the road beneath the streetlights and beat against the windows with the undulations of the wind.

Pou did what came naturally and what she would do many times over the coming days. She prayed.

DAY TWO
MONDAY, AUGUST 29, 2005

2:11 A.M., WWL New Orleans Radio:

"Let's go to Alan. Alan you're on the sixth floor of Baptist Hospital. I bet those windows are doing a little shimmy shake right now, aren't they?"

"Yes, sir, and I've been on the watch since around twelve forty five and it's been a heck of a show. [. . .] We've had about three good squalls come through in that time."

"The windows are already doing the shimmy shake on the sixth floor? You know the winds are much higher where you're at than they are down at ground level."

"Yeah. That's one thing everybody in the hospital is really, really aware of. And, um, most of the patients who we're taking critical care of are actually moved away from windows."

"Any idea what those windows can take?"

"No, and I'm not going to find out, either."

"Well, you might. We might find out."

The news announcers reported that three people had died on a bus on the long exodus from a New Orleans nursing home to a Baton Rouge church. Many of the survivors were dehydrated. Other details weren't yet available.

Katrina shed some of its fury over the Gulf and spun north before beginning to envelop the coast in its massive grip. Area residents called in, concerned about what would happen over the coming hours. Would this be merely the worst storm they'd seen, the announcers asked, or would it cause a true worst-case scenario, with significant flooding? The National Guard was estimating that more than 25,000 people who wouldn't or couldn't leave New Orleans were packed into the Superdome. They were among those awaiting the answer.

———

4:30 A.M., FOURTH FLOOR, MEMORIAL MEDICAL CENTER

A LOUD CRACK startled Susan Mulderick awake, and she jumped up and ducked away from the floor-to-ceiling windows. She and her family members scrambled to gather their belongings and ran out of her office into the corridor. Mulderick's seventy-six-year-old mother, a gray-haired widow in a billowy housedress, had never moved so quickly.

Mulderick slammed her office door shut behind them to protect passersby from flying glass in case the windows shattered completely. The sturdy building shook violently. The sounds of the wind stealing through invisible crevices added to the aura of terror, a moaning, like a ghost, up and down the musical scale.

In the corridor, a panicked crew from plant operations ran toward Mulderick. "Glass is shattering all over the building!" they yelled. She was in charge. What did she want them to do?

It had fallen to Mulderick, the rotating hospital manager on call, to lead the hurricane response at Memorial as "incident commander." She felt responsible for every patient, staff member, and visitor. Her job was to oversee all emergency operations, lead meetings, and make decisions with the hospital's top executives. The fifty-four-year-old nursing director appeared well qualified for this job, with the authority of her thirty-two years of employment at the hospital—decades more than CEO L. René Goux, also present, who had been sent by Tenet to run Memorial only in 2003. Mulderick directed sixteen nursing departments and had more than fifteen years of experience on the hospital emergency committee, which she now led. When Hurricane Ivan had menaced and missed New Orleans a year earlier, she had also been at the helm, although Memorial's emergency management plan called for the CEO, typically, to assume the role of incident commander.

Mulderick had another sort of crisis-management experience—the family kind. Like Pou, she belonged to a large, Catholic school–raised New Orleans brood. But as she grew up, despite the outings to City Park in perfect, matching Easter dresses and bonnets, beyond the swingset and white shingles, beneath the high ceilings and crystal chandeliers, a certain chaos reigned. The third of seven children, the care of her younger siblings had often fallen to her, and she emerged from childhood remarkably strong and calm, a manager, an emergency responder.

Mulderick began her nursing career in the ICU at Baptist in 1973 and never left. She raised her own children and painted as a hobby, but for more than three decades, she had given almost everything else of herself to the hospital. She rarely took a break and once, when she did, a deadly storm nearly ended her life. In 1982, after spending five years planning a trip to Las Vegas with friends from Southern Baptist and another local hospital, she and they were bumped off an overbooked flight at the last minute, leaving their suitcases behind on Pan Am 759. The 145 people on board that airplane plus eight more on the ground were lost when a violent form of wind shear, a microburst, blew the Boeing 727-200 back down to the ground soon after takeoff. Mulderick saw smoke billowing out of the trees from a window of the plane her group had boarded fifteen minutes later. True to her coolheaded nature, Mulderick did not tell her friends what she saw so as not to make them worry.

Hospital life and family life intertwined. One of Mulderick's brothers died at Memorial after back surgery. A sister, with help from Dr. Horace Baltz, had been saved there from a bleeding brain aneurysm. Another sister worked at the hospital as an executive assistant, and Mulderick's housemate, as a nursing coordinator. Mulderick held on to her position as a nursing director for more than a decade, through significant changes. Under financial pressure, Southern Baptist Hospital merged with a New Orleans Catholic hospital, Mercy, in the early 1990s and then both were sold to giant, for-profit Tenet Healthcare Corporation in 1995. Mercy-Baptist's president didn't hide his lack of enthusiasm for the sale when he announced it in prophetic terms: "Due to market-driven health-care reform, the days of stand-alone community hospitals are limited."

Christmas decorating contests and the decades-old motto "Healing Humanity's Hurt" disappeared. Gone, on paper, was the Baptist name; calling it that became a satisfying, if minor, form of rebellion. Now press releases extolled Memorial Medical Center's "fiscally sound partnerships," and "stronger financial performance." Patient-care managers were given monthly budgets and productivity goals and took a beating if they failed to meet them. Success was rewarded with progressively tighter budgets. Mulderick adapted and survived.

Tall and fair-skinned, with straight red hair cut short in a pageboy, she had a tough, no-nonsense manner that intimidated some employees. She was known as calm and cool, even cold, under pressure.

After the maintenance crew came running to announce the breaking windows, Mulderick got on the phone with Cheri Landry. The senior intensive care nurse was camping in the new surgery building across Magnolia Street where Pou and her group were. Mulderick told Landry to get everyone out of there before the bridge linking the two buildings collapsed or its windows shattered. The staff members and their families would have to make a terrifying dash across its swaying, rattling expanse.

Anna Pou called one of her sisters before making the trip. "The walkway's about to collapse. I have to run across it," she said. "Just checking to make sure you all got out." She learned that one sister, a dialysis nurse, had not left the city, staying instead in the flood-prone Lakeview neighborhood near Lake Pontchartrain. Pou knew she was tough, but she prayed for her anyway.

Mulderick went with the maintenance men to survey the hospital. They roped off the danger zones and moved patients out of exposed areas into interior hallways. In the ICU on the top floor, where Jannie Burgess and around twenty other patients were staying, the small patient rooms were arrayed along the building's outer walls. Most patients were attached to oxygen tubing, IV pumps, and EKG monitors plugged into outlets and would be difficult to move away from windows. Instead, for the first time anyone could remember, maintenance crews had boarded up the windows with plywood from the inside.

The exposed sides of the windows shattered under a hail of rocks launched from nearby rooftops. The ICU filled with screams. Plywood grew wet and buckled. Water slipped inside to pool on the floors, creating another hazard. The father of one of the nurses on duty, who had taken shelter in the hospital with her, tried to stop his daughter from entering the area to do her work. The metal window frames strained and creaked like the *Titanic,* it seemed to one doctor, who finished up his work and headed to a lower floor. Several policemen were camping at the hospital, and a patient's son brought one upstairs to insist his mother be moved into the corridor for safety. "If I had someplace else to move her, I would," the nurse manager of the ICU, Karen Wynn, said, exasperated. "This is a clinical decision. This is not a decision he can make. We have to keep the patient safe, but also do what's clinically appropriate." The policeman understood, but the son didn't. His rage threatened to ripple chaos into the calamity. "If you're going to continue to be a problem, we will have you removed by the same cops you got," Wynn told him. There was enough going on without this.

At 4:55 a.m., the supply of city power to the hospital failed. Televisions in patient rooms flicked off. Memorial's auxiliary generators had already thumped to life and were playing counterpoint to the shrieks of the storm. The system was designed to supply only emergency lights, certain critical equipment, and a handful of outlets on each floor; the air-conditioning system shut down. Nurses trained box fans on their patients. There weren't enough to go around.

On the sixth floor in the newly renovated family waiting room outside of Labor and Delivery, the windows shimmy shook so hard they blew themselves out with a sound like a sonic boom. Rain sheeted onto the carpeting. Elsewhere, winds funneled through broken windows and scrambled narrow aluminum blinds. In their offices, doctors drew drapes across picture windows and stanched leaks with hospital gowns and bed sheets, the scene outside black and thundery.

At just after six in the morning, Katrina's eye slid over land as a Category Three hurricane, glancing at New Orleans from Buras, Louisiana, about sixty miles southeast of the city. The storm raged after daybreak. The view outside Memorial, for those who dared to get close enough to a window to look, was an impenetrable white blanket. Gusts of 135 miles per hour were expected by nine thirty.

Between squalls it was possible to stand outside on the emergency room ramp and peek out from behind a heavy post. The US and Louisiana flags flapped madly on their flagpoles against a gray sky. Water raced like a river down Clara Street. A red car and a red van were bathed to the middle of their wheel wells. The wind kicked up whitecaps and spray.

The basement began taking water. It was, as it had been in 1926, full of food—three to five days' worth, five to seven if it was rationed. Incident commander Mulderick helped pack the supplies onto rolling dollies and move them upstairs, an arduous process that took hours because of the limited number of hand trucks.

The possibility that the floodwaters could reach the first floor raised fears for the ten patients in the emergency room and the Noah's ark of pets in the medical records department. For now, the emergency patients stayed put. Surgeon Anna Pou joined a chain of hospital volunteers and National Guard soldiers to help pass kennels up a staircase to the eighth floor and place them in the old, unused surgical suites behind the ICU. The area filled up with cages and the earsplitting barking and the stench of frightened animals.

Mulderick's first-floor command center was relocated to a fourth-floor nurse training room. Another concern was drug reserves. Memorial, like many modern hospitals, did not maintain a large supply of medications on hand, opting instead for a "just in time delivery" system. The head pharmacist had requested an emergency cache of medicines from supplier McKesson on Saturday, but the company's workers seemed to have already left their local warehouse ahead of the storm. They never delivered the drugs. Now, Monday morning, only about a day's worth of certain medicines remained. Memorial would need more supplies by Tuesday morning.

Memorial CEO René Goux was on-site and asked his community relations manager, Sandra Cordray, to share these issues with corporate executives at Tenet Healthcare in Dallas. "Rene's major concern is patient care after storm and high flood waters and continued loss of power," she wrote in an e-mail to Tenet's chief operating officer and other officials.

"We will consider options for patient evacuation—that we may not have to use."

Some patients were not being seen because their doctors were off-site and unreachable by phone. The medical staff president, Reuben L. Chrestman III, was on vacation. In his absence, Dr. Richard E. Deichmann, chairman of medical services, one of Memorial's three clinical departments, took the lead in organizing the physicians. Most of them were, like Anna Pou, university doctors or private contractors credentialed to admit patients, but not employed by the hospital. Memorial didn't specifically require most medical specialists to be present for hurricanes. These doctors had stayed either because they were on call for the weekend like Pou or had, like Dr. John Thiele, grown accustomed over years of hurricane warnings and near misses to spending storms in their offices.

More doctors seemed to be on hand than in any previous hurricane, perhaps because the storm had fallen on a weekend and those on call had simply stayed. Several, Deichmann and Baltz among them, were internists. Thiele was one of three lung specialists present who treated critically ill patients in the ICU. Others included a kidney specialist, an infectious diseases doctor, emergency medicine doctors, and neonatologists who took care of the youngest, sickest babies. There were several surgeons, including Pou, and three anesthesiologists. Deichmann assigned these clinical doctors to different nursing stations so that someone would be in charge of each of the fifteen patient units.

Katrina rapidly lost strength after moving onto land. The rain lessened and the winds began to ease by late morning. The water level outside Memorial stabilized at about three feet. Maintenance crews began to survey roof damage and broken windows, downed ceiling tiles, and sodden carpets that, in the growing heat, invited mold.

By midafternoon, the waters outside began to recede. Pets and food were carried back downstairs. Nurses mopped floors for hours until the rain and the ceiling leaks stopped completely. Patients tried to call loved ones to check on them and let them know they had come through all right. Emmett Everett, the 380-pound patient up in LifeCare who had been moved from Chalmette in St. Bernard Parish, was unable to reach his wife on her cell phone and told his nurse he was worried about her.

By evening, the flooding was gone, and it was possible to walk dogs outside. Some doctors who lived nearby navigated the debris-filled streets to check on their property and even stay the night at home. Other staff crossed back to their campsites in the new surgery building. Katrina had weakened before arrival, buffeting the city with only Category One or Two winds, not the Category Five tempests envisioned by the doom-prophesying weathermen. "We dodged a bullet," people said to one another with weary relief. Memorial had sustained damage but remained functional on backup power. The hospital seemed to have weathered one more storm.

CHAPTER 4

DAY THREE
TUESDAY, AUGUST 30, 2005

"CODE BLUE, ER."

Karen Wynn's eyes opened in the dark room. She felt around for her shoes and socks, but could only find her teenage daughter's flip-flops. She shoved them on her feet and ran the length of two city blocks from the new surgery building over the footbridge into the main hospital and down to the first-floor emergency room, struggling not to trip or cut her feet on broken glass.

Along the way, the ICU nurse manager tried to sort through her confusion. It had to be four or five in the morning. Why were they summoning her to a Code Blue in the emergency room? The ER staff members could resuscitate patients by themselves. Besides, who would be coming into the hospital when most of the city had been evacuated?

She arrived, panting. Blood was everywhere. A woman was lying on a gurney. She looked to be in her late sixties. The story came from her grandson, who had carried her up the ER ramp. There had been drinking. A fight. The woman's daughter stabbed her in the chest with a kitchen knife. The grandson ran for help and found policemen, but they told him there were no ambulances running and he would have to find some other way to get her to the hospital.

The knife-and-gun club hadn't taken a break, even within hours of a major hurricane.

The page operator called overhead for all doctors to come to the emergency room. Internist Horace Baltz appeared in a white coat, with bare legs. In an effort to get there quickly, the senior doctor had thrown the coat on over his shorts, then tied on his black Oxford shoes and run downstairs.

The patient, at first conscious and communicative, began struggling to breathe. Wynn knew air might have followed the knife's path into her chest and collapsed her lungs. The woman's blood-pressure measurements were falling.

Blood could be collecting in the sac around her heart, constricting it and limiting its ability to fill and pump. Someone called for an ultrasound machine technician to check this, but for now there was no time to await answers. A doctor made a cut in the skin between two of the woman's ribs, spread the tissues with a blunt instrument, and pushed a tube into her chest cavity to release any built-up air. Another tube went into her throat and was attached to a mechanical ventilator to help her breathe.

Fortunately, the ultrasound exam showed that the knife had not penetrated the membrane around the woman's heart. Open-chest surgery wouldn't be necessary. The team hadn't liked the thought of attempting it on backup generator power. Wynn's ICU had one available bed. The woman was taken by elevator to the eighth floor.

The ICU nurses on the overnight shift received their new patient at about six a.m. and began positioning the tangle of equipment that had taken over for many of her bodily systems. The machines breathed for her, checked her blood pressure at regular intervals, measured her pulse, pumped fluid into her veins, and monitored the oxygen level in her capillaries—all just as if a hurricane had never happened.

A nurse rolled a cart with a computer up to the woman's bedside and began documenting her progress. Some of the ICU nurses had radios on their carts. They tuned them to WWL, a popular 50,000-watt talk radio station that was broadcasting on generator power.

On the radio, the president of neighboring Jefferson Parish announced that martial law had been declared. The hosts aired his message repeatedly, but martial law—an extremely rare assumption of police powers by the military typically requiring an act of Congress—had not, in fact, been declared in the disaster zone.

A caller complained that looters were ravaging New Orleans. She didn't say how she knew this, but the radio host took her at her word and amplified her outrage to thousands of listeners. "If someone is breaking into businesses and looting merchandise, these people should be shot," he said. "We're under martial law here."

Throughout the early morning, callers began describing something even more ominous. Water from the storm was still sitting in the streets. One resident was mystified because he could hear the city's drainage pumps running. "My question is," he said to the host, "if you live a block away from the pumping station, and the pumping station is working, why would you have water in your house?" The host had no answer.

"We're very frightened," a man named Freddy said calmly, and described his situation. He was sitting in the attic of his home in the Gentilly neighborhood near Lake Pontchartrain, surrounded by about nine feet of water. The area, one of those that had flooded badly in the 1927 storm, was several miles northeast of Memorial. With him were four other people, including a baby. They had punched a hole through the roof and, using candles, a lantern, and a flashlight, had tried for four hours to signal a helicopter.

"And is the water rising anymore?" the host asked him.

"Yes, it's steady rising, yes."

"The water's rising?" one nurse asked aloud in the medical ICU at Memorial. It made no sense. The street flooding around the hospital had gone away. Anyone who had taken a break and ventured outside during the night knew it was clear and still. The news was confusing and worrisome, but there was work to do.

The sun rose, and around Memorial the streets remained dry. The sky outside the windows was blue. At seven a.m., after the stabbed patient was settled in, nurse manager Karen Wynn went downstairs to the relocated command center on the fourth floor for the day's first meeting of the disaster leadership team.

The meeting took place in a large, rectangular room marked NURSING RESOURCE CENTER. White linoleum tables held a bank of computers normally used for training nurses. The computers were connected to the Internet and plugged into the red emergency outlets that operated off the generator system.

The room offered a sense of remove. Homey pink, pleated valances framed windows overlooking a courtyard enclosed by the reddish-brown tapestry brick of the old hospital building. There were mismatched sofas, brown cabinets, and a sink. The hospital's chief financial officer, Curtis Dosch, had brought over a television set with a rabbit-ear antenna, placed it on a low table, and plugged it into a red outlet. Staff hunched down to peer at it, though it showed mainly static.

Susan Mulderick, Wynn's longtime boss, ran the meeting. Wynn trusted Mulderick, who had hired her as a staff nurse when she started her career in the 1980s, then promoted her to manager when Wynn was pregnant and on bed rest. While others saw only the professional, intimidating Mulderick, Wynn knew inside she was a marshmallow, a cream puff. She had always set clear expectations and given Wynn the freedom and support she needed to meet them. Wynn adored Mulderick and admired her intelligence and creativity.

The command team announced a shift in hospital operations from "assault mode" to "survival mode." This unofficial designation reflected news they had received minutes before the meeting. An Acadian ambulance worker on-site had confirmed with his dispatchers that one of the canals in New Orleans had been breached. That meant water could be headed toward the hospital. Memorial's workers might be exhausted, but they were beginning to realize that rather than signing out their patients to the returning "B" team and going home, they could be stuck at the hospital for a while.

Wynn and the other department heads checked in. Their reports were relatively upbeat. The hospital was functioning almost normally, in spite of the heat. Maintenance workers were picking up debris, taking down floodgates, and patching holes in the roof exposed when the wind ripped away ducts and flashing. Kitchen employees were handing out Styrofoam cups filled with scrambled eggs and bacon. (The sight of low-wage cooks tending the stoves in the swelter with tied-up hair and cut-off sleeves and scrub pants had awed one executive who came down to the kitchen seeking extra food for a patient. An employee turned and asked, "What you need, baby?" as if it were any other day.)

Feeding not only the patients but also everyone else, it was thought, might help calm the hundreds of family members and hospital neighbors who had taken shelter at Memorial and were getting antsy. With downed trees and power lines on the streets and reports of flooding only blocks away, it wasn't safe for people to leave, though many were trying. Some headed to a darkened Winn-Dixie supermarket about eight blocks away and returned, arms laden with diapers, food, and drinks. One described this as "soul surviving, surviving for the soul." Others considered it looting.

After the meeting broke up, a memo went out to reinforce what the command team had decided: "Incident Command has declared Survival Mode for Memorial Medical Center."

All staff and physicians were instructed to stay at the hospital. Family members were advised to stay too. The hospital could expect flooding. There would be no elective surgery and no MRIs, PET scans, or CTs.

Medically stable patients were to be discharged, even though they may not have had anyplace to go or any way of leaving. Some were taken to the lobby in wheelchairs to wait. The head pharmacist was still scrambling to arrange for a drop-off from his supplier to replace the dwindling stores of medicines.

Each department had to report to the command team by noon with a list of employees and family members present and an inventory of available medicines, supplies, equipment, and cell phones, as the hospital's landlines worked only intermittently. The command team also sought any nurse with experience performing kidney dialysis. Patients in renal failure needed hours of dialysis every few days to clean their blood and remove fluid from their bodies, but the city's dialysis clinics were closed. Their clients were showing up at the hospital, where there was only one dialysis nurse on hand for Memorial and LifeCare patients, including some of the new patients transferred from Chalmette. A nursing director from LifeCare and another nurse volunteered to help, and they tutored the kidney specialist, who was adept at ordering dialysis, not providing it.

The dialysis procedure required water, but the city water was reportedly so heavily contaminated with chemicals and bacteria that it would be dangerous to bathe in it. The doctor faced a decision. The patients would die without dialysis, and it was unclear how quickly they could be transferred out of Memorial. Workers would filter the water and hope for the best. Staff members formed an assembly line to boil water in the microwave and stockpile it for other uses.

Within view of the hospital windows people were ransacking a Walgreens. One Memorial administrator wrote an e-mail to her family at ten twenty in the morning describing what she had heard from the security supervisor.

> They are locking down the whole hospital to keep the looters out. We are under marshall law so our security officers can shoot to kill if they want.

A NATIONAL GUARD soldier jogged up to a group of people mingling outside the hospital.

"Who's in charge?" he asked.

"I am," a short, muscular man in his early forties answered. Eric Yancovich was Memorial's plant operations director and a member of the
hospital's emergency leadership team. He was outside snapping photographs to document the damage Katrina had caused the hospital. Blown-
out windows and light fixtures. A collapsed penthouse. Bent antennas
and exposed roof joints.

The National Guardsman told him the levees protecting New Orleans had been breached. "You need to prepare for fifteen feet of water,"
he said. "Yeah right," Yancovich muttered. Then he saw the soldier
wasn't kidding. "Will you come into the command center?" Yancovich
asked. "Because I'm not bringing this news in by myself."

Yancovich knew they were in trouble. The design of Memorial's
backup power system had a flaw all too common in flood zones, the one
that the state and federal emergency officials had discussed in their conference call immediately before the storm. When Tropical Storm Allison
inundated Houston in 2001, hospitals in the nation's largest medical complex, Texas Medical Center, lost power because either emergency generators or their various electrical components were located below flood
level. News of the incident had alarmed New Orleans's health director,
Dr. Kevin Stephens. The following year, he had surveyed representatives
of every hospital in the city, asking whether they could withstand a flood
with fifteen feet of water, how much it would cost to elevate generators
if needed, and whether there was interest in having the city look into the
possibility of federal funding to make improvements. One letter went to
Memorial's emergency committee head, Susan Mulderick.

The response from the hospitals was unenthusiastic. It would cost
much more than they had to spend, millions of dollars in at least one

case. The initiative never went anywhere, and that was why, the day before Katrina made landfall, the federal emergency management officer had been told that all but two of the hospitals in New Orleans had either generators, electrical switches, or both at ground level.

That was the case at Memorial. After Hurricane Ivan's near miss in September 2004, the hospital's leaders had reviewed hurricane plans. Eric Yancovich himself attended a meeting with the US Army Corps of Engineers and studied government storm-surge models—known as "SLOSH" for sea, lake, and overland surges from hurricanes—which estimated the height of a wall of water driven onto land by a hurricane's winds. He learned that if a Category Four or Five storm hit the city and caused the lake or the river to flood it, a massive twelve to fifteen feet of water could rise up around Memorial.

By hand, on a piece of lined paper after the Army Corps of Engineers meeting, Yancovich had sketched out the elevation of various hospital entrances and critical outdoor equipment in relation to the center of Magnolia Street, a narrow road perpendicular to Napoleon Avenue that ran along the back side of the hospital. His calculations showed it would take less than four feet of street flooding for water to flow over the load-ing dock and into the hospital. He knew that while the hospital's backup generators on the second floor were at a safe elevation, some critical parts of the emergency power distribution system were located below ground level or only inches to a few feet above it.

The story this told was clear and grim. "Based on these readings it won't take much water in height to disable the majority of the Medi-cal Center," Yancovich had written in a note to his supervisor several months before Katrina. He predicted that power would be lost in the main hospital and all patients would have to be moved to the newer Clara Wing, where he believed the electrical circuitry was better protected.

Yancovich's department had taken a few steps to harden the hospi-tal's defenses, including adding floodgates and raising the vent for the underground diesel fuel tanks. But more extensive work needed to be done. Yancovich had recommended elevating basement and ground-level emergency power transfer switches and the pumps that supplied most of the hospital with medical air and vacuum suction, needed by patients with respiratory problems. A partial bid for the electrical work came to more than a quarter of a million dollars. "Due to the lack of capital, I don't anticipate anything being approved right now," Yancovich had concluded in his recent memo. "I'll keep it on file for future consideration."

The backup generator system was only as robust as its weakest part. Now, with floodwaters heading for Memorial, it was the hospital's Achilles' heel. They all needed to get out of the hospital. Yancovich knew it. Susan Mulderick knew it. She advised Memorial CEO René Goux, who spoke with his bosses at Tenet, in Dallas. He told them that evacuation looked likely.

———

"WHERE'S VINCE?"

The nurse asking about Dr. Anna Pou's husband looked concerned. Vince Panepinto had surprised Pou the previous evening by showing up at the hospital. A security guard had paged her through the overhead speakers. Panepinto had spent the night with Pou and the surgical nurses in the endoscopy suite, his tall frame squeezed onto a little stretcher. He charmed the nurses with his dark good looks, and they agreed Pou had done well after the breakup with her former boyfriend.

Panepinto left the hospital that morning to take care of their recently purchased home about a mile from Memorial. He had wanted Pou to join him, but she still had patients at the hospital, and the staff was not supposed to leave. "I'll be home before you know it," she'd told him.

"Oh my God, you need to get him," the nurse said. "Look outside." Pou joined her at the windows overlooking Clara Street. Water was gushing out of the sewer vents. They stared in disbelief. Then they jogged up three flights of stairs to the eighth floor to get a better look at the neighborhood. Water was flowing up Claiborne Avenue, a main city artery just north of the hospital.

Faces appeared at windows all over Memorial. Some doctors would later say the sight of the water advancing toward the hospital, pushing the hurricane debris ahead of it, was like something out of a movie: a glob of murderous slime from a '60s sci-fi thriller, or the mist-cloaked Angel of Death wafting down Egyptian streets to envelop the homes of firstborn sons in Cecil B. DeMille's *The Ten Commandments*. To a Life-Care patient's daughter, Angela McManus, who was standing on Memorial's smoking balcony, the blackness overtaking the ground looked like the shadow of a cloud.

A doctor told ICU nurse Cathy Green the water was coming back. "The water's coming back?" she asked. "From the river?" No, the doctor told her, not from the Mississippi River, from the lake. "From the lake? Our lake? Lake Pontchartrain, our lake?"

The doctor told Green that water from the massive saltwater estuary north of the city had already reached Claiborne Avenue. Green attempted a calculation. The intersection was probably fifty city blocks from the lakefront.

This told her that the water wasn't a meandering stream. It was like something she had watched on television the previous December, video footage of curious Indian Ocean beachgoers staring at a distant, muscular wave that failed to subside after breaking and instead punched across the sand, the gathering torrent of a tsunami about to flatten them.

There were certain signs, devastating signs, that told Green that an ICU patient was "crashing" toward death. This was that sign. We did not dodge a bullet, she thought. Lake Pontchartrain is emptying into our city. Very bad news is coming. It was the moment that everything changed.

Anna Pou kept calling her husband's cell phone. There was no answer.

NEWS OF THE waters prompted an unplanned midmorning meeting in the command center. It was hot, and someone bashed out the windows with a two-foot-high metal oxygen tank. Susan Mulderick announced that up to fifteen feet was expected around the hospital. Despite Memorial's flood-prone electrical system, its voluminous set of emergency plans did not contemplate the precise scenario they were facing, almost as if it would have been too horrible to countenance. Mulderick's emergency committee had ranked hurricanes, floods, and power outages among the highest-priority emergencies, but the hospital's preparedness plan for hurricanes did not anticipate flooding. The flooding plan did not anticipate the need to evacuate. The evacuation plan did not anticipate a potential loss of power or communications. Most critically, the hurricane plan relied on the assumption that the hospital's generators would keep working for a minimum of seventy-two hours, although they were never tested to run that long. The entire 273-page set of twenty separate plans offered no guidance for dealing with a complete power failure or for how to evacuate the hospital if the streets were flooded. There was no mention of using helicopters to evacuate the hospital. There was no contract or arrangement for a company to supply them.

Surveyors from the organization that accredited Memorial, known then as the Joint Commission on Accreditation of Healthcare Organizations, or JCAHO, had fanned out across the hospital for three days in late May of that year, examining everything from the signs in the stairwells to the details in patient medical records. They identified nearly two dozen areas of required or suggested improvement, a fairly typical number.

None of the deficiencies concerned Memorial's emergency plans. While it was possible to discern that a Memorial physician had failed to document a patient's informed consent for treatment, or failed to write progress notes and orders for care that were legible to nurses, or had left an anesthesia cart full of controlled substances open and unsecured—all of which had been noted in the last survey—when it came to emergency management plans, it was difficult to properly assess them until they were actually needed. "There's really no good way to test them rigorously," Dr. Robert Wise, who introduced national standards for emergency management at JCAHO's headquarters near Chicago, would say.

JCAHO was a nonprofit organization that Memorial, like most hospitals in the United States, hired to accredit it every third year. A "Gold Seal of Approval" from the organization paved the way for state licensure and Medicare and Medicaid reimbursement for treating patients. The Gold Seal was not a rarefied designation. Some 99 percent of hospitals achieved it, and details of their inspection deficiencies were hidden from public view. Most of JCAHO's revenues came from fees paid by the very hospitals it accredited. In some cases, its survey teams missed serious problems at hospitals that law enforcement investigators later uncovered.

Detailed emergency management standards were a relatively recent development. In the 1990s, disaster experts from the Department of Defense and Veterans Administration warned JCAHO that hospitals needed to prepare for a growing threat of attack on American soil. The existence of a Soviet bioweapons program was disclosed in 1992. The first assault on the World Trade Center occurred the next year, followed by the 1995 Oklahoma City bombing and the Aum Shinrikyo sarin gas subway attacks in Tokyo that killed thirteen and sent thousands to hospitals. Bombings of American assets outside the country, including the US embassies in Kenya and Tanzania in August 1998 and the naval destroyer USS *Cole* in Yemen in October 2000, raised worries about future incidents at home.

In the 1990s, less than a page of JCAHO's thick book of hospital accreditation standards was devoted to emergency preparedness, which was a decidedly unsexy field. Disaster managers were thought of as earnest, basement-dwelling creatures who drew up emergency plans and imposed fire drills that interrupted other people's work. Hospital leaders kept their distance.

When JCAHO proposed new emergency standards for the new millennium, hospital executives around the country protested them, fearing a costly, unfunded mandate. "Leave us alone!" was their message to JCAHO officials. "We're prepared."

JCAHO's governing board could veto proposed standards, and most of its members represented powerful industry organizations, including the American Hospital Association and the American Medical Association. Still, the board recognized the importance of better preparedness for hospital crises, and the proposed emergency standards went into effect in January 2001, nine months before the September 11, 2001, terrorist attacks.

Robert Wise, their author, had to admit that the standards were not based on much evidence. He was not convinced that they would make the hospitals that implemented them better prepared. He and his colleagues decided to wait until disasters happened, then debrief affected hospitals to figure out how much was vaporware and how much was real.

The new standards required hospitals to set up an incident command system for emergencies like the one Mulderick was currently heading for Katrina. Hospitals were also expected to coordinate plans with the wider community. Preparing for a flood in isolation did not make sense when there might be citywide power and water failures.

The 9/11 attacks and the subsequent mailings of anthrax-laced letters to politicians, media organizations, and others, which sickened nearly two dozen people and killed five of them, led to a narrowing of focus on particular types of hospital readiness. By 2005, more than a billion dollars had been made available to the nation's roughly five thousand hospitals to promote bioterrorism preparedness. Memorial's most detailed and by far its longest emergency planning scenario was written shortly after the 2001 attacks. This bioterrorism plan ran 101 pages, as opposed to the 11 pages devoted to hurricanes.

JCAHO had nothing to say about how realistic emergency plans had to be. Like biblical passages, the standards were written in a way that invited a generous range of interpretations. For the most part, surveyors did not check whether a hospital had the resources to do what it said it would do. Still, JCAHO's new standards far exceeded federal requirements, meaning that hospital leaders looking to avoid meeting the new mandates could seek accreditation from one of JCAHO's competitors.

Hospital emergency plans were supposed to be based on a yearly analysis of vulnerability to a variety of potential emergencies or "hazards." Every year since 2001, Mulderick had convened Memorial's emergency preparedness committee to go over a three-page form covering some forty-seven events, from volcanic eruptions to nonfunctioning fire alarms and an undefined "VIP situation." Unlike some other hospitals, Memorial had never hired a consultant for this task. Instead, Mulderick and her committee evaluated their own preparedness at a time they were under pressure from above to save money. The template the committee used could be downloaded for free from the Internet, and other New Orleans hospitals also used it. Mulderick and her committee produced a matrix of scores estimating probability, risk, and preparedness for each event. The latest rendering was rife with multiplication errors.

Mulderick's committee had rated the hospital's preparedness for power outages, generator failure, and floods as "good"—the top ranking on the scale. In designing their plans, committee members would later say they thought more about the constellation of emergencies that *had* happened rather than the worst things that *could* happen.

Whether scoring the "probability," "risk," and "preparedness" for volcano eruptions in Louisiana was a true contribution to disaster preparedness could certainly be questioned.

Years after Katrina, Bob Wise would look critically at Memorial's twenty separate emergency preparedness plans. "They have nothing to do with each other," he would say. "Nobody can know this many plans." Memorial, he felt, had missed the point of JCAHO's new preparedness standards, putting down on paper what was needed to pass accreditation inspection rather than focusing on cross-cutting "all hazards" preparedness. "It's not the guts of what you're supposed to be doing. It's covering your ass, is what it's doing." He found this all too often.

Memorial was now facing its first real crisis. Despite years of emergency preparedness committee meetings and revisions of the hospital's disaster plans, in many ways the hospital would have to wing it.

———

TO ICU NURSE manager Karen Wynn, the moment Susan Mulderick announced in their hastily organized meeting that floodwaters were headed their way, the atmosphere in the command room shifted from a hospital emergency to a military operation. There was one objective: act quickly before the power failed.

Nearly two hundred Memorial patients needed to be brought to safety. Mulderick suggested that the sickest, the ones most dependent on life support or mechanical aids, should go out first. That meant around two dozen patients in the ICUs, a similar number in the newborn nursery, high-risk pregnant mothers, and around a half dozen dialysis patients, with more showing up since the storm. There were also two bone marrow transplant patients highly vulnerable to developing infections. It would be difficult to care for them if all power was lost. Others at the command meeting agreed.

The tougher question was how to move them. Susan Mulderick knew the looming catastrophe was bigger than the staff at Memorial could handle alone. A National Guard unit had spent the hurricane at Memorial, and a few Acadian ambulances were parked on the ER ramp. Mulderick asked if Acadian could provide more ambulances and even helicopters. She sent an e-mail to her ex-husband, a buyer at a helicopter-transport company, asking if his firm could help get a helicopter to fly in medications and fly out patients. He wrote back to tell her that the company had already been hired to evacuate people from another private hospital, Tulane. He sent her the phone number of an Air National Guard major with a Baton Rouge exchange who was, he wrote, coordinating all civil and military evacuation efforts.

Karen Wynn wondered about the feasibility of an evacuation by helicopter. Memorial's heliport hadn't been used in years. The last time she could remember going up there was for an emergency drill in 1987, when Pope John Paul II visited New Orleans. She left that for others to contemplate and returned to the ICU to let the staff know that evacuation was imminent and they would need to get the patients' medical records and medications ready.

———

A CALL WENT out over the public address system. "Prayer service . . . ten thirty a.m." Everyone at the hospital was invited to attend.

Father John Marse was the only chaplain present at Memorial during the storm. He had decided to stay after hearing the voice of God calling him to serve. Now the Catholic father carried his sacramentary and lectionary out of the dim Myron C. Madden Chapel, windowless but for the narrow, stained-glass strips that decorated its two wooden doors. He stood with several dozen people in the well-lit hospital entrance lobby. Father Marse, who spoke quickly in a Southern drawl, began reading from Matthew:

And, behold, there arose a great tempest in the sea, insomuch that the ship was covered with the waves: but he was asleep. And his disciples came to him, and woke him, saying, Lord, save us: we perish. And he saith unto them, Why are ye fearful, O ye of little faith? Then he arose, and rebuked the winds and the sea; and there was a great calm.

We're in this storm, Marse said in a brief homily for those gathered before him. And Jesus is with us, no matter what the outcome is.

Marse couldn't help noticing that the water outside the windows of the entrance rose halfway up the side of a fire hydrant during the time he spoke.

Sandra Cordray, a community relations manager who was the designated communications leader for Katrina, asked Marse to attend all future command meetings. Memorial needed help from every possible power.

Memorial had another power at its disposal by virtue of having been swallowed by a hospital chain. Cordray took charge of communicating with executives at Memorial's parent company, Tenet Healthcare. With phone connections difficult to make, but e-mail still functioning, she wrote for help, explaining that water was rising in Memorial's basement and was expected to keep rising for days. The hospital was locked down because of reports of looting in the area, and other hospitals were evacuating. She said that the National Guard was present at the hospital, and she forwarded the phone number of the Air National Guard major identified by Mulderick's ex-husband in the hopes that someone at headquarters could contact him. She also shared what she was hearing about the increasingly frightening situation in New Orleans.

From: Cordray, Sandra

Sent: Tuesday, August 30, 2005 11:00 AM

Subject: reports

>We are receiving reports that the inmates at the prison near Tulane have taken over.

From: Cordray, Sandra

Sent: Tuesday, August 30, 2005 11:07 AM

Subject: RE: reports

>Break in the 17th street canal levee—200 feet wide flooding New Orleans

Cordray's e-mails to Tenet's Dallas headquarters grew more panicked by the minute. Sean Fowler, Memorial's chief operating officer, pulled his chair up to hers and instructed her as she typed. Memorial needed to evacuate its patients. Memorial needed medicines and blood products. What did Tenet have in terms of supplies, medicines, water, and food? How quickly could the company deliver them? What kind of airlift and ground resources was the corporate office coordinating?

WE NEED PATIENTS OUT OF HERE NOW!
Please can you take patients.
Is anyone out there?

Michael Arvin, an executive at Tenet headquarters, finally responded. "We have been told getting into the city is not going to happen," he wrote. "Have you contacted the National Guard?" It was an odd question. Cordray had already informed Arvin that Guard members were at the hospital. That contingent alone could not solve all these problems.

Arvin, in Texas, had no background in emergency management. His normal job was to direct business development for Tenet in the Gulf Coast region, which he referred to as "the market." It was amazing how quickly his duties had changed. Two days earlier, Arvin had interrupted a tennis match with his kids at a Dallas country club to join a conference call with the CEOs of Tenet hospitals in the Gulf region as Katrina took aim at the coastline. Now, three of Tenet's six hurricane-affected hospitals needed to evacuate.

Tenet did not have preexisting contracts with medical transport companies. The corporate headquarters did not have an incident command system in place for emergencies. One of its executives had served in the National Guard and knew something about crisis management, but he was on vacation and offered tips by cell phone from a secluded beach retreat in Oregon.

Arvin let Cordray know that the company was working on securing medicines and blood for Memorial, but he was not sure how to get anything to her. Again he mentioned the National Guard, explaining that Memorial's sister hospital, Tenet's Lindy Boggs Medical Center, the former Catholic hospital Mercy, was waiting for troops to arrive.

> We suggest you do the same. If you are beginning your plans to evacuate it is our understanding the National Guard is coordinating. Good luck.

Cordray wrote back, incredulous:

> Are you telling us we are on our own and you cannot help?

———

AT 12:28 P.M., Memorial's director of case management took matters into her own hands. She typed "HELP!!!!" in the subject line of an e-mail and sent it to colleagues at other Tenet hospitals outside New Orleans. She told them the hospital was expecting fifteen feet of water and it needed to find places for its current census of 187 patients. Hospitals that might accept them should contact Arvin at Tenet headquarters.

Arvin was quickly inundated with responses. Many hospitals offered space and at least one offered to send relief staff. But Arvin, too, had been busy trying to line up assistance, contacting Tenet hospitals in Houston and Nacogdoches. His message back to the Memorial administrator who sounded the alarm was brusque:

> please route any requests through to me and Bob Smith. We are getting overwhelmed with your MAY DAY to the entire company!!

Among the hospitals that responded was Atlanta Medical Center. Like Memorial, Atlanta was a former Baptist hospital founded in the early 1900s and now owned by Tenet. By e-mail and phone, its hospital executives offered support, including aeromedical helicopters to help evacuate Memorial's patients.

Michael Arvin reined them in, saying that the National Guard was coordinating all relief efforts. The Atlanta CEO felt the bit.

> Michael, per our conversation, we will "sit tight" unless we hear from you or someone at the Dallas office regarding the need for assistance in the evacuation of patients.

———

AT MEMORIAL, word spread that all available doctors and nurse managers should report to the ER ambulance ramp, which overlooked Clara Street. Anna Pou walked out of the hot hospital into a bright, slightly breezy day. In a small parking lot across the street, water was rising up the wheel wells of the cars.

Dr. Richard Deichmann, the head of the internal medicine department, told the doctors that the hospital was going to be evacuated. They needed to work on getting patients transferred, the sickest first.

Deichmann took stock of who was present and reassigned two physicians to cover each of the fifteen patient wards. At the suggestion of Dr. Horace Baltz, to avoid duplicating work, doctors would no longer visit their own private patients unless they were on the designated ward. The doctors were to categorize every patient and to prepare a count by four p.m. Patients would be marked down for transfer to one of several types of care settings: an ICU, a general hospital ward, a rehabilitation facility, or a nursing home. Patients ready to be discharged could be given a week's worth of medications and sent on to an evacuation center. The medical staff should get the patients packed up and work on transfer orders.

Pou paired up with a thirty-five-year-old internist, Kathleen Fournier, and went to the fourth floor, where Pou had several surgical patients. She knew the nurses well, and one confided in her that many of the staff and patients were frightened and worried about their homes and their loved ones outside the hospital. Pou met with the nurses and offered what reassurance she could.

Pou and Fournier walked from patient to patient, evaluating and classifying them. There were around two dozen, a full complement. Many had been put in wheelchairs and pushed to a central nursing station to sit with fans blowing on them.

Nurses began photocopying charts and readying a few of the sicker patients to go out first. Throughout the day, Pou shuttled back and forth to the fourth floor, bringing the nurses whatever news she heard.

One of Memorial's veteran critical care doctors was Ewing Cook, a pulmonologist who was Dr. John Thiele's former partner. Cook took responsibility for another section of the fourth floor, replacing his son, also a doctor, who had gone home the previous night and was prevented from returning by the flooding. To ease the load on nurses, Cook decided all but the most essential treatments and care should be discontinued. Bryant King, a thirty-five-year-old internist who had recently joined Memorial as part of its new inpatient hospitalist program, caring for other doctors' patients during their hospital stays, came to check on one of his patients there. Bucking the directive to see only patients in assigned wards, he still planned to submit billing claims on his existing patients as usual. He canceled the senior doctor's order to turn off his patient's heart monitor. Cook found out and was furious. He thought that the junior doctor did not understand the circumstances, and he directed the nurse to reinstate his instructions. "I'm in charge of this floor," he told the nurse in front of King. "I told you what to do; I don't care what any other doctor says. Do it."

Outside on the ER ramp, maintenance workers watched a fuel truck approach to top off the generator tanks. The shiny chrome truck inched toward the hospital along the wrong side of Napoleon Avenue in the lane where the water was shallower. As the tanker turned the corner onto Magnolia Street a hundred yards away from the hospital it stopped, backed up, and left. "Oh jeez," an electrician said, disheartened. The driver seemed to have judged he couldn't make it the rest of the way without flooding his vehicle.

Workers paddled one of the small, flat-bottomed boats kept for minor street flooding to the ER and carried it to the top of the ambulance ramp, which was dry. With dark humor, Susan Mulderick jumped in with chief financial officer Curtis Dosch and hammed for the maintenance chief's camera, pretending to row. Behind them, Clara Street was a rising lake, calm enough to bear an image of the dappled blue sky, to double the stature of twisty-limbed oaks along Napoleon and add two reflected floors to the cancer institute across the street while now engulfing the cars in its parking lot to their door handles.

Downstairs in the basement, puddles expanded on the floor. Maintenance staff shut off some lighting and electrical panels to try to prevent a fire. An electrician heard the sound of a waterfall pouring through the breached seals of a ground-level window. Two carpenters raced to buttress the loading dock against flooding with custom-built plywood walls. They layered duct tape around a vulnerable set of doors, but water sought its level, spurting through cracks ten feet into the hospital shop.

The supplies that Mulderick and the maintenance crew had moved out of the basement during the storm had been restored shortly after it. Now teams of volunteers rushed to remove them again as water flowed up the drains, a reprise of 1926.

The pets, too, had been moved back down and were now being taken up to the parking garage facing Magnolia Street. Dr. Ewing Cook and his wife, Minnie, joined a procession bearing creatures and cages. The Cooks and their children and pets always stayed for hurricanes. Recently, not long after his son graduated from medical school, Ewing had retired from clinical practice. He now served as chief medical officer after working at the hospital for a quarter century. Minnie was one of several Baptist nurses who gave birth to daughters who grew up, studied nursing, and replaced them. Her daughter now worked in one of the ICUs with another second-generation RN, Lori Budo, whose mother had once been nursing director there.

The Cook entourage included their daughter's three cats and Rolfie, her giant, furry Newfoundland. Minnie walked ahead with one of the cats and Rolfie on the leash, while Ewing followed dragging the dog's four-foot-long, folded metal cage.

At the top of the staircase, Minnie turned and waited for Ewing, but he and the cage didn't appear. "Dr. Cook's down in the security office," someone came up and told her. "You might want to go see about him."

The sixty-one-year-old doctor had nearly passed out in the heat on his way upstairs lugging the forty-pound cage. A security guard had grabbed him and brought him to his office by the stairwell.

Minnie thought Ewing was having another heart attack. He'd had two, the most recent one only months earlier when he'd borne the pain like a stoic, continuing to load floor tiles into his car at Home Depot until she noticed he was gray and insisted he go to the hospital.

This time heat exhaustion had caused his symptoms. Cook rested, drank fluids, and recovered.

———

A RUSTING HELIPAD sat atop the hospital's Magnolia Street parking garage on the southwest side of the campus, 114 feet above sea level. Memories of its use had faded like the blue letters painted on its tarmac: SBH, for Southern Baptist Hospital—the name the hospital hadn't officially carried in more than a decade.

The helipad, known as a Helistop, had been opened with fanfare in

1985. In what only a hospital marketing newsletter would proclaim as a "time-saving, potentially life-saving feat of logistics," the building project had involved extending the garage elevator two floors higher to allow direct helipad access from the hospital's emergency room and sixth-floor maternity unit.

The Helistop had special features. Pilots could illuminate the landing lights remotely by setting their VHF radios to a particular frequency and pulsing the switch on their microphones. The lights alerted hospital staff to prepare for an arrival. Landings could take place day or night in most types of weather.

The elevators and the landing lights relied on electricity. From that standpoint, the helipad design no longer represented a time-saving or lifesaving feat. The garage elevators had not been wired to the backup electrical system, rendering them useless without utility power. It was now impossible to take a patient directly from within the hospital to the helipad.

Several hospital administrators and others trudged up the seemingly endless garage staircase to assess the situation. The picture of decrepitude that met them raised a more serious question about the Helistop. Would it buckle under the weight of a helicopter? The engineers in the group were unsure. Whereas the platform once could accommodate an aircraft weight of 20,000 pounds, the hospital had recently spent upward of $100,000 in repairs merely to keep it from collapsing onto the eight-story parking garage below.

One doctor lingered on the helipad after everyone else departed. Paul Primeaux, an anesthesiologist in a hospital where surgery was no longer being performed, was one of several physicians who had no clinical responsibilities because of the situation. (Others included two radiologists and a pathologist, doctors who didn't normally see patients but provided critical services to them.) Primeaux had never been up to the helipad before and had joined the group out of curiosity.

Standing atop the thin platform was dizzying. Its flat edges dropped away to nothingness as breezes whooshed across it, unhindered by almost any other structure as tall as it for miles. Before him, to the west, the flooded streets of the Freret neighborhood stretched out like long mirrors, reflecting treetops and the top halves of double-shotgun homes. Southward, the land sloped up to the banks of the Mississippi River. Church steeples rose above debris-strewn rooftops. To the northeast, beyond the upper stories of the main hospital, he could see the skyscrapers of downtown a mile or so away and the Superdome, the city's shelter of last resort. The storm had ripped away most of the gleaming white outer layers of its roof. The north side of the helipad led to the elevator tower through a tunnel full of glass from broken windows.

Primeaux heard the thrum of helicopter rotors and looked up at the sky. He saw a massive, dark-olive military helicopter with the numbers "585" painted in white across its nose. It looked like a Black Hawk. Primeaux gave it a casual, friendly wave. He did not mean to signal it, but the pilot began lowering his aircraft toward the spindly-legged helipad.

The Black Hawk, weighing more than 11,000 pounds empty, touched down. It sat, rotors spinning, framed by blue sky and wispy clouds. The helipad held.

The pilot asked Primeaux if there were people who needed to be evacuated. Primeaux said yes and suggested a sick newborn. The pilot checked with his commander and received permission to take one. Primeaux ran down the parking garage stairway and into the hospital to alert the incident command team. Then he went up to the neonatal ICU, where critically ill babies were being tucked into portable incubators, cradles, and cribs in preparation for transport.

The lack of functioning garage elevators turned the journey between the maternity unit and the Helistop from "immediate access" to long and circuitous. When the first baby finally reached the helipad, the waiting pilot was unhappy. "That took too long," he said. Thousands of people needed help across the city. He had spoken with his commander and wouldn't be returning. "You've got to figure out a better system."

———

"OUR HELIPORT IS operational. We can receive air," Memorial emergency communications leader Sandra Cordray wrote just after noon to Tenet's regional business development director Michael Arvin at Tenet headquarters. The panicked calls and e-mails to make transport plans began to produce results. A hospital in Baton Rouge agreed to take all of Memorial's babies; sixteen were critically ill. Coast Guard helicopters were expected to arrive in the afternoon to transport them and several adult ICU patients. The plan was coordinated with the help of a nurse's husband who happened to be a junior grade lieutenant and medic working at the Coast Guard's emergency command center in Alexandria, Louisiana. The National Guard promised to move thirty-five medical and surgical patients to a Tenet hospital in Texas via high-water troop hauler trucks with big tires and high platforms.

That would still leave well over one hundred Memorial patients and hundreds of other people in the hospital, and there were signs that government assistance might not be sustained. In the midafternoon, Arvin and his boss, Bob Smith—Tenet's senior vice president for operations in the Texas–Gulf Coast region, a top official who reported to the company's chief operations officer—received an e-mail with a desperate plea for help from the Federation of American Hospitals. "Senator Landrieu's office called and is begging us to help them fill in emergency rescue gaps in Louisiana," it said. "Apparently the state's emergency response capability is falling woefully short." Louisiana senator Mary Landrieu was asking hospitals in surrounding areas to lend their Medevac helicopters to help evacuate patients in the coming day. The author of the e-mail asked hospitals to respond "asap."

Despite the request, and the fact that executives from some Tenet hospitals, like Atlanta, had already expressed a willingness to provide evacuation support, Tenet officials continued to rely on governmental resources to respond to the emergency.

———

BY MIDAFTERNOON, the waters around Memorial had climbed partway up the sloping emergency room ramp, where a camouflage-green National Guard troop hauler stood. Patients emerged from the ER, some pushed in wheelchairs, others using walkers, and were guided to the truck by hospital staff with sweat-soaked shirts and hair wet with perspiration. Anna Pou worked among them.

Pou and her colleagues loaded about a dozen people onto the open truck bed. They sat squeezed together along its sides on simple metal benches beneath a green metal frame. Hospital security personnel wearing blue bulletproof vests joined the effort to lift patients onto the chest-high platform. Several nurses climbed aboard to accompany the patients out of the city. One still wore her neat white tights despite the heat.

Beyond the truck, a man in a striped shirt waded along Napoleon Avenue in water up to his chest. One of the Memorial security guards walked atop the raised brick siding to the submerged end of the ramp. Gripping a traffic sign for balance, he leaned out over the water in the direction of the wading man and gestured away from the hospital. Even if the man didn't hear what was said, the message seemed clear: he was being warned away from the hospital, not welcomed there.

The platform of the truck wasn't much higher than the water level. A limited time remained to rescue patients by road.

At about four p.m., the truck's large wheels churned through the water, rolled past downed crepe myrtle trees at the front of the old hospital building, and then headed west. Hospital leaders had arranged for the patients to be accepted at a hospital in Nacogdoches, Texas. They planned to send twenty-seven more patients there when a second truck arrived.

—

"IT'S TIME TO GO!" In the neonatal ICU, portable plastic bassinets, normally used to carry babies to their mothers' rooms, were lined up on the ground with two babies each and their recent medical records. To the relief of the nurses, the NICU had not yet switched to computerized charts, which would have taken a long time to print and compile. A nurse's husband sat in a chair cradling a skinny, diapered neonate against his chest to comfort it; one of its tiny brown feet stretched down to balance atop the man's beer gut as someone snapped a picture. The man was one of many family members who were now volunteering with important nonmedical tasks.

The sickest babies were placed in transport isolettes—large, self-contained incubators on wheels complete with oxygen tanks, warming pads, and battery-powered pumps that administered IV fluids. The staff rolled one of them carrying two very sick babies to the single elevator working on backup power in the medical center's newer Clara Wing. The incubator was too tall to travel through the garage on the back of a pickup truck, so staff pushed the wheeled machine up the parking garage's down ramp, circling to the ninth story. Then five men in sweat-soaked T-shirts squeezed around the incubator and began to heave it up three sets of fire-escape stairs to the helipad. The machine that provided oxygen to one of the babies wasn't working, so a nurse climbed the staircase beside the men, pushing oxygen from a small tank into the baby's airways by repeatedly compressing a self-inflating bag the size and shape of a large lemon. She worked with a worried expression, her hand inserted in a round opening in the incubator.

When they reached the top, none of the expected Coast Guard helicopters awaited the babies. In the late afternoon someone at Memorial forwarded approach maps and geographic coordinates to a Coast Guard representative. Pilots from out of town were having trouble locating Memorial Medical Center. The helipad still bore markings indicating the old name of the hospital, Southern Baptist, and it hadn't been certified for use in years.

The babies waited for the Coast Guard helicopters in the covered tunnel, their incubators plugged into a power outlet supplied by a hospital generator. A neonatal specialist wearing green scrubs paced from the holding area to the helipad, growing increasingly worried as time passed. The babies were hot; one was having complications that might require urgent surgery. The neonatologist, Dr. Juan Jorge Gershanik, looked down at the water surrounding Memorial and imagined what it would be like if all power went out. The children would be goners. It would be a death sentence. He felt like he was in a movie.

He went to speak with internal medicine department chairman Richard Deichmann, who was outfitted with a two-way radio to communicate with other hospital employees as he directed movements on the helipad. Small private helicopters were landing, including one that dropped off the long-awaited drug supplies. Other pilots were willing to take sick elderly patients but not sick neonates, who typically required more specialized care.

Could Deichmann convince the pilots to transport babies instead? "We can't wait any longer," Gershanik said. "Please, Richard, see if any of them can take us."

"I'm at their mercy," Deichmann replied, but when another helicopter landed, he turned and gave Gershanik a pointed look. The neonatologist didn't know what the look meant, but he rushed toward the helicopter, pushing the incubator ahead of him.

"No way," the pilot said. The giant incubator couldn't fit in his three-seat helicopter. The babies would have to wait.

"They can't wait," Gershanik said. More than an hour had passed on the helipad. It was getting close to sunset. "I really think they're running out of time," Gershanik said.

They were also running out of backup oxygen tanks on the helipad, and the nursery staff had to trek back into the hospital several times to get more. Some of the tanks went to elderly ICU patients also arriving on the helipad.

On the eighth floor in the ICU, nurse manager Karen Wynn, a blur of motion in wrinkled blue scrubs, was helping get them there. With the air-conditioning off for more than a full day and the ICU equipment producing heat, it was getting unbearable. The windows that hadn't broken were sealed shut, some were still covered in plywood, and it was moist inside, humid. People were sweating. She told her staff they could change from their scrubs to shorts if they had them.

White box fans were moved back and forth between patients. Some in the unit weren't terribly sick, but others were fragile and lacked resilience. The tiniest change in their environment threatened their homeostasis. The heat menaced them.

Wynn helped pry boards off of the inside of the windows, hoping to uncover cracked and broken panes that would let in some air. Male nurses and the housekeeping director took turns battering the windows Katrina had left intact with a tall metal pole normally used for hanging bags of intravenous fluid, finally shattering them.

When Karen Wynn put a patient on the elevator she heard a sound like Niagara Falls. The shaft was filling. A security guard stayed in the elevator to ensure that nobody pressed the button for the basement. Wynn wanted to get her patients off the eighth floor. Time was of the essence. Even if the generator power didn't go out, they were going to have to shut down the elevator soon for safety.

The ICU had received a call for more patients on the helipad: "We need some more! Helicopters are waiting!" It was taking about forty-five minutes to get each patient to the helipad. Veteran surgical ICU nurse Cheri Landry, entrusted with the radio on the eighth floor, passed the word to her colleagues. "We're losing helicopters, we have to move faster."

Wynn's staff, helped by some of their accompanying relatives, worked furiously. It was taking so long for the single elevator to arrive that they started carrying some patients down the stairwells. They rolled patients onto their sides, pushed a blanket up against their sweaty backs, then rolled them the other way and pulled the blanket out so it was lying underneath them. Volunteers grabbed onto the sides of the blankets, gathered up the slack, and lifted the patients from their beds.

Another surgical ICU nurse, Lori Budo, gripped a flashlight under her chin as she navigated the dark stairwell alongside a patient. When she came back up, she collected flashlights and tape and directed a volunteer to fix them to the railings.

One of the sickest patients in the ICU was seventy-seven-year-old Helen Breckenridge, a former drapery maker and interior decorator who had been a patient at Memorial for about a week. Breckenridge had developed complications of lung and heart disease and diabetes, and had been in hospice care at another hospital. That meant that the treatments she was receiving had been focused on affording her comfort rather than extending her life. She was receiving morphine and powerful sedatives and, when she stopped eating, perhaps as a result of the sedation or her worsening disease, the hospice had not provided nutrition or fluids. Her brother, a physician at another New Orleans hospital, couldn't stand to watch her wither away. He believed she had been forced to sign paperwork that led to her hospice admittance and that she didn't really want to be there. He went to court to have her removed from hospice and transferred to Memorial for aggressive treatment in the ICU.

Now, a team of medical workers labored to move Breckenridge. One squeezed air into her lungs by hand and others kept an eye on the multiple battery-powered pumps that delivered drugs into her veins to regulate her fragile circulatory system. They traveled downstairs from the eighth floor.

"Bring her back up," a doctor said when she arrived downstairs. "She can't go in the first sweep."

Memorial's doctors, meeting earlier, had established an exception to the protocol of prioritizing the sickest patients and those whose lives relied on machines. They had decided that all patients with Do Not Resuscitate orders would be prioritized last for evacuation. There were four DNR patients in the ICU, including Breckenridge and Jannie Burgess, the African American nurse who had once cared for patients at hospitals where she herself could not be treated.

A DNR order was signed by a doctor, almost always with the informed consent of a patient or health-care proxy. Informed consent was a legal concept established beginning in the 1950s in the United States. It was designed to protect patient autonomy in medical decision making, in the context of historical abuses. Doctors were required to disclose the nature, risks, benefits, and alternatives of the medical interventions they proposed. A DNR order meant one thing: a patient whose heartbeat or breathing had stopped should not be revived. A DNR order was different from a living will, which under Louisiana law allowed patients with a "terminal and irreversible condition" to request in advance that "life-sustaining procedures" be withheld or withdrawn.

But the doctor who suggested at the meeting that DNR patients go last had a different understanding, he later explained. Medical chairman Richard Deichmann said that he thought the law required patients with DNR orders to have a certified terminal or irreversible condition, and at Memorial he believed they should go last because they would have had the "least to lose" compared with other patients if calamity struck.

Other doctors at the meeting had agreed with Deichmann's plan. Bill Armington, a neuroradiologist, later said he thought that patients who did not wish their lives to be prolonged by extraordinary measures wouldn't want to be saved at the expense of others—though there was nothing in the orders or in Memorial's disaster plans that stated this. This decision about evacuation priorities would perhaps not be a momentous one—as long as the hospital was emptied quickly.

Nurse manager Karen Wynn learned of the doctors' decision from two doctors, Ewing Cook and Roy Culotta, and shared the information with Susan Mulderick. The plan was also made clear to a nurse helping transport Breckenridge: first "the most salvageable had to go."

By the time Breckenridge was returned to the ICU, she was barely alive. They plugged her pumps and drips back into the emergency wall outlets and restored her mechanical ventilator, but she soon died, a death perhaps imminent but nonetheless seemingly the first in the hospital to be hastened by Katrina. A staff member summoned Dr. Horace Baltz to pronounce her death, and the white-haired doctor came panting up the staircase.

Rodney Scott, a sixty-three-year-old licensed practical nurse who'd once worked at Baptist, was brought down from the ICU, where he was recovering from a heart attack and multiple surgeries. But he weighed well over three hundred pounds, and a doctor feared he might get stuck in the narrow passageway being used to funnel patients into the garage. Worried this would back up the evacuation line, the doctor decided Scott should be the last patient to leave the hospital. Scott was taken to a patient unit on the fourth floor to wait.

———

UP ON THE HELIPAD, neonatologist Gershanik was deciding what to do about the two sick babies whose incubator didn't fit on the small helicopter. Gershanik depended heavily on technology to keep his critically ill newborns alive. Transporting babies this sick without an incubator was unthinkable.

And then it wasn't. Gershanik decided to take the risk. He climbed into the seat next to the pilot and cradled a six-week-old preemie wrapped in blankets in his arms. "Baby Boy S" had been born at twenty-four weeks with severely underdeveloped lungs and still weighed less than a kilogram. Gershanik dispensed rapid puffs of oxygen with squeezes of the reinflating bag, attempting to replicate the work of a sophisticated machine that sent oscillating waves of oxygen into the baby's lungs. Someone placed the other tiny baby from the incubator into the arms of a nurse, who folded herself into the backseat of the helicopter. She slid the baby under her scrub shirt, decorated with pink and blue baby footprints.

As soon as they lifted off, Gershanik grew afraid. A cold draft circulated through the helicopter, and he tried to shield the baby with his body. It was getting dark. He could easily, without knowing it, dislodge the tiny tube in the baby's windpipe. He had brought no machine to check the level of oxygen in the baby's blood. The cacophony of the helicopter blades rendered his stethoscope useless. It would be impossible to listen to the baby's chest for breath sounds. What did I do? he wondered. Did I make the right decision? Practically the only way to know whether the baby was still alive was to use his free hand to pinch the baby's foot and feel whether he withdrew it. Gershanik's other hand was getting cramped from rapidly squeezing the oxygen bag. He made a silent promise: If this baby lives, I'll never complain about anything again.

The pilot announced that he had to stop for fuel. Gershanik couldn't believe it. They landed at a refueling site for petroleum-industry helicopters. A planned five-minute stop stretched into ten, then fifteen, then twenty-five minutes. Gershanik pulled out his penlight and shined it on the baby. Still alive. He swung the light to the baby's oxygen tank. Nearly empty. Two US Army helicopters had landed after them, but were getting served first. Gershanik protested to the pilot. "Sir, the babies are not going to make it." The pilot told him the Army helicopters were rescuing people from rooftops. "Otherwise they'll die as well."

For a moment, Gershanik considered the larger reality, the competing priorities that had emerged as waters suffocated an entire city. He was only doing what is ingrained in a doctor—advocating for his own patients—but now he saw that the struggle to save lives extended far beyond the two critically ill neonates in the helicopter, or Memorial's entire population of sick babies, or even the whole hospital, much as it had seemed like the universe when he was back there. He used the delay to switch oxygen tanks with some difficulty. He apologized for his impatience.

Back on the helipad at Memorial, some of the remaining neonatal-ICU nurses had taken to waving down passing helicopters like hitchhikers putting out a thumb. The activity on the helipad drew the attention of a mass of hospital onlookers, who had climbed upstairs to watch. They were hot and had only time on their hands. The air of chaos surprised a newly arrived coordinator for Acadian, who was moving from hospital to hospital with several small medical helicopters to evacuate critical patients. Other hospitals had been more organized. On the northeast edge of Memorial's helipad, he put down a cooler filled with sandwiches for his hardworking flight crews. It was promptly ransacked and emptied by Memorial staff and strangers loitering on the tarmac.

The doctors on the helipad had gone from practicing medicine to, at least in one case, arguing with a Coast Guard pilot about how many patients could fit in his helicopter. The pilot flew away to rescue people elsewhere. A nurse who was also an Air Force captain witnessed the scene and was upset at losing a helicopter. She knew that these pilots ruled the air and, having logged thousands of search-and-rescue flight hours, could be trusted to know their capacity. She approached Dr. Richard Deichmann, the chairman of medical services managing the helipad, and told him the Air Force had trained her to run a flight line in an emergency. He put her in charge, and she cleared the helipad of doctors and patients, sending them to wait in the wind-protection tunnel. She shooed people off the hospital rooftops so that the pilots could keep landing.

Memorial staff members began loading the last group of critically ill babies onto a helicopter. Its pilot had a flight plan for a hospital west of

Baton Rouge instead of the hospital that had agreed to accept Memorial's neonates.

The neonatal ICU nurses resisted. They had no idea whether the other hospital was prepared to support the lives of their fragile charges. Richard Deichmann said the babies could leave. "The babies will be taken to wherever the pilot is going," he told the nurses and, via walkie-talkie, their director in the hospital. "This is a disaster."

"Then we will remove the babies from the helicopter," the nursing director in charge of the neonates radioed back, contradicting him in spite of the unwritten hospital hierarchy that put doctors on top. She told Deichmann that the pilot had to find a way to fly to Baton Rouge or she would not allow him to take the neonates. Within minutes the pilot received approval for a flight plan to Baton Rouge.

A text message arrived a few hours later from Baton Rouge. All the babies had made it, including Gershanik's. Baby Boy S's oxygen level on arrival matched what it had been on the high-tech machines, thanks to the doctor's life-support improvisations. The babies were more resilient than the doctor had imagined.

———

AS SOON AS Anna Pou walked back into the hospital after helping load patients onto the National Guard trucks, a nurse came to tell her that a Code Blue medical emergency had been called on LifeCare, the long-term acute care hospital that leased the seventh floor. "I think you better go, because I don't think they have doctors up there," the nurse said.

The stairs were slippery with condensation, but Pou ran up six flights in the heat rather than wait for the one working elevator. A seventy-three-year-old man had developed a very slow heartbeat just before three p.m. and had stopped breathing. A team of nurses had surrounded his bed and pulled up a crash cart filled with the supplies needed to try to resuscitate him. As the only doctor present, Pou took charge.

She stepped behind the man's bed and, with the help of a LifeCare respiratory therapist, tipped his head back with some difficulty. The man was extremely thin, and his neck was stiff and bent. Using the metal blade of a laryngoscope, she scooped his tongue and pulled his jaw up. Then, with a battery-powered light on the scope to guide her, she carefully inserted a tube between his vocal cords and into his airway. The tube was connected to a ventilator plugged into a red emergency outlet. It pumped oxygen into the man's lungs from a supply that ran through pipes in the hospital's walls, fed by a giant tank of pressurized gas that did not depend on electricity.

The electrocardiograph showed that the lower chambers of the man's heart had stopped beating effectively and begun quivering—fibrillation—which could result in death in minutes. The team that gathered had initiated a code, a prescribed sequence of drugs and electric shocks, interspersed with CPR, to attempt to restore a more normal heart rhythm. An ER doctor arrived and took over for Pou. Resuscitating patients was not a typical job for a head and neck surgeon. Despite all their attempts to save the man, he did not survive. He was Dr. John Thiele's patient, and with no doctors specifically assigned to LifeCare, Thiele had come upstairs and examined him late that morning, finding his condition stable.

After they called off the code, Pou introduced herself to the respiratory therapist who had assisted her. "How y'all doing?" she asked. "Making out OK up here?" They were, albeit feeling somewhat forgotten. While LifeCare's medical director and the doctors who admitted the most patients to LifeCare were absent for the storm, none of the physicians who were present had been eager to take responsibility for the seventh floor when dividing up the wards, even though one, Roy Culotta, had pressed LifeCare staff into finding extra room for his grandmother for safety before the storm because her nursing home did not evacuate. "What about us?" a senior LifeCare manager, nurse executive Therese Mendez, had asked at one doctors' meeting. A female doctor had given

Mendez her phone number and location. "Don't call me for a runny nose," she said. A male doctor told the woman, "You don't have to do that. You're not under any obligation at all."

That the doctors would feel more of a duty to care for Memorial patients versus LifeCare patients during the disaster surprised some LifeCare employees. Many of the available doctors were on staff at both hospitals. Some had patients on LifeCare, as Thiele did, and also Pou, who had checked on a man with a jaw tumor over the weekend.

LifeCare's leaders were grateful for the Code Blue efforts. "Great response from team and MD's," one typed on a notepad computer in LifeCare's pharmacy. Since midday, LifeCare staff had "talked" to corporate colleagues in Shreveport in real time via a software program, pcAnywhere, normally employed by help-desk specialists to access computers remotely. As the day progressed, confusion had deepened over LifeCare's evacuation prospects.

Diane Robichaux, an assistant administrator who was seven months pregnant, had shouldered the role of incident commander for LifeCare's New Orleans hospitals to allow the senior administrator to leave the city before the storm with his family, which included a child with special needs. Now, on backup power with limited phone and Internet connectivity, Robichaux was attempting to manage evacuations for LifeCare's patients not only at Memorial, where she was, but also at another LifeCare campus near the New Orleans airport.

In the late morning, she had gone downstairs to Memorial's incident command leaders, provided a list of LifeCare's most critical patients, and told them that LifeCare was trying to do whatever was possible to move its own patients. An Acadian ambulance paramedic on-site at Memorial registered surprise that LifeCare was awaiting direction from corporate officials, as he believed Acadian had a transportation contract with LifeCare, and he wanted to help them.

In the command center, Memorial's leaders informed Robichaux that the helipad was operational and LifeCare could land helicopters on it.

Robichaux came back upstairs and shared the news via the chat connection with a corporate contact in Shreveport, Robbye Dubois, LifeCare's senior vice president for clinical services. Robichaux sent Dubois a list of fifty-three LifeCare patients who needed to leave Memorial (two of the original fifty-five had died). Most critically, seven relied on ventilators, one on an assisted-breathing device, and five needed dialysis.

The reply from Shreveport appeared letter by letter on the screen, tracking backward, excruciatingly, whenever a typed mistake was corrected. Shreveport employees were in contact with a man named Knox Andress, who, they believed, worked with FEMA in Baton Rouge. He'd said FEMA and the Louisiana Department of Health and Hospitals were aware of LifeCare's situation and planned to evacuate patients on ventilators first. Because all of the hospitals needed help, he could not tell them when, exactly, the cavalry would arrive.

They waited. An employee in Shreveport offered to make calls for LifeCare staff members in New Orleans who wanted to let their families know they were OK. Some had been unable to contact loved ones for almost two days. Phone numbers and messages were passed on the chat connection: "Yvette is alive, love you guys"; "I'm alright cant reach you, tell Marvin that I love him."

Then, in the midafternoon, came an urgent offer from Memorial, followed by confusion. LifeCare patients could go out on the Coast Guard helicopters heading for Baton Rouge. LifeCare had twenty minutes to decide whether to send patients this way.

Before they could answer, the offer was withdrawn. The Memorial representative had assumed that LifeCare's patients were included in the patient count sent to the Coast Guard, but it wasn't true. When Memorial incident commander Susan Mulderick had reached an air evacuation coordinator at the Coast Guard's emergency command center in Alexandria, Louisiana, by phone in the early afternoon, he had logged her request to transport two hundred people—just slightly more than the number of Memorial patients. "LifeCare patients were not included. Repeat NOT included," Robichaux typed to her Shreveport colleagues.

Memorial, Robichaux wrote, had worked on the assumption that FEMA was coordinating LifeCare's transport, an understanding that seemed to have stemmed, like in a game of telephone, from the conversation between LifeCare's Shreveport representatives and Andress, the man they believed worked with FEMA. Only, as they would find out much later, Knox Andress was a nurse at a Catholic hospital in Shreveport who had volunteered as a hospital disaster-preparedness coordinator for his region of northwest Louisiana after 9/11. His volunteer title, "HRSA District Regional Coordinator," was based on the federal hospital bioterrorism preparedness grant to the state. He displayed it proudly on his CV, and he took his role very seriously, participating in local and national training programs as a student and speaker. He did not, however, work for FEMA.

The most important message was this: "MMC told us that they are going first. First the critical then the other patients." That meant even Memorial's less sick patients were being prioritized over LifeCare's generally very sick ones.

Robbye Dubois, in Shreveport, said that she thought the helicopters heading to Memorial were coming for both Memorial and LifeCare patients. "We have spoken to the folks at FEMA and we were supposed to be included in the move." It was hard to imagine that FEMA and the Coast Guard wouldn't be coordinating with each other. Besides, these were federal resources. How could Memorial monopolize them? If the goal was to get the critically ill patients out first, then why should Memorial's noncritical patients go out before LifeCare's critical ones?

At around five p.m., Robichaux spoke with the LifeCare New Orleans administrator who had evacuated with his family. She told him Tenet's patients were being lined up for evacuation, which was a little depressing for the LifeCare staff. From the pharmacy computer on the hospital's seventh floor, Robichaux also pressed her colleagues in Shreveport for specifics. Had FEMA actually said that the Coast Guard airlift at Memorial could include LifeCare?

A LifeCare staff member in Shreveport called Knox Andress again to check. "All he is telling me is that they have our information and will get back to us," she wrote to Robichaux. "I specifically asked several times if we were to be included with MMC and all I got is they have our information and will be evacuating all hospitals." The hospitals were, Andress had told her, going to be evacuated in a certain order, though it was unclear what that order would be.

Corporate Senior Vice President Robbye Dubois would keep making calls from Shreveport, trying to reach whomever she could who might help. "Please keep pushing from your end," she wrote to Robichaux, urging her to go to the helipad and explain to the Coast Guard that Life-Care was a hospital within Memorial and also needed to be evacuated.

Dubois was working at a disadvantage. LifeCare had employed her for many years, and she commuted between its corporate headquarters in Plano, Texas, and her home two hundred miles away in Shreveport, where she was now, working out of a hospital. But her superiors were new, part of a management team appointed by the investment firm The Carlyle Group, which had acquired LifeCare earlier in the month. Most of them, including her new boss, LifeCare's corporate COO, happened to be traveling and out of the office that day.

Dubois was not inclined to turn to her new boss for help in any case. The morning before Katrina struck, he had questioned whether evacuating the Chalmette campus of LifeCare alone was doing enough given the strength of the coming storm. He wanted suggestions on what might be done to help the other two New Orleans–area campuses after the hurricane hit, such as bringing in additional staff from Shreveport or Dallas to help. Dubois had sent him a terse reply. Hospital evacuations weren't being recommended, the campuses were well staffed and supplied, and she had compiled a list of staff who could go to New Orleans from Shreveport.

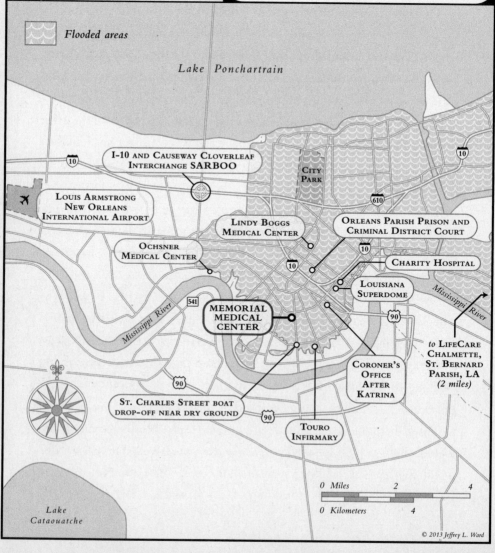

HURRICANE KATRINA FLOOD INUNDATION

•

NEW ORLEANS, LOUISIANA

LOUISIANA

ARKANSAS

Mississippi River

MISSISSIPPI

TEXAS

Baton Rouge

area of detail

New Orleans

Gulf of Mexico

0 Miles 100

0 Kilometers 200

Flooded areas

Lake Ponchartrain

I-10 AND CAUSEWAY CLOVERLEAF INTERCHANGE SARBOO

CITY PARK

LOUIS ARMSTRONG NEW ORLEANS INTERNATIONAL AIRPORT

LINDY BOGGS MEDICAL CENTER

ORLEANS PARISH PRISON AND CRIMINAL DISTRICT COURT

OCHSNER MEDICAL CENTER

CHARITY HOSPITAL

LOUISIANA SUPERDOME

Mississippi River

MEMORIAL MEDICAL CENTER

Mississippi River

to LifeCare CHALMETTE, St. Bernard PARISH, LA (2 miles)

CORONER'S OFFICE AFTER KATRINA

ST. CHARLES STREET boat DROP-OFF NEAR DRY GROUND

TOURO INFIRMARY

0 Miles 2 4

0 Kilometers 4

Lake Cataouatche

© 2013 Jeffrey L. Ward

Now, as conditions deteriorated, there was no way she was going to bring more LifeCare staff into danger to relieve the exhausted staff, which was what she believed her superiors wanted. When she floated the idea of hiring buses to aid in the evacuation, they did not seem enthusiastic. She decided to head up the corporate disaster response alone, assisted mainly by a LifeCare quality management director and an information technology specialist with her at the hospital in Shreveport. She would do whatever it took to aid these hospitals, to the best of her abilities, and ask permission later. She did not turn to higher-ups at the multibillion-dollar firm, who might have had more influence or resources at their disposal, because she felt she wouldn't get help from them.

Back in New Orleans, Diane Robichaux went downstairs to Memorial's command center. When she returned, she seemed to have accepted the status quo out of a sense that LifeCare was covered by at least one of the federal agencies. "OK got clarification again," she wrote. A Memorial representative said the hospital was not using FEMA to evacuate its patients. It was using the Coast Guard to get patients to Baton Rouge on the way to other Tenet facilities.

> I told her that we spoke with our FEMA contact and that he said we are on the list. She said that is good and that Fema is getting all the other hospitals out in the area as well, but not them. SO, if we are on the list that means that FEMA has a plan to get to us.

It was unclear whether Robichaux or her interlocutor at Memorial realized that FEMA itself does not operate rescue helicopters. "If we run into trouble [Memorial] will help coordinate with us to get our patients out."

Robichaux returned to typing out employees' messages to loved ones on the pharmacy computer. At about five thirty p.m. the connection failed. The power had gone down in part of the hospital. She rushed to the bedsides of two patients on ventilators on the west side of the building, where power had been expected to go out first. The plan was to move them to the north side of the floor, which was supplied by a different generator.

The lights came back on after just a few minutes, but the team moved the two patients anyway.

"We lost all power on the West side for a few minutes," LifeCare's pharmacist texted.

"I'm glad you are back," someone on the outside replied. "Scared us for a little while."

The gravity of the situation was becoming clearer. Even the elevator had stopped working, perhaps taken offline to avoid the possibility of someone getting stuck. Two of LifeCare's patients still needed to go downstairs for dialysis.

"We are now pushing for MMC to take at least some of the most critical patients if possible," Robichaux wrote.

Dubois wrote back that she and her colleagues would arrange transport from wherever the helicopters dropped the LifeCare patients, using ambulances or Angel Flight, a company that provides free air medical transport. The important thing was to get the ventilator- and dialysis-dependent patients out quickly.

On that front, Robichaux had disappointing news. "MMC is wanting a list of ambulatory patients first." Patients who could walk. It was another shift from the original idea of maintaining a singular focus on getting the most vulnerable and dependent out first. By this point the patient Anna Pou had tried to resuscitate had died. Only seven of Life-Care's surviving fifty-two patients made the list. Perhaps they could be transported by boat. "I know it is not our critical but at least it will get some out for now."

The news grew grimmer. Memorial's CEO warned that an additional fifteen feet of water was expected around the hospital. A rumor had started that the Army Corps of Engineers was considering blowing up a levee, causing even deeper flooding in the city. And the LifeCare employees in Shreveport had spoken with a tearful Knox Andress. They texted to say they had learned from him that the situation in other hospitals might be even worse. "It is a total mess. Hospitals are out of oxygen. People being bagged for eighteen hours, patients in the water."

At close to sunset, an orange-and-white Coast Guard Jayhawk helicopter descended onto Memorial's helipad, landing beside a smaller private aircraft. The roar of the rotors and the odor of fuel carried into LifeCare. Any employee could look out the windows of the nursing station on the west side of LifeCare and watch the evacuations. Patients who remained on the west side could see the helicopters from their beds. A huddle of hospital volunteers, including family members of patients and staff who had been organized into transport teams, lifted a patient into the Jayhawk, then jogged away from its whirring rotor blades, heads bent.

Still, LifeCare patients had not moved. What Memorial offered was this: the corporate overseers at Tenet would be asked for permission to transport LifeCare patients with the Coast Guard. "I hope and pray this is not a long process for getting their approval," Robichaux wrote to her colleagues. Why Tenet corporate permission should be required for Life-Care to use federal rescue assets was unclear. From Memorial's fourth-floor command center, community relations manager Sandra Cordray typed a message to Michael Arvin at Tenet about LifeCare. Her message did not sound a note of urgency.

> We are priotorizing our patients -can you work directly with LifeCare corp? Thanks.

If Memorial could get LifeCare's fifty-two patients to a staging area just outside New Orleans, she told him, LifeCare could meet them with ambulances and take them to Baton Rouge.

At around seven thirty p.m., Cordray followed up with Arvin, sending him contact information for LifeCare's Robbye Dubois. There would be no more National Guard trucks that day, she added. The water had risen too high. The second set of patients had left for Nacogdoches around six thirty. "Let me know what is worked out for Lifecare patients regarding how will leave. Thanks."

More than an hour came and went. LifeCare's Robbye Dubois wrote Cordray from Shreveport to say she was awaiting approval to get ambulances en route, a process she expected to take hours. Arvin had not called her. She requested his phone number and finally spoke with him after nine p.m. "Been on the phone with Tenet," she reported back to Robichaux. "Will eventually be to our patients. May be in the morning because the water has risen to the point they cannot get trucks to you. I will have ambulances to the staging area. Critical will go first. They will contact me when first patient leaves LifeCare."

Robichaux confirmed that if the backup power went down and they lost the computer connection, they would proceed with the plan, sending patients to the staging area in the morning, critical ones first with staff to care for them. They expected the patients would start moving between three and eight a.m.

Nobody wrote it directly in a message, but some employees began to worry that the choice of which patients went out first could affect their medical outcomes. A realization dawned on Memorial's incident commander, Susan Mulderick, that day. The variability in the sizes of helicopters that were landing and the length of time it was taking to move patients to the helipad left her with one conclusion: not all of the patients would be getting out alive.

———

IT HAD BEEN a grueling few hours for the Memorial command team. During the brief power outage that also affected LifeCare, they had temporarily abandoned the command center and regrouped in an area of the first floor used by security guards. Then most of the radios that they'd been using to communicate across the hospital's vast campus had stopped working. So, too, did one of the few ventilation systems left functioning, in the unit for vulnerable bone marrow transplant patients. It was now blowing hot air.

The command staff and Arvin in Texas had worked for hours and found a receiving hospital for those patients, in vain it seemed. At around nine p.m., a call from the Coast Guard to the incident command staff left the impression that the governor had instructed helicopter pilots to take patients to any hospital that would accept them. "We no longer have any control over destinations," Cordray wrote to Arvin.

What the command staff didn't seem to have considered, perhaps hadn't even been aware of, was the relatively small number of medical transport helicopters flying in the region and the large number of hospitals in New Orleans that now needed to be evacuated. Flying a patient or two to a Tenet hospital out of state would take a helicopter out of commission for hours, even as it might provide the best possible care for those patients. Some pilots wanted to make only quick trips to a highway interchange. The cloverleaf at Interstate 10 and Causeway Boulevard served as a staging area just west of the city. The idea that patients would be dropped off on "lily pads" on their way to more definitive care had been part of the Hurricane Pam exercise. The lily pads were known as SARBOOs—search-and-rescue bases of operations. However, a system to supply the sites and transport patients from them remained to be planned.

At this point, the hospital's command team believed that Memorial had only hours to go before losing generator power.

The hospital received another stabbing victim at around ten p.m. He waded up to Memorial's ER ramp. He was taken in for treatment and needed urgently to go out by air. The helicopters taking people out of the hospital complex were highly visible. They attracted other desperate people. "We've had to secure all egress," one Memorial employee wrote to Tenet colleagues in the evening, "as the community is trudging through three feet of water to try to find shelter here."

Anesthesiologist Paul Primeaux showed up at the incident command office to report that the situation outside the emergency department was "getting ugly." Around a dozen people had arrived in boats with their children and were arrayed outside the hospital in need of food and assistance. The National Guard had left. A contingent from the New Orleans Police Department was about to leave. Its officers offered no advice to the hospital's security guards about where to send these people.

Cordray reported to Tenet that Primeaux and security officers would give the families food and tell them that the hospital wasn't evacuating any more patients, that they should go to the Superdome—the "shelter of last resort" downtown—to get evacuated more quickly. But this might not have been wise advice. The Superdome was more than two miles away, and on WWL, which Cordray was monitoring, news reports suggested the situation there was abysmal. A reporter described people jumping barricades into the floodwaters trying to flee.

> They said the conditions in the Superdome are breaking down, and it is a madhouse. Now, again, this is all hearsay from the folks who are leaving the 'dome, that there have been a couple of murders, people committing suicide jumping from the balconies, rapes, everything.

The New Orleans police captain called in on the radio to say those reports were false. Still, Gov. Kathleen Blanco announced at a nighttime news conference that roughly 20,000 people were stranded in the Superdome with no power and deteriorating sanitary conditions, and the building needed to be evacuated, particularly those with medical conditions who had been told to take shelter there. "The 'dome is degenerating, the conditions are degenerating rapidly, and there are too many people in there," she said.

Memorial's security concerns were relayed to Louisiana's 911 system by Michael Arvin in Dallas, who stressed that the evacuation of Memorial needed to be expedited. He wrote back to Cordray to reassure her that the person heading up "all air evac coordination" said there would be a reinforced crew of helicopters at first light. Arvin may have misinterpreted. The EMS coordinator had logged the conversation as a request for help, not a promise to give it.

Before eleven p.m., a Coast Guard officer called the command center at Memorial with an offer. The Guard would continue sending helicopters and boats to Memorial. "They are deploying as many as five helicopters in a renewed effort to evacuate all patients this evening," Cordray reported in an e-mail to Arvin and others. When the Coast Guard offered to extend the rescues, anesthesiologist Paul Primeaux was the only clinical employee in the command center, and he gave his wholehearted backing to the plan. "Let's go, absolutely!" he said. The chaplain agreed. "Fuckin' A!" Primeaux would remember him saying. Primeaux didn't have a radio, so he ran downstairs, into the garage, and up to the helipad to alert the evacuation team.

Gunshots punctuated an oddly quiet, dark night lacking in the swoosh of traffic, the buzz of air-conditioners, and the glare of streetlights. The voices of people from the nearby flooded houses, the splashing sounds of swimming, were magnified over water. The staff on the helipad had rigged up industrial lantern flashlights along the perimeter with plastic zip-ties to mark the landing spot, not realizing white light could almost blind pilots using night vision goggles.

The Coast Guard's offer had arrived before Primeaux had and been declined. Someone had tripped in the dark and nearly plunged off of the helipad. Primeaux understood the danger. Earlier, he had stepped on the ancient flat fencing that extended around the helipad as a safety net, and he had worried it might not hold his weight. Still, the decision to turn away rescuers aggravated him.

The hospital's sixteen critically ill babies and most of its critically ill adult patients had been flown away—twenty-five in all, and the stabbing victim, too—before a fog set in that made it difficult to fly. The Acadian Ambulance flight coordinator did not plan to return with his growing fleet of private medical air ambulances on Wednesday. Their charge was to evacuate critically ill people who had a reasonable chance of survival, and as far as he knew, that had been accomplished at Memorial. Other hospitals were still waiting. He packed up his satellite phone and waited out the passing fog, then began looking for a helicopter to wave lights at and flag down to take him to Tulane Hospital downtown. He had no desire to stay at Memorial overnight. He had been down to the emergency room, where it was dark and seemed dangerous. He had only his .45 pistol.

Sometime around eleven p.m., a massive Coast Guard Jayhawk helicopter descended. The Acadian coordinator thought he had signaled it, but in fact its crew had been diverted to Memorial by a C-130 turboprop plane flying overhead, relaying search-and-rescue requests from the ground. The Coast Guard crew's mission was to begin the medevac of all remaining patients. However, someone on the helipad said that there were no more patients who needed to leave and that it would be best if the Coast Guard could return after daylight. A crew member communicated that back up the chain and received permission to fly instead to Tulane Hospital with the Acadian coordinator and about a thousand pounds of medical equipment that had been pulled from private helicopters throughout the day to make room for more patients. They lifted off, and the Coast Guard Jayhawk flew away from Memorial with no patients on board.

Memorial had shaved its patient census from 187 to about 130. Staff counted 460 Memorial employees, 447 family members, and 52 Life-Care employees left in the building. On the seventh floor, all 52 LifeCare patients, including seven who relied on ventilators to breathe, remained.

CHAPTER 5

DAY FOUR

WEDNESDAY, AUGUST 31, 2005, EARLY MORNING

AFTER MIDNIGHT, the intensive care nurses gathered in the unit on the eighth floor. They slapped palms, clapped backs, and congratulated one another. They had managed to get all of their non-DNR patients out safely, despite the smothering heat, confusion, and physical hardship. Overnight, two nurses cared for the two surviving DNR patients who remained.

Some staff found the strength to clean up and arrange mattresses, and the employees and their family members settled down together for the night. They passed around an oxygen mask, taking hits of the gas and letting it cool their faces. Some, beginning to grasp the enormity of the disaster and how it might scatter them, wondered aloud if they would ever again work at the hospital where so many of the nurses had grown up together as professionals. Nurse manager Karen Wynn feared they never would. One of her staff nurses, Lori Budo, disagreed. Her mother, the retired ICU nurse, had trained many of the current set of nurses. "I'll be back," Budo said.

Someone suggested the day's events had the makings of a good television movie. Budo, dark-haired with a heart-shaped face and thick eyebrows, said she wanted Demi Moore to play her. Her longtime colleague on the night shift, Cheri Landry, short and stout, with hooded eyes, arched brows, and an air of wisdom, would be portrayed by Kathy Bates. Ben Affleck, Matt Damon, and Junior Seau—the star linebacker who was still alive at that time and playing for the Miami Dolphins— had roles as male ICU nurses: tough heroes who had carried patients up to the helipad in the heat.

Budo had her eighteen-year-old daughter with her. Their striped kitten, Honey, was in a kennel in the garage. Budo and her daughter went to sneak Honey upstairs in the dark. Animals were now forbidden to be in the hospital itself, but by this point Budo had worked the Saturday night shift before the storm, stayed awake packing on Sunday, and then spent more than two exhausting days on hurricane duty. She felt that she, her daughter, and their cat needed to be together. Honey was part of the family. As she climbed back upstairs to rejoin her colleagues, Budo turned and aimed her flashlight beam behind them. She would later write of having the sense that a menacing presence was following them.

———

IN THE COMMAND center, the few working cell phones kept ringing. The Coast Guard members held fast to the idea of continuing rescues overnight, particularly after learning about the seven LifeCare patients on ventilators, the rising water, and the possibility of a power cut within hours. A doctor sent a security guard to wake Dr. Richard Deichmann and ask him what to tell a Coast Guard officer about sending more helicopters for the LifeCare patients. "Tell him to send them in the morning," Deichmann said. As if we have any control, he thought. Deichmann considered it too dangerous to reopen the helipad. The staff needed rest.

Memorial incident commander Susan Mulderick discussed the matter with LifeCare incident commander Diane Robichaux. With all elevators now out of commission, Robichaux felt her staff would need extra hands to carry these most critical patients downstairs safely, but Mulderick said the men she could offer to help had gone to bed. Robichaux agreed to wait for daybreak. That would also allow time for LifeCare to send ambulances to pick up the patients and take them to other LifeCare hospitals, creating a smoother transition for the patients at a time when regional hospitals were jammed and, whether or not Robichaux thought of it, serving the interests of the company by keeping LifeCare patients within the LifeCare system.

⌒

FOR ICU NURSE manager Karen Wynn, the day's reward was one small luxury, a trip to the doctors' lounge down the hallway from the ICU to take a shower. There was just enough pressure to nudge a trickle of water out of the showerhead, water that had been declared contaminated and dangerous to drink. It felt fantastic.

"Mom! Mom!" The voice of Wynn's teenage daughter interrupted the Calgon moment. "There's a guy out saying, 'We need to move patients, we need to move patients.'" He was calling out for women and children.

"Wait a minute, nobody's moving anywhere," Wynn said. She felt responsible for the staff members she had called in to work. She felt responsible for their families, too. With most of the intensive care patients on the eighth floor gone, she wasn't inclined to send her staff out to transport patients from other units. "Nobody on the eighth floor is moving anywhere," she said. She quickly toweled off. "We're not doing this willy-nilly, we need direction." The one person she trusted to give that was Susan Mulderick. "I'm going to find Susan," she said.

In other parts of the hospital, the sound of a man shouting stirred groggy adults and children from mattresses, sofas, and the odd examination table. "Everybody up! Everybody, get up!" The noise pierced the slumber of Dr. Ewing Cook, lying in his office with his wife and colleagues. They clicked on their flashlights and caught sight of a white man in fatigues yelling as he moved through the dimly lit respiratory care department at around one a.m.: *The boats are here! Get down there! You can take one bag! No animals! Go to the first floor! Boats are here and leaving in thirty minutes!*

People screamed back at the man—how could he expect them to leave their pets behind? An Indian-born respiratory therapist and his wife had secreted a pair of golden retrievers in the hospital where they weren't allowed. At home, the cossetted pets slept like children in their own room on individual recliner beds and were never permitted to trot outside without a quartet of boots placed over their paws. What was to become of them now?

Staff members scrambled to consolidate insurance certificates, needed medicines, important papers they had with them for safekeeping. Who had a single bag packed? They had brought enough to sustain themselves for days.

The Cooks and a group of other employees and family members tromped down the stairs by flashlight. They came to a halt at the sight of Susan Mulderick. She faced them, tall and authoritative, on a staircase landing. "What are y'all doing here?" she asked. They said they had been told to come downstairs. The boats that people had been expecting were ready to take them away. "What boats?" Mulderick asked. "There aren't any boats." Others told her they'd heard helicopters were waiting. Mulderick left to investigate.

The groups wound back upstairs to their mattresses in a sleepy fog. What little peace the night might have brought had been shattered. Word spread that some people couldn't find belongings they had stowed and left behind. Had the man stolen from them? Was it all a hoax built on their hopes of rescue?

The night was wasted. Now even the most exhausted found it impossible to sleep. After the futile jaunt downstairs, Ewing Cook felt a new level of anxiety, not good for his damaged heart. He lay awake in his office near the hospital's engineering plant and listened to the roar of its diesel generators, the ticking of Memorial's own weakening heart.

———

A BATTLE WAS under way to keep the generators running. Each of the three teal-colored generators was taller than a typical adult and pumped electricity into a complex circulatory system of feed lines, riser circuits, and transfer switches. Normally an outside company serviced the 750 kW generators, each producing the power of about six engines from one of the year's most popular cars, a Toyota Camry. The hospital's maintenance staff did little more than change the oil and run tests once a month in the middle of the night. The tests were brief, in keeping with national codes that treated hospital generators like heart-lung bypass machines used during surgeries, meant to support vital functions for a period of only minutes to hours. Despite the fact that the generators were not built for prolonged work, Memorial's disaster plans called for them to shore up the hospital for at least three days. They had already been running for two.

None of the Memorial electricians or engineers on-site was a generator mechanic. Earlier, when one of the generator engines had shut down, casting part of the hospital into darkness and sending staff scrambling to move patients, maintenance workers concluded it was overheated. Laboring by flashlight, they added water to the radiator and were able to restart it.

Hours later, the problems multiplied. Low oil pressure appeared to be the cause; the men brought barrels of diesel to try to prime the motors with fresh fuel and restart them. Maintenance men crossed the bridge to the surgery building to retrieve more diesel from a generator there. Some sections of the hospital were losing power. In parts where there was light, it seemed to be dimming, strangling.

Over the years, the original 1926 hospital had received additions, and the electrical system now resembled the blood supply of conjoined twins, separate but overlapping and, as a whole, unique to itself and mysterious.

One generator failed. Unable to restart it, the engineers tried to tie some of the lines it supplied to another generator. They pulled on rubber boots and ran down to the basement, splashing into knee-deep water, then climbed up a few steps to the mezzanine of the core electrical building.

They tried to determine the reason for the partial outages throughout the hospital. The depth of the water offered a clue. About a third of the automatic transfer switches, which allowed the generators to power the hospital when normal utility power was lost, were on a low level of the building, and it looked like they and their associated distribution panels might be submerged, much as plant operations director Eric Yancovich had predicted several months earlier.

Like in a scene from *The Poseidon Adventure,* the men waded through a narrow hallway bordered by electrical panels and a sign with two lightning bolts that read CAUTION: HAZARDOUS VOLTAGE INSIDE. Using a flashlight, they located a metal lever with a yellow rubber–coated handle above their heads marked "bypass handle." Praying not to get electrocuted, one flipped it, grafting the load of the nonworking generator to a working one.

Soon a gauge showed that the working engine was drawing too much current, a sign of a short circuit. The men tried to back off and untie the two loads to avoid a fire, a terrifying possibility given that the sprinkler system's pumps were now underwater and city fire trucks were presumably out of commission. To further adjust the load, they went around the hospital shutting off scattered branch circuits serving unused fixtures and devices.

Another generator failed. This time, the workers had an idea of what caused the problem, but no spare parts to fix it. They tried to scavenge from the failed generator, but the attempted repair was unsuccessful.

The battle for the generators raged for two hours. At about two a.m. on Wednesday, August 31, 2005—nearly forty-eight hours after Katrina made landfall near New Orleans—the last backup generator surged and then died.

The sudden silence struck Dr. Ewing Cook, lying in his office on the second floor, trying to rest, as the sickest sound of his life.

———

ALARMS HERALDED the power loss. They flashed and wailed on the eighth floor, where the ICU nurses had settled for the night in the rooms of their rescued patients. Nurse manager Karen Wynn stepped up on a chair and clobbered an alarm panel with her shoe to quiet it. She told her nurses to try to get some sleep.

On the seventh floor below them, the LifeCare notepad computer lost its text-messaging connection. The special mattress supporting Emmett Everett's massive body deflated. Mechanical breaths still hissed rhythmically in the rooms of patients on life support. They would cease when the battery backupus on the ventilators were exhausted.

———

MEMORIAL'S FIFTH FLOOR was bathed only in the dim, bluish light from Toshiba Satellite laptop monitors. A night shift nurse, Michelle Pitre-Ryals, quickly typed notes into her patients' electronic charts before the computer batteries died, despite the fact that once that happened, the electronic medical records system would be useless. Paper was high technology in a disaster. The electronic medication dispensing cart, new to Pitre-Ryals's unit, would also shut down, its stock of medicines locked securely inside it.

Pitre-Ryals was carrying a cell phone belonging to the nurse whose husband was at the Coast Guard station. It rang. "We have sent three helicopters and someone is waving them away," a Coast Guard auxiliary member said. Pitre-Ryals took the phone downstairs in the dark to the command team. "Is that that guy again from the Coast Guard?" a nursing director asked, and she disappeared with the phone to speak with him. On return she instructed Pitre-Ryals not to bring it down again. The man, she said, was "not part of our evacuation plan."

Pitre-Ryals made her way back upstairs, but then a Louisiana health department official and a Coast Guard lieutenant called. The latter commanded her to disregard her instructions and bring the phone immediately to someone in charge. Pitre-Ryals descended the unlit staircase again, and the nursing director berated her before taking the phone. A male doctor said no more patients were being evacuated because it was too hard to see. Pitre-Ryals suggested waking people up and putting flashlights in the stairwell, but she was ignored. After she returned to the fifth floor, the phone rang again. A more senior Coast Guard lieutenant insisted on speaking with a hospital leader. Pitre-Ryals gave the phone to a nurse's husband to carry back downstairs while she went to care for her patients. She couldn't believe hospital leaders were yelling at the Coast Guard for trying to send rescuers. "With these people in charge," she told a fellow nurse, "we may very well die here."

———

UP ON THE eighth floor in the ICU, it wasn't easy to sleep. Battery-powered fans agitating the hot air lost their will and sighed into silence.

Nurse Manager Karen Wynn lay awake on an air mattress that her

ICU staff had prepared for her. Her daughter, lying beside her, seemed to be the only one asleep.

After a time, Wynn stood up in the darkened room.

"Where are you going?" one of the nurses from the medical ICU, Thao Lam, asked.

"I'm just gonna go see what's going on," Wynn told her. "I'm not asleep, might as well get up and do something, be productive."

"Can I come with you?"

"Sure. Come join the party."

Wynn shined her flashlight, and the two nurses walked to a staircase near the elevator lobby on the eighth floor. They didn't have to descend more than one story to find action. On the seventh floor, LifeCare staff members were carrying ventilator-dependent patients into the stairwell as nurses dispensed huffs of oxygen from football-shaped Ambu-bags compressed like bellows between their fingers. Word had come that the Coast Guard was on the pad again and could evacuate patients if they were brought there immediately.

Wynn and Lam offered their help. They and the other workers helped roll patients onto their sides in bed and then roll them back atop stiff spine boards. They slid the spine boards onto waiting stretchers and wheeled the patients down the corridors toward the staircase by the elevator bank. They lifted the spine boards off the stretchers and began carrying the patients downstairs.

Lam held on to the front end of a spine board and lit the way with a flashlight. Wynn carried the back end and managed to shine hers. Two or three other volunteers stood at each side. Every few steps, they reached a landing that marked a turn in the narrow staircase. They lifted the patient above the handrails and rotated the board into position to continue down to the next flight. All the while someone continued to pump oxygen into the patient's lungs and tried to ensure that the breathing tube didn't get dislodged from the airway. Down five stories they went, to the second-floor lobby and through a hallway to the power plant, with its now silenced generators.

No doorway existed between the hospital and the parking garage beneath the helipad. Without the elevators working, Wynn assumed they would have had to go outside to access the garage—clearly impossible now with the flooding. Plant operations director Eric Yancovich had talked about busting a hole in a hospital wall to create a direct conduit. In fact, they could have carried the patients down to the first floor, through two doorways into a separate stairwell and up to its second-floor landing, which opened into the garage, a taxing journey. But one of Yancovich's workers recalled a hidden passage. Inside the machine room, halfway up the wall to the right of the entrance beneath a massive water pipe, stood a rectangular three-by-three-and-a-quarter-foot opening lined by rough concrete. It was normally covered by a piece of hinged metal. Yancovich thought the opening might have been created to allow equipment to be serviced directly from the garage.

Wynn and Lam passed the patient through the opening and into the hands of other volunteers stationed in the parking garage. A welcome breeze tunneled through the passageway. Wynn had no idea why it existed. Perhaps God had said there needed to be a hole there.

Each time Wynn returned to LifeCare to roll a patient onto a backboard, she was surprised at how hot the patient felt to her touch. My God, she thought, someone could fry an egg on them. She knew elderly bodies had trouble regulating heat. Certain medical conditions, such as a stroke or a head injury, as well as some commonly used drugs, interfered with the process. Dehydration, heart disease, a little extra weight—all could impair the body's ability to rid itself of heat through sweating and other mechanisms. The extra heat, in turn, could complicate other critical illnesses.

It was likely that over the two days since the air-conditioning cut out, these patients' core temperatures had risen. Their bodies would have failed to buffer the heat as sweat production paradoxically ceased. This was heat stroke, widespread inflammation in the body and dysfunction of multiple organs, particularly the brain, causing a range of effects from confusion to coma. Ice baths could reverse it, or wetting the skin and fanning the patient, along with giving oxygen and sometimes fluids. Nine times out of ten the person would survive. But Karen Wynn worried about the potentially irreversible damage the heat might be causing in the cells and organs of the patients she carried. We're going to have fried brains here, she thought.

Even those without medical training worried about the effect of the heat on the LifeCare patients. A woman who had been hired to sit at the bedside of patient Elvira "Vera" LeBlanc reached her charge's daughter-in-law by cell phone at around four on Wednesday morning. The sitter described how hot it was. "The nurses are starting to freak out," she said. "People are dying. There's no place to put them." LeBlanc's daughter-in-law Sandra was a paramedic. She said she was trying to get into New Orleans and back to the hospital. "When are you coming?" the sitter asked, sounding desperate.

—

AT THE COAST GUARD emergency command center in Alexandria, LTJG Shelley Decker, a former Army pilot who had recently joined the Guard, had been fighting to get helicopters to Memorial for LifeCare's ventilator patients. She learned that at least three had gone to Memorial and were waved away. "No, they want them to land," she said to a contact at the air station. "You have to go back." The auxiliary member beside her, Michael Richard, spoke by cell phone with a nurse leader atop the helipad. She seemed to be panicking, waving her arms over her head, believing she was signaling the pilots, not turning them off. "When those helicopters come," he told her, "stand clear!"

Each air rescue crew had only eight hours to fly within any twenty-four-hour period; thousands of people in the city needed help. Every minute was precious. The same was true for the fragile LifeCare patients on life support. Decker kept trying to reach Susan Mulderick on the nurse's cell phone to give a play-by-play of the helicopters' arrivals. The rescue effort needed to proceed. She'd been told that one ventilator patient had already died waiting. Yet the pilots weren't seeing patients on the pad. How can we keep missing these people? Decker wondered. She and two colleagues engaged in a complicated chain of communications, maintaining contact with three cell phones at Memorial, while talking to the air stations, and, via HF radio patch, to the crew of the C-130 flying over New Orleans, which then tasked the helicopter pilots.

The Jayhawk that had flown away from Memorial to Tulane Hospital hours earlier with the Acadian Ambulance coordinator was diverted again by the C-130 and directed back to Memorial to rescue the critically ill LifeCare patients. In the intervening hours, crew members had hoisted several people from the rooftops of flooded homes, depositing them at the cloverleaf highway interchange west of New Orleans. One elderly woman couldn't walk, and the rescue swimmer on board had carried her across a field of grass to emergency workers. What he saw concerned him: thousands of people camped out on the south side of the highway, surrounded by refuse, no buses in sight.

The pilots flew to Memorial as instructed and executed a challenging maneuver at night, using a slight tailwind to position the helicopter properly on the helipad. Crew members were again told that there were no critical patients to rescue but that non-patients and staff were anxious to leave and were becoming unmanageable. One member of the flight team took to the radio again to ask what to do next. Back came the word that, according to contacts inside the hospital, the patients were indeed still there awaiting rescue.

Incident commander Susan Mulderick had climbed up to the helipad in the dark to see what was really happening with the Coast Guard. She passed people who were clearly non-patients, perhaps extended families and community members who had taken shelter at Memorial before the storm. They snaked up the stairwell and into the covered, enclosed walkway she had purchased years earlier when the helipad was still in use. The tunnel was designed to protect against the hurricane-force winds unleashed by helicopter rotors. Dozens and dozens of people were up here clamoring to leave, no doubt roused and alarmed by the man who had run through the hospital.

The pilot kept his rotors going to avoid stressing the pad with the full weight of the aircraft, and it was loud. Mulderick stood to the side of the helipad and discussed the situation with the Coast Guard flight mechanic, who shouted questions at her over the din. Was there food and water? Was it dry inside the hospital? Mulderick shouted back, yes. "Listen, you've got food, you've got to stay here, because where I'm going to take you, it's not good!" the flight mechanic screamed. "We're going to dump you off in a field!" There was no infrastructure set up at the cloverleaf. It was basically a point in the highway. It looked to him like Woodstock after the concert. The civilians were better off staying at Memorial.

Over the side of the helipad, Mulderick and the flight mechanic could see a patient being carried up the metal steps. There was barely any lighting. It struck Mulderick as extremely dangerous to have untrained staff performing this work. She told the flight crew to take the patient but not return again to Memorial.

A group of workers approached with the patient, manually ventilating her. They'd had to run a Code Blue resuscitation on the way to the helipad, and the patient needed to go directly to a hospital in Baton Rouge. After spending a long time spinning on Memorial's helipad, the Jayhawk was approaching bingo—it didn't have enough fuel to make it all the way to Baton Rouge. The crew, too, was running out of flight time.

In desperation, a doctor threatened to leave the patient unattended on the helipad if the patient wasn't allowed aboard the Jayhawk. A plan was hatched—they would fly the woman to the hurricane-battered Coast

Guard New Orleans air station and transfer her to another aircraft. They loaded her and a LifeCare nurse and left Memorial at five fifteen in the morning.

Inside the roaring, shaking military helicopter, the accompanying nurse looked terrified to the point of inaction. The Coast Guard rescue swimmer, along with a young freelance cameraman accompanying the crew, took over the care of the patient. Somehow they made it.

Mulderick's decision to end the airlift hadn't yet reached everyone. A fresh Jayhawk crew that had taken flight from a Coast Guard air training station in Mobile at three thirty a.m. had also received a call for assistance over the radio. Power has been lost at Baptist Memorial. Patients need help. Could the aircraft transport two ventilator patients at once? "Hell yeah," the crew's rescue swimmer told the pilot. "Let's go get it, man."

The pilot kept the helicopter aloft, concerned the helipad might not hold his Jayhawk's weight, as the swimmer lowered himself onto Memorial's helipad, where he was swarmed by frantic hospital personnel. This time the LifeCare patients were ready to go. He saw they were so fragile and required so much medical equipment, it would be dangerous to "package" them in the litter used for rooftop rescues and hoist them. He radioed the pilot, orbiting overhead, who set up for an approach, his flight mechanic lying on the deck with his head to the ground to help them land light on the wheels, holding power to the rotors to maintain some lift. They landed safely. The staff rushed the two patients to the helicopter, and the swimmer put up troop seats to make room on deck. He unloaded bottled water and ready-to-eat meals for the hospital staff. "You need to nourish yourselves," he, a seasoned emergency responder, advised, "or you're not going to do anybody any good." He handed the doctor something perhaps even more needed—a portable Coast Guard drop radio around the size of a cell phone that he could use to communicate on emergency channel sixteen.

The helicopter lifted off with the two patients. The pilot headed directly for a hospital in Lafayette, more than an hour's flight. To the rescue swimmer, every moment felt like forever. He kept bagging and monitoring the patients' vital signs and praying.

Back inside the hospital, more ventilator patients from LifeCare had been brought downstairs and were lined up waiting to be carried through the hole in the machine-room wall.

One of those patients, wrapped in sheets, was passed through the hole with the help of a LifeCare respiratory therapist. On the garage side, a team maneuvered the patient onto a mattress on the bed of a truck that would drive to the helipad. "We need more viable patients," the therapist heard a voice say in the dark. "Y'all can't keep bringing patients like this to us." The comment struck the therapist as snide and offended him. The patients he cared for on LifeCare were "like this."

Susan Mulderick's decision to stop the airlift reached LTJG Shelley Decker at the Coast Guard command center in Alexandria before six in the morning. By that time, three sorties had occured, and only three of the LifeCare ventilator patients and one patient on a special oxygen device had been rescued. The Memorial nurses explained to Decker that it was dark; they were moving patients by hand up and down the stairs, with a nurse standing by them and bagging them constantly. "We're tired," they said. Decker had assumed there was emergency lighting. She tried to picture what they were seeing, but found it difficult. She sat in a well-lit room with running water, electricity, and working phone lines. It was surreal; she imagined a weird B movie, the dystopian, post-disaster world depicted in the film *Escape from L.A.*

The Memorial nurses told her that the remaining vent patients "were DNR"—although that was not true of all of them—and that operations had to stop for now and could resume at nine in the morning. A Memorial nurse assured Decker that the patients would continue to be bagged, ventilated by hand. Decker understood, but it was hard for her to swallow. She could get rescue assets to Memorial if only its staff could get the patients to the helipad.

The Coast Guard auxiliary volunteer working beside her, Michael Richard, had an even harder time accepting the decision. As Memorial's generators failed one by one, he had spent hours finding hospitals to take the patients and laboring to convince hospital leaders to allow the rescues to proceed. It had shocked him when one told him that the hospital's priority was to evacuate first its own patients—her responsibility was to them, not to these sickest patients belonging to another company who were going to die anyway. Holy crap, he thought. She wants to walk away and let them die. Was it all a question of money? "Hold on," he'd told her. He put the phone down and pretended to consult a superior about this decision. He didn't feel he had to speak with anyone. He knew exactly what was right. He picked the phone up again. "Absolutely not," he said. "You're going to take the most critical out first." She insisted it was her choice to make. He told her it wasn't. Maybe it wasn't his, either, but he didn't care. He couldn't imagine her making this call and living with it later. He thought the decision would scar her conscience. He was raised Christian; he was raised to take care of those most in need.

Back at Memorial, the number of LifeCare patients being ventilated by hand grew by one: eighty-year-old John Russell, a Korean War veteran who liked to joke with his caregivers. Russell, who was being treated for a bad skin infection on his leg, had a history of cardiac disease. He was found not breathing, with no heartbeat, at about five thirty in the morning, within hours of the backup power failing. The staff called a Code Blue, intubated him, and injected him with drugs that restored a livable heart rhythm. Then they carried him downstairs.

LifeCare director of nursing Gina Isbell stood beside him now on the second floor, pulsing air through a one-way valve into his breathing tube with squeezes of a reinflatable Ambu-bag. In previous disasters, hospital workers had ventilated patients this way for hours, just as Gershanik had done with the neonate on the helicopter. However breaths given by hand were not as precise in volume or pressure as those that would have been dispensed by a machine, likely making them less effective.

Isbell's hands grew tired and her white scrub shirt stuck to her generous frame. Russell was twitching and largely unresponsive, signs that he wasn't getting enough oxygen to his brain in spite of her efforts. The wait in the hot corridor went on for nearly an hour before Russell was advanced into the machine room on the way to the heliport. A physician stopped by the stretcher and shined a flashlight into Russell's eyes, a crude check of his neurological function. "You do know that he needs oxygen," he said to Isbell.

"Yes, sir."

The doctor said the hospital didn't have any more oxygen, and couldn't get any. "You have to let him go."

It was not true that there was no oxygen in the hospital, but Isbell was not in a position to know this. She did not know that the ICU nurses had passed around an oxygen mask like a marijuana bong just hours earlier (oxygen from the wall supply was not available in the machine room). She did not know where the stores of portable oxygen tanks were at the hospital. Did the doctor? Perhaps he felt that searching for tanks wasn't practical. Perhaps he'd heard there weren't any. Or perhaps he felt the man was too far gone, or that oxygen needed to be saved for other patients, or that the airlift wouldn't start again in time to save the man.

The oxygen problem was also recorded in the state's emergency medical services logs a few hours later: "Baptist Hospital has now run out of O2—Priority has been given to moving their vent patients."

Isbell believed the doctor when he said there was no more oxygen. She stood for a moment by her patient and wondered, How do I just let him go? Then she stopped pumping the Ambu-bag. She hugged the elderly man and stroked his hair as he died.

Isbell pulled a sheet over Russell's face and rolled him out of the machine room. She sat on the ground by his feet waiting for LifeCare's nurse executive, Therese Mendez, to tell her where to take his body. The main morgue was all the way up on the eighth floor, no longer refrigerated, and possibly full. People passed Isbell and asked for the dead man's gurney. The requests bothered her. It was all she could do not to snap back in anger. Find your own gurney, she wanted to say. Leave us alone. The man deserves respect.

Almost an hour passed, and then hospital chaplain John Marse approached.

"Come on with me," he said. Isbell stood up, and Marse guided her and the gurney through a nearby door with stained-glass windows. Therese Mendez pushed chairs to the side of the empty chapel to make space. Inside, Isbell cried in the chaplain's arms. They prayed together. She had seen patients die before, but this death felt different. Normally, she had what she needed to give people a chance to survive.

The chaplain left and Isbell sat alone for a while in the chapel, composing herself. Then she and Mendez walked to the fourth floor of one of the parking garages and sat in Isbell's SUV with the air-conditioning blowing. They took a short break. Isbell didn't want to leave.

In the early morning, Dr. Anna Pou, too, also took a turn on the second floor squeezing a reinflatable Ambu-bag to ventilate a LifeCare patient. She switched off with a nurse and another staff member as they waited. When Pou returned to relieve one of them, the patient had died.

"What are we gonna do here?" Pou and her colleagues asked one another. It hit her that there was not much she could accomplish without the tools she relied on, without basics, including electricity and running water. As a specialist in head and neck disorders, Pou was particularly attuned to another problem: the loss of hospital suction. Normally the negative airflow—running from an outdoor vacuum pump through a vein-like system in the hospital's walls—had an outlet in each patient's room, where an aspirator could be used to clear congestion from patients' upper airways, helping them to breathe. Overnight Pou had been reduced to tickling the back of one patient's throat, stimulating a cough. It took about an hour before a nurse found a portable, battery-powered suction device.

Pou was the kind of cancer surgeon who fought to give patients with poor prognoses the latest treatments and every last possible chance to survive. Sometimes she fought after other physicians would have given up hope. Now, robbed of her armamentarium, Pou's sense of efficacy as a doctor was diminished. She, like Mulderick, had concluded the sickest remaining patients and those on ventilators might not make it out of Memorial alive.

The four LifeCare patients who left on Coast Guard helicopters were successfully transferred to other hospitals. The remaining five ventilator-dependent patients did not make it out of Memorial. One patient died being carried down the staircase. Another, a fifty-one-year-old woman in a deep coma who had a DNR order, never left the seventh floor. Memorial staff members came up to say patients with DNR orders could not go.

———

WEDNESDAY, AUGUST 31, 2005—MORNING

THE SUN ROSE and with it the temperature. The hospital was stifling, its walls sweating. Water had stopped flowing from taps, toilets were backed up, and the stench of sewage mixed with the odor of hundreds of unwashed bodies. Interior corridors were enveloped in darkness penetrated only by dancing flashlight beams. Without working phones, televisions, computers, and overhead pagers, information was scarce. Critical messages passed voice to voice up and down the staircases.

Plant manager Eric Yancovich came to tell Susan Mulderick that an official had arrived at the hospital saying he was the cavalry. Mulderick met the very tall, bald man, who wore black pants and a yellow shirt and carried a radio. He introduced himself as a representative of the state's Department of Health and Hospitals, and in the press of the emergency, Mulderick quickly forgot his name. He said he was going to get the hospital cleared out by the end of the day. He told Mulderick to get everybody ready to go.

The incident command team met at about seven a.m. They adopted a plan to consolidate resources and patients by moving them to staging areas near exit points on the first and second floors. A nurse was sent to the emergency room to find the color-coded triage armbands the hospital kept in case of emergencies. She was to distribute the bands to each nursing unit and explain how to use them. Patients who could walk would be given green bands, those who needed assistance would get yellow bands, and those who depended completely on care given by others would get red bands. Patients with DNR orders were to get a black band.

———

LIFECARE NURSING DIRECTOR Gina Isbell and nurse executive Therese Mendez left the cool peace of Isbell's car to return to work on the seventh floor. Isbell carried with her the medical chart of the patient who had died in her hands, John Russell. She gave the chart to a young, dark-haired doctor whom she had seen frequently on the Life-Care floor, Dr. Roy Culotta, the one who had brought his grandmother to the hospital for safety during the storm and entrusted her to the Life-Care nurses. Culotta was a pulmonary physician at the hospital who had inherited Ewing Cook's patients when Cook retired from clinical practice earlier in the year. Isbell told Culotta that Russell had died on the second floor and had been moved to the chapel.

Although it was still early in the morning, by the time Isbell returned to the floor, workers had helped many of the LifeCare patients into wheelchairs and wheeled them toward the stairwells. Boats were expected to arrive and ferry patients to dry ground. The patients would be staged on the ambulance ramp outside the emergency room to await them. Isbell, though she hadn't slept overnight, went back downstairs at around nine thirty a.m. to oversee their care.

AN AMPED-UP, motorized roar drew dozens of Memorial's inmates to the hospital windows. Cheers, applause, and shouts erupted from the crowds massed atop the flooded ambulance ramp on Clara Street. Deliverance!

"Thank God!" someone yelled in the direction of two flat-bottomed airboats wafting up to the hospital on propellers nearly the size of Ferris wheels. "How did y'all know we were here?" How in the hell would we *not* know you're here? Sandra LeBlanc, in one of the airboats, wondered. The hospital had guarded the corner of Napoleon and Clara streets for seventy-nine years.

LeBlanc, whose bright-yellow Louisiana State University baseball cap stood out on the metallic airboat, was a paramedic and the coordinator of the Emergency Medical Technology program at Elaine P. Nunez Community College in nearby Chalmette. The journey she and her husband had taken to Memorial, despite knowing its location well, qualified as an odyssey. It had begun a full day earlier, on Tuesday, with news that the city had flooded. Mark and Sandra loaded up their six-cylinder Chevy Silverado and left a relative's house in northern Louisiana, where they had sheltered from the storm after evacuating from New Orleans. Their goal was to rescue Mark's mother, LifeCare patient Vera LeBlanc, and her sitter. That meant finding a way to get into the city. They drove first to check in at the state's Bureau of Emergency Medical Services in the capital, Baton Rouge, to pick up volunteer identification badges. The offices, rented from the Jimmy Swaggart Ministries, faced a vast parking lot filled with ambulances and medics who seemed to be awaiting direction. New Orleans was about seventy-five miles to the southeast.

Sandra had a loose connection with government by virtue of having once administered state EMT exams. At the EMS registration desk, she wrote her name on a piece of paper and the name of her next of kin. That officials were requesting this detail scared her. "Where are you going?" a worker asked. "Where are you sending us?" Sandra replied. The worker told her there was a triage center on a freeway interchange just west of New Orleans. Sandra said they would go there.

The bureau had run out of ID badges, and Sandra had mistakenly left her credentials behind before Katrina. Concerned about possible checkpoints, Sandra and Mark drove their Chevy to a fire station about forty miles from New Orleans, hoping to tag along with rescue crews. The LeBlancs found dozens of firefighters there, but then waited all day for them to be sent toward the city to replace tiring crews. The call never came. Finally, close to evening, a few frustrated firefighters and their chief decided to drive to the triage point. The LeBlancs joined them, and the group was waved through toward the city.

They reached the cloverleaf highway interchange west of New Orleans at Causeway Boulevard. Thousands of people came into sight, sitting, standing, and lying on land bristling with debris and light poles, downed to facilitate helicopter landings. To Sandra it looked like a war zone, unfathomable. They stopped and watched helicopters descend and pour more people onto the grass.

The SARBOO, search-and-rescue base of operations, allowed pilots to make quick loops in and out of the flood zone. Officials had managed to execute only half of the concept described in the Hurricane Pam exercises, however, as they had failed to provide the 600 buses and 1,200 drivers needed to pick up the people being dropped there.

Sandra searched for other medical personnel and found the leader of an ambulance company shouting into his cell phone. "I don't give a shit!" he said. "I need bathrooms, I need food, I need water, I need it now! I need buses, I need cots . . ." Sandra saw a few of her former EMT students. They looked exhausted, and she joined them in helping to sort patients. Sandra examined injured people, sick people, diabetics missing limbs. She directed some of them to ambulances heading to Baton Rouge.

For the vast majority of people camped on the freeway interchange, she could do nothing. Many, Sandra learned, had experienced a terrifying day and night on their rooftops and urgently needed shelter, food, and water. When one approached with a polite request, "Please give me a bottle for my mom over there," Sandra said no. The medical teams had hidden their own food and water in supply trailers for fear of being overrun. "If I give you a bottle, then I have to give everybody a bottle, and then we won't have water to take care of you people," Sandra told the petitioner. She felt horrible. It was crazy. Why wasn't there water for the people?

As she worked, Sandra combed the crowds for someone who could tell her about rescue plans for the city's hospitals. Early that afternoon, officials had called on the radio for anyone who had a boat to bring it to a nearby Sam's Club in a suburb of New Orleans. "We desperately need these boats, we've got deputies that need to be rescued," Aaron Broussard, the president of neighboring Jefferson Parish, had told a radio host. Hospitals, too, could be evacuated by water. But as evening fell and light drained away from the disaster zone, Sandra LeBlanc saw boats lined up on the interstate, on trailers.

While Sandra worked on Tuesday evening, five hundred miles away, in Dallas, Tenet's regional business director, Michael Arvin, phoned the EMS bureau in Baton Rouge and left a message for its director. He reported that floodwater was rising quickly around Memorial and another of the company's hospitals, Lindy Boggs Medical Center. One of the hospitals had lost electricity, he said, and he asked the state for help. Within an hour, at 8:30 p.m. on Tuesday, a worker had noted in the state EMS logs that the two hospitals would become a high priority to evacuate: "Mission 1."

Twenty minutes later the EMS bureau dispatched a volunteer, Carl Cramer, from Baton Rouge toward New Orleans. His mission was to meet up with fifty-five boats and evacuate the two hospitals. He checked in with the bureau after midnight on Wednesday morning, and his update was dutifully recorded in the logs in Baton Rouge. "Never did hook up with the boats. Was told they stopped the boats because of snipers and darkness." Instead, Cramer joined the other EMS workers at the cloverleaf on Causeway Boulevard.

When Vera LeBlanc's sitter called Sandra LeBlanc in the middle of the night from Memorial, Sandra carried the phone out of the trailer and saw Cramer. She knew him from his work with the state's EMS program. "Can you get the command center on the radio?" she asked. If EMS officials could hear the sitter's desperation, she thought, they might focus harder on rescuing people at the hospital. Sandra's plea was recorded in the EMS logs at 4:45 a.m. on Wednesday: "Frantic call from her mother in law—the nurses are starting to panic—they are in Memorial Hospital on Napoleon."

LeBlanc was told, inexplicably, that the hospital was now considered *second* priority. Its best hope of rescue, it seemed, lay with her, an EMT teacher who wasn't even on contract with the state anymore. The person on the other side of the radio said Sandra should go with the boats at sunrise, find the best place to launch them, and do what she could to help empty the hospital.

At daylight on Wednesday, the LeBlancs drove six miles south on Causeway Boulevard to the Sam's Club parking lot near where the floodwaters started. The lot was filled with people and boats. The LeBlancs struck up a conversation with two men. The blunted vowels and head-spinning pace of their patois marked them as Louisiana Cajuns, descendants of the French via Nova Scotia and centuries-long residents of southern Acadiana, a land of marshes and languid bayous that tilted along the Gulf Coast and was best traversed by boat.

"We're here to rescue people out of the hospitals. That's what we're going to do," one said. Each man had an airboat and was looking for someone to tell him where to go. The LeBlancs told them about Mark's mother and the horrible conditions the sitter had described at Memorial. The men said they thought Memorial might be one of the hospitals where volunteers would be sent. One of them went to look for information. He returned and said, "They're fixing to make an announcement."

The boat pilots in the parking lot gathered around a woman who climbed up on a tailgate to speak to them. She announced that she needed volunteers to scout out routes to an initial set of destinations. She shouted out the names of several hospitals—other hospitals, not Memorial.

When the woman finished, the LeBlancs raised their hands and asked, what about Memorial, what about Baptist? The woman said it was being prioritized *last* among the hospitals. Why, she didn't know.

The LeBlancs couldn't understand it. Didn't officials realize that Memorial had lost power and that people there were panicking, getting desperate, even dying? Were the other hospitals in New Orleans somehow worse off? Who was in charge? Where were the answers?

One of the two Cajun men asked the LeBlancs if they knew how to get to the hospital. "Well, sure," Mark said. He had been born there when it was known as Baptist. It was the hospital where his family always went for care. He had visited his mother there just the other day. The two men said they would pilot their airboats to Memorial if the LeBlancs could show them the way.

"We don't need much water to launch," one of the airboat captains said. They piled into pickup trucks and explored one potential route to the flood zone, then looped back and hit water on Jefferson Highway just east of Ochsner Medical Center, near a set of railroad tracks and the Orleans Parish line. The LeBlancs explained that from there it was a straight shot to Memorial along the highway, which turned into Claiborne Avenue. It was the route, in reverse, that the LeBlancs had used to evacuate the city days earlier. The men backed their trailers into the water and launched the boats from there.

The giant fans at the back of the boats stirred the air with a roar and propelled them. As they floated over the highway, Mark LeBlanc imagined cars, from clunkers to the fanciest Jaguars and Mercedes-Benzes, parked in the medians, now drowned. The deeper they ventured into the city, the more intense and frantic the scene. They saw people wading through water up to their necks who turned to look and gesture at the airboats loudening the midmorning. The LeBlancs had only advice to dispense. "There's dry land that way! We can't stop. We're on our way to the hospital."

Two small aluminum boats joined them as they went. When they arrived at Memorial, Mark borrowed a flashlight from a nurse and bounded up seven flights of stairs to LifeCare. What hit him first was the heat, then the stillness. Nursing assistants loitered at a desk, looking worn, not tending to patients. Some of them registered shock when they saw him, knowing he had not stayed at Memorial for the storm. The patients he passed were almost naked. He found his eighty-two-year-old mother covered in sweat, lying on a wet bed. She greeted him with a smile and told him she was thirsty. She was, she said calmly, "in a mess."

The sight infuriated Mark, and he left to get Sandra. They comforted his mother and then went to find out what the hell was happening. Diane Robichaux, the visibly pregnant senior leader on the floor, met with them in her office and said she didn't have much information. The LeBlancs told her they had brought airboats to Memorial and planned to round up more. They explained the location of the launch site where patients could be dropped. "You're going to have to have ambulances to pick them up there," Sandra said.

Robichaux no longer had, she explained, a way to contact her corporate office to request the ambulances. The LeBlancs, struck by how resigned everyone at the hospital seemed, offered to try to arrange ambulances themselves with their working cell phone. "Of course," Robichaux said, "any help you can give us, we'll take."

The LeBlancs called an ambulance company and put Robichaux on the phone. She described the location of the site by the railroad tracks near Ochsner Medical Center. "We need an exact address," the person on the line told her. "Without an exact address, I can't send anybody out."

"Well, I don't have an exact address," Robichaux said.

"Ma'am, we can't help you. We can't help you unless you have an exact address." While Robichaux's colleagues wrestled with a pile of phone books, looking for some kind of address or at least the name of a cross street, the call with the ambulance company dropped. Robichaux was unable to reconnect.

She reached a LifeCare corporate representative in Shreveport. Speaking quickly, so as not to lose another call, Robichaux asked if LifeCare could divert some of the ambulances that were heading to the staging area they had previously discussed, and send them instead to the boat location near Ochsner. The corporate representative said she would try. She and her colleagues would also try to locate the ventilator patients who had gone out earlier and arrange for their transfer to other LifeCare hospitals.

The LeBlancs headed back downstairs. Mark was upset. He believed his mother needed an IV to hydrate her and deliver antibiotics for a stubborn urinary infection, but he'd been told the hospital could no longer provide intravenous fluids. Though his mother was a LifeCare patient, Mark complained to a Memorial administrator, who explained that the hospital was in a survival mode now, not a treating mode. "Do you just flip a switch and you're not a hospital anymore?" Mark asked.

⁓

THAT MORNING, after having difficulty locating a sufficient supply of official, color-coded triage armbands, doctors and nurses settled on a new method for categorizing the many more than one hundred remaining Memorial and LifeCare patients as they were brought downstairs. They were divided into three groups to help speed the evacuation. Those in fairly good health who could sit up or walk would be categorized "1's" and prioritized first for evacuation. Those who were sicker and would need more assistance were "2's." A final group of patients were assigned "3's" and were slated to be evacuated last. That group included those whom doctors judged to be very ill and also, as doctors had agreed on Tuesday, those with DNR orders.

Dr. Anna Pou, always one to take on the most difficult tasks, jumped in to help coordinate the mass movement of patients. Every breath she took of the rancid air burned the back of her throat. She considered the unsanitary conditions in the hospital nearly unbearable, the pitch-black interior rooms exceptionally dangerous. She worried that even healthy people were getting sick and having difficulty breathing in the heat.

Pou and other workers scoured the hospital floor by floor for every last cot and stretcher and dragged them down to the second-floor lobby. Throughout the morning, makeshift teams of medical staff and family members carried many of the remaining Memorial and LifeCare patients there. Pou rolled the short sleeves of her scrub shirt up to her shoulders and stood ready to receive them.

In the dim light, a ranking began. Nurses opened each chart and read the diagnoses, using flashlights sparingly to save batteries. Pou and the nurses assigned a category to each patient. A nurse wrote "1," "2," or "3" on a sheet of paper with a Marks-A-Lot pen and taped it to the clothing over a patient's chest. Other patients had numbers written on their hospital gowns. Many of the 1's—roughly three dozen in total from Memorial and LifeCare—were guided down to the emergency room ramp. The airboat flotilla was beginning to make runs to dry ground, and the plan at first was for these patients to go out on them. LifeCare nursing director Gina Isbell and Memorial nurse manager Karen Wynn took charge of the patients' care while they waited on the ramp.

The 2's—perhaps seventy in all throughout the day—were generally placed along the corridor on the way to the hole in the machine-room wall that was a shortcut to the parking garage and, ultimately, the helipad. A dozen and a half or so 3's were moved to a corner of the second-floor lobby near a Hibernia Bank ATM and a planter filled with striped green dieffenbachia. Patients awaiting evacuation would continue to be cared for—their diapers would be changed, they would be fanned, often by family members of the staff, and given sips of water if they could drink—but once the patients were moved out of their rooms on Wednesday, most other medical interventions were limited. The idea of indicating somebody's destiny by a number struck at least one passing doctor, neuroradiologist Bill Armington, as expeditious but distasteful.

Pou and her coworkers were performing triage, a word once used by the French in reference to the sorting of coffee beans and later applied to the battlefield by Napoleon Bonaparte's chief surgeon, Baron Dominique-Jean Larrey. Triage came to be used in accidents and disasters when the number of those injured exceeded available resources. Surprisingly, perhaps, there was no consensus on how best to do this.

Concepts of triage and medical rationing are a barometer of how those in power in a society value human life. During World War II, the British military limited the use of scarce penicillin to pilots and bomber crews. Before lifesaving kidney dialysis became widely available in the United States, some hospital committees secretly factored age, gender, marital status, education, occupation, and "future potential" into treatment decisions to promote the "greatest good" for the community. When this practice attracted broader public attention in the 1960s, academics condemned one Seattle clinic for ruling out "creative non-conformists . . . [who] have historically contributed so much to the making of America. The Pacific Northwest is no place for a Henry David Thoreau with bad kidneys."

A story in *LIFE* magazine by Shana Alexander exposed the practices and led to public outcry. Lawmakers created a system in which Americans who needed dialysis would be entitled to it, typically at the government's expense. However, in countries such as South Africa, dialysis rationing persisted for patients receiving care in public hospitals. With the number of those who could benefit far exceeding the number of treatment slots, doctors struggled at weekly meetings to choose who lived and who died. Would it be ethical to weigh "social-worth criteria"

like a person's job, parental status, or drug-abuse history alongside medical criteria? Should patients be informed of the decisions and given the
opportunity to appeal? After years of decisions that favored white South
Africans, how could the process itself be made more just? Eventually
doctors sought input from patients themselves in constructing a more
standardized rationing system; the dreadful process of selecting patients
was made more accountable as advocates campaigned to expand dialysis
programs for low-income South Africans and to prevent kidney disease.

In the United States at the time of Katrina, at least nine well-
recognized triage systems existed to prioritize patients in the case of
mass casualties. Because of the difficulty of investigating outcomes, including deaths, in emergencies—and perhaps because of the potential for
political embarrassment or due to a lack of financial incentives—almost
no research had been done to see whether any of the commonly used
triage systems achieved their intended goals or even that they didn't
paradoxically worsen overall survival. Most systems called for people
with relatively minor injuries to wait while medical personnel attended
to patients in the worst shape. This was Baron Larrey's original concept
of triage as described in his memoirs of an October 1806 battle in Jena,
Prussia, between Napoleon's forces and the Fourth Coalition. "They
who are injured in a less degree may wait until their brethren in arms,
who are badly mutilated, have been operated on and dressed," he wrote.
"Those who are dangerously wounded should receive the first attention, without regard to rank or distinction," an idea in keeping with the
French Revolutionary concept of *égalité*.

British naval surgeon John Wilson introduced another triage tier several decades later in 1846 when he decided to withhold surgery from
patients for whom it would likely be unsuccessful. In 2005, a few triage systems incorporated this idea, calling for medical workers to forgo
treating or evacuating injured patients who were seen as having little
chance of survival given the resources at hand. That category was in-

tended for use during a devastating event such as a war-zone truck bombing in which there were far more severely injured victims than ambulances or medics.

Consigning certain sicker patients to go last has its risks, however. Predicting how a patient will fare is inexact and subject to biases. In one very small study of triage, experienced rescuers were asked to categorize the same patients and came up with widely different lists. Many patients who could have survived were mistakenly deemed unsalvageable by some rescuers. And patients' conditions can change; more resources can become available to help those whose situations at first appear hopeless. The importance of reassessing each person is easy to forget once a ranking is assigned.

Designating a category of patients as beyond help creates the tragic possibility that a patient with a chance of survival will be miscategorized and left to die. To avoid this, some experts have concluded that patients seen to have little chance of survival must still be treated or evacuated— after those with severe injuries who need immediate attention to survive, but before those with significant injuries who can wait.

Pou and her colleagues had little if any training in triage systems and were not guided by any particular protocol. Pou viewed the sorting system they developed as heart-wrenching. To her, changing the evacuation order from sickest first to sickest last resulted from a sense among the doctors that they would not be able to save everyone.

———

POU WOULD LATER SAY that the goal in a disaster must be to do "the greatest good for the greatest number of people," the same phrase used by public servants, including New Orleans Sewerage and Water Board superintendent George G. Earl when he decided which parts of New Orleans to protect from flooding with his limited budget in the 1920s.

But what does the "greatest good" mean when it comes to medicine? Is it the number of lives saved? Years of life saved? Best "quality" years of life saved? Or something else?

The goal of maximizing net good for a population has its roots in the utilitarian philosophy developed by Jeremy Bentham and John Stuart Mill in the eighteenth and nineteenth centuries. More recent philosophers have warned that this approach, if applied to lifesaving medical care in disasters, may require an unacceptable level of sacrifice from those most in need of assistance. These thinkers favor an approach modeled on the principles of justice set out by John Rawls in the late twentieth century (although Rawls himself did not apply them to medical care). The idea is to distribute care based on need. Those in the most imminent danger of dying without care have a bigger claim to the pool of aid, much as French surgeon Larrey articulated, even if that inconveniences a larger number of patients with less urgent conditions who have to wait. This is the approach taken in most American emergency rooms in non-disaster settings.

Other philosophers have gone further afield, arguing that potentially lifesaving resources should be allocated randomly, because everyone deserves an equal chance to survive, and because it is dangerous to endow groups of people with the power to assign who lives and who dies. This argument sparked a debate that played out in the pages of philosophy journals for a decade beginning in the late 1970s. Proponents rejected the popular idea that the number of lives saved should be a central consideration when prioritizing rescues. The writer of an influential paper, John M. Taurek, also argued that suffering is not cumulative between individuals—for example, that it is impossible to add up the suffering of a large number of people with minor headaches to equal the suffering of a single person with a migraine, as a utilitarian might do. This concept was also elegantly expressed many years earlier by the author C. S. Lewis, who wrote:

There is no such thing as a sum of suffering, for no one suffers it. When we have reached the maximum that a single person can suffer, we have, no doubt, reached something very horrible, but we have reached all the suffering there can ever be in the universe. The addition of a million fellow-sufferers adds no more pain.

The quandary of disaster triage had an analogue in everyday American medicine: the allocation of transplant organs. The United Network for Organ Sharing invited both doctors and laypeople to help design allocation schemes as part of an ethics committee. According to medical ethicist Robert M. Veatch, members of the general public typically favored giving organs to those in the direst need, even if these patients were less likely to survive or lived at a greater distance from where organs became available. In contrast, health professionals tended to favor systems aimed at directing available organs to the patients most likely to benefit medically from them. To achieve this, the professionals were more willing to accept that many of the sickest patients would die without transplants, as would patients who had less of a chance of acquiring a well-matched organ because they were members of ethnic groups that had a higher rate of need or a lower rate of donation (a problem mitigated by the development of newer antirejection drugs). The approach could also disadvantage members of groups whose outcomes tended to be poorer, including, in the case of kidney transplants, those of lower socioeconomic status.

Although no allocation method could ever enlist universal agreement, the process of devising a method, at least, can be made more just. In the case of organ transplantation, including both doctors and laypeople in decision making resulted in policies that prioritized a mixture of both justice and efficiency. Who decides how care is allocated is critically important because it is, at its heart, a question of moral priorities.

At Memorial, however, in the disaster's vise, only medical professionals had a say in how patients would be categorized for evacuation. Once the decisions were made, no system was established to share the information with the people who would be most affected by it.

In some cases it was actively kept from them.

On a fifth-floor hallway in Memorial's Clara Wing, transporters rolled a bed-bound patient toward the stairwell for evacuation, but after seeing she had a DNR order, they stopped and repeatedly maneuvered other patients around her. Nurses were instructed not to tell the patient's daughter that this was because her mother had a DNR order. To calm her, they said her mother wasn't the only patient left on the floor, failing to mention that the only other patient was dead. His son had taken him to Memorial's emergency room before the storm for a cough, but the ninety-seven-year-old man with Alzheimer's disease, James Lafayette, was discharged and had spent two days lying on the floor of Memorial's lobby before being admitted. Hours later, nurse Michelle Pitre-Ryals found him pulseless in his bed. Doctors and nurses appeared from everywhere, lighting his room like a Christmas tree with their flashlights. They ran a Code Blue, but extraordinary measures, after the lack of ordinary measures, failed to revive him. Pitre-Ryals was distraught. In her five years as a professional, no patient had died unexpectedly on her watch.

Now a man with a walkie-talkie appeared and told staff members they had to leave the floor. "What are you talking about?" Pitre-Ryals asked. Nobody had come for the DNR patient. The hot, exhausted nurse couldn't believe she and her colleagues were being told to abandon her and they refused. Pitre-Ryals informed the woman's daughter of her right to request that the DNR order be discontinued, just as she had approved it after her oxygen-dependent mother was admitted for the storm. "If she goes into cardiac arrest, let her go," the daughter had said, reasoning it wouldn't make sense for her mother to be resuscitated at age ninety-three. This situation struck the daughter as entirely different. "I didn't mean for her to be left up here," she told Pitre-Ryals. "When I made my mother a DNR, I did not know it meant 'do not rescue.'"

The daughter asked for the DNR order to be canceled. She even appealed to the self-interest of the nurses who insisted on staying with her despite being ordered to leave. "You people have to get out, and we're keeping you." Someone went to find a doctor to remove the DNR order, and the patient was moved downstairs and out into the parking garage on the way to the helipad and rescue, surviving her immediate ordeal.

On a seventh-floor hallway at LifeCare, Angela McManus, another patient's daughter, panicked when she overheard workers discussing the decision to defer evacuation for DNR patients. She had expected that her frail seventy-year-old mother, Wilda, would soon be rescued, but her mother, too, had a DNR order. "I've got to rescind that order," Angela begged the LifeCare staff. They told her that there were no doctors available to do it.

Wilda McManus stayed upstairs in LifeCare. The doctors in the second-floor staging area told LifeCare staff to stop sending down patients. There was, they said, no more room.

CHAPTER 6

WEDNESDAY, AUGUST 31, 2005—AFTERNOON

IN A PRIVATE PATIENT room on the fourth floor of the Clara Wing at Memorial, Karen Lagasse watched four men take hold of the corners of her mother's hospital bed sheet and lift her. The men carried Merle Lagasse toward the staircase. Karen and a nurse followed, holding an oxygen cylinder and the single bag Karen had stuffed with belongings.

Merle was, until recent months, a vivacious seventy-six-year-old. She had volunteered in the schools and worked reception at a beauty salon, and was a lover, rescuer, and collector of feral cats.

Dr. Ewing Cook had treated Merle for emphysema until his recent retirement. Merle adored him. She would dress up for appointments at his office. She had an Elizabeth Taylor aura, her brows arched, a corona of mascara radiating around her richly lined eyes, her lipstick bright. Cook would greet her with a huge smile. "Merle," he'd say, "you're gonna make a beautiful corpse." The comment irked her daughter, Karen. But Merle heard only "beautiful."

The tall, balding doctor had been sober with them from the beginning. Merle had emphysema. There was not much to be done. Cook prescribed a home oxygen machine and Merle opted for the longest cord so she could walk freely through the house. She went out sometimes with a portable tank. But she was weak. Karen wished Cook would be more proactive. Could physical therapy help?

More recently Merle had learned she had lung cancer—not the curable kind. A little more than a week before Katrina, her new doctor, Roy Culotta, had admitted her to Memorial after she had a bad reaction to a pain medicine patch.

During Merle's hospital stay, Culotta had worked to relieve her pain, her shortness of breath, and the existential anxiety that grips patients whose hunger for air goes chronically unsatisfied. Before the hurricane, he had prescribed treatment with a Vapotherm machine that directed a high flow of oxygen from the supply in Memorial's walls into Merle's nose.

Culotta had another idea he said would help Merle breathe easier. Fluid on the left side of her chest cavity was constricting a lung. He could tap the fluid in her thorax using a sterile needle and a flexible tube, allowing the lung to expand again. This thoracentesis procedure promised temporary relief, perhaps for days or weeks, until the fluid built up again.

Culotta ordered a thoracentesis kit to be placed at Merle's bedside, but he had not yet come to perform the procedure. On Monday afternoon, after the intermittent bands of wind and rain from Katrina had abated, Karen saw him in the parking garage. He told her he was on his way home to take a shower. She had not encountered him since then. The kit sat at Merle's bedside still wrapped in plastic as it had been since the day before the hurricane.

After the air-conditioning cut out on Monday, Karen had lifted a box fan to the bedside table and pointed it at her mother. She covered her in ice packs. She ran downstairs to pray in the dark, empty chapel for her mother and their cats, whom she had left at her mother's house with food and water. She feared they might have drowned.

Overnight on Tuesday, the alarm on the high-flow oxygen machine began ringing. The respiratory therapist had stopped making visits. To Karen, it seemed to take the nurses on the fourth floor a remarkably long time to figure out the reason for the alarm—the power loss.

They took away the failing Vapotherm machine and replaced it with a less-effective alternative—a mask that connected to the hospital's bulk oxygen supply, still flowing miraculously from the wall. Karen felt anxious. Her mother's breathing seemed more effortful. Karen tried to cool her by fanning her with a piece of cardboard printed with the hospital company logo that a hospital worker had distributed.

The nurses said Merle would be one of the first patients to leave Memorial because she relied on equipment to help her breathe. Then a doctor came to ask whether Merle could sit in a wheelchair. Karen didn't think so. Karen realized the plan for her mother had changed when the patients who could walk or sit in wheelchairs began leaving the floor first.

When it was finally Merle's turn, a nurse detached the oxygen tubing from a nozzle on the wall and slid it onto a regulator atop a green metal gas cylinder. Karen noticed that the kit for removing the fluid around her mother's lungs was still sitting at the bedside. She asked the nurse whether to take it along. "Oh, they're not going to do that now," she replied.

Several volunteers gripped the sides of Merle's bed sheets, lifted her, and carried her to a stairwell. They began their descent with Merle facing headfirst. Realizing the peril of this approach, they backed up and turned her feet-forward before continuing.

When they emerged from the stairwell two flights below, they laid her down in a line of patients leading to the machine room on the second floor. Lying flat made it even harder for Merle to breathe. A nurse whom Karen recognized came to check on Merle. "She's got to go now!" the nurse said, and twisted the knob on the regulator to maximize the flow of oxygen.

No kidding, Karen thought. Staff members descended on Merle to begin moving her to the heliport, and Karen was told she had to leave the area. She started to walk away, but heard her mother's voice. "Karen," Merle gulped, "I can't breathe." Karen turned around and saw the oxygen tank had been disconnected and her mother was about to be passed through the narrow opening in the wall leading to the parking garage.

"She can't breathe without the oxygen!" Karen yelled at a woman in scrubs who looked like a doctor and seemed to be in charge. "You have to put it back on her!"

"You don't know what's going on," the woman said. Others stood and stared. Karen argued with the woman, even as she was reassured that her mother would receive oxygen on the other side of the hole in the parking garage. Karen was told she needed to leave the area. She was so hot and angry she felt ready to kill the woman speaking to her so insensitively. She knew she had to get out of there and her mother did too. She turned and rushed down to the ER ramp to try to get on a boat so she could begin searching for wherever her mother might be taken. She did not want her to be alone.

—

ON THE OTHER side of the wall, on the helipad above the parking garage, a fortunate few were being helped aboard helicopters. Among the first to lift off were a pregnant ICU nurse and several patients with kidney failure who needed dialysis. In the bright sunlight on the open pad, hospital volunteers mopped their brows with small white towels that they wore on their heads or tucked around the necks of their scrub shirts. In the helipad's shadow, wheelchair-bound patients were staged on the gravel-covered roof of the parking garage so that volunteers could bring them to helicopters quickly.

A Coast Guard lieutenant reached Susan Mulderick by phone. His colleagues had been trying to put Memorial staff in touch with state emergency officials but had difficulty reaching anyone at the hospital.

The overnight rescue operation had come in for some official criticism. At least one Coast Guard commander said the local sector and its junior grade lieutenants had stepped on toes by responding directly to Memorial, taking initiative when they received no response from higher officials or those stationed at the State Emergency Operations center.

The lieutenant on the phone asked Mulderick whether the hospital had water and food. When she told him it did, he said he needed to pull helicopters away for a period of time to rescue people stranded on rooftops, something that had been more difficult to do overnight in the dark. Coast Guard pilots, entering New Orleans airspace at night on the way to Memorial, had seen what appeared to be a sea of light through their night vision goggles. With no streetlights or headlights, every source of those lights likely represented a person with a candle, flashlight, or lighter, signaling for help. Additional search-and-rescue assets were being sought from around the nation. The number in the area was inadequate to the need. Pilots nearing Memorial could see people desperately waving their arms and flapping sheets and towels out of the windows of a nearby apartment building and from the back of a flooded pickup truck. Near the intersection of Claiborne and Napoleon Avenues, some people attempted to wade through rainbow-sheened water nearly up to their necks, pushing tires and coolers ahead of them as flotation devices.

Private air ambulance companies now had to request special permission to enter the New Orleans airspace, and those present were focusing on critical patients at other hospitals. Even as the number of aircraft operating over the city grew, the limited or absent air traffic control radar and air-to-ground communications, and the presence of aboveground power and phone lines, made flying extremely dangerous. Only a few private and military choppers arrived at Memorial on Wednesday morning after daylight. Some of the pilots seemed to be under the mistaken impression that only a handful of patients remained. Several National Guard pilots landed to *drop off* patients at Memorial.

At least the Coast Guard emergency radio proved helpful. To conserve its batteries, every hour, at a quarter to the hour, the nurse who was also an Air Force Reserve captain asked someone to find the CEO and Susan Mulderick and see if the hospital needed anything. She then turned on the radio, checked in with emergency officials, and made requests for supplies, which helicopters dropped on the pad. Later, someone took the radio and gave Memorial two satellite phones to use instead, but nobody could make them work. Reliable communications with the world outside were lost.

Overhead, the sky pulsed with a war-zone soundtrack of low-flying aircraft. During the day President George W. Bush, too, cutting short his Crawford, Texas, ranch vacation two days after the storm, overflew the devastation in *Air Force One* on his way back to the White House.

Inside the plane, photographers Jim Watson and Mannie Garcia captured the president in profile as he leaned toward a window. Daylight sharpened the maze of creases on his face and illuminated the frown on his lips. Another photographer, Susan Walsh, caught the president from a different angle, behind a shoulder of his monogrammed blue flight jacket as he rested on crossed forearms, gazing out at a body of water, hands balled into fists.

Some would later accuse the president's peregrination of grounding rescue flights. Exceptions to presidential airspace restrictions were, however, typically granted for lifesaving medical flights. Whatever its causes, the slowdown in the arrival of rescue helicopters compared with the previous day frustrated the staff and volunteers on Memorial's helipad, who were now organized, eager to work, and surrounded by patients awaiting transport. A doctor on the helipad aimed his Treo cell phone skyward and snapped a picture of what appeared to be the Boeing 747 body silhouetted against bright clouds as it glided overhead, less than half a mile above the hospital.

GREEN VINES SPILLED over the side of a smoking balcony, where several people watched as evacuees were helped down from the top of the emergency room ramp onto the bow of an airboat. Other onlookers took to hospital windows, and still others watched suspended from a double-deck bridge over flooded Clara Street.

Each of the two airboats fit three or four people in addition to its pilot. Several adult patients whose breathing relied on a tracheostomy— a surgical hole in the neck—or who had cancer went aboard, including the two relatively young people who had recently received bone marrow transplants and whom Memorial staff had hoped to transfer out on Tuesday. They were highly susceptible to infections but were able-bodied enough to wade through shallow water at the drop-off point. They and the other passengers put on earmuffs or stuffed their ears with gauze to protect against the din of the airboat propellers.

An aluminum flatboat, its motor singing a gentler vibrato, took five newborn babies cradled in slings against their mothers. A World War II veteran with leukemia, who had once seen an American ship explode at sea, put on his Merchant Marine cap for the journey. A young man warned him to take it off so the wind wouldn't steal it as they shoved off from shipwreck Memorial.

Nurse manager Karen Wynn didn't like to pull rank or beg favors, but she was determined not to let all the first boats leave without her other pregnant ICU nurses. One, less than a month from her due date, had started having contractions the previous day, but she resisted getting on a boat without her grandmother. Her colleagues told her she had to go. Wynn said she couldn't put her unborn child at risk for the sake of the elderly woman. Wynn and nurse Cheri Landry would look after the nurse's grandmother and an elderly aunt who had also accompanied her. The nurse climbed aboard.

The giant fan at the back of one of the airboats roared. Its pilot, high above his passengers on a metal chair, steered through the murky water on Clara Street, leaving a small wake. The boat floated past the domes of several vehicles in the parking lot of Memorial's Cancer Institute and a trunk door that had popped open in the water. Where the hell her nurses were heading, Wynn had no idea. Somewhere, she thought, somebody out there has this organized, has this under control. She was sure.

At the drop site, the airboat pilots transferred these first evacuees into waiting ambulances and began the more than three-mile journey back to Memorial. They glided slowly to avoid hitting debris. The round-trip took more than an hour.

Sandra LeBlanc scouted out a closer dry-drop location near a Rite Aid and a Copeland's Restaurant nine blocks south of Memorial. Along the city's southwest border, the "sliver by the river" was dry, and it connected to roads out of town. The airboat pilots, whose efforts were soon bolstered by the arrival of a much larger vessel, began ferrying people to the new site, but they found no ambulances there. Perhaps nobody had tried to get a call through and redirect them. Also, disembarking there required wading through dirty shallow water to dry ground.

The evacuation strategy underwent another subtle shift. Now only the relatively few patients who were well enough to be discharged were put onto the boats. Several doctors had taken over loading the boats, trading the hot hospital and its very sick patients for the open-air emergency room ramp, where they oversaw the process. They began allowing hospital employees to leave along with their own and the patients' family members, hundreds of whom still remained at Memorial. The evacuation line wound from the ramp back through the emergency room and into the hospital's reception area.

As they neared the boats, many people asked questions of Karen Wynn. "Where we goin'? Where we goin'?" She didn't know where. It frustrated her when people on the cusp of freedom suddenly hesitated to leave the hospital. They seemed more comfortable with the hell they knew than with the unknown journey that awaited them. One woman refused to get on a boat when told she couldn't bring her purse for space reasons. Her and her husband's "whole life" was in that purse, she said, and she was willing to be separated from him, a discharged patient, to hold on to it. *Give me the fricking purse!* Wynn wanted to tell her. Wynn offered to take responsibility for it, as she had taken responsibility for the pregnant nurse's grandmother, if that would convince the woman to go. But it didn't. The woman wasn't having it. She would not give up the purse, and so she wouldn't leave.

The stress of the disaster narrowed people's fields of vision, as if they wore blinders to anyone's experience but their own. Again and again, Wynn saw signs that others were not appreciating the gravity of the situation inside Memorial. Early in the morning, an outpatient somehow made it through the floodwaters to the hospital for a regularly scheduled chemotherapy appointment. The water had stabilized at about five to six feet around the sloping hospital grounds; the feared additional fifteen feet had not come. "Sweetheart, we're not giving chemo today," Wynn told her.

A representative of the Women's Hospital in Baton Rouge called Wynn to complain that a male psychiatric patient from Memorial had been transported there along with the neonates on Tuesday. *Just what do you want me to do?* Wynn wanted to ask. The staff at Women's could simply put him in an ambulance and send him to a hospital that accepted men. At least she assumed they could. She wasn't thinking about how many patients from New Orleans might have been dropped in the capital. She couldn't imagine the situation outside the walls of Memorial was anywhere near as bad as it was inside them.

While the boats made runs to dry ground with hospital staff and family members, Wynn helped care for the patients categorized as 1's from LifeCare and Memorial who had been carried down to the first floor in anticipation of rescue. They waited on the down-sloping sides of the ambulance ramp, the brakes of their wheelchairs locked. Throughout the hot afternoon, Wynn memorized the faces of her "little bodies" so as not to lose a soul, and then an unfamiliar one appeared. Where'd he come from? she wondered. He's not one of mine. The man was wet, and she noticed a dialysis catheter hanging from his chest just below one shoulder. It dangled from him, lacking the protection of a sterile dressing. The man told Wynn he lived in the neighborhood, had stayed for the storm, and was overdue for a dialysis treatment. As it was a matter of life and death, he had waded to Memorial in the foul, chest- or neck-high brew; Wynn could only imagine what little trolls had trekked into the catheter, which opened into a major vein, putting him at risk of a deadly blood infection.

Wynn called out to one of the doctors manning the boat launch. "Dr. Casey?" She pointed to the man. "Dialysis. He's gotta go. He's gotta go on the next boat." She had no idea what awaited the man at the other end of his boat ride, but she prayed she was giving him a chance to survive.

⁓

SOMETIME ON WEDNESDAY, people on the ER ramp noticed the strange sight of a mattress floating up Napoleon Avenue. The mattress made a turn onto Clara Street and neared the hospital. On it lay an ill-appearing black woman, with several men swimming through the fetid water, propelling her. "The hospital is closed!" someone shouted. "We're not accepting anybody."

René Goux, the hospital's chief executive, had decided for reasons of safety that people approaching Memorial should generally be directed to the dry ground at Napoleon Avenue and St. Charles Avenue nine blocks away, the same place Sandra LeBlanc had identified for discharging boat passengers from Memorial. Even the previous day, the Coast Guard auxiliary member in Alexandria had instructed Memorial staff by phone to secure the premises, station men at the doors and windows, and bar entry to anyone not in uniform. Nonetheless, after a heated exchange, a sympathetic doctor convinced administrators to take in the woman and her husband, but the men who'd swum in the toxic soup to deliver her were told to leave. The woman was lifted onto a stretcher and moved indoors into the emergency room hallway. Whadda we have here? Karen Wynn wondered. It was all well and good of the doctors to insist on accepting this patient, but now somebody had to care for her. Wynn had more than enough work with her charges on the ambulance ramp. Still, she couldn't leave the situation alone. She had to go inside and see about this lady.

The gaunt-faced woman, wrapped in covers on a stretcher against the wall, looked dead. Wynn pulled back her covers to assess her. The elderly lady was still breathing, but barely. She was emaciated. Her husband, who had arrived with her, told a confused story that suggested his wife had been in hospice care, suffering from some condition from which she was expected to die soon.

Wynn reached a hand beneath the woman's tiny frame and felt wetness. A tube had been placed into her bladder to drain her urine, but it had detached from its sterile collection bag. Wynn reattached the bag, even though it was no longer sterile and could eventually cause an infection. "So much for aseptic technique," she said to herself. She gathered up the wet bed linens. At least the woman would be dry.

"Have you all eaten today?" she asked the woman's husband. When he said no, Wynn went outside to rummage through her small cache of food. She returned, popped open a can of nutritional supplement, drew some into a straw, and dripped it into the woman's mouth. The woman swallowed. At least she could do that. Wynn turned the can and straw over to her husband, who coaxed his wife to drink.

Wynn found food for the man, too, and after he finished eating, he told her he was worried about looters. "I gotta go back and lock my house," he said. Wynn spent about twenty minutes trying to convince him that returning home wasn't possible. "Sweetheart, you can't go back home," she told him. "It's too dangerous. There's water and it's just too dangerous."

One couple with small children rowed up to Memorial, and the family was told to "go away." Dr. Bryant King, the young hospital-based physician who had recently come to work at Memorial, lost his temper. "You can't do this!" he shouted at CEO Goux. "You gotta help people!"

Karen Wynn saw that the hospital had all the people it could handle. She did not detect a note of racism in the refusals, even as the people being turned away were nearly all African American, as was she. King, by contrast, was offended largely because the people they were turning away had dark skin. As the only African American doctor on duty and one of very few who worked at the hospital, race had not been an issue for him until now. He believed introducing color into his argument would only make everyone touchy, and so he did not. This was a universal issue: the hospital was harboring dogs and cats while babies floated over polluted water on unsteady skiffs.

The family was refused in spite of King's advocacy.

To Dr. Ewing Cook, watching from the ambulance ramp, the episode reinforced the impression of King he'd developed the previous day when King resisted discontinuing treatments that weren't absolutely necessary. King was, Cook thought, out of touch with reality. Memorial wasn't so much a hospital anymore but a shelter that was running out of supplies and needed to be emptied. Cook also worried that intruders from the neighborhood might ransack the hospital for drugs and valuables. He'd had his semiautomatic Beretta in a pocket of his scrub pants since he'd heard rumors that a nurse was assaulted while walking her dog near the hospital on Monday. The CEO had told him to take the damn thing out of his briefcase and wear it.

Now, Wednesday afternoon, a day after his heat-exhaustion episode, Cook was physically and mentally drained, filthy, and forlorn. A painful boil was growing under his wristwatch, and bladder spasms drove him repeatedly into a ghastly-smelling bathroom with a nonflushing toilet.

Cook had also been contending with the illnesses of various family pets. His adult daughter's massive, ursine Newfoundland had at first frolicked in the floodwater and later began panting heavily in the heat. His daughter, ICU nurse Stephanie Meibaum, wanted to try giving Rolfie oxygen from the wall supply in the empty surgical building across the pedestrian bridge from the main hospital. The dog lumbered there obediently on shaking legs. As he stepped inside, he collapsed on the floor and convulsed.

Cook wrote a prescription for "Rolfe Meibaum" for five 100 mg tablets of the antiseizure medicine phenobarbital from the hospital pharmacy. On the same prescription form, Cook ordered eight syringes of the powerful anesthetic drug Pentothal, a half gram each. In Louisiana, only licensed veterinarians typically could prescribe medicine for animals. In the context of the disaster, the pharmacist let this go, but he insisted on the prescription as documentation in order to give Cook the controlled substances.

Cook began injecting Rolfie with Pentothal. It took multiple doses before he died. Cook also euthanized one of his daughter's three cats, which was suffering from a tooth abscess.

Pets weren't being allowed on the boats and helicopters, leading people to fear they would not be rescued. The owners of the two coddled golden retrievers had departed by boat, leaving them in Cook's office with instructions not to abandon them to suffer alone. Cook euthanized them, too.

After Rolfie's death, Dr. Horace Baltz noticed Cook's wife and daughter weeping and asked what was wrong. Ewing Cook described what had occurred with characteristic bluster, hiding any sadness behind what struck Baltz as a devilish laugh.

At around two p.m., Cook climbed slowly upstairs to check what was happening on the eighth floor in the ICU, where he had worked for many years. Most of the ICU patients had been airlifted on Tuesday, but the four with DNR orders who had been kept behind had not.

"What's going on here?" he asked the four nurses he found in the unit. "Whaddya have left?" The nurses were down to one patient with advanced uterine cancer, the seventy-nine-year-old woman who had worked as a nurse in segregation-era New Orleans.

The disaster had interrupted plans to move Jannie Burgess into a general medical ward for comfort care. Instead, the ICU nurses were giving her small doses of morphine every few hours as needed for pain. Cook opened Burgess's medical chart. According to the notes, on Monday night after the storm she had cried and was agitated. Her surgeon had visited on Tuesday and wrote that Burgess had stable vital signs and responded when he spoke to her. At one fifteen on this morning, her electronic monitors had stopped working when the emergency power failed in their section of the hospital. Intravenous pumps continued to drip fluids, sugar, electrolytes, and medicines into her veins for another two hours until they drained their batteries. Nurses then ran the fluids by gravity through Burgess's IV tubing, controlling the flow with a slide clamp.

After daylight, her eyes had remained closed. The rhythm of her shallow breaths was irregular, like the tick of a slowing clock with a dying battery. Sometimes ten to fifteen seconds would go by without an inspiration.

Cook examined Burgess. She was so weighted down by fluid from her diseases that he sized her up at more than three hundred pounds, much more than her normal weight. He arrived at certain conclusions: (1) Given how difficult it had been for him to climb the steps in the heat, there was no way he could make it back to the ICU again. (2) Given how exhausted everyone was and how much this woman weighed, it would be "impossible to drag her down six flights of stairs." (3) Even in the best of circumstances, the patient probably had a day or so to live. And frankly, the four nurses he found upstairs with her were needed elsewhere, although it was not up to him to tell them where to go.

To Cook, a drug that had been on Burgess's medication list for several days provided an answer. Morphine, a powerful narcotic, was frequently used to control severe pain or discomfort. But the drug could also slow breathing, and suddenly introducing much higher doses could lead to death.

nurses, and clinical researchers who specialized in treating
near the end of their lives would say that this "double effect"
d little danger when the drug was administered properly. To Cook,
it was not that clear. Any doctor who thought that giving a person a
lot of morphine was not prematurely sending that patient to the grave
was a very naïve doctor. "We kill 'em" was, in all bluntness, how he
described it.

In fact the distinction between murder and medical care often came
down to the intent of the person administering the drug. Cook walked
this line often as a pulmonologist, and he prided himself as the go-to
man for difficult end-of-life situations. When a very sick patient or the
patient's family made the decision to disconnect a ventilator, for example, Cook would prescribe morphine to make sure the patient wasn't
gasping for breath as mechanical assistance was withdrawn.

Achieving this level of comfort often required enough morphine that
the drug markedly suppressed the patient's breathing. The intent was to
provide comfort, but the result was to hasten death, and Cook knew it.
The difference between something ethical and something illegal was, as
Cook would put it, "so fine as to be imperceivable."

Burgess's situation was a little different, Cook had to admit. Being comatose and on occasional doses of painkillers, she appeared comfortable.
But the worst thing he could imagine would be for the drugs to wear off
and for Burgess to wake up and find herself in her ravaged condition as
she was being moved. Cook turned to Burgess's nurse. "Do you mind
just increasing the morphine and giving her enough until she goes?"

Cook returned to Burgess's patient chart. A sticker on its front cover
listed allergies to "egg/poultry" and a sticker on its back cover said
"DNR." Cook turned to an empty lined page of her progress record and
scribbled "No respirations or cardiac activity." He added, "Pronounced
dead @," left the time blank, and signed the note "ECook" in a large
squiggle. Then he walked back down the stairs, believing that he had
done the right thing for Burgess. He would later call that choice "a no-

brainer" and reflect on it. "I gave her medicine so I could get rid of her faster, get the nurses off the floor," he would say, perhaps to cover up the deeper emotions of a man who had devoted his career to the sickest of patients and was loath to let them suffer. "There's no question I hastened her demise."

The question of what to do with the hospital's sickest patients was also being raised by others. By the afternoon, with few helicopters landing, these patients were languishing. Incident commander Susan Mulderick, who had worked with Cook for decades, shared her own concerns with him. He would later remember her telling him, "We gotta do something about this. We're never going to get these people out."

Cook sat on the emergency room ramp smoking cigars with another doctor, John Kokemor. The patients were lined up in wheelchairs or sitting before their walkers on mismatched chairs. In their similar blue-patterned hospital gowns, they reminded Cook of a church choir. Help was coming too slowly. There were too many people who needed to leave and weren't going to make it. It was a desperate situation and Cook saw only two choices: quicken their deaths or abandon them. It had gotten to that point. You couldn't just leave them. The humane thing seemed to be to put 'em out.

Cook went to the staging area on the second floor, where Anna Pou and two other doctors were directing care. The area was broiling. Only some older wings of the hospital, built to be "productive of coolness" in the age before ubiquitous air-conditioning, had windows that opened. At first, some staff members had been warned they could be charged with destroying hospital property if they broke windows. Now, patients were moved back, and uniformed men and other eager volunteers crashed chairs, two-by-fours, and an oxygen tank through the tall glass panes into the surrounding moat, punishing the building that had failed to protect them.

Cots and stretchers appeared to cover every inch of floor space. An immense patient lay motionless on a stretcher, covered in sweat and almost nothing else. Cook thought the man was dead, and he touched him to make sure, but the man turned over and looked at him.

"I'm OK, Doc," Rodney Scott said. "Go take care of somebody else." He was the licensed practical nurse who had once worked at the hospital and who had been designated, because of his size, to leave the hospital last.

Despite how miserable the patients looked, Cook would later say he felt there was no way, in this crowded room, to do what he and Kokemor had discussed over cigars. "We didn't do it because we had too many witnesses. That's the honest-to-God truth." A different memory of their interactions would be held by Kokemor, who would say he never talked about euthanasia, and, regardless, was not involved in hospital decision making.

The scene in the second-floor lobby also rattled registered nurse Cathy Green. Like many of the other ICU nurses who no longer had their own patients to treat, she had volunteered to help care for others.

Green stood between the rows of recumbent patients and waved a bit of cardboard over them, agitating the dankness. "Help me," patients said. She offered sips of water.

Separated from their medications and treatments, and the nurses who knew them, they looked so sick. For all her experience with critical care medicine, this scene broke her heart. She couldn't bear it. She had to leave.

Green went up to the parking garage. Patients were arrayed on the asphalt awaiting helicopter rescue. An elderly lady lying on the ground was wheezing and looked distressed. Her lungs sounded as if they were choked with fluid. The oxygen tank beside her was empty. Green found a partially used tank. She recruited a few other people to help prop up the lady to a partial sitting position, making it easier for her to breathe. Green set up an inhalation treatment to help clear the woman's lungs. She talked to the woman softly, trying to reassure her.

A doctor came and peered at the lady's chart. "She has lung cancer," he said quietly. He turned to Green and closed the woman's chart. "She's not going anywhere." He looked at the oxygen tank and shook his head no. "That's it," he said, and chopped the air with his hand. There would be no more respiratory treatments. This oxygen cylinder, its gauge indicating a quarter tank left, would be the last.

Green felt numb. She took the lady's hand and held it. The decision not to evacuate her or support her with oxygen felt personal. Two dozen or so of Green's relatives were in St. Bernard Parish, an area she'd heard on the radio was the worst and first hit by the flooding. Several times, Green's young adult daughter, who lived in a different state, had reached her on a cell phone. "Mommy," she cried, "I really think something happened to Granny. I just have this horrible feeling."

Green saw the sick lady before her as somebody's mother, somebody's grandmother. Many people probably loved this lady. Green felt love for her and she didn't even know her. The woman was precious, whether she had six months to live, or a year to live, whatever it was.

Green stood up and walked to another patient. She couldn't stand to watch this lady die on the ground, in a parking garage, in an American city, because nobody came to get her. She didn't want to know this lady's name.

———

WEDNESDAY, AUGUST 31, 2005—LATE AFTERNOON

THE UPTURNED BOWS of the airboats cast longer shadows on the water as they bobbed alongside the emergency room ramp. Sandra LeBlanc had spent hours helping to load them. Hospital visitors, technicians, nurses, even doctors had left throughout the day. LeBlanc's yellow-billed Louisiana State University baseball cap was stuck to her head, and sweat darkened her blue T-shirt.

LeBlanc looked for her husband, Mark. She found him caring for his mother, LifeCare patient Vera LeBlanc, in the second-floor lobby. "We got to get Mom out," she told him, surprised her mother-in-law had not already been rescued. With helicopters landing only rarely and ambulances failing to arrive at the boat drop-off, only a few patients had left Memorial all day. Vera had been placed far from the head of the line.

Vera's hospital gown was covered with the family names and phone numbers Mark and Sandra had scrawled on it after they had been told she would leave Memorial by helicopter. Instead, she was lying near the ATM and the planter full of green-striped leaves. The patients around her had DNR orders, as did she. Vera's Do Not Resuscitate status was not the recent wish of a dying woman, but rather the result of a request she had made more than a decade earlier so that her heart would not be restarted if it stopped. Her heart was still beating.

Earlier a staff member had tried to block Mark and Sandra from entering this patient-care area. It took a threat to gain admittance. We brought the boats, Mark warned, and we can take them away.

The patients lying cot to cot, partially uncovered, looked terrible to the LeBlancs. Most were deathly quiet, but not Vera. "Give me water," she demanded in a voice fit for a stage. The volunteers fanning other patients turned to stare. Mark found a five-gallon plastic jug of Kentwood water he figured belonged to the hospital staff. He filled a cup, deciding that the need to keep his mother hydrated trumped the risk that she might choke on the water because she had difficulty swallowing. "Oh, the water tastes so good, Mark," Vera crooned. "More water! More water!" A female doctor yelled for a nurse to give Vera a medicine to quiet her, but no nurse came.

Mark and Sandra discussed what to do with Vera. The boats were running low on fuel, and their pilots had heard that people were shooting at rescuers. These volunteers from the Louisiana swamplands had no plans to return with their vessels on Thursday, despite the fact that hundreds of people remained at Memorial.

No hoofbeats had been heard from the cavalry promised by the imposing man with the handheld radio. He seemed to have accomplished nothing. He told Sandra LeBlanc that no more helicopters would be coming for the day.

The LeBlancs didn't know where they might take Vera, but anywhere else seemed better than another night here. They decided to carry her down to the first floor and put her on one of the airboats they had directed to Memorial.

They picked up the ends of her cot. Instead of holding firm, it bent in the middle and began to sandwich Vera. They tried to readjust. Several doctors came to tell the LeBlancs they couldn't take Vera. "The hell we can't," Sandra said. "You can either help or get out of the way."

At first Sandra thought that the doctors were just being protective of their patient, but it seemed ironic that they didn't want to let Vera go when they had clearly decided there was nothing they could do to help her. Or were the doctors upset that a patient they had designated to leave last was cutting the line?

The LeBlancs readjusted their grip on Vera's cot and, with the help of two volunteers, carried her down to the ambulance ramp. Looking as pleased as a queen held aloft on a litter, she chattered away as they made their procession. They lifted her over the edge of the ramp where hospital workers had removed a pane of Plexiglas. "I'm on a boat!" she said, stentorian, and they fitted her with a set of earmuffs.

There was one more thing Sandra LeBlanc had promised to do before they left. She turned back to guide a burly hospital security guard onto the boat. They had worked together that day on the emergency ramp. He was desperate to leave Memorial. She'd offered to help him, too, escape.

———

AS THE ABLE-BODIED left Memorial, two dozen or so of the category 1 patients, "the choir," remained grouped in their wheelchairs on the ER ramp, watching and waiting for their turn at rescue.

Nutrition. Hydration. Elimination. Memorial's Karen Wynn and LifeCare's Gina Isbell worked with other staff to meet the patients' basic needs. Medical care, for the most part, was not provided.

One partially paralyzed stroke patient had diarrhea. Wynn repeatedly rolled her wheelchair into the privacy of the darkened emergency room, went with a flashlight to search the supply room for bottles of sterile water and saline, returned, put down the flashlight, and helped hoist the heavy woman to a standing position to be cleaned.

Wynn and Isbell rummaged for bedpans and changed adult diapers. Outside, they held up sheets around the patients to provide a semblance of privacy. At times, nature's urgency outpaced the nurses' alacrity. Wynn covered one accident on the emergency room ramp with a piece of cardboard.

The bathrooms in the hospital were offensive. People had continued to use the backed-up toilets, spreading feces onto the floor. No cleanup appeared to be happening. The spirit of volunteerism seemed to have retreated at the bathroom door.

The prospect of having to use a toilet took away Gina Isbell's hunger and thirst. Once, she brought a patient's elderly sister inside the hospital to a bathroom. When she returned for her, the woman was gone. Isbell lumbered as fast as she could down a dim, crowded corridor searching for her. She found the lady being led by the arm away from a door she had tried to exit. "She's mine," Isbell said. "I got her. I'll take her."

Some nurses said she was a Holocaust survivor, and as the day progressed, she grew more confused about where she was. "I need to get my sister out of here," she said, and unlocked the brakes of her sister's wheelchair, sending it rolling down the sloping pavement toward the floodwater. Isbell ran to catch the patient, but her sister kept repeating the trick. "You're killing me!" Isbell told her. Karen Wynn caught the woman trying to wander off with her sister's medical chart.

When evening came and the boats left, Isbell and Wynn wheeled the patients back inside the hospital's first-floor lobby for safety and settled them down on cots and stretchers to rest for the night. Father John Marse came to offer prayers, and the elderly sister swung her cane at him, asking "Why are *you* in such a place like this?" He answered: "'Cause God sent me here." She swung her cane at a nurse. She seemed to think she needed to protect her sister. A security guard took away her cane.

One male patient refused to get out of his wheelchair for the night; he wanted to be first in line to leave in the morning and thought being ready to move would give him an advantage.

Patients weren't the only fearful ones. National Guardsmen and local policemen had left for the night. Many in the hospital sensed danger in the coming darkness. Some employees from St. Bernard Parish, expecting that their houses might be flooded, had brought along their entire gun collections for safekeeping. Memorial CEO René Goux distributed the firearms to security and maintenance staff, who cordoned off the hospital's entrances.

Karen Wynn went to find her ICU nurses to tell them there would need to be a night shift to care for the estimated 115 remaining Memorial and LifeCare patients. Her nurses, anticipating this, had already volunteered to cover patients in the second-floor lobby, despite the fact that most of them had worked all day fanning and carrying. Wynn broke down in tears when she told her staff she had been watching them and was so proud of them.

She slipped back outside to decompress. The heavy air, though it couldn't be described as fresh, seemed to shift against itself in the barest of muggy breezes.

Wynn stared out at Clara Street as the darkness deepened. Her gaze lifted above the flooded parking lot across the street to fix on the outpatient cancer center beyond it. What she saw momentarily perplexed her: a light was on inside the building.

Just a light, she told herself. It was a newer building, and it must have a different generator that supplied the lights. She thought no more of it.

The emergency room manager was resting on the ambulance ramp nearby. A call came in on his cell phone at about eight p.m. It was a Tenet executive in Dallas trying to reach Memorial's CEO to say that the company was sending rescuers. Everyone should be ready to leave the hospital at seven a.m. on Thursday. Wynn had trouble believing it.

———

IN DALLAS, dozens of Tenet employees had spent the day scrambling to support the company's six hurricane-affected Gulf Coast hospitals. The ground floor of corporate headquarters had been given over to banks of phones and computers manned by dozens of employees from various departments. They had little experience in disaster management.

Early that Wednesday morning, business development director Michael Arvin and his colleagues had been unable to make contact with staff at Memorial and another New Orleans hospital in the flood zone. They began calling authorities in search of information.

The one who leveled with them was Cynthia Matherne, a seasoned hospital emergency manager with military experience who sat in a warren of desks at New Orleans City Hall. The municipal building had been transformed into an emergency operations center, but it, too, was surrounded by several feet of floodwater. Phones trilled and people in uniforms and mufti shuffled together and apart for meetings.

Matherne was responsible for learning what was happening at the region's hospitals and nursing homes and relaying that to emergency officials. Her usual job was as a bioterrorism preparedness coordinator for the local hospital association. That position had been created after the 9/11 terrorist attacks and anthrax mailings in September and October 2001, when federal appropriations flowed from the crisis. The program's mandate had only recently been expanded to allow the funds to be used to prepare for natural disasters—a belated acknowledgment that these occurred far more frequently and inevitably than bioterrorism attacks.

Matherne had attended the mock "Hurricane Pam" workshop. It was hard to believe it was just the previous week; in a follow-up meeting two days later, she had jotted "Katrina" in the margin of a handout as the storm approached Florida, noting that its track was moving westward along the Gulf Coast. Still, when she'd been asked to consider what to do when "each hospital in the affected area has become an island," she'd had no idea she was in a dress rehearsal for that precise calamity. "Which patients should be extracted first? Second? Will you focus on those that could make the trip?" Those questions on paper were now a reality.

Matherne knew there were no plans setting out how New Orleans hospitals would be evacuated after hurricanes. What agency, if any, was now in charge of that was unclear to her. The Pam scenario had assumed that flight resources would be limited and, for at least the first five days, applied "to save life and limb of those clinging to rooftops and trees. Hospitals should be prepared for 7 days." That number of days had surprised Matherne, as it had previously been three, but hospitals had indeed long been instructed to prepare to be on their own.

When Matherne discovered that at least two hospitals had lost power on Tuesday, she made her best guess about who could help. She searched out liaisons from the Coast Guard and National Guard and asked them to rescue the hospitals' trapped occupants.

One serviceman told her they were in a safe building. They had supplies. Matherne hadn't expected to have to do any convincing. "They don't have electricity!" she said. "You can't take care of patients without electricity."

She noticed the people in uniforms at the command center avoiding her after that. She knew her outburst had violated the emergency officials' code of cool. It occurred to her that the Guardsmen had resigned themselves to the idea that some flood victims were going to die. These officials, too, felt helpless. They were performing an awful triage of their own.

The local Coast Guard air station where the helicopters were staging had been damaged by Katrina. Its radio antenna was down. Its generators undulated through states of failure and temporary repair. Fixed telephone lines were out, and the station's commanders had only intermittent contact with superiors via satellite and cell phones. Their old Nextels worked. The new Treos didn't.

A rigid command protocol was therefore impracticable. Commanders sent down few tasks and had not yet divided the city into a grid to execute a systematic rescue plan. With so many people waving rags on rooftops, the Coast Guard air-response units, which could talk to one another when flying, worked freelance, setting their own priorities, often rescuing people as they saw them.

By Wednesday morning, when Tenet regional senior vice president Bob Smith reached Matherne, she had concluded that the best hope for the rapid evacuation of private hospitals was to use "private assets."

Smith was incredulous. His company had no experience mounting rescue operations. The corporate jet couldn't land on a hospital rooftop, and the company had no corporate helicopters. It had no pre-storm disaster plan. He and his colleagues were still setting up the command center in the ground-floor conference room with phoned-in advice from Tenet's regional chief medical officer, the executive with National Guard experience who was on vacation in Oregon talking on speakerphone while his wife went down to the beach without him.

Smith jotted down notes as he spoke with Matherne. "Boats," he wrote. "Wildlife and fish," for the state's Department of Wildlife and Fisheries, which had a fleet of swamp boats that, Matherne supposed, might be able to help. "Staging and pontoon boats."

From Matherne, Smith learned that Tulane University Hospital's parent company, Hospital Corporation of America, a corporate competitor, had started hiring helicopters to assist in that hospital's evacuation on Tuesday morning as soon as it became clear the city was flooding. When Smith finished speaking with Matherne, he contacted HCA for advice. The HCA executives wished him luck. Contracting with privately owned helicopters and bringing them into the disaster zone had taken time, and communications problems in New Orleans had made the process more difficult.

Smith wondered how to begin arranging an airlift. Michael Arvin told him about a phone message he had received late Tuesday from the representative of an air logistics company in a Dallas suburb. It was an offer of assistance.

"Call them," Smith said.

Meanwhile, other Tenet executives attempted to convince government officials to prioritize the evacuation of Memorial and the company's other marooned hospitals. Staff at every agency seemed happy to nudge another agency. Someone from a senator's office offered to appeal to Gov. Kathleen Blanco and the Centers for Medicare & Medicaid Services. But people at the Centers for Medicare & Medicaid Services directed Tenet to contact the head of the appropriate hospital association. That association, the Federation of American Hospitals, appealed to the US Department of Health and Human Services, which appealed back, on behalf of patients in general, to the Federation, the American Hospital Association, the nation's hospitals, and the Federal Emergency Management Agency. Billionaire Ross Perot, whose son was a Tenet contractor, appealed to the Coast Guard and the Navy. There was no locus of responsibility. Fingers pointed every which way, much as they had when New Orleans flooded in the 1920s.

To make matters more confusing, the federal, state, and local communications systems were not interoperable, much as the city's electrical systems had not been interoperable in the 1927 flood, when the utility NOPSI couldn't supply emergency power to the city's drainage pumping plant because it ran on a different frequency. Also, the software that authorities were attempting to use to manage the current disaster didn't sort information in a shareable way. Multiple agencies and officials appeared to be maintaining separate priority lists for hospital evacuations, which perhaps explained why Memorial was variously first, second, or last on "the list." The bureaucratic complexities were incomprehensible to key Tenet officials and bred panic in them. "We are in dire need of help from the Navy!!!!" Michael Arvin wrote in an e-mail to a woman in California, asking her to seek assistance from a particular admiral she knew. "We are getting runaround from local USCG and US Navy."

"Admiral Mike retired . . ." came the woman's reply.

On Tuesday evening, EMS officials in the state capital had supposedly made the evacuation of Memorial a top priority. However, by Wednesday morning, Matherne, at the emergency operations center in New Orleans, told Tenet's Bob Smith that Memorial was among the lowest on her list of eight local hospitals that needed help evacuating. Tenet officials later discovered yet another prioritization list was being managed by state public health officials. On it Memorial ranked sixth out of seven.

"Evacuation is going SLOWLY," a state official explained in an e-mail sent to staff of Louisiana's US Senators and congressional Representatives, who had been hearing from constituents trapped at hospitals. "Please ask your folks to be patient."

According to the e-mail, critical care patients were "going out first." Memorial's critical care patients had been airlifted out on Tuesday evening.

The message also said: "The hospitals that are flooded and without generators are being evacuated FIRST." Presumably news of Memorial's power loss over a dozen hours earlier hadn't reached this particular set of officials, despite the daylong presence at Memorial of the tall man who introduced himself as a state health officer.

Tenet executives, generally out of touch with the hospital since the previous evening, hadn't mentioned in their missives for help that the hospital had lost power. They could have inferred that from the sudden loss of electronic communications and Sandra Cordray's warnings about an impending power loss the previous evening.

One Tenet official wrote to Tenet's general counsel:

Our number one priority for the last two days is getting our hospital's evacuated. . . . For some reason no one seems to want ot help us with this. We have 2000 people at Memeorial (150 patients) but we do not seem to be a priority. We need help on this one from any angle.

The lead agency coordinating the federal public health and medical response was among the most hamstrung. The US Department of Health and Human Services (HHS) had an official emergency coordinator assigned to a five-state region that included Louisiana. However, in her four months on the job, she had not visited the state, communicated with its emergency health officials, or participated in the recent Hurricane Pam exercises. Still, the state of Louisiana requested that the federal officials take charge.

When a Tenet employee contacted the HHS coordinator to ask how to enter the disaster area, she directed him to the Louisiana Hospital Association. A Tenet official's appeal to the HHS deputy secretary resulted only in a promise to pass word to FEMA.

Rather than providing assistance to Tenet, HHS officials were requesting it. Tenet officials, along with hospital CEOs around the country, participated in a call with the head of the agency, HHS secretary Michael O. Leavitt, early in the afternoon. Leavitt asked the nation's hospitals for medicines and staff to establish federal emergency field hospitals in the disaster region.

The conference call left one Tenet official angry. "Field hospitals are great, but we can't get people out," he wrote to the head of the Federation of American Hospitals, Charles N. Kahn III, asking for an immediate conference call with HHS. "Today has been a complete wreck. I don't know how much clearer it can be said."

"HHS is only a side player here," Kahn responded. "We have to get them to push FEMA and the locals. I am working on that."

LifeCare's corporate chief financial officer was also on the conference call with HHS. The company was making as poor progress as Tenet was in getting its patients to safety. Senior vice president Dubois had spent much of Wednesday trying to locate the four LifeCare patients flown out of Memorial by the Coast Guard early that morning, and to move them to other LifeCare locations.

Dubois had engaged a fleet of ambulances from Lone Star Ambulance in Texas, where LifeCare had a contract, to pick up patients being flown or boated out of Memorial and a LifeCare hospital near the New Orleans airport, which was not flooded but was having power issues. She sought permission for the ambulances to go to the city but did not get it. Dubois advised the LifeCare staff at Memorial to send the patients with whatever transport officials arranged for them. Dubois was upset to learn, late in the day, that four LifeCare patients and seven LifeCare staff members from Memorial were stranded on the corner of Napoleon and St. Charles Streets. She worked the phones in the evening to seek help for them from the Coast Guard and Knox Andress—the disaster preparedness coordinator she still thought worked for FEMA.

The Federation of American Hospitals's Charles Kahn sent an appeal to an HHS official in the early evening. "I cannot over emphasize the urgency of these situations," Kahn wrote. He included a list of the immediate needs of area hospitals, but left out several hospitals, including New Orleans's biggest medical center, the public Charity Hospital, which was not a Federation member. Kahn's message also failed to mention the power situation at any of the hospitals. The status update for Memorial that appeared in his appeal had been written nearly twenty-four hours earlier.

At Tenet headquarters in Dallas, Michael Arvin's contact with the private air logistics company proved fruitful, and the company began lining up helicopters to arrive in New Orleans on Thursday morning. Though these were regular helicopters normally used for firefighting and other purposes, Tenet executives began referring to them as "air ambulances."

As Tenet planners sought flight clearances, they told officials they would be rescuing their own patients. What they really needed help with, they said, was moving out "800 community members" who had sought refuge at Memorial. "Our real need is to get the local residents out of the hospital by boat," a Tenet vice president wrote to Sen. Mary Landrieu's staff. Landrieu offered to intervene with the governor on behalf of the hospitals—another pivot in the circular game of telephone.

Corporate officials seemed fixed on safety concerns at Memorial. "Our last communication with them indicated they were also having security problems with the local citizens," Tenet's Bob Smith wrote to a Navy captain. "This situation is getting to a critical point with no security."

Tenet distributed an update for communications managers to upload to each affected hospital's website. It said: "Martial law is in place in New Orleans." It was as untrue as it had been when the radio announcers had said it.

By the time a Tenet official reached Memorial's emergency room manager on Wednesday evening as Karen Wynn stood watching, there was better news to share. Though the details were vague, Tenet had received word that Louisiana's Department of Wildlife and Fisheries would send boats to Memorial.

Just before ten p.m. the private aviation services company confirmed that it had received Tenet's signed contracts for a half dozen helicopters of various sizes. They would converge from around the country to begin arriving at Memorial early Thursday morning, one as early as six a.m.

But the news from Memorial to Tenet was grave. Tenet vice president Bob Smith summarized in an e-mail to Tenet leaders what he said he learned via HF radio communications. "They have 115 pts. in-house, 30 bed bound and 40+ wheelchair bound. Expect up to 60 are fragile and may die within the next 24 hours."

Smith's business development director, Michael Arvin, the other main point of contact with the hospital, shared similar conclusions with company employees who had offered assistance with the evacuation.

> Conditions in Memorial are deteriating fast. We may lose 30-45 patients overnight. There is rampant looting in the streets and the hospitals do not have security to protect. It has become our priority to get all patients and employees/families out of Memorial.

CHAPTER 7

WEDNESDAY, AUGUST 31, 2005—NIGHT

NURSE MANAGER KAREN WYNN lay awake beside her sleeping teenage daughter in an operating-room hallway on the eighth floor. It was so hot, it hurt to breathe. The air stirred only with the complaints of an older woman, the girlfriend of an ICU nurse's father. "We never gonna get out of here," she moaned. "We gonna die in here."

The woman's cries threatened to wake Wynn's daughter. Wynn worried the panic would spread to the other people resting in the room. Maybe, she thought, there's just that little seed in the back of their brain, and I don't want this to grow into an acorn and an oak tree. Wynn stood up and steered the woman to a stairwell to sit, breathe, and quiet down.

The floor was full of glass, and Wynn had gone barefoot in her haste. Exhaustion played on her perceptions and emotions. Through the open windows, Wynn could hear amplified movement and conversations outside the building over the water, eerie in the dark.

When she returned to her pallet, Wynn had the sense the fearful woman was right. They were never going to get out of Memorial. Thoughts of her sleeping daughter uprooted the feeling. They would get out. They had to.

One story below Wynn, in LifeCare, shattered windows also opened onto the stage of the shattered city, echoing with gunshots, shouts, and blaring car alarms. Staff members, convinced the hospital had been broken into, blockaded the stairwells for the night.

Just before midnight, a nurse pushed a dose of the sedative drug Ativan through a syringe into LifeCare patient Wilda McManus's IV line. It wasn't a drug McManus normally took. Her daughter Angela had made sure of that because Wilda had once had a bad reaction to the drug, growing more agitated instead of calmer.

McManus was lying on a bed by a doorway near the nurse's station, uncharacteristically alone. Late Wednesday morning, she'd been "en route," according to a note in her medical chart, "to the heliport." She had never even made it off the floor. All day she had waited, Angela by her side, asking in vain for a doctor to rescind her mother's DNR order.

Angela served as the voice and advocate for her mother. Wilda had been the longtime patient information manager at Charity Hospital, the first person visitors would see when they walked beneath an ornate metallic screen through that hospital's Art Deco entranceway. Wilda could still smile sweetly but couldn't always make herself understood due to a stroke and the brain-muddying effects of certain medicines. A note in her hospital admission paperwork said "daughter stays with patient at all times." Angela had quit her job and spent more than a year as her caregiver. She had not put limits on her sacrifices. Tending to her mother and ensuring her dignity was her life's current purpose.

Living on a cot or reclining chair for days under unremitting fluorescent hospital lights, frequently being awakened at night, making life-and-death decisions, watching mistakes being made, and being buffeted again and again by new test results was stressful, even unhinging. Hospital life was so different from normal life that it could be jarring to step outside and see people smiling and laughing, apparently carefree.

Though it was difficult for Angela McManus to accept that death might come soon for seventy-year-old Wilda, she was not unreasonable about this. Carefully counseled by the infectious diseases specialist on duty the day Katrina hit and Wilda's infection worsened, Angela had opted against surgical intervention in an operating room on backup power. She also agreed that if her mother's heart or lungs shut down there was no sense in trying to revive her with breathing tubes, electric shocks, or chest compressions—interventions that would have no effect on chronic, underlying health problems. But the role Angela McManus had chosen was not to preside over her mother's dying process. She found value even in Wilda's less active life. Angela's role was to ensure that for every last moment her mother would be well cared for, and, until this latest setback, that she would be given every chance modern American medicine could afford her to survive.

All day Wednesday, the McManuses had watched dozens of other LifeCare patients bundled into cocoons of sheets and carried into the stairwells ahead of Wilda. More than once, nurses returned crying after patients had died in transit.

The day brought Wilda no closer to the heliport, but helicopter rotors washed wind and the smell of fuel into the unit. Although reaching the helipad involved an arduous journey—down five flights of stairs, through the hole in the machine-room wall, up the parking garage ramp and three stories' worth of metal steps—from the windows across the hallway, the helipad looked almost touchable, framed like a picture in the windows.

A radio played in the corridor, transmitting tales that alarmed the LifeCare staff: hostage situations, prison breaks, someone shooting at police. Looters had used AK-47 assault rifles to commandeer postal vehicles, filling them with stolen goods, according to a councilman from Jefferson Parish, which shared a border with the city. A deputy sheriff said on air that he saw a shark swimming around a hotel—or perhaps it was just debris that looked like a shark fin; he wasn't sure.

"The hunger, the anger, the rage is growing among people who have nothing, and if they have nothing they get violent and they get angry,"

Jefferson Parish president Aaron Broussard said, appealing to the governor for more armed military police: "Basic jungle human insticts are beginning to creep in because they lack food, they lack a decent environment, a shelter."

WWL announcer Dave Cohen denounced the looting on the station's marathon ad-free, call-in broadcast, being fed out to AM and FM stations all over southeast Louisiana. "It's such a big problem that state police have sent in a tactical team—two task forces [. . .] The governor is making it so clear," Cohen said. "It's time for a full evacuation of the city of New Orleans."

Officials and civilians called into the station and stopped by its makeshift studio in the basement of an emergency operations center near New Orleans. Two guests referred to the people remaining in the city as zombies. Cohen described them as "a mass of humanity, slowly wandering."

"It's like *Night of the Living Dead*," Oliver Thomas, the city council president of New Orleans, said. "And you look at the look in their eyes; they're stressed, they're hungry, they're thirsty. The governor has asked for armed reinforcements."

An organized group of criminals, "hordes of 'em," Thomas said, seemed to have waited out the storm in order to start breaking and entering. "I heard one lady say maybe this is Sodom and Gomorrah."

Some of the staff on the seventh floor at LifeCare seemed to be taking the stories to heart, freaking out, Angela McManus thought as she listened to them cry out what amounted to, *Oh Lord, the world's coming to an end!* Nurses worried aloud about their children and roamed the halls for a spot where their cell phones would work to try to locate their families. Employees who had visitors were beset by requests for water and other necessities. A poodle owned by Wilda McManus's nurse barked and barked from a nearby room. "Shut that dog up!" Wilda said to her daughter. Angela's own eyes and throat were scratchy from pet allergies. A cat escaped its quarters in a shower stall and the nurse's dog pinned it behind a cage. The nurse, frantic with worry about leaving her dog behind to be euthanized, spent more time feeding and doting on it in the room next door than she did caring for Wilda, Angela thought. She overheard nursing assistants argue over whose turn it was to do the un-enviable work of cleaning and toileting patients in the awful heat.

Angela, exhausted, dizzy, and anxious about a sibling who lived close to the levees, nonetheless found the strength to nurse her mother herself. She nourished Wilda through her feeding tube, removed and replaced the colostomy bag that collected her feces, and ran her hand under her mother's backside after her fever broke to find it slick with sweat and wound discharge. There was no running water to bathe her. It took hours for Angela to recruit a nurse to help her wipe Wilda down with alcohol, dry her, and change her wound dressing. All the while Angela talked, sang, and prayed with her mother. Wilda had been fond of recit-ing the Lord's Prayer and the Twenty-Third and Ninety-First Psalms. Before the storm, LifeCare staff members would bow their heads as she prayed in sessions the staff had come to call "church."

It encouraged Angela when she overheard staff members lamenting that they couldn't leave the hospital until every patient was gone. In her mind, that meant they would not leave the patients behind. Finally in the late afternoon on Wednesday, Angela was told that the remaining patients would soon be on their way and it was time for her to leave the hospital by boat. Before agreeing to leave, she asked where her mother would be taken. "I don't have any idea where your mom is going to end up," LifeCare's nurse executive Therese Mendez told her. "But where are you going? Let's put that number on your mom." They tried to inscribe her with a permanent marker, but her skin was too wet. Instead they wrote contact phone numbers with a brief message on pieces of gauze and wrapped them around Wilda McManus's right arm and right leg below her hospital gown: DAUGHTER—ANGELA MCMANUS, ASAP.

Angela was taken downstairs and put in line for a boat, as was another devoted daughter, Kathryn Nelson, whose mother, Elaine, was a gravely ill LifeCare patient.

Hours later, in the evening, the infectious diseases doctor who had made Wilda McManus a Do Not Resuscitate patient after the storm came up to LifeCare. She surveyed the ragged, fearful nurses, pronounced the death of the ventilator-dependent patient with a DNR order, who had passed away earlier, and checked on all the remaining patients. McManus was one of them. "Are you in pain?" she asked each one. "Do you feel anxious?" Some of the patients said no, including Rose Savoie and her remaining roommate, "Miss Alice" Hutzler, and McManus. Others could not answer. None of the patients said they needed anything, but the doctor was struck by how weak they appeared in the heat. She was sure that the gravely ill lady, Elaine Nelson, would die overnight. Her eyes had been glazed, and she seemed to be breathing with great difficulty. The doctor was sad to find her alone in a room at the end of a hallway, her daughter absent. She asked the staff to move Nelson closer to the other patients.

The doctor had no intention of staying the night on the seventh floor, and she saw that the LifeCare nurses would have no easy way to contact a physician. She left standing orders for nurses to give small injections of morphine and Ativan to any patient who might become agitated or restless. The nurses could also have Xanax pills to quell their own anxiety.

The drugs were federally controlled substances, kept locked away and signed out when needed, their misuse subject to criminal penalty. But these were extraordinary times. Even the firmest rules softened in the intense heat. The LifeCare pharmacist did not feel safe when he went back into the pharmacy. He gathered two boxes of morphine, each with twenty-five glass vials of the powerful drug, and one smaller box of Ativan vials, and handed the drugs to one of the nurses on duty to use on the honor system.

The nurse, Cindy Chatelain, had struggled with narcotics addiction and had previously had her license suspended for prescription painkiller abuse. Two weeks before the storm, the nursing board had put her on probation for treating patients with drugs that had not been ordered by a doctor. She was supposed to be closely supervised, to "work in a restrictive environment," but here she was working with great autonomy, shouldering extra shifts with the assistance of her teenage daughter while some other colleagues wilted into inaction in the heat. Chatelain had severe chronic back pain, and eventually the temptation of the drugs, which she had placed at the nursing station under cover of torn-up rags, was too great. She gave herself an injection of the morphine.

She saw that her patient Wilda McManus also seemed like she could use something—in McManus's case to calm and quiet her. This was how, just before midnight, McManus came to receive a small dose of Ativan. Her daughter Angela wasn't there to warn the nurse about the drug's previous paradoxical effect. And even if it worked like magic, no drug could replace the comfort and reassurance of a daughter, of Angela, who had been told to leave her.

—

DAY FIVE, THURSDAY, SEPTEMBER 1, 2005

From: Tim Burke [administrator, LifeCare Hospitals of New Orleans]
Sent: Thursday, September 1, 2005 12:09 AM
To: Robbye Dubois [LifeCare senior vice president of clinical services]
Cc: Chase Finley [LifeCare assistant vice president of operations]
Subject: I am really worried about Baptist . . .
>No one I talk to has had any contact today—trying constantly with no luck.
>Starting to wonder if generator out . . .
>Gangs roming the streets (as per news and contacts down there)
>Fatigue, stress, anxiety, supplies—all are issues by now
>I can't stand it
>Tim

—

MAYBE THE WORLD *was* ending. A large, dark shadow moved over the water toward the hospital at around midnight. The approaching craft was noticed by arms-bearing volunteers stationed at the hospital's perimeter.

"Stay away!" one screamed from the main hospital.

"Stay away!" another shouted from the pedestrian bridge over Clara Street. "Don't come close to the hospital!"

The commotion brought nurses and security personnel to windows all over Memorial. Beams lighted upon a huge boat filled with dark figures as it angled toward the hospital's emergency ramp.

"Turn off the fucking lights!" a man shouted from the boat. Blinding beacons glared back at the hospital.

"Identify yourself!" someone at the hospital yelled. "Stay away! Don't come to the building."

"Turn off the fucking lights!"

"Identify yourself!"

The boat turned up the ER ramp. Machine gun–bearing figures disembarked and ran inside in a two-by-two formation, about twenty in all. They wore night-vision goggles, helmets, and dark uniforms with bulletproof jackets.

Police. The masses at Memorial met them with emotions ranging from fear to relief to anger. A nurse peeping out a second-story window as they approached ran out of her room, leaped over a doctor sleeping with a gun on his chest, and descended the staircase to see if the troops had come because of her SOS calls to well-connected family members.

The police said that they were responding to a call that thugs from the neighborhood had overrun the hospital and were trying to loot its pharmacy. "That's what it took to get you here?" the hospital locksmith asked. He knew the looting report wasn't true, but he was upset that the job of staying up all night to protect everyone had fallen to civilian duck hunters like him rather than trained law enforcement officials. The SWAT team soon returned to the boat and sped away from Memorial.

AROUND THE TIME the police arrived, Dr. Anna Pou excused herself from the second-floor lobby to take a nap. She returned an hour later and shooed away the infectious diseases doctor, who was anxious and having stomach problems. Pou told her to go get some rest.

Pou found clean scrubs to change into each day, but she was drenched and dirty, and for the third night in a row, she worked on scarcely an hour's sleep. She had assumed an attitude of blindness, navigating dark corridors with the run of fingers along humid walls and ascending invisible staircases by kicking the steps ahead as she went and counting. With several doctors and crews of nurses, she changed patients' diapers and dipped rags into water to make cool compresses. She said prayers with anxious nurses whose faith in their skills was shaken.

Pou still had not reached one of her sisters, a dialysis nurse who had stayed at her home in Lakeview, a picturesque neighborhood bordering Lake Pontchartrain. Pou had spoken with her soon after the storm, but the phone had cut off and she had not reached her since then. Pou and the nurses had been saying prayers for her well-being.

Pou's husband was also presumably somewhere out in the flooded city. She took comfort in the fact that he was a big, strong outdoorsman, and she sublimated her concerns about both family members into patient care. To avoid distraction from her work, she tried not to focus on the rumored dangers that surrounded the hospital.

All around her on the second floor, dozens of LifeCare and Memorial patients lay on dirty, sweaty cots. It was so crowded there was barely enough space to walk between them. Most of the nonmedical volunteers who had fanned and offered sips of water to the patients had gone elsewhere, dismissed and told to take a break by the doctors, who said too many people were present. Workers had included little girls, the "PBJ and cracker brigade," who made snacks for diabetic patients.

Another doctor passed through the second floor, Memorial's surgery chairman John Walsh. The tableau reminded him of the Civil War–era Atlanta railway-station scene from *Gone with the Wind*, when the music swells and the camera draws back to reveal row upon row of patients in misery. "Thank heaven you're here, I need every pair of hands," a doctor, his face glistening with sweat, tells Scarlett O'Hara. Her eyes widen as she takes in the moaning soldiers who surround and reach for her. "Now come, child, wake up. We got work to do," the doctor says. "Look at them, bleeding to death in front of my eyes. No chloroform, no bandages, nothing. Nothing to even ease their pain."

Memorial's conditions were an improvement on the Civil War, even if it didn't feel that way. For one thing, ice had miraculously appeared. Nurses slipped chunks into exam gloves and wore them tucked under their clothes.

The more important development was almost an afterthought: the belated discovery and repair of two small generators by the director of plant operations and his staff after he returned Wednesday evening from ferrying passengers in his fishing boat. One of his electricians, who feared being shot or having to shoot someone on a security shift, busied himself instead setting up a generator in the parking garage. If the generators had been employed earlier, perhaps they could have saved some of the patients who depended on electrical equipment. Now, he ran an extension cord through the stairwell and into the lobby to power a high-speed centrifugal "squirrel cage" blower. Usually used to dry floors, here it cooled patients and staff. The new power source led to the reemergence of box fans and lamps collected from around the hospital. These supplemented the repository of cardboard fans and Coleman camping lanterns. The generators also lit a handful of ancient incandescent bulbs on the long-unused helipad, the few bulbs with working filaments out of about thirty.

A battery-powered CD player in a small room on the second floor belted out oldies to the accompaniment of a whimpering dog, caterwauling cats, and a dozen or so ICU nurses and others, who joked and sang along between fanning shifts on the second floor. They trooped in and out to use a bucket toilet. They rested stretched across one another's limbs and belongings. Dr. Ewing Cook's daughter owned the CD player and the two cats, her surviving pets. The elder Cook had retreated from his office near a hospital exit, warned about possible encroachment. He dragged a cot outside the noisy room, flopped down on it, and fell into a slumber within moments, oblivious to the commotion.

The main pharmacy was fortuitously located down the hallway from the patient-filled lobby and well stocked because of the post-storm helicopter drop. A retinue of pharmacists took turns sitting on chairs outside the dark pharmacy awaiting orders, then disappearing inside with a headlamp. Even now the pharmacists documented each dose they dispensed and asked doctors to write out paper prescriptions; they were giving out medicines that could be dangerous if used improperly or put into the wrong hands. They had, unlike Scarlett O'Hara's Civil War doctor, ample medicine to ease pain—including morphine.

Pou had ordered morphine for a fifty-year-old woman with cancer, the patient of a colleague for whom she was covering during the storm. The patient had long received the drug. A pump had pushed it continuously through her intravenous line before the power cut. But the pump relied on electricity.

She was moaning. A nurse brought this to Pou's attention, and Pou ordered a shot of the painkiller through the patient's blocked-off intravenous line. Pou was careful, prescribing a dose of morphine that was lower than the patient's usual dose per hour, since she would be getting it all at once. A pharmacist filled the prescription. A nurse who knew the patient gave the injection, and it seemed to ease her pain.

Pou's priority was to keep the patients comfortable. As for anything else, "There's not a whole lot we can really do for those people," she and other staff members agreed.

Nurses were told not to give patients IV fluids, or even their usual medicines, because the hospital was in "emergency mode," and the lighting was so dim it wouldn't be safe.

Overnight, a patient stopped breathing and died on the floor where Pou was fanning. We live, Pou would later remember thinking, in the greatest country in the world and yet the sick could basically be abandoned like this. As she, too, awaited rescue, she felt sad, frustrated, and helpless.

While care was limited, it was still desired. Some patients asked and even cried for the medicines they knew they needed but the doctors had decided should not be given. Carrie Mae Hall, the seventy-eight-year-old LifeCare patient with long, braided hair whose vast family called her Ma'Dear, managed to reach out to a passing nurse and indicate that she needed him to clear out the phlegm from her tracheostomy. The nurse was surprised at how fiercely Hall was battling to stay alive, lying beside the Hibernia Bank ATM among some of the sickest patients—most of whom had been assigned to triage category 3. He suctioned Hall's airway with a portable machine and told her to fight hard.

On the other side of the lobby, a nurse called her supervisor over to Rodney Scott, the ICU patient whose rescue had been deferred because of his immense size, and whom Ewing Cook had earlier taken for dead. "Am I going to make it out?" Scott asked. "They said they can't get my size out." The nurse supervisor tried to reassure him. "We're going to get you out, just like everyone else." She hadn't realized patients feared being abandoned.

While patient deaths demoralized some health workers, they inspired others to try to systemize care. Dr. Bryant King sent a group of nurses from one end of the lobby to the other to check the blood pressures of hypertensive patients and blood-sugar levels of diabetic patients. "If we need to give them medications, we will," he said, and he and the nurses dispensed insulin and other drugs as needed. From the beginning of the disaster, when he had tussled with Ewing Cook over discontinuing a patient's heart monitor, King had maintained the sense that they could do more. Under King's direction, nurses lifted photocopied medical charts out of manila envelopes and scoured them for diagnoses and issues that required urgent attention or monitoring, which they wrote on sheets of paper and taped to the patients. This way the next shift of nurses could more easily discern medical needs.

Working overnight on the second floor of Memorial, as uncomfortable and foul-smelling as it was, was a whole lot better than sleeping in the rain and mud in South Carolina during Army Reserve boot camp in high school; King's father, a military sergeant, had insisted that Bryant and his three younger siblings—who grew up in East Chicago, Indiana, sometimes on welfare, their parents divorced—learn military discipline. In medical school, King had cared for patients without sophisticated machinery or even an X-ray machine during a two-month rotation in Jamaica. He had learned there to make the best of what was available; to rely on his clinical skills. King had also practiced medicine in the somewhat austere environment of the public Charity Hospital in downtown New Orleans during his internal medicine residency. He had ascended to chief resident the year before Katrina, an honor indicating high achievement. King had strong opinions, and he sometimes chafed against authority and did not take well to criticism or rejection. He had quit halfway through his chief's year over a disagreement with those in charge about how he should fulfill his administrative duties.

Here, even King recognized Katrina's shattering of the sterile, digital, odorless, dehumidified, gloved, and gowned illusion of mastery over death and suffering doctors typically maintained. The smashed windows and lack of power left them exposed, like an army field hospital, to the elements. Knitted together for safety overnight, they felt as isolated as if they were under fire. King was as eager as anyone to get out of this motherfucker, and he said that. The task, in his mind, was figuring out the best way to keep caring for the sickest patients.

King left the second floor for a nap and returned an hour or so before sunrise. He examined a large African American man in a green-and-blue patterned hospital gown, lying unmoving in the lobby. King pronounced him dead and documented this on a page of his medical chart.

The man, in his early sixties, had a close-cropped beard and mustache and a history of heart disease. He had come to the hospital with symptoms of pneumonia as the storm approached. His wife had accompanied him, but like some other patients' family members was separated and escorted away to the boat line by armed security guards after he was carried down to the second floor. Now, with the help of the family members of staff, King lifted his body and carried it into the chapel.

A nurse had earlier coaxed Father John Marse to an empty cot on the first floor, telling him it had his name on it and ordering him to rest. Standing in for him in the chapel, the nurse chanted a Hail Mary, Our Father, and Glory Be over the dead. King counted five other bodies arrayed before the altar.

———

EARLY IN THE MORNING on Thursday, September 1—seventy-two hours after the hurricane struck—a small group of doctors gathered in a radiology suite on the second floor. Surgery chief John Walsh described the scene he had witnessed in the lobby overnight. How rough the night had been for staff who had stayed awake to care for patients. Many were demoralized and some complained that one physician was being obnoxious and upsetting them.

The doctors at the meeting were unhappy that hospital leaders had turned down the chance to continue the helicopter rescue on Tuesday night into Wednesday morning. Few patients—unlike family members, other visitors, and staff—had departed Memorial since then. Prospects for a prompt, government-organized rescue appeared dim. The helicopters organized by Tenet, if they came, might not effect a quick rescue.

"We need to have a little bit more of a surgeon's attitude," Walsh said. Surgeons were men and women of action. The group of doctors in the suite opted for insubordination over inaction. Rather than await the scheduled morning meeting to discuss options, Walsh left after first light with an anesthesiologist on the plant-operations director's fishing boat to try to organize a more concerted rescue effort. Another anesthesiologist went to find Drs. Anna Pou and Roy Culotta to see if they would re-triage the patients who remained. The message that day needed to be a positive one: everyone would be getting out.

———

SOON AFTER SUNRISE, hospital staff gathered on the emergency room ramp. Incident commander Susan Mulderick stepped up on a curb to begin the meeting, with CEO Goux beside her, and medical chairman Deichmann also present. Doctors, nursing managers, maintenance workers, and security staff jostled and shushed one another. It was difficult to hear.

Mulderick went over what remained of food, water, and people at the hospital. Few participants took special note when she mentioned the LifeCare patients who were still on the seventh floor.

The conversation moved in other directions. Food-service employees fretted over the remaining food stocks, having spent days filling Styrofoam cups with grits, sausage, and spaghetti prepared with propane stoves and Sterno, and serving juice, bagels, and mystery meat from a temporary kitchen above the flooded basement.

One doctor asked what was being done to dispose of human waste; the smell in the hospital was bestial. The hospital's elder statesman, Horace Baltz, formally commended his colleagues for their hard work. He told them to pull together and they would all get out alive. The crowd applauded him.

Memorial's chief financial officer, Curtis Dosch, returned to the ramp as the meeting started to disperse. He had just used a working cell phone to speak with Tenet official Bob Smith in Dallas and received confirmation that Tenet was dispatching the fleet of privately hired helicopters and a satellite phone that morning. "Everybody shut up for a minute," someone shouted. "We got an update." Mulderick asked Dosch to share the good news. Some of the worn, anxious staff members seemed to disbelieve him. They wanted to know exactly when and how they were getting out of the hospital, answers Dosch and Mulderick couldn't provide. All the leaders could do was reinforce the idea that they were awaiting more boats and helicopters and, somehow, they were going to get everybody out of Memorial that day.

———

From: Bob Smith [regional senior vice president, Tenet Healthcare]
Sent: Thursday, September 1, 2005, 8:56 AM
To: Captain John Andrews, Navy Second Fleet
Subject: Tenethealth Prioities in NOLA

> Since my communication yesterday we have a dire situation at Memorial Hospital in NOLA. This facility is unsecure and we need immediate assistance. We are unable to evacuate our patients and staff due to gun fire in the area. The facility is compromised and there are people dying in the building. There are people with weapons in and/or around the building. We believe lives are in immediate danger. Memorial Medical Center 2700 Napoleon Ave.

———

Louisiana Bureau of Emergency Medical Services phone call log, Thursday, September 1, 2005, 9:33AM:

... 60 patients that need a move by stretcher are at Memorial Medical Center.

———

US Coast Guard LTJG Shelley Decker notes on Thursday, September 1, 2005:

Tenant Memorial Hospital-Presidential tasking to evac immediately

IT SMELLED WORSE on the second-floor lobby than Susan Mulderick remembered from having walked through the area on Wednesday. Despite the broken windows, the air stayed stubbornly still near the
bathrooms. The fecal stench was intense.

Nobody, she thought, should have to bear such conditions, particularly not fragile patients. Some called for help, looking up from their cots
along the hallway, dazed and fearful as people streamed past them.

Mulderick knelt beside an elderly woman. She peeled the pads away
from her backside and began to wipe away her feces. The woman cried.
The heat and a shortage of diapers and fresh linens had defeated the nursing staff's efforts to keep patients dry and clean. Her skin was raw. Mulderick found a fresh red sore above her buttocks. It looked as if the skin
had broken down as the woman lay sweating into her cot. The slight-
est touch caused her to yell out in pain, and as Mulderick took in the
woman's misery and extrapolated it to the dozens lying around her, the
normally stoic nurse executive was profoundly shaken.

When Mulderick stood up from her work, Dr. Kathleen Fournier approached her, looking equally upset. She was worried about her cat, she
told Mulderick. It was sick and suffering, no longer eating or drinking.
She took Mulderick to see "Tabby." Fournier was torn up by the prospect of putting her pet down. What did Mulderick think?

Mulderick wanted to slap her. How could the doctor express more
concern for a cat than for the patients all around her? Pets were everywhere—everywhere!—in spite of Mulderick's exhortations to keep
them out of the hospital. Staff members simply ignored the rules, walking their dogs through the areas where patients were lying and telling
her they wouldn't leave their pets behind. *For Christ's sake! Where's your
damn common sense?* she wanted to ask. It angered her to see them attending to pets around the corner from where the sickest patients lay.

A short time later, Mulderick shared these frustrations with a radiologist on the ER ramp. "We are talking about euthanizing the animals," she said, "but not about what we can do to help the patients." Mulderick asked him to communicate her concerns to the medical chief, Dr. Richard Deichmann, who was holding daily meetings with the doctors.

She would later recall that her idea was to rid the patients of their pain and dull their senses to the point they would no longer care that they were smelling the feces they were lying in, that panting dogs were weaving past and licking their hands. But the radiologist seemed to interpret her intentions differently. A physician colleague heard him ask Deichmann if they could convene a meeting to discuss euthanasia, because some of the staff were concerned about the patients and wanted to consider it. The radiologist thought it would be best to get the discussion out in the open and not have the decision made by a few people in a dark corner. Deichmann said no. The idea shouldn't even be considered.

The physician colleague watching the interaction figured that staff inside the hospital didn't want to see patients suffering and were at a loss for what to do; while medicine had, of late, been overtaken by a fad of standardization, no guidelines existed for this situation. The idea of euthanizing patients, however, struck him as dangerous, and he shared his opinion with the radiologist. "I can't imagine getting through all this—with all we've been through and all we've done—and having a physician go to jail because they were trying to help a patient and did something illegal."

What would stick with Dr. Richard Deichmann years later would be not this conversation, but another one: He and Mulderick speaking in a quiet hallway alone; she asking him whether it would be "humane" to euthanize the hospital's DNR patients (a word and an idea Mulderick would deny, through her attorney, ever having spoken of with Deichmann or anyone else at Memorial); and Deichmann replying, "Euthanasia's illegal." Throughout the disaster, he and Mulderick had expressed minor differences about how the evacuation should proceed, which sometimes frustrated the employees, who were confused about whose direction they should follow. But this question, if Deichmann understood it correctly, represented a major difference. "There's not any need to euthanize anyone," he would recall telling Mulderick. "I don't think we should be doing anything like that." He had figured the DNR patients should go last, but the plan, he told Mulderick, was still to evacuate them, eventually.

One of the emergency medicine doctors, Karen Cockerham, interpreted Mulderick's words the same way as Richard Deichmann did and as the radiologist did. However, Cockerham agreed with the idea of euthanizing patients, which was what she was sure was being proposed when she listened to Mulderick on the ER ramp. *When is somebody going to say it?* she'd been thinking. *It's the thing nobody wants to say.* The ER doctor looked around and saw others nod and noticed that nobody was objecting. This is the United States, she thought, and was surprised at what was being said so frankly, out in the open, with maybe a couple dozen people around. She wondered how smart that was, but she thought that euthanasia needed to be considered. It was obvious to her, although she couldn't, in her normal life, have imagined it being a viable option. Now it seemed, while not the only option, perhaps the only humane one. She felt confident it was the right thing even before this conversation, and no doubt, she thought, others were thinking it, too.

Why? Because time had come to feel magnified. She was no longer able to envision what would happen when life returned to normal; many people seemed to be wondering whether that would ever happen. Having an end would give them a reference point for their options. Yes, she had heard they would all get out that day, but she couldn't see it, couldn't believe it, wasn't convinced by the CEO or by Susan.

Conditions seemed increasingly unstable. The doctor felt not only unsafe, but also vulnerable. She had fleeting thoughts that at any moment prior to being saved something even more catastrophic would occur—perhaps some sudden, secondary natural consequence of the disaster. This building could explode, she thought, or somebody could come in and hold us up and take everything we have and decide to shoot us. Her two-year-old was safe with her husband out of town, and she worried increasingly about putting herself in harm's way when she had a responsibility to return to them. She'd heard gunshots outside the hospital, which she knew was turning away neighbors seeking rescue, and she envisioned racial tensions rising. She was sure these existed because once she—a pale blonde student craving a late night biscuit—had stopped at a chicken restaurant a half-mile from the hospital near the Magnolia public housing project, and a lady warned her, honey, to get on out of here.

In the second-floor lobby, where she stopped several times to help, the temperature felt like more than a hundred degrees. Even breaking windows in the glass oven had not improved air circulation that much. *This is awful.* She saw skinny patients lying almost naked, which was so that the people tending to them could keep them cooler and could more quickly clean up their waste. Some of the patients looked like the cadavers she recalled from gross anatomy in medical school. She was sure they had no idea what was going on, and that they had bedsores from lying in place without a good mattress and someone regularly shifting their bodies from side to side.

She knew what she would want in their place, she would say. "If I were one of those little bitty, skinny, debilitated, confused poor little ladies, I mean let me go to heaven. Don't do that to me. I've lived my life, I'm not going to be watching TV or reading a book or even carrying on a conversation. I got to look forward to being in bed anyway, please don't do that to me."

Somebody had already made that choice for the dogs. *Why should we treat the dogs better than we treat the people?*

She thought it almost criminal what they were doing to these people, putting them through a torturous process of suffering. And these were people, she would later explain, "who in the best-case scenario might be able to nod or something, but not people who can look forward to going through this horrible ordeal and enjoying anything or being aware of life." They were the type of people she thought shouldn't be resuscitated anyway, "people who have no quality of life in the best case scenario, even if they make it through this horrible ordeal. And then to put them through this horrible ordeal." Didn't military guys take a cyanide capsule to war, to have an option to avoid torture? And those, she reflected, would be people who would have hope for a meaningful life after their horrible torture. The people she saw on the second floor would, she thought, "have horrible torture and no meaningful life." She knew it was torture, because the heat was hard enough on her, too, that, when she took breaks from working, she sought refuge in her air-conditioned car, grateful for having topped off her gas tank before the storm.

The ER doctor said something to Susan Mulderick, but Mulderick told her it was being taken care of.

———

MULDERICK'S IDEA to medicate the patients found a champion in Dr. Anna Pou.

The two had met for the first time only the previous day when Pou informed Mulderick that the chapel had been converted into a morgue for the LifeCare ventilator-dependent patients who died after staff put an end to the Coast Guard evacuation. Like Mulderick, Pou had also been pressed for advice by a distraught animal owner deciding whether or not to put down his pet. Mulderick had seen Pou directing patient care on the second floor.

Mulderick shared her feelings with Pou now and repeated her statement. They were talking about euthanizing the animals, but not about what they could do to help the patients. She would later remember Pou saying the men and women lying before her were much like many of her cancer patients—at some point there was nothing else to do for them but try to make them comfortable. Pou said she would use pain medications to do that, though she wasn't sure what to give the patients.

What to give them? Dr. Ewing Cook would know. Mulderick had worked with Cook for two decades, going back to her time as head nurse in the ICU. She knew he believed that certain drugs exist to relieve suffering. Unlike many doctors, he didn't shy away from ordering them. For years as a pulmonologist he had helped patients who were taken off life support die without pain and anxiety. Cook believed in making dying patients comfortable.

Mulderick said she would ask Dr. Cook to speak with Pou about what to give the patients. Mulderick found Cook readying his gun. He was preparing to leave the hospital by boat to rescue his son, the doctor who had gone home after the storm and been trapped since Tuesday's flooding. She asked Cook to talk to Pou before he left.

Cook spoke with Pou on the second floor. He had interacted with her during the year she worked at Memorial and thought highly of her. The weary doctors discussed the category 3 patients. These included some of the patients from Memorial and LifeCare who remained in the staging areas, and nine patients who had never been brought down from LifeCare. To Cook, Pou seemed worried that they wouldn't be able to get them out. Cook hadn't been to LifeCare since Katrina struck, and that was on purpose. He had not been asked to go there, had no patients there, and knew that any doctor brave enough to venture upstairs would face difficult, gut-wrenching decisions. He considered LifeCare patients to be "chronically deathbound" at the best of times and knew they would have been horribly affected by the heat. Plenty of staff and volunteers remained at Memorial, but they were exhausted, and Cook couldn't imagine how they would carry nine patients down five flights of stairs before the end of the day. Nobody from outside had arrived to help with that task. If there were other ways to evacuate these patients, other ways to care for them, Cook wasn't seeing them.

Cook told Pou how to administer a combination of morphine and a benzodiazepine sedative. He later said he believed that Pou understood that he was telling her how to help the patients "go to sleep and die." That was different from what she and her colleagues on the second floor already knew how to do and were doing: treat patients for comfort. Over the previous hours, nurses had alerted Pou, Fournier, or King when a patient in the staging area appeared to be in pain or anxious, and the doctors prescribed doses of medicine. Pharmacists had dispensed Ambien, Ativan, diphenhydramine, Geodon, and Restoril to help patients relax and sleep; and morphine, OxyContin, and Vicodin for pain.

What Cook was describing to Pou was something else entirely. The drug combination "cuts down your respiration so you gradually stop breathing and go out," he would say. He viewed it as a way to ease the patients out of a terrible situation.

Pou wrote out large prescriptions for morphine for three of the patients lying in the second-floor lobby. She ordered nine vials each of a concentrated form of IV morphine, totaling 90 mg for each patient. The highest dose Pou had prescribed for pain in the last two days for her colleague's patient, the one with cancer who was already on morphine and tolerant to its effects, had been 10 mg of morphine—nine times less than what she was prescribing for each patient now. In terms of how the drug would be given, Pou wrote only: "as directed." At the bottom of the prescriptions, she filled in her Drug Enforcement Agency number, as required, which authorized her to prescribe legally controlled substances.

One of Pou's prescriptions was for LifeCare patient Wilmer Cooley, an eighty-two-year-old African American former truck driver with heart problems and a serious infection, who required dialysis and had a Do Not Resuscitate order. Another was for Carrie Hall—"Ma'Dear"— the LifeCare patient with a tracheostomy who had so impressed a nurse the previous night with her will to survive. The third was for Memorial patient Donna Cotham, the forty-one-year-old mother of four with liver disease. The day after the hurricane, her condition had worsened, and doctors planned to transfer her to the intensive care unit. But the unit had been evacuating, and she hadn't gone. She wasn't expected to survive. She had looked particularly bad overnight to the nurses fanning her on the second-floor lobby.

Two female doctors approached the pharmacist on duty across the hall. He took the three pieces of paper and filled Pou's prescriptions.

⁓

DR. KATHLEEN FOURNIER had been present, listening, when Susan Mulderick spoke with Anna Pou about giving the patients medication.

"I just disagree with this," Fournier had said.

"OK, don't order it," Mulderick responded. "Don't give it. I'm just asking. If you don't want to give it, don't worry about it."

Mulderick hadn't known Fournier before the storm, but after the cat incident she was coming to share the opinion some nurses had of her. They found her aggravating. Fournier didn't shy away from letting nurses know when she was upset about something, often in a loud voice with colorful curses and comments that struck some as inappropriate. She didn't filter.

Fournier didn't have her own medical practice. Dr. Richard Deichmann paid her a flat fee to cover his group's internal medicine practice, including Memorial and LifeCare inpatients, whenever his turn came up to take call on weekends. Fatefully, while it was not her turn, Fournier had agreed to work because the doctor on the schedule had wanted to throw a birthday party for her daughter. Deichmann had suggested she leave the hospital after Katrina passed. He would later recall that even her physical appearance was concerning. A large patch over an irritated left eye was fixed with a piece of ragged tape whose grip, in the terrarium-like humidity, grew progressively more tenuous.

Fournier had decided to stay and had worked harder than most, often alongside Anna Pou. That morning, Fournier had sprawled on the second-floor lobby carpet amid the patients in front of a box fan with blades, powered by the overloaded generator, that moved in slow motion. The long extension cords and high loads kept tripping the generator's breaker, and someone had to run to the parking garage repeatedly to reset it. The doctors who met in the radiology room had decided to try to convince Fournier to leave the hospital as soon as transportation arrived. One was dispatched to encourage her to do so, but he thought she seemed fine and hadn't pressed the issue.

Fournier grappled with the implications of Mulderick's request as she interpreted it. She did what she typically did when she had concerns— shared them freely. Fournier asked a nurse manager, Fran Butler, what she thought of the talk going around about putting people to sleep or out of their misery. "That is not an option," Butler said. She'd held that view for a quarter century—personally, professionally, and spiritually— since becoming a nurse. She didn't turn up the morphine unless a patient looked uncomfortable. She'd trained at Charity, knew how to work in the trenches, and while Memorial "wasn't the Taj Mahal," she'd say, she didn't think the conditions were unbearable. Back upstairs there had been a breeze through the broken-out windows, she'd cut her uniform pants into shorts, put on her flip-flops, slung a tied-together pair of ice-filled gloves around her neck—and worked; she was heavyset, sweat-slicked, flushed, and not the youngest of nurses, but she thought everyone should have stayed on their wards and "maintained" until the water went down around them.

Kathleen Fournier solicited another opinion later, as she and pulmonologist John Thiele struggled to euthanize two Siamese cats around a corner from where the patients lay on the second floor. The cats belonged to a pharmacist who lived alone and considered them her children. She had asked Fournier to euthanize them, convinced she would have to abandon them.

Fournier held one of the cats as Thiele trained a needle toward its heart. While they worked, Fournier told Thiele she did not want to participate in putting patients out of their misery. Thiele told her he understood, and that he and others would handle it. She wasn't sure what that meant.

Before Thiele could inject the heart-stopping medicine, potassium chloride, the cat struggled out of Fournier's hands. It clawed at Thiele, ripping his sweaty scrub shirt. Someone else injected another cat and threw it out a broken window into the floodwaters.

Fournier polled another of the doctors, Bryant King, whom she knew from Tulane Medical School. She pulled him aside on the second floor. "This is between me, you, and the fence post," she told him.

The words tumbled out. Her concerns about her cat. Her concerns about the patients. The patients were suffering miserably, she said, and she asked King what he thought about helping to end their suffering.

He said if they could find some way to turn on the air-conditioning or more fans, that might help.

"No," Fournier said. That wasn't what she meant. She told him about her conversation with Susan Mulderick and Anna Pou.

"I can't be a part of anything like that," King said. "I disagree one hundred percent." The idea was stupidity itself. They had only been there two days since the floodwaters rose, and they were dry and had food and water.

He told her that hastening death was not a doctor's job. He knew the situation was grave. He'd carried the man's body to the chapel before sunrise. But he, unlike Pou, Fournier, and Mulderick, had gone upstairs and visited every patient on the seventh floor to assign a triage category. The remaining patients were hot and uncomfortable, and a few might be terminally ill, but he didn't think they were in the kind of pain that called for sedation, let alone mercy killing.

In normal times, doctors occasionally sedated very sick patients to unconsciousness in cases of intractable anxiety, breathlessness, and pain, and sometimes even to make caring for certain patients less taxing on nurses who would otherwise constantly need to monitor patients' suffering or guard against the possibility that their movements would disrupt a spaghetti-like mass of tubes and lines. But taking away patients' ability to monitor their own well-being and express themselves could render them even more helpless than a baby or an animal to communicate when something was wrong. And they might seem less alive, less worth saving.

"I'm a Catholic," Fournier said, "but not a great Catholic."

"Well that's between you and your God," King replied.

The conversation deepened King's desperation to escape Memorial. He was nearly ready to swim out, despite having watched nurses foul the murky water with the contents of bedpans. He sent text messages to his sister and his best friend telling them that "evil entities" were discussing euthanizing patients. He begged them to send someone to get him out of there. Contact CNN, the National Guard, anyone, he wrote.

———

Handwritten note by Aviation Services, Inc., on-site flight manager, Memorial helipad

Pilot's log book with leatherette cover

Please pass to Aviation Services in Dallas

1) AVS 3 lifts so far 2 Slidell & 1 to Kenner

2) Coast Guard shuttling 3 HH65 aircraft. 5 lifts so far moving amb, children, women to (about 5-6 per lift) ambulance ground site near Superdome

3) Per Admin-total population as of 1000 CT/1 Sep is at 450. Repeat 450

4) Total pop includes ~120 patients from this hospital (Memorial) & associated hospital

5) Population was ~1500 but surface water craft moved many yesterday

6) Criticals were moved Mon & Tue [. . .]

7) CG shuttling about every 15 minutes w/ 5-6 pax per lift.

———

AFTER A DAY and night working downstairs, LifeCare nursing director Gina Isbell returned to the seventh floor and was surprised to see "Miss Alice" Hutzler and her roommate Rose Savoie still in their shared room instead of in an evacuation line. Hutzler looked dehydrated and barely responded to her. Isbell felt guilty. She remembered she had promised Hutzler's daughter she'd take good care of her.

Isbell took a short break in an empty room, peeling off the thick white T-shirt, blue scrub pants, and tennis shoes she had worn for days. She washed herself down as best as she could with baby wipes and put on a clean pair of jean shorts and a light gray T-shirt she had picked up from her car, where she had enjoyed another burst of air-conditioning. She sat down to have a Ding Dong and make some instant iced tea. A doctor passed the room. Isbell didn't know her name, but she recognized the short woman with the fluffy hair, having seen her on the floor earlier in the week.

Isbell offered Anna Pou a packet of powdered iced tea for her water. "I think I will have a tea," Pou said softly. She wore a scrub shirt with the arms ripped off and little shoes. She looked sad as she walked away.

One of Isbell's favorite nurses, a friend from school, Andre Gremillion, approached her looking upset. He had been down to the second floor. The other workers, he said, didn't seem to realize there were still patients on the seventh floor. One told him they were under martial law, that "Baptist" was evacuating its employees, and anyone who could walk needed to go. "From what they telling me downstairs," he said, "everybody's leaving." He was afraid LifeCare staff members would soon be the only ones there, with nine patients still to transport from the seventh floor. "If everybody leaves, who's gonna move the patients?"

Several LifeCare leaders went down to find Susan Mulderick.

"IF YOU WANT your suitcase that badly, you'll have to swim out with it!"

Mulderick lost her temper with a hospital employee's family member who insisted on the right to carry a very large suitcase onto an evacuation boat. The rule was at the most one small bag, sometimes just a wallet, no suitcase, no pets.

Mulderick couldn't take two steps without running into someone having a conniption and who felt the need to share it with her. She had walked the floors for two days, shouldering people's tension, anxiety, and panic. Two nurses who had brought teenage children to Memorial had come to her in tears saying they had to get out. When she told them there were still patients to be cared for, they had yelled at her. Other nurses had been allowed to leave. Why not them? Mulderick defended the departed nurses—they had gone to help people at the boat drop-off point—even though she had asked them, too, to stay at the hospital.

When Mulderick passed through the second floor, people sitting with their animals and their packed bags asked her when they could leave. A therapist erupted when she told him he had to stay; there were still many patients to move. He yelled at her. He had a bad back. Carrying patients was a job for younger men. Mulderick walked away. There was too much happening to argue with every person who was upset.

After the fight over the suitcase, three senior staff members from LifeCare approached her. They said they were getting low on rubbing alcohol and a few other supplies and wanted to know what the plan was for nine patients who remained on the seventh floor—as if they expected her to tell them what to do! They said they weren't sure they could move the patients on their own, including a large paraplegic patient. One of the LifeCare staff members had told Mulderick earlier that two of their patients were in grave condition, running extremely high temperatures of 104 and 105 degrees.

Mulderick told the LifeCare team the plan was not to leave any living patients behind. She asked them to talk to Dr. Pou. After all, the doctors working on the second floor were the ones who had stopped LifeCare's DNR patients from being brought down to the staging areas on Wednesday, saying it was too crowded. Were the patients dying, would they not attempt to move them; or would they proceed with getting them in the staging area for evacuation? Whatever the LifeCare leaders were going to do, Mulderick told them, they needed to decide and get it done.

During their conversation, a uniformed man began yelling, "All women and children!" More boats had arrived, and people streamed toward the ER ambulance ramp as if the man had announced the last one was leaving.

One of the LifeCare staff members, physical medicine director Kristy Johnson, excused herself to fight through the crowds. She wanted to bring the news of the family evacuations to the seventh floor, where two daughters of LifeCare patients remained.

CEO René Goux came to the ramp and asked the doctors why the hell they were loading family members onto boats. The doctors who had gone out that morning to the drop-off point had marshaled resources, including ambulances. "We're trying to get the patients out!" he said.

"Everybody's a patient, including us," Dr. John Kokemor said. He, like many others, had been concerned for his life. He kept a credit card on him to use if he made it out of the hospital and a driver's license for others to identify him in case he did not. Patients were slow getting onto the ramp. If the boats quit at five thirty as he expected, they would all be there another night. Kokemor's goal was to get as many people on board each boat as quickly as possible; that included two of Memorial's oldest doctors, one of whom was Horace Baltz. Kokemor wanted to get Baltz's older sister out too, and her daughter, an ICU nurse. They had medical problems, and Kokemor didn't think they were doing well. "I'll move you to the front of the line," Kokemor told them, "and you guys get out of here."

Baltz accepted the offer even though he had not asked to leave. His longtime colleagues Dr. Ewing Cook and Susan Mulderick both hugged him and told him tearfully that they loved him. Their uncharacteristic emotion surprised the elder doctor. This wasn't a normal good-bye.

Two men in camouflage caps who appeared to be National Guard soldiers helped Baltz step down into the unstable boat. Baltz, in shorts with white socks, held one young man's rifle for him while the man helped others aboard. Baltz looked back at his beloved hospital. He was sure he was watching it die.

⁓

ANGELA McMANUS couldn't believe that three men who looked like police, holding sawed-off shotguns, could be demanding that she leave her mother's bedside near the nursing station on the LifeCare floor. They told her they were evacuating the hospital and she had to go.

"You're going to stand over my mom's bed with a gun pointed at me? Have you lost your mind? Shoot me!"

After staff had said her mother was being evacuated on Wednesday, McManus had waited in the boat line and had spent the night downstairs. This morning she had run into her mother's nursing aide, whom she'd befriended.

"Angela, Mama's doing good," the aide said. "She's a *strong* woman."

"What do you mean?" McManus asked. "She's still here?"

She climbed back up to the seventh floor and found her mother in the hallway near the nursing station where her bed had been rolled after Angela left her. Her mother was being given a cooling alcohol rubdown. "What's going on here?" Angela McManus asked. "Why's she so lethargic?" Angela was told patients had been given Ativan. "She can't take Ativan!" she said, even while noticing that this time the drug seemed to have achieved its intended effect of calming rather than exciting Wilda.

Wilda was a little too calm for Angela's liking. She kept dozing off, and Angela repeatedly woke her to make sure she was OK.

Now, as the policemen told Angela she had to go, she refused.

"I'm not leaving my mom," she said. "I'm not leaving until they get her out of here."

"Oh no, you're leaving," one of the policemen said. He lowered his gun, which had been pointed up at the ceiling, and Angela screamed. She noticed her mama didn't awaken. Something seemed very wrong. Was it the Ativan?

"I need to talk to my mom," Angela told the police. "Y'all move so she can't see you." The men moved behind the head of Wilda's bed.

Angela roused her mother. "Mom," she said, "the police are making me leave the hospital. They're evacuating."

Wilda McManus asked what was happening.

"They want us to get out of the hospital," Angela said. "I can't go with you."

Angela tried to soothe her mother with words she used frequently. "It's OK for you to go and be with Jesus. Daddy's waiting for you, Grandma and Grandpa, Auntie Elois, waiting for you." She had a sense that she was not only leaving her mother, her mother was about to leave her.

Wilda McManus couldn't sit up, but she raised herself a little, looked intently at Angela, and screamed.

Angela kept calming her. "Mama, do you understand what I just told you?"

"I'm going home."

"Yes, you're going home."

Wilda McManus asked her daughter to sing. Angela sang again like she always did, like it was church. She sang the gospel song "Near the Cross," about the soul finding rest, and Wilda shut her eyes.

Angela asked her mother's nursing aide to make sure her mother continued to receive nutrition through her feeding tube. "I'm going to be with her," the nursing assistant said, "no matter what happens."

Angela cried so hard during the walk downstairs that she had trouble seeing. In the heat, carrying her belongings, she quickly grew winded.

LifeCare physical medicine director Kristy Johnson, who had come up to get her, guided her down the dim staircase with a flashlight and helped carry her bags. They walked slowly, taking rests between floors. When they reached the first floor, Johnson bulldozed Angela through the crowds to the front of the boat line. Because Angela was traveling alone, a spot on a boat was quickly found for her.

———

KATHRYN NELSON also didn't want to leave her mother. Life-Care nurse executive Therese Mendez was trying to convince her to go now or she'd never get out of the hospital. Nelson had inscribed Mendez in the "Especially Nice to Mother" list she had maintained throughout her mother's hospital stay. Mendez was listed twice, meaning the smart, take-charge executive had been especially nice to Mother on at least two occasions. When Nelson told Mendez she didn't care about missing the boats, Mendez responded so sharply Nelson felt that she had undergone a Jekyll-and-Hyde switch. "Your mother is dying!" Mendez said, after days without sleep, having worked overnight on what she called "First Floor Beirut." She was worried it was Nelson's last chance to leave.

"I'm dying too!" Nelson said, and told Mendez she had cancer. She didn't, and later she would wonder how she had come up with something so ridiculous. She would say or do anything to protect her mother.

If her mother really was dying, then why would Nelson want to leave her now after she had been with her every day in the hospital for more than a month and a half? When she had first been told to leave, on Tuesday, she had asked if she could be admitted as a patient so they could travel together. Nelson looked the part of a patient. She had taken to wearing hospital gowns during her mother's stay.

The last time she had been made to go downstairs, she hadn't stayed away long. She couldn't bear to be separated from her mother. Though she had been told on Wednesday her mother would soon be evacuated, she'd had a sense that her mother and the other bed-bound LifeCare patients would be staying for a while. She had peered at the helipad through a window and watched people, including a male nurse she recognized, boarding helicopters. The able-bodied were leaving, not the sick.

Nelson had gathered her ample belongings, bundled in a sheet like a cartoon hobo's, and dragged them back up the stairwell Wednesday evening, but she ran into blockades: first a LifeCare nurse and then three men who seemed to be guards or police. The guards told her she couldn't go back upstairs. They called her a "security risk."

The security risk, all five-feet-four and 108 pounds of her, had stood her ground, arguing with the guards until a woman arrived who had just received word that her own children, not in the hospital with her, had survived the disaster. Whoever she was, she took pity on Kathryn and, with authority, told her to go ahead upstairs and spend as much time as she wanted with her mother.

Nelson found her mother in a new room—she'd been moved closer to the nursing station after the doctor's visit—with a nurse at her bedside fanning her. A makeshift suction device, a plastic tube attached to a syringe, was being used to remove secretions from her airways. Her eyes were glazed and she was breathing with what seemed like great effort.

Kathryn requested medication to help her mother breathe more easily. The nurse agreed, saying she thought Nelson's mother needed a bit of comfort. Her temperature, 106 degrees, was extremely high, and her chest was congested. The nurse administered a small dose of morphine and Ativan according to the orders the infectious diseases doctor had left earlier Wednesday night in case any patients needed them. Afterward, the nurse told Kathryn Nelson that the drugs sometimes made patients like her mother stop breathing altogether. This so upset and alarmed Kathryn that she kept vigil at her mother's side all night, not sleeping.

Overnight, Elaine Nelson's high fever broke. In the morning her body felt cooler to the touch, her color was better, and her eyes were open but no longer glazed. The nurse did not hear congestion in her lungs. Kathryn still had a hangover of worry, but the roar of helicopters landing one after the other on the helipad cheered her. The intensity of the rescue made her feel proud of whoever had come to save them.

Therese Mendez returned with reinforcements, some sort of security guard or policeman who might or might not have been armed. Kathryn was given a few minutes to bid her mother good-bye.

Kathryn had been trained as a registered nurse and knew from working in the ICU that even patients in comas could hear and remember what was said to them. She told her mother she was the best mom any girl could have and she was proud to be her daughter. At around eleven fifteen a.m. she kissed her mother good-bye, said a prayer over her, and, with the nurse executive, departed LifeCare.

———

AROUND A CORNER from Elaine Nelson's room, on the other side of a long corridor, LifeCare nursing director Gina Isbell walked into a meeting in progress between several other staff members and the fluffy-haired doctor with whom she'd shared her tea. Her staff nurse and friend Andre Gremillion was crying and shaking his head. He brushed past Isbell into the hallway, and she followed, grabbing his arm and guiding him to an empty room.

"I can't do this," he kept saying.

"Do what?" Isbell asked. When Gremillion wouldn't answer, Isbell hugged him and tried to comfort him. "It's going to be OK," she said. "Everything's going to be all right."

Isbell searched for her boss, LifeCare's pregnant assistant administrator, Diane Robichaux. "What is going on?" Isbell asked, frantic.

Robichaux told her that staff members from Memorial had arrived and were taking over the care of their patients.

"Are they going to do something with these patients?"

"Yeah, they are," Robichaux said, in tears. "Our patients aren't going to be evacuated. They aren't going to leave."

Isbell swore. She cried. She asked Robichaux why no one was coming to help. Robichaux didn't have an answer.

Robichaux said the task now was to get all the staff off the floor except the core leadership team. Isbell tried not to think about what was going to happen. For five days she and her colleagues had tried so hard to keep everyone alive. She didn't want to accept that they couldn't save everyone who had made it this far. A colleague told her that they were under martial law. Isbell believed she had to follow orders. She did what she was instructed to do.

Isbell, Robichaux, and other LifeCare leaders split into two groups and headed for different parts of the floor. "Everybody get out of here now," they told the nurses who were on duty. "Get your stuff, we got to go now. Let's go!" Cindy Chatelain, about to pass medicines to Elaine Nelson, was told to drop everything and leave without so much as signing off her patients to another caregiver. Andre Gremillion, who was tending to two patients, was told to go. He asked if someone would care for the patients. "Yeah," he was told. "Get your bags and go ahead and evacuate now."

As the LifeCare administrators cleared the floor of all but a few senior staff members, Robichaux sent Isbell to the back staircase to make sure nobody reentered. It was quiet there, and Isbell was grateful to sink into a chair. She sat alone, itching from a heat rash, aching from oozing skin wounds, drained and upset. Isbell let the occasional staff member through to retrieve belongings from the closets. She saw the fluffy-haired doctor walking back and forth for a while, and then noticed that she had gone. She thought again of her promise to Alice Hutzler's daughter and felt a pang of guilt. She prayed that help would come before her patients died; she didn't want to believe that no one would come.

It was close to noon when Isbell and the LifeCare leaders left the seventh floor to join the evacuation lines. On the way down, they passed the other LifeCare nursing director. He wanted to know what was happening. Isbell avoided his eyes. Tenet people had come up to LifeCare, she told him. Their patients were, she said in a near whisper, "gone."

Their intention was to stop on the second floor to check on "Ma'Dear" Carrie Hall and several other LifeCare patients who had been moved downstairs on Wednesday. From there the LifeCare leaders planned to proceed through the hole in the machine-room wall to the garage with a dose of Ativan for a staff member they had heard was having a breakdown there. But a Memorial employee blocked the LifeCare team at the stairwell exit on the second floor. A doctor had told certain staff members to direct people away from the patient area on the second floor where the DNR patients lay.

"Should we just make a break for it and just go looking?" one of Therese Mendez's coworkers whispered in her ear. "Don't do it," Mendez said. "We're going to end up shot or arrested."

For now only the LifeCare pharmacist was allowed onto the second floor, to go directly to the garage with the medicine. The Memorial employee blocking the entrance gave the others an e-mail address they could use later to find out which of their patients had died. Someone took a pen and wrote the address on Mendez's scrub shirt.

———

DR. KATHLEEN FOURNIER walked back into the second-floor lobby at around noon. Her acquaintance from medical school Bryant King was grabbing his bag, looking upset and angry. "I'm getting out of here," he said. "This is crazy." She asked him for a hug. She was upset and angry, too. She told him she knew why he was leaving.

———

CFO CURTIS DOSCH saw a doctor administer drugs to a patient and then flap a hand around the patient's mouth for some reason he couldn't discern. Was the doctor trying to cool the patient? Something else? Susan Mulderick had called Dosch to the side of the second-floor lobby and told him that some people felt that there were patients who wouldn't make it. He gathered from her that the patients were being medicated to help make them comfortable in the process of dying. "Really?" Dosch asked her. He was surprised because the patients already looked comfortable to him—comatose even, though he wasn't medically trained. Also, the evacuation was well under way. Pilots had also delivered oxygen tanks and food supplies (although nobody seemed to be able to find a wrench to open the oxygen tank valves), and Memorial's pharmacy was so well-stocked now with the delivery of its emergency cache, that its drugs were being flown to a Tenet hospital across Lake Pontchartrain where some of the patients were going.

Dosch's job was to keep tabs on how many people remained at the hospital, updating Tenet officials in Dallas every half hour using the satellite phone that had arrived as promised with the first helicopter. One of the helicopter crewmen had at first said that only patients who could walk would be permitted onboard, but Dosch had called Tenet to clarify and was told that the information was wrong. The helicopters were to take any and all.

Dosch returned to counting people after the conversation with Mulderick. As the hospital cleared quickly, he was "a man on a mission," as he phrased it, but the conversation concerned him enough that he stopped to talk with CEO René Goux. Dosch asked Goux if he knew what the staff was up to on the second floor. Goux indicated he didn't. "I think you ought to go talk to Susan," Dosch told him and described what she had said. Dosch entered a staircase off of the second-floor lobby and heard the hospital's chief nursing officer wailing; several nurses surrounded her. He believed she had just learned what had been decided.

ICU NURSE MANAGER Karen Wynn arrived on the second floor
after having spent the morning helping clear the first floor of the wheelchair-bound patients who had spent the night there. The plan for these
patients had changed as hospital leaders disagreed with one another and
with the state police over how best to evacuate them from Memorial.

Rather than going out by boat from the ambulance ramp, most were
carried up to the second floor and through the hole in the wall to be
evacuated by helicopter. Others were taken, surreptitiously, out by boat
from the gently sloping parking garage ramp. The police had opposed
the use of this second boat launch, saying it was too insecure.

Several people heard the police say they would be leaving by five p.m.
and everyone needed to be out of the hospital because of civil unrest in
New Orleans. The police would not stay later to protect the hospital.
They stood stone-faced on the emergency ramp, shotguns on their hips,
barking threats at anyone who came too close, only increasing the sense
of urgency. People felt intimidated, not protected, by them. A large airboat they had brought to Memorial was not used to help transport anyone. A policeman sat in it chain-smoking and taking naps.

Hospital visitors and staff continued to leave from the ER ramp. The
surgery chief, anesthesiologist, and plant-operations chief who had left
early in the morning returned with an additional boat they had found,
and maintenance workers hotwired it. Now staff members were permitted to leave with their pets. It was too late for many. It hadn't been necessary to euthanize them after all.

Over the course of the morning as Wynn encountered her ICU
nurses, she instructed them to leave Memorial, telling them she would
not go until they were all on their way. She felt no particular urgency
for herself. She had in fact been greatly encouraged by the words of a patient that morning. The woman, Janice Jenkins, had two fractured legs

at the knee joint and was in large casts, having been hit at a bus stop after leaving her job as a nursing assistant at another hospital. Shortly before the storm she'd had surgery and was confined to bed, legs elevated, unable even to sit. Then on Tuesday night, when she was still on the fifth-floor medical ward, her heart had developed a dangerous arrhythmia. Dr. Baltz had run into her room, lab coat thrown over his boxer shorts as he answered the emergency overhead page. He and his colleagues had treated Jenkins successfully, and now Wynn helped her slide with difficulty onto a bedpan and held up a sheet to give the long-suffering woman some privacy. But Jenkins wasn't thinking about herself. "Y'all going to get this done," she told Wynn, "because you're nurses."

What cheered Wynn even more was knowing that her daughter was now safe, having boarded a helicopter with another nurse's teenage daughter. They carried money from Wynn's purse, a cell phone, and instructions to call Wynn's parents wherever they arrived. Wynn had watched them go from a window in the seventh-floor stairwell.

Wynn hadn't left the stairwell to go into LifeCare. She had assumed all the patients there were gone. It later surprised her when one of her most experienced surgical ICU nurses, Cheri Landry, told Wynn she was going up to the seventh floor with Dr. Pou to make patients comfortable. Wynn told her that was fine, but then she wondered: Seventh floor? There's still patients on the seventh floor?

Wynn could see there was still work to do on the second floor, too. About a dozen patients who were designated as 3's remained near the ATM wearing big tags that said "DNR." Other patients were lined up on stretchers and cots on the other side of the lobby and along the corridor to the machine room, awaiting transfer through the opening into the garage. One young male amputee was complaining loudly and repeatedly about the conditions. Wynn wished they could get him out. All it took was one person to spread panic.

Wynn wandered over to a small group of doctors and nurses gathered near the DNR patients. The makeshift unit had an open-air feel.

What had been an alcove on the northern side of the lobby was surrounded now by crashed-out floor-to-ceiling windows, a precipice over the floodwaters. Wynn's nurse Cheri Landry returned from LifeCare. She told Wynn they were giving sedatives to the patients there on the second floor. "What can I do?" Wynn asked.

"Just check on people," Landry said, as Wynn would later remember. "See how they are."

Wynn focused on four women lying in a row adjacent to the corridor. One, an elderly white lady, was breathing slowly with apparent difficulty. "She looks really bad," Wynn said. "She's breathing really, really hard. She could probably use some."

Wynn walked over to a table in the corner that was covered with medical supplies, some of which she had helped organize. "What are we giving?" Wynn asked. There were vials of morphine and the sedative midazolam, known by its brand name, Versed, on the table.

It was a combination Wynn was accustomed to giving to patients on ventilators in the ICU. In that context, it would sedate the patients and, when indicated, reduce their drive to breathe, allowing the ventilator to do the work of breathing for them. The combination was also given to minimize any potential sense of pain, discomfort, or air hunger prior to removing a breathing tube when the decision had been made to withdraw life support and allow a patient to die.

The drugs were meant to be given by vein, but many of the patients didn't have IVs. Wynn and Pou requested several boxes of IV catheters, but not IV fluids and tubing, which would have been needed if the goal were to hydrate hot patients who had difficulty drinking on their own. Pou called for someone with a light, and a male nurse came with a flashlight and held it for her while she started an IV.

Another very young nurse working on the scene found it strange to see doctors and nurses placing IVs in the eight to ten still-living DNR patients; she had been told by Fournier the previous night not to start IVs in these patients because the hospital was in "emergency mode." Now a female doctor with short brown hair who had been in charge of triaging patients told the young nurse to get out of the area and go pack up her things upstairs; the nurse didn't know her name, but she followed her direction.

Dr. John Thiele turned to Karen Wynn and asked, "Can we do this?"

It wasn't a question of could or couldn't. In Wynn's opinion, medicating the patients was something they *needed* to do. The patients needed to be comfortable.

When Cheri Landry had told Wynn she was going upstairs to the seventh floor, Wynn had already heard rumors that patients were being euthanized. Wynn passed them on. "Did you hear that they're euthanizing patients?" she had asked a colleague, who had cried.

Wynn didn't cry. OK, so what if they are euthanizing? she'd thought. Unlike that nurse, who managed a regular medical unit, Wynn lived in the world of the ICU, where many patients didn't get better. Death was often scheduled, orchestrated, the result of decisions to switch off machines.

Withdrawing life support was something Wynn had grown extremely comfortable with from her work in the ICU under the tutelage of Dr. Ewing Cook. She considered him masterful and compassionate in his approach to end-of-life care. They both served on Memorial's bioethics committee, of which she was the longtime chair because, she sometimes told people, nobody else wanted to do it. Committee members were called in to consult in cases where end-of-life treatment dilemmas arose. The situation seemed analogous now, the only difference being that family members were usually there to receive the message that Wynn had heard Cook, unafraid of bearing bad news, deliver so many times: "We've done everything possible for her. Now the only option is to make her comfortable."

Wynn had, many times, told the same thing to other doctors. One Memorial oncologist performed bone-marrow transplants and was crushed whenever he couldn't make his patients better. A pretty young woman had grown so bloated and bruised she looked like a monster, no longer human, struggling and holding on to the last bit of life on the ventilator. When patients like this were so disfigured they appeared to be dying cell by cell from the inside out—so bad that Wynn couldn't bear going into their rooms to examine them—she would approach the doctor. "It's time," she'd say. "We need to go and talk to the family."

Wynn knew what type of patients she and her colleagues regularly discharged from Memorial to be admitted to LifeCare for long-term care. Many had multiple medical problems, their bodily systems failing. If on ventilators, they had poor chances, she thought, of ever breathing without them. Wynn remembered how the LifeCare patients had appeared when she had helped carry some of them downstairs on stretchers on Wednesday, her knuckles brushing against frying-pan-hot skin. She'd believed that if they didn't get out soon, they would be brain dead.

She was also haunted by what a nurse had told her about one of the four ICU patients who were not evacuated on Tuesday. Tesfalidet Ewale was a sixty-six-year-old Eritrean political asylee. Soon after he was admitted to Memorial in mid-August suffering from a presumed heart infection on top of chronic illnesses, he had been politely turned down for a transfer to LifeCare because the company did not accept Medicaid patients. Ewale had stayed a patient at Memorial, and on Tuesday an ICU nurse had reassured his daughter by phone that Ewale, who was drowsy but arousable and could grasp hands, would be airlifted out of Memorial, possibly to a hospital in Atlanta. But he was considered DNR—a designation his daughter had at first resisted.

Ewale had been resuscitated once several days earlier when he was at the point of dying. He had since come off of the ventilator and stabilized with the use of a special oxygen mask, but he still had grave medical problems and his doctors, including Roy Culotta, had felt strongly that resuscitating again someone as sick as he, with such a poor prognosis, would be futile. After the power went out and the vacuum lines failed, medical workers had not figured out how to suction his airways effectively. Ewale had been given, at Culotta's direction, injections of the sedative Ativan and morphine for comfort. He had been pronounced dead shortly before two p.m. on Wednesday after having choked on his secretions for hours.

Ewale had been comatose and unresponsive during those hours, but Karen Wynn believed that even when patients weren't conscious, they could still feel things. As a young staff nurse, she'd had a patient with liver failure who was unresponsive for weeks. One day he awoke and asked for pizza and a Pepsi. He said that the whole time he was unconscious he had heard everything the nurses were saying to him. If he could hear, Wynn had concluded, he could probably feel as well, and this inference had informed her practice ever after.

The patients lying before Wynn on the second floor looked bad. They appeared to be struggling and working for each breath, when breathing should be effortless. In the incredible heat, even if they were not conscious, in Wynn's mind they were suffering.

Wynn believed giving morphine and Versed would probably speed up these patients' deaths, a process of dying she felt was already under way. Although she didn't examine all the patients, her sense from seeing and hearing them, after decades of experience, was that they weren't going to survive. She believed the outcome would be the same with or without the drugs even if the time frame would likely be different.

Besides, if the patients were working this hard to breathe when lying still, how would they fare if the staff attempted to move them? Shoving them through the hole in the machine-room wall, putting them on the back of a pickup truck, and bumping them up to the eighth floor of the garage seemed to her a more active means of precipitating their demise. Even then, it would be appropriate to sedate them for the journey.

All she and her colleagues had were means to provide comfort, peace, and what little dignity remained possible. Wynn turned to the elderly white woman with labored breathing. She diluted what she later remembered was a 10 mg vial of morphine and a small amount of midazolam in 10 ml of saline. She drew it up in a syringe and pushed it slowly into the woman's IV catheter, then flushed the line with saline. The woman seemed to stop struggling so hard to breathe. She died within about half an hour.

Wynn saw one of her ICU nurses with Anna Pou attending to patients near the supply table. Another group comprising Dr. Thiele and several nurses had gathered near the broken windows. Wynn joined them beside a heavyset African American patient whose mouth was open in an O. Everyone could hear his awful death rattle.

The man had already received morphine, but to Wynn he looked and sounded dreadful, his breathing raggedy, like he was obviously suffering. "I've done everything I can do to make him comfortable," Thiele said.

Thiele tried more morphine. He tried prayer. He put his hand on the man's forehead; Wynn and another nurse manager took the man's hands in theirs. Together they chanted: *"Hail Mary, full of grace. The Lord is with thee."* They recited the Lord's Prayer. They prayed for the man to die.

The man kept breathing.

"It's hot! I wanna drink!" the young male amputee groused from the opposite side of the lobby. Thiele stood up from the heavyset man he'd been praying over and strode furiously toward the grumping and griping man. "He's gotta get out of here!" Thiele said. Another staff member intervened to prevent the situation from escalating. The complaining patient was moved toward the head of the evacuation line.

A nurse approached to ask if anyone working in the lobby needed a break. She saw a group of colleagues gathered around a patient she knew well. "Oh good, you're giving her some fluids," she told a nurse. It was starting to hit her that what was really causing the patients to decline was dehydration. How easy it had been to lose presence of mind in an emergency, addled from nights without sleep. Of course you could run an IV without an electric pump. You could hang a bag of fluids above the patient and, with the right kind of tubing, allow gravity to do the work of dripping it into a vein.

As the hours had passed with patients sweating out their vital fluids, dehydration posed the most lethal threat to those who could not drink on their own. The initial goal had been to discontinue all treatments that could interfere with marshaling the patients up to the helipad as quickly as possible. But now that a day or two had passed, depriving these patients of liquids was undermining their chance of surviving.

From the shake of her colleague's head, "No," the nurse perceived that it was not IV fluids that her former patient, Ms. Essie Cavalier, was being given. The seventy-nine-year-old lady had been unable to walk or speak more than a few words since a stroke in her sixties. However, she'd had no acute health issues that would mean she could not survive. In fact, as the storm approached she was being discharged back to her nursing home after treatment for a urinary infection, but the nursing home was evacuating and could not accommodate her.

She had been a frequent patient at Memorial. A tall lady who had once played semi-professional basketball, Cavalier had grown up picking cotton and sweet potatoes, and had met her husband while working as a Rosie Riveter on the Higgins amphibious boats that originated in the Louisiana swamps and had helped win World War II. Recently, during her hospital admissions, some staff members would get annoyed with her because of her difficulty communicating. She could do little for herself but was well aware of her own needs and did what she had to do to draw attention to them, including scream. She would repeat the few words she could still form, including "Mama, Mama" and "my, my, my," at a loud volume and nod and shake her head to indicate when she was uncomfortable and needed to be shifted in bed.

Here in the open lobby, these outbursts had disquieted those around her. After she was first carried downstairs, Dr. Pou ordered a dose of medicine to relax her, which a nurse gave her. Dr. Bryant King had done the same for her twice, most recently early this morning. He had been concerned that people like her were getting a little delirious, starting to yell out—some staff members were, too. King, like Karen Wynn, believed that fear was contagious. Now Ms. Cavalier's eyes were open, looking around, but she appeared calm and was silent.

The nurse tried to find out what was happening. She noticed another patient, surrounded by caregivers trying to comfort him, who was struggling to breathe after receiving an injection. The nurse panicked and searched in vain for someone to do something, write an order to reverse the drugs, inject an antidote. Later her recollection of it would all be a blur that left her with the discomfiting sense that, at least in some people's minds, the medicines were being given "for the greater good," to get the exhausted, frightened employees out more quickly because there were too many patients who were immobile. "This is what needs to be done," one colleague told her when she asked what could be done to stop it. Several staff members said that Dr. Pou had ordered the drugs, though the nurse had no idea if that was true or what her intentions might have been.

As the patients on the second floor died, and word spread about what was happening, the nurse wasn't the only one who felt the way she did. Several nurses familiar with the patients who were injected believed that after they had survived everything so far, there was no reason they couldn't still make it to safety. One employee acted like those who objected to patients being given the medicines weren't being realistic and needed to grow up; most of the other employees milling around the second floor seemed to think what was happening was horrible but necessary.

Because no one was willing to try to reverse the drugs, a group of nurses carried the man who was still struggling to breathe toward the parking garage, hoping that getting him quickly up to the helipad might give him a chance to survive.

The very young nurse who had been told to go pack her things returned to the second-floor lobby about an hour later. She noticed one of the patients she had been caring for looked weirdly whitish. A nurse who accompanied her placed a sensor on the patient's finger to measure her blood-oxygen level with a battery-powered pulse oximeter. The reading was extremely low, around 65 percent. The young nurse, Julie Couvillon, scanned the lobby and noticed that a few of the patients definitely didn't look right. The female doctor with the brown hair who had told her to leave now came to tell her and her fellow nurses to stop what they were doing and cease all care for the patients. The young nurse saw other staff putting sheets over the patients. She was frightened. She was only twenty-two years old and three months out of nursing school, and she had never seen a patient die. The previous evening she had broken down in fear for her own life. Now the doctor asked her to help carry dead patients and line them up inside the chapel. The young nurse began assisting.

———

From: Ben Russo [Tenet Healthcare business development and man-aged care director]
Sent: Thursday, September 1, 2005 1:25 PM
To: Michael Arvin [Tenet Healthcare regional business development director]
Cc: Steven Campanini [Tenet Healthcare media relations director]
Subject: Fw: Fw: New Orleans Bound
    Mike or Steve, can you call Mitch or me regarding having fox news and john hammerly follow our clinical team to evacuate personal. This would be a huge pr play for Tenet. Mr. Hammerly is near Baton Rouge and would like to do a story on evacuation efforts.

———

AS THE PATIENTS who had been injected died, Wynn and her colleagues helped cover them with sheets and move them into the chapel. They tried to move discreetly to avoid attracting the notice of more cognizant patients still waiting in the evacuation line. Someone unlocked the chapel for them to enter and relocked it when they left.

Throughout the day, boats and helicopters drained the hospital of nearly all of its patients and visitors. Wynn and a group of other female nurses helped lift the last few patients through the hole in the machine-room wall.

———

From: Denise Beltran on Behalf of Earl Reed [LifeCare CEO]

Sent: Thursday, September 1, 2005 4:02 PM

To: All LifeCare Locations' Employees

Subject: New Orleans Update – Sept 1

> [. . .] Our patients in the Tenet hospital are still being evacuated. We are exploring private means of evacuating those patients. [. . .]

———

AS THE LAST patients were brought to the top of the garage in the waning daylight, Merle Lagasse continued to await rescue there. A day had passed since the wrenching separation from her daughter as Lagasse was conveyed through the machine-room hole. Lying for days in the heat, suffering from advanced cancer and emphysema, Lagasse was far from the glamorous lady she had once been. A nurse noticed her gasping for air, breathing in a pattern that often heralds death. The nurse asked Lagasse's physician, Roy Culotta, to give her something to ease her respirations.

Culotta saw Lagasse was in respiratory distress and believed she was actively dying. He took her out of the evacuation line. He asked an ICU nurse to retrieve painkillers and sedatives from the hospital.

A shortcut led from the garage back into the seventh floor of the main hospital over the rooftop of an intervening building. A wooden pallet bridged the gap between the garage and rooftop, with a hose to grip for balance, allowing those staffing the helipad to go back and forth easily to retrieve supplies. The ICU nurse returned with a mix of painkillers and sedatives Culotta assumed came from a lockbox in the ICU; they included morphine, Versed, and Ativan.

Culotta had been treating Lagasse with narcotics for weeks because she had pain and anxiety from her spreading cancer, so he knew her tolerance was high. It would take a large amount of morphine, he felt, to relieve her gasping and suffering. It would also, he believed, undoubtedly hasten her death. While she and her daughter had not agreed to a DNR order, he, as her doctor, had felt during her hospitalization that her therapeutic options were limited, and a central goal of his care was keeping her pain and anxiety in check.

The nurse gave the drugs Culotta ordered. They put Lagasse in the back of the truck, and Culotta drove back down with her and brought her into the hospital. He was with her when she died.

———

SUSAN MULDERICK surveyed the emergency room. She had been told hours earlier that the two patients lying in its waiting room—one of them the elderly lady who had arrived with her husband and was cared for by Karen Wynn—were not being moved because they were dying. The two were still present and alive. "What are we doing with these people?" she asked the ER doctor. Mulderick told him they needed to make a decision about the two. Were they expected to die soon, or was it time to move them upstairs? The doctor said, "OK," that he'd take care of it.

———

IT HAD BEEN a long day on the helipad. Some helicopter pilots refused to take bed-bound patients. To get around this, doctors lifted some of these patients into wheelchairs and tied sheets around their midsection and chest to convert them to "sitting patients."

At around nine p.m., the obese ICU patient Rodney Scott was hoisted up the open metal steps to the helipad. He was apprehensive about being carried up a narrow passageway by inexperienced volunteers but relieved to be outside of the dark, airless hospital. Sudeep Reddy, a reporter from Tenet's hometown newspaper, the *Dallas Morning News,* tracked Scott's progress toward rescue. Reddy had begged a ride from the aviation services company supplying leased helicopters to Tenet and flown in with a photographer, Brad Loper, late that afternoon. Reddy had counted eighteen people, many of them women, helping slide Scott through the machine-room wall on a count of three. Six others received him on the garage side, discussed how much oxygen he needed, and loaded him onto the back of a Ford F-150 pickup truck for a ride to the top. As Reddy ascended to the upper level of the parking garage, he was surprised to see patients in obviously terrible condition still lying in the heat on the ground. Some looked so bad that Reddy took doctors and nurses aside and asked in a low voice whether the patients were alive. The medical staff said they were, but that others had died on the ground in the horrific conditions. Reddy could not piece together why these very sickest patients had not yet been airlifted.

Reddy watched clusters of volunteers hoist stretchers on their shoulders and carry patients up the narrow metal steps to the helipad. He scribbled in his notepad. "Urine and feces rolled off the beds and onto the workers, forcing them all to wipe down with sanitizing liquid every time," his story would say.

Now four men surrounding Rodney Scott shouted, "Push! Push!" and rolled his heavy wheelchair into a Coast Guard helicopter. When this was done, one of the male ICU nurses collapsed to the ground. He'd been pinned against the helicopter by the wheelchair and his colleagues hadn't heard him yell for them to stop.

The ICU nurse seemed to be having trouble breathing and it looked like he would need to be evacuated, too, perhaps in place of Scott. Dr. Roy Culotta bent to examine his chest and other workers screamed for ICU nurse manager Karen Wynn, who had helped lift Scott through the machine-room wall and then grabbed her purse and hiked to the top of the eight-story garage. What can I do? she wondered. She was like a mother to her nurses, even as they scattered from Baptist and New Orleans, perhaps forever.

Another helicopter hovered overhead. It could take the injured nurse and Culotta, who would accompany him, ready to insert a chest tube in midair if necessary to help him breathe.

As they devised this plan, the helicopter carrying Rodney Scott lifted away. Weighing more than three hundred pounds, recovering from surgery and heart trouble, and unable to walk, Scott had been designated the last to go through the hole in the wall because of his weight. Ewing Cook had mistaken him for dead the previous day. And yet he had been successfully airlifted, alive. Scott was the last living patient to leave Memorial.

PART 2

RECKONING

Yesterday we could see, today we can't, tomorrow we shall see again. . . .

—José Saramago, *Blindness*

THE CAMERA WENT LIVE, showing some of the thousands of people trapped on the stinking, trash-filled Interstate 10 cloverleaf on Thursday night. The reporter estimated that 90 percent of them came from inner-city housing projects. "But then there are the others," she said. She introduced two Memorial Medical Center employees, describing them as very scared.

"You could have gotten out. You could be in a nice, warm bed tonight, but instead, you're out here," the reporter said. Her made-up face looked, to the tattered survivors, out of place in the disaster.

Memorial's director of maternal-child nursing, Marirose Bernard, had agreed to go on camera in exchange for what she thought was a promise from the news crew to help rescue her children, husband, and mother, who had left Memorial on Wednesday only to end up hungry, thirsty, and terrified at the New Orleans Convention Center.

The nursing director described the five days at Memorial. She said doctors and nurses had worked with, at most, an hour of sleep a night. She spoke of learning to triage and explained how employees and visitors carried each patient down the stairwell in the dark.

The reporter asked whether she had any regrets for having stayed at Memorial for the hurricane. "No regrets whatsoever," the nursing director replied. "I don't regret it at all because I'm a nurse, and that's what nurses do."

———

IN ATLANTA, GEORGIA, a tall, slender man with graying hair watched the interview and felt a swell of emotion. Arthur "Butch" Schafer lived and worked in Louisiana and was crushed by the vast wasteland he saw on television. This nurse was a hero.

The death and devastation mirrored a personal tragedy. He and his wife were in Georgia with family because one of their daughters, Shelly—a thirty-one-year-old with a sweet smile and a giving nature— had recently died.

Schafer interrupted his mourning to return to Louisiana where he was also needed. In his professional life, he fought to protect the lives of elderly and disabled hospital patients and nursing-home residents. Schafer worked as an assistant attorney general in the state's Medicaid Fraud Control Unit, charged not only with rooting out fraud but also investigating abuse, neglect, and exploitation of Louisiana's most vulnerable—a population now displaced by the thousands and scattered across the state.

———

LIKE MANY RELATIVES of hospital and nursing home patients, Carrie Everett could not locate her husband, Emmett, the heavyset paraplegic patient in LifeCare. Carrie had spent Katrina in the Ninth Ward of New Orleans, trapped in a house as the waters rose. A boat pilot rescued her, and she ended up in Houston. Everyone she reached by phone to ask about Emmett passed her to someone else. Day after day she worried.

Carrie had cared for Emmett ever since a freak spinal cord stroke had disabled the Honduran-born, blue-collar laborer a decade earlier at the age of fifty. She was a small woman, but every day she had dutifully helped transfer Emmett to a wheelchair so that he could sit in their yard, read the Bible, play with their dog, and clown around with his seven-year-old granddaughter, his "eyes," riding on his knees.

Emmett had been in LifeCare awaiting colostomy surgery to ease chronic bowel obstruction. Carrie had visited him in the hospital every day, but she'd been told to stay at home when the LifeCare patients on the Chalmette campus were transferred to Memorial Medical Center. Emmett had called her to let her know that he had made it there with no problems, brought a photograph of his granddaughter with him, and was safe. That was the last she had heard from him.

———

LINETTE BURGESS GUIDI searched the Internet for news of her mother, Jannie Burgess, the licensed practical nurse with advanced uterine cancer whom she had flown in from Europe to visit in the ICU as the storm approached. Burgess Guidi and her mother's caring niece enlisted every relative from Louisiana, Chicago, Holland, and Italy to make calls, comb missing persons listings, and try to find her.

———

AS FAMILIES SEARCHED FOR loved ones, bodies lay decomposing in the flooded city. Days passed as government officials argued about whose responsibility it was to recover them. On Tuesday, September 6, MSNBC cameraman Tony Zumbado paddled to Memorial Medical Center in a kayak and followed the overpowering smell of death to the Myron C. Madden Chapel. A small piece of yellow lined paper reading DO NOT ENTER was duct-taped to the wooden door. Inside, Zumbado's camera panned to take in more than a dozen bodies lying on low cots and on the ground, shrouded in white sheets. Here, a wisp of gray hair peeked out. There, a knee was flung akimbo. A pallid hand reached across a blue gown.

For days more, Memorial's deceased underwent a sort of wake—a viewing attended by, among others, a passing battalion of National Guardsmen from San Diego assigned to aid and secure the neighborhood, Tenet-contracted DynCorp security guards recently returned from Iraq and Afghanistan, a *Christianity Today* magazine reporter, and a relief worker who vomited from the stench.

A chaplain who came to search for survivors compared what he saw when he entered Memorial's chapel with Dante's *The Divine Comedy.* "It was like a picture of hell," he said on CNN. When members of a disaster mortuary team finally arrived on Sunday, September 11, more than a week after the last living patients and staff members had departed, they recovered forty-five bodies from the chapel, morgues, hallways, Life-Care floor, and the emergency room.

It was the largest number of bodies found at any Katrina-struck hospital or nursing home. Major news outlets covered the shocking discovery. Dr. Anna Pou agreed to an interview with a Baton Rouge television reporter. Pou put on a simple white V-neck blouse. Her cinnamon-colored hair was well coiffed, but the camera showed shadows under her eyes and a hollowness beneath her cheekbones. She struggled to explain why so many at Memorial had died.

"There were some patients there that, who were critically ill, and regardless of the storm were, uh, had the orders of Do Not Resuscitate, in other words that if they died to allow them to die naturally, and not to, um, use any heroic methods to resuscitate them." As she spoke, she nodded emphatically, as if to bring along her interviewer or her audience, or perhaps to convince herself. "We all did everything in our power to give the best treatment that we could to the patients in the hospital, to make them comfortable."

WHILE MORE PATIENTS had died on the grounds of Memorial than anywhere else, horrible stories were beginning to emerge from health facilities around the flooded region. At St. Rita's, a single-story nursing home near failed levees in St. Bernard Parish, more than thirty residents had apparently drowned. The owners, a married couple who had been urged to evacuate their facility before the storm, were nowhere to be found. It began to appear that people in hospitals and nursing homes accounted for a significant proportion of all deaths from the massive disaster.

As the outlines of this medical tragedy sharpened, there was an urgent need to understand its causes before the next catastrophe occurred in New Orleans or elsewhere in the country. Were deaths at hospitals and nursing homes regrettable results of an act of nature, a chaotic government response, and poorly constructed flood protection overlaid on a degraded environment? Or had lax oversight allowed individual or corporate greed to play a role? Did some hospital and nursing home leaders decide not to evacuate before the storm primarily to avoid the substantial costs of emptying and closing health facilities? Were emergency plans not followed, important pre-storm investments not made, and health workers not properly prepared?

These were questions Butch Schafer, returning home from mourning his daughter's death, began to probe. He was an experienced criminal prosecutor who specialized in complex cases. His boss, first-term Louisiana attorney general Charles Foti, had served for thirty years as elected sheriff of Orleans Parish and had a strong constituency among the elderly. White-haired himself, Foti had taken care of his own father until he died that May at ninety-two, driving him out of the predicted path of several hurricanes. Foti pledged in public to investigate fully what he called a horrific tragedy at St. Rita's, and his Medicaid Fraud Control

Unit opened investigations into every one of the hospitals and nursing homes where patients had died.

The unit, supported by state and federal funds, had jurisdiction over hospitals and other health facilities that participated in Medicaid, one of the programs that Southern Baptist Hospital's leaders had, four decades earlier, resisted joining in part to avoid government meddling. Now Memorial Medical Center's current corporate owners received a request by phone from a government investigator for a list of deceased patients and a copy of the hospital's disaster plan.

If the company could show the disaster plan had been followed, there was every reason to expect the case could quickly be closed and the locus of blame for the deaths could be pursued elsewhere. New Orleans mayor Ray Nagin's pre-storm evacuation order had not applied to hospitals, which had been ordered to stay open and staffed.

Almost immediately, however, suspicious signs emerged. A Tenet attorney responded to the phoned-in questions defensively, by requesting them in writing. He faxed a corporate summary of events, copies of newspaper articles highlighting the heroism of Memorial's employees, and a set of press releases blaming the deaths on forces beyond the hospital's control:

> During more than four days with poor sanitation, without power, air-conditioning and running water, and with temperatures in the building approaching 110 degrees, some patients simply did not survive despite the heroic efforts of our physicians and nurses. [. . .] By Sept. 2, we were able to evacuate every living patient from the hospital, often using private helicopters hired by Tenet after government rescue efforts were overwhelmed.

A day later, a fax came into the unit from an attorney for LifeCare Hospitals of New Orleans. It reported that nine LifeCare patients on the seventh floor at Memorial had died under suspicious circumstances.

Although we are just beginning to collect the relevant facts, we have information that the patients involved were administered morphine by a physician (Dr. Poe, whom we believe is not an employee of LifeCare) at a time when it appeared that the patients could not be successfully evacuated.

Allegations of intentional killings at health facilities were almost unheard of in the unit. Even deaths as a result of abuse emerged only rarely. Of all the potential crimes Schafer and his coworkers were planning to pursue, this one was completely unexpected and seemed, at first, almost outlandish.

Schafer and his new partner, Special Agent Virginia Rider, knew that the allegations needed to be investigated. Rider was a ten-year veteran of the unit, where prosecutor-investigator teams worked cases. Rider had a top-notch reputation: thorough, diligent, and smart. Fact-gathering and public service ran in her blood—her father, a mapmaker, had served in army intelligence in the Korean War and then worked for decades on the interstate highway system. Rider had followed her mother in becoming an accountant.

Rider loved poring through financial transactions—a case that left her buried in paper bank records made her "as happy as a pig in mud"—but she hadn't been satisfied keeping the books at a real estate development firm, her first job. Only a few months after starting, she netted an embezzler and discovered she had a knack for lifting the numerical fingerprints of fraud. The employee had stolen $400,000 from the small company over a period of years and nobody noticed. Rider had found her passion—pursuing fraudsters. What had led her to her current, hazardous duty investigator position, which had required police-academy training, was a passion and talent for helping bring wrongdoers who harmed others to justice.

Rider was a tenacious worker who loved her job just north of the Louisiana state capitol complex, where a fraud investigator could work surrounded by reminders of the unbroken strain of patronage running through Louisiana political history. Legendary governor Huey P. Long, known as "Kingfish," both convinced legislators to build the limestone and marble capitol during the Depression and was assassinated there in 1935. Thirty-four stories high and Art Deco in its details, it remained the nation's tallest state capitol. Both Rider and Schafer lived about an hour away from Baton Rouge and made the drive to work in state-issued Impalas. Rider kept an ancient blue Thunderbird at home.

Rider was twenty-four years younger and a foot shorter than Schafer. He was newer to the unit and had had only one previous interaction with her, a year earlier, when she led an investigation of combined money laundering and Medicaid fraud and came to testify at trial. She had dimples when she smiled, but she cultivated the conservative look of someone dedicated to a life behind the scenes, with a medium build, gray-blue eyes, and natural hair she called dishwater blond. It was the first time she had ever been called before a jury, and she was nervous about going onstage. Schafer, by contrast, was a frustrated actor who loved the sanctioned confrontation of the courtroom; it was practically the reason he had gone to law school. He'd advised Rider to hold on to a pen in her lap and fidget with it to avoid telegraphing insecurity to the jury. She did well, and Schafer saw that Rider worked hard because she believed in what she did, not out of a desire to get out in front of others and be recognized for it.

Upon receiving the fax from LifeCare, Rider immediately requested copies of the patients' medical records from Tenet, which controlled access to Memorial, where the records were still likely to be. Tenet officials were vague about the location of the records. They might have been removed with the bodies to the coroner's office or might still be in the hospital. Rider, Schafer, and several colleagues drove to New Orleans with subpoenas to attempt to retrieve them. Security guards denied them entry to the hospital, insisting they needed protective gear. Federal investigators accompanying the group located two hazardous-materials suits and went into Memorial, but found little in the way of records for the nine patients.

Butch Schafer had visited many hospitals in his life. He had never heard of one that lacked current records. That struck him as curious. Interesting, too, was the presence of heavily armed guards intent on blocking the group.

The number of complaints arriving at the attorney general's office about other hospitals and nursing homes was also surprising. The CEO of Touro Infirmary in New Orleans, Les Hirsch, bragged after the storm about his hospital's performance. In an essay for *Modern Healthcare,* he wrote that even after a fire department superintendent gave Touro's staff an hour to leave the hospital because violence was breaking out in the city, there was "no way" they would leave patients behind. His employees stayed until the last patient was safely evacuated.

An anonymous letter writer took issue with Hirsch's story and copied the attorney general. A patient at Touro had been found "alive and abandoned" on Friday, September 2, 2005, by workers from a nearby hospital.

One of the nurses helping with the hospital evacuation came upon 16 bodies in your building. It was reported that numerous morphine vials were found littering the floor. One of these bodies was still alive and is currently receiving treatment in another hospital. Why were these patients left to die? Were they euthanized? How did you decide which ones to leave, based it on ability to pay? I find the actions of this hospital deplorable. No patient should be left to die or euthanized.

"Someday," the letter writer warned, "the truth will be told."

MEMORIAL PATHOLOGIST Dr. John Skinner had recorded the names, birth dates, and locations of the dead before leaving Memorial. He had faxed the handwritten scraps of paper to Tenet officials in Texas, who entrusted them to the company's regional chief medical officer, the man who had worked from vacation in Oregon as the disaster unfolded. During the week and a half that the bodies of the dead remained in the hospital and were not yet in the hands of the coroner, little was done with this information. Tenet telephone operators took down messages from dozens of frantic families, and these were entered into a database. If a patient's relatives somehow reached the medical officer directly, he told them what he knew. Not until after the bodies were retrieved and the attorney general's office launched an investigation did Tenet officials print out medical chart "face sheets" with names, addresses, and family contacts of the dead, and assign various employees to notify them. The callers received a set of instructions:

1. Speak in general terms.
2. Never give opinions!
3. May be first time family has had contact with anyone about loved one.
4. The loved ones know nothing except news media information.
5. Loved ones are usually angry.
6. Tell truth, i.e., Patient may have died due to lack of electricity or high temperatures, etc.

The employee was to introduce himself or herself, verify the family member's relationship with the patient, and: "Reveal information: patient expired between the hurricane and evacuation of patients from the facility."

The document included guidance for handling tough questions, including why notification was occurring more than two weeks after the deaths: "All information electronic; however, computer server stored in New Orleans. Did not ever plan for a whole city to shut down."

The employee was to tell each family: "Your loved one was cared for throughout. Your loved one was identified and shrouded and placed in our chapel area. Your loved one was treated with dignity."

If a family member questioned the decision not to evacuate before the hurricane, it was based on "risk to the patient." The decision to evacuate after Katrina had been mandated by government officials: "In situations like this disaster, the government takes control. The state retrieved your loved one and brought to the parish's coroner office. Eventually, all deceased will be taken to St. Gabriel, LA (southwest of Baton Rouge), where a thorough medical exam will be performed and a cause of death will be identified. A death certificate will be available. Once a cause of death has been determined, state officials will contact the family."

The eight members of the call team included ICU nurse manager Karen Wynn and incident commander Susan Mulderick. Both women had spent the night of Thursday, September 1, on Memorial's open helipad with about fifty other staff and family members, including Mulderick's aged mother, still wearing her housedress. Rescue helicopters had stopped coming after dark, and the group did not reenter the hospital for fear of encountering looters. Armed staff members blockaded the staircases. When a group of people appeared at a hospital window, including wide-eyed children, the armed employees threatened to shoot "the looters" if they came closer.

The next morning, Wynn flew out on a helicopter to the New Orleans airport. It angered and disheartened her to see Mr. Rodney Scott sitting on the concourse in his wheelchair, shivering in a paper gown, without a soul taking care of him. Many of the last push of Memorial patients from the previous evening had not gone far after leaving the hospital. Her injured ICU nurse, however, had been flown directly to a Baton Rouge hospital at the insistence of Dr. Roy Culotta and another accompanying doctor, with a Coast Guard pilot's knife at the ready for one of them to extemporize the insertion of a chest tube. Fortunately it was not necessary, and X-rays showed the nurse had sustained only severe bruises to his ribs and the area around his spleen. He spent three nights at the hospital being treated for dehydration developed over days of moving patients in the heat.

Susan Mulderick's harrowing hegira from Memorial had ended in the state of Delaware and included a day at a crowded refugee-collection point at the small New Orleans Lakefront Airport. She and her exhausted colleagues had been asked to care for people there. A sympathetic official ushered them to an airplane ahead of others who had waited longer, and they feared for their lives that the desperate mob would attack them to avoid being left behind. By contrast, a few of the hospital's executives, she later learned, had been helicoptered to a nearby Tenet hospital and given a hot meal and a room to shower, shave, and change before being picked up in a helicopter and taken to Hattiesburg, Mississippi, then flown in a private jet to their preferred destinations. Memorial CFO Curtis Dosch, a beneficiary of this arrangement, had learned of it from Tenet's Bob Smith by phone on Thursday. Dosch's wife had spent the week making repeated calls to Tenet's COO, a longtime friend, asking when Tenet would get Dosch out of there and insisting that he not go by ground. "You can't put my husband on a bus with all them people" was how Dosch phrased it when he told the story.

In fact, the buses leased by Tenet weren't bad. They drove to Dallas, where the company had reserved and paid for rooms at the upscale Anatole Hotel, complete with toiletry amenity packs, free food vouchers, and assistance reuniting with loves ones. Memorial staff, family members, and even LifeCare employees lucky enough to be rescued via Tenet-hired helicopters and taken to the nearby Tenet hospital also received meals and showers there and could take advantage of the arrangement.

Mulderick called her assigned sets of family numbers for three of the

deceased patients repeatedly, reaching full voice-mail boxes and auto-
mated recordings announcing network difficulties. After several hours,
she made contact with the son and daughter-in-law of one elderly Life-
Care patient. Mulderick tried to give context to their mother's death.
Water never reached the patient-care areas, but the basement flooded and
there was no electricity or air-conditioning. The woman had been cared
for by MDs and nurses, but was very ill.

The following Monday, September 19, Mulderick received a call from
Dr. Anna Pou. Pou had read that the state was investigating the deaths at
Memorial. CNN reporters had phoned her to say they were preparing a
report on possible euthanasia at the hospital, and they pressed her to tell
her side of the story. She didn't know what to do. She asked Mulderick
for help. Mulderick told her to sit tight and someone from Tenet would
call her.

———

ANNA POU had climbed into a helicopter on Memorial's helipad
around six p.m. on Thursday, several hours before the last patients were
airlifted. She looked down, disoriented by the water covering familiar
landmarks, and felt heartbroken for her city. Pou's New Orleans home
on high ground near the river had been spared from flooding. Less than a
week after leaving Memorial, with the hospitals still closed and patients
displaced, she had agreed to work for her employer, LSU, at a public
hospital in Baton Rouge.

With several hospital workers extremely upset about the patient injections and the many deaths, word quickly made it to reporters. When
CNN and other media contacted Pou, she reached out first to fellow
Memorial doctors. She phoned chief medical officer Ewing Cook, the
pulmonologist whom Susan Mulderick had asked to advise Pou about
what drugs to give the patients. He was in Houston after the disaster, and
she told him that people in Louisiana were looking into things. She asked

if he had been contacted. He had, by the news media. CNN was looking for him, too. He wanted nothing of it. He wished to remain completely unknown. When it came to issues of medical ethics and helping people die—good Gertie, there were people with opinions all over the place! "Anna," he said, "don't talk to the news media. Say nothing." A reporter looking for sensationalism could twist their words in any way. "Hide," he advised.

Pou also called John Walsh, Memorial's surgery department chair, a smart and kindhearted general surgeon whom she had come to know when they chatted during breaks between operations in the year she had worked at the hospital. On the afternoon of Thursday, September 1, she had stopped to speak with him about what happened on the seventh floor, where she had injected patients and many there had died. Walsh now urged Pou to get an attorney, be forthcoming, and contact Memorial CEO René Goux. She left messages on Goux's cell phone and with his mother. When she couldn't reach him, she called Mulderick and asked for help.

Tenet's corporate communications director, Steven Campanini, called Pou back on her cell phone. He asked if she was somewhere near a landline. She assumed he wanted a more secure connection. When he called Pou again, he had Tenet assistant general counsel Audrey Andrews on the line.

Pou spoke with them for more than an hour. Andrews clarified during the conversation that she worked for the corporation and not individuals. She advised Pou to get her own attorney, and Campanini suggested she draw up a general statement for the media. Pou called him the next day to go over it, and he phoned back with Andrews. They advised Pou, in fact, not to send it to the media. Andrews started to ask more questions, but Pou said she wanted to get her own lawyer before answering.

Richard T. Simmons Jr., a criminal and civil defense lawyer who specialized in white-collar offenses, worked in a wealthy suburb of New Orleans at Hailey, McNamara, Hall, Larmann & Papale. Formerly an assistant US attorney in New Orleans and a US Army JAG Corps officer during and after the Vietnam War, Simmons was well connected. He had helped represent commanding officer Lt. William Calley on an appeal in the My Lai massacre case and successfully helped defend a business partner of one of Louisiana's most corrupt recent governors, Edwin Edwards, in a racketeering case. Simmons was turning sixty that month. He wore a few long strands of shoe-polish-black hair stretched over his balding pate. Pou hired him on the advice of her employer, the Louisiana State University Healthcare Network, which had used Simmons's services in another matter. The network agreed to pay Simmons at the same rate, $275 an hour, to defend Pou.

One of the first things Simmons did was to contact one of Tenet's attorneys and insist that whatever Pou had told Andrews and Campanini be treated in confidence, as if Andrews had actually been Pou's attorney, not Tenet's, and the conversations had been covered by attorney-client privilege. Simmons wanted to ensure that nobody else had the chance to discover what Pou had confided. There would be no more unrestricted discussions with people aside from him, no more unmediated forays into the media. Even Pou's husband would be kept, to a certain extent, in the dark.

Protecting Pou would mean marshaling the facts and safeguarding them until the time was appropriate to release them. Simmons began constructing what he would refer to as her "defense camp," and Pou retreated into it. Lines were being drawn.

Those seeking to discover and expose the truth were on the other side.

———

ON THE SAME day that Pou called Mulderick, Prosecutor Butch Schafer and Special Agent Virginia Rider sat down to interview the first of four LifeCare witnesses about their allegations of suspicious deaths on the seventh floor of the hospital. A lawyer for LifeCare scheduled the interviews at their request. Joining Schafer and Rider was a friend of Rider's from the police academy, Artie Delaneuville, a federal investigator with the US Department of Health and Human Services who had previously been employed in the Medicaid Fraud Control Unit. He often worked cases with Rider. The US attorney for southeast Louisiana had opened concurrent investigations into the hospital and nursing-home deaths as potential criminal violations of the federal health-care fraud statute.

The witness was LifeCare's pregnant assistant administrator Diane Robichaux, who joined them by phone with two LifeCare attorneys. She recounted her experiences during the storm, how by Wednesday the smells of the unrefrigerated morgue on the eighth floor had drifted down the staircase in the furnace-hot air, the way the staff labored all night with rubbing alcohol and gravity-drip IVs—uncommon elsewhere in the hospital—to cool the patients and keep them alive, and finally what she said had happened the morning of Thursday, September 1. Robichaux had gone downstairs with two colleagues to speak with Susan Mulderick, who had told them, Robichaux recalled, "The plan is not to leave any living patients behind."

Robichaux found Pou on the seventh floor when she returned to Life-Care. "We said, 'Are you Dr. Pou?' And she says, 'Yeah, I'm Dr. Pou.' And I said, 'Ms. Susan told us we need to talk with you.' Robichaux introduced herself and Pou said she had already spoken with LifeCare's nurse leader and had some nurses coming up to meet her. "I'm trying my hardest to remember the exact words she said to me, but she, she just, she said that, ah, 'We, we're here, these patients,' ah, you know, 'are not gonna survive,' or, or something like that." Pou had asked Robichaux to make a choice. "'You need to make a decision whether you want your, your staff on the unit or not.' And at that point I mean, just things are going through your mind and, and I just, I remember saying, 'Well, absolutely not I, I don't want my staff on the unit.' Now, she was a little bit more specific with Therese, ah, when she spoke with her, you know, in terms of."

"Let me ask you," Delaneuville interrupted her. "What did Therese relate to you that Dr. Pou told her?"

"She said that, ah, Dr. Pou said that, she came up and said, 'These patients aren't going to survive,' or you know, 'these patients aren't going to survive,' something like that. And, ah, 'a decision has been made to administer lethal doses to these patients.'"

It was a harrowing story, but a confusing one. Robichaux hadn't directly heard Pou say she was going to give the patients "lethal doses." She had only heard that from her colleague, Therese Mendez, LifeCare's nurse executive. Perhaps Pou had been misheard and her intentions misjudged. (Pou's lawyer would later strongly deny that she had used those words.)

The interview continued. Robichaux said she told Pou about sixty-one-year-old Emmett Everett, who was aware of his surroundings, but weighed 380 pounds and was paralyzed. Pou replied she hadn't known that any of the patients were "aware"—that is, conscious. Two Memorial nurses joined Pou on the seventh floor. Robichaux didn't know their names. Together, they discussed the situation.

"We kind of went back and forth with scenarios if, ah, of whether or not he'll be able to be evacuated in terms of, whether someone could physically or people could physically get him down the stairs and lift him through that hole to get on the helicopter and, ah, and you know, it, it was said that they, they didn't think that, that was possible and, ah, then she said, 'Will one of your staff members be willing,' you know, 'somebody that, that he feels comfortable with, to go in and, and, and sedate him,' and ah, at the time, you know, we said, 'We, we have one very strong nurse here and, ah, his name is Andre,' and we, we pulled Andre in at that point, but something just at that point clicked in, ah, I just see Andre hearing this and, ah, I said, 'No, Andre is not going to do it.'"

Robichaux had gathered her staff and left the floor. She remembered

Pou coming to speak with her before they went downstairs. "And she said to me, 'I know this is hard for y'all, I don't want anybody to feel responsible, this is nothing to do with LifeCare,' ah, she said, something like, 'I take full responsibility for, I don't want anybody to worry about their license,' or, you know, something along those lines."

After being airlifted to another Tenet hospital on Thursday afternoon, Robichaux and several colleagues took a Tenet-hired bus to Baton Rouge, where LifeCare senior vice president Robbye Dubois helped arrange a flight for them to Shreveport.

Robichaux stayed overnight at Dubois's home. The next morning they sat together in the kitchen and cried as Robichaux described what had happened. This was how corporate officials learned of the events. From there Robichaux and other senior LifeCare leaders were called to the company's headquarters in Plano, Texas, where they received support and counseling over the weekend. After Labor Day, the company's lawyers discussed the situation and decided the best approach would be to self-report the potentially criminal events to government officials and offer full cooperation. Getting to the government quickly and disclosing all that was known was the best insurance against criminal charges for the corporation, it was thought.

The attorneys interviewed Robichaux and other witnesses and counseled them that they had little to fear in terms of their own exposure to criminal prosecution. They told them to be honest when they spoke with law enforcement officials. However, they advised them not to answer anything they weren't asked.

In Plano, Robichaux happened to be in the room when a call came in from Memorial pathologist Dr. John Skinner. He shared the names of patients he had documented as deceased before leaving the hospital. He was calling in case any of them were LifeCare patients. The names Skinner mentioned included all nine patients on the seventh floor and some additional patients who the LifeCare staff hadn't been aware had died. Robichaux's colleague took the information from Skinner. Robichaux passed her a note with a question for him: "Does he know cause of death?" She wanted to know, were these natural deaths? Or something else? Skinner said he didn't know.

Robichaux's interviewers remained skeptical that something illegal had happened at Memorial. It could all be a case of misunderstanding. Two days later the three colleagues interviewed LifeCare nurse executive Therese Mendez, who joined them by cell phone from an evacuated house. She had crawled through a window and was squatting in a back room until she could reenter her home. Mendez had left a hotel room and driven eight hours only to discover, nearing New Orleans, that the mayor had changed his mind and residents would not yet be allowed back into her neighborhood. Meanwhile a new Category Five hurricane, Rita, was mustering in the Gulf. One of the strongest ever recorded, it had a bead on Louisiana, and Mendez, spooked by hysterical television news reports, worried she'd be forced to evacuate again.

To save Mendez time, the investigators asked her to begin her account with the morning of Thursday, September 1, her last day at the hospital. Mendez said she had worked overnight on the first floor. After daybreak she heard the sound of helicopters. "We're just getting one right after the other. The air was just filled with helicopters." It made her think of the rush to the evacuation helicopters on the American embassy rooftop during the 1975 North Vietnamese capture of Saigon. She returned to the seventh floor at around eight or nine a.m. and walked along a corridor of LifeCare, overpowered by the smell of diesel fumes from the helipad washing into the unit. The patients she saw looked bad. Several were unconscious, frothing at the mouth, and breathing in an irregular way that often heralds death. Still, while two patients had died on the LifeCare floor on Wednesday, the others had lived through the night against the expectations of the infectious diseases doctor who had come upstairs on Wednesday night and examined them. Only a few were given small doses of morphine or the sedative Ativan for comfort.

Mendez said she heard her colleagues hollering for her through the ducts. "I got up and came down the hall and Dr. Pou was coming up toward the north side." Mendez sat down with Pou in a back office with an open window. "She said that, um, the patients that I had left on the floor will probably not survive or were not going to survive. And having seen what I had just seen when I looked around, well, you know, 'I think you're right.'" Mendez was amazed that her staff had been able to keep these sickest patients, relegated to be rescued last, alive this long.

Mendez paused. HHS special agent Delaneuville asked what happened next. "The patients that I had seen, you know, when I was looking at them, I was wondering how much longer it was going to go on because they, it was just so horrible. And, um, in the meantime you have the helicopters and the gunshots and windows crashing and people screaming and, you know, it's just like total chaos."

Mendez stopped talking again. A long time passed. Delaneuville asked her, "Well, what did she say next after she says they're not going to, probably not going to survive?"

"She said the decision had been made to administer lethal doses." Mendez paused again.

"Of what?" Delaneuville asked.

Mendez said she had asked Pou that question "and she listed off the drugs and I asked her to repeat it and she repeated it," but now Mendez couldn't remember exactly what drugs Pou had mentioned. "Morphine was one of them, Ativan, um, I don't know. I'm—I'm guessing after that."

Mendez had asked Pou if the plan applied only to LifeCare patients "because, you know, why would they just do that to our patients?" Pou said no. Staff members from another part of the hospital were coming to assist, and LifeCare employees should pack up their belongings and leave. Mendez, in tears, went to gather her colleagues. After having worked so hard to keep their patients alive to be rescued, the floor nurses and aides could not be allowed to see what was going to take place; she felt they would never recover.

Hearing the word *lethal* had given Mendez the sensation of stepping off a curb the wrong way. The investigators did not press her on why she—a smart, forceful advocate for her patients—had not challenged Pou. Nurses had the duty as professionals, no less as humans, to refuse to implement doctors' orders that they considered wrong. Mendez explained how her perception of the nexus of control had guided her actions.

"I'm under the impression here that, you know, that she [had], you know, gotten her orders from a higher authority and she's acting under these military orders. OK?" Pou said the doctors were having a hard time with the decision to medicate the patients. "I mean, I've been told that this is, uh, martial law and the military is making all the decisions now and, you know, we're having one helicopter after another just, you know, taking out hundreds of people."

Mendez had seen this on TV once and had a name for it, a "bug out," a decision to retreat at once in the face of the enemy, leaving everything— and potentially everyone less fortunate—behind. Saigon.

Mendez's account seemed, to her interviewers, consistent with Robichaux's in every important way. It was remarkable. It had enough minor differences to be credible; a fabricated story was more likely to sound identical. What was surprising was that the alleged plan was put into action not when the staff was desperately awaiting rescue, but rather when the evacuation was at last under way.

Days after the interview with Mendez, more misery visited Louisiana. Hurricane Rita plowed into the western part of the state and Texas on September 24. This time massive pre-storm evacuations took place. Roads clogged in the storm's projected path. A charter bus with an illegal license, driven by an undocumented Mexican national, caught fire on its way from Brighton Gardens of Bellaire, a nursing home near Houston, Texas, to a sister facility in Dallas. Oxygen tanks in the luggage bays exploded. Twenty-three of the thirty-eight elderly people aboard the bus burned to death. In the end, the storm spared Houston.

"I told you so," James A. Cobb Jr., the attorney for the owners of St. Rita's nursing home, wrote in an e-mail to the producers of a network news show. Days earlier he had gone on air to defend his clients' choice not to evacuate for Katrina when all three other nursing homes in St. Bernard Parish had moved patients ahead of the storm. The Texas deaths made his clients' bad decision look a little more reasonable. St. Rita's owners, Sal and Mabel Mangano, and their family had, contrary to popular assumption, stayed at St. Rita's and tried to save their residents. Before a planned meeting between Medicaid fraud investigators and the married couple, the attorney general issued a warrant for the arrests of the pair on thirty-four counts each of negligent homicide for failing to evacuate prior to Katrina. The Manganos surrendered to authorities and Attorney General Foti took to the media, condemning them. Cobb fired back, savaging Foti for acting before he knew the whole story. He called his clients heroes.

Cobb's point was that moving residents before a storm also carried risks. Investigators were looking into transportation-related deaths that had occurred prior to Katrina, too, but been quickly forgotten by the public. Ferncrest Manor Living Center was the unnamed subject of the brief WWL radio report about three deaths that occurred en route to Baton Rouge before Katrina. The residents had apparently died of complications from heat exposure in the course of evacuating on buses that lacked functioning air-conditioning, drinking water, and, in some cases, nurses. They had spent up to four hours boarding and six hours traveling the clogged route from New Orleans to Baton Rouge. Many survivors were treated in a hospital for dehydration.

Mayor Nagin had mandated evacuations of nursing homes because many homes occupied single-story buildings with marginal electrical backup. However, his order was not enforced. Many homes were not prepared and did not receive needed support to relocate in the less than a day between his order and predicted landfall. About two-thirds of the affected nursing homes had kept residents in place. In Jefferson Parish at

Chateau Living Center, the home where the contracted tour company had refused to provide buses before the storm, thirteen died in the heat after power failed.

In another extreme case, nineteen residents perished in an inundated nursing home, Lafon, run by the Sisters of the Holy Family, a New Orleans congregation of African American Catholic Sisters. The congregation had evacuated its members, including residents of the nursing home, in advance of Katrina, but left the nursing-home residents who were not congregants, and the staff of sisters and non-sisters who cared for them, in place.

All of the resident rooms were on the first floor, but their occupants had not drowned. The valiant staff had carried everyone who could not walk up to the second floor out of the floodwaters, only to watch many die in the heat and darkness despite the fact that the water had quickly receded. First responders had rolled by on the highway, ignoring roadside entreaties from the staff. The administrator went out dressed in her religious habit to seek help, but rescue came too late.

———

THE WEEK AFTER Hurricane Rita, Special Agent Virginia Rider interviewed another witness, LifeCare physical medicine director Kristy Johnson, who had supervised the hospital's rehabilitation-therapy programs. Despite Rider's preference, as an accountant, for interrogating numerical databases over questioning people, she often conducted interviews; her colleagues were out for the day and she spoke with the thirty-one-year-old physical therapist alone.

Johnson's memory for detail at first seemed excellent. She, too, recounted the ways the LifeCare staff labored Wednesday night to hydrate and cool patients, including pouring Kentwood mineral water onto cut-up blankets to wet their skin, helping keep all of them alive. Johnson said on Thursday morning she heard Susan Mulderick say at a meeting that she didn't think the LifeCare patients would make it. Along with Diane Robichaux and LifeCare pharmacist Steven Harris, Johnson spoke with Mulderick after the meeting to ask about the plan. "She's like, 'We need to talk to Dr. Pou.'" Johnson recalled Mulderick saying: "The plan is that we're not going to leave any living patients behind." It was the same phrase Robichaux had remembered.

Johnson painted the chaos on the first floor as rescuers arrived and called for women and children to evacuate, and she told of how she ran back up to LifeCare and guided Wilda McManus's tearful daughter Angela down to the first-floor ER ramp to get on a boat. She heard Therese Mendez calling for her through the crowds.

"I just heard 'LifeCare, Kristy Johnson.' She's screaming my name and, you know, I'm like, 'Here I am!' And I'm way down the hall and she's like, grabbed me, she's like, 'Come on, we got to go.' So, we're running up the stairs, I'm like, 'What's wrong, what's going on?' And that's when she told me, um, that our patients were going to be given a lethal dose and, I mean, I just stopped and, I was like, 'What?!' And I knew the day before that, you know, a physician had told Therese we were under martial law, so I just was thinking, I can't believe it's come to this, that they're ordering, you know, that our patients are going to be given a lethal dose."

Johnson was in the room for the discussion with Pou about evacuating Emmett Everett. "She was saying, 'There's no way; he couldn't fit through the hole.' He was triaged to three. I knew he was sick, he was either a quadriplegic or paraplegic, but um, you know, he could talk and everything. So, she wanted someone to sedate him and Diane told her that—"

Rider interrupted Johnson. This was a key point. "OK, you heard, you heard Dr. Pou ask for someone to sedate him?" Johnson admitted that she wasn't sure whether she had heard Pou say it or had heard this particular detail from her colleagues while they waited in the evacuation line. "I did hear this part, I mean, she, she said you know, 'Y'all need to evacuate. The patients are going to be in our care now.'

"I did see Dr. Pou, like, as she was walking down the hall. She was nervous, and she had two nurses with her." Johnson described the two women, saying they were familiar faces from the seven years she had worked at the hospital.

Agent Rider named twenty-three deceased LifeCare patients one by one, and Johnson was able to tell her either when they had died or where they were—on the first, second, or seventh floor—when she had last seen them alive.

The day after the interview, Schafer, Rider, and their partners spoke with LifeCare pharmacist Steven Harris. He told a similar story: he had heard Mulderick say at the Thursday morning emergency meeting that she didn't expect the LifeCare patients would be evacuated. He approached her with Johnson and Robichaux after the meeting to discuss what the plan was. She said they needed to talk with Pou. He and Robichaux found Pou on the seventh floor, and, he said, Pou told them "lethal doses" would be given to the patients. Robichaux told Pou that Emmett Everett was oriented and aware of what was happening at the hospital. Pou requested someone to talk with him or sedate him, but a nurse who was asked to do it refused.

Robichaux in her interview hadn't remembered hearing the phrase "lethal doses" directly from Pou. Harris offered other distinct recollections. When he had asked Pou what medications she was going to give the patients, she had shown him a large package of morphine vials and some loose vials. She requested supplies including syringes and vials of sterile saltwater used to chase a drug through an intravenous catheter and into a patient's bloodstream. Harris had provided these supplies.

Pou and the two nurses who accompanied her prepared to draw up morphine into the syringes. Harris didn't know the names of the nurses, but he thought he might be able to identify them. Later, he saw them entering the rooms of the remaining patients, and after that he saw Pou and the two nurses heading for a staircase carrying one or more translucent garbage bags. They had said they would return. Johnson told him that Pou had asked them to check on the patients and pull up sheets over those who had died.

Harris went downstairs with the other LifeCare administrative staff. They were prevented from walking through the area where the patients were lying on the second floor. He caught a glimpse of Pou and the same two nurses in the blocked-off area when he was allowed to pass quickly to the parking garage with antianxiety medicines for a LifeCare nurse who "was kind of losing it."

Harris's attorney suggested his client might have something more to add to the story. The attorney wanted to meet with prosecutor Schafer first. They made plans to do so later in the week.

The LifeCare witnesses had confirmed one another's stories. They all alleged that Dr. Pou had come up to the seventh floor to end the lives of the nine surviving patients, and two recalled that Pou had told them directly that "lethal" was her intention. The patients had all indeed died. But had the plan actually been carried out? Why, and who was involved besides Pou? Who were the unnamed nurses? What Rider and Schafer needed to see was whether physical evidence corroborated the allegations. Rider drew up a wish list, including items she had requested and Tenet had not yet supplied: medical records for all the deceased patients; evacuation plans; computer hard drives; names and contact details of hospital employees; pharmacy records; and medical waste, which might contain discarded drug vials and syringes.

They needed to search the hospital. Given the unwelcome response to their previous appearance, it was unlikely to be a consensual search. To get a warrant, they had to convince an Orleans Parish District Court judge that a crime was likely to have occurred there. Schafer discussed potential charges with his bosses, and Rider pulled up the Louisiana statute, because she wasn't used to dealing with alleged murders. In the state, the difference between first- and second-degree murder had to do with the nature of the victims, not premeditation. She wrote up an affidavit summarizing the key events described by Robichaux, Mendez, Johnson, and Harris. She submitted it with an application for a warrant to search for items "necessary in order to prove the crime of second-degree murder." Louisiana's legal definition of second-degree murder included murder with the specific intent to kill. Everyone seemed to agree, in light of the circumstances of Katrina, that they weren't going to seek the death penalty and thus there was no need to charge first-degree murder. Lesser charges of manslaughter or negligent homicide could always be brought.

The judge granted the search warrant. The next day, Saturday, October 1, Rider and Schafer joined twenty-two special agents, including nearly every agent from the Medicaid Fraud Control Unit and many others from the US Department of Health and Human Services Office of the Inspector General. Accompanying them were two crime-scene investigators from the Louisiana State Police. They drove an hour from Baton Rouge, descending on the hospital at around nine a.m. Rider participated in searches about once a month. This was the largest search team in which Rider had ever participated.

The agents approached with their badges on display, and Rider handed Memorial's security supervisor a copy of the search warrant. Infectious diseases experts from the US Centers for Disease Control and Prevention evaluated the air and determined it was safe for the agents to enter.

The hospital spanned two city blocks and still had no electricity. It would be a challenge to search. Rider carried a duty belt around her waist laden with flashlights, a radio, handcuffs, pepper spray, and firearms with extra magazines—her typical search-warrant raid gear. Some colleagues wore blue gloves and breathed in the faintly medical smell of a respirator mask that covered their noses and mouths and made each breath feel somewhat suffocating. It was hard to walk, let alone climb stairs in the heat, and Rider and Schafer left their masks around their necks. Rider had high blood pressure and was out of shape, so she left the seventh floor for the others to search. Schafer and others were clamoring to go there, and they clomped upstairs in their heavy boots. When everyone else wanted to do something, Rider was inclined to do something different.

She trekked through a maze of rooms on several floors. Once she stepped into what appeared to be a nursery. Blooms of black mold spread like creepers over the cheerily painted walls.

The security guard's passkey opened most doors, but it took a battering ram to breach the Memorial and LifeCare pharmacies. A forensic scientist prepared an inventory of morphine. Agents seized pharmacy records, including the three prescriptions for large amounts of morphine dated September 1, 2005, and signed by Dr. Anna Pou.

What struck Schafer the most was the smell of death. It was everywhere in the hospital; if you'd smelled it, you could never forget it.

Some news stories had suggested the hospital had run out of food and water. It astounded Schafer to see water bottles stacked to the ceiling. There were canned goods in the kitchen and food and beverages stashed and scattered throughout the hospital. After hearing the stories of looting in New Orleans, it shocked him to see that nobody had even been desperate enough to clean out a vending machine. Those sheltering at Memorial had come supplied like good south Louisianans, with more to eat than they could possibly consume.

Search-team members traced the paths used to rescue patients. Later, putting together the pieces, they would have a hard time understanding why the staff had used the hole in the second-floor machine room wall exclusively when there seemed to be other ways to reach the parking garage, including the route over the rooftop directly from the seventh floor.

It amazed Rider to see the hospital's main generators sitting well above flood level. She assumed they were functional. Why hadn't the staff figured out how to bypass the submerged parts of the electrical system and drive power to important patient-care areas and equipment? She

couldn't help thinking her self-reliant family of South Central Louisianans would have figured out a way. Some people depended too much on
the government to help them.

The search team found plenty of medical records, but not the particular ones Rider had requested and not yet received from the Tenet attorneys. Schafer wondered if the company was hiding them out of fear of
criminal culpability. Perhaps company officials, not only a rogue doctor,
had a hand in what had happened.

While the absence of the medical records was disappointing, other
evidence appeared to back up the witnesses' stories. The agents seized
boxes of morphine ampoules from the nursing station on the west side
of LifeCare, a desk that sat beneath windows facing the helipad. The
controlled drug was sitting out in the open instead of locked away. Elsewhere on the seventh floor, in the garbage can of Room 7305, the room
Rose Savoie and Alice Hutzler had shared, they found a translucent bag
like the one pharmacist Harris had described, full of syringes. Next door
in what was Emmett Everett's room, the agents seized a saline push syringe from a bedside table next to a box fan. Near it, a cafeteria meal tray
still had its plate, mug, and bowl. In the second-floor lobby, multiple
morphine vials and boxes sat in the open on a blue tray.

Computers and a server were removed and would go to the state's
High Technology Crimes Unit in the hopes that important records
might be found. The agents documented the search with photographs
and videotape.

That evening, Rider turned the seized medical items over to the
state police crime laboratory to analyze for fingerprints and traces of
controlled drugs. On the official request form, under the line marked
"Subject," she wrote Anna Pou's name, birth date, and driver's license
number. She scribbled: "Suspect may have euthanised multiple patients
in Memorial Medical Center (MMC) following Hurricane Katrina."

Rider and several others returned to the hospital four days later, this
time with permission from Tenet officials, accompanied by a Tenet at-

torney. They went to the seventh floor and found more syringes and medical waste in the LifeCare therapy charting room, where the witnesses had described sitting and speaking with Pou about Emmett Everett. Elsewhere at Memorial they located Pou's employment agreement, a staff roster, and a set of the hospital's emergency policies and procedures.

In the days after the searches, Rider and Schafer interviewed family members of three of the deceased LifeCare patients. Doug Savoie was the grandson of Rose Savoie, Alice Hutzler's roommate. Both women had been aware enough on Wednesday night to tell the infectious diseases doctor who visited LifeCare that they were not in pain or anxious. A daughter of Savoie's, Lou Ann Savoie Jacob, had come to New Orleans to visit her and had been with her until the storm approached. Rose was sitting up and talking, with no IVs, recovering well, it seemed to her. Learning of her death, after a difficult search, had surprised the family.

Wilda McManus's daughter Angela, and Elaine Nelson's daughter, Kathryn—the two who had stayed with their mothers on the LifeCare floor until Thursday, September 1—were also eager to assist the investigators. Kathryn Nelson, who had blurted out, "I'm dying too," when she was forced from her mother's bedside, had waited downstairs as long as possible before leaving Memorial. When she finally climbed into a boat, a young woman behind her asked who she was and told her that her gravely ill mother, Elaine, had died.

Kathryn had, after the boat ride to dry ground, been picked up by a brother. Then, with tunnel vision, she had walked to her home in polluted, chest-high water to save her cats. She, and one of them, spent a night sleeping atop her flooded car—there was nothing dry to lie on inside her toxic-smelling home. Kathryn ended up in a Shreveport hospital with suicidal thoughts and a bout of depression. When Rider, Schafer, and another special agent interviewed her by speakerphone on October 3, her family had only recently located her mother's body at a massive temporary morgue set up in a town named for Saint Gabriel, the "archangel of death," between New Orleans and Baton Rouge. A volunteer coroner from Wisconsin had told Nelson an autopsy had been performed on her mother. Nelson asked why. The coroner said euthanasia was suspected.

"I don't think that any circumstance justifies euthanasia," she told Rider and Schafer, even though her mother had been close to death. Killing someone was breaking God's law. Kathryn, her mother's longtime caregiver, would have known more than anyone what Elaine would have wanted and whether she was suffering. Nobody had asked her opinion. Her mother was extremely strong and believed in always doing right, the kind of lady who slipped a dollar into each purse she donated to Goodwill so that whoever ended up with it would have a little something extra. Kathryn had no doubt her mother would want the truth to emerge.

She offered to write down everything she remembered from the time of the storm until she was forced to leave the seventh floor on Thursday, September 1, and provide it to the investigators. "I appreciate what you are doing," she said. "I think this is extremely important."

Butch Schafer sympathized with Nelson, even given her mother's short life expectancy. Weeks earlier, looking down at his daughter's coffin, speaking at her funeral, he'd said he would give everything that he owned, everything that he would ever have, everything that he was, for five minutes more with her right then.

He could not allow his personal grief to influence the investigation, but that grief always accompanied him, always awaited him as he filled his time and his mind with work. In Nelson's loss, he recognized his own, and he experienced it again. This occurred each time he spoke with a bereaved family member. It was like a knife, death. Always waiting to cut.

The Wisconsin coroner Nelson had spoken with had been right about the autopsy. At first, Orleans Parish coroner Frank Minyard told Special Agent Virginia Rider it would be useless to examine the bodies from Memorial, which had decomposed in the heat for more than a week before being recovered. There was no way to take a blood sample, for example, to check for lethal levels of drugs.

The news was upsetting. Rider and Schafer would need more than eyewitness testimony and empty morphine vials to prove a crime. But a volunteer pathologist told Rider that drugs could leave traces in other, hardier, tissues, such as liver, brain, and muscle, or in the fluid that pooled in the abdomen after death. At the attorney general's request, overburdened coroner Minyard grudgingly agreed to ask a federal disaster mortuary team to perform autopsies and take tissue samples from all the hospital and nursing-home patients who had died in Orleans Parish after Katrina—about one hundred in total, it first appeared. The attorney general's office had received allegations of wrongdoing at several of the facilities.

On September 22, state and federal investigators flew north with sets of tissue samples from eighteen of the Memorial Medical Center bodies and delivered them to National Medical Services, Inc., a forensic toxicology laboratory in Willow Grove, Pennsylvania. In an acidic-smelling corner of a long, open room with scuffed walls, technicians extracted the samples into tiny, metal-capped containers shaped like medicine vials and sent them through gas chromatography/mass spectrometry machines bearing nicknames, including "Morticia" and "Gomez."

Two weeks later, on October 6, the head of the laboratory, Dr. Robert Middleberg, called the attorney general's office with preliminary results. Virginia Rider put him on speakerphone so prosecutor Butch Schafer and another special agent could hear. The strength of their case depended on the news the forensic toxicologist was about to deliver, the answer to whether the LifeCare patients had died with detectable levels of morphine and other sedative drugs in their bodies.

Middleberg began by qualifying his findings in the language of a careful scientist. He said the samples the laboratory had received were less than ideal because of decomposition.

"So that's just one of the reasons why there has been a slight delay in us getting back to you. In fact, we're still working on these cases; we are not complete. We wanted to give you an update as to where we are."

"OK," Rider said.

"Thank you, Doctor," Schafer said.

"Ah . . . of the eighteen cases today, nine of them are positive for morphine and a number of them, I guess about another five or six, are positive for midazolam."

"Doctor, you're going to have to forgive me," Schafer interrupted. "I don't know what that is."

"OK, I'll be happy to tell you. Morphine obviously you've heard of?"

"Yes sir."

"Midazolam is, the brand name is Versed, V-E-R-S-E-D. And it belongs to what's known as the class of compounds called benzo, B-E-N-Z-O diazepines, D-I-A-Z-E-P-I-N-E-S. And the one you are most familiar with in that family would be Valium, but the difference here is that midazolam is not a compound that people are routinely put on. It's a compound generally used in operating suites or when someone is going to be intubated; someone may be given midazolam, but it's not one of these compounds that you'll find somebody getting a prescription for at home."

"Yes sir," Schafer said.

Middleberg explained that the lab had also detected a number of common medicines in the bodies, as expected, including antidepressants and drugs for gastric reflux. "Certainly the midazolam I'm finding is a little bit disconcerting," he continued, "and I understand the difficulty, but medical records are going to be very, very important now."

"Doctor, are these drugs such that they could have accumulated in a person?" Schafer asked.

Middleberg said midazolam shouldn't be given on a repetitive basis. "Unless somebody is consistently being intubated and extubated or consistently going into the operating suite, there would be no reason for somebody to accumulate midazolam over periods of time."

"Yes sir," Schafer said.

"Morphine, certainly you can accumulate over time. But the concentrations we're finding—and you have to understand that the specimens we have, again, were not ideal—some of the concentrations with morphine that we're finding are, are pretty darn high."

"If you were here," Schafer said, "I'll give you a kiss."

"Ah . . . well, I'll have to see you first." Middleberg joked.

"OK," Rider chimed in. "*I* would give you a kiss if you were here."

"That would be more pleasurable," Schafer said.

"All right," Middleberg agreed.

"Thank you very much, Dr. Middleberg," Rider said.

"Ah . . . you said, there were nine positive for morphine," Schafer said. "Would you have the body numbers or some identifying number that we could go by and check out?"

"Yes, we can. Yes, we do. We will give you names of people, how about that?"

"Wonderful, oh great!" Schafer said.

"First one where morphine is found is a Harold Dupas, D-U-P-A-S."

"Yes sir," Schafer said. Dupas was one of the nine patients the Life-Care staff had believed were injected by Dr. Pou or the two Memorial nurses who came up to the seventh floor on Thursday, September 1.

"Next is a Hollis Ford [Hollis Alford]; Wilda McManus; Elaine Nelson; Emmett Everett; Alice Hutzler, H-U-T-Z-L-E-R; Rose Savoie, S-A-V-O-I-E; Ireatha, I-R-E-T-H-A [sic], Watson; and George Huard, H-U-A-R-D. I apologize for the pronunciation."

It was stunning. Of the eighteen samples tested, those positive for the two drugs coincided exactly with the names on the attorney's list of suspicious deaths. And the laboratory hadn't been told which names were on the list.

They said good-bye and Middleberg wished them a good afternoon. It certainly was. It was rare that everything lined up so neatly. Middleberg had called the morphine concentrations "pretty darn high." Rider and Schafer would remember those words.

———

AS UPLIFTING as it was to gather the evidence needed to pursue justice, much remained ahead of them, and Butch Schafer knew from experience that even the most promising new case usually doesn't end up the way you think it might. "Don't. Get. Emotionally. Involved," he warned Virginia Rider.

It could easily have been a subconscious warning to himself. Only weeks had passed since he lost his daughter. She had lived with an aggressive form of rheumatoid arthritis and died in her sleep after too many doctors prescribed too many drugs to treat her pain. Toxicology results suggested that the medicines, magnifying one another's actions, had killed her in an accidental overdose. Schafer was furious to learn that the pharmacy that had filled nearly all of her prescriptions had not cross-checked them.

The same day as the phone call with Middleberg, October 6, brought another first—an interview with a medical professional not employed by LifeCare. Rider and Schafer spoke with Dr. Bryant King briefly by phone and then drove to his undamaged home in a part of New Orleans that hadn't flooded. King had walked there after being boated out of Memorial. "My plants were dying, so that was my biggest tragedy. Everything has actually worked out really well other than the fact that I don't have a job," he said.

Unlike the LifeCare witnesses, who had come to be interviewed through the company's lawyer, King had contacted the attorney general's office after seeing television coverage of mortuary workers recovering bodies from Memorial. He was disturbed by the number of bodies found in Memorial's chapel. He told them about the man he had pronounced dead early Thursday morning and carried to the chapel. "That person made the sixth patient. I'm willing to go to my grave on that because I was counting in my head," he said. "After that, nobody else died on my second-floor area before I left the hospital. I left the hospital between twelve thirty and one thirty."

Including the bodies in the chapel, King said, the total number of deceased patients in the hospital had been twenty or twenty-one when he left. When he learned from news reports that forty-five bodies were recovered in total, "I was like, That's way too many. That's the first thought that came to mind. There's no way that that many people died in the time frame in between the time I left and the following day because . . ." He paused. "They were sick, they were really sick, but they weren't sick enough that, well, they weren't sick enough collectively, that twenty of them would die in a day. I mean, come on! What hospital loses twenty patients in a day? I mean, really! If you lose twenty patients in a day, somebody is coming to investigate because there is something abnormal going on."

The "something" he had in mind was more abnormal than the heat and loss of power that followed Katrina. King suggested Rider and Schafer speak with the person who "controlled everything" at the hospital during the storm. "I would expect that the CEO would, you know, kind of conduct what happened, but he didn't." Instead it was a tall woman with striking red hair. "She conducted every meeting. I mean, that was strange to me, for someone that I'd never seen before."

He knew her only as Susan. "I didn't know who she was, other than the fact that she rolled with a lot of clout. Everybody responded to her. She walked in a room and said, 'OK, let's go ahead and get started.' Everybody shut up and started the meeting."

On Thursday morning, September 1, King had spoken with Dr. Kathleen Fournier, his acquaintance from medical school, who told him about a conversation with Susan and Dr. Anna Pou. The conversation was about ending patients' suffering, and King recalled that, according to Fournier, "Anna said, 'Oh yeah, I don't have a problem with it.'"

Fournier had asked for King's opinion on eliminating patients' suffering. "In my mind, I'm thinking, it's not normal. That's not what we're paid to do. We're paid to do this until either everybody dies or everybody leaves."

The investigators pressed him later in the interview. "You knew what she meant, but you didn't question it?"

"I kind of . . . we . . . the conversation was . . . It's a little murky . . . But I was like, 'What are you talking about?' 'Well, they're suffering, da-da-da.' Nothing was explicitly said other than I can't be a part of anything like that."

He hadn't thought his opinion would make a difference. Whereas some people had been scared of the people outside of the hospital, King was wary of the people in it. He was a six-foot-tall, two-hundred-pound man, but all he'd brought to the hospital were apples, oranges, and some almonds. Not a weapon. The person with the weapon was the boss, the law. He'd thought this on the ER ramp when he'd seen people being turned away and had argued with the CEO. Well hell, they've got all the guns. They could throw me in the water and say, "You can no longer come inside." When he saw what was happening on the second floor, he figured: There's only so much I can do or say. There were armed security guards everywhere. Obviously they wouldn't have shot him in front of everyone, but he was sure they would have removed him. He was the last doctor hired there. The newbie. He grew up in East Chicago. He often spoke his mind, but he knew, in the end, when to shut his mouth.

King said he had sent messages to his best friend telling him that "evil entities" were planning to euthanize patients.

"You were talking about 'evil entities'?"

"Because I couldn't call them people anymore. When you talk about killing people you're—talk about killing people who've done nothing wrong—you're not . . . to me that's not really a 'person.' Humans don't do that. We don't do that to each other. So, I was like . . . These . . . these . . . these . . . the correct word would have been, 'These mother-fuckers are talking about killing people!'"

King's best friend had taken the messages to National Public Radio, and reporter Joanne Silberner had described the texts on air on the pro-gram *All Things Considered* the very afternoon the injections were taking place. "King said some of the staff was starting to panic, even talking about helping some of the long-term acute care patients, those close to death, die."

King said that after telling Fournier he disagreed with the idea and sending the texts, he helped carry patients to the parking garage for evac-uation. The hospital was no longer functioning as a hospital. "The whole formal structure of it had broken down." When he returned to the second floor, the helpers who had been invited to fan the patients were mostly gone. They had been told to leave. "A guy came in and asked, 'Would you like to join us in prayer?' I was like, 'No.' There's no reason . . . we've never prayed before. This is Thursday at noon, I mean, what's this?"

King said he looked around and saw Anna Pou standing on the other side of the walkway by the bathrooms and the ATM. "She had a hand-ful of 10 cc syringes with the pink needle—which is our eighteen- to twenty-one gauges—she had a handful of them and she said verbatim to a patient, 'I'm going to give you something to make you feel better.'" King said it was highly unusual for a doctor to be handling syringes. "I don't know what was in the syringes; I don't know why she had them because we don't ever inject anybody if we don't have to. I mean, call a nurse to do that. We don't do it. Not to say it that way, but that's how we function." King wasn't just being flippant. He saw a reason for that division of responsibility. A doctor's order was checked by a pharmacist and checked again by a nurse. Even those trappings of medical formality and quality control hadn't broken down at Memorial until that moment.

King hadn't seen Pou inject a patient. He had drawn his conclusions by piecing together earlier events. "So when she had a handful of syringes, it

really startled me. It's like: prayer . . . la-la-la . . . conversation this morning. . . . This is not a normal situation. I should probably not be here.

"As I'm leaving I'm thinking, This is crazy. Why are they praying in
the middle of the day? Why does a physician have a handful of syringes?
Because we haven't been giving medicine that way." He didn't know
what had happened after he left by boat and reached shallow water at the
drop-off point. "I took all my stuff and took my bag I had upstairs and
put it in one of the red contamination bags, waded through the water,
took it out of the bag, changed socks, and went home. Walked from Memorial to this location right here."

Rider and Schafer showed King photographs and he identified several people. "That's Anna," he said of the first one.

Before leaving, Schafer asked whether they could contact him again.
"Absolutely," King agreed. "By all means, call me, contact me, knock
on my door. . . . My take on this is that something wrong occurred, and
I don't know how, why, or who decided it, but they need to answer to
the family members, because somebody lost family members because of
whatever decisions were made."

King said the only other people he'd spoken with about events in
the hospital were his girlfriend, best friend, sister, and a producer from
CNN, with whom he'd had an on-camera interview several weeks earlier. It hadn't yet aired. He said he was telling Schafer and Rider the same
things he had told the producer.

"How has my information contributed?" King asked Rider. "Was it
telling you things that you already knew, things you didn't know? One
direction or another?"

"Learned some things from you that I didn't know," Rider told him.

———

SUSAN MULDERICK had moved back to the city in early autumn
and was cleaning out her home when she received a call from a Tenet at-

torney. Mulderick spoke with him at length before he told her she should get her own lawyer, and he doubted that Tenet, her employer, would pay for one. In tears, Mulderick walked to the nearby house of an attorney she trusted, who took a break from cleaning her own house to sit on the porch and talk. The attorney was furious and thought what the Tenet lawyer had done—milking Mulderick for information, then telling her to get an attorney—was unethical.

Mulderick had half a dozen siblings, many of whom worked at other hospitals in New Orleans, and it had recently become clear how different each one of their experiences had been. One night, soon after returning to the city, they sat in a circle in the backyard drinking wine and taking turns telling stories. Mulderick shared the anecdote about Dr. Fournier and her cat and spoke of the smells and the suffering. Another sister described how St. Bernard's Chalmette Medical Center, where ambulances had failed to return to complete a pre-storm evacuation, had flooded in a matter of hours to the ceiling of its first floor. It only had two stories. The hospital's several dozen patients had been moved upstairs and then transferred by boat to the care of doctors at a nearby prison, on higher ground. Several strong men had lifted a patient who weighed roughly five hundred pounds through a window on a bed sheet and lowered him successfully onto a boat from the second floor. Several patients had died.

Another sister had worked at Tulane Hospital in downtown New Orleans. Tulane was also dark, hot, and surrounded by water, but officials at its parent corporation, HCA, had been proactive about arranging for private helicopters and buses to rescue patients, employees, and their families, betting correctly that government assets would prove insufficient. The process of an orderly if slow evacuation had kept panic at bay. She knew of no patients who had died at Tulane. This sister was able to laugh and joke about her experiences.

After the phone call from the Tenet attorney, Mulderick hired her own lawyer, and he advised her to stop talking about what had happened.

He quickly learned of the attorney general's confidential search-warrant affidavit. A well-connected criminal attorney for Tenet in Louisiana, Harry Rosenberg, had obtained a copy of it and described it to him.

Mulderick's attorney said LifeCare had "put the hat" on Tenet for the deaths and pointed fingers at Mulderick and Dr. Pou. He encouraged Mulderick not to worry. A search-warrant application, he explained, has to convince a judge that a crime was likely to have been committed and that the search location could have evidence of it. The allegations could include hearsay—evidence someone heard from someone else rather than witnessed directly—which likely would be inadmissible should there ever be a trial.

Again he reassured her. Asking for patients to be given morphine to make them comfortable was something the lawyer's wife had done for his ailing mother-in-law. Hospice had even suggested it.

Tenet attorney Rosenberg had been promised that the attorney general's people would not take action against anyone without talking to him first. Mulderick and her lawyer could consider working together with Tenet's attorneys, given their overlapping interests. It was in fact possible the corporation would pay for her defense.

Anger at Tenet began to swell among the hospital's employees. At the end of September, Memorial's CEO had sent out a legally required notice that the hospital would be closed for at least six months and the employment of most staff members was officially ending. The hospital would provide relief pay until early November, plus a bonus to those who worked the hurricane, and would try to accommodate staff members who were willing to relocate. Long-term staff members were infuriated by the short notice of their termination and the lack of a severance package and continued benefits. Some shared their feelings with Memorial and Tenet leaders. Why had other hospitals, not Memorial, posted thank-you letters to their staff in the newspaper? Why had another hospital continued to pay full salaries for months instead of providing only partial "relief" checks? Tenet president and CEO Trevor Fetter forwarded complaint letters to his regional human resources director and asked her to respond for him.

In one letter, Marirose Bernard, the nursing director for women's and infants' services who had appeared on Fox News, accused Fetter of having said on cable television that Tenet had the situation at its hospitals under control on Wednesday, August 31; all the most severe patients had been evacuated; and replacement workers from throughout the country were prepared to go into New Orleans:

> Where did those "replacement workers" go to? [. . .] Virtually ALL of these patients were "severe" and deserved to have been evacuated long before Thursday night when the last of the patients were finally evacuated. I recall as we picked up one patient to move him along the line to the helicopters and told him that he would be leaving soon he screamed out "Oh God—are you throwing me away??!!!" He said he had been told for so long that he was going to get out that he just knew we were throwing him away. This memory will be with me forever. Another patient called out "Mama, Mama, Mama" constantly, others were in terrible pain and agony—how dare you give this nation the impression that you were providing for these patients and for your employees.

Some workers recalled the sense of abandonment they had felt during the disaster both before and after leaving the hospital. Upon being airlifted or boated from Memorial, many had been left to fend for themselves on threatening street corners, highway intersections, and at the teeming Ernest N. Morial Convention Center, which Mayor Nagin had opened as a second mass shelter after the storm but had not supplied with food, water, or adequate staffing.

"Frankly, I believe Tenet had a duty during Hurricane Katrina to protect employees such as me and failed to fulfill its obligation," one ICU nurse, Dawn Marie Gieck, wrote to Fetter. "When I consider how others and I put ourselves in harm's way for Tenet, I feel a sense of indignation that the company wasn't there to take care of those taking care of its patients." She added that she had served in the military during Operation Desert Storm and agreed with comparisons between post-Katrina Memorial and a war zone. She argued that it was easy for individuals and organizations to point to the floundering of local and federal governments after a natural disaster as a way of excusing their own failures.

One of Memorial's administrators did blame the government, copying company officials on an aggrieved letter to US president George W. Bush. "I want to express how deeply proud I am to have been associated with such a courageous and compassionate group of caregivers at Memorial Medical Center, and how disappointed and ashamed I am in my government that failed each and every one of us."

Three nurses from the medical and surgical unit on the fifth floor also wrote to Tenet. They had been accused of abandonment and fired. One was the nurse whose husband was the Coast Guard junior grade lieutenant who had helped organize the evacuation of Memorial's neonates and ICU patients. Another was her close friend Michelle Pitre-Ryals, the nurse who had repeatedly carried a cell phone downstairs on Tuesday night when Coast Guard officials called trying to continue Memorial's evacuation overnight.

The commander of the New Orleans Coast Guard sector had authorized the lieutenant to land on Memorial's helipad late on Wednesday afternoon and rescue his wife. The nurse and her two close friends made a split-second decision to go against their manager's instructions. Although all except one of the patients were off the floor and the nurses had not been assigned to care for others, some of their coworkers were furious at them for leaving. For their part, the three nurses wondered how Tenet could fire them after all their hard work, when the hospital itself was pitifully unprepared for the disaster. They were reinstated and their relief pay was restored, but another nurse who had left her post as soon as the water began rising, saying "I'm getting out of here," and telling colleagues she was concerned about her pets, was permanently fired.

ON OCTOBER 12, 2005, Rider and Schafer came to New Orleans from Baton Rouge to reinterview the main LifeCare witnesses in person and go over photographs with them. After they finished their work, they found a bar where they could watch CNN.

"Good evening," anchor Anderson Cooper said to hundreds of thousands of viewers. "We begin tonight at a moment when Hurricane Katrina went from being a disaster to a tragedy, when people began making choices that leave a mark on the soul. Now, as the water and the mud recede, secrets are coming to light, whispers of life-and-death decisions and talk, heard here for the first time anywhere, of more, of mercy killing. Authorities in Louisiana are investigating. Tonight, we know this for certain: at a bare minimum, the question was on the table inside a hospital."

Reporter Jonathan Freed described the horrific conditions at Memorial and introduced Dr. Bryant King. "Most people know that something—something happened that shouldn't have happened." Without naming names, King described what he had heard and seen, much as he had told Virginia Rider and Butch Schafer the previous week. He said he had spoken with one doctor about putting patients out of their misery and saw another one holding syringes.

"The only thing I heard her say is, 'I'm going to give you something to make you feel better.'"

The network took care to protect Pou's name. Airing accusations of murder with little evidence could have put the news organization in danger of a libel suit, and Pou now had an aggressive defense attorney. If nothing else, exposing Pou's identity would have alienated her, and producers at the channel still hoped to convince her to tell her side of the story on camera. Reporter Freed said that, when told of King's allegations, the doctor in question would not comment either way. Freed quoted Pou anonymously from what he described as several phone conversations:

"We did everything humanly possible to save these patients. The government totally abandoned us to die, in the houses, in the streets, in the hospitals. Maybe a lot of us made mistakes, but we made the best decisions we could at the time."

Memorial nurse manager, Fran Butler, also appeared in the piece. "Did they say to put people out of their misery? Yes." She said she, too, had learned of a discussion about euthanasia. "I kind of blew it off because of the person who said it," she said, describing, but not naming, Dr. Kathleen Fournier. Could it all have been a misunderstanding?

In the broadcast, Attorney General Foti predicted the investigation would be complete in two weeks and asked all who had information to come forward. "We're looking at probably thirteen nursing homes and six hospitals scattered through the greater New Orleans region. So we are operating on many fronts at the same time."

A parade of experts discussed the issues on various CNN news segments. Forensic pathologist Cyril Wecht spoke of the challenges of wresting evidence from decomposed bodies. Randy Cohen, then the *New York Times Magazine* ethics columnist, questioned the hospital's preparedness. "Why weren't there plans to cope with these patients when you knew a storm was coming? Sometimes the ethical—the most important ethical question sometimes is the one you ask not at the moment of crisis, but the duty you have to anticipate certain kinds of crises and avoid them."

Bioethicist Arthur Caplan, then at the University of Pennsylvania, said American juries rarely sent doctors to jail for hastening deaths. "The culture that we live in does not want doctors killing, to be very clear about that. But it will listen closely and you might be able to make a defense of a mercy killing, if you will, under very, very extenuating circumstances. Whether New Orleans meets that, we'll have to see."

Versions of the report ran for days on the twenty-four-hour news channel. CNN's anchors rehashed the story, verging into sensationalism. "Did an angel of death stalk the halls of Memorial Medical there in Louisiana?" Nancy Grace asked on her Friday-evening news show. "No one knows for sure." When a guest began describing the loss of power, rising fears, and delayed rescue that preceded the injections, giving context to them, Grace cut him off: "Sean, Sean, Sean—I don't want to relive Katrina. I want to find out if there was an angel of death stalking the halls of Memorial Medical! That's what I want to find out."

Grace seemed frustrated that Bryant King hadn't stayed around to find out what happened, if only so he could return to report it on her show. "I find it fantastical in this case, and in many others, where witnesses can lead you up to the brink of an alleged crime, and then suddenly they turn away, they leave the room. Here they're saying that there's a doctor with a handful of syringes with liquid in it, saying, 'This will make you all feel better,' to patients. But they don't know what happened after that? I would have been doing a backflip to see what was going on."

The major television networks excerpted CNN's report on their own news shows and added new details. NBC reported that a family had filed suit against the hospital for the death of a loved one. Several Memorial doctors rushed to defend their colleagues on television. "There was no way we were going to hasten anyone's demise," Memorial internist John Kokemor said on NBC.

Jannie Burgess's daughter, Linette Burgess Guidi, the former Playboy Bunny who had come from Holland to visit her mother before the storm, knew only that her mother had died during the evacuation. She had been informed of this, via e-mail, many days later. The images of Memorial on CNN looked familiar. She screamed, covered her ears, and pulled the bedcovers over her head. She heard enough to know she did not want to hear more. She refused to believe her mother was one of the patients injected. Who would want to believe that?

One network reported on an article that had appeared in the British tabloid *The Mail on Sunday* almost two weeks after the hurricane, quoting from an interview with an unnamed female doctor at an unnamed hospital.

I didn't know if I was doing the right thing. But I did not have time. I had to make snap decisions, under the most appalling circumstances, and I did what I thought was right.

I injected morphine into those patients who were dying and in agony. If the first dose was not enough, I gave a double dose. And at night I prayed to God to have mercy on my soul.

This was not murder, this was compassion. They would have been dead within hours, if not days. We did not put people down. What we did was give comfort to the end.

On the third day of the media binge, a memo went out by e-mail addressed to all Memorial Medical Center personnel and marked "Attorney-Client Privileged and Confidential." It said employees contacted by government or media representatives should "feel free to speak with the hospital's lawyer at the below-listed number."

If you decide that it is in your best interests to be interviewed by the government or the media, you have a right to request that a hospital representative appear with you. It is often prudent to have a third party present in such situations to ensure that your words are not inadvertently misconstrued or taken out of context.

Because it is not appropriate to discuss publicly these matters, the hospital asks that you refrain from talking about these issues with other employees and people outside the employ of the hospital. If you need any information or have any questions, or if the government or the media contacts you, we would appreciate it if you would call me. Please feel free to call collect: Audrey Andrews

⌒

THE SAME DAY, the Medicaid Fraud Control Unit's chief prosecutor received a fax from Tenet attorney Harry Rosenberg. He requested that before questioning Tenet employees, government officials inform them that they had the right to confer with him or another Tenet attorney and have an attorney or a hospital representative present. Rider and Schafer complied. Ethics required this. They also wanted to ensure the information they obtained would be admissible in court. At the same time Schafer saw how strategic it was for Tenet to offer to represent its employees. What company, facing potential lawsuits, wouldn't want to know what its workers had to say about it?

———

ON OCTOBER 18, a few days after the CNN stories ran, LifeCare nursing director Gina Isbell met the attorney general's representatives in a private room at LifeCare's Kenner hospital, near the New Orleans airport. An attorney for LifeCare joined them on the phone.

Isbell described the events of the hurricane. She glossed over the details of what she had learned on the seventh floor when three medical professionals from Memorial arrived on Thursday morning and asked the LifeCare staff to leave. "I guess I thought they were just going to take care of our patients, but, you know, and round on our patients and take care of them, but I don't know if it was something that somebody said, that made me believe that it was something different. I don't know. I was just assuming, but I honestly don't know."

Isbell didn't want to get anyone in trouble. She was angry about the criminal investigation and the accusatory news coverage. She viewed everyone at the hospital as heroes.

Schafer asked whether the LifeCare nurses kept up medical charts, recording what drugs they gave their patients during the disaster.

"Yes. I mean, we were giving medications up until Wednesday morning and [were] charting everything and we basically went into survival mode and were just trying to keep them alive with food and water. There was just no way we could do everything."

"We've all been on that floor," Schafer said, having searched it. "We know what it looked like. I can just imagine what you guys went through."

How dare he say that? Isbell felt a flash of anger so strong she could imagine her head spinning like the child possessed by the devil in the horror film *The Exorcist*. "You *can't* imagine," she said, coughing. "It was unbelievable. We tried so hard to keep them alive, and I would like to know why it took so long for people to come in and help us to get those patients out. We wouldn't have lost so many patients." The government hadn't been there to step in and help. That, to her, was the real crime. That was why most of the lives were lost. The investigators should be going after President Bush, not a doctor in the hospital. Leave the people who stayed and worked through the storm alone. Let the doctor who had tried to comfort people and take away their pain be a hero, not a villain, in a situation Isbell compared to being simultaneously on the *Titanic* and in war.

"LifeCare, our company, had resources to come in, get my patients out, my employees out." She blamed government officials for dissuading LifeCare executives from sending in help. "It's just not fair. I don't know, it's just not fair. It's just not. I'm sorry."

Schafer suggested they take a break, but Isbell composed herself and said she wanted to continue. She tried to recall a specific detail.

"Tomorrow at three it will come to me because I can only sleep till two or three in the morning and then I'm up," she told them. Isbell was sleeping poorly, her hair was falling out, she was having nightmares in which she saw the faces of her patients. Her roommate was worried— Isbell always looked sad; a force had gone out of her. She had left Memorial in a small flat boat, with a weeping heat rash, mentally and physically drained, only to discover she had lost her home and her entire community in devastated St. Bernard Parish. She felt guilty about every staff member she had picked to work the hurricane with her. She felt terrible about the patients who had died.

"Take a pad with you to bed and as you think of things write them down," Rider suggested.

"That's when our questions will come to us," Schafer joked. "So we'll just give you a call at three tomorrow morning."

"You have my cell phone number! Give me a call!"

They finished the interview and Schafer thanked Isbell. "I know it was painful to relive this, but I appreciate it."

"I'll tell you, every day is a challenge," Isbell replied.

———

ISBELL'S GUARDED, angry reaction to the prosecutor and investigator was typical. The CNN stories and the Tenet lawyers' letters marked a turning point. While the first few interviewees had seemed eager to speak with Rider and Schafer, now that the story and the investigation were public and Rider began conversations with a legal disclaimer, most potential witnesses were wary and uncooperative.

"I wanted to talk to you about what happened at Memorial Hospital after the storm," Rider said in a phone call to one Memorial pharmacist who might have had important information about how Anna Pou came into possession of controlled drugs. "Are you OK with talking with me?"

"Yes, OK," the pharmacist said.

"Because you are still an employee of the hospital, I have to inform you that you have the right to have a hospital representative or an attorney present when I ask you any questions."

The pharmacist reconsidered. "I guess I probably should call them, huh? I think that it might be better, I mean, obviously I would be willing to talk to you, but since you said something, I guess maybe I should talk to someone beforehand, just . . . I really don't think I need an attorney. I think, just to make sure, I'll call them."

The pharmacist eventually called back, but suddenly the main people Rider and Schafer wanted to speak with were lawyered-up and unwilling to talk. When employees did agree to interviews, Schafer, drawing on more than three decades of legal practice, sensed in their guarded responses that their attorneys had schooled them on what they could and could not say. There wasn't a lot he and Rider could do when an interview subject answered, "I can't recall," even when the question concerned an event it would seem that no one could ever forget.

"Did you ever remember hearing any rumors about what happened to those patients on the seventh floor?" one of the Medicaid fraud prosecutors asked in a phone interview with a nurse who had worked at Memorial for ten years and was now working for another Tenet hospital.

"Um . . . I'm sorry, during, during the hospital I may have heard something."

"What did you hear?"

"I really can't recall everything that I heard."

"The things that you can, let's start there."

"It's just a rumor that I heard. I think there was like seven patients supposedly, I think, that were supposedly euthanized. That was the rumor."

"Where did you hear that?" Virginia Rider picked up the questioning.

"In the hospital."

"Where in the hospital?"

"I can't recall what particular spot I was standing in at the time. I mean, just in the hospital in general."

"What day?"

"Um . . . I can't recall that."

"Who told you?"

"Um . . . I can't . . . I can't recall."

"Was it a nurse?"

"Um . . . possibly?"

"Was it a doctor?"

"No."

"Had you heard why they were euthanized?" the prosecutor asked.

"Um . . . if I did hear anything, it probably was because they probably weren't gonna make it."

The employee later said he thought he had heard the rumor from several people at several different times. "Was it on the last day that you were there?" the prosecutor asked.

"I don't believe."

"Was it on the Wednesday before you left?"

"Could have been."

Rider knew that the nurse had, shortly after the storm, openly told a journalism student that people at the hospital were "euthanizing" and "putting people to sleep." The journalism student happened to work part-time for a district attorney's office in another part of Louisiana and reported it to her boss.

Schafer was familiar with what attorneys did when they represented defense witnesses, and he had to admire the good lawyering of the competition. Their work energized him, made him play his "A" game, even as he saw that it only angered Rider, who seemed to see it as a form of withholding evidence.

Now that some allegations were out in the media, there was another concern. News reports could trigger memories. They could also, perhaps, manufacture them. Researchers had shown that recollections of alleged crimes, as of all events, were fallible, malleable, and subject to possible contamination by new information and discussions with other witnesses. Nearly three out of four convictions later reversed based on DNA evidence with the help of the US nonprofit group the Innocence Project were based on faulty eyewitness identification. It was also potentially significant that several of the LifeCare witnesses had spoken after the evacuation and consulted on a written time line of their experiences.

To help mitigate the problems, Schafer, Rider, and their colleagues needed to interview more witnesses, taking care to avoid leading them or suggesting ideas, and to collect as much physical and written information as possible from the time of the events.

The investigation was stalling. The initial interviews had been unfocused. Rider and Schafer had been unsure of what information they needed.

LifeCare's attorneys were prompt and helpful in answering requests for documents and details, but Tenet's were taking a more defensive and protective tack. One of Rider's earliest and most important requests had been for the medical records of the deceased patients. Weeks later, she still had only some of them. Rider had learned from Tenet's chief of security that Tenet attorney Audrey Andrews had directed him to secure any medical records relating to deceased patients on September 14, which was the day after the attorney general's investigation began. The records were brought to another Tenet hospital, but it had taken until October 7 before investigators were able to retrieve them, and they were far from complete.

Rider and Schafer also lacked key facts. Who were the nurses who allegedly accompanied Pou to the seventh floor on Thursday morning? None of the witnesses had as yet been able to name them. During the search, investigators had found and seized papers listing everyone present at Memorial by department. They focused in on staff who might have had the most contact with Pou.

The last week of October, agents fanned out to serve subpoenas on seventy-three Tenet employees, compelling them to appear for interviews. Under the law, willfully disobeying could be punishable as contempt of court. The subpoenas could serve another purpose: they would flush out people who invoked their Fifth Amendment right not to incriminate themselves—the people who might have something to hide.

CNN reported on the subpoenas and the attorney general's frustration over Tenet's letter and its "chilling effect" on the investigation. "We had no choice but to issue these subpoenas," Foti said. Tenet attorney Harry Rosenberg sent a chastening letter to the Medicaid Fraud Control Unit's longtime director: "We were disappointed that your office served subpoenas upon Memorial personnel—many of whom

are displaced from their homes and facing the hardships caused by
Hurricane Katrina—particularly when I had indicated to you that Memorial will cooperate and has been cooperating with the attorney general's office."

Notwithstanding the displeasure they caused, the subpoenas quickly
did their work. Interviews began in earnest. Eddie Castaing, a New Orleans attorney whose services were paid for by Tenet, was brought on to
represent most of the Memorial employees and accompany them during
their interviews. On November 1, he sat down with Rider, Schafer, and
their supervisors for an important meeting. Rider summarized their discussion in a memo dated November 7, writing that Castaing was seeking
immunity for two nurses, Lori Budo and Mary Jo D'Amico:

> One of his clients was present on the seventh floor when injections were
> made for the purposes of mercy killing and participated with the doctor
> in administering morphine and versed. Two other nurses were also pres-
> ent, but CASTAING does not represent these nurses. CASTAING also
> advised that LIFECARE HOSPITALS personnel were present during
> or right after the event and were aware of what was happening. Later
> CASTAING's client returned to the second floor and observed similar
> activities in the area where patients who had been triaged as threes (in-
> dicating that they were more critical). There was a male doctor present
> when this incident occurred on the second floor. CASTAING advised
> that he does not represent the other two nurses, but believes he could
> persuade them to come in if they were offered immunity. CASTAING
> also advised that he had spoken with one of the other two nurses and ad-
> vised her to seek another attorney and that he had been unable to make
> contact with the other nurse.
>
> CASTAING advised that his other client was asked to go up to the
> seventh floor later in the afternoon. There was one patient who was
> still alive on the seventh floor at that time but was experiencing agonal

breathing. CASTAING's client observed DR. ANNA POU inject the patient.

As Rider and Schafer understood it, the nurses were essentially offering to help the state prosecute Pou in exchange for their own protection. And it looked like three nurses were involved, not two as recalled by the LifeCare employees, and a fourth nurse was a witness. Rider and Schafer now believed they had the names of two of the nurses who had come to the seventh floor with Pou; their lawyer's opinion that injecting the patients was intended to kill them; and new details about what had occurred on the second floor, including the possibility that another doctor had played a key role.

Rider and Schafer's problem was that they could not offer immunity, interview these women, and learn even more. The attorney general's office was investigating potential murders, but it was unclear whether it would be prosecuting them. Control of criminal proceedings generally rested with local officials, in this case the district attorney of Orleans Parish, Eddie J. Jordan Jr. He would choose whether to step aside and allow the attorney general's office to prosecute after its investigation. District attorneys considered it their duty to prosecute the cases in their parish. Recusals were relatively rare, usually stemming from ethical conflicts, and early signs were that Jordan would keep the complicated, high-profile case for himself, even though his office was considered by many to have been inept even before the chaos of Katrina, with a poor rate of convictions. The attorney general's staff were under instructions not to communicate with the district attorney's staff about the case.

Because it appeared that prosecution of any alleged murders might ultimately fall to the district attorney, Schafer, Rider, and their colleagues from the attorney general's office didn't believe they could provide anyone with full immunity. That would be up to District Attorney Jordan. For now, based on the usual terms of a legal proffer, anything the prosecutors and investigators might gain from what Castaing had told them would be tainted, in attorney parlance, like "fruit of the poisonous tree." The information couldn't be used in any way to incriminate the nurses, even if Schafer and Rider confirmed it from other sources, unless they could prove they would have discovered it through an alternative and natural course of the investigation.

Castaing would, years later, say he had spoken with the attorney general's staff and requested assurances that anyone being interviewed would not be prosecuted, but he denied that he had sought immunity for the nurses, "because immunity means you did something wrong and you're immunized for it. I never made any admission like that." He would specifically deny and strenuously disagree that he had given an account of what allegedly happened on the seventh and second floors, although he said he did not keep notes on the meeting. "They already had those facts," he would say of the investigators. "They told me."

Castaing added: "It didn't make sense for me to go in there and tell them all this incriminating stuff and say, 'You can't prosecute.'" However offering information in advance of any non-prosecution guarantee is just what another attorney did the following month. She took over representing Mary Jo D'Amico and made an oral proffer to Schafer and another assistant attorney general, detailing what D'Amico would say if given immunity from prosecution in the case. The lawyer wrote a letter emphasizing that the proffer was made off the record and could not be used against D'Amico either directly or derivatively. D'Amico's new attorney even said she would, if requested, provide the proffer directly to the district attorney, too, and she had also reached out to the feds, who still had a case open on Memorial.

Schafer, Rider, and their colleagues had visited the US Attorney in New Orleans, Jim Letten, to see what federal statutes might apply. Murders were typically prosecuted by local authorities, and federal jurisdiction over them was limited. The Memorial deaths had not occurred on federal land, or during the commission of another federal crime, and none of the deceased seemed to fall within a category—for example, that of high government officials—that would make their alleged murders prosecutable under federal law. Causing a death in the course of "depriving the person of his or her civil rights under color of law" could be considered a federal crime, as could murder to further a drug offense, but these were not seen, for the moment, to apply to the Memorial cases.

The most serious federal charge the group could imagine applying was quickly rejected. A conviction for inappropriately prescribing narcotics would carry perhaps a five-year sentence, akin to punishing a hit-and-run killer for having expired license tags.

Unable to use information from any attorney proffers, Schafer and Rider pursued other avenues. As a law enforcement official, Rider had the right to demand that the companies turn over whatever they might have discovered in their internal investigations. She sent requests to Tenet and LifeCare and subpoenas for various pieces of information. LifeCare turned over a file with summaries of debriefing interviews conducted with LifeCare leaders in the days after the evacuation.

Tenet, however, did not turn over information from its own interviews with medical staff. Rider received a legal notice stating that "certain Tenet attorneys" had spoken with Dr. Anna Pou, but Pou's lawyer, Richard Simmons, had requested that the information Pou had given be kept confidential in light of her "reasonable belief" that what she had disclosed would be protected under law from being released. An attorney for a second doctor made a similar request. Dr. John Thiele, his lawyer said in a letter, had spoken with Tenet attorneys not realizing that they did not represent him, and he had "discussed facts with these attorneys that he would not have discussed had he known."

—

UNWELCOME ATTENTION from the attorney general's minions and CNN reporters was only the latest in a string of tribulations that had dogged Johnny Thiele since Thursday, September 1, the day he had stood beside Karen Wynn on the second floor of Memorial and asked, "Can we do this?"

Flying away from Memorial that sunset, a sense of relief had settled over him with the realization that he had in fact survived what he'd been sure he wouldn't. He landed at Louis Armstrong New Orleans International Airport with a posse of other Memorial staff and walked into a concourse teeming with hot, dirty, thirsty, antsy evacuees, some of them patients. No Tenet-dispatched buses awaited them as they had hoped. Fear returned and squeezed his insides. He kept it there, not wanting to alarm his colleagues. He lay down on cardboard and tucked a pliant military meal-ready-to-eat beneath his head as a pillow.

The next day he waited hours in the swirl of chaos with the small hospital group. They swayed in the pushing, pulling crowds. Teenage National Guardsmen armed with semiautomatic weapons failed to impose a sense of order. People skirmished. A nurse companion fainted. He maintained his doctor's mien, bucking up his colleagues, but inside himself grew sure they would not make it out, that they were on the cusp of death, that any moment gunfire would erupt. "This is crazy." He was white, his colleagues, too, and those around them were nearly all "Afro American." And, he feared, desperate.

At last they climbed into the gaping bay of an Air Force cargo plane, where tanks had surely gone before them. It was hot. Nobody would say where they were going. The big African American man who sat across from him noticed Thiele's silver acupressure bracelet, magnetic spheres at each end, admired it, and asked the woman next to him, honey, would you like one like that? *Oh Lord, this guy's going to . . .* Thiele steeled himself. "You Dr. Thiele?" The woman interrupted his imaginings. "Ya." She, a relative of a hospital security officer, didn't want his bracelet. She told the man, "You let him keep it." They landed near San Antonio in a storm and surrendered their bags to sniffer dogs and inspectors who worked under the shelter of an airplane wing while they stood on the tarmac, the heavens swiping them with rain. "We gotta get out of here," the fainting nurse declared. They spoke with an Air Force somebody who put them in a cab on the way to a Holiday Inn. The Spanish-speaking driver prayed with them in the parking lot.

The next day Thiele paid $1,200 for a ticket to Atlanta to reunite with family. Two days later, on Labor Day, he awoke unable to speak clearly or lift his right arm. How would he ever practice medicine again? He thought for the third time in less than a week he was going to die. He looked out the window of the hospital where he was taken. "God, you've got my attention." It was a stroke. He was only fifty-three. The doctor could find no reason. "It just had to be the stress of the storm."

He had dropped twelve pounds over the period of the disaster and its aftermath. Slowly, his abilities returned. He learned to speak again, proud of his rapid, slurring, New Orleans blue-collar brogue.

A couple of weeks later, someone called from CNN—"I hear you're one of the heroes of the storm"—wanting Thiele's story. Let me think about it, he said. Memorial's media director was one of his airport kin. She had prepared him for this: If anyone contacts you, call this number. Thiele called and spoke with Tenet media in Dallas, then Tenet attorneys. He told them his story.

Later he would remember it this way. Wednesday, August 31, had its upsides. He had made two valuable discoveries. One was that the soda machines in the basement cafeteria at Memorial still worked. He took off his shoes and waded into ankle-deep water to fill his cup.

The other discovery: the cancer institute, with its lights, relative coolness, and its miraculous electrical outlets powered by a still-working generator. Thiele walked across a bridge from the hospital to a medical office building and followed its hallways to the cancer institute. He spent many hours there. Hospital administrators came and went, made coffee, charged cell phones, sat in front of fans. He had a breezy talk with the chief financial officer, a rangy, gray-haired, and affable good ol' boy who reminded Thiele of Buddy Ebsen's Jed Clampett from *The Beverly*

Hillbillies. They spoke about their children, their home lives, and nothing about hospital administration, which Thiele found weird. Thiele fell asleep in a recliner chair for chemotherapy patients.

Over that day, Wednesday, August 31, Thiele also spent hours on the emergency ramp. Another doctor, John Kokemor, joined him to puff on cigars from the humidor Thiele had thought to bring to the hospital for safekeeping. Brown-leaf brothers, they called themselves, laughing. When do you suppose we'll get out of here? Doctors are being asked to stay until last. Why?

That's when Thiele's friend had used his index finger to make the sign of an injection in the crook of his opposite elbow, and Thiele had said, "Man, I hope we don't come to that." It was an exchange his friend would say had never happened.

Overall, Wednesday had been frightening. Another doctor on the emergency room ramp said rescuers weren't coming and the hospital was on its own. Thiele panicked at the sounds of shouting, and gunshots coming from the neighborhood scared him.

Returning to his office at night, he passed a plainclothes sentry posted for protection. "They gave me a gun," the man said, "but I've never shot a gun before." That didn't inspire Thiele's confidence. Climbing a stairwell in the pitch-dark, Thiele lost sense of where the steps and the railing lay. Disoriented, he took a friend's cell phone to the garage and sat in the gusty, air-conditioned sanctuary of his car. He reached his family in Georgia and tried to prepare them for the worst. "I may never see you again," he said.

That was the first time he felt sure he would not survive. They had no way to defend themselves. The long-repressed masses outside the hospital, brandishing looted guns and rifles, would revolt and overtake them. The enemy was near. A rowdy gang squatted in the credit union building across the street from Memorial. Thiele's colleagues kept asking one another what anyone had to gain by killing people trying to evacuate a hospital. On the phone with his wife, Thiele heard his daughter rage in the background, "Why is he there? . . . He didn't have to be there!"

Thiele had spent nearly every hurricane at Baptist. He stayed even though he wasn't a hospital-based doctor and didn't need to do so. He had practiced for twenty-one years, but there was nothing in his experience, nothing in anyone's experience there at Memorial, to prepare them to solve the problems they were facing. They were, he thought, in a war zone.

Daylight, Thursday morning, had refocused him. Susan Mulderick, taller, more confident than he, walked toward him from the emergency room. "John, everybody has to be out of here tonight." He heard the same from CEO Goux. Their words suggested the possibility of survival. He felt encouraged.

Evacuations had resumed by the time he began euthanizing the pharmacist's cats. When Dr. Kathleen Fournier asked him about putting patients out of their misery, it was hard not to draw a parallel. Thiele felt that pet owners were right to euthanize their pets when the animals were close to death. As a doctor who worked with critically ill patients in the ICU, his beliefs about euthanasia had changed over the years. He no longer opposed it. He had seen people try and fail to commit suicide when they were in pain near the end and no longer wished to live.

Thiele looked at the scene on the second floor, lit naturally through vacant window frames—the dozen or so supine patients, the nurses and doctors attending them, the fans and water bottles, and the refuse thrown everywhere. Thiele saw morphine, midazolam, and syringes set up on a table near the ATM. He remembered his friend's gesture on the emergency ramp, miming an injection. This is happening, he thought.

Thiele didn't know Pou by name, but she looked like the physician in charge on the second floor. She told him the category 3 patients were too sick to be moved, and without looking at their medical charts, he believed her. Some were sweaty, others slack with dehydration, breathing quickly. From some came unearthly rasps, then silence, rhapsodic frog song, the cadence of the dying. He was sure they wouldn't survive a trip to safety.

"Can I help you?" he asked Pou several times.

She told him no, he didn't have to be there.

"I want to be here," Thiele insisted. "I want to help you."

Pou and several nurses took care of the patients lying near the hallway. He took charge of the four closest to the windows—three elderly white women and a heavyset black man—trying to start IVs for those who didn't have them. The patients' blood pressures were so low, their veins had collapsed like empty fire hoses. Apart from their breathing and the soft moans of one, they appeared lifeless and did not respond to him.

A nurse cleaned a patient's IV port with an alcohol swab before giving an injection. The unintentional irony of the gesture struck him. What infection could have time to develop in a patient about to die?

Moral clarity was easier to maintain in concept than in execution. When the moment of truth came, he wavered. That's when he turned to nurse manager Karen Wynn, trusting her experience in the ICU and her leadership of the hospital's ethics committee. "Can we do this?" he asked. He was grateful for her assent.

Thiele gave patients a shot of morphine and midazolam at doses higher than what he normally used in the ICU. He held their hands and reassured them, "It's all right to go." Most patients died within minutes of being medicated. But the heavyset African American man with the labored breathing hadn't.

Thiele gave additional shots of morphine. He thought it must have amounted to 100 mg. He chanted Hail Marys with Karen Wynn. The man kept breathing. Perhaps his circulation was so poor that the drug wasn't getting into him.

Thiele covered his face with a towel.

He remembered it took less than a minute for the man to stop breathing and die.

It had gone against every fiber in his body to smother the man. It was something he had never thought he would ever have to do in any circumstance, was not in his "database." Though he'd felt what he had done was right, immediately afterward the question of whether it was indeed right continued to play in his mind. *Can we do this?* If the man was unaware of what was going on, if he would have died in an hour anyway, how cruel was it to have suffocated him?

Thiele left the hospital that Thursday evening by helicopter and landed at the airport, where the patients he had injected—had they survived—would have gone.

Beneath a skylight in an open concourse, patients lay everywhere on litters and on the carpeted ground. They sat propped in wheelchairs and in hard airport seats, some moaning, most motionless. The stench of urine, overflowing diapers, and feces-soiled garments suffused the swampy air. Brain-surgery patients. Transplant-surgery patients. Patients with breathing tubes in their throats who needed oxygen, respiratory therapists, and ventilators. Hundreds had arrived and continued to arrive from the city's hospitals and nursing homes. Thousands of hungry, thirsty, sodden evacuees, separated from their medicines for hypertension, diabetes, schizophrenia, and other ailments, camped under signs for Jesters Bar and Grill, Back Alley Jazz, and other airport concessions. Their voices swelled and rose, as did, in many cases, their blood pressures and their blood-sugar levels. The skeleton medical staff of doctors, nurses, and paramedics, many at work for more than two days without sleep, ranted at one another in exhaustion.

Thiele and a nurse who had accompanied him offered to help. *Stay outta the area;* a female doctor shooed them. *We got it covered.* The intermittent federal employees—members of Disaster Medical Assistance Teams, or DMATs, who underwent specialized training—were not supposed to work with unvetted outsiders. There was no good system for checking whether or not someone who walked up to offer medical assistance might be qualified. Per protocol, the teams at the airport turned away Thiele and other doctors and nurses, even as their members were utterly overwhelmed.

A DMAT had arrived that Thursday to join three other DMATs that had established the field hospital early Wednesday morning. Three dozen paramedics, nurses, and a few doctors who had trained and drilled and volunteered to respond in times of national emergency toured the site in disbelief. Many cried. Their supply caches, driven rather than flown from the West Coast, were late and short. Minute after minute, the helicopters landed and the patients kept arriving from hospitals and nursing homes, many times more than the volunteers had been told would come, ten times more than anyone who worked with a DMAT knew could possibly be cared for. Where were the departing flights to take these patients to real hospitals? Supplies ran out within a day. And they had no communications with superiors, no provisions for resupply.

Federal officials outside New Orleans touted the work of the DMATs in news interviews.

That Thursday night passed in moans and screams and death. No time to move the bodies. Thiele lay listening. His moral clarity returned. If the patients he had injected with morphine and midazolam at Memorial had come, instead, to this place, they would only have suffered and died.

Can we do this? After the disaster, the question had shifted for Thiele from a moral to a legal one, the price of conviction in the currency of consequences. His attorney warded off the attorney general's advances while Thiele—his home destroyed, and out of a job because of the hospital's closure—sought the means to pay him.

In December, he attended a meeting of Memorial Medical Center doctors planning for an eventual reopening of the hospital. Thiele read aloud from a letter his lawyer had sent to the medical staff president. "Tenet, through its attorneys, has not agreed to pay the legal fees and costs incurred and to be incurred by John S. Thiele, MD, in connection with an ongoing inquiry by the state Attorney General." Thiele's attorney argued that Tenet had the authority to pay, even though Thiele, as a physician contractor, was not a direct employee. Thiele wanted his colleagues' support.

"Did you do anything you'd need a lawyer for?" a doctor, Brobson Lutz, asked Thiele.

"Let's just say what I did I thought was right. Others think it was wrong."

A gasp escaped from Dr. Horace Baltz, the senior doctor who had served during the storm. "Oh my God, John. I pray for you."

Baltz had been an evacuee in northern Alabama when Dr. Bryant King appeared on CNN. Baltz had turned off the television and sat in a daze. This couldn't be true. He fretted about the tarnished reputation of the hospital where he had invested his entire career, the sterling reputation so many colleagues had worked hard and long to build and uphold at Baptist and Memorial. How could he show his face after this, especially having recounted his hurricane experiences with pride at the small, rural hospital that served the region where he had taken refuge?

Baltz had only encountered King once, at an emergency meeting before the storm, and the young doctor had impressed him as conscientious and participatory, a team player. Why would he want to stir up a mess? Other colleagues spoke of King in terms of treachery. Rumor spread that he had fled the hospital soon after the floodwaters rose and was not even present on Thursday, September 1, despite the people who recalled interacting with him on that day. As hard as it was, Baltz had to believe that King was reporting events as he had seen them, events that he'd thought were wrong.

Baltz searched his memory for clues and settled on a conversation he had overheard. The scene: Thursday morning, September 1, in a doctor's office on the second floor of Memorial. Three doctors in conversation. One said: "Our most difficult job will be to convince the nurses that what we ask them to do is all right." Baltz stopped and asked what his colleagues were discussing, and one of the three said that some of the patients couldn't make it out on their own and would need to be "helped." Baltz had wondered for a moment whether the doctor was talking about euthanasia. He dismissed the thought as absurd. This was loose and crazy talk, talk in which he did not care to be involved. He departed.

Dr. John Kokemor had, a short time later, guided Baltz and his elderly sister to the head of the boat evacuation line. Baltz was sure Kokemor knew his opinion of euthanasia. He was one of the colleagues Baltz believed espoused the "Governor Lamm philosophy." Baltz and Kokemor, who had practiced together briefly in the early 1980s and then split, held low opinions of each other. Kokemor would later ridicule the idea that he had put Baltz on a boat to get him out of the way so that euthanasia could proceed. Kokemor called the idea a "fabrication," a product of Baltz's guilt over the death of one of his longtime patients.

The seventy-eight-year-old woman with an advanced case of the movement disorder Parkinson's disease had died that Thursday at Memorial after Baltz had last seen her. She hadn't been acutely ill. He had admitted her for safety before the storm because she relied on electrical equipment for her care. He did this whenever hurricanes approached, throughout the eight years of her illness. And at her request, he always gave her a Do Not Resuscitate order, because she did not want any heroics in case her heart or her respiratory system failed unexpectedly. Her caregiver, a loyal sister, had been separated from her at Memorial.

The death of Baltz's patient had surprised him. Her vocal cords were paralyzed. She couldn't speak for herself. Could she have been euthanized? He resolved to find out what had happened and who was responsible. He resolved not to be silent about it.

———

SPECIAL AGENT Virginia Rider harbored a similar moral outrage. What had happened at Memorial was wrong. It was as basic as the tenets of her Catholic religion, but she wasn't a rigid thinker. While she wouldn't ever want to be euthanized, she could understand that some people in some circumstances would. She had no problem with the illegal acts of the then-imprisoned Dr. Jack Kevorkian, who had built a killing machine and helped patients die, patients with advanced cancers, with progressive dementias that robbed them of their memories and independence. The difference was that they had requested his services. The doctors at Memorial, as far as Rider knew, had acted without consent. Rider spoke with the doctor who had treated Emmett Everett before the storm. Despite his years of paralysis and many medical problems, Everett had seemed content with his lot and had told his medical team to do "whatever it takes," including surgery, so he could get as well as possible and return home to the grandkids who visited him often and the wife who would never agree to put him in a nursing home.

According to his caregivers, Everett's passion for life had remained strong throughout the disaster. One of his nurses, Cindy Chatelain, told investigators that she had helped round up food for Everett on Thursday morning. (It was tuna fish, crackers, and relish, according to another staff member.) Chatelain said Everett had eaten his breakfast and was alert and oriented. He had worried aloud about his wife and asked if the three other patients who had been his roommates, who had left, were OK. He also expressed concern about himself. "Cindy, don't let them leave me behind," she remembered him saying. She had promised him she wouldn't. She lived now with a heavy burden of guilt and leaned harder on alcohol and prescription painkillers.

Rider spoke with his wife, Carrie, who told Rider that he had desired to live. She also gave the investigators a copy of a picture of him, the only one she had. In his photograph, Emmett Everett sat in front of a Coca-Cola machine in a cafeteria, holding a fork and a plate of food. He wore a tie and a white dress shirt across his broad shoulders. His eyes sparkled in the flash, giving him a boyish look even with a closely cropped gray goatee. Schafer, who was fond of nicknaming, began calling Everett the case's "poster child." The name stuck.

Schafer was also raised Catholic, like Rider, and he also was not an absolutist on matters of life and death. As an attorney, he had drawn up living wills for many people who wished to document their end-of-life preferences in advance of any problems. He, too, had done this, after getting older and thinking more about the issue. If he was a "vegetable," he wanted that life-support plug pulled. But that was his decision. He didn't want someone else making it for him.

While he felt it wasn't his place to form opinions, given their medical conditions, he could perhaps understand why some of the patients at Memorial had been given the drugs. Others, like Everett, made him say "No way." The point was that there were so very many cases, and each one was different. When some members of the public said, "If it was my mother, I'd want them to do that," he wanted to ask, "How about *this* mother, this daddy, this uncle, this grandpa, this one over here?" How many people had to be injected before they'd no longer think, "It's OK to do that."

In 1979, Schafer's father had spent two or three weeks at the hospital, sick with what his doctor described as "everything natural at one time." Some people just wore out. Daddy was wearing out. Schafer had been with him, holding his hand, until he died. It never would have occurred to him to ask the doctor, "Why don't you just kill him?"

It was hard not to be personally affected by the case. Schafer had developed the famous "Katrina cough" that seemed to strike everyone who spent time in New Orleans. He traced it to their tours of Memorial without masks; God knew what had come up from the sewers and drains.

The people Schafer spoke with—whether it was the family members of the dead or the nurses and doctors—had so much more on their minds than talking to investigators. He found himself feeling sympathy for nearly all of them; they were heroes.

As the scale and complexity of the case grew, Schafer saw that Rider in particular as lead investigator was spending a huge amount of time ramrodding it. It had become so big that she had been taken off all other hospital and nursing-home investigations. She said that even at night, at home, she thought about the case. Only the two of them, investigative partners and allies, fully understood and shared each other's passion.

They lived the case from early in the morning until nighttime. Every day. Every day. Every day. They held conclaves in his office with a big notepad on an easel. They brainstormed in the smoking area outside the building. They made frequent trips to New Orleans, where the blue tarp roofs everywhere were an inescapable reminder of tragedy.

They bounced ideas off of each other. It was never prosecutor-investigator. It was never him or her. It was them. Their case, their situation, what were they going to do. They got to the point where they almost thought alike. They talked constantly about the case. Theirs was a rare partnership, a great friendship. Schafer had never had one like it. He enjoyed every minute of it.

He thought the way they got along was like Rosalind Russell and Cary Grant in *His Girl Friday*. She, tenacious and idealistic in the pursuit of truth. He, a wily plotter who knows he needs her. Both addicted to their callings—two opinionated people who got along best when they were focused on their work—finishing each other's sentences, lighting each other's cigarettes (well, Rider didn't smoke), knowing what the other was thinking.

They were perfect together. He couldn't type. She could type a thousand words a minute. He loved seeing Rider, because seeing her meant it was going to be an exciting day. He knew it was unusual for two people to enjoy working together as much as they did.

Schafer felt Rider was the only person with whom he could discuss everything. He thought he couldn't share details of the high-profile case with his wife. You just didn't talk about those things with a spouse or with anyone else outside of the unit. You didn't want secrets to be passed on to the grocer, the neighbor, whomever.

He knew his wife saw that he was caught up in something, and that she worried about him working too hard. She worried that he might injure his health.

Schafer and his wife were dealing separately with an accumulation of family losses: first their daughter, then his wife's cousin who was like a sister to her, and most recently his wife's father—all in under five months. Schafer received a call about his father-in-law's death while he was in the middle of an interview with a Memorial doctor, and he finished the interview. He plunged into work and tried to fill his time with the Memorial investigation. His wife retreated, sitting for hours in solitude on the back patio in their quiet subdivision, immersed in mourning. Schafer thought she grieved better by herself.

Schafer's wife was a painter who also ran an art gallery that specialized in images of angels—a career launched years earlier when their now-deceased daughter had dreamed of an angel. Schafer admired his wife as an active and outgoing woman. The change in her was drastic.

Schafer grieved, but differently. He drove his daughter's Honda Accord around the neighborhood. He patted the shift lever as if it were her hand.

As Rider and Schafer interviewed the employees who had received subpoenas, they had other investigators make screening phone calls to dozens more Memorial employees to assess where they were assigned to work during the storm and whether they had been on the seventh or second floor on Thursday, September 1. Most were storm-displaced and unreachable, or refused to talk, or requested lawyers, who often made their clients unavailable for interviews.

Rider prepared subpoenas for several doctors who might have worked on the seventh floor. Among them was young Roy Culotta, whom Butch Schafer began referring to as Doogie Howser, MD, referring to the child medical prodigy from the eponymous TV show.

People in the unit came up with nicknames for all the major players in the case. Several of the opposing attorneys were "Mr. Wonderful." Tenet, "the Evil Empire." Suspects were "the Cajun Injectors," after the

Louisiana food brand of injectable meat marinades, which came pack-
aged with a gargantuan needle and syringe. One syringe, available in
chrome-plated copper, was called the "Fat Boy Injector." Like doctors,
law enforcement officials sometimes made tasteless jokes as a means of
coping with tragedy.

Culotta came to his interview without a lawyer and spoke confi-
dently. He had dark hair, darker eyes, and a youthful face.

Rider asked him to begin with the night of Wednesday, August 31.

"I remember being in the respiratory area," he said. This was on the
second floor. "We all took oxygen tubing from the wall and just . . . had
it just blowing all over me because it was so hot."

Did he realize how terrible this could sound when Dr. Bryant King
and others had spoken of running out of oxygen for patients in the
second-floor lobby? Why weren't patients who needed oxygen carried to
wherever it was, on the same floor, that oxygen could so easily be had?

Rider and Schafer did not ask these questions. If they had even thought
of them they would have had to interrupt Culotta, who spoke for many
minutes without another word from them, instead posing questions to
himself and answering them. How was euthanasia first raised? In the
context of pets. Was he aware of any patient deaths? "There were at least
two patients who they brought all the way onto the, ah . . . at the top of
the parking garage, who, you know, sitting there waiting for helicopters,
went into respiratory distress and, you know, we decided that there was
no way that they could make the trip."

One was an African American man. Culotta didn't know him, but
"he was in really bad shape . . . and it was me and a nurse and essentially
we gave him pain medicine, ah . . . as he was taking his last breaths."

The other patient who went into distress atop the parking garage was
one he had cared for in the hospital for the preceding two weeks, Merle
Lagasse, who had end-stage lung cancer.

"I was trying to get her evacuated and she basically went into, ah . . .
call . . . it's called Cheyne-Stokes respiration where . . . it's just, ah . . . it's

kind of . . . it's . . . it's before you die and you start breathing in a certain pattern and, ah . . . and we, you know, we did everything we could to make her comfortable."

Culotta's monologue drifted to other events. Schafer politely brought him back to the deaths in the parking garage. "I hope you don't read anything into this line of questioning, but you're the first one that I've listened to that has had firsthand knowledge of this."

"I knew she was dying." When Merle Lagasse went into a breathing crisis, he had sent a nurse from the parking garage across the rooftop into a hospital window on the seventh story to go up and fetch medicines from the ICU. "I said go in the back, get some . . . some morphine and Ativan."

The nurse returned with several drugs—Culotta recalled morphine, Ativan, and Versed. "Morphine is . . . it relieves that sense of, you know, gasping and yeah, it does hasten death, I mean, it's no doubt about it but at that point it's . . . the intention is to relieve any suffering, ah . . . and that's what we did."

He remembered being with Lagasse when she died. "The other gentleman, I was with him and I assessed him, gave him medicines, I went back fifteen, twenty minutes later, he was still struggling, we gave him some more medicine."

Schafer asked how this differed from normal medical practice. Normally, Culotta said, the patient would have an intravenous line, and an electric pump would dispense precisely controlled amounts of the drug over time. "You can easily titrate the medicine, you know, so you start someone off at ten milligrams an hour and, you know, you feel like they're struggling or in pain, you can easily go up to twenty."

Without electricity, at the top of the parking garage, the nurse had simply injected a bolus of the drugs into the patients' veins. Culotta didn't remember the exact dose he ordered for Lagasse other than that it was a high one. She had been taking narcotic pills for pain and had developed tolerance to their effects.

"When we went to give her morphine, it ended her life." Culotta's matter-of-factness surprised his interviewers. Was it standard practice to administer high doses of narcotics and sedatives when a patient developed the irregular breathing pattern Culotta had described? After the interview, one of the investigators researched the question and shared the results with Rider and her team. The revving and stalling pattern of Cheyne-Stokes breathing could precede death, but also occurred in numerous other situations—for example, when certain people, especially those with heart failure or brain damage, were sleeping. This suggested there was at least some possibility that the patients Culotta had medicated were not about to die.

The agent found an article about a different type of breathing they had been hearing about in their interviews, called "agonal"—a gasping reflex that often occurs just minutes or moments before death when the level of oxygen in the body drops extremely low and the brain stem, a hardy and evolutionarily ancient part of the brain, is left in charge. "Given our current knowledge of pain, suffering, and brain function, patients who are gasping are probably not experiencing pain or suffering." That is because so little oxygen is reaching their brains.

Still, the gasping *looks* uncomfortable, a sharp contraction that rocks the body as if the patient is struggling to breathe, horrifying family members and even nurses when it persists. Some medical experts believed it was ethical to treat potential pain and suffering in these dying patients with morphine and other drugs, even if this could suppress breathing and quicken death, because it was impossible to know whether the patient experienced discomfort. Moral and legal culpability for the deaths rested on the wisps of contrast between wanting, foreseeing, and intending death.

ANNA POU was the focus of Rider's every day. She began as a ghost, a dim presence haunting the seventh floor. Soon Rider had a sketch of the woman. She knew her vital statistics. Name. Birth date. Last known address. She kept her driver's-license photograph in a binder of others she passed before the eyes of hospital workers to identify.

Rider knew Pou's signature, the round, generous cursive inked on a job relocation agreement setting out her employment at Louisiana State University with benefits contributed by Memorial a year before the storm. The same signature appeared beneath the words "morphine sulfate" on the three prescription forms dated Thursday, September 1, 2005, neat and assured in the foreground of chaos.

Rider knew that one of Pou's older brothers, Frederick, named after their physician father but using the aliases "Johnny Morales" and "Cecilio Romero," was a federal fugitive on the US Drug Enforcement Administration's Most Wanted list, indicted for drug running with a last known address in Mexico.

Rider also knew Pou by proxy: a sketchy, phantom Pou, conjured at interviews conducted in hospital offices smelling of antiseptic and bathed in fluorescence; in a slideshow of living rooms; in the familiar formality of her building's conference room, or at her or Butch's desk, in Baton Rouge. She gleaned descriptions of the woman: "Fluffy-haired." "Nervous." "Incredibly dedicated." Dabs and brushes of color on canvas.

Rider knew Pou's allegedly used objects, collected and submitted to the crime lab, awaiting analysis for fingerprints. A plastic tray. A Sterilite drawer. Empty morphine vials. Discarded syringes.

Most of all, Pou materialized each time Rider returned to the dank cavern of Memorial in person or in her mind, retracing the doctor's steps by light of day or in dreams at night. Rider tracked her, drawing nearer.

In early December, Rider, Schafer, and their team returned to Memorial with LifeCare's pharmacist, Steven Harris. Three months had elapsed since the hurricane, and the buildings were full of restoration workers, administrators, and other short-term visitors like them. Former employees and doctors returned to pick up personal property and medical records. Contractors arrived each day to tear out stained carpets, mop floors, pump out elevator wells, and replace wires corroded by the muck that had swamped up from the sewer grates. They drilled away mold-spangled drywall like caries from a bad tooth. Each day each contract worker signed a sheet of paper beneath a bold-faced warning from Tenet Healthcare: "The Property is not in safe condition and entry into the property may subject the undersigned to a substantial risk of personal injury or death." The workers agreed that they were entering at their own risk and would not sue the hospital.

The proud old hospital was now ringed by a fence. Camouflage-clad officers from the security firm DynCorp closed any gaps they found with plastic ties. DynCorp had more lucrative business in war-torn Iraq and Afghanistan, but Rider and Schafer learned the company had taken this commission for Tenet within days of the evacuation. Its first assignment had been to assist anyone who might have been left behind alive. Now, carrying long-necked automatic rifles, the guards patrolled the perimeter by foot and vehicle once an hour, staggering the start times. At night they checked on the buildings and escorted away drunks.

The attorney general's staff and pharmacist Harris and his attorney signed an entry log at entry gate number 1. They went upstairs to the Life-Care pharmacy. Harris confirmed that his entire stock of morphine—125 10 mg vials—was missing, along with dozens of Versed and Ativan injection vials. Other controlled drugs were still present, suggesting the pharmacy had been selectively pilfered, not burglarized.

Also touring the shuttered hospital that afternoon, escorted by a Tenet attorney, were three women. Harris pulled prosecutor Butch Schafer aside to say he recognized them from the LifeCare physical therapy charting room on Thursday, September 1. He identified them as the doctor and two Memorial nurses who had joined her.

Anna Pou and Virginia Rider looked at each other from roughly the same height. They were introduced. They reached out and shook each other's hands.

Here Pou was, at last, standing where Rider and Schafer had for months imagined her. It was typical to meet a target in the course of an investigation, but they hadn't until now met Pou, who spoke in the open to her lawyer, Rick Simmons. Here were words that might help explain what they still could not fully understand. They were hungry for the least clue.

⁓

POU TOURED MEMORIAL with Simmons and nurses Cheri Landry and Lori Budo, pinning locations to memories. They circulated throughout the hospital where both nurses had been born, and then above it, to the top of the parking garage, climbing two rickety metal staircases to the helipad. Pou took Simmons to Room 7312 on the Life-Care floor, where she had rushed to answer a "Code Blue" early in the disaster. The moment was frozen in the evidence that remained: a crash cart with medicines for resuscitating patients, a ventilator, and a monitor. In the sepia wash of indirect daylight, in the noticed quiet, disconnected from the normally ubiquitous cycling electrical buzz, the most modern equipment could appear oddly obsolete.

Down the hallway at the nursing station, a box held a metal laryngoscope with a folded beak that Pou had snapped open and pushed into the patient's mouth, sliding away his tongue, clearing a path for her other hand to curve the breathing tube into his throat. Here was evidence that she had tried to save, not take away, a life. If only she could brandish it before a public that was, despite Simmons's efforts at suppression, days away from learning her name.

⁓

"TONIGHT, A CNN EXCLUSIVE, from an act of God, to playing God, accusations of intentional killings in the wake of Katrina, as one doctor is worried a colleague may have done the unthinkable." Anchor John King teased the story on a Wednesday night in late December.

Angela McManus appeared. Her eyelids looked heavy. She spoke of her mother, LifeCare patient Wilda McManus. "I think she died from the infection. I don't know. I really don't know. And, you know, hearing—this doctor was saying about euthanasia—euthanasia at the hospital, I just don't know where to go."

Dr. Bryant King said he had seen a doctor holding a handful of syringes on the second-floor lobby.

"Dr. Anna Pou," the reporter, Drew Griffin, interrupted, identifying her.

"The words that I heard her say were, 'I'm going to give you something to make you feel better.'"

Griffin read a statement from Pou's attorney, Rick Simmons. "We feel confident that the facts will reveal heroic efforts by the physicians and the staff in a desperate situation."

Pou was overcome by anger, grief, and outrage. Simmons counseled her not to watch the news, but that was hardly what mattered. Dozens of reporters called her and appeared at her home and the hospital where she had gone to work in Baton Rouge. They somehow found her family members. The curtain separating strangers from her private life was a scrim.

Pou considered herself harassed by the reporters, "terrorized," she called it. One day a resident at her hospital summoned her to see a visitor, a woman who claimed to represent a pharmaceutical company. "I don't think she's a drug rep," the resident said.

Pou assumed the woman was a reporter. "Tell her to quit interfering with the care of my patients," she told the resident. Pou could not abide this. Simmons, too, was worried. Imagine an operation went poorly: "You're *that* doctor." It was a bad environment for her to practice in, and she needed to let it cool.

Simmons, Pou, and the head of her department at Louisiana State University all drew the same conclusion. Days earlier it would have been unthinkable. She had to stop performing surgery.

Notifying her patients, some with advanced cancer, was heartbreaking. Pou called one of them, James O'Bryant, to tell him and his wife, Brenda, he would need to see someone else for an upcoming operation, the third she would have performed on him.

From the first time Pou met him, that January, she had worried about him. James O'Bryant was a busy working father of two who lived on a bayou off the Pearl River, far from a big city. Months earlier, thinking the pain in his mouth was from bad teeth, he'd put off going to see a doctor. He wasn't a smoker or a drinker like most of Pou's other patients with disfiguring facial cancers.

Pou gave the terrified couple her cell-phone number with instructions to call anytime, day or night, to talk about anything at all. They used it frequently.

Before the first surgery Pou had come into the hospital room and enveloped O'Bryant's family members—including his children, James Lawrence and Tabatha—in kisses and embraces. "We're all going to pray and we're not going to stop praying," she'd said. She rehearsed each step of the surgery with them, describing how she would remove the large tumor from the sinus above O'Bryant's teeth and reconstruct his face. She hugged and kissed them again and disappeared through a door to scrub for the surgery, leaving O'Bryant's brother-in-law in tears. He cried at Pou's tenderness. He had a history of health problems and had never had a doctor treat him this way. The operation lasted more than twenty hours.

At follow-up appointments over months of radiation therapy, the O'Bryants would wait three or four hours to see Pou. Once they were in, she checked James "up one side and down the other," Brenda would joke. The couple stayed as long as they needed, asked any questions they liked.

The month before the storm, Pou had lifted a flap of skin from O'Bryant's forehead and swung it on a pedicle across his nose to fill in a hole under his right eye where the skin broke down after radiation therapy. The flap took root in its new location, and a new surgery was planned to sever the stalklike connection. But with Katrina bearing down, Pou had decided to delay it. She told the O'Bryants she didn't want to put James in the hospital with the storm coming at them.

She had promised always to be there for him. Now she said she couldn't practice and needed some time away; there were questions about what had gone on during the hurricane. She told Brenda her experiences had been horrifying, that anyone who was not there could never, ever understand. That words could never explain it.

———

BY DECEMBER, Rider, Schafer, and their small team of coworkers had gathered all the pieces of information—detailed toxicology reports, medical records, and autopsies—that an expert would need to determine causes of death for four of the LifeCare patients on the seventh floor. The New Orleans coroner, Frank Minyard, was a gynecologist, not trained to interpret these results to a level of certainty that could verify the prosecutors' suspicions, so he recommended a forensic pathologist, Cyril Wecht, a longtime friend and colleague who had worked on the John F. Kennedy assassination case and the O.J. Simpson murder trial.

The fast-talking coroner of Allegheny County, Pennsylvania, was a media fixture and had commented on the Memorial investigation on CNN weeks before he was hired. "If you find any morphine in a patient for whom morphine had never been ordered, now, in my opinion, from a forensic, scientific, legal, investigative standpoint, that's enough, because what are they doing with morphine?"

Wecht reported back to Butch Schafer by phone in early December. "Mr. Schafer, I have reviewed the four cases you sent to me," he said. All four patients had been found with drugs in their bodies that had not been prescribed for them in the medical records. "I believe that they can be said to have caused or to have substantially contributed to the deaths of the individuals."

Schafer asked if the drug levels found by the laboratory were abnormally high. Wecht said that didn't matter.

"When you talk about morphine and you talk about Demerol, any amount when it is not prescribed is significant."

"Yes sir."

"Especially with somebody who was severely compromised to begin with . . ."

"Oh, I agree with you."

"Morphine is a central nervous system depressant drug that slows down respiration, slows down GI motility, slow down heart rate, lower blood pressure. That is the last thing in the world that they need."

Still, Schafer homed in on a potential defense. Could the drugs at the levels detected have been given with the intention of relieving pain and not of causing death?

"I see your point," Wecht said, as if the possibility hadn't occurred to him. "Let me do this. Let me go back to the levels and deal with that. That is a very good question and yeah, right, absolutely. Let me do that and then I will get back to you on that, whether or not they could be said to be present in therapeutic doses."

Wecht supplied his answer by fax two days before Christmas. He had found, in a respected textbook, Randall C. Baselt's *Disposition of Toxic Drugs and Chemicals in Man*, a range of morphine concentrations associated with previous fatalities. Wecht compared them with the drug levels found in the tissues of the four LifeCare patients. "In all four of the cases it appears that a lethal amount of morphine was administered," he wrote.

Wecht's findings seemed to supply the probable cause needed to prosecute Pou and two of the Memorial nurses who the prosecutors believed had first accompanied her on the seventh floor, Cheri Landry and Lori Budo. They had not accumulated enough evidence on a third ICU nurse they were investigating. Rider and her colleagues began preparing arrest warrants.

In January, Wecht sent a $7,500 bill to the attorney general's office for fifteen hours of work at $500 an hour on the Memorial case. The same day a federal grand jury indicted him on eighty-four counts of alleged wrongdoing, including mixing expenses from his public office and private consulting work. Some argued that the charges were politically motivated, elements of a wave of prosecutions of outspoken Democratic elected officials under the Justice Department of Republican president George W. Bush.

USA Today quoted the Louisiana attorney general's spokesperson saying that another expert would probably be appointed to review toxicology reports related to more than two hundred hospital and nursing-home deaths across the state. Wecht interpreted that to mean he would no longer be used as a consultant. Famously thin-skinned, he shot Butch Schafer—who had been as effusive with him as with toxicologist Middleberg—an excoriating letter. "I recall that when I informed you about my conclusions, you stated that you 'would like to give me a big hug and a kiss.' Instead, you have quite unnecessarily and callously thrust a dagger into my heart."

———

THE CHARGES against Wecht concerned his business ethics, not his competency as a forensic pathologist. For now, as toxicology reports on other patients continued to arrive from the laboratory, Rider and Schafer's team relied on his determinations in the first four cases.

What they were missing was an eyewitness who had seen these patients being injected on the seventh floor. LifeCare pharmacist Steven Harris, reinterviewed in December, said he had seen Pou standing by Emmett Everett's bed. His attorney had also said, in a secret proffer, that Harris had supplied Pou with additional morphine and midazolam.

Prosecutor Schafer and Special Agent Rider needed more to seal their case. They and their colleagues did another round of interviews with the key LifeCare witnesses and with others. As a prosecutor, Schafer was thinking ahead to the possibility of taking his witnesses to court. He wanted to make sure their testimony would be credible and believable, and part of that was seeing whether they were consistent from interview to interview.

Over time he also came to suspect that some of the witnesses had held back in their original interviews. He confronted the LifeCare attorneys, offering an example. "Butch, you didn't ask that question," one responded. In the first stages of the investigation, the witnesses had dutifully answered the questions that were asked of them, but had not volunteered more. Now that trust had grown between Schafer and LifeCare, the lawyers advised the witnesses to tell the whole story. In these next interviews, the questioners focused more on what had happened to Emmett Everett, and they coaxed more from the witnesses than they had originally recalled or been willing to share.

A new witness, LifeCare respiratory therapist Terence Stahelin, offered compelling details. He said that he had spoken with Everett when volunteers came up to help carry LifeCare patients downstairs for evacuation. "He called me into his room and shook my hand and thanked me for all that we—not me personally—but what we had all done for him." Stahelin said the volunteers then told him they weren't going to carry Everett downstairs because he was too heavy. "I find that really hard to believe," he told Rider and her colleagues. "There's a big flat roof next to the seventh floor. They could have knocked a window out and passed him through a window and then across to the helicopter pad." Stahelin did not say, and the investigators did not ask, whether he had suggested this to anyone. Why did Stahelin think some of the smaller patients weren't carried downstairs? "Because they were little old ladies who were either Alzheimer's patients, senile dementia," he said. "These were the 'expendable' patients. The ones who someone decided that"—he paused—"had no quality of life."

Stahelin said he had left the LifeCare floor on Thursday, September 1, after an armed, uniformed man he believed was a National Guardsman came to the respiratory area and told everyone they had to leave. At the boat drop-off point, Stahelin said, he saw the infectious diseases doctor who had come to LifeCare the previous evening. He asked her what she thought would happen to the patients left on the seventh floor. "She broke down and cried and said, 'Terry, they're going to help them find their way to heaven.'"

The investigators spoke again with LifeCare's incident commander, assistant administrator Diane Robichaux, who had now had her baby. She recalled that on the morning of Thursday, September 1, 2005, she and physical medicine director Kristy Johnson had tried to figure out how they could get Everett, who was so heavy, out of the hospital.

"Let's go talk to him," Johnson had told Robichaux that morning, "see how he's doing." They went into Room 7307 and asked Everett how he was. He said he felt a little dizzy. "I might need some oxygen or something," he told the women.

"Well, you are already hooked up to the oxygen," Robichaux said. "We got your window open." The air was blowing through and it was loud with the sounds from outside. They spoke about the noise.

"So are we ready to rock and roll?" Everett asked.

"We are working on it," Robichaux told him.

Later that morning, Anna Pou came upstairs and they discussed Everett's prospects in the physical therapy charting room. One of Everett's nurses, Andre Gremillion, joined the discussion and was asked to sedate him. He backed out of the room crying.

Rider, Schafer, and their colleagues had interviewed Gremillion several times early in the investigation. In another interview in late December, Gremillion said he remembered one of the main reasons he was so upset by the request to sedate Everett. A recent chat with his nursing director, Gina Isbell, had sparked his memory.

He recalled Pou had turned to him in the physical therapy charting room after asking him to medicate Everett and said something like: "If you don't feel comfortable, don't do it, because it will come back and haunt you. The first time I did it, I wasn't ready and it haunted me for two years."

Gremillion had left the room and walked past Isbell, who saw he was upset and tried to put her arm around him. He kept going down the hallway to a nursing station in an alcove. He walked up to the corner of a wall and hit it to try to get a handle on himself. Pou's comment, Gremillion told the investigators, had made him think "they were going to give Mr. Everett something to let him go."

Still, Schafer and Rider were missing a true eyewitness who could link Pou's words directly to the injections of LifeCare patients. In January, an attorney for LifeCare called Butch Schafer to say that physical medicine director Kristy Johnson had remembered something more, something she wanted to share. Schafer got on the phone with her on a Thursday evening. When he told Rider what he'd learned, she arranged to talk with Johnson, too. What Johnson had come forward to say was so potentially important to the case, so revelatory, that Rider needed to hear it for herself.

With both Rider and Schafer, Johnson began by talking about Mr. Everett. She said she had accompanied Pou to the entrance of Everett's room. Johnson couldn't remember if Pou was holding syringes then. Johnson said she had never seen a physician look as nervous as Pou did. As they walked, Pou said to Johnson that she planned to tell Everett she would give him something "to help him with his dizziness."

"What do you think?" Pou had asked, Johnson recalled.

"I don't know," Johnson had said. "I guess."

They reached Room 7307. One of the nurses from Memorial was outside. "Are you going to be OK?" the nurse asked Pou. "Do you need me to go in with you?"

"No, I am OK," Pou said.

Pou disappeared into Everett's room and shut the door.

Johnson mentioned several other important details she had not yet told the attorney general's team. She had witnessed Pou drawing fluid from vials into syringes. She had seen Pou and nurses from Memorial carrying syringes in their hands. She had escorted the health professionals to each of the patients' bedsides and, most crucial of all, had been present for some of the injections. Johnson held some of the patients' hands and said a prayer.

Johnson stood across from Pou at Wilda McManus's bedside after Wilda's daughter Angela had been ordered to leave. Johnson had walked her downstairs and reassured her they would do everything for her mother.

"I am going to give you something to make you feel better," Pou told Wilda, according to Johnson. It was the same phrase Bryant King had mentioned hearing Pou say on CNN. Johnson said she didn't glance down at what Pou was doing to McManus on the opposite side of her bed. Instead, Johnson looked right into McManus's eyes and spoke to her.

"Mrs. McManus, I just want you to know, your daughter got out safely and she's going to be OK," Johnson had said.

The seventy-year-old woman, who had been feverish and drifting in and out of consciousness, didn't say anything in reply. "She is really fighting," Johnson thought she recalled Pou telling her later. "I had to give her three doses." (Pou's attorney Rick Simmons would later emphatically deny Pou ever said something like this.)

Johnson accompanied the taller of the Memorial nurses into Room 7305. "This is Ms. Hutzler," Johnson said, touching the woman's hand and saying a "little prayer." Johnson tried not to look down at what the nurse was doing, but she saw the nurse inject Hutzler's remaining roommate, Rose Savoie, a ninety-year-old woman who had a case of acute bronchitis and a history of kidney problems. A LifeCare nurse later told the investigators that both women were alert and stable as of late that morning. "That burns," Savoie murmured. Johnson looked down and saw her arm was puffy.

By that afternoon, Savoie was dead, as were the rest of the nine remaining LifeCare patients. Rider and Schafer had their eyewitness.

They had another one in Memorial pathologist Dr. John Skinner. He, and his lab director David Heikamp, had some of the answers as to what happened on the seventh floor after Johnson and her LifeCare colleagues had left. On Thursday afternoon, Skinner and Heikamp walked through the hospital to ensure everyone was gone and to write down the names of the dead and their locations. Medicine chairman Richard Deichmann and CEO René Goux had asked Skinner earlier in the week to keep track of any deaths.

The notes the men took and their recollections were now important evidence in establishing the timing of the deaths.

On the seventh floor the two encountered Anna Pou and a nurse manager Heikamp knew well, Mary Jo D'Amico, with a patient, a heavyset black woman lying on a bed in the hallway near a nursing station. Skinner and Heikamp didn't name her, but by location and description she was likely to have been Wilda McManus. The woman appeared unconscious and was taking occasional, labored breaths.

The sight and sound of her upset Heikamp. His mother had breathed like that for hours before she died the previous year. Skinner explained that it was agonal breathing, assuring him that patients like that had so little brain function they didn't experience pain.

It looked to Skinner like Pou was trying to get the woman's IV to work, toggling the valve and readjusting the catheter in her vein. Unsuccessful, she took a syringe and tried to inject medicine into the woman's thigh.

Skinner asked to speak with Pou privately, away from Heikamp and the nurse. "I told her that I thought this patient was still living and that we should evacuate this patient. And that I would like to go and get appropriate help; find someone to help us carry her."

Skinner's assistant Heikamp remembered Pou asking if one of them could go to the helipad and tell the doctor in charge that there was one more patient who needed to be evacuated. Heikamp left to do that.

Skinner went with Pou into the room of an African American female patient. Pou tried to get her IV working too, and asked Skinner if he thought the patient was still alive. She was, just barely. Skinner noticed a cardboard box filled with what appeared to be syringes, gloves, tubing, and several unopened medicine vials. Skinner picked one up to see what it was. Morphine.

Pou said she wanted to talk with a particular anesthesiologist before moving the female patient in the hallway. Skinner went downstairs with Pou and instead they found the chairman of surgical services, John Walsh. Walsh later recalled that Pou sat down beside him on a bench and put her head in her hands. She looked upset.

"What's wrong?" he asked. She mentioned something about a patient, or patients, dying and about someone, or some people, questioning her.

Walsh had known Pou for only about a year, but he thought of her fondly as a "medical loser," devoted to a fault to her patients. "I'm sure you did the right thing. It'll work itself out. It'll all turn out OK."

Skinner's name and description had come up in an interview Rider and several colleagues did with LifeCare nurse Cindy Chatelain, in November. She said a tall, thin, light-haired doctor she thought was named Skinner had appeared on the seventh floor with a short, stocky man on Thursday morning, when she was on her shift caring for the remaining nine patients. The doctor told her the situation was grave, that there were no more resources to get these patients out. "These little people," she remembered him saying, "were not going to make it" and were "Do Not Resuscitate." Chatelain had corrected him—at least one of them wasn't DNR, just extremely obese. The doctor said the helicopters couldn't carry patients of his weight, which was not generally true (although some Acadian air ambulances had stretchers that could hold only four hundred pounds, just over his weight). "He said that what was going to have to happen was that the law of nature would take over. Only the strong could survive this. Um, he told me that, um, you know that Mother Nature's course would have to be hastened."

Rider didn't ask Skinner about the Mother Nature comment. It was difficult to tell whether Nurse Chatelain had identified the right doctor. Years later in an interview, Skinner would say the nurse was not referring to him. He did not recall having spoken with a LifeCare nurse on the seventh floor or having conveyed a message of that sort. He felt he would not have referred to patients as "little people" or said that Mother Nature's course would have to be hastened. It didn't sound at all like him.

Rider later learned Chatelain had a troubled history and had been put on probation by the nursing board shortly before the storm. Skinner fit the physical description Chatelain had provided, and he was head of the hospital's infection control committee. But Chatelain said he had introduced himself as "Dr. Skinner with the CDC," the federal infectious diseases center.

The interviews with hospital workers were full of such small, important, and maddening inconsistencies, memory's transmogrifications. Rider's job was as impossible as collecting fragments of a fractured mirror and then, somehow, inferring what image had once appeared there.

———

SUSAN MULDERICK had a sense of what the attorney general's investigators might ask at her interview with them in early January 2006. She knew there were things others had heard her say at the hospital that were being interpreted as suspicious or incriminating. She knew this from the copy of the secret search-warrant affidavit that had been sent to Tenet attorney Harry Rosenberg, which set out the allegations.

At the interview, a short investigator with dark blond hair asked Mulderick about her conversations with LifeCare employees the morning of Thursday, September 1, 2005.

"Did you make a statement to them to the effect that no living patients would be left behind?" Virginia Rider asked.

Mulderick said she might have. "I'm sure I said it to dozens of people," she said. Staff and family members were concerned they would never get out of the hospital, that they would die there. Many stopped her to ask whether and how they would ever get all the patients and themselves to safety.

"So, I was always trying to reinforce with everyone that we are all going. Everybody's going, every patient is going. We will get out of here." Mulderick said she viewed Anna Pou as the primary doctor on the second floor. She had several discussions with Pou on Thursday morning. "What was the substance of those discussions?" Rider asked.

"Um . . . One of those discussions had to do with um, asking her if some of these patients could be given something for, what I considered was their suffering, their anxiety, their pain." Mulderick said that Pou had agreed and said, "I'm not sure what to give them." That was when Mulderick had said she would ask Dr. Cook to talk with Pou, which Mulderick had done. Mulderick said she had not seen the medications being given. "I don't even know if she followed up on it. I just left it at that."

"Did you have any discussions with anybody regarding euthanasia of the patients?" Rider asked later.

"Specifically euthanizing patients? No."

"What about discussions of giving them palliative care that might result in their deaths?" Rider asked, and then clarified the question when Mulderick seemed to hesitate. "Something that would ease their pain, but might also speed up the dying process?"

"No," Mulderick said. "My discussions with, well, had to do with palliative care. Comfort patients, certainly not to speed up a process like that."

Mulderick's interview revealed that the idea of medicating patients at Memorial that Thursday came from her. She portrayed her intentions as having wanted to provide comfort. "You give them some Ativan or something," she offered as an example, to relax patients. However the prescriptions seized from the pharmacy during the search had shown that Ativan and other normal drugs for comfort were already being prescribed for these patients by Pou and other doctors throughout the disaster. The idea that Pou would need Cook to tell her about them made little sense.

Mulderick appeared extremely well prepared for her interview. But at least she presented herself as knowledgeable and involved in leading the response to the disaster. That wasn't the case for all of the "uppity-ups," as Butch Schafer referred to the hospital's major players. CEO René Goux, whom Rider and a colleague had interviewed in November, claimed to have known almost nothing about what had gone on in his hospital after the storm, even though he had stayed there the entire time. Months later, interviews with two of the CEO's fellow uppity-ups, Memorial CFO Curtis Dosch and Memorial COO Sean Fowler, stunned Schafer and Rider when the men casually mentioned that the cancer institute connected to Memorial via sky bridges had a working generator and electricity throughout the disaster. Hospital executives went there to make phone calls and coffee, and their interviews revealed something of the executive mind-set. "We sat there and watched TV for a little bit," Fowler said. Dosch described discovering that the place had power and going back to get the rabbit-ear antenna. "I'm feeling pretty good, 'cause I got a fan, I got a recliner, and I got TV, and I rummaged around and found a can of chicken noodle soup." He said he hooked up a microwave and had a hot meal. "I want to tell you, it tasted pretty good!"

Dosch had not kept all the goodies for himself. He made coffee for the nurses and brought the fans to the hospital's second-floor lobby, where they could be powered by the small generators and positioned to blow on patients. The investigators were left to wonder why, however, the patients weren't lifted onto gurneys and rolled into the more comfortable cancer center (or to air-conditioned cars and trucks).

Dosch had recently been promoted to interim CEO of Memorial in advance of its reopening. He spoke benignly to Schafer and Rider about Susan Mulderick's expression of concern regarding the patients' ability to survive. Mulderick had told him that they were being made comfortable, he said. Schafer and Rider did not press him hard for specifics, and Dosch did not volunteer that he had seen a doctor inject a patient on the second floor, had asked CEO Goux if he knew what was happening, or had seen the chief nursing officer crying.

In fact, until Dosch returned home one day to find two CNN employees on his porch, he hadn't realized "what a big deal it might become," he'd later say. Dosch had confronted Susan Mulderick after the disaster, and she had denied having spoken of medicating the patients. People from Memorial shunned conversation about the events of Thursday, September 1, and he felt they were trying to protect themselves. He wondered whether the patients might have lived if they had gotten out. And was it someone else's right to decide for them that they wouldn't make it?

Dosch was not the only person to notice and be disturbed by a general refusal to acknowledge and discuss what had occurred. Nurses referred to it as a Code of Silence, which was adopted almost immediately upon departure from the hospital. "We're not talking about it. . . . And by the way, nothing happened," was how one would describe it. Circle the wagons. Don't get anyone in trouble.

Whereas the LifeCare attorneys had eventually advised their clients to be open in their interviews about what happened, even to volunteer facts that the investigators might not know or ask about, other lawyers had a different take on the wisdom of being more forthcoming than the law required.

Pou's attorney called another lawyer involved in the events and said, as the other lawyer would remember it: "It's in nobody's interest for these things to see the light of day."

———

THE INVESTIGATORS turned increasingly to the corporation that owned the hospital and employed these executives. What had Pou meant when she had allegedly told Therese Mendez that "the decision had been made" to give lethal doses to the patients? Who was behind that? Rider and Schafer had not yet interviewed anybody who would admit to being a decision maker.

The grudging cooperation of Tenet's attorneys, the delays, and the failure to produce certain pieces of potential evidence raised Schafer's suspicions in particular. Tenet attorneys insisted that copies of all medical records in the company's possession had been provided to the attorney general's office, but Schafer and Rider believed some were still missing.

Tenet had also refused to allow LifeCare representatives to enter the hospital in the first weeks after the storm. In the interim, certain patient records, computer servers, and computer tapes had gone missing and Life-Care nurses' lockers were cut open, their property removed. LifeCare had filed a restraining order and injunction against Tenet seeking the return of the materials.

Schafer's suspicions had only grown stronger as interviewees intimated that when a "decision was made" about giving the injections, it appeared to have come from a higher place. He wondered whether Tenet corporate officials might have been aware of or even issued an order to euthanize the sickest patients and quickly clear the remaining workers on Thursday, September 1, to protect them from the feared, rampaging mobs, or, as far-fetched as it sounded, even to avoid having to pay for another day of staff overtime and leased helicopters. After all, this was a corporation that had, the year before Katrina, paid nearly $400 million to settle claims that doctors at one of its hospitals performed unnecessary heart surgeries and procedures on healthy patients. That didn't speak well of corporate ethics.

Higher-ups in the Medicaid Fraud Control Unit did not encourage Rider to go to Tenet's corporate headquarters in Dallas to interview officials there. At least, not now. One of the most important interviews she could do in Dallas was with Steven Campanini, Tenet's media chief, who had received Pou's urgent call for advice days after she left Memorial and spoken with her extensively. Pou's attorney, Rick Simmons, had gone to court to block the attorney general's staff from interviewing Campanini. Because Tenet's attorney, Audrey Andrews, had been involved in some of the phone conversations, and she did not immediately warn Pou that she did not represent her, Simmons argued, all the information should be protected as attorney-client privileged and confidential. Campanini could not speak to it.

Assistant Attorney General Schafer fought back against Simmons's motion, arguing that Pou couldn't have possibly thought a Tenet lawyer represented her. The evidence was right there in the employment contract she had inked a year before the storm. While the hospital had supported her recruitment and first year's salary, she was an employee of Louisiana State University—not Memorial, not Tenet.

A ruling by the district court pleased neither side, and the motion was now with the Louisiana Supreme Court on expedited appeal. Lawyers for Dr. John Thiele and nurse Cheri Landry also asked Schafer to await the court's decision before seeking to learn what their clients had told Tenet personnel. As there was no official case against Pou yet, and perhaps because both sides wished to avoid alerting the media to the dispute, the motion was entitled "IN RE: A MATTER OF AN OFFENSE UNDER INVESTIGATION."

Rider and Schafer wanted to interview others at Tenet headquarters, including those who had staffed the hastily established command center and communicated for some time by e-mail and cell phone with the panicked Memorial employees as the waters rose. But higher officials at the AG's office told Schafer that it would probably be a waste of time now that the company was lawyered-up—if they went to Dallas, they would presumably only get to speak with lawyers. And besides, Tenet's attorneys had said they would fully cooperate and send whatever materials were requested.

An observer might have wondered whether politics and high-level personal relationships were at play in lightening the pressure on the corporation. "Tenet is a major health-care provider in our state and has contributed to campaigns of most of our federal elected officials," a spokesman for US senator Mary Landrieu of Louisiana was quoted as saying in the *Baton Rouge Advocate* in March. The quote seemed aimed at reassuring the company that it was valued in Louisiana. A minor group of dissident Tenet shareholders led by a doctor with a personal grudge hoped, the article reported, to pressure the company to reform. Toward that end, the group was demanding that Senator Landrieu donate to charity the $29,000 she had received from Tenet in campaign contributions. The shareholders cited the AG's investigation of events at Memorial as evidence against a company with a trail of fraud and abuse suits and settlements. The group pointed out that Landrieu's aunt had received nearly a million dollars for lobbying on behalf of the company. Tenet's Steven Campanini was quoted in the article saying that the company was not a target of the AG's investigation. "Euthanasia is never permissible under any circumstances."

The senator's spokesperson said she would not be giving up the contributions.

Schafer tacked up the article in his office. He didn't honestly think that Senator Landrieu had called Attorney General Foti to protect Tenet, but seeing something in the news that backed his cynical view of the company made him giddy.

———

THE NEWS MEDIA continued to fan public interest in the story. CNN reporter Drew Griffin and producer Kathleen Johnson extracted morsels of information from an array of sources and broadcast a new story on the investigation every few weeks, garnishing tiny discoveries

("More than one medical professional is under scrutiny as a possible person of interest"; "Dr. Cyril Wecht [. . .] has been hired as a consultant") with footage from earlier interviews.

Angela McManus followed the news closely from temporary lodgings in Baton Rouge, many miles away from her flooded family home. McManus made sure her new phone number was listed. She wanted investigators and reporters to be able to find her to talk about her mother, Wilda.

"I don't know what God's will is," she told National Public Radio's Carrie Kahn in a story that aired late that winter. "I don't know when He was calling her home. If He did in fact do it, OK. But if man decided that, I want to know that. My family needs peace about that."

McManus's siblings had retained a lawyer to help them find answers. The family members of several other deceased patients did too. Many family members wrote to the attorney general's office seeking information. Some complained that coroner Frank Minyard had not responded to requests to release death certificates needed for successions. When the certificates were received, the cause of death was often marked "pending investigation," leaving open the possibility that insurance company payouts would be denied.

On NPR, Kahn gave the public the first details of the case being built against Anna Pou. A male actor read aloud Virginia Rider's words from a leaked copy of the previous October's search-warrant affidavit. "Dr. Pou informed them that it had been decided that they were going to administer lethal doses to the LifeCare patients."

In the broadcast, Kahn said attorney Rick Simmons was asked if Pou had euthanized any patients. "Dr. Pou did not engage in any criminal actions," he told NPR.

Reaction to the story was swift. The anti-euthanasia group Not Dead Yet issued a statement full of outraged speculation: "The only way the staff could evacuate was if they could report there were no more living patients to take care of. This was not about compassion or mercy. It was about throwing someone else over the side of the lifeboat in order to save themselves."

———

ALTHOUGH THE NPR story laid out the version of events Rider had pieced together, she was furious that her affidavit, with the names of victims and witnesses, had leaked. She was determined to find the source. The reporter had allegedly told someone it came from Tenet. Rider knew that Tenet attorney Harry Rosenberg had received the search-warrant materials by order of court the previous October, agreeing that he would keep them confidential. Rider served him with a subpoena commanding him to identify everyone to whom he had disclosed the information. Then she was told by her superiors to back off. Perhaps they were protecting a friend. Or perhaps the leak had come from the attorney general's side.

———

ON MEMORIAL DAY WEEKEND, workers raised white tents on the outdoor parking lot across Clara Street from Memorial's emergency room ramp and prepared a crawfish boil for former employees and staff. Servers dumped steaming piles of crustaceans before guests, who snapped them in half and tugged out their tails. Some doctors had returned to practice at their outpatient offices in the complex, and Tenet had announced plans to reopen the new surgery building where Anna Pou, Karen Wynn, and the intensive care nurses had tried to sleep the night Katrina struck. The main hospital, however, would remain closed. The music was upbeat, the faces downcast, even tearful. Dr. Horace Baltz saw it as an occasion for emotional closure. He came to bid colleagues and his forty-three-year career at the hospital good-bye. The clash of the festive and funereal reminded him of a wake, the darkened hospital lying corpselike before them.

Baltz didn't hear anyone speculate on what might have happened to the patients after the storm. Several partygoers did, however, excoriate the absent Dr. Bryant King in a way Baltz considered a racially prejudiced "verbal lynching," calling him untrustworthy, not a team player, and a troublemaker for having spoken out on CNN. King had moved out of the state after the uproar began against him.

Baltz departed without thanking his hosts. The next month, Tenet announced intentions to sell Memorial Medical Center and what remained of its other hospitals in the region.

———

AS THE SPRING months passed, Rider and Schafer found little of significance to add to the evidence against Pou for the LifeCare deaths on the seventh floor or against nurses Cheri Landry and Lori Budo, whom they believed had accompanied Pou. When would the agents be allowed to make arrests? "Not now," they were told, without explanation.

In June, Schafer received a letter from a lawyer for the family of John Russell, the LifeCare patient whom Gina Isbell had tried to save by hand-ventilating him as he was carried downstairs after the power failed. She had stood by his body after he died and taken him to the chapel, the first patient placed there and blessed by Father Marse. The lawyer was writing to Schafer because—nearly a year later—the woman to whom Russell had been married for forty-two years and her daughter had learned none of this. They had received a death certificate from the coroner's office, but had not been given any conclusive proof as to what date Russell died and how he died. "He appeared to be in relatively good health and lucid shortly before the Hurricane," the lawyer wrote. "That is when they last saw him. I attempted to contact the Coroner's Office in New Orleans and my call was not answered." The death certificate marked "pending investigation," listing no cause of death, made them worry, made them think that maybe the attorney general was right and patients at Memorial had been injected.

The urge to learn what had become of a loved one who perished in a large disaster or crisis was so essentially human that it had led to the development of a special field of DNA identification focused on mass casualties. The techniques drew from anthropology, forensics, molecular biology, genetics, and computer science. They had been applied, at great cost, to the jumbled bones from mass graves in Bosnia-Herzegovina; waterlogged corpses from the beaches of post-tsunami Phuket, Thailand; and the fragments—sifted through for years—from Ground Zero in New York City. A DNA sample from Russell's left tibia had been taken to help confirm the identity of his body. Unique skin marks were also noted, and a skull and crossbones tattoo on Russell's left arm seemed to have been wryly placed for the occasion. It said: AS YOU ARE I WAS. AS I AM YOU WILL BE.

It had taken Russell's widow three weeks to locate his body, and she was never able to see it because it was too badly decomposed. It was held for investigation and released to a funeral home well over two months after the storm. Russell's widow felt the need to know more. Although Schafer didn't know it, she had suffered from severe post-traumatic stress disorder after the storm, imagining her husband suffering in the heat. She was not aware that he had died before the worst of the ordeal recounted in the news. Schafer called the attorney the very next day and made arrangements to get Russell's medical records to him.

Also in June, Schafer and Rider interviewed the nursing director in charge of women's and infants' services at Memorial, Marirose Bernard. She described the successful transfer of the neonates the first day the waters rose. After this, she said she had taken charge of organizing two-hour nursing shifts to care for the adult patients staged on the second floor. She had seen patients die in the heat, and had given doses of the sedative Ativan to the one who looked uncomfortable and was crying out, "Mama."

She denied hearing anyone talk about euthanasia, and Rider and Schafer did not press her on this. She said when she had left Memorial on Thursday afternoon with other nurses, about fifteen "pretty sick, pretty sick, awful" patients remained on the second floor under the care of Drs. Pou and Thiele and several nurses. She said she left in a boat, was allowed to take her cat, and hoped to find family members who had departed the previous day and were stuck in the New Orleans Convention Center. Instead, she spent the night on the I-10 cloverleaf, huddled with other staff "because our lives were being threatened."

Butch Schafer had a flash of memory. "Were you interviewed by a news . . . ?"

She said she had been interviewed by a Fox News correspondent. "She says, 'Why did you stay, if you had the choice of being in your bed? Why did you stay?' I said, 'Because I am a nurse.'"

"You are the one," Schafer said.

"I said I am a nurse, and that is what nurses do."

Bernard was the one Schafer had been quoting ever since he was in Atlanta with his family and saw her interview after his daughter's death. Bernard had evoked memories of his mama, a dedicated, white-capped nurse in the 1940s. "You are the one. I remember it now. Absolutely."

"We did the best we could," Bernard said. Schafer walked around the table and asked her lawyer for permission to hug her. The lawyer said it was up to his client. The nurse stood up, and they embraced.

———

LATE JUNE BROUGHT a major development in the case Rider and Schafer were assembling against Pou. The Louisiana Supreme Court had, in May, denied the investigators access to anything Pou had told Tenet attorney Audrey Andrews prior to Andrews informing her she was exclusively Tenet's attorney. However anything Pou said subsequently to Andrews or Tenet's media relations chief was fair game. Rider and Schafer quickly moved to interview the two Tenet employees, and Tenet offered to make them available, but Pou's attorney, Rick Simmons, filed new motions in court attempting to block them.

Although he wasn't required to do so, Schafer agreed to a hearing to determine the answer to a single question: at exactly what point in the conversation had the Tenet lawyer informed Pou that she was not Pou's attorney? Schafer's gentlemanly decision proved to be a critical mistake. He had been outfoxed. Simmons used the hearing to argue for broader protections against disclosure of what Pou had said. On June 26, the lower court ruled that anything Pou had discussed prior to being notified, even if Pou revealed it again in the later conversations, was protected. The Tenet lawyer's eight pages of notes on the conversation would, consequently, be protected too.

Schafer planned to appeal this decision on behalf of the attorney general's office, but for now, the decision frustrated Rider and Schafer's efforts to get key evidence of Pou's unguarded conversation with the Tenet employees. After months of waiting, it seemed that their case would have to go forward without the information.

One weekday afternoon in July, several weeks after the court's decision, Rider received a call from her chief, telling her the arrests of Anna Pou, Cheri Landry, and Lori Budo could take place the next week. The timing disappointed her. She was at last heading to Dallas to interview a Tenet official and then planned to fly to Las Vegas to take a Certified Forensic Accountant exam. She'd had to postpone the test once to search the hospital the previous year.

She had already written up a draft arrest warrant. She offered to take it down to the courthouse on Friday before she left town. Another special agent could then execute it and make the arrests.

No, she was told. Attorney General Foti wants *you* to execute the warrant.

She said she could still take the affidavit to the court on Friday, get it signed before her trip, and then return on the red-eye flight from Las

Vegas, arriving in New Orleans by ten thirty a.m. the following Thursday. Someone could pick her up at the airport and they could execute the warrant. Rider assumed arrangements would be made with Pou's lawyer for Pou to turn herself in and be booked. This was, most of the time, the way things were done, particularly when the target was a professional not deemed a flight risk.

"You can't get the warrant signed early."

Rider wondered why. Her boss directed her to get the warrant signed at six p.m. on Monday. She was to execute it the same day, after the ten o'clock news. She would have to cancel her trips. These would be surprise arrests. The director's job was on the line if the "targets" were lost.

That weekend, Rider began surveillance on Anna Pou, Cheri Landry, and Lori Budo.

ANNA POU HAD FINALLY and quietly returned to performing surgery. Months had passed since her name was broadcast, and little seemed to be happening with the investigation at the attorney general's office, although rumor had it something might soon emerge.

James O'Bryant, her patient before Katrina, had developed facial pain again. A scan showed the cancer had grown back behind his left eye and needed to be removed. He said he wasn't sure he wanted to undergo another extensive operation. The chairman of Pou's department, Dr. Dan Nuss, believed he could remove the whole tumor, and O'Bryant decided to let him try. Pou would work alongside Nuss to reconstruct O'Bryant's face.

The operation took place on Thursday, July 6. The surgeons painstakingly removed bits of tissue, sending them for a rough initial check under a microscope for cancer cells before cutting deeper. Over many hours, they pursued the tumor's tentacles only to discover that it had invaded a bone around a previously removed blood vessel. The scan had not shown this. To get all the cancer, they would need to open O'Bryant's skull, something they felt he could not withstand. Twenty hours into the operation, they closed his face as best as possible and left part of the tumor inside him.

A nurse walked into O'Bryant's room after the operation. "Oh my God," she said. "What do they expect me to do with this?"

"Please just act like you know what the hell you're doing," O'Bryant's wife, Brenda, said. "He's frightened to death."

Patients with shocking facial deformities were new to Our Lady of the Lake Regional Medical Center, a Franciscan-run hospital in Baton Rouge. Pou and her Louisiana State University head and neck surgery colleagues were operating there now because the New Orleans hospitals where their department had been based had not reopened.

After Pou learned from Brenda O'Bryant about how the nurses were treating James, she called a meeting with the staff members. They crowded into a room with a computer, and Pou showed them step-by-step what procedures had been done and how James had reached his current condition. She explained why following every last detail of her care instructions was so important to helping the fragile tissues of his reconstructed face heal.

Pou worried about O'Bryant's recovery. She posted signs in the intensive care unit warning anyone caring for him not to put pressure on the left side of his face, head, neck, shoulder, or arm.

FRIDAY, JULY 14, 2006

DEPARTMENT CHAIRMAN NUSS had friends in high places. Through him, Pou and her attorney, Rick Simmons, learned that Foti was likely to release the findings of his investigation, and they would not be good for Pou. Someone from the attorney general's office called the department asking for Pou's address, a worrisome development.

On Friday afternoon, Simmons phoned the attorney general's office. "Are you going to arrest my client?" he asked. "No, not right now," prosecutor Butch Schafer said, somewhat honestly. "We can self-surrender," Simmons reminded him. They had discussed this before. Simmons would deliver Pou to be booked in order to avoid the indignity of a surprise arrest. Attorneys for Lori Budo and Cheri Landry had also expressed a preference for self-surrender. Simmons assumed they all had a deal.

Simmons asked Schafer to give him a call so he could bring Pou in and avoid a "perp walk." He didn't want news crews tipped off, snapping photographs of his client being led to jail in handcuffs. Schafer assured him that wasn't going to happen.

Simmons placed a few other phone calls and told Pou to keep her surgery schedule. Pou had plans to spend a long weekend off in New Orleans with her mother. She gave that up, instead picking up her mom and driving the seventy-five miles back to the capital where Pou now stayed part-time at a home she did not own. Throughout the weekend, she checked on O'Bryant in the ICU, spoke with his nurses, and sat with Brenda, consoling her.

SUNDAY, JULY 16, 2006

THE ARREST TEAMS had printed out Yahoo! maps on Friday and checked their targets' work schedules. On Sunday afternoon they met to learn the surveillance plan. Pairs of agents began watching Anna Pou, Lori Budo, and Cheri Landry in four-hour shifts, following them between their homes and worksites. They were instructed to "maintain visual" and know the women's whereabouts at all times in preparation for the planned arrests of all three women on Monday.

Anna Pou's cell phone rang on Sunday evening. It was Brenda O'Bryant calling about James. Hours earlier at the hospital, a doctor in training had tugged at what he thought was a stitch that needed to be removed. He had in fact torn away part of a scab, but James had seemed all right. He was discharged as planned and the couple drove two hours home to Bogalusa, a paper mill town on the Pearl River at the Louisiana-Mississippi border. In 1995, a chemical accident in Bogalusa poisoned thousands and led to a class action lawsuit that was settled months before Hurricane Katrina. Brenda figured that the orange cloud that had hovered over the city for several days had caused James's cancer.

At around seven thirty p.m., Brenda noticed blood pooling beneath James's face and called Pou, who instructed her to put something cold on his wound and head to the nearest emergency room. Pou asked to speak with the ER doctor on Brenda's cell phone. At first he refused to take the call. Brenda insisted and handed him her phone. Pou asked him to check several things. He seemed annoyed and gave the phone back to Brenda.

Pou kept Brenda on the line, even when a security guard escorted her out of the ER for violating the hospital's no-cell-phone policy. Pou convinced her not to hang up. "I need to know what's going on," she said.

The bleeding seemed to have stopped. If it started again, it could be catastrophic. Pou told Brenda to make sure James was observed for at least an hour in the ER, then taken back to Our Lady of the Lake in Baton Rouge by car or ambulance. "I can't do anything without seeing him," Pou said. "You've got to bring him back here."

James was experiencing more pain. He began praying aloud. Then his wound started gushing.

The ER doctor put a stitch in his face to stop the bleeding. It seemed to work, but Pou wasn't yet comfortable letting Brenda drive James to Baton Rouge. Blood might be gathering in a confined space beneath the surface, a hematoma, its pressure growing.

James said his pain was getting worse. The doctor didn't seem to believe him. He acted as if James were an addict seeking narcotics.

Then James's face erupted. The staff rushed him into an ambulance. He was bleeding so profusely that on the way to Baton Rouge, they transfused him with two units of blood.

Pou prepared the operating room. She called her chairman, Dan Nuss, telling him he had to come in on a Sunday night. The surgical nurses arrived, and the staff scrubbed their hands and arms and donned sterile gowns and gloves. They operated on O'Bryant through the night.

THE SAME NIGHT, Attorney General Foti met by speakerphone with agents and prosecutors to go over the arrest plan for Monday. One prosecutor suggested upping the charges from second- to first-degree murder. Murdering with the specific intent to kill someone older than sixty-five, or more than one person of any age, fit the state's definition of the more serious crime.

"No!" Foti's public information director Kris Wartelle nearly shouted. The idea of prosecuting Katrina health professionals for first-degree murder was crazy. Merely investigating them for second-degree murder had provoked angry letters from the public. A second-degree murder conviction would carry a lifetime sentence of hard labor without parole in Louisiana. The only thing to gain from first-degree charges was the option to pursue the death penalty.

One attorney on the call suggested dialing down the charges to man-slaughter; murders committed in "sudden passion" with loss of self-control after a provocation, or in cases where there was no intent to kill, carried a maximum sentence of forty years' imprisonment. The voices advocating for second-degree murder prevailed.

Wartelle sensed that sending agents out to arrest the women was a terrible idea from a PR standpoint. She gave Attorney General Foti advice on how to avoid media attention during the arrests, so the television cameras did not catch the women in a perp walk and broadcast the footage on the popular "Live at Five" evening or ten o'clock nightly television news. She asked him to slow down, to go over with her the questions he might face at a press conference after the arrests. He did not.

Prosecutor Butch Schafer and Special Agent Virginia Rider also disliked the idea of surprise arrests. Rider bore responsibility for organizing them, and Schafer knew she was not enthusiastic about slapping hand-cuffs onto suspects' wrists. Schafer made his opinion known in the strongest possible terms within the attorney general's office. Letting people turn themselves in was done every day; it hadn't occurred to Schafer these arrests would go any other way. He knew the women's attorneys expected they would be allowed to deliver their clients to be booked. He had given them his word he would contact them if their clients were going to be arrested, and a Southern gentleman didn't violate a gentleman's promise. But it was the attorney general who had the power to make this decision. Perhaps he wanted to use the case to establish his strength as a prosecutor after spending three decades as a sheriff.

Rider often lay awake the night before an arrest, wondering if what she was about to do was wrong. Whether by surprise or self-surrender, she knew it would change the suspect's life forever. In this case, evidence to warrant the arrests before a judge had been present for months. It was time for justice to advance.

Schafer did not wrestle with his conscience over prosecuting the women. Given what he knew about what happened at Memorial, he felt, absolutely, it was right.

MONDAY, JULY 17, 2006

ANNA POU and Dan Nuss succeeded in closing James O'Bryant's facial defect after operating all Sunday night. They transfused him with more blood to replace what he had lost.

Pou tried to calm Brenda, who was furious at the ER doctor. "It's not his fault that it started bleeding," Pou said. "The hematoma may have happened anyway." If James hadn't stopped at that emergency room, the crisis might have occurred in their car on the way to Baton Rouge. "He could have died then," Pou said. "Things happen for a reason. We just have to believe that God put you there and that's where you needed to be at that time."

When James was settled in the intensive care unit to recover from surgery on Monday morning, Pou left for the other hospital where she worked. She had not slept, and she had another long operation on her schedule.

⸻

THAT AFTERNOON, Virginia Rider drove to New Orleans with affidavits and warrants of arrest for Anna Pou, Cheri Landry, and Lori Budo.

Rider's affidavit was a concise and potent narrative of the alleged crimes, concatenating the salient evidence she had gathered. It drew mainly from interviews with the four initial LifeCare witnesses: Diane Robichaux, Therese Mendez, Kristy Johnson, and Steven Harris. They had heard from Susan Mulderick that the LifeCare patients weren't expected to make it out, that staff members were "not going to leave any living patients behind," and that the LifeCare leaders needed to talk with Dr. Pou. Dr. Pou had appeared on the seventh floor and told Mendez that the patients would be given a "lethal dose" and LifeCare staff should leave. Pou was told that one of the patients was aware but weighed 380 pounds. She asked for him to be sedated, but the LifeCare staff refused. Steven Harris had given Pou morphine, Versed, and injection supplies, and Kristy Johnson had shown Pou and two Memorial nurses to the patients' rooms, watching a nurse, later identified as Lori Budo, inject Rose Savoie, who responded, "That burns." Toxicology tests revealed morphine and midazolam in the four patients named in the affidavit. They included Emmett Everett, Rose Savoie, and two other LifeCare patients from the seventh floor for whom toxicology results had first become available and whose cases were reviewed by pathologist Cyril Wecht. Ireatha Watson, age eighty-nine, who had dementia, had been treated for gangrenous toes; and Hollis Alford, age sixty-six, who had a history of schizophrenia, was gravely ill from a blood infection. Wecht deemed all four to have died from a lethal amount of the drugs. Criminal District Court Judge Calvin Johnson asked Rider a few questions and signed the arrest warrants at about six p.m. They alleged that the women had violated the state's second-degree murder statute by intentionally killing the four patients.

Rider gave the warrants for nurses Cheri Landry and Lori Budo to the leaders of their arrest teams in New Orleans. She drove back to Baton Rouge, and at about eight thirty in the evening had a rendezvous with other agents at a shopping center about a mile from Anna Pou's Baton Rouge home to coordinate final details.

They reached Pou's house around nine p.m. Rider walked to the door with a male colleague. She wore body armor and a gun that weighed down the bottoms of her pantsuit, pinned at the waist, a reminder of the weight she had lost in recent months of hard work and marital problems; she had not had time to go shopping for new clothes.

Rider's colleague knocked. Moments later, a woman's voice asked who was there. Pou opened the door and stood without shoes in rumpled surgical scrubs.

Rider reintroduced herself. Seven months had passed since they had met one another while touring Memorial. The agents told Pou she was being arrested and several entered the house. Pou was alone. They asked if she had any weapons and patted her down. Pou asked permission to change into fresh scrubs. Rider agreed and followed Pou into her bedroom with another female agent. They watched as the short, compact woman changed, brushed her teeth, and put on deodorant in the attached bathroom.

"What about my patients?" Pou asked. She told the officers she couldn't leave home because she was awaiting a stat laboratory result. Rider asked which doctor covered her patients when she was not available and allowed her to phone him. "I can't tell you what's going on," Pou told the doctor. She asked him to check the calcium level on one of her patients, and she described the other issues she needed him to track. "Please cancel all my surgeries this week."

Pou was told to take off any jewelry and bring only her driver's license with her to the prison. She said she wasn't wearing jewelry, and her driver's license was in her bag. Rider told her not to reach into the bag, to pour its contents out instead. She watched while Pou did this and removed what appeared to be her wallet.

Rider read Pou her rights. Pou signed "Anna Maria Pou" on a form indicating she understood them, and she initialed the line "No" where it asked if she was willing to answer questions without her lawyer. Then Rider slipped a pair of handcuffs over Pou's hands, checking, as she had learned in police academy, for a space of two fingers' width between the metal and Pou's wrists for comfort before double-locking the cuffs.

Rider escorted Pou to the backseat of the car and made sure she did not hit her head as she entered. With the help of a colleague, Rider fastened Pou's seat belt.

They drove thirteen miles, with other agents following them, to the East Baton Rouge Parish Prison in Scotlandville, where Rider told Pou she would be booked as a fugitive. The sound of this concerned Pou, whose brother was a federal fugitive. Rider explained that it didn't mean Pou was running from the law, only that she was being picked up in East Baton Rouge on a warrant from another parish.

At the prison Pou was booked, fingerprinted, and photographed. It was nearly ten thirty p.m. She looked straight into the camera with wide eyes, questioning brows, and lips closed and downturned like a child stunned by an unjust punishment. It was a look that communicated shock and devastation. It was an accusatory look. It was a look that asked: *How could you?*

———

HER HANDS that had just performed surgery were being cuffed again and hooked to a chain attached to a loop at the front of a belt at her waist. Rider and a male agent escorted her back to the car. The male agent asked if she was OK and offered her a water bottle, opening it for her. She found she could drink from it while shackled.

Small things made her grateful. They didn't cuff her behind her back for the ninety-mile journey. "I don't think you'd be comfortable going all that way with your hands behind your back like that," one of the officers said.

During the trip, Pou prayed quietly. She prayed for God to help her family get through this. The agents seemed courteous; they asked her several times if she was all right. One, after speaking with a colleague by phone, told her that her lawyer, Rick Simmons, had been notified and would meet them at the Orleans Parish Prison. They arrived just before midnight.

She had to go to the bathroom, but even this she was not free to do on her own. The short agent with the dirty-blond hair accompanied her. When Pou finished on the toilet, she asked for assistance. Virginia Rider helped Pou pull up her scrub pants.

Rick Simmons wasn't there yet. Pou was booked. It shocked her to read "PRINCIPAL TO SECOND DEGREE MURDER 4 COUNTS," handwritten on the booking form. She was made to sit for another photograph under a harsh overhead light. This time she looked into the distance, not meeting the camera's gaze. Assistant Attorney General Butch Schafer offered her his phone, and she chose to call her mother first, then her husband, Vince. Schafer kept her off to the side so she wouldn't be sent to a holding cell with other prisoners. She signed a property bond for $100,000 and was given a subpoena requiring her to return with that sum of money and her passport by Thursday. Simmons arrived, and Pou was released on her own recognizance forty-five minutes after being booked, after midnight on Tuesday, July 18.

Pou went to stay at her mother's house in New Orleans. After the arrest, her mother advised her to entrust herself to the Sacred Heart of Jesus. She told her to hope and to trust. Pou's husband, Vince Panepinto, told her how hurt he was for her. "I've watched you work so hard and sacrifice so much and always be there for everybody, not just patients," he said, Pou would later tell reporter Julie Scelfo. "It hurts me so much to see this happen to you of all people." On the morning after Pou's arrest, two friends arrived. They gave her a silver charm with the image of Our Lady of Prompt Succor, which was a statue of the Virgin Mary that had been sculpted in France and brought to an Ursuline convent in New Orleans in the early nineteenth century. Prayers to Our Lady of Prompt Succor were thought to result in quick intercession. Pou's friends told her to put on the medal, never remove it, and never underestimate the power of her family.

TUESDAY, JULY 18, 2006

VIRGINIA RIDER wore a light summer suit to the afternoon press conference at the attorney general's office in Baton Rouge. She went to stand, hands crossed before her, in a gaggle of tall male colleagues gathered in a conference room already abuzz with reporters. Butch Schafer walked in behind her wearing a polo shirt with a patch over his heart in the shape of the "Louisiana boot," the attorney general's office logo. He was the only man not in a dark suit and tie. He had stayed behind in New Orleans overnight to monitor the booking process and ensure the arrest paperwork was correct. He had only just walked back into the building in Baton Rouge. A riot of microphones was perched atop a podium emblazoned with the state seal and surrounded by flags. Attorney General Foti's media staff passed out copies of the arrest warrants in dark-blue folders and asked reporters to add their names to a sign-in sheet.

The gray-haired attorney general entered the room, ambled in front of Rider, and walked stiffly to the podium amid strobelike flashes and the clatter of camera shutters. "Afternoon, everybody," he began without notes, slowly scanning the room as he spoke.

"Memorial Hospital is a hospital in the city of New Orleans—a big hospital, been there a long time. Inside that hospital, they have another hospital called Lakeside. Lakeside has acute care patients."

"LifeCare," his spokeswoman, Kris Wartelle, whispered from a chair beside the podium. He halted, turned, and peered at her through rimless glasses. "LifeCare," she corrected him. He craned his neck to bring his ear closer to her, and she said the word a third time, a little louder. "LifeCare."

"Has acute care patients," he repeated, not acknowledging his mistake. "These were some of the people that it was alleged that they were killed by lethal injection."

Foti turned to his notes and announced the arrests the previous evening of Pou and two nurses, Cheri Landry and Lori Budo, for four counts of principal to second-degree murder. "'Principal' means that you assisted or participated with the act," he said, explaining later that it was not yet clear exactly who had injected which patient with morphine and what he called "mazdolome," a mispronunciation of the drug midazolam, or Versed. He held up two fingers. "Either one of them can kill you, but when you use *both* of them together it becomes a lethal cocktail that *guarantees* they are going to die." He paused, blinking, for emphasis.

The reporters recognized a good quote, a quote that telegraphed Foti's message succinctly and provocatively. The problem was that viewers with any medical training knew that it was false. The drug combination could indeed be fatal, but could also be used safely if given with care.

"We feel that they had abused their rights as medical professionals," Foti added, pointing out that the arrests had nothing to do with the other doctors and nurses who had cared for patients under the most adverse conditions. These three were different. "We're talking about people that pretended that maybe they were God."

He explained why his office had worked so hard on the case. "We are entrusted to look after the safety of our senior citizens, our children, people that need help.

"For those voices that cannot speak, we will speak." He thanked several members of the team by name, including lead case agent Virginia Rider.

Foti took questions. He asked the reporters to speak up because he had a head cold and his ears were blocked. When a reporter mentioned the word "euthanasia," he stopped her short.

"This is not euthanasia. This is plain-and-simple homicide," he said, careful to note that it was subject to being proved in court. "We have probable cause to say that this was homicide." Most of the reporters used the inflammatory quote without including the attorney general's caveats.

Foti emphasized that the women gave the injections just as helicopters and boats were emptying the hospital. "During all this time, there were people getting out of there," he said, placing his hands in front of him as if holding the scene. "Do not all of us deserve the best chance we have to live?" he asked.

Foti warned that more counts might be brought against the women. "This case is by no means finished." Other health-care workers were still being investigated. "I would probably say there will be more arrests," he said.

"I want to say that this is an allegation. Every person, under our Constitution, has a right to trial and is presumed to be innocent." Now that the three women had been arrested, prosecuting them was up to Orleans Parish district attorney Eddie Jordan and, if he chose to pursue indictments for murder, a grand jury.

"Thank you very much. I appreciate your indulgence," Foti concluded, leaving the podium after thirty minutes.

⌒

LATER IN THE AFTERNOON, Rick Simmons sat before a smaller cluster of microphones at a conference table in his high-rise office in a New Orleans suburb. Although there had been no perp walk,

Simmons accused Foti of arresting the three women to get mug shots for a "media event" that would bolster his reputation. Law enforcement officials would be better used "patrolling the streets of New Orleans," Simmons sneered.

He emphasized there had been no formal charges against Anna Pou and that the power to prosecute rested not with Foti but with the office of Orleans Parish district attorney Eddie Jordan. "Mr. Jordan has agreed to my request to be able to meet with him and present any evidence we might wish to present," he said, noting that while that was unusual, this was not a usual case. "I certainly intend to try to dissuade him from taking any action."

Simmons held up a copy of the affidavit. "It's just a piece of paper with allegations on it," he said. "Like every piece of paper, it has two sides."

He leaned on his forearms toward the microphones. "There's no motive here"—he shook his head—"and there's no homicide."

He spoke of the deteriorating conditions at Memorial.

"It sounds as if you're saying there were extenuating circumstances," one reporter said.

"Oh, by all means. More than just extenuating. I think there were circumstances tantamount to a defense."

Simmons explained that twenty elderly LifeCare patients had been moved from Chalmette in St. Bernard Parish to higher ground at Memorial before the storm, creating a concentration of acutely ill patients with what he called Relocation Stress Syndrome. "It's a phenomenon, that people in elderly positions, if you move them around a lot, they get disoriented, it creates more problems, not to mention your medication problems, et cetera, et cetera." As evidence, he said, "a lot" of the patients who had left Memorial alive had since died (at least six, he would later say in another forum).

Some reporters seemed interested; others tried to keep Simmons on point. "Is your client innocent?" one had asked earlier in the conference.

"Yes. No doubt. Absolutely."

"Well, was there euthanasia if there wasn't homicide?"

Simmons refused to answer. "There's no criminal misconduct. That's, I mean, I hate to start using the definitions other people use, 'cause it's used for so many contexts of end-of-life issues and things like that, so. There's no criminal conduct."

"Were people injected with morphine and other drugs?"

"Again, I have to get into the facts of the affidavit and talk about it." He shook his head. "There are circumstances in which we will present our side of the case of what happened and that's all I can say at this point."

"Who are you guys blaming? Do you feel abandoned by the state?"

"Yes. If you look at what happened on Wednesday to Thursday when a lot of these events occurred, the state of Louisiana *abandoned* the hospitals," he said, lacing his words with a tone of acid disgust. "Where was the state of Louisiana on September first? It wasn't at Memorial Hospital, I can tell you that!"

He defended Tenet, with whose lawyers he was cooperating, saying the hospital company had rescued patients from Memorial and the state had not.

———

THE ISSUE of larger responsibility and blame, regardless of whether it would be admissible in a court of law, was on many people's minds. Individual decisions at the hospital had occurred in a context of failures of every sort. Over the eleven months since the storm, government agencies, private organizations, and journalists had churned out reports that analyzed and found fault with actions and inaction at nearly every level of every system. There were echoes of the 1920s, with advance warnings unheeded, investments not made, and aid being turned away. At least this time, some of the officials pointing fingers appeared to be pointing at themselves.

Why had the city flooded? A bad storm. The loss of a wetlands buffer.

Most of all, around New Orleans, the levee and flood control system—increasingly federalized after the 1927 Mississippi River floods and managed by the US Army Corps of Engineers—was grievously and predictably faulty. The failure to address its known weaknesses had saved money in the short term and now appeared outrageous.

Why, in the end, had more than a thousand died immediately in New Orleans—many of them in medical facilities, and many others poor and elderly—and an unknown number of others suffered and died in the aftermath due to stress and disruption of health care? So many reasons. The mayor's delayed evacuation order. The lack of buses and drivers to move people out of town who had no cars of their own. Stubborn decisions to stay by people with the means to leave. Uncoordinated rescue efforts. Confusion and turf battles between different agencies and levels of government. Poor communications, not interoperable. Hospitals and nursing homes that didn't evacuate before the storm and had not invested in backup power systems and backup water systems robust enough to withstand a prolonged emergency. Fears of violence interrupting rescues. It soon became clear that the fear of violence outweighed the actual violence, and that fear itself had compounded tragedy, as when first responders, including medical workers at the Superdome, were instructed to abandon their posts and their patients out of concern for their safety. "Most of the worst crimes reported at the time never happened," *Times-Picayune* reporters asserted in an investigative story, part of a group that won a Pulitzer Prize.

Although real and troubling lawlessness and several murders and violent crimes occurred, rumors of homicidal gangs and "zombies" that had swirled from WWL to the rescue boat pilots to the halls of Memorial were revealed as overblown. Looters were sometimes foragers, searching for food and water. Gunshots assumed to have been aimed at rescuers may have been gunshots aimed, however misguidedly, at alerting those rescuers to the presence of desperate survivors. In the wake of the rumors, journalists began uncovering real and troubling evidence of several white vigilante attacks on unarmed black men after the storm, and of police misconduct, questionable shootings, and a cover-up.

Underlying the official response to the crisis was a lack of situational awareness—a view of the larger picture of what was happening and what needed to be done.

All of this had occurred against the backdrop of the knowledge, for years, that exactly such a scenario could occur. The *Times-Picayune* had written about it. The Hurricane Pam exercises had modeled it.

The hospital was a microcosm of these larger failures, with compromised physical infrastructure, compromised operating systems, and compromised individuals. And also instances of heroism.

The scenario was familiar to every student of mass disasters around the world. Systems always failed. The official response was always unconscionably slow. Coordination and communication were particularly bad. These were truths Americans had come to accept about other people's disasters. It was shocking to see the scenario play out at home.

Life and death in the critical first hours of a calamity typically hinged on the preparedness, resources, and abilities of those in the affected community with the power to help themselves and others in their vicinity. Those who did better were those who didn't wait idly for help to arrive. In the end, with systems crashing and failing, what mattered most and had the greatest immediate effects were the actions and decisions made in the midst of a crisis by individuals.

E-MAILS AND CALLS of support flooded into Pou's home and Simmons's office. The arrests of all three women had occurred well after the evening news, but they were amply covered the next day in New Orleans and around the world, complete with pitiful black-and-white mug shots. CNN carried much of Foti's press conference live. The online discussion threads of the *Times-Picayune* website filled with comments mostly favorable toward the medical professionals.

"I know if I was in a nasty hospital like that with 100 degree temperatures and I was suffering in pain, I would want them to off me too," Timothy of Luling, Louisiana, wrote.

"To the family members whose loved ones died in Memorial, (and who I'm sure are suing the hospital), I have one question. Where were you? You obviously weren't with your loved one while they were trapped in that hospital," nurse Mark C. of Metairie, Louisiana, wrote.

Anonymous A of New Orleans blamed others: "Instead of arresting three women for alleged murder, we should put our Local, State and Federal Government on trial for this atrocity."

J. Nisis of New Orleans went even further: "Enjoy your press conferences and photo-ops, Mr. Foti. I certainly won't forget this incident the next time you're up for re-election."

But not everyone was sympathetic to Pou and the nurses. Writer DM Edwards of Marrero, who described having worked at another New Orleans hospital during the disaster, wondered exactly whose pain the medical workers had been trying to relieve: "Our whole purpose for being here was to aid the patients; not to kill them because we wanted them out of our misery."

A debate on this question broke out on the medical blog *KevinMD:*

What were they supposed to do, let their patients suffer and die in misery?

Who are you to decide whether or not my misery is enough for you to put me out of it without my consent or permission?

As a RN I support Dr. Pou and the nurses. I have seen Drs order lethal doses of IV medications to be given every hour to utimatley cause death. Good for Dr. Pou, let the patients die with dignity and not any further suffering.

It's really unnerving to see how many healthcare professionals have granted themselves the right to kill when they are upset.

"Might we all make questionable judgments if we were hungry, dehydrated and sleep deprived?" asked a writer who self-identified as a doctor in Kansas City.

Two of Pou's siblings spoke with CNN in her defense, referring to her and the two arrested nurses as heroes. A sister, Peggy Perino, said Pou had told her little about what had happened in the hospital. Perino said a Memorial nurse she knew considered Pou an incredible person and had said that nobody would have made it out of the hospital without her. "She took complete control of the whole situation," Perino said the nurse told her. "She gave orders."

AFTER THE ARRESTS, the lawyer for Dr. Ewing Cook, the retired pulmonologist and Memorial chief medical officer, phoned to say that under no circumstances should Cook speak voluntarily with investigators. Six days before the arrests, Virginia Rider had come to Cook's house and handed him a subpoena to appear for an interview at the attorney general's office. Butch Schafer was waiting in the car.

Cook had told his lawyer then, "I'll be very glad to go. I can say what I saw."

Cook's attorney was one of the city's top criminal lawyers and had been appointed by Tenet. He would tell the attorney general's office that Cook would plead his Fifth Amendment rights and not divulge anything if he was called for an interview.

Cook was sorry about that. He had wanted to paint the scenario, explain how bad the situation had been at the hospital. They'd had the feeling they might not get out alive, and that the sick had even less of a chance. They'd felt desperate.

The lawyer's response stuck with Cook. "For God's sake, *never* say that! They'll *seize* in the court on the fact that desperate people do desperate things, and you're dead!"

Cook should volunteer nothing, keep a low profile, and speak of this to no one. "You don't want to talk to these people," the lawyer said, even to try to defend Pou and the two nurses. "Whatever you say has no bearing. Whatever you'd say is not going to help them anyway." If reporters showed up, he shouldn't talk to them, either.

This discussion made Cook feel unimportant. He wanted to help defend Pou and the nurses! It could have been he who was arrested. The only difference, he was convinced, was that the nurses who worked with him to hasten Jannie Burgess's death had protected him in their discussions with the attorney general's representatives.

The lawyer would tell the people seeking to interview Cook that he would be happy to testify at the grand jury. Even Cook knew no fool would bring someone to a grand jury without knowing in advance that he had something helpful to say for the prosecution.

———

WHEN SENIOR INTERNIST Dr. Horace Baltz saw the mug shots of Cheri Landry and Lori Budo flash across his television screen as he dressed for work, he fell forward onto his bed. He had a hard time believing they had been arrested as he slept. He adored them, knew them as principled professionals who cared for his ICU patients on the night shift with excellent judgment and skill. His heart bled especially for Budo, whose mother he'd regarded as a standard-bearer in nursing.

Baltz called her and offered to be a character witness if it ever came to that. A Memorial nurse phoned back to ask if he would be willing to speak to the press on the nurses' behalf. He agreed, as long as he could be assured the women were being candid with the authorities. Some LifeCare employees had by their own admission facilitated the giving of "lethal doses," and they had not engaged in cowardly obfuscation but instead bravely told the truth to law enforcement. The Memorial nurses who had any part in what happened should do the same. "Oh Dr. Baltz, we can't do that," the nurse who had called him said, suggesting that was because Tenet was paying for their attorneys.

Baltz felt nauseated. He prayed. His mind kept returning to the conversation he had overheard in the doctor's office early the morning of Thursday, September 1: "Our most difficult job will be to convince the nurses . . ." Had one of the persuasive male physicians he'd overheard devised the evil deeds in the Stygian hospital? Had the girls, as he still thought of the middle-aged nurses, succumbed, obeying a doctor's orders like Eves seduced by Satan in the Garden of Eden?

———

ANNA POU'S ARREST sickened Dr. Dan Nuss, her compassionate department chairman, who saw it as a pathetic political move by the attorney general. Nuss hadn't been at Memorial to witness the events, and Pou hadn't spoken much about what had happened after Katrina, but that didn't matter. He felt he knew her so well as a dedicated, ethical doctor; there was no chance she had done anything to harm anyone.

Nuss believed the same of the nurses, with whom he had worked for many years. The idea that the three had formed a renegade team roaming the hospital bumping people off was inconsistent with their personalities and lives' work. He viewed their accusers as disgruntled, less capable professionals who had disagreed with decisions during the disaster and ended up with an ax to grind. Pou, Landry, and Budo had his complete support.

As news of Pou's arrest spread, Nuss was inundated with phone calls and offers to help Pou from her former colleagues and even doctors who were total strangers. They, too, seemed outraged and unwilling to believe that three health professionals who had pledged to save lives had snapped under pressure and conspired to kill.

Over the ensuing days, Nuss discussed the offers with Pou's attorney, Simmons. Nuss believed he should use his position as a Louisiana State University medical department chairman to help generate an army of support for Pou, and he took time away from work to organize a legal defense fund through his office at the public university.

"One of our dear friends and most respected colleagues, Dr. Anna Maria Pou, is in urgent need of your support," he wrote in an appeal.

He described how Pou had worked heroically "without sleep and without nourishment" to help others after Katrina at Memorial, where "the prevailing conditions were absolutely desperate."

> At great self-sacrifice, she prevented further loss of life and has been credited with saving multiple people from dying.
>
> Apparently there were a few individuals at the hospital who could not understand why so many people were dying. Allegations were made, egregiously accusing Dr. Pou and the others of giving too much narcotic pain medication, even using the word "euthanasia". This attracted national news coverage which became absurdly sensationalistic.

He surmised that news coverage had triggered the attorney general's investigation. Nuss was confident Pou's name would be cleared, but her defense, not covered by malpractice insurance because of the criminal allegations, would be costly.

> Therefore Dr. Pou's professional reputation AND her personal assets are at substantial risk. Remember, this kind of thing could happen to any of us who happen to be on call when a disaster strikes.

Nuss asked for donations to the Anna Pou MD Defense Fund, to be sent to him at his office. Even secretaries in the department spent their off hours spreading the word in a letter and e-mail campaign. Within a week they had collected about $30,000.

The money would be used both for Pou's legal defense and the defense of her reputation. The effort now turned to making the allegations disappear by attracting attention to a radiant image of Pou. Her supporters would highlight the virtuous, heroic aspects of her career and personality in the public's mind, which would carry into the DA's office and the grand jury room. They would act as if the allegations did not exist—a sleight of hand. They would savage the reputation of the attorney general and chastise reporters who sought to learn the truth about the alleged crimes.

In large circles of New Orleans society it became impolite to discuss the events as if they had happened. It was no longer a question of whether what the women did was right or wrong. It simply could never have occurred. There was absolutely no basis in the claims that patients had been injected and died, no matter the intent.

Partners of the New Orleans public relations agency Beuerman Miller Fitzgerald ("The strength to shout; the wisdom to whisper") took up Pou's case. Greg Beuerman—a tall, perpetually tan veteran oil-company spokesman and former Republican Party state director—had spent Katrina volunteering at another marooned, Tenet-owned hospital, Lindy Boggs Medical Center. His colleague Virginia Miller told potential clients that one of the goals of successful crisis communications was: "Control!" For now, control meant keeping Pou herself out of the public eye in spite of an avalanche of media requests seeking her side of the story.

Nurses who had worked with Budo and Landry launched their own support fund with the help of a lawyer relative of Landry's. Landry was single, had lost nearly all her possessions to Katrina's floodwaters, and had an elderly mother to support. Agents had arrested her at work at a local hospital and arrested Budo at home with her husband and two teen-age children.

The two nurses were just weeks away from starting jobs again at the soon-to-reopen surgical institute at Memorial when they were arrested.

Tenet representatives told them that their services would no longer be needed, although the company was covering their legal expenses.

Tenet released a statement after the arrests disclaiming responsibility for the alleged crimes. "We have assisted the Louisiana attorney general in all aspects of his investigation," it said. "If the allegations are proven true, the doctor and nurses named by the attorney general made these decisions without the knowledge, approval, or acquiescence of the hospital or their key physician leaders."

Hours before Foti's press conference, Tenet had announced it would be selling Memorial to a local nonprofit hospital system, a deal that had been in process for months. The sale of Memorial and other Tenet New Orleans hospitals for $56.8 million was to be used to help fund a nearly billion-dollar settlement to end investigations for overcharging Medicare in Louisiana and other states. The hospital system also disclosed that its insurers had agreed to pay the company $340 million for Katrina-related damage and business interruption at five of the company's hospitals.

The nurses' coworkers received the news of their arrests with pain and disbelief. Fear spread through the tight community. Who would the witch hunt bring down next? They rallied, sent e-mails, compiled call lists, and sought doctors and hospital leaders willing to talk to the media. They aimed high, leveraging connections to oil-business executives who had plenty of money and experience with crises.

ICU nurse Cathy Green took action as soon as Budo's daughter called her about the arrests. Green was appalled and panic-stricken for her friends. She mustered her colleagues—"We have to do something about this!"—arguing that Foti had attacked the integrity of every one of them who had worked during the storm. And where had his helicopters and boats been when they needed help?

Green went on an errand with Budo and met her lawyer, Eddie Castaing. A criminal lawyer. It was unbelievable. She sat down beside him and looked him in the eyes. She asked him if he had any idea who he was representing. "These are not ordinary people, these are *great* people. Truly, I will not live long enough to be as good a nurse as they are."

Most of the other nurses now shied from the media, but Green went on the record with reporters, unafraid of sounding hyperbolic: "They are, bar none, the best nurses we have. If my daughter had been in that storm and needed care, those are the nurses I would have handpicked to take care of her. And had she died in the storm, I would never have looked at them and said, 'You did the wrong thing,' ever."

The nurses' supporters filled an Internet home page with testimonials to their exemplary careers and a description of the horrors of Katrina at Memorial and the personal sacrifices made.

"Tragically, the rescue helicopters and boats that finally arrived were too few in number and far too late to save some of our patients—and THAT is the crime that happened in our hospital," the website said. "Please join us as we offer our full support and love to Cheri and Lori. They are not criminals, they are battlefield heroes!"

⌒

ONE DOCTOR who was certainly not on the support team was Cyril Wecht, the well-known forensic pathologist from Pittsburgh whose determinations of homicide had cinched the arrests. About a month after they occurred, on a Sunday evening in August, Virginia Rider picked him up at the airport for a three-day meeting with Orleans Parish coroner Frank Minyard.

Wecht had come to assist Minyard in classifying the cause and manner of all of the suspicious Memorial and LifeCare deaths, and Minyard promised in return to leaven his New Orleans nights with wine and oysters. Minyard, a loyal friend, kept Wecht involved in the case even as the pathologist awaited trial on the federal charges of public corruption brought against him months earlier (years later all charges would be dropped). Perhaps in part because of this cloud over Wecht's reputation, Minyard had also invited to the meeting and oysterfest Dr. Michael Baden, another prominent forensic pathologist.

The men gathered that Monday morning in Minyard's new quarters at the vacant Good Citizens Rhodes Funeral Home, a single-story concrete building with boarded-up row houses and a wig shop as neighbors. Minyard's ruined offices in the basement of the stately criminal courts building had not been repaired.

The importance of the meeting was clear. Attorney General Foti was not in charge of prosecuting the cases, District Attorney Jordan was, and he had made it plain that he wanted the coroner's classification of the deaths before bringing the cases to a grand jury for possible indictments. As of that moment, Minyard and his assistants had kept most of the patient death certificates from LifeCare and Memorial "Pending Investigation" or, less commonly, "Accident" by a tick in a checkbox. "Hurr. Katrina Related Death," some said.

The experts sat around a large table and began considering evidence. Rider and two nurses who had worked the case in the fraud unit with her had prepared charts and tables depicting the drugs found in each body. Robert Middleberg, the director of the Pennsylvania toxicology laboratory where the autopsy samples were tested for drugs, joined them to present his results.

Pou, Budo, and Landry had been arrested on the basis of four deaths, but twenty-three of the forty-one bodies from Memorial and Life-Care analyzed by Middleberg's lab had tested positive for morphine or midazolam, or both. Middleberg had handled thousands of cases in his career, and the drug concentrations found in many of these patients seemed high to him, made him think: these numbers are sticking out, sort of like a sore thumb.

Still, interpreting toxicology results from tests on postmortem tissues was not as straightforward as interpreting blood tests in living patients. The fact that the bodies had sat out in the heat for so long before being sampled could have changed the concentrations of the drugs. Middleberg advised his colleagues to consider each patient's clinical history in conjunction with the lab numbers. The group began poring through the available medical records, case by case.

There were many questions to consider. Did the findings suggest that the patients received a single massive dose of the drugs shortly before death, or repeated doses that allowed the drugs to accumulate, particularly in patients with problems like kidney failure or liver disease, which would have made it difficult for their bodies to process certain drugs? Would the morphine-midazolam drug combination have been contraindicated in patients with these medical problems? Would large doses of these drugs, known to suppress breathing, be dangerous to any patient not on a respirator? How long would it take for the drugs to decrease the breathing rate and blood pressure, and did this match up with the times of the deaths, to the extent these were known?

The experts went over evidence related to LifeCare patient "Miss Alice" Hutzler, the ninety-year-old nursing-home resident who was being treated for pneumonia. Morphine and midazolam were found in her liver, brain, and muscle tissue, but neither drug had been prescribed, according to her chart, which was kept current until a few hours before her death was recorded on Thursday, September 1, by pathologist Skinner. She had been "resting comfortably" on Wednesday afternoon, and that night her nurses didn't document any complaints of pain or distress that indicated a need for the drugs.

Hutzler was one of the nine LifeCare patients found on the seventh floor with one or both drugs in their systems. All were seen alive the morning of September 1, and all were listed as dead by Memorial's pathologist that afternoon.

"Homicide," Wecht wrote on a sheet of paper under Hutzler's name, underlining it twice. "Homicide," he wrote for seven of the eight other seventh-floor patients, including Emmett Everett, Wilda McManus, and Rose Savoie. The last patient, Kathryn Nelson's mother, Elaine, whose records indicated she was close to death on Thursday morning, he marked as "Undetermined." Baden thought all nine were homicides.

The group also considered the deaths on the eighth floor in the ICU. Jannie Burgess was the seventy-nine-year-old nurse with advanced metastatic uterine cancer who had been found by Dr. Ewing Cook when he climbed the stairs in the heat on Wednesday, August 31. Burgess's medical chart showed that a nurse gave her 15 mg of morphine seven times on Wednesday between 2:10 p.m. and 3:35 p.m., based on spoken orders from Cook. This amount—105 mg over one and a half hours—was more than five times the maximum she had ever received in an entire day during her hospitalization, according to her chart. She had received morphine only irregularly in small doses as needed for pain, at most once an hour and typically only two to four times a day. The largest dose a nurse had ever documented giving her at once was 6 mg. From seven that morning until Cook's arrival that afternoon, a nurse had only seen the need to give her a single injection of 4 mg. But because she had already been receiving some amount of morphine and because of her advanced cancer, she was "not a clear, strong case," Wecht wrote in his notes. He marked her death as undetermined and recommended that she not be included in any legal case. The bodies of two of the three other ICU patients who were left behind with Burgess after the other ICU patients were airlifted also tested positive for morphine, but at lower concentrations, and Wecht did not consider these homicides.

Besides the nine patients who remained on the LifeCare floor and Burgess, the group also reviewed nine Memorial and LifeCare patients whose deaths were recorded by pathologist Skinner on the second-floor lobby during the evacuation on Thursday, September 1. Every one of them, plus a tenth, Merle Lagasse, tested positive for midazolam and five of them for morphine, too. Among the dead were the three patients whose prescriptions for large amounts of morphine were signed by Anna Pou and found during the search warrant, including Carrie "Ma'Dear" Hall, former truck driver Wilmer Cooley, and forty-one-year-old engaged mother of four Donna Cotham. (Despite their morphine prescriptions, two of the three tested positive for midazolam only, not morphine.) On the autopsy report the experts reviewed, Cotham had a recent needle-puncture wound in the crook of her left arm, but her decomposed body revealed little evidence of her severe liver disease.

Essie Cavalier, the stroke patient who said "Mama" and whose former nurse had been upset by what she saw being done to her on the second floor, had also died and had what Wecht considered high levels of morphine and midazolam in her tissues. Wecht marked her death and many of the other second-floor patients' death as likely homicides, too, pending review of hospital records. But Rider and her colleagues still had not managed to obtain many of those records. Tenet had turned over most of the LifeCare charts but, according to correspondence from one of its attorneys, had been "unable to locate" records of many of the Memorial patients who died on the second floor "despite diligent efforts." He suggested the charts might have been removed with the patients' remains. Rider had checked with a mortuary worker who had helped remove the bodies and was told the records were not taken.

Dr. Horace Baltz's longtime patient was found not to have had morphine or midazolam in her system. Only traces of Tylenol and her anti-Parkinson's drug were found, suggesting that her death had been a natural, if unexpected, one. About five of the forty-five bodies found at the hospital had, available evidence suggested, been of patients whose deaths occurred just before the disaster. In addition to the forty-five adult bodies, seven apparently stillborn specimens had been recovered from the hospital—they did not consider them.

Five patient bodies did not have toxicology test results. At least one of those, a Memorial patient, had been found deceased on the second floor by the ATM on Thursday afternoon, September 1, after having been seen alive there by the infectious diseases doctor that morning. She had an IV catheter in her right forearm at autopsy. It was frustrating to think they might never know whether she, too, had received the drugs.

The first day of the meeting passed with no participation from the district attorney's office. Hearing firsthand from the experts was apparently not a priority for those who might be presenting the case to the grand jury. On the second day, two assistant district attorneys finally showed up. The lead prosecutor on the Memorial case was a young, dark-haired man with slightly crossed eyes, Assistant District Attorney Michael Morales. He had prosecuted homicides for only about two years and arrived at the coroner's office with his boss, ADA Craig Famularo.

"Whaddya have?" one of them asked.

Their manner—particularly the short, testy Famularo's—struck Rider and the two forensic pathologists as unusually hostile. The experts were accustomed to ass-kissing from prosecutors, but these attorneys acted suspicious, skeptical, and uninterested. The lawyers left after about half an hour. "Obviously these guys don't want to do anything," pathologist Baden commented to coroner Minyard. Minyard, in contrast, seemed to agree with the experts that many deaths at Memorial were homicides. What was striking was the pattern. Almost every patient who died after the helicopters and boats arrived on Thursday morning and whose bodies were tested—including all nine patients on the LifeCare floor, nine on the second-floor lobby, and Merle Lagasse—were positive for the drugs.

———

MICHAEL MORALES HAD been following the pleadings in the case for his boss, District Attorney Eddie Jordan, since the previous fall when Pou's attorney, Simmons, had sued to keep her post-storm conversations with the Tenet attorney private. While Simmons sent Morales courtesy copies of his filings in the case as it proceeded, the attorney general's office usually did not. Unlike in the Medicaid fraud unit, where investigators and prosecutors worked in teams, at the district attorney's office, prosecutors typically did not get involved in the investigation of a case—usually conducted by police—unless specifically requested to do so by the investigative agency. The attorney general's office had not sought to involve Morales in the Memorial investigation. Now he was realizing what a big job lay ahead of him.

He had mixed feelings about it. After Katrina's floodwaters ravaged the DA's building, the staff had decamped to a cramped office suite with stained carpets and folding tables for desks. Morales saw his new surroundings as improved—the carpet in the DA's old office had been held together with duct tape. Morales was only five years out of law school and punctuated his sentences with the occasional snort, exasperated sigh, or other sound effect. He was one of a few homicide prosecutors in a city with one of the highest murder rates per capita and a poor record of bringing perpetrators to justice. He was also smart and well regarded by his colleagues. The high-profile Memorial case was starting to absorb all of his time.

While the attorney general's office had kept the DA's office in the dark throughout the yearlong investigation, now DA Jordan, in his first term in an elected position, was receiving nasty letters from the public for being associated with it. Jordan hardly needed another unpopular cause. Soon after taking office as the first African American district attorney in Orleans Parish in 2003, he had fired dozens of white employees and replaced them with black ones. Now he was fighting a federal judgment against him for racial discrimination.

Jordan was caught between powerful forces in the Memorial case. Tenet had money invested in the New Orleans political scene. Pou's lawyer, Simmons, as well as several of the Tenet lawyers, were, like Jordan, former US attorneys. On the other side, the attorney general had saddled the case with his reputation. Foti and Jordan had markedly different interests. Foti needed to prove he had done the right thing by arresting the three. Jordan would benefit if the case just went away.

But Jordan didn't tell Morales to make the case disappear, and the young ADA had his own reasons for lacking enthusiasm. Under Louisiana law, intentionally killing someone as alleged in the arrest affidavit was murder. Morales understood why the deaths at Memorial had merited an investigation. Still, these weren't typical homicides. The military had been called in to restore order in the city, with Governor Blanco warning that their M-16s were "locked and loaded," the troops more than willing to shoot and kill, "and I expect they will." Morales felt he was being asked to apply civilian law to a war zone.

This feeling was both professional and personal. Morales's former student clerk, a New Orleans police sergeant who studied law in night school, was under investigation in the shootings of unarmed civilians on New Orleans's Danziger Bridge on the tense, chaotic, sixth day after the storm. It first appeared he had been responding to a call to assist police who had been shot there. Morales considered him a very good cop and a very promising budding attorney. Good people, Morales thought, shouldn't necessarily be charged for the bad things they did in a crisis.

Morales's ambivalent feelings about the Memorial case contrasted with Rider and Schafer's undimmed enthusiasm for it. In August they had slapped Pou's outspoken boss, Dr. Dan Nuss, with a subpoena seeking to find out what he knew.

Morales did not view this as helpful collaboration. As prosecutor of the case, it was he who should be signing subpoenas. They had stepped on his toes and irritated him. Just as the AG's staff had not cared to involve the DA's office while investigating the Memorial deaths, the DA would now return the favor. Morales drafted a letter from DA Jordan to AG Foti asking his office to cease investigating because it "would not be advantageous to the case" until the grand jury investigation was under way.

———

THE ORDER to stop investigating came as a severe blow to Virginia Rider and Butch Schafer. They had hoped that even after the DA claimed his right to prosecute Pou, Landry, and Budo, he would invite the AG's team to assist. Moreover, Schafer regarded the investigation as having spider-webbed out in multiple directions, and he wanted to follow the radii out to other doctors, nurses, and staff, to explore the potential for additional charges and arrests. Schafer also wanted to probe a potential corporate thread of responsibility for the deaths, even a conspiracy. He and Rider hoped the DA would grant immunity to some of the health workers who had proffered potentially critical testimony.

By the time of the arrests, Rider and her partners had accumulated on the order of 50,000 pages of documentary evidence. The Orleans Parish DA's office requested a case summary, and Rider set about preparing it with the help of other agents. The report grew longer and longer as she worked on it.

Rider's colleagues, who'd had previous dealings with the DA's office, told her that people there would not be interested in receiving something so detailed, but Rider insisted on being thorough. If the DA's prosecutors were serious about seeking indictments, why wouldn't they want as much information as possible? Attorney General Foti caught wind of the internal disagreement and called Rider into his office to broker a compromise. She would write a brief executive summary as well as a more detailed report keyed to the records. The task of organizing the documents began to monopolize her days.

———

AS THE FIRST ANNIVERSARY of Katrina approached, Dr. Horace Baltz turned each day to a new installment of a five-part *Times-Picayune* "tick tock" story about events at Memorial by reporter Jeffrey

Meitrodt. The series was based on more than three dozen interviews with people at the hospital and others, including Anna Pou's eighty-three-year-old mother, Jeanette, who said she had once thought her daughter "too tenderhearted" to become a doctor. What Anna Pou was being accused of having done, the elder Pou said, was out of character. "Maybe one of my other children could have done something like this, but not this one. Not Mrs. Soft Heart." The articles also introduced readers to rescuers Mark and Sandra LeBlanc and the story of Mark's mother, Vera LeBlanc, whom they had come to Memorial to save.

One of the articles said incident commander Susan Mulderick had declined a request for an interview through her attorney. Without Mulderick's voice, reporter Meitrodt had little way to offer her perspective. He wrote that she had provided her colleagues with "appallingly incorrect information" at Thursday morning's meeting by "telling them that they could expect no rescue that day," something his sources contended, but which others would later suggest was not true. He also repeated what the LifeCare nurses had said about Mulderick, from the affidavit.

Baltz realized Mulderick would be upset and called her to offer his support. He had worked with her for decades, thought highly of her, and was close to her family, having long ago helped save one of her younger sisters from dying of a brain aneurysm. That sister's gift of an Audubon print depicting waterfowl was one of his few possessions to survive Katrina's destruction.

The tough nurse had bawled like a child after reading the article. She was a proud administrator, fiercely loyal to the hospital, and the accusations in the attorney general's affidavit devastated her. Baltz consoled her as best he could.

Baltz met again with fellow Memorial Medical Center staff doctors planning for the possibility of the hospital's reopening under new ownership. While the subject of what had happened after the storm remained off limits, one colleague detailed his efforts to ensure the attorney general's defeat in the next election. Some of the doctors positioning themselves for leadership on the hospital staff were ones Baltz had overheard talking conspiratorially, he'd thought, about the need to "convince the nurses" on Thursday morning, September 1. Baltz opposed the idea of a cover-up. He felt that his value systems and ethics were no longer in step with those of his colleagues. There was a new aroma in the air, and he disliked it. On the back of a news story printout about Tenet's fraud settlements, Baltz scribbled a note for medical staff president Reuben Chrestman. It was Baltz's note of resignation from the medical staff of the hospital where he had worked more than forty years.

Baltz heard a rumor that there was an invitation-only memorial service and catered reception on the Katrina anniversary in one of Memorial's garages. After briefly smarting over having been left out, he resolved to organize a simpler, more respectful way of memorializing the victims a few days later.

On September 1, the anniversary of the deaths, he laid two small wreaths at the corner of Napoleon and Clara Streets. He held hands with his sister/receptionist to pray for the dead. A few security guards came to join them.

The hospital was weeks from its partial reopening and Baltz caught sight of its new CEO, Curtis Dosch, the tall, reedy former CFO who had reminded Dr. John Thiele of Jed Clampett when they had rested together in the cancer center during the disaster. Baltz thought Dosch looked ill at ease as he raced past their small congregation.

———

IN THE DAYS leading up to the anniversary, lawyers filed petitions in the names of the Memorial and LifeCare dead. Medical malpractice claims and personal-injury actions typically had to be made within a year of an incident. Just weeks after the disaster, eager attorneys had begun soliciting potential clients. Advertisements ran in newspapers, on television, and on billboards as far away as Houston and Atlanta. One lawyer had even ridden around New Orleans on her scooter planting campaign-style lawn signs on street medians and near hospitals. "I know black people—I was raised by black women," the attorney, Tammie Holley, a white woman, wrote in an e-mail to colleagues. The families, she wrote, "would drive by the hospital to see 'where mama died' in search of answers." She also obtained a mailing list of displaced voters from the NAACP. "The rest is history." She wrote that a fellow attorney came into her office and said, "I can smell the money."

The law allowed family members to seek compensation not only for the damages caused to them by their loved one's wrongful death, including loss of love and affection, but also for the pain and suffering the patient experienced before dying. The first suit related to Memorial had been filed just over a month after the storm. In January 2006, the plaintiffs' lawyers amended the claim, seeking status as a class action on behalf of all patients who died or were injured by the allegedly poor design of Memorial's backup electrical system, and the inadequacy of its evacuation plan and patient care during the disaster. A judge would determine whether to certify the class over any objections from the defendants. LifeCare, made a defendant alongside Memorial and Tenet, sought to have the case heard in federal instead of state court. Some attorneys viewed federal courts as more favorable to out-of-state corporations. In support of this move, the company's lawyers argued that as New Orleans flooded, a federal official, Knox Andress, had advised LifeCare administrators that FEMA would rescue their patients. During the litigation Andress clarified that he was in fact a nurse in Shreveport who did regional disaster-preparedness work under a federal grant, but that FEMA had never employed him. The court ruled he did not qualify as a federal officer. The case was remanded to Louisiana district court.

Many families filed their own claims outside of the proposed class action. Merle Lagasse's daughter Karen described in her suit how an unknown health-care worker, "Jane Doe," had removed her mother's oxygen mask before she was passed through the machine-room wall.

The clinical language of the petition only heightened its pathos. "At that time, decedent yelled out that she could not breathe," it said. Both Merle Lagasse and her daughter pleaded for the mask to be replaced, "but Jane Doe refused such a directive."

Karen Lagasse had made it out of Memorial by boat only to end up at the overcrowded New Orleans Convention Center where, in fear for her life, she slept outside on the street.

Someone told her there that her mother had died at the hospital, but she refused to believe it. She recruited friends to call emergency rooms from Louisiana to Texas, searching for ten frantic days before she finally received a call from a Tenet official who told her that her mother was on a list of people thought to have died during the evacuation. Months later, she was allowed to return to the hospital garage to sift through debris for her mother's personal effects, surviving artifacts of the life they had shared in a Lakeview neighborhood now lost to flooding.

She buried her mother on Valentine's Day, in a metal coffin the funeral home workers sealed with a rubber gasket to confine the odor of decomposition. Lagasse argued with them to remove the body bag before placing her in the coffin. They refused. The indignity of this upset her, as did the thought that her mother had not, at the very least, become the "beautiful corpse" of Ewing Cook's morbid imagination.

A full year later, Karen Lagasse had still not been told what had happened to her mother after their traumatic separation. The interview the attorney general's investigators had conducted with her mother's doctor, Roy Culotta, was not shared with her. She believed her mother to have died from his negligence and that of the hospital that had failed to prepare properly for a disaster. She wondered how long her mother had suffered in the heat and whether she had continued to receive oxygen and pain medicines.

Karen Lagasse sued Culotta; the hospital; its CEO, René Goux; "Jane Doe"; and internal medicine department director Dr. Richard Deichmann, whom her lawyer found had written and self-published a book,

Code Blue: A Katrina Physician's Memoir, revealing his key role in the evacuations. Deichmann was Karen Lagasse's own internist and she was at first surprised to learn her attorney had sued him in her name.

The family of stroke patient Essie Cavalier also sued the hospital. Her daughter, who had worked as a medical malpractice attorney, became depressed after obtaining Cavalier's toxicology results. She wondered aloud how someone could have decided for her mother that she wasn't going to make it. Where were the checks and balances?

Families of three of the four LifeCare patients mentioned in the arrest affidavit—including Emmett Everett and Rose Savoie—filed civil suits not only against Memorial and LifeCare but also against Pou, Budo, and Landry and, in two cases, Susan Mulderick and Steven Harris, the LifeCare pharmacist. The suits variously alleged euthanasia, inadequate backup power supply, failed evacuation policies, and abandonment.

Emmett Everett's wife, son, and daughter also named Pou's employer, Louisiana State University. "He was awake, alert and oriented throughout the relevant time period," the suit said.

"Who gave them the right to play God?" Carrie Everett asked on a CNN Katrina anniversary broadcast. "Who gave them the right?"

The Everetts had not learned of Emmett's death until fifteen days after it occurred. They asked for a trial by jury. Kathryn Nelson's mother, Elaine, was not one of the four patients whose deaths were attributed to the injections in the arrest affidavit. However, her family knew from interactions with the attorney general's office, and from having obtained the toxicology reports, that the laboratory had found a large concentration of morphine in her tissues. They were outraged that after living an upstanding life and doing so much to help others, she had apparently died as if her remaining moments had no value. Kathryn's brother Craig was an experienced white-collar and health-care attorney nearing retirement who had the knowhow, resources, time, and motivation to find out exactly what had happened to his mother—and make someone pay.

Angela McManus, Wilda's daughter, felt differently. The prospect of having to talk to a lawyer on a regular basis about her experiences at Memorial was too upsetting, and she left it to a sibling to file a lawsuit. She needed to focus on getting well. She had little energy. Anhedonic, she found it difficult to escape the narcosis of her television screen.

Instead of suing, she had done what felt more important to her, though it nearly destroyed her—she spoke publicly about what had happened to her seventy-year-old mother, became again her mother's voice. She was outraged at suggestions that the health workers were relieving suffering in the last moments of life—who told them it was the patients' last moments, patients they had never even treated?

She felt her family and her mother had been violated even though her mother might not have had much time left. Family members had been deprived of the chance to be with her when she died, to see her body and sit vigil over it at a wake—it was so badly decayed, the family had decided to have it cremated. As a result, Wilda McManus could not have the kind of funeral she merited, at the church, St. Raymond's Catholic on Paris Avenue, around the corner from their house, where she had sung in the choir and everybody knew her. It would have been, Angela knew, a standing-room-only crowd.

After the arrests, Angela believed that having listed her phone number made her the only LifeCare family member the media could readily find in Baton Rouge.

"I gotta tell this," Angela said to herself, and took calls from radio reporters on the phone. She allowed television reporters to troop in and out and aim their bright lights on her framed family photographs. She posed, gazing off the patio balcony, for them to record their background B roll.

"I don't believe that a person with a sane mind could make this decision," she told an ABC reporter for *Good Morning America*.

"At least now I'll be able to get some answers," McManus said to an Associated Press reporter after the arrests. "For months, I haven't known what happened to my mom. I need some answers just to be able to function.

"Euthanasia is something you do to a horse, or to an animal. When you do it to people, it's called murder."

Reporters engaged her from morning until night the day after the arrests, working her last nerve. They lined up in the parking lot of the Baton Rouge apartment where she was staying; the two-story New Orleans duplex where she had grown up was destroyed. The wind had blown the roof down into the bedrooms, and floodwaters had come up from below. She had stopped paying insurance on it after she left her job to become her ill mother's caretaker.

She brooked no challenge, no skepticism or disrespect. She knew exactly what story she wanted to tell, the story she had lived with from the day she had been forced to leave her mother's bedside, the story the world finally wanted to hear. "I'm going to play the devil's advocate," a male reporter said.

"No, you're not," McManus told him. She threw him out. "Neither the devil or his advocates are welcome here."

The families' suits stalled pending the outcome of a challenge to a similar lawsuit at another hospital, Pendleton Memorial Methodist in New Orleans East. The suit alleged that the hospital had been negligent in preparing for and responding to the storm, a premises liability claim that one uninvolved insurance attorney described as "a new theory of liability against health-care institutions—lack of emergency preparedness." The hospital's lawyers were arguing that the case should proceed instead as a medical malpractice claim. That would advantage the hospital: Louisiana medical malpractice law required a panel of three doctors to review each case before it could proceed, and it capped compensation at $500,000 per hospital or other health-care provider—most of which was typically covered by a patient compensation fund.

Patients and their families weren't the only ones seeking legal recourse. While Louisiana workers' compensation law protected employers from claims by their employees, some Memorial workers, including a group of neonatal ICU nurses, nevertheless sued, variously attempting to hold parent company Tenet responsible or to exploit the law's exception for intentional tort. LifeCare staff and their families at the hospital also sued Memorial, as they were not its employees.

The ICU nurse who had previously written a critical letter to Tenet's CEO, Dawn Marie Gieck, claimed in her suit that Memorial and Tenet had failed "to see to the care and safety of the people stranded at the Hospital" and failed to evacuate properly: "Since Katrina I have experienced emotional distress, which makes it impossible for me to work as an ICU nurse or [in] any other kind of nursing. I have been diagnosed with post-traumatic stress disorder. Although I have attempted to work nursing jobs, I could not stay on."

However, some Memorial evacuees were grateful, not bitter. The premature neonate whom Dr. Juan Gershanik, earning the nickname "the Argentinian Kangaroo," had held against his body and ventilated by hand in a rescue helicopter, had thrived over the year at his new home in Houston. Baby Boy S's mother returned with him to New Orleans to reunite with the doctors and staff who had saved him, on the first anniversary of the storm, initiating a yearly tradition.

———

THE NBC TELEVISION news magazine *Dateline* carried an anniversary report about Memorial's sister hospital, Tenet-owned Lindy Boggs Medical Center. The conditions had been similar to those at Memorial—no power, almost no communications, delayed rescue. Water had poured over the hospital's floodgates with the drama and variegation of a natural waterfall.

With no helipad and no assurance of ambulances a boat ride away on dry ground, hospital staff at first ferried only able-bodied non-patients

from Lindy Boggs. On Wednesday, firefighters arrived and began directing drivers of the small dinghies and pleasure boats to take patients to a
berm by a nearby post office to be picked up by helicopters. The roughly
150 patients were divided into categories: A, B, and C. Some doctors
and nurses thought the C's, the most critical patients, should be rescued
first. But the doctors and firefighters in charge decided to leave them for
last. The concern might have been that there would not be medical care
for them at the drop points. For the *Dateline* story, reporter Hoda Kotb
asked firefighter Chris Shamburger the reason for the triage protocol. He
offered little explanation: "That's the way things are done."

Dr. Glenn Johnson, acting chief of staff, described drawing letters on
people's foreheads with a permanent marker. "I'm just having horrible
thoughts, like, Is this what happened, like, at Auschwitz or something?
You know, where people were just marked like cattle."

Johnson took pity on a paralyzed patient whose husband offered to
carry her—Johnson turned her C into an A, "my one act of mercy for
the day." Lindy Boggs staff helped carry patients down multiple flights
of stairs in sheets. The firemen were instructed to retreat before sundown
due to safety concerns. They left critically ill, hospice, and long-term
acute care patients behind and never returned. A handful of medical staff
and other rescuers came back on Thursday, September 1, and began taking survivors out on a small, stolen flatboat. Other patients went out on
Friday.

The story focused on Dr. Johnson's agony over the decision making, his
outrage at the dearth of outside help, his ingenuity in replenishing medicines, and the intensity of his work in the deadly, sapping heat. When he
flew out on Wednesday, August 31, rather than being delivered to safety,
he was dropped off with his patients on the I-10 freeway cloverleaf.

Anna Pou thought the *Dateline* program was phenomenal. It gave the
public a sense of what it felt like to be trapped as a doctor and face such
difficult decisions. Many people, including one of her sisters, called her
to say they had not appreciated what she had gone through until watch-

ing it. The report painted a sympathetic picture of the medical professionals. The flooding itself was the enemy.

The story mentioned that the attorney general's office was looking into events at Lindy Boggs. Virginia Rider had originally helped out on the investigation, which uncovered an even more troubling story than what *Dateline* had portrayed.

The criminal inquiry centered on what had happened after nearly all of the 175 staff members escaped. At the fire officials' suggestion, they had put on gowns and drawn the triage symbol "C" on themselves to look like patients so they could be evacuated by military helicopter. Some took pictures of one another grinning, patient gowns tied loosely over their scrubs, bright-red triage letters marking their chests, hands, and foreheads.

A respiratory therapist asked what would happen to the patients being left behind. She was told: "At some point, someone will have to euthanize them." An anesthesiologist, James Riopelle, was approached about euthanizing patients and said the idea was crazy. This isn't the *Titanic,* he thought, Lindy Boggs isn't going down. We're only a mile from dry ground, with plenty of drinking water. Official rescue efforts had been slow, but he knew they would eventually gain traction, despite rumors that officials were turning away civilian rescuers with boats at the border of the city out of security concerns.

Riopelle, a past president of the state humane society coalition, had quietly decided earlier in the day to disobey the authorities and stay. There was no way he was leaving behind the sixty or seventy pets at the hospital, including his own, just because some twenty-year-old fireman from Shreveport had ordered him to go. He'd made a pledge to himself years earlier, after touring the Holocaust concentration camp Dachau, to refuse to comply with misdirection. Two other hospital staff members with pets—a nurse director and a respiratory therapist—decided to stay behind with him.

It had never occurred to Riopelle that the rescuers wouldn't take all the patients, but he and his two colleagues found themselves alone with the pets and roughly twenty-five patients who were extremely fragile, many with DNR orders. Riopelle saw some patients die, and he dragged three bodies to the hospital's entrance to deter looters.

The first evening, Riopelle went to see a twenty-eight-year-old patient who was awaiting a liver transplant. Her mother was with her, having also disobeyed the order to leave, and she said her daughter was in pain. The pharmacy was locked, but another staff member had given Riopelle morphine to use in case any pets needed to be euthanized.

Having nothing else, he offered the woman, Elaine Bias, a 10 mg dose of morphine she could use on her daughter. He told her bluntly that the drug might kill her daughter, because she had liver failure and the liver was needed to break down the drug. He did not know what a safe dose would be, and he wanted Bias to be very cautious about giving her daughter the medicine, which he said would help her sleep.

Bias recalled, contradictorily, that Riopelle said she should *put* her daughter to sleep and demonstrated how to inject the morphine into her IV line. Bias refused. Her reaction was colored by an earlier conversation, she told investigators. She had learned from a staff member after an administrative meeting that certain patients were not going to be evacuated. The woman allegedly told her, "They will give them morphine to put them to sleep."

Jessie Lynn LaSalle, the wife of another young patient, one who had just undergone a liver transplant, also recalled being offered morphine by Riopelle repeatedly, something Riopelle later said he did not recall. She said he had told her nobody was coming to rescue her husband and she should let Riopelle give him morphine so he could "go at ease." Furious, she sent Riopelle out of the room. She said he told her if she changed her mind she could find him upstairs with the animals.

LaSalle's husband was on a ventilator rigged to operate pneumatically on the hospital's supply of oxygen now that the power was out. Because of this, Riopelle later pointed out, morphine—even if he had offered it—would not have depressed the man's breathing or posed a danger to him.

Riopelle denied having euthanized any patients or given any morphine, and he told investigators that Bias and LaSalle might have misunderstood his intentions because they were feeling abandoned. Several of the patients who remained in the hospital were on life support, breathing with the help of ventilators powered by compressed gas. Bias alleged that she saw these being turned off and patients without accompanying family members being injected with what she believed was morphine, then dying.

Approximately twenty-seven bodies were recovered at Lindy Boggs, including many from a separately owned long-term acute care hospital, Genesis Specialty (a few patients had died before the storm). While the total number of deaths in the building was lower than at Memorial, the proportion was similar, as there were fewer patients overall. Toxicology tests revealed the presence of morphine in nearly a quarter of twenty-one bodies tested; however, only one had levels that appeared to be unusually high.

Both of the young transplant patients went out by boat the next day, but they died weeks later of infections that their families believed stemmed from the abandonment and lack of care. They filed medical malpractice claims against Riopelle and the transplant doctor—both of which were later dismissed—as well as the hospital and its owner, Tenet. The claims mentioned the "strong suggestion" that the patients be euthanized.

———

THE ATTORNEY GENERAL'S staff had also continued to look into the case of the patient who had been abandoned for dead and later found alive at Touro Infirmary. This was the patient mentioned in a letter to Touro's CEO, copied to the attorney general's office, predicting: "Someday the truth will be told." The patient in question was Odun

Arechaga, a seventy-year-old man with a regal face who had suffered a heart attack before the hurricane, falling unconscious and sustaining brain damage while awaiting rescuers who had difficulty finding his house. Neurologists had advised his daughter to "let him die." She refused, and in the days before the storm, he regained the ability to breathe on his own and became somewhat more responsive.

In the 1960s Arechaga had founded the occult Sabaean Religious Order in Chicago. He imbued its practices with ancient philosophies and mysteries and referred to himself as a priest of the Am'n, the hidden and deep. In her book *Drawing Down the Moon,* NPR reporter Margot Adler compared a fantastic Sabaean marriage feast at his temple in 1975 with Fellini's *Satyricon,* which, Arechaga playfully reminded her, was "merely a movie." He had been a brilliant storyteller fascinated by disasters. He wrote and produced elaborate plays for holiday festivals where the children of his order would reenact cities being destroyed by Sumerian earthquakes and the eruption of Mt. Vesuvius.

Witnesses told investigators they had found Arechaga on a soiled gurney on Touro's third floor on Friday, September 2, with small Styrofoam coffee cups inexplicably taped over his ears, and his medical record at his feet. National Guardsmen wheeled him out of Touro and summoned medical staff from a smaller hospital across the street, screaming that they had a patient who needed help. When rescuers examined him, they found his airway nearly completely blocked and the tracheotomy collar around his neck saturated with dried, crusted green-and-yellow sputum. His heart was beating slowly, his extremities were cold, and his oxygen level was low, his body failing.

The rescuers suctioned his airway, changed the collar, and removed his soiled clothing. Arechaga opened his eyes as he was loaded into an ambulance.

Touro Infirmary's staff, not knowing how high the waters would rise, or how quickly, had carried eighteen critical patients like Arechaga in the heat from the ground floor, which still had backup power, to the third floor, which had lost power when the hospital's generators—some of them decades-old—began failing. They had not been tested to work for such a long period, were running on possibly tainted fuel from the government, and were not configured in many areas to support the air-conditioning system (which also relied on the crippled city water system for its chillers). When the battery backups on ventilators were exhausted, patients were bagged by hand, but many didn't tolerate being off the machines, and died.

Some staff later described a unique and horrifying triage system: those patients who could not say their names were not given IVs—an allegation that haunted the family members of a man with advanced Parkinson's disease who could not speak and had died unexpectedly at the hospital. A number of patients were tagged "black"—too sick to move—and were not taken to the helipad.

Touro Infirmary had remained reachable by land after Katrina, unlike Memorial and Lindy Boggs, but its workers had been similarly frightened by reports that violence was breaking out in the city. Medical workers from Touro and a separately owned long-term acute care unit within it, Specialty Hospital of New Orleans, told the investigators that while many of their colleagues worked heroically and tirelessly to rescue patients, even returning to the hospital to do so, some units' entire staff had driven out of the hospital garage, leaving their patients behind. After the storm, some nurses were fired and were reported to the nursing board for abandonment.

A Touro emergency room nurse who was put in charge of triage later said that members of the National Guard arrived at the end and commanded the last remaining staff to leave for their safety, reassuring them that soldiers would stay behind to protect the remaining two dozen or so patients. Cars lined up with snipers at the lead. "At some point you just have to save yourself," the nurse, Brent Becnel said. Although the professionals were upset and didn't want to leave, they resigned themselves to the situation. "If you get hurt, when the hospital can open again and you're not there, what good are you?"

A Touro doctor, writing anonymously to the attorney general's office, described being told by a military commander who had supervised Touro's evacuation that Arechaga was among fourteen patients considered "too critical." Medical workers "shot them full of morphine and left them behind."

Toxicology tests on some of the bodies found at Touro and at Specialty Hospital of New Orleans revealed high levels of morphine and midazolam, the same drug combination used at Memorial.

—

THE STORIES from Memorial, Lindy Boggs, and Touro hospitals stood in contrast to the reaction of staff at New Orleans's public Charity Hospital. Charity had flooded; lost power, functioning plumbing, computers, telephones, and elevators; lacked a helipad; and had no corporate overseers to assist, however belatedly. It had taken until Friday afternoon, September 2, to transfer all the patients from there, compared with Thursday, September 1, at Memorial. Approximately twice as many patients were present at the public hospital's two campuses as compared with Memorial, with a lower ratio of staff to patients. However, only three patients died.

Doctors said that staff continued to provide medical care to patients in their rooms until the end, despite similar or even worse conditions of existential threat, including a gunman reported to be on a nearby roof, disrupting the evacuation, and the presence of more than a hundred psychiatric patients inside. People urinated on stair landings. Convoys attempting to reach the hospital over water were reportedly shot at and looted. News reports suggested the hospital had been evacuated when it hadn't. Soldiers had brought additional ventilator-dependent patients *to* the hospital.

In articles and conversations, hospital workers chalked up their resilience to a number of factors, including morale-building—leaders held meetings every four hours in the lobby for everyone from doctors to janitorial staff. They put on a talent show by flashlight. They painted and laughed.

Hospital officials had drilled for a Category Three hurricane and levee failure and purchased, with the help of federal preparedness funds made available after the 9/11 attacks, several portable generators, oxygen-powered ventilators, and a ham radio system. Special disaster training had been provided to hospital security officers.

The Charity staff was populated by crusty characters accustomed to the comparatively Spartan, chaotic, and occasionally threatening conditions of an inner-city government hospital. Workers included Vietnam War–era ER doctors known for their bravado and machismo. Nearly everyone had experience getting creative with all-too-common resource limitations.

At Charity, workers siphoned gas from cars to fuel ten small portable generators. These were used to power ventilators and cardiac monitors in the ICUs, keeping critically ill people alive, including a very premature baby. This contrasted with Memorial, where patients were ventilated by hand with Ambu-bags after the power failed, as two similar generators were only later put to use for powering lights and fans in common areas and the helipad, not medical equipment.

Charity staff also kept up the hospital routine despite the bizarre conditions, continuing to provide services like physical and occupational therapy and encouraging workers to maintain shifts and a regular sleep schedule. This signaled that the situation was under some degree of control and kept panic to a minimum. There was an active effort to stem rumors. "You can only say it if you've seen it," staff were told.

Perhaps most important, Charity's leaders avoided categorizing a group of patients as too ill to rescue. The sickest were taken out first instead of last.

RICK SIMMONS'S EFFORTS to construct a defense for Anna Pou were unflagging but handicapped by a deficit of evidence from the prosecution. In mid-September he wrote Assistant District Attorney Michael Morales, asking for the umpteenth time for copies of the forensic test results performed on the bodies. Simmons referred to it as an exchange: in return for being given the laboratory and autopsy results, he would offer his own experts' input on the case.

ADA Morales declined the offer, reminding Simmons that Pou had not yet been indicted. When and if she was, her attorney could move under Louisiana law to gain access to certain evidence that the DA had amassed. But they were not yet at this point in the process. Morales was happy to look at Simmons's hand if he wanted to show it, but he wasn't prepared to show his.

Simmons repeatedly reminded Morales that the DA's office had "absolute discretion" in the case, could reject it out of hand, could simply send it back to the attorney general as a refusal. As Morales underwent a crash course in medical care under crisis, Simmons seemed always at the ready to supplement his information, sharing the defense's concepts of the case.

Morales was learning so many new terms, he began to keep a glossary: Agonal Breathing; Double Effect; Euthanasia; Palliative Care; Triage. Special prosecutors, division chiefs, and the attorney general had the glossary at hand for reference whenever they met to discuss the evidence and what remained to be done. In a normal case, one charging conference would be held. The Memorial case was on its way to five.

As hard as Morales found it to apply civilian criminal law to a "war zone," he was impressed at how well the medical ethical concept of the double effect tracked with the legal concept of specific criminal intent, which was required to prove murder in Louisiana. Were the injections intended to harm and kill, or to palliate? He began to view the case from this perspective.

Simmons continued to move aggressively to ensure that Pou's conversations with the Tenet attorney and media relations chief after Katrina would not be heard. At the end of September, a Louisiana appeals court sided with him and allowed the lower court's decision to stand. The information would remain protected from disclosure.

Simmons also guided Pou, who now harbored great enmity for the media, through an interview with the influential CBS television magazine show *60 Minutes*. The camera crew and producer arrived to film Pou twice. Nervous, she changed her mind and refused to see them the first time.

Simmons arranged for an audio recording of her entire interview with Morley Safer so that nothing could later be taken out of context in court should *60 Minutes* be served with a subpoena. As the broadcast date approached, he was confident the segment would paint her in a good light, and he helped orchestrate a chorus of support from professional medical organizations to appear in the days after it aired. Befitting his role as mastermind of Pou's defense, Simmons even took issue with a plan by the American Medical Association—an influential membership organization of doctors—to release a statement the day after Sunday night's show, arguing that a much-anticipated *Monday Night Football* broadcast marking the return of the New Orleans Saints to the restored Superdome would draw local news attention away from it.

Meanwhile, Attorney General Foti's public information director, Kris Wartelle, had also helped organize an interview with her boss, confident that the broadcast would be a hard-hitting investigative work that would fairly present his side of the story. She had been impressed by *60 Minutes* reporter Ed Bradley's work with her office on a story examining why police in the majority white suburb of Gretna prevented a largely black crowd of New Orleans residents from crossing a bridge to relative safety there after Katrina. It took Wartelle by surprise to learn that Morley Safer, not Bradley, would be reporting the Memorial story after what she believed to have been an internal fight. Safer's young producer assured Wartelle the story would still portray Foti as a hero.

Safer arrived to conduct the interview. "Morley's in a bad mood," the producer warned Wartelle.

When Safer began questioning the attorney general under the klieg lights, it became apparent the story would be critical toward him. Foti was angry at Wartelle, who argued with Safer for about an hour after the interview and sent a scathing e-mail to a top CBS network official. She felt she had been lied to about the reporter's intentions.

The segment aired Sunday night, September 24, 2006. Pou's appearance was a sensation.

The camera closed in on her attractive face. Her lips trembled slightly, their corners turned down in a pained grimace as she stared intently at Safer. "I want everybody to know that I am not a murderer," she told him, speaking slowly and nodding her head to emphasize her words, as if the American public were a child whom she needed to make understand something vital.

Safer's face showed pity and sympathy. He asked what it was like going from being a respected surgeon to an accused criminal. "It completely ripped my heart out," she said, on the verge of tears. "My entire life I have tried to do good." She argued that she had done the best she could under dreadful conditions that resulted from being abandoned. She didn't believe in euthanasia, she said, but in comfort care—ensuring that patients don't suffer pain. Asked by Safer if she ever lost hope, Pou was indignant. As a cancer specialist, she said, "I am hope."

The attorney general, meanwhile, appeared stiff and distant behind thick glasses, his face shiny and lit from the side, highlighting his wrinkles. Safer asked him, "Would you not think that in case of murder, the perpetrators would try to conceal their actions?"

"Maybe they just didn't think that anybody would ever find out," Foti replied, crooked teeth showing between chapped lips.

Doctors from around the country were incensed. "Your Attorney General, Mr. Foti, is a complete buffoon for prosecuting these professionals," a doctor from Virginia, John M. Kellum, wrote to the web-master of the attorney general's website during the broadcast.

Spokeswoman Wartelle filed a complaint with Kellum's medical school dean, describing his e-mail as "rude and unprofessional," and she sent a message back to Kellum. "If you don't want allegations of wrong doing investigated, then maybe you should contact the hundreds of eye-witnesses we interviewed [. . .] We cannot comment on the evidence which puts us at a disadvantage when viewers lash out without one inkling of the evidence in this case."

As Simmons had helped orchestrate (albeit on the Monday) the American Medical Association released a statement describing Pou as a member in good standing and the case against her as complex and sharply contested. One of the organization's top executives was a head and neck surgeon like Pou and worked on her behalf behind the scenes. "The AMA is very proud of the many heroic physicians and other health care professionals who sacrificed and distinguished themselves in the aftermath of Hurricane Katrina," the statement said.

Meanwhile, a doctor on the board of the Louisiana State Medical Society who had known Pou since childhood lobbied for her within that organization. Members pressured the group to donate to Pou's support fund, and when legal strictures precluded that, employees posted information about Pou's defense fund on the organization's website, which carried a statement suggesting that the strength of Pou's television performance be used to gauge her innocence.

Following the airing of the *60 Minutes* interview with Dr. Anna Pou, the Louisiana State Medical Society (LSMS) is confident that Dr. Pou performed courageously under the most challenging and horrific conditions and made decisions in the best interest of her patients. Her recent statements regarding the events clearly show her dedication to providing care and hope to her patients when all hope seemed abandoned.

It concluded by commending her "valiant efforts" during and after Katrina.

—

WAS IT HER trembling lips? Her appealing eyes? The fact that the entire medical community to which coroner Frank Minyard belonged appeared to support her?

Something about the *60 Minutes* broadcast gave Minyard the urge to meet this lady, to chat over a cup of coffee and try to get a handle on her. He had done this before with people accused of crimes he was investigating.

At some point in a case he felt he had to go beyond science, go instead by his gut, which sometimes aligned conveniently with political interests and the interests of his buddies. Once, in 1990, he had suggested that a criminal who had died after being badly beaten while in the custody of Minyard's policeman friend, could have sustained his injuries because he "slipped on the floor."

Minyard was now seventy-six years old, had served as elected coroner for thirty-one years, and had recently garnered another term (after going to court to get his sole challenger disqualified), but community opinion and his image still mattered greatly to him. An obstetrician-gynecologist by training, Minyard was inspired by a Catholic nun to devote his life to what he called "the business of serving suffering humanity." He gave up his private doctor salary and gained a measure of public adulation. For decades, he peered into bodies in the basement office of the colonnaded criminal courthouse, emerging in cowboy boots to play jazz trumpet at city charity events. He kept posters of his younger self in a white suit playing trumpet on a levee and would sign them for visiting reporters.

Minyard was proud of his office and its history and liked to tell people that "coroner" meant "keeper of the crown," the person who collected money for the king when someone died. "It's in the *Magna Carta*," he'd say. He considered his job to be different from that of medical examiners or pathologists who use "pure science with blinkers" to draw conclusions about the causes and manner of suspicious deaths. He, being elected, was a man of the people. He felt it was his duty to take into consideration the potential effect of his rulings on the community.

Minyard received calls after the *60 Minutes* piece asking why he was even investigating and why the attorney general was doing what he was doing to "that good woman." Minyard had watched his close friend Dr. John Kokemor, a former member of his staff, appear on *60 Minutes* and in other media to defend Pou and the honor of the hospital.

Minyard invited Pou's lawyer to bring her to his office for a visit.

Pou sat across from Minyard. On his desk was a Bible, on his wall a crucifix. All around them were framed pictures of life in their native city. Soon it was Old Home Week as they discovered mutual friends and chatted about several members of Pou's large Catholic family with whom Minyard was close. They reminisced about Pou's deceased father, the family doctor, who had been especially kind to Minyard and had referred patients to him when Minyard opened his ob-gyn practice.

They talked for about an hour and Pou enchanted him. He considered her a "very ladylike lady, a real, real Southern charming lady." She told him that she had been trying to alleviate pain and suffering. Pou's lawyer was there, and Minyard was careful not to put her on the spot with direct questions about what she had done. The conditions she described at Memorial took Minyard back to the days he spent trapped in the criminal courthouse after Katrina. The city had flooded as he was driving back to work. He got out of his car and made it there by wading, swimming, and hitching a ride on a boat. He was stuck for four days. How precious food and water had seemed. How impossible it was to sleep at night with gunshots echoing all around him.

Minyard's feelings were less sympathetic than he let Pou know. He believed he would have at least tried to save Emmett Everett. There must have been a way to get the 380-pound man downstairs. It also bothered Minyard that few of the elderly patients who died had been receiving or seemed to have required pain medication before they were injected.

The first week of October, the expert consultants submitted their reports on the Memorial and LifeCare deaths. In their letters, forensic pathologists Wecht and Baden formalized the strong opinions they had expressed in Minyard's office in August. The LifeCare deaths were the result of drug injections. Minyard, seeking additional information to help him make his decision, had also sent the patients' medical, autopsy, and toxicology records to three other experts for an independent review.

"Homicide," Dr. Frank Brescia, an oncologist and specialist in palliative care, concluded in each of the nine cases. "Homicide," wrote Dr. James Young, the former chief coroner of Ontario, Canada, who was then president of the American Academy of Forensic Sciences. "All these patients survived the adverse events of the previous days, and for every patient on a floor to have died in one three-and-a-half-hour period with drug toxicity is beyond coincidence."

A local internist concluded that while medical records and autopsies for several of the patients revealed medical issues that could reasonably have led to their deaths, most of the patients' records did not. In his report to Minyard, he wrote that it was "evident" that Emmett Everett was "in stable medical status with no clear evidence that death was imminent or impending." (Pou's lawyer said that Everett almost certainly died of an enlarged heart, not an overdose of medication.)

The day after the last of the forensic reports was received in late October, Pou's attorney, Rick Simmons, documented spending close to two and a half hours and $360 in expenses at Minyard's office. Perhaps the sympathetic coroner had allowed him to make photocopies of the lab results that Simmons had been trying to get from the assistant district attorney. Two weeks later, Pou's brother Michael, a trustee of her defense fund, which had been moved after LSU had warned it could not legally be operated from the public university, wrote a $3,300 check from her fund to William J. George, PhD, a toxicologist brought on to analyze the evidence.

Simmons's dogged efforts to protect Pou met with more success in early November. The Louisiana Supreme Court denied the attorney general's appeal of the lower court's decision protecting Pou's initial post-storm discussions with Tenet's attorney and media relations chief. That case was finished. Whatever Pou had told the Tenet employees at a point less clouded by the passage of time and the pressures of prosecution—perhaps an honest accounting of her decisions and actions—would, it seemed, remain forever hidden.

⸺

ANOTHER VISITOR to coroner Minyard's office was Dr. Horace Baltz. He came in mid-November after Minyard called him one day and asked if they could meet. Minyard had seen a copy of a letter Baltz had sent to the attorney general's investigators encouraging them to continue looking into potential mercy killings at the hospital.

The men shared that they were having sleepless nights. Baltz, too, had known Pou's father. As a high school delivery boy, Baltz had fetched prescriptions for him. Minyard felt obligated to him, Baltz gathered, but was swayed by the fact that five independent forensic experts had agreed that the deaths Pou was accused of were homicides. The case would be going to a grand jury and then, presumably, to trial, which, judging by the calls Minyard was getting every day from around the world about the case, would attract the media in droves. "It would be the biggest thing since the Super Bowl in New Orleans." To Baltz, the coroner appeared to be juggling a hot potato. Emotionally, Minyard felt bound to Pou's father. Politically, Minyard was loath to court controversy. Intellectually, like Baltz, he seemed to think the deaths were homicides. It was odd that the coroner shared so many details about the case with a stranger. The next day Baltz sent Minyard an article about Memorial and a letter of thanks:

> For months—like a voice in the wilderness—I have felt out of synch with my professional peers, as relates to the Memorial situation. Like the lyrics of the popular Christmas song [. . .] I asked, "do you hear what I hear; do you see what I see?" I began to question my moral values and ethics. However, yesterday's visit was most therapeutic, has restored confidence in my judgement, and strengthened my resolve. Thank you. Last night was my first full night's REM sleep.

Baltz, like Minyard, cared deeply about his city and his place in it. He expressed that by clinging to high moral virtue, even if that necessitated an occasional confrontation. As a local nonprofit hospital chain, Ochsner Health System, completed its purchase of Memorial and partially reopened it under the Baptist name, Richard Deichmann sent a letter of appreciation to Memorial's medical staff. This incensed Baltz, particularly given that he himself had not received an invitation to the anniversary memorial ceremony. His pointed, two-page reply to Deichmann began by calling his compliments "kind, but inappropriate." Baltz had worked at Baptist for every hurricane except Betsy, when he had volunteered at a high school medical station. To him, service in a disaster was pro forma, not "valorous or uncommon."

> True valor would have been to oppose euthanasia; to lock all narcotics and sedatives securely; to erase all orders "DNR"; to dissuade naive nurses enlisted to execute orders that ordinarily would have been rejected; to assure that evacuees have secure destinations before being dispatched; to adhere to professional ethics at all times; to guard against aberrant behavior of staff members; to demand the Chief Executive Officer and staff be held responsible and visible; and to pray that Devine guidance grace us with sound judgement, serenity, and composure.

The scenario at Memorial, he wrote, was a horror, but an instance of the horror others faced throughout the Central Gulf Coast region. "Our situation was not unique, but somehow our reactions and responses regrettably were," he wrote. "Other hospitals with similar stress had more success than we. Was there some inherent flaw in our leadership? Look to ourselves and our behavior. Don't indict government abandonment, while ignoring corporate neglect. Don't cite the dread of lawlessness surrounding the hospital, when internally dreadful disregard for law and ethics may have become endorsed policy."

On New Year's Eve at a local restaurant, Baltz spotted ICU nurse Cathy Green and her sister, whom he also knew, at an adjoining table. He shared how disturbed he was over what her nurse colleagues had been accused of doing, and Green turned kinetic. Oh no, she blasted back, they did the right thing. She was helping rally support for them. He saw she was a true believer.

—

AROUND THE TURN of the New Year, New Orleans was rocked by two widely publicized killings. Dinerral Shavers was a well-known jazz musician, teacher, and father in his twenties who spoke out against gun violence and was starting a high school marching band to help disadvantaged teenagers. He was shot when picking up his stepson who had called for help. Helen Hill was a Harvard-educated independent filmmaker who had returned to New Orleans after losing her home to Katrina. She was shot by an intruder just feet away from her toddler son and doctor husband, who was also shot but survived. Hill's murder was the sixth in the city in twenty-four hours. Both her and Shavers's killers escaped justice. After some witnesses refused to testify against the suspect in the Shavers case, he was found not guilty and released.

The two deaths drew public attention to extreme dysfunction in the district attorney's office and police department and led to calls for reform. In 2006 the city had the highest murder rate in the nation at 72.6 per 100,000. Gary, Indiana, was a distant number two, with only 48.3 per 100,000. Of the 162 homicides that year, only a third were followed by arrests, which had thus far led to very few convictions. Nearly 3,000 suspected felons were released automatically by state law simply because the district attorney and his overburdened assistants had not charged them within the allotted sixty days, sometimes for lack of evidence from the police. Serving two months in prison for allegedly committing a serious offense in New Orleans was common: "Sixty days and I'm out," the saying went. There was even the very occasional "misdemeanor murder."

District Attorney Jordan had reportedly never tried a criminal case before taking office. His homicide unit was struggling to get a handle on the murder problem as its staff left in droves for better-paying work.

Signs along the avenues posted by a pastor read:

THOU

SHALT

NOT

KILL

It frustrated the chief prosecutor in the Memorial case, Michael Morales, to think about how much effort and attention were going into prosecuting the doctor and nurses from Memorial when so many violent criminals were menacing the public.

⸻

ON A FOGGY day in late December, Anna Pou hit traffic on her way to a hospital in New Orleans. She called Brenda O'Bryant. "I don't know if I'll get there before they take him to surgery."

James O'Bryant had another major operation planned for his facial cancer. It was nearly six months after Pou's arrest, and there appeared to be no movement on her case, but Pou had not ventured back to practicing medicine and performing surgery. Her days were occupied instead with teaching and administrative duties in Baton Rouge, part of helping revamp the Louisiana State University training program for head and neck surgery now that the major teaching hospitals in New Orleans were closed.

Pou reached the hospital and raced to where she thought the O'Bryants would be waiting. She rounded a corner to see James on a transport gurney being wheeled down the hallway toward the operating room. "She's here!" he shouted, and sat up on the cot to greet her. She hugged him.

"I'm going to be right here when you come out," she said. She sat in the waiting room with Brenda and the family. Hours later, they rejoiced when James made it through all right.

This couple whose problems were so much greater than her own treated Pou with awe, gratitude, and reverence. They didn't seem to mind that Pou had never told them what happened at Memorial. "My lawyer won't let me get into conversations about this, but I can tell you this," Pou had said to them: "I loved all my patients. I would never do anything to hurt any one of them."

The O'Bryants believed her and not the allegations. The attorney general had punished them, too, by taking away the doctor they trusted in their hour of need. Brenda O'Bryant—a bright, well-spoken woman convinced that she was neither—told coworkers at the lace factory where she worked that she would not believe that Pou had killed her patients even if Pou herself confessed she had done it; she knew Pou as a Christian who looked to God for guidance, and someone like that did not take other people's lives.

If being arrested like a criminal had completely ripped Pou's heart out, the O'Bryants and her other friends, coworkers, and family members were helping to restore it.

Pou needed support in this winter of uncertainty. Not knowing what would happen was, she would later tell reporter Julie Scelfo, "the most effective form of torture." The first days of 2007 brought a new drama. A "spoiler blog" predicted that an upcoming episode of the popular television series *Boston Legal* would feature a doctor accused of killing patients after Hurricane Katrina in New Orleans. Pou was about to be tried by a jury of television writers.

Rick Simmons badgered the producers before the broadcast. Believing he could not influence the script, he argued instead that the very idea of the program was insensitive, not only to Dr. Pou but also to the family members of the dead. The timing was inappropriate, airing only a little over a year after the alleged events, with a grand jury investigation about to get under way.

The producer refused to disclose the verdict, saying only that the show's attorneys rarely lost a case. Simmons asked for a disclaimer to be broadcast in the local area to help blunt any negative effect on potential jurors.

A last-minute campaign to stop the network from airing the episode was launched by Pou supporters including Dr. Michael Ellis, an influential fellow otolaryngologist and the former president of the state medical society. Ellis attempted to rally colleagues in an interview for a Louisiana medical newsletter. He noted that public pressure had recently resulted in the cancellation of a book and a two-part television special, *O.J. Simpson: If I Did It, Here's How It Happened*. Simpson had been arrested for the murder of his wife and her friend and acquitted in a criminal trial, but was viewed by many members of the public as responsible for the deaths.

"It's abhorrent to all of us in the medical family that some of our most respected colleagues, well known personally to so many of us, could be so horribly and unjustly attacked in such a vicious and inappropriate manner," Ellis said to the *Louisiana Medical News* reporter. He had taught Pou and known her since she was a child, although the article did not mention this. "Shame on our entire legal community for allowing such a travesty to occur."

The day before the *Boston Legal* episode was set to air, Simmons spent hours making calls and writing e-mails. On show day, he went to the local ABC station for an interview. It wasn't until he saw the program that he learned its conclusion.

The doctor on the show—Donna, not Anna, a middle-aged white woman with the same haircut as Pou—"had five patients faced with very painful deaths if she didn't do something," one of her television lawyers said. "I need somebody to first establish my client as an underdog—not easy, because she's a doctor—and then, keep her out of prison." Just what Simmons was trying to do.

Looters had stolen drugs. Corpses were rotting. "The hospital was like a death camp." In his closing argument, TV attorney Alan Shore claimed that New Orleans was not part of America after Katrina. Different norms applied. "During that horrendous week, the United States of America was nowhere to be found." Only the doctor, by helping the patients go peacefully, retained her "innate sense of humanity."

When Simmons saw the program he ripped up his copy of the unused version of the show's ending. The jury in the television case found the doctor not guilty of first-degree murder.

After the broadcast, medical professional organizations released more statements of support for Pou and the two nurses, as if the fictional show proved their innocence. "Their acts were those of heroism," said the American College of Surgeons. The chairman of the department where Pou had trained, a grandfatherly man who was deeply fond of her, had written the statement. It went so far as to assert that Pou, who had voluntarily stopped performing surgery, had been denied her constitutional right to due process because she was "forbidden to practice—a situation that gives the impression that she has been deemed guilty without review of the records."

DR. EWING COOK was elated by the *Boston Legal* episode. "Boy, that's good for her," he said aloud when he watched it. "I hope that's what goes on in the grand jury in New Orleans." The writers had captured what he felt. Nobody who was not there at Baptist could judge.

Cook was still feeling the effects of his time at Memorial. He'd had surgery, for kidney stones that he attributed to dehydration. He had tried not to drink much while at the sweltering hospital to avoid having to go to the bathroom.

Cook's lawyer had managed to keep him out of trouble. After the subpoena, he had never been called in for an interview. Cook worked a couple of hours a day now at two rural hospitals. He and his wife had moved far west of New Orleans and 110 feet above sea level, out of range of any storm surge a hurricane might cast against the earth again.

———

WHILE FRANK MINYARD had commissioned many forensic reports on the Memorial dead, he lacked the views of an ethicist, someone who could situate the alleged acts of the health professionals in a panorama of history, philosophy, law, and ever-changing societal norms. This was a perspective Minyard wanted, even though his job by law was merely to decide whether the deaths were technically homicides—caused by human intervention. In advance of a grand jury, he was doing his own unnecessary, unbidden—but, he felt, vital—investigation.

Minyard reached out to the noted bioethicist Arthur Caplan, who had appeared on CNN soon after the allegations emerged and opined that a jury might consider "very, very extenuating circumstances" a defense for mercy killing. Now Caplan reviewed the records of the nine LifeCare patients on the seventh floor and concluded that all were euthanized, and that the way the drugs were given was "not consistent with the ethical standards of palliative care that prevail in the United States."

Those standards make clear, Caplan wrote, that the death of a patient cannot be the goal of a doctor's treatment.

Caplan knew that the history of thought, law, and policy on aid in dying could be arrayed along two axes. One was whether or not the patient had requested to die, making him or her either a voluntary or involuntary participant. The other was whether the aid in dying came in an active form, such as the giving of drugs, versus what was referred to as "passive" withdrawal or non-initiation of life-sustaining treatment. The poles of these two axes were known as voluntary, involuntary, active, and passive euthanasia.

Whether killing someone who wishes to be killed is an act of mercy or an act of murder was a question that had divided humanity from ancient times, millennia before the advent of critical care medicine focused the modern mind on it. In a story related in the Bible, King Saul, injured in battle, asked his armor bearer to finish him off. He refused, "for he was sore afraid." Saul then fell on his own sword and called out to a passing young man, "Stand over me and kill me! I am in the throes of death, but I'm still alive." The young man did so and later told the story to King David, saying, "I knew that after he had fallen he could not survive." David condemned the young man to death for his actions.

Physician involvement in killing had also long divided opinion, back to the time of ancient Greece and Rome. Hippocrates's thoughts eventually held sway, and many medical schools still honor his tradition by having graduating doctors swear an oath descended from the one attributed to him: "I will not give a lethal drug to anyone if I am asked, nor will I advise such a plan. . . ."

This marked an important transition in medicine. "For the first time in our tradition there was a complete separation between killing and curing," anthropologist Margaret Mead told the eminent psychiatrist Maurice Levine, who recounted their conversation in a widely quoted 1961 lecture reprinted in his book *Psychiatry & Ethics*. "Throughout the primitive world, the doctor and the sorcerer tended to be the same person. He with the power to kill had power to cure, including specially the undoing of his own killing activities. He who had the power to cure would necessarily also be able to kill [. . . .] With the Greeks the distinction was made clear. One profession, the followers of Asclepius, were to be dedicated completely to life under all circumstances, regardless of rank, age or intellect—the life of a slave, the life of the Emperor, the life of a foreign man, the life of a defective child."

Mead added: "This is a priceless possession which we cannot afford to tarnish, but society always is attempting to make the physician into a killer—to kill the defective child at birth, to leave the sleeping pills beside the bed of the cancer patient." Mead was convinced, Levine said, that "it is the duty of society to protect the physician from such requests."

The Christian acceptance of mortal suffering as redemptive only solidified the Hippocratic stance. In notable historical cases even the exigencies of the battlefield could not shake doctors' exclusive commitment to preserve life. After Napoleon I's troops were struck by plague in Jaffa, in May of 1799 the emperor told his army's chief medical officer, René-Nicolas Dufriche Desgenettes, that if he were a doctor, he'd put an end to the sufferings of the plague patients and the danger they represented to the army. He would give them an overdose of opium, a product of poppies that contains the opiate painkiller morphine. Bonaparte would, he said, want the same done for him. The doctor recalled later in his memoirs that he disagreed, in part on principle and in part because some patients survived the disease. "My duty is to preserve life," he wrote.

Less than two weeks later, Turkish troops closed in on their position. Bonaparte ordered that those in the hospital not strong enough to join the retreat be poisoned with laudanum, a tincture of opium. Dr. Desgenettes refused. The fifty or so patients left in the hospital, seemingly close to death, were poisoned instead by the chief pharmacist, but apparently he gave an insufficient dose. The Turks found several alive in the hospital and protected them.

Although stories of wartime mercy killings of injured soldiers frequently appear in fictional novels and movies, it is extremely difficult to find a real, documented case of physician involvement. In the nineteenth century, however, a movement arose to challenge the physicians' absolutist views on preserving life. In the United States and Europe, some non-physicians criticized doctors' penchant for prolonging lives at all costs. They advocated using anesthetic drugs developed in the 1800s not only to ease the pain of dying but also to help it along. Known as "euthanasiasts," these advocates called their proposal "euthanasia"—a Greek-derived term (*eu* = "good," *thanatos* = "death") that English-language writers had for centuries used to mean "a soft quiet death, or an easy passage out of this world."

Many doctors argued against the proposed use of their skills to bring about dying, fearing the public would lose trust in the profession. Allowing death to claim patients naturally struck them as far different from causing patients' deaths. "To surrender to superior forces is not the same thing as to lead an attack of the enemy upon one's own friends," editors of the *Boston Medical and Surgical Journal* opined in 1884.

Still, the movement for euthanasia grew in the United States and Europe, and it morphed. Some advocates noted the great burdens the sick, mentally ill, and dying placed on their families and society. Helping them die would be both merciful and a contribution to the greater collectivist good. Why not, some asked, extend to terminally ill people what few would deny their sick animals, regardless of whether they were capable of expressing the wish to die? These were lives not worthy of living.

These ideas found particular resonance at a time of widespread economic privation, suffering, and hunger in post–World War I Germany. Attention focused on the costs of caring for the elderly, disabled, mentally ill, and other dependent individuals, many warehoused in church-run asylums. (Also couched in terms of public health was the growing international support for eugenics—improving the gene pool of the society—and these individuals were seen as a threat to the purity and superiority of the German race.)

In an effort to save money and resources during wartime in the early 1940s, the Nazis took the ideas to their logical extreme and implemented programs of *involuntary* euthanasia of these populations. By some counts up to 200,000 people with mental illnesses or physical disabilities were executed, the Darwinian notion of survival of the fittest employed to justify the murders. After these programs were shut down, their administrators were sent to orchestrate mass killings of Jews and others in extermination camps in Poland.

Doctor and nurse mass murderers of more recent ilk, some who have killed many dozens of patients before being stopped—Howard Shipman, Michael Swango, and Arnfinn Nesset among them—have similarly targeted the very sick and elderly, as well as those unable to communicate and neglected by their families. On arrest, some have invoked similar justifications, claiming to have euthanized suffering patients to put them out of their misery.

Psychiatrists have profiled these killers, identifying them as grandiose narcissists who tend to bristle at criticism, or to see themselves as saviors or gods unable to do wrong, or who get a thrill out of ending suffering and deciding when somebody should die.

Decades after World War II, arguments for legalizing voluntary euthanasia again gained traction in several European countries. In 1973, a Dutch court ruled that euthanasia and physician-assisted suicide (whereby a doctor provides medicine that a person can take to commit suicide) were not punishable under certain circumstances, and imposed only a symbolic, suspended sentence. These acts were decriminalized in the 1980s and formally legalized by a vote of the Dutch parliament in 2001. Similar laws passed in Belgium in 2002 and Luxembourg in 2009. In Belgium, one pharmacy chain made home euthanasia kits available for about €45, complete with the sedative drug used at Memorial, midazolam; along with the anesthetic drug sodium thiopental (Pentothal), which Dr. Ewing Cook used at Memorial to euthanize pets; and a paralyzing agent that stops breathing. The kits were intended for use by doctors in patients' homes. Doctors could prescribe them for specific patients who had signed a request for euthanasia at least a month in advance, after having discussed it with two independent doctors. The Dutch and Belgian laws did not require a terminal medical condition for a euthanasia request to be granted.

In each country, legality rested on different guidelines, which at first appeared to offer important safeguards. For example, in the Netherlands, euthanasia was supposed to be limited to people who made repeated requests to die and were experiencing, as certified by two doctors, unbearable suffering without the possibility of improvement. However, a study of the program showed these rules were not always followed, and a small proportion of people were killed each year without having made an explicit request. There were few prosecutions in these cases. Were the Dutch merely more honest about their practices? Or did the legalization of one form of euthanasia bleed, inexorably, into the other, darker kind?

While it was a problem that some ill or injured people had no option of participating in the program because they could not speak for themselves and had not let their wishes be known, involuntary, active euthanasia was, at the time Caplan made his review of the LifeCare deaths, not legal anywhere. Taking the life of someone who had not expressed the wish to die would contravene the principle that people have a right to decide what doctors can do to their bodies. It would also put the physician or other decision maker in the position of judging what quality of life is acceptable to another human being. The possibility of abuse (for example, insurance payouts for family members) was too great.

However, while not legal, in practice what was considered acceptable in the Netherlands had expanded to include this type of active euthanasia. The 2002 Groningen Protocol for Euthanasia in Newborns, devised by leading Dutch medical authorities, outlined conditions for taking the lives of very ill or brain-damaged babies with the substituted consent of their parents. While this was not explicitly legal, doctors who followed the guidelines were not prosecuted. Babies—albeit sick, disabled babies, but babies nonetheless—were being euthanized openly again in Europe.

The Netherlands's premier advocacy and counseling organization for euthanasia and choice in dying, the NVVE, promoted social acceptance of euthanasia under conditions that were not yet legal in the hopes that they someday would be. People, particularly the elderly, who were reasonably healthy, but who were becoming an increasingly dependent burden on their families, had a profoundly diminished "quality of life," and felt "after many years on this earth, life has been completed," should be entitled to aid in dying, according to the group. So, too, should people with dementia and difficult-to-treat chronic psychiatric illnesses. A Dutch court approved of euthanasia for a woman with advanced dementia who repeatedly communicated her wish to die.

In contrast with the European countries that formally legalized euthanasia in the first decade of the twenty-first century, in the United States, intentionally ending a life to relieve suffering remained illegal. The American Medical Association's influential *Code of Medical Ethics* continued to prohibit active euthanasia.

The debate in the United States focused instead on what some call passive euthanasia, the withdrawal of life support and withholding of medical treatment. In 1975, not long after the widespread adoption of high-tech intensive care medicine and only a decade and a half after the trial of Nazi leader Adolf Eichmann in Jerusalem had focused attention on the horrors of mass euthanasia, the parents of a comatose young woman, Karen Ann Quinlan, asked doctors in New Jersey to remove her from a ventilator. She had stopped breathing and suffered brain damage after taking the sedative Valium and drinking several gin and tonics with friends. She was not expected ever to recover, and friends and family recalled her having said she would never want to be kept alive that way. Doctors refused to discontinue life support, but the New Jersey Supreme Court ruled that this could be done on the basis of Quinlan's constitutional rights to privacy and liberty, as exercised by her father. The respirator was turned off.

Quinlan breathed on her own and survived nine more years, but her case proved a landmark. Subsequently, state courts ruled in other cases that the right to refuse treatment flowed from established rights to privacy, liberty, self-determination, and informed consent. The right to refuse treatment had already been established, in the case of some Jehovah's Witnesses, on the basis of freedom of religion.

The climate of American medicine had changed since the Clarence Herbert case Dr. Baltz and his colleagues had discussed at Memorial in the 1980s. Doctors treating the comatose Mr. Herbert had been charged with murder for withdrawing life support and intravenous fluids, even as they contended that this accorded with his prior wishes and the requests of his family members, who did not want him on "machines." A California appeals court decided the case should be dismissed because the burdens to Mr. Herbert of continued treatment, although minimal, outweighed its benefits to him, as his prognosis was "virtually hopeless for any significant improvement in condition." Stopping treatment, the court ruled, taking its lead from a presidential ethics commission, was indistinct from never having started it and was not in this case equivalent to active euthanasia. Shutting off an ordinary IV, the court likewise decided, was no different from shutting off a ventilator, as long as the treatment was legitimately refused by a patient or surrogate decision maker.

The case set a binding precedent only in part of California, but these concepts had gained wide acceptance by the time of Katrina. The US Supreme Court in 1990 considered the case of thirty-three-year-old Nancy Cruzan, severely brain damaged in a Missouri car accident years earlier, whose parents sought to remove the feeding tube that nourished her. The Court agreed by a five-to-four margin that the right to liberty included the right to refuse life-sustaining medical care and die. However, the ruling allowed states to require clear and convincing proof of the patient's wishes to discontinue care, not just what was believed to be in the patient's best interest. A Missouri judge allowed Cruzan's nutrition to be discontinued after acquaintances gave evidence this would have been her wish. The case led to increased adoption of living wills and advance directives that documented treatment preferences prior to a catastrophe.

The next battleground was assisted suicide: whether it should be legal for doctors to prescribe drugs certain patients could take to end their lives. Having the option of a painless death at a time of one's choosing could ease the senses of terror, loss of control, and existential suffering experienced by people with grave progressive diseases such as metastatic cancer, advocates argued. They questioned why only people who relied on life support or medical treatments that could be withdrawn should have the freedom to choose a dignified death with medical assistance.

Opponents countered that removing life support allows nature to take its course whereas assisting suicide is intended to shorten life, long considered unethical and akin to active euthanasia. Hundreds of years after sorcery's amputation from medicine, did Americans want doctors again to conjure death? Could the societal embrace of suicide for terminally ill or disabled people lead members of those groups to feel more worthless, devalued, and abandoned? Would it discount the meaning to be had from family reconnections, insights, and various forms of spiritual enrichment and personal growth that may accompany death's approach?

Physician-assisted suicide became legal in Oregon in the 1990s (and later in Washington and Vermont, and was deemed by Montana's state supreme court as not legally forbidden there), but at the time of Caplan's review, most American doctors continued to reject the practice as unethical. To address the very real issues of pain and suffering in the last stages of deadly illnesses, hospitals and doctors increasingly offered palliative and hospice care programs. These employed an array of medical treatments, counseling, and support to address symptoms and keep patients comfortable rather than to attempt to cure them. Hospice was considered a philosophy and a movement to care for the terminally ill and their families, which took root in the United States in the 1970s after being developed in Britain. Because patients had to agree to forgo treatments aimed at extending their lives, caring for them was thought to be cheaper, too, and Medicare covered hospice care beginning in 1982.

For the minority of patients whose suffering failed to yield even to the most determined efforts to treat it, another strategy had emerged: terminal sedation. The idea was to render patients unconscious until death. A proposal that would have explicitly legalized the practice upon request of "mortally injured and diseased persons" had been made and voted down by the Ohio legislature in the first decade of the 1900s, but interest in it surged again in the 1990s.

Terminal sedation seemingly fulfilled the goal of relieving terminally ill patients' discomfort without intending to kill them, but it did not do away with all ethical bugbears. A sedated person was unable to eat and drink, which would eventually lead to death, and unless the drugs were withdrawn and the patient awakened, it would be impossible to know whether the symptoms had abated. Still, in a 1997 decision that there was no constitutional right to physician-assisted suicide, the US Supreme Court supported the legality of terminal sedation. While Dr. Minyard deliberated about Memorial, the American Medical Association's top ethics body was considering a proposal to endorse terminal sedation as a last resort under the more palatable term "palliative sedation." (It later backed the practice in 2008.)

Some observers suggested the Memorial health professionals, if indicted, could claim palliative sedation as their defense. However, Pou's attorney, Rick Simmons, had for the time being decided not to have Pou publicly wade into a discussion of end-of-life care issues. Louisiana, he felt, was too fundamentally Christian for the kind of discussion that would entail. It was too risky, too hot a topic.

Simmons had been frustrated to find no useful guidelines for comfort care in disasters from the American Medical Association. "I'm defending a doctor here," he'd told leaders of the organization. "I don't see any standards. There's nothing there for me to go to a courtroom and say she followed these standards." The AMA did have guidelines on palliative care, but they called for consultation with family members and documentation of the medications given, neither of which Pou had done. "Why is it that you can't do something," Simmons asked, "that addresses the situation when you cannot document the file, when you cannot talk with the relatives?"

Ethicist Arthur Caplan concluded that what had happened at Memorial did not fit within the purview of palliative sedation precisely because of these guidelines. If the women had intended solely to ease pain and discomfort on Thursday, September 1, then he would expect at least some documentation that the medicines were given gradually and with care. The fact that doctors, including Pou, had recorded some medication orders by hand throughout the disaster before midday on Thursday meant that, while difficult, this was not impossible. Even war hospitals kept records. The apparently rapid introduction of large amounts of drugs known to be lethal, without any prior use in these patients, concerned him. It also disturbed him that at least some of the patients did not appear to have been terminally ill. No effort seemed to have been made to consult with the family members who were present at Memorial.

He was unconvinced that the sole option to relieve any pain or suffering was to kill.

Caplan had told CNN viewers that judges and juries rarely convicted physicians and non-physicians for murder when they believed the motive for hastening a death was compassionate. Studies in 1973 and in 1987 of twenty cases of alleged euthanasia found that only three resulted in prison sentences, and those were marked by unusual circumstances including that the victim may not have been terminally ill and suffering. Similarly, juries have acquitted—sometimes on technicalities—physicians who have intentionally killed patients with air emboli, potassium chloride lethal injections, and expired Amytal Sodium sedatives. One of the few doctors to see jail time was Jack Kevorkian. He escaped conviction for first-degree murder several times in the 1990s, even as he hooked up more than 100 suicidal patients to his death machines. Kevorkian finally goaded a judge to send him to prison for second-degree murder after he videotaped himself injecting drugs into Lou Gehrig's disease patient Thomas Youk in 1998 to put him to sleep, paralyze his muscles, and stop his heart, killing him. Previously the patients themselves, not Kevorkian, would press a button or handle on his machines to release a sequence of deadly drugs or carbon monoxide gas. Kevorkian later said he wanted to go to jail to make a point and shift public debate from assisted suicide to euthanasia.

———

THE HEADLINE of the February 1, 2007, New Orleans daily newspaper the *Times-Picayune* reported that coroner Frank Minyard had made his decision on the Memorial cases: "N.O. coroner finds no evidence of homicide."

Virginia Rider heard the news on the radio on her way to work and couldn't believe it. She stopped to buy the paper. What she read made her cry. A successful murder prosecution in Orleans Parish typically required a coroner's medical determination of homicide—simply that a death was caused by the actions of another human being—without regard to fault or legal responsibility. It was a step toward a criminal finding of homicide, in which a Louisiana court assigns fault for a killing. The DA's people had told Rider more than once that they wouldn't pursue this case without a homicide ruling from the coroner.

At the office Rider handed the article to her colleague Butch Schafer, shaking. "Get your purse," he said. "We're going to New Orleans."

Rider slapped the paper on Minyard's desk. She sat down before him in tears. She was convinced by everything he'd told her that he believed the deaths were homicides. "How could you do this?" she asked. "How could you say this?"

There was so much local support for Pou, Minyard explained. A public homicide declaration would stir the media into a frenzy. That would look bad for the city.

What will it look like for New Orleans when this all comes out, Rider asked, when the world knows that the truth was swept under the rug? A coroner's job was to discover and report the truth!

Minyard told her he had to consider what was best for his city, whose reputation had already suffered so much damage.

But did his own reputation concern him more?

Rider had never witnessed the level of politics that she had seen in this case. At the most, when Rider would investigate a well-connected doctor, a legislator might call on his or her behalf.

After the arrests, she had participated in a meeting with Attorney General Foti and District Attorney Jordan that Minyard had organized. One of the men suggested that if the deaths were proven to have resulted from the intentional acts of individual health professionals, this might hurt the survivors' chances of collecting compensation from corporate defendants like Tenet in civil suits.

Rider had interviewed the family members and believed that people like Mrs. Everett weren't motivated by money. She wanted justice for her husband. "Would you like to meet her?" Rider asked. "I'll go get her and bring her here so y'all can meet her." Almost before she had asked the question, the officials in the room said, "No!" That would have made the victim real. It was easier to avoid doing the just thing if the victim was only a name.

Rider was taking the case personally, while she knew she shouldn't. A foundation of her life was crumbling. Growing up in a state where politicians exploited every opportunity for corruption, she had deposited her faith in the burnished version of the American justice system her teachers had described in school. She believed in it. She believed, even to her ripe old early forties, that good would prevail over evil. She had given so much of herself to this ideal.

This case was not the usual Medicaid fraud case involving graft with public monies; it had to do with people's lives and seeking justice for victims. Shouldn't that be the motivation? Shouldn't that trump politics?

In one of their bull sessions in the smoking area outside of the office, Schafer called her a "naïve little girl." The way he saw it, she was used to going into a nursing home, finding someone stealing out of purses, and arresting that person. This wasn't a case of investigate, arrest, and you're done. Look at the overall picture here, he'd tell her: a city underwater, politics in the background, multimillion-dollar corporate interests, the medical profession on trial. She wanted two plus two to equal four. She had never thought two plus two could equal five. But that's what she got. She would not accept it. She would keep digging to find that extra "one." He had tried to warn her not to get emotionally involved, that the case would tear her heart out. And now it had.

The truth was that he greatly respected her. He watched her cry, a woman who'd been to the police academy, who toted two pistols, who had many years of experience as an investigator, whose quality of work on this case had been peerless all the way.

She had collected overwhelming evidence of homicides. She had earned the right to be disappointed, to be devastated.

Rider began applying for new jobs, a dozen in one week. On Valentine's Day she had a promising meeting that evolved into an offer. Schafer didn't see the emotion behind her departure as much as he saw that it would make her more money and give her the chance to become a CPA. She had ambition. He thought the move made good sense for her career. She shouldn't stay pigeonholed in state government. In the end Schafer wasn't Cary Grant, fighting to rekindle the passion of his jaded girl Friday for the work she clearly still loved. He let her go.

She accepted the job and left her position.

CORONER MINYARD took several phone calls from upset colleagues after the article appeared. When a *New York Times* reporter interviewed him about his determinations, he was coyer. He said he had not *yet* found evidence that the cases were homicides, but suggested he was awaiting more evidence and expert reports before he classified them. In fact, he could still make a determination of homicide when he went before the grand jury. Their proceedings were secret; what he said there would make fewer waves. Locally, though, the original *Times-Picayune* version of the story held sway. Pou's attorney and members of her public relations juggernaut repeated over and over again that the coroner had found no evidence of homicide.

Minyard was, even still, struggling with what to tell the grand jury. He consulted one more expert, Dr. Steven B. Karch.

Karch had staked his career on advancing the argument that the level of drugs found in a cadaver may have no relationship to the levels just before death. Minyard had come across Karch's name as the author of a well-known textbook on the signs of drug-induced deaths. He also came recommended by one of Pou's most vocal supporters, Dr. John Kokemor, Minyard's former coroner assistant and Dr. John Thiele's "brown leaf brother" in smoking cigars on the ER ramp at Memorial. Kokemor had recently helped reopen the hospital.

Karch flew to New Orleans, where he had studied medicine and had once as a student attended a party at Minyard's house. He examined the evidence and concluded that it was absurd to try to determine causes of death in bodies that had sat at 100 degrees for ten days. In all of the cases, he advised, the medical cause of death should remain undetermined.

To Karch, Minyard appeared convinced by his argument, which undermined those of the other experts. He seemed to agree with Karch in all cases except perhaps one.

Indeed, Minyard put great weight in Karch's opinion, which was shared by the prominent local toxicologist retained by Pou's attorney. However, Dr. Michael Baden considered their main point moot.

Whether or not it was possible to deduce the dose of drugs given to the patients, there was no arguing with the fact that the drugs were present. "These people were given Versed and morphine shortly before they died," he explained to Minyard, "and there's no other competing cause of death."

Cyril Wecht went even further in rebutting Karch. The levels detected in some of the bodies in question weren't borderline high, he told Minyard, they were huge. He put Karch's theory that drug levels change in decomposed tissue to the test, subjecting samples from patients who had died of drug overdoses to days of hot, humid conditions. Wecht compared the drug levels in these samples with others that had been refrigerated and found no significant differences. It was a small study, far from definitive and never vetted by other scientists or published, but it produced one more shard of evidence to consider.

Minyard imagined the case going to trial, provoking a battle royal of these forensic experts. The parish would lose the case over reasonable doubt. This, in his estimation, would not be good for the city, for the recovery. This was the bigger picture that he felt he had to consider beyond what pure basic science suggested about the deaths.

Minyard agonized. He was a man whose Catholic faith guided him. Willfully taking a life was a very bad thing. "Only God knows when you're going to die," he would tell his students.

The case occupied Minyard's life, his thoughts, and the dreams that awoke him at night. He called his experts again and again for support and advice.

———

IN FEBRUARY 2007, Mardi Gras season returned to New Orleans, lifting spirits lowered by lingering struggles to claim insurance payouts, find honest contractors, and file and file again the often-lost applications for "Road Home" public rebuilding funds. Mardi Gras krewes paraded in the evenings, and revelers dressed for balls, but it would be hard for Anna Pou to celebrate. Her case had returned to the news.

The *Times-Picayune*'s Gwen Filosa reported on the selection of a new special grand jury for Orleans Parish. The previous jury had worked through a backlog of cases after Hurricane Katrina. The new one was supposed to consider the Memorial deaths. The young lead prosecutor, ADA Michael Morales, intended to use the grand jury as an "investigative tool," a highly unusual move, Filosa reported. Rather than presenting the evidence to the jurors and seeking an indictment, as he typically did, he planned to invite the jurors to act as investigators in conjunction with the DA's office and decide what evidence they wanted to consider. Morales said this was because the case was very complicated.

The coroner's public comments and Rick Simmons's lobbying had not jammed the gears of the prosecution. Now that it was clear that members of the public would decide Pou's fate, Simmons, the publicists, and other backers began orchestrating more vocal support for Pou, though selectively so as not to incite a backlash. Leaders of the national professional organization for head and neck cancer surgery castigated the prosecutors in a press release for going forward with the grand jury despite the coroner's public statement: "Dr. Pou's heroism should be rewarded, not punished," it said, suggesting that doctors and other health-care professionals would refuse to volunteer in future emergencies. "These accusations are completely incompatible with what is known of her character and her history of exceptional care."

The kind words boosted Pou emotionally, but in the days before the grand jury was set to convene, she felt "very alone, very abandoned and very betrayed," she would later say. She ran into an old friend she hadn't seen in a quarter century. The woman invited her to come to Father Seelos's. "What's Father Seelos's?" Pou asked her. The woman said it was a place for healing. "Get in my car," she offered.

She drove Pou to a downtrodden corner of New Orleans's Irish Channel neighborhood on Constance Street, where a redbrick church, St. Mary's Assumption, rose up before them.

On its grounds was a shrine to Father Francis Xavier Seelos, "the Cheerful Ascetic," who had served briefly there as a Redemptorist Catholic pastor in the nineteenth century and was known for his concern for the poor and abandoned. He had cared for yellow-fever victims and died of the disease himself in 1867, a year after coming to the city. Pope John Paul II beatified him in 2000.

Pou began to visit almost daily when she was in New Orleans. The workers at the shrine taught her again to have faith. God had sent people to help her, and she came to believe in Father Seelos's ability to heal the body and soul. She needed "a lot of healing of soul and heart," she'd say. There were times she was depressed, moments she found it difficult to continue, days when friends, hearing despair in her voice, suggested gently that maybe she should "talk to somebody." Her steel magnolia mother told her God would take care of her. Pou prayed with the people at the shrine and found the strength to go on, she said, "thanks to the grace of God, the greatest healer."

Pou spoke nearly every day with Rick Simmons. She shared her anxiety and details she could discuss with nobody else in often lengthy, tearful conversations. She followed his advice not to watch the news, and she let him handle media inquiries and a stack of interview and book proposals. He had not yet committed to any of the offers, instead advising Pou to explore options for marketing her story if she was indicted, because the legal costs would be huge.

Pou knew the local public was behind her and the two nurses because Simmons had commissioned a poll of the potential jury pool to help him decide whether to move for a change of venue. He found, as he described it, that 76 percent of Orleans Parish residents supported the health professionals and opposed an indictment. Only 8 percent wanted them to be indicted, and the rest were undecided.

That backing was reflected in the letters that arrived in a post office box for Cheri Landry and Lori Budo, full of kind words: I wasn't there, but I'm a nurse, too; or my relative's a nurse; or I'm a former patient or coworker or doctor, and I know you did the best you could. On the nurses' support fund website, ICU nurse Cathy Green solicited not only money for Budo and Landry, but also "cards, letters and words of encouragement" to help cheer the nurses.

The accused women also uplifted each other. When Landry's house had to be demolished due to flood damage, Budo went to pick a few items out of the putrid muck, taking them home, washing and sterilizing them for her friend—a couple of boxes' worth salvaged from the belongings of a lifetime.

Far worse than losing everything she owned, Landry told Green, was losing her job. Landry questioned whether they would ever be able to be nurses again.

Not working was difficult both professionally and existentially. Tenet continued to pay the nurses' legal fees, but in many ways, their position after the arrests was more difficult than Anna Pou's. Unlike Pou, Landry and Budo did not have a university job to fall back on when they could not practice clinically. Landry had lost her home to Katrina and was the primary caregiver for her ailing mother. Budo was the major breadwinner in her family with two children in college. The nurses were middle class, with mortgages, rent, and car loans to pay.

Colleagues from the Memorial ICU sold plastic bracelets and car magnets to raise money for the two nurses. They organized a committee to deliver food and perform "other acts of kindness" for them. At the request of their friends, Landry and Budo drew up itemized budgets and received a monthly allowance from the support fund to cover bills, food, and clothing. Landry told a reporter for the local *Gambit Weekly* that she was grateful, but having her bills paid this way was very humbling and weird. "It's like someone else's life." The reporter wrote that Budo wept during the joint interview.

The women's supporters worked to keep a three-month cushion of funds in the bank. One particularly generous donor said that if the treasury ever fell short, he would pick up the slack. The medical staff of the hospital gave each of the two nurses a gift of $10,000.

Getting together with Budo or Landry reminded Green of being at a funeral. They could be talking calmly one moment, and someone would start crying the next. They asked, "Why me?" Green felt terrible knowing that her friend Lori awoke every morning thinking, *I could lose my husband and my children. I could go to jail for the rest of my life for staying at the hospital.* Green believed the nurses' lives would never be all right again. She saw the toll their plight was taking on their families.

Anna Pou, in contrast, had kept her job and quietly returned to operating again, although her PR force did nothing to dispel the public's perception that the arrest had stilled the hands of one of Louisiana's great surgeons. She restricted her clinical work to the public hospital in Baton Rouge, Earl K. Long (named after Gov. Huey Long's younger brother, who also served as governor), a limping structure with two aluminum-clad cylindrical towers some doctors referred to as the "twin trash cans." Among other things, Rick Simmons feared the potential for "frivolous lawsuits" lodged by private pay patients. Some attorneys in New Orleans believed that poor patients had less wherewithal to sue their doctors.

LSU had not reopened Charity Hospital in New Orleans after Katrina, lobbying instead for state and federal support to build a long-hoped-for new hospital, and Earl K. Long was picking up some of the slack. The air-conditioner in the operating room didn't work reliably, and Pou operated sometimes under the light of hunting headlamps. Pou questioned her surgical academy's practice of sending surgeons overseas when Louisiana was, to her mind, "as Third World as any place you want to visit."

The state medical board had not sanctioned or investigated Pou. She even received something of a promotion, being named director of Louisiana State University's residency training program for her specialty, which required the approval of national medical organizations.

———

ON MAY 19, 2007, secretaries, nurses, and doctors who had once worked with Pou in Texas spent hours dressing up a windowless exhibit room in the basement of the Hyatt Regency in Houston, covering concrete walls with cardboard cutouts in the shape of the New Orleans symbol, the fleur-de-lis, slipping black polyester sheaths over dozens of ugly metal chairs, and placing tall candles into hurricane glasses. They had organized a disaster-preparedness seminar and dinner dance fundraiser for Pou far from New Orleans, where a fancy celebration to raise money for her defense might seem inappropriate.

As her friends worked, Pou paid a visit to her old hairdresser, Raoul, who created a poufy shag for the occasion. Another stylist tended to her eighty-three-year-old mother, who had ridden in with her for the event along with many of her brothers and sisters. They were staying at the hotel, some sharing beds.

Before the disaster seminar, well-wishers crowded around to ask about her ongoing legal travails. Pou compared them to purgatory. "Now I know what the nuns were talking about in Catholic School," she said, and laughed bitterly. "I know exactly what it feels like." She recalled the little white snowmen the nuns had said represented the soul and had marked in black to symbolize sins. Pou had thought her soul was white. "Apparently not," she said to her admirers. "I have a feeling I must have had some black marks I didn't know about."

She stood with a phalanx of siblings, and many attendees remarked on the diminutive women's striking resemblance. Pou and her sisters even finished one another's stories. When the subject of conversation drifted to the hurricane, the sisters stopped themselves lightly. "We won't even go back there," Pou said. Her older sister Jeannie—the dialysis nurse whose phone conversation with Pou had cut out after the Seventeenth Street drainage canal split open and began filling her Lakeview neighborhood with Katrina's floodwaters—picked up the riff. "We can't, we're not goin' back there," she agreed.

As they discussed disaster preparedness that afternoon, Rick Simmons argued that Katrina showed what worked best was a central, top-to-bottom command. He gave the example of the Coast Guard, perhaps not knowing that many in the Guard attributed their Katrina successes, conversely, to the initiative of ground-level crew members who were empowered to solve problems impromptu and worked with great autonomy.

"Well, there was a problem with the Coast Guard," Pou asserted. "The Coast Guard do not fly at night. When you have a disaster, you need people who can fly at night. That's absurd that that can't happen, in my opinion."

Of course the contention wasn't true. In the days after Katrina, Coast Guard air crews had donned night-vision equipment and risked tangling themselves in power lines to land on rooftops, hack into attics, and rescue people, including patients at Memorial. The Coast Guard had specific policies and procedures for flying at night.

Pou could fix on an idea and be absolutely convinced of it, and convince others of it, even without all the evidence. "Trust me, they don't fly at night," she said to the audience. "Ask Vince." Her husband, a pharmacist who was a recreational pilot, had heard this.

What "really rescued people in Katrina" was "the military," she said, as if discounting the Coast Guard as part of the military. "It was the Night Hawks," she said, meaning Black Hawks, "those big, giant Black Hawk military helicopters that came in and got everybody."

"It was dangerous to fly at night because there were so many unlit towers," Vince Panepinto said. He had become a legend among Pou's friends for having reportedly made his way north to Hammond, Louisiana, after Katrina's floodwaters rose, and from there flown helicopters to rescue people.

One of the seminar presenters, Dr. Neil Ward, gently cited a report suggesting the Coast Guard had in fact flown at night. "They make the point that they did, with night-vision goggles, make some rescues."

Pou expressed similarly unshaded, Manichaean views on other matters. The LSU Medical Center employees working with her to serve the poor at the rundown public hospital in Baton Rouge were heroic. "I tell you, the courage. They are so courageous," she said. "I've never seen such altruism."

By contrast, those at the rival medical school, Tulane, had "abandoned all indigent care" for the uninsured poor, she said, even as a system of clinics set up by Tulane doctors in New Orleans after Katrina was continuing to treat thousands of residents for free.

Pou had told many friends she would never return to practicing in New Orleans after what had happened to her, but at the seminar she said she hoped other doctors would stay there, despite conditions she compared to "Civil War Reconstruction," to help bring back the city.

"We just have to give people a shot of hope," she said without irony.

Before the seminar ended, Pou's former chairman from Galveston complimented her. "There's never been a stronger patient advocate in our department than Anna Pou," he said. He lauded the work she was doing now at Louisiana State University to reorganize its residency program. "All of us are praying for you," he said.

Pou thanked her friends at the seminar for helping her through her ordeal. "I know that phenomenal good is going to come of this. I've been through some very dark places in my mind. I wouldn't be here without all of you. The courage and strength all of you have given me are a gift from God."

A FEW HOURS later in the transformed hotel basement ballroom, a former colleague of Pou's welcomed around two hundred guests who had donated up to $2,000 per couple to attend and support her. "Doing the right thing sometimes isn't the most popular thing to do," he said into a microphone. "But it certainly is not a crime. And so I think all of us are here today to celebrate doing the right thing. So that's what I want the emphasis of this evening to be, is to be a celebration."

Pou took the microphone in tears. "If it would not be for you," she told her supporters, "I would not be standing here today." She thanked them from the bottom of her heart and told them their love and support got her out of bed every day. "I consider myself one of the luckiest people that I've known because people have been so wonderful."

The organizers kicked off the entertainment with a country ditty about Pou, sung raspy and gravelly to an untuned guitar, written and recorded by a patient whose voice box Pou had reconstructed. Waiters served steak and poured wine. A local band, the DarDans, played Creedence Clearwater Revival's "Born on the Bayou" and invited the "bayou folks" to dance. Pou and around a dozen others obliged, drinking and dominating the dance floor throughout the night.

Pou wore a diaphanous gown with a deep V-neck that disappeared into a high empire waist, exposing a broad expanse of pink chest. The look, Southern Lady, Prêt-à-Party, was enhanced by a small gold cross dangling from a strand of pearls.

Even Rick Simmons let loose on the dance floor in a sweat-soaked dress shirt and tie; the heavyset lawyer had a dripping comb-over plastered to his scalp. One of Pou's friends thought it improper for "Disco Dick" to be enjoying himself so visibly—after all, the purpose of the dinner was to raise money to pay him. "I'm telling her to get a new lawyer," she said.

Pou let her girlish side take over, donning a fake grass skirt for "Margaritaville," erupting in chirpy whoops, and pushing her hair back, Vogue style, with jerks of alternating arms.

Pou's husband, Vince Panepinto, stood watching as his wife danced with her former colleagues and Simmons. "I wish I knew all the things he knows," he mused. Pou and her lawyer were speaking every day as the case progressed, but Panepinto said that he didn't ask her for details of their conversations. "Attorney-client privilege; they take it seriously."

Panepinto had tried to walk back to Memorial after the city began flooding. But the sight of two menacing men on his way there had made him turn around. Without a gun, he felt vulnerable. While he had not been at the hospital to witness what happened there, he knew his wife would never kill anyone, and he was convinced Foti had arrested her and accused her of killing elderly patients to impress other seniors, a constituency Foti had long courted. Now Panepinto said he didn't know what his and Pou's future would be.

From the dance floor, Pou summoned her tall, handsome husband. He gestured no and stayed to the side, watching. She didn't press him.

Attendees browsed auction tables laden with treats of a distinctly high-low flavor. A Chanel purse, a spa package, a hunting vacation . . . a hooked rug by a friend's mother, an awkward metal wall hanging, an enormous wooden cross hewn by a sick little girl, according to its auction tag. Peggy Perino, one of Pou's sisters, bid on and won a giant basket filled with supplies for making margaritas, then had trouble fitting it into the family's car the next day. "Peggy did this to us," Pou sighed.

———

THE EVENT RAISED close to $100,000 and Pou emerged from it enriched in more than one way. During the seminar on disaster preparedness, she jotted occasional notes on the record pages of her checkbook, having forgotten a notepad. A presenter read a quote from the World Medical Association, an organization founded after World War II to set ethical guidelines for doctors. In a disaster, "patients whose condition exceeds the available therapeutic resources," the organization said, "may be classified as 'beyond emergency care.'" Rather than maintaining their lives at all costs, "the physician must show such patients compassion and respect for their dignity, for example by separating them from others and administering appropriate pain relief and sedatives."

Pou scrounged in her purse for more paper to record the quote. After the event, she went on the Internet to find the full WMA policy on disaster medical ethics and e-mailed it to Rick Simmons.

Simmons was thrilled. They had found a respected medical organization stating that a disaster doctor could ethically designate a class of patients as not savable and treat them only with painkillers and sedatives. It sounded exactly like the decision Anna Pou had made.

There were, in fact, crucial differences. The policy defined "beyond emergency care" as applying to patients who had "extremely severe injuries" such as radiation burns that were not survivable, or who would require a long operation that would oblige a surgeon to choose between them and other patients. It also said that if any patient was categorized in this way, the decision had to be "regularly reassessed" in case the resources available—such as the helicopters that began arriving in force at Memorial Medical Center on Thursday morning—or the patient's condition changed.

Still, Simmons thought, this is something I can use. He met with WMA representatives in Chicago. A jury, he felt, could readily understand the concept of "beyond emergency care," and from now on he and Pou would refer to this in all publicity materials and public statements.

If the case went to trial, he and Pou might also need to justify one of the more controversial choices made at Memorial, that the healthier patients should be helped before the sicker ones. He and Pou adopted the term "battlefield triage." That would say it all to a layperson, portray the conditions as Pou had perceived them, regardless of the fact that this method of triage was not typical practice on the battlefield.

They also took to calling the concept "reverse triage," as in the reverse of what a layperson would expect. The term was used, albeit rarely, to refer to theoretical wartime situations where treating the most able-bodied first to get them back on the battlefield could help ensure the group's survival.

Simmons was devoting nearly his entire practice to the goal of preventing the grand jury from indicting Pou, and he expressed great confidence in the case. He taught himself about triage and end-of-life issues, interviewed or took statements from more than a hundred potential witnesses, filed motions to protect evidence and keep her statements to Tenet officials confidential, and, though money flowing in from her support website had been tucked away and Louisiana State University was paying for some things, he was prepared to sue the state to pay his legal fees if Pou, technically a state employee of the public university, was not indicted. He was still working by the hour. As the weeks passed, he became confident enough to draw up a motion to wipe her record clean in the event that the charges were refused by the grand jury.

He took pride in having written statements of support for Anna Pou adopted by and released in the name of several professional organizations. He also collaborated with the attorney for the owners of St. Rita's Nursing Home, James Cobb, in a public relations campaign to undermine the image of the man who'd had their clients arrested—an accusation AG Foti would lob, referring to their efforts as a "nefarious conspiracy," one to which Cobb would later happily admit. Cobb was impressed by the Pou team members' "deep pockets" and took turns with them feeding the media negative stories about Foti. The nursing home's owners were months away from standing trial for negligent homicide in the drowning deaths of their residents at the home, which had been named for Mabel Mangano's grandmother Rita, who was named for St. Rita of Cascia, the patron saint of lost and impossible causes.

Cobb and his colleagues planned to call Gov. Kathleen Babineaux Blanco to the stand and lay the blame on the government for failed levees and failed evacuation plans for the most vulnerable residents. How could the state scapegoat his clients at the same time it was attempting to hold the Army Corps of Engineers and its deficient levees responsible for an estimated $200 billion in damages, using the same language of negligence—willful, wanton, and reckless—that Foti was using against the Manganos?

Simmons also coordinated with a team of roughly two dozen lawyers representing other Memorial staff members, who shared information with one another. In late April, as the grand jury was preparing to hear testimony in the Memorial case, the attorneys had gathered to plot media strategy. They wanted to make the point that health workers wouldn't stay in New Orleans if the prosecution went forward.

The plan was to push for health worker immunity in future disasters; Simmons wanted statutory protections. Pou derived meaning from a new life goal—ensuring that what had happened to her and the others at Memorial would never happen again. The group would consider increasing the visibility of their public relations activities as hurricane season approached—it was a time of year when it would look particularly bad to indict doctors.

———

THE WEEK AFTER Pou's fund-raiser, the district attorney served subpoenas on Cheri Landry, Lori Budo, and Memorial nurse manager Mary Jo D'Amico through their lawyers. The good news in an accompanying letter was that the district attorney had decided not to prosecute them. The bad news was that he was compelling the women to testify without counsel before the grand jury so he could find out what they knew about Anna Pou.

The deal was this: in light of their Fifth Amendment privilege against self-incrimination, the women's testimony and any information derived from it could not be used against them in a criminal case, except if they gave false statements or otherwise failed to comply. Judge Calvin Johnson of Orleans Parish criminal district court, who had signed the arrest warrants in the case, now signed the order for the nurses to testify. The women's lawyers fought the subpoenas all the way to the state supreme court. With no statute of limitations for murder, the women could always be prosecuted in the future. Cases against them could be built on other evidence. Their lawyers pointed to an ongoing case with similarities to Memorial. Seven New Orleans policemen stood accused of shooting unarmed civilians on the Danziger Bridge after the storm, seriously injuring four and killing two. Police then attempted to cover up the events. Three of the seven accused officers, including the former night student and law clerk for ADA Michael Morales, had been forced to testify under similar conditions of immunity. However, all seven were eventually indicted by the special grand jury that had heard their testimony—the special grand jury that had sat before this one. The same could happen to the Memorial nurses, their lawyers contended.

Supporters of the Danziger Bridge Seven, just like supporters of the Memorial Three, argued that their actions should be judged by a different standard from the one normally applied because they occurred in the confusing, dangerous environment of a disaster. The supporters' arguments echoed those of the television attorney defending the fictionalized Anna Pou character on *Boston Legal:* New Orleans at the time of Katrina had not been America, so the accused should not be held to America's laws and professional norms. Colleagues had come out strongly in favor of the accused police officers, chanting "Heroes!" and applauding them in front of news reporters as the men walked into jail to be booked on murder and attempted-murder charges, and clearing them in an internal police department investigation. At the rally, the local police association handed out forms asking fellow officers to donate part of their paychecks to the men's families while they were being prosecuted, the *Times-Picayune's* Laura Maggi and Brendan McCarthy reported.

On June 13, 2007, Louisiana Supreme Court judges denied an appeal challenging the subpoenas for Lori Budo, Cheri Landry, and Mary Jo D'Amico. The nurses would have to testify before the special grand jury.

———

A FOURTH MEMORIAL nurse received word from her lawyer that she, too, would be asked to testify. It was Budo and Landry's supervisor at Memorial, nurse manager Karen Wynn. One of Wynn's colleagues had told the attorney general's investigators that Wynn had spoken to her about people being euthanized on the seventh floor. Wynn wouldn't deny it. "Even if it had been euthanasia," she would say, "it's not something we don't really do every day—it just goes under a different name."

After having helped inject patients on the second floor, Wynn had emerged from the disaster confident in what they had done for the patients. "We did the best we could do," she would say. "It was the right thing to do under the circumstances."

The only decision she questioned was having put her sixteen-year-old daughter on a helicopter out of Memorial without her. The child had experienced a difficult journey to safety, and Wynn heard her tell others it made her question her belief in God. That broke Wynn's heart.

Wynn was also concerned about her two arrested nurses. Their lawyers had told the women under scrutiny not to talk to one another—they could be accused of colluding—but Wynn and others ignored that advice, checking in to see how the others were doing.

In advance of Wynn's possible grand jury date, her attorney prepared her to testify. She told her what types of questions to expect and made sure Wynn's message was clear and consistent. The lawyer was patient and kept her up to date on the legal proceedings. She was fierce and protective, and Wynn came to love her, but talking about the events felt like reliving them. Sometimes after their meetings, it took weeks to find her way back to feeling OK, to move forward in a different direction and get beyond what had happened.

Wynn supposed it was post-traumatic stress disorder. She recognized its symptoms in herself and in her colleagues, figured they were there for life.

For the moment, the dedicated nurse didn't want to be one anymore. She made light of this, joking that she wanted to grow up and sell shoes at Saks Fifth Avenue instead, but she felt she had given up a part of her soul at the hospital, sacrificed it. She thought of the many times in her quarter century of work there that she had put patients and her career as a manager ahead of time with family. She recalled the fifty- or sixty-hour work weeks and the fact that it was she who had called Cheri Landry and Lori Budo to tell them they were on the schedule for the storm. She no longer wanted that kind of responsibility; that feeling had been building even before Katrina. She felt worn.

After everything they had been through in those five days, to have their integrity questioned, to be facing the possibility of going before a criminal grand jury investigating a colleague for murder, was unbearable. Wynn awaited the call to testify, but for her, unlike the others, it didn't come.

———

THE SAME DAY the other nurses were scheduled to testify, Anna Pou's patient James O'Bryant was given a choice. A scan showed that his cancer had advanced through the bones of his face and reached his brain. Pou was still practicing only at the public hospital, not the private hospital where O'Bryant was being treated, and her colleague Dan Nuss, who had recently performed another extensive operation on O'Bryant, told her about it. Nuss had cried when he gave the news to O'Bryant, only fifty-three years old, who touched him on the shoulder and told him he knew Nuss had done everything he could. It was the day before the O'Bryants' thirty-second wedding anniversary. The choice was between chemotherapy, which Nuss felt would only make him sick, or stopping anti-cancer treatment altogether and going into hospice, meaning O'Bryant would receive care focused on controlling his symptoms and keeping him as comfortable as possible until he died. O'Bryant chose hospice.

Pou called his wife, Brenda. "How did he take it?" she asked. Brenda said they weren't happy but were kind of OK. Pou invited Brenda to call her morning or night, any day of the week, twenty-four hours a day. Pou phoned repeatedly to check on them. She told Brenda she would try to visit.

———

AS THE ANNIVERSARY of the arrests approached, the American Medical Association published the first issue of a new journal on disaster medicine, with a photograph of a post-Katrina shelter on its cover and a preliminary report suggesting the death rate in New Orleans had risen dramatically after the storm. Several articles cited Pou's case as an argument for new disaster-medicine policies.

In late June, prominent doctors from across the country converged in Chicago for the AMA's annual meeting. Inspired by Anna Pou's case, the AMA's ethics council, whose appointed members served as custodians of the organization's code of ethics for the medical profession, held an open forum to consider whether and how normal medical standards should be altered in disasters. AMA policymakers also planned to vote on a proposed campaign for state laws that would make doctors automatically immune from liability in disasters unless they acted maliciously, even if their care was grossly negligent. Only a minority of American physicians were said to claim membership in the AMA, and many opposed its policies, but the professional organization exerted considerable legislative influence through richly funded lobbying and political donation wings.

Rick Simmons appeared at the Hilton Chicago to speak in favor of both proposals. Wearing a dark suit with cufflinks and a sapphire tie, a matching handkerchief in his left breast pocket, he took the microphone beneath immense chandeliers in the hotel's international ballroom. Simmons warned that when medical resources were overwhelmed, some patients would have to go untreated and die, their lives sacrificed for the greater good based on factors including DNR orders and physicians' fears for their own safety. Family members would inevitably sue, meaning doctors were in peril all over the country, at all times, should any number of emergencies caused by nature or terrorists occur. If doctors were to "answer the call" in such situations, they would need to be protected. Simmons reminded the crowd of the AMA's long-standing opposition to criminalization of doctors' medical judgment.

He argued that national guidelines on end-of-life care, which included post-Nazi protections such as seeking consent of patients or their proxies and documenting decisions and actions, weren't appropriate for a time of catastrophe when those steps were "not available," and it was up to doctors to exercise their own judgment in good faith.

Simmons held up the example of the World Medical Association guidelines Pou had sent him after the Houston symposium. Doctors could ethically separate "beyond emergency care" patients from others and sedate them.

Public officials, he pointed out, were immune from prosecution for certain mistakes in judgment. Why not legislate the same immunity for medical workers in disasters?

Simmons proposed a federal law to rein in state prosecutors and bereaved family members by mandating that any complaints about a doctor's actions in a disaster be reviewed by other doctors instead of lawyers and judges. To temper the appearance of self-interest, he suggested including a victim-compensation fund to satisfy the family members of the dead.

He concluded, thanking the AMA on behalf of Dr. Pou and expressing his and her hope that no more doctors would have to endure an ordeal such as hers.

The AMA delegates voted to create model legislation to shield disaster doctors from civil and criminal prosecution. Members would be encouraged to lobby nationwide for a new standard for conviction that would require proving a doctor set out with malice to hurt a patient. The

AMA would also strengthen existing efforts to oppose criminal prosecution of doctors by adding an emphasis on doctors in emergencies.

Without a jury or a judge having yet ruled on Pou's case, without Pou having shared publicly what she had done, organized medicine's main response to the alleged murders at Memorial was to close ranks and defend itself.

———

THE DAY BEFORE the first anniversary of Pou's arrest, Simmons launched an attack on the attorney general, filing an invective-filled lawsuit on behalf of Pou and distributing copies to the media.

As an LSU physician, Pou was a state employee, and the suit demanded that the state pay Simmons's legal fees for her defense in several civil cases brought by families of the dead, including Emmett Everett. "The State of Louisiana abandoned Dr. Pou and others during Hurricane Katrina and now she is being abandoned again by the State's denial of a civil defense," Simmons wrote, accusing the state of forcing the doctors to "save who they could save."

Simmons's petition circumambulated, veering from legal arguments to a personal takedown of Attorney General Foti. It called his conduct in arresting Pou and the two nurses improper and unethical, drawing parallels with a sensational case in another state.

Days earlier, Michael B. Nifong, a North Carolina district attorney who had prosecuted several Duke University lacrosse players for allegedly raping a stripper, had been disbarred for having tried his case in the media and misleading the public about evidence that was later revealed as false.

Nifong's case "demonstrates the dangers in extra-judicial comments by prosecutors," Pou's suit said, suggesting that many of the charges against Nifong could be made against Foti, who had vehemently criticized the women he arrested and whose press conference caveats had been edited out of news coverage.

Pou's suit alleged that Foti, like Nifong, sought to capitalize on a high-profile case to bolster an upcoming reelection bid. As evidence, Simmons attached a copy of an invitation to a $500-per-head cocktail fund-raiser at the fancy Windsor Court Hotel in New Orleans, held three days after the arrests, which perhaps explained Foti's insistence to his staff that the arrests take place when they did.

Attorney General Foti's public information director, Kris Wartelle, didn't need the Nifong case to put a scare in her. She already girded her tongue when speaking with the media. She often lamented to reporters that Pou's people were free to say anything they wanted about the events at Memorial, and did, while the prosecutors were bound to say nothing about all the evidence they possessed.

Rick Simmons also kept up the pressure on coroner Frank Minyard and about a dozen of the attorney general's and district attorney's prosecutors and investigators by regularly calling them. He obtained information from them as he developed his defense strategy. His toxicologist and pathologist were ready to engage in a forensic fight over the evidence.

———

MINYARD LIKED to interact with defense attorneys, and he particularly liked Rick Simmons. The men were from the same part of New Orleans, downtown. That inspired a kinship, though Simmons was younger. Most people were younger. Minyard tried to give defense attorneys what they wanted, do what they wanted. He never wanted it to be said that he was acting as a doctor for the police or the DA. He wanted it said that he was a doctor for truth. He called his office his palace of truth. He'd told that to Mike Wallace years ago in an interview on *60 Minutes*, a tale he never tired of recounting.

That made it all the more difficult now that the day of decision had arrived after many agonizing months. The grand jury called him to testify. Nurses who worked on the case at the attorney general's office and some of his own office staff helped the septuagenarian prepare a Power-Point computer presentation.

Normally Minyard loved an audience. He considered himself the one person the grand jury had listened to in New Orleans for thirty-five years. He liked to say that he'd had more time before a grand jury than Jack the Ripper. He'd grown to enjoy the prospect of coffee and doughnuts, the relaxed repartee, the aura of pride and concern most citizens exuded when exercising their civic duty. He might be one witness of several, but he knew his opinion on the manner of death was pivotal in a murder case.

Today he didn't want to go. This case was different. He felt pressure from family and friends who opposed Pou's prosecution. He felt pressured by the bad publicity the city was getting.

On the other side were his religious convictions. In his years as coroner, he regularly saw people die who had no reason to die and people survive accidents that should have left no one alive. He had seen the young perish quickly and the old live unexpectedly. You could never figure out God's plan. You just had to try to fit into it, like water taking the shape of its vessel. He liked to tell that to young people. The secret to life is learning what God has planned for you.

He would sing a bar or two of one of his favorite hymns: *"When the roll is called up yonder I'll be there."* Respecting life was the most important thing. The road to heaven was paved by God's grace.

There was plenty of evidence in this case that disturbed him. "Leave no living patients behind," Susan Mulderick's alleged directive. What did that mean? He didn't know, but he thought it would make a hell of a movie title.

Someone told him that other doctors at Memorial had done the same thing Pou did. Christ! Minyard couldn't bring himself to follow up and investigate additional deaths and alleged perpetrators. It was taking every bit of his energy to go through what he was going through with this lady.

Someone asked him, "What would you have done if you were working at the hospital under those conditions?" And he knew exactly what "those conditions" were, could imagine them from his four days trapped at the courthouse in the heat, hustling for water and food, smelling urine, his bare feet slipping on the damp floor, his boots stuck back in his flooded truck.

What would he have done? He would have done what he thought was best for each person. And, by his ethic, sick people came before non-sick people. One thing he wouldn't do if they told him to leave the hospital, that they were closing it down at five p.m., everybody out, he wouldn't walk around with two syringes and shoot up nine people to kill them because they couldn't get them off the seventh floor. "I know I wouldn't do that," he said. Not that he was saying Pou had done it.

His heart was torn. Yes, the patients died. And yes, she gave some of them the medicines. But pathologist Karch had described morphine redistributing in the body after death, making murder difficult to prove.

Had Pou meant to kill? Minyard didn't have strong evidence either way, just a feeling about her. He couldn't believe it. He *wouldn't* believe it. She was no Dr. Harold Fredrick Shipman, an extremely popular British physician who, prosecutors eventually concluded, had secretly killed hundreds of his patients with injections of morphine or heroin. Minyard had to believe that Pou's intention really was to sedate the patients. Some she might have helped. Some she might have hurt. In the end they all died. He didn't believe she had planned to kill anybody, he would say, "but it looks like she did."

Where did this leave him? He could easily call six or seven of the nine deaths on the LifeCare floor homicides, the administered drugs being the technical cause of death. In some of the other cases, the people were extremely ill and he just couldn't, in his own mind, call them homicides, but he could imagine another doctor saying that being so ill made these patients even more susceptible to morphine, knocking them off even quicker. This kind of thinking, these arguments, chased circles in Minyard's mind like they did in the public's, and he knew they would for years and years to come. His typical cases were 100 percent clear. The Memorial case remained a mystery to him.

Mr. Everett. He was the problem. He was an outright homicide. Minyard would stake his life on it. He considered making it clear to the grand jury that Everett had died unequivocally from the drugs. He could be a little fuzzier on the other deaths, telling them that some, like Rose Savoie, *might* be homicides, but he couldn't be sure. If the grand jury indicted Pou on just Everett's count and the case went to trial, Minyard imagined Mr. Simmons could easily defend her. Pou could say she was trying to sedate everybody, and because of Mr. Everett's great size she, not being an anesthesiologist or pharmacologist, had overestimated how much sedation he would need.

This was the solution Minyard settled on. It came closest to satisfying his warring convictions and loyalties.

He looked out at the jurors and imagined he saw the larger public sentiment reflected in their eyes. Pou was Mother Teresa. Florence Nightingale. He looked into these citizens' hearts and saw they were not interested in bringing charges against her. That was how he would later describe it.

———

DESPAIR INFECTED the Justice Department in Baton Rouge. Virginia Rider had been gone for months, but in her place were others consumed with the Memorial deaths and so troubled by the course of the grand jury's investigation of them, monitored by the forceful head of Foti's criminal division, Julie Cullen, that they drafted a scathing letter to the New Orleans district attorney on behalf of Charles Foti protesting that "essential evidence in this case is being ignored."

The grand jury's exposure to the evidence had been in their estimation far from thorough. Problems had emerged from the beginning. One of Pou's publicity messages had clearly reached its mark. When Butch Schafer met with the jurors to summarize the case, they spoke as if they assumed LifeCare staff had failed to care for their patients and not tried to evacuate them. "Many on the grand jury appear to believe this case is merely a conspiracy on the part of Life Care to escape liability for abandoning their patients," the attorney general's draft letter said.

There was plenty of evidence to the contrary, but according to the letter, the grand jurors had not been provided with e-mail and text messages showing how LifeCare staff inside and outside the hospital had worked to try to arrange for an evacuation, and how confusing the mixed messages were that they received from Memorial. Prosecutors had not made it clear to the grand jury that the LifeCare witnesses had reported the events voluntarily, giving statements without immunity. "LifeCare employees and administrators are ready and willing to testify about their efforts to save lives, to try to evacuate their patients, and about the directions/orders by MMC staff (Pou, Mulderick, and others). None of these witnesses have been called."

Instead, the jurors heard, early in their investigation, from the Memorial nurses. It was unusual for a prosecutor to grant immunity before knowing what a witness would say.

Cheri Landry, the shorter of the two nurses (who had, early in the disaster, imagined Kathy Bates would play her in the movie version of the heroic ICU evacuation), told the jurors that she had injected up to four of the LifeCare patients on the seventh floor and two patients on the second floor, according to the letter. She acknowledged she was not familiar with the medical condition of the patients on the seventh floor and had not asked about their medications, but believed all of them were going to die. She assumed the patients she injected had DNR orders. She suggested that most had the gasping, automaton-like agonal breathing pattern of the dying.

Landry emerged from her testimony impressed by how kindly the jurors spoke to her. She told her lawyer she sensed they were on her side. One looked somewhat familiar.

Lori Budo's story was much the same. She told the jurors she was unaware of the medical conditions of the patients on the seventh floor or their DNR statuses, but they appeared to be dying, the letter said. She said she had injected two of them with morphine and midazolam.

By the nurses' own testimony, according to the missive, they had violated in numerous ways Memorial's policy on administering sedatives; it required an initial assessment of the patient by a doctor, informed consent, a medical order recorded in the patient chart, and continuous monitoring with emergency equipment at the ready in case resuscitation was needed. Not all of those steps should have been impossible during the disaster if the goal had been to sedate the patients. The jurors were not made aware that a policy even existed, the letter said.

Mary Jo D'Amico, the nurse manager of the operating room, who had accompanied Pou on a trip to the LifeCare floor, used her grand jury appearance to disparage LifeCare, the letter said, suggesting that their nurses were "sleeping on the job" on the second floor on Tuesday night.

The attorney general's team feared the grand jury would not hear from any LifeCare witnesses at all, leaving them no chance to correct what the Memorial nurses had wrongly assumed about the condition of the patients and the LifeCare staff's actions. "When will they be allowed to tell their stories?"

Moreover, the state had expended "considerable funds" for expert analyses performed by pathologists, toxicologists, coroners, and the medical ethicist—Frank Minyard's forensic all-stars. While it was hard for Minyard to be the heavy, living in the community with Pou's supporters and feeling indebted to her father, he had specifically recommended that the grand jury hear from all of the experts, most of whom believed all the deaths were homicides. The experts had received notice to prepare to come testify, but not one had been called to do so.

The same was true of Emmett Everett's wife, Carrie, and of Angela McManus and Kathryn Nelson—daughters of the dead, who had been made to leave LifeCare just before the injections took place. "Testimony from these family members who were present as late as 9/1, is essential to the presentation of an accurate picture of the realities of the situation and the care being provided."

One draft of the letter urged that Memorial doctors, too, be called to testify without immunity. "Someone in that hospital made decisions about who would be evacuated and who would not be evacuated. The patients who died on the 7th floor died as a result of that decision."

The grand jury seemed unaware that some doctors had contacted prosecutors in support of the case, including Horace Baltz. He, too, had not appeared. The attorney general's draft letter raised this issue and said, "I am very concerned that many of the grand jurors have already made a decision in this case." Julie Cullen expressed these views in multiple, jalapeño-hot meetings with ADA Morales.

At a grand jury, hearsay was admissible. It was common for the lead investigating agent to summarize the evidence before the jurors. Virginia Rider, who knew every detail, was not called.

———

ON JULY 17, 2007, one of New Orleans's most popular talk-radio hosts, WWL's Garland Robinette, urged his listeners to rally in support of Pou that evening at City Park. "Say to the attorney general and the DA, 'Drop this case. We got more important things to do in this city!'" Robinette urged.

In mid-July, Foti had called in to Robinette's *Think Tank* show, and the emotional host accused him of driving nurses and doctors out of the state. Foti hung up. "This whole city is angered by what you've done to that doctor and those two nurses," Robinette said, his deep voice cracking as he sobbed.

Robinette, a hero of the marathon Katrina broadcast and a post-storm crusader for accountability, was a relative newcomer to radio, but the disaster had taught him its power to incite the public. He believed if he showed people how a problem could affect them, they would take care of it. He was outraged by what was done to Pou, Landry, and Budo "for trying to save lives." He hoped to bring Foti down as low as Duke prosecutor Nifong.

It was a warm day, with thunderclouds chasing sunshine. Cicadas droned and red-faced ducks paddled in a pond behind the pillars of City Park's peristyle, where hundreds of people gathered, spilling outside and opening umbrellas against the intermittent rain. The downpours stayed just light enough to avoid forcing a cancellation of the sort that scuttled the 1926 May Day fête in the very same spot, where moss-draped live oaks had stood rooted for hundreds of years.

Several supporters of Buddy Caldwell, one of Attorney General Foti's opponents in the upcoming election, stood to the side wearing campaign stickers. Other attendees held cardboard signs: THEY STAYED. And: FOTI IS ANOTHER NIFONG.

ICU nurse Cathy Green walked up to the podium in blue scrubs and looked down at her prepared remarks. "Many of you worked at Baptist during the storm with Dr. Pou. I know you thought our rescue work was done. The storm was almost two years ago. But we are not done. We are called to another mission. We must seek justice and exoneration for the one person who is carrying a burden for our whole hospital, Dr. Anna Pou."

Speakers included a nurse, a clergyman, one of Pou's brothers, and Dr. Dan Nuss. Some of them aimed their comments directly at the grand jury members, who had not been sequestered and could freely watch news coverage. The speakers warned that medical professionals, whose ranks had already been depleted by Katrina, would flee Louisiana in droves if a doctor was indicted after serving in a disaster. They read aloud a joint statement from the American Medical Association and American Nursing Association urging "that strong consideration be given to the harmful repercussions of continuing the prosecution of this case."

———

DR. JOHN THIELE stood in the crowd, well aware of those repercussions. He had endured an even more punishing year than Pou, although few people had learned about his role in the Memorial deaths, namely that he had injected patients beside her.

After the arrests of the three women, Thiele's attorney had told him, "If someone rings the doorbell, be ready." Sitting across from Thiele in a small office, the lawyer had outlined four possible charges: first-degree murder, second-degree murder, manslaughter, and negligent homicide. All were felonies. A conviction on any one of them would mean the loss of his medical license. "Prepare what you're going to do," the lawyer advised.

"I'll fight it," Thiele said at first, but if the jury found him guilty, he would go to jail, losing his freedom and his family. He knew he could not live in jail. He was too family oriented and had too many friends and relatives. The lawyer asked what he thought about a plea bargain that might get the charges reduced to negligent homicide. That would still mean losing his medical license. If that happens, Thiele wondered, how can I do what I was born to do? His vocation was to care for people, help people, make a difference in their lives.

All year whenever his doorbell rang, he seized up with the thought, I'm going to jail. In his gut he felt he should fight the charges, but if his attorney could plead him down to a lesser charge with no prison time, he would grab that. He could live without his medical license, he decided, but not without his freedom. He would find something to substitute for doctoring.

He'd been able at times to laugh about the storm, once gathering with a few other Memorial kin for a night of drinking and reminiscing. Sitting out on a colleague's dock on a canal just off of Lake Pontchartrain, Thiele read aloud a top-ten list of memories he had drawn up in the style of David Letterman's late-night television comedy show. Number six: eating peanut-butter-and-jelly sandwiches by candlelight, serenaded by a nurse on violin. Another was coaxing a friend's dog to pee in the parking garage by peeing there himself, and lying on the carpet of a medical office, petting the dog, looking into her eyes, "both of us thinking, 'I don't need this shit.'"

Thiele recalled taking turns with friends sitting in his car to cool off, listen to classical music, and recharge their cell phones from the car battery with the motor running, while they wondered if they were in a good spot not to get shot by snipers . . . then discovering at the gas station after the storm that from the Saturday before the hurricane to the Thursday after it, the car had averaged 0.7 miles per gallon.

Number one on his top-ten list was an expression of gratitude. "Thanking God over and over again for surrounding me with such great and special people facing this hellacious ordeal."

Thiele's life had remained stressful. As his lawyer fought to keep his statements to Tenet from being released to the attorney general's office, his legal bills mounted, far exceeding the total in the medical staff slush fund, normally used for banquets, that had been set aside to help several doctors after Thiele's appeal for support at the medical staff meeting the previous December. Tenet higher-ups balked at paying to defend him, arguing that he wasn't an employee and hadn't been required to stay for the storm. How absurd, when he had been called upon to care for Memorial patients whose doctors were unreachable after the storm hit.

He worried he would have to mortgage his home, and it was not clear whether threatening to tell his story might convince the company to pay.

Thiele had recovered from the stroke he experienced days after leaving Memorial, but over the course of the year, he lost a great deal of weight. He chalked it up to the stress of the investigation. He skipped a colonoscopy, recommended for men his age.

In February, the month the grand jury was selected, he'd experienced a few days of pain in the lower left side of his abdomen. He thought it might be a hernia or diverticulitis, a painful infection in an outpouching of the intestinal lining. He was admitted to a hospital.

"Suppose you had cancer?" his wife, Patricia, asked.

"Whatever it is, we'll handle it," he told her before being wheeled to the operating theater.

His surgeon, Dr. John Walsh, whom he knew from Memorial, discovered a tumor that had blocked off and killed a large portion of bowel and seeded his liver and spleen. It was advanced, metastatic colon cancer. Walsh marveled at how tuned out of himself Thiele had to have been not to notice how sick he was. He attributed it to the stress Thiele had been enduring as a subject of the attorney general's investigation, his worries over becoming the next Anna Pou.

Thiele did not awaken that day. He developed a life-threatening infection in his abdomen that spread to his blood. He was taken five times to the operating room, given blood transfusions, and kept sedated and mostly unconscious for weeks with a milky, hypnotic drug called propofol.

There were awful ironies. Thiele, a lung specialist, developed severe breathing problems and lay in the ICU on a ventilator attached to his neck through a tracheostomy.

Since well before the storm, after his mother died peacefully of lung cancer at his home on hospice, he'd had a passion for caring for patients at the end of life and counseling their families about "when to say when,"

when cure was not possible and another test or procedure made no sense. Now his own wife was being warned of his grave condition and asked about their end-of-life preferences.

By all accounts, Thiele had very little chance of surviving or, if he did, emerging without significant damage to his brain and other major organs. As his health problems mounted in the foreground of advanced cancer, it was time to consider whether to keep treating him aggressively.

His wife had no question about what she wanted for him—the most aggressive treatment possible. The doctors and nurses, many of whom knew him, concurred.

As Thiele passed weeks in a half-conscious limbo, there were certain things that even a drug known for causing amnesia could not erase. He experienced what he later described as nightmarish distortions, visions of monsters and pods. Many times he was underwater, struggling to surface, only to feel someone pushing him down.

Rarely during this period of sedation did he communicate with the people around him. Dr. Horace Baltz's niece was a nurse who tended to Thiele in the ICU and had also served at Memorial after the storm. Thiele seemed terrified to her. When they spoke briefly during his hospitalization about the events at Memorial and his role in them, she believed he was remorseful, that he'd thought he was doing something compassionate for the patients he injected, but wished he could do things differently.

Thiele later said that was not true. He did not recall ever having felt that way. No, he was confident in what he had done. After a month in death's shadow, he still saw a difference between himself and the people he had helped inject at Memorial. True, in twenty-five years of practicing in the intensive care unit, he had rarely if ever seen a patient go through what he did and live. He had developed nearly every sign known to predict poor survival in the ICU. Still, and this was crucial, every problem he had was potentially reversible.

If the family members of a patient in a similar condition had come to him for doctorly advice, he would have painted a hell of a bad picture for them, letting them know, realistically, that recovery was unlikely. But he would have kept going, kept treating a patient like himself because there was nothing that happened to him that couldn't get better with good fortune and the grace of God. Potential reversibility, that was key; it differentiated his constellation of illnesses from those of some of the patients at Memorial.

"You got special care," someone suggested. "You're a doctor."

"This wasn't in the hands of man," Thiele replied. "This was in the hands of God. I shouldn't be here. The fact that I came out with my kidneys intact, my brain intact, and went back to some degree of normalcy is just miraculous. There's no other word for it."

The ironies continued. During the disaster, Memorial's cancer institute, with its working lights and fans and power, and its comfortable chemotherapy recliners, had been a source of refuge. Now chemotherapy from another cancer center was keeping him alive.

As the grand jury process progressed and Thiele recovered, his well-connected attorney asked for permission to use the fact of Thiele's illness to try to forestall any attempts to involve him. "Hell yes," Thiele told him, "if it will keep me from being prosecuted."

Thiele's dedication to his medical practice was prodigious. He returned to work, making rounds to see patients wearing his chemotherapy pack.

Later he learned that one of the nurses had been asked about him at the grand jury. From what he heard, she'd simply acknowledged that she knew him and said he was a good doctor. She hadn't spilled the beans.

His attorney had forbidden him to communicate directly with Pou and the nurses out of a fear that they could be accused of conspiring. He felt for Pou and felt terribly guilty that he was not sharing her angst as the jury considered her fate. He was happy to attend the rally to support her.

DR. HORACE BALTZ resented the thrust of what he began calling the "euthanasia rally." By warning that an indictment would lead medical professionals to leave New Orleans, Pou's supporters were threatening to abandon their patients if the issue wasn't resolved to their satisfaction. It was ridiculous, irrational. It undermined the trust of society in the medical profession. How dare these educated professionals hold a gun to the head of the community and say, "You do what we want!" Never had he seen such a constructed, hysterical response to serious allegations.

Anna Pou did not appear at the rally, but it was infused with her presence. While friends speculated that the events had "really taken a toll" on Pou's marriage, her husband, Vince Panepinto, came to support her as he had at the Houston fund-raiser. Pou was watching, in a sense, through him as he stood with a video recorder in the crowds. Pou spoke to her faithful in a statement read by her brother Michael that quoted from Isaiah: "'For I am the Lord your God, who takes hold of your right hand and says to you, Do not fear, I will help you' . . . and this is exactly what God has done for me."

Pou was, that day, performing surgery at the public hospital in Baton Rouge, two complicated operations that lasted from the morning of the rally until midday the following day. She returned to the hospital that night when one patient developed a complication.

Her former patient James O'Bryant was also on her mind. Over the previous week, she'd spoken with Brenda, who said he had stopped eating much, grown so weak he could barely walk, and had trouble sleeping. The hospice nurse measured his remaining life in days.

Pou told Brenda she had been so busy with the rally planning and other work that she'd had a hard time making time to get there. Her colleague Dr. Dan Nuss had visited, and the day before the rally, Pou asked for directions. "I'll be there this evening," she said, and took a long detour on her trip from New Orleans to Baton Rouge to stop at the O'Bryants' little red house on the bayou.

"Dr. Pou is here!" Brenda said to James. Pou climbed onto his bed and hugged and kissed him. He opened his good right eye. The left socket gaped downward toward a reconstructed cheek several shades lighter than the rest of his skin. Below, an area of black nothingness bordered his nose.

"Do I see a grin on your face?" Pou asked.

James said something Pou couldn't understand, in a morphine-garbled voice further handicapped by his disfigurement. Brenda, thrilled to see him smile, translated: "How are you doing? Are you OK?"

"Don't you worry about me," Pou said. "I'm gonna be all right. I'm gonna be OK."

It was what she always said. But James had worried about her, even cried over her situation. "It's just not fair," he'd say. Brenda wanted more than anything for James to know the uncertainty was over for Pou before he died.

Brenda asked after Pou's husband, saying it must be as hard for him as it was for her. Pou said they had their good and their bad days, but they were doing all right.

⁓

THE GRAND JURY met again that week of the rally as storms lashed the city, hard rain and lightning strikes so strong they made the ground tremble, made clapboard homes shudder. New Orleans felt cursed.

The weather was one more punishment to a population fading into the malaise that inevitably follows an early jolt of post-disaster optimism and solidarity, people's fight ebbing in the face of mounting evidence that rebuilding and repairing would take years, and what was lost could never fully be regained. Whereas the rest of the country had largely moved on, people in New Orleans still spoke of Katrina every day, and not a day went by without the once-innocent girl's name appearing on the *Times-Picayune*'s front page, often within stories recounting an outrageous abuse or failure of official power.

At their meeting, the members of the special grand jury stopped hearing evidence and signaled that they were ready to decide. They had taken an oath to make "all indictable offenses triable"—to indict when warranted, allowing a trial to take place—and keep secret what had gone on there. The assistant district attorney, who had examined witnesses in front of them, was their legal advisor, but they were to deliberate and vote alone. In his closing instructions, he urged them to act on what they believed. If you believe these facts, then this is what you should do. If, on the other hand, you believe this other thing happened, do that.

An indictment required nine grand jurors to agree. The jury consisted of twelve members when all were present. They had broad latitude. They were to indict if they believed the evidence warranted conviction. There were very few grounds on which an indictment by a grand jury could be quashed.

The evening before the grand jury return was scheduled, the medical staff of the partially reopened hospital, now owned by Ochsner and once again called Baptist, gathered at the New Orleans Country Club for the first medical staff banquet since Katrina. The banquet slush fund seemed to have been replenished. The *Times-Picayune*'s social columnist reported on the foie gras canapés, turtle soup and boiled shrimp, main courses of Chateaubriand and crabmeat-topped trout, and mini French pastries.

The next morning, July 24, 2007, ten grand jurors arrived at the New Orleans criminal courts building, where Minyard had survived Katrina. The structure's high ambition and modest upkeep were evident even with the gloss of FEMA funding after the storm. In its soaring, marble-paneled second story, the jurors gathered in the Section E courtroom beneath vaulted ceilings, massive windows, and Art Deco chandeliers with missing lightbulbs that swayed in the air-conditioning. Fading letters high up beside the entry door were painted between black marble pillars, quoting the eighteenth-century English legal scholar Sir William Blackstone: HVMAN LAWS ARE ONLY DECLAMATORY OF AND ACT IN SVBORDINATION TO DIVINE LAW.

Eight women and two men appeared for the vote. Six were white and four were black. One grand juror had died and been replaced. Observers gathered in the churchlike pews facing the words of the Louisiana state motto: "Union, Justice, Confidence."

The district attorney's office had prepared a ten-count bill of indictment against Pou for the grand jury to consider: one count of second-degree murder in Emmett Everett's case and nine counts of the lesser conspiracy to commit second-degree murder, one for each of the Life-Care patients on the seventh floor, including Everett.

This meant that the grand jurors had been asked to decide whether the evidence they heard persuaded them that Pou had "a specific intent to kill"—part of Louisiana's definition of second-degree murder.

Judge Calvin Johnson read aloud the ten counts of indictment. Then he turned over the paperwork to read what the grand jury foreman had handwritten. "Not a true bill." The grand jury had declined to indict Pou on every charge.

———

A CROWD of reporters, already at the courthouse covering the acquittal of a former police officer accused in the videotaped beating of a man after Katrina, was tipped off in advance of the hearing. The journalists surrounded Assistant Attorney General Julie Cullen as she exited the courthouse steps. "It's our position that it was homicide," she said.

Reporters trod the stained carpets of District Attorney Eddie Jordan's temporary offices to hear his contradictory view. "We respect the decision of the grand jury," he said in a press conference. "I agree with the grand jury." The case, in New Orleans, was over.

That evening, prosecutor Michael Morales looked over at the boxed-up evidence from the case in a corner of his small office. This was the last homicide he would prosecute in New Orleans. His unit had been disbanded and another was taking over. He was being sent to work on other felonies. He insisted he didn't feel one way or another about the outcome of the case, didn't care. The abiding lesson he took from it was the need to evacuate in advance of future storms.

His office had received condemnatory letters every day for bringing a case against Pou. He would later admit that he and DA Jordan "weren't gung-ho" about prosecuting the case and that his direct boss, the gruff ADA Famularo, had not hidden his ambivalence. "We were going to give some deference to the defendant. We weren't going to just rush in and indict her," Morales said, because Pou wasn't the usual career criminal accused of murder. At the same time, because a judge had signed a warrant to arrest Pou and multiple witnesses were willing to testify, "we weren't going to shirk our duties and tank it."

He believed he knew what had happened at Memorial and that the special grand jury did too. Why else would they have signaled they needed no more evidence and were ready to vote?

What he wished, as a former history major, was that the information the grand jury had collected did not have to be kept secret from the public. Perhaps a congressional hearing would have been a better way to reveal the truth, he reflected. He believed there would never be an open debate about what happened.

———

ATTORNEY GENERAL FOTI held a press conference that day in Baton Rouge. His staff handed out copies of the forensic expert reports concluding the Memorial deaths were homicides. He criticized the grand jury for failing to hear from the experts and from family members of the dead.

Several days later, he published an op-ed in *USA Today*:

While you may argue that Dr. Pou was under immense pressure, is this an excuse for her alleged actions? I cannot accept this argument. What is the value of human life? What circumstances justify taking human lives? These are the questions this case raises.

For my part, I will stand for human life and the victims of crime.

Weeks later, in September, a jury in St. Francisville, Louisiana, acquitted the owners of St. Rita's nursing home, Sal and Mabel Mangano, on all thirty-five counts of negligent homicide and twenty-four counts of cruelty to the infirm that Foti had brought against them. Six weeks after that, following a campaign by Pou's supporters to unseat him, Foti lost his reelection bid. He ran last in a primary field of three.

Before Foti left office, his Medicaid Fraud Control Unit closed the post-Katrina investigations into other health-care facilities, including Lindy Boggs Medical Center, where the sickest patients were left behind with the pets and three medical professionals; and Touro Infirmary, where Odun Arechaga was abandoned for dead and later found alive. "A successful prosecution is unlikely," two of the closing memos said. Federal officials also shut down their part of the joint hospital and nursing home investigations, noting the "unsuccessful results" of the Memorial and St. Rita's cases.

⁓

AT A PRESS CONFERENCE the day of the grand jury return, a reporter asked Pou what she thought of the attorney general. "I'm putting Mr. Foti in God's hands," she said with the grace of a martyr. "I'm praying every day."

The reporters had come to a hotel meeting room anxious to hear what Pou had to say as she broke a nearly yearlong silence. Her family lined the walls behind her. Her press representative, Greg Beuerman, and her attorney, Rick Simmons, stood on either side of her.

Pou looked angelic in a pale peach suit. She described being at home with her husband, Vince, when she received the news from the grand jury. "I fell to my knees and thanked God for helping me."

She thanked her family in tears and expressed her hopes. "No health-care professional should ever be accused in a rush for judgment."

What the reporters really wanted to know, Pou refused to share. She would not say whether she had injected patients or what her motivation might have been. Her defense team raised the ongoing civil cases like a shield against the questions. Besides, another grand jury could always reconsider murder charges. It was unclear whether Pou would ever tell the world exactly what she had done and why.

Away from the reporters, she called Brenda O'Bryant to share the news. James was still hanging on, sleeping all the time, no longer visibly conscious. The medical people had said there was no reason he should still be alive. Brenda took to calling him "the bionic man."

"Be sure to tell him right in his ear," Pou said, "so he'll know."

She thanked Brenda for all the prayers James had said for her. "Tell him I'm praying for him."

Pou continued to practice surgery and went on to become a popular national lecturer on "ethical considerations" in disaster medicine. In her talks, she rewrote history. "FEMA called us and said we're taking the airboats at noon," she said as the keynote speaker at a conference register-ing nearly a thousand California hospital executives and health profes-sionals, who gave her a long ovation. "So whatever you can get out of the hospital get out because they can no longer stay." In all the months Virginia Rider and Butch Schafer had investigated events at Memorial, and in all the years of stories journalists had written about the disaster, nobody had made that claim.

Standing on stage, her voice booming through the large hall, Pou said that in addition to no running water there was "no clean water" at Memorial—though investigators found a large amount of bottled water left over after the evacuation—and she asked audience members to put themselves in the position of deciding who should get the last bottle of

drinking water—an employee or a patient, "Who gets it? Who gets the
one bottle of water?"—a decision that was never necessary at Memorial.

"The Coast Guard helicopters did arrive," she said, "late Thursday
afternoon." She spoke as if helicopters had not arrived early on Thursday
morning—documented by the pilots, cacophonous, and later recalled
by LifeCare staff members present as Pou gathered drugs and supplies
to inject the patients (Pou's attorney, Rick Simmons, counters in a letter: "The obvious effect of that type of contention would be that the
helicopters were awaiting right outside and ready to evacuate patients
[. . .] We flatly deny this new contention of 'loud helicopters' during
the morning hours"). Pou also did not say that the Coast Guard came to
rescue patients on Tuesday afternoon, the day the floodwaters rose, and
throughout Tuesday night, and into Wednesday morning—despite Memorial employees having tried repeatedly to send the helicopters away
after deciding it was too dangerous to conduct the evacuation in the dark
and that staff needed rest. "I should note that, something I didn't know:
Helicopters cannot fly at night," Pou told the audience, years after a colleague at her Houston fund-raiser had gently tried to relieve her of this
mumpsimus. ·

Embellishing the profound hardships she experienced might have
been inconsequential except for the fact that as Pou lectured to medical groups around the country, she used these stories—juxtaposed with
the fact of her arrest—to convince her audiences of the need to crusade
for immunity laws that would prevent people from suing and prosecuting medical professionals in future emergencies. In her talks, Pou sometimes flashed her mug shot on the screen, but she did not say that she was
arrested for having allegedly murdered patients, not for having made
the challenging and controversial triage decisions she discussed. In fact,
she left out mention of injecting patients entirely. In lectures to hospital executives in Sacramento, disaster preparedness planners in Chicago,
doctors in Texas, and attorneys in New Orleans, she did not discuss or
explain the decision she and her colleagues made to medicate at least

nineteen patients on Thursday, September 1, all of whom died as helicopters and boats emptied Memorial.

Pou took issue with the AMA's ethical directive for doctors to serve
in emergencies "even in the face of greater than usual risk." Pou said,
"The duty to care sounds easy, great. It's not always so; it's more roman-
tic on paper." Pou concluded her Sacramento talk by sharing her views
on handling the media in disasters: "Restrict them and use them to the
best of your ability."

After Attorney General Charles Foti released the forensic experts'
findings to the media, litigation ensued, with dozens of hospital employees fighting—as "Jane Does" and "John Does"—to protect the balance
of the Medicaid Fraud Control Unit's thousands of pages of investigative
case records from public disclosure on grounds of privacy and grand jury
secrecy. The *Times-Picayune* and CNN led a multiyear effort to force the
state to produce what the organizations viewed as public records. Anna
Pou filed a brief supporting the Jane and John Does' position that the records should be kept secret. A lower court's ruling that the records should
be released was reversed on appeal, and—after numerous actions that led
the Louisiana Supreme Court to consider the issues—in 2012, the Jane
and John Does prevailed. The files remain sealed from public view.

In fiscal year 2009–2010, at Anna Pou's request, the general fund of
the state of Louisiana paid $456,979.41 in legal fees and expenses for her
successful defense, reimbursing the LSU Health Network and the Dr.
Anna Pou Defense Fund.

Claims brought against Tenet Healthcare and Memorial Medical
Center for deaths and personal injuries as a result of insufficiencies in
Memorial's electrical systems, preparedness, and evacuation plans were
certified as a class action and reached jury selection in 2011. Post-Katrina
suits against hospitals, numbering about two hundred, had been allowed
to proceed as general negligence actions, as opposed to medical malpractice actions that would have capped damages. The class action suit
against Memorial and Tenet was settled before trial for $25 million with

no admission of wrongdoing. The settlement was to be divided among patients, visitors, family members, and others at the hospital during and after Katrina who wished to take part, including LifeCare staff (Memorial employees were excluded according to provisions of Louisiana workers' compensation law). It took until 2013 for the checks to be distributed—more than seven years after Katrina, in a case some referred to as a "full employment act" for disaster-struck New Orleans attorneys. Many families objected in court to what they considered meager compensation for the suffering they and their loved ones endured.

In order to receive money, those eligible had to submit a notarized claim form indicating whether physical or emotional injuries were suffered. Funds were divided among three categories: patients who died, patients who survived, and non-patients. Each claim effectively reduced the payout to other claimants in the same category.

Anna Pou, an employee of LSU, opted in for a share of the settlement. According to the guidelines, she qualified for $2,090.37 for each day she was at Memorial.

———

THE SPECIAL GRAND jury's decision in 2007 raised spirits in unexpected quarters. Some LifeCare nurses rejoiced, perhaps because lifting a cloud on Pou lifted a cloud on them, too. If she was not guilty of murder, then they were not guilty for having entrusted their patients to her.

A friend from nursing school called Gina Isbell with the news. She was at work with another former LifeCare nurse. They screamed, hollered, and jumped up and down in celebration.

Isbell wore a necklace with a pendant in the shape of a hurricane symbol. She still saw the faces of her Katrina patients in nightmares and was angry and bitter—not at Pou but at the thought that help came too slowly. She considered herself a different person after the storm, forever changed by the trauma of those days and how they had ended.

Sometimes she took comfort in a memory from her last hours on the helipad at Memorial. Dr. Roy Culotta's eighty-seven-year-old grandmother reached out and grabbed her arm. "If I'm alive tomorrow," the woman told Isbell, "it's because of you."

Isbell clung to the belief that she and her LifeCare and Memorial colleagues had done the best they could. She would serve again in a storm if she was asked. It was her job, her oath.

———

CATHY GREEN was still a true believer. Nothing could shake the ICU nurse's faith in her accused colleagues and her pride in Baptist Hospital and the nursing and medical professions. The grand jury's decision pleased her, but it was not enough. She wished she could erase the idea Foti had implanted in the public that health-care workers would willingly do harm to their patients.

Memorial staff had been criticized for playing God. Green knew they were asked to play God every day in the ICU. She didn't believe in killing people, but she saw no valor in prolonging death by not giving painkillers. At Memorial's ICU, doctors like Ewing Cook wrote orders that gave nurses like her a great deal of leeway with "a whole arsenal of stuff." That was the culture, and she embraced it, having seen, early in her career, a woman die a "lingering death." When Memorial's long closure forced Green to work in other hospitals, she noticed that the approach was different. Patients weren't given as much sedation.

It pained Green to watch the sharp contractions of agonal breathing. When a young doctor reassured her once that patients at that point weren't in pain, she told him to try breathing like that himself and see how comfortable it was. The doctor's point was that the patients had too little brain function to be uncomfortable, but Green thought "young mind doctors" and "young mind nurses" didn't get it.

Green didn't want a protracted ending for herself. She told her daughter that if that time came, "You just take me to Holland."

What was it about death in the United States? Why did it seem like Americans were so unprepared for it when it occurred? She had seen it again and again working in the ICU. People often did not want to talk about death with the dying, or be there with a relative when it happened.

Why did we celebrate every milestone in life except this one? she wondered. Everyone wanted to be there to witness the beginning of life, but the ratio of birth to death was one to one. We all had to learn to say good-bye and give our loved ones the dignity to acknowledge we knew they were going. She would ask, "If your best one got on the slow boat to China, you would not be at the dock saying good-bye?"

Green had once been extremely sick on a ventilator in an ICU. She knew that the softness provided by a caring nurse like her was meaningful. But what she did not like about her job was the way she and her colleagues, with their drugs and machines, forced some suffering people to be alive for many months. People who chose ICU care did not realize this could happen, she believed. Death was not always the enemy, she felt, especially when somebody was elderly. She thought that most of her patients did not want the high-tech care that their families wanted for them. The effect of ICU treatment on quality of life should be considered. She knew what her next battle was, now that the one for her colleagues was won.

"We're so frightened of 'euthanasia,' " she would say. "It's the race card of medicine. It's like the word 'lynching.' " She wanted that to change.

———

FRANK MINYARD would later say he felt a little betrayed, a little hurt. It wasn't often that he called a death a homicide and the grand jury failed to indict. Their decision had stemmed, he concluded, from the harsh way that Attorney General Foti had treated the women, as well as the persuasive power of the media. He did not consider the role of his own media statements.

He thought someone would pick up the case again, perhaps a federal prosecutor. He didn't believe the story was over. It would lie dormant and come back roaring.

—

FORENSIC EXPERT Cyril Wecht did not care if Pou was punished. What he cared about was the truth and what could be learned from it. For heaven's sake, he thought, Memorial wasn't on a goddamn battlefield with enemy shells coming in. This was New Orleans, and there were helicopters and boats. And really, were they saying they couldn't get patients off the seventh floor? Given a choice, would someone rather die a painless death or live after being lowered, however uncomfortably, from a window? A great disservice was being done to the field of medicine, because the events were covered up and medical leaders reacted emotionally, without knowledge about what had happened. For now the lessons seemed to be that in a disaster if you're a doctor, you're in charge. If you feel giving large doses of morphine and Versed are appropriate, go ahead. It's your call. "Is this what we want young doctors to learn?" he asked. "It's a goddamn precedent, a very dangerous, bad precedent."

—

ARTHUR CAPLAN, the ethicist, worried that without formal analysis, the case would remain "an unsettled moral toothache." Bioethicists, not usually shrinking violets, had generally shied from sharing their opinions on this case. Perhaps some thought there was an underground practice of assisted suicide and euthanasia in America that seemed to be working and nobody wanted to shine a big spotlight on it. Many ethicists felt the conditions at Memorial were so horrible that moral judgments could not be made about what happened there.

Caplan felt differently. "Why not there?" he would ask. He never received a satisfactory answer.

———

VIRGINIA RIDER and Butch Schafer did not believe justice had reached its end in the case. Justice did not require, ultimately, a conviction. It could be served in a retelling through the court process.

Pou, Budo, and Landry symbolized the people in whose hands everyone places their lives in times of sickness. It was imperative to know how they would react under pressure, to learn that simply because people were medical professionals did not mean they would always act in the interest of their patients, whether from a self-serving motive or muddled thinking.

This case had changed the way Rider looked at the world more than almost anything in her life besides her children. It had led her to set out her own end-of-life preferences very clearly in an advance directive: for example, that she should be removed from life support only if two doctors and a sister she had designated as her health-care proxy agreed; that she would want pain medicines, yes, but no more than necessary for pain, and not in an amount that would carry a great risk of killing her. Members of the public deserved to know the story, so that they, too, could use its lessons to make informed choices.

Most of all, the victims deserved to have their stories told. Rider's position on Pou herself would soften slightly after the surgeon performed a daylong operation on a relative with cancer. Perhaps God was telling her she shouldn't be so quick to judge people.

Schafer could understand Rider's feelings about the case, but he was more sanguine. He knew what had really happened at Memorial. Whether anyone else knew it was not his concern. As a prosecutor, you learned that many of the people you bring to trial won't be found guilty. You couldn't spend your life sulking about it.

Years later, Dr. Ewing Cook would walk into a room at a small, rural hospital where Schafer had been admitted for the treatment of a possible lung infection. As Schafer lay helpless on the bed, hooked up to monitors and drug infusions, he marveled at the irony of the situation—his life now in Cook's hands. To his relief, the doctor did not seem to recognize him from the day he had sat outside Cook's door in the car while Rider handed him a subpoena. In the hospital, Cook was nice, cordial, with a dry sense of humor—a great guy, Schafer thought. Cook told Schafer there was nothing wrong with him. Schafer recovered.

Schafer believed the small, underresourced Medicaid fraud team had done the best they possibly could with the resources that they had. He was proud of the whole unit. They did not cheat. They had nothing to be ashamed of, contrary to public opinion. They'd been good. He would always have that.

———

ANGELA McMANUS spent the entire day of the grand jury return crying. She phoned family members to let them know. "Now what?" they asked. McManus had no answer. She wished the grand jury had called her to testify. She still believed Pou was her mother's murderer.

———

KATHRYN NELSON, Elaine's daughter, didn't feel angry; she didn't necessarily want to see Pou in prison, but she didn't believe she should keep her medical license. She had broken her primary oath. The nurses had too. What was to stop them from doing it again?

She thought of the wars going on across the ocean in Iraq and Afghanistan. Americans didn't leave their dead troops behind, no matter how intolerable the situation. But here at home a war against nature had been lost because some people were killed and left behind.

Her brother Craig moved forward aggressively with his civil case.

⸺

CARRIE EVERETT wanted to see justice done, to see Pou accept responsibility for her actions. Even though her husband, Emmett, had lost the use of his legs and the control of his bladder, and had depended on her care for nine years, she would still rather be bathing him, putting a diaper on him, laughing and clowning and arguing like every couple did—she would still rather have him there.

She wanted to know, what was the reason, what was the purpose? She didn't know what happened; she wasn't there to see Pou, to place her hands on the woman and say, "Don't do this." If she had been there, instead of trapped with her children and grandchildren in the flooded Ninth Ward, she was sure Pou would never have come into the room. Whatever had happened would not have happened. She would still have her husband.

⸺

RODNEY SCOTT, the patient whom Ewing Cook once took for dead, had made it home. He had suffered during the disaster, designated to go last because he weighed more than 300 pounds. He was frightened and hot and uncomfortable. He had hit his head in the helicopter, and had been left for two days in a paper gown at the New Orleans airport, in his feces, in pain. The trauma had lasted: the next time he'd had to be in a hospital, he refused to remove his street clothes. Still—and despite lingering medical problems that kept him from getting around much, that put him squarely in the camp of "the disabled"—there was no question in his mind that it was worth going through all of that to survive and reunite with his family.

If nothing else was learned, what he hoped people took from Memorial's misfortune was simple: "Every time you can save a life, save it." If they could get him out, they could get everyone out. What had happened need not have happened. "There's a way for everything," he would say. Every option should have been explored.

When he was younger and healthier, he had worked as a nurse. He did not know whether euthanasia had occurred at Memorial, but if it had, he wondered what the doctors and nurses could have been thinking in deciding who would die that day. "How can you say euthanasia is better than evacuation? If they had vital signs, you could evacuate them . . . get 'em out. Let God make that decision."

———

FATHER JOHN MARSE, as hospital chaplain, was careful to tell people that he was not present when the alleged acts occurred. And he was not a bioethicist. What he would say was that people faced with bad choices should make choices that are in the best interests of patients and family members, not their own egos. He believed in comfort and felt that the staff at Memorial did the best they could to offer that. He believed that God was merciful and forgiving.

———

DR. BRYANT KING had stayed far away from New Orleans, turning down later CNN interview requests out of concerns for his safety. A friend warned him that the moneyed people who were trying to discredit him could sweep him under the rug and get rid of him. "Don't say a word," the friend said. "Go somewhere. If you've got shade, go in it." Keep it low. You don't want anyone hunting you down.

King had worked closely with Anna Pou throughout the disaster, switching off caring for patients on the second floor. He'd thought she was doing a yeoman's job. What troubled him later was how easily someone with whom he'd had a cordial relationship could be turned to do something so horrible. No matter how tired a doctor was, the initial reaction to the proposal should have been to take a step back and say, "Are you kidding me? Oh no, that just doesn't sound right." He wondered what words someone could possibly have used to make Pou and others say instead, in essence, "We know this is not how we usually function, but today we're going to do it and pretend it never happened." He could not wrap his mind around it. And he could not believe that Pou was allowed to continue practicing medicine.

DR. HORACE BALTZ shook his head when he heard Pou's remarks from the press conference. He was still violently upset over the euthanasia, considered it totally unethical and unnecessary. It haunted him. Pou's alleged actions, he felt, destroyed the trust in the medical profession that is a foundation of society. That trust was further eroded by the lockstep defense of the medical community.

Pou had genuflected to thank God that she wasn't going to prison? He longed to hear that she had taken to her knees to do something different: beg forgiveness for having violated the commandment "Thou shalt not kill."

Just after Katrina, Britain's *Mail on Sunday* tabloid newspaper had reported that a doctor had done exactly this. The doctor had been quoted anonymously. She was, in fact, a more repentant-sounding Anna Pou:

I did not know if I was doing the right thing. But I did not have time. I had to make snap decisions, under the most appalling circumstances, and I did what I thought was right. I injected morphine into those patients who were dying and in agony. If the first dose was not enough, I gave a double dose. And at night I prayed to God to have mercy on my soul.

———

"DOES ANYONE FEEL that they're making a mistake?" a man on the special grand jury had asked his fellow jurors before they took their final vote in July 2007. None of them said they did. The Memorial nurses had been very sad and cried throughout their testimony. The coroner struck one juror as a "cute old man" who spoke calmly and whose opinion in large part contradicted those of his experts.

What that juror couldn't understand was where the LifeCare staff members had been on Thursday, September 1, 2005, when the patients were medicated. It was only at the final meeting of the grand jury that two LifeCare leaders—assistant administrator Diane Robichaux and nurse executive Therese Mendez—were called to testify. The prosecutor did not ask the women very detailed questions. Mendez described how Pou came upstairs to LifeCare and said that she was assuming responsibility for the patients and that they would be given a lethal dose of drugs. Neither Mendez nor Robichaux, however, had seen what happened next, because they had gone to clear staff off the floor.

There was, of course, a witness, who had stood at the bedsides of the patients as Pou and the nurses injected them. Kristy Johnson. Two people close to Johnson would later recall that she was scheduled to appear before the special grand jury the same day as her colleagues—perhaps later in the day, because of a work schedule conflict. She was not, however, called by the prosecutors when she was available.

What sank the case in the one juror's mind was that nobody stood before the jury and testified to seeing Anna Pou actually inject a patient. The fundamental evidence needed to pin the deaths on the woman whose name was on the indictment papers was, in this juror's opinion, lacking.

The juror was a devotee of forensic pathologist Michael Baden's documentary television series *Autopsy*. What particularly struck her was the fact that so many patients who had been alive in the morning were dead by the afternoon. And Emmett Everett, he would stay with her. She would recall, years later, the vision of him eating his breakfast that Thursday morning and asking the staff when they were going to rock and roll. She believed the experts' reports that concluded that the deaths at Memorial were homicides.

The juror was convinced—and, she believed, all of her fellow jurors were too—that a crime had occurred on that fifth day at Memorial.

EPILOGUE

HOURS BEFORE HURRICANE ISAAC'S expected arrival in New Orleans on August 29, 2012, I opened a wooden door inset with a stained-glass window and entered a small chapel. There, almost exactly seven years earlier, the bodies of men and women had been blessed after they died in the hot, darkened, powerless hospital surrounded by floodwaters.

Walking the quiet corridors of what was now known as Ochsner Baptist, I looked for someone to ask about preparations for the current storm. The sound of voices led me to a patient room. The door was open, the light was on, and balled-up sheets were strewn on the bed. A partially eaten meal tray sat on a rolling cart beside an IV pump on a tall metal pole, but the room was empty; the talk I'd heard droned only from the television.

Across the long-repaired walkway where nurse manager Karen Wynn had run in flip-flops to answer a Code Blue, and Dr. Anna Pou had girded herself with a call to her family before flying across its swaying, windowed expanse, was the surgery building, the site of the current ICU. Nurses Cheri Landry and Lori Budo again cared for patients here; their faces smiled from pictures on the bulletin board in the staff room.

The ICU was a hive of light and monitors, but it was filled with only ghosts. Every few seconds a dissonant croak issued from a disconnected machine. The building creaked in a gust of wind from a band of the approaching hurricane. The patient bays were vacant, the nurses gone, the hospital evacuated before the storm. Electrical transfer switches still sat in the basement, but one lesson from Katrina had been learned.

———

HAD IT ONLY been learned in New Orleans? Two months later, on the night of Monday, October 29, I watched a health executive burst into a meeting of doctors at the command center for Long Island's North Shore-LIJ Health System. Ceiling tiles rattled in the wind and television screens showed images of Superstorm Sandy raging over New York City.

"NYU called," the executive said. "They want to evacuate. I don't know how to help them right now. They're in a panic mode." Officials at New York University's Langone Medical Center were asking for ambulances in the midst of the storm to pick up four critically ill babies from the neonatal intensive care unit.

Like Mayor Ray Nagin in New Orleans before Katrina, New York City mayor Michael Bloomberg had exempted hospitals in low-lying "Zone A" areas of the city from his pre-storm evacuation order. He made this decision even though city and state health officials knew that many of them had backup generator systems that could fail if towering, wind-swept tides slammed into the coastline. After everything that should have been learned about those horrific days in New Orleans, another hospital in a major American city now found itself without power, its staff fighting to keep alive their most desperately sick patients.

The North Shore-LIJ executive had his own hospitals to worry about—sixteen of them spread across New York and Long Island. Minutes later, a member of his team delivered an alarming report about one of them, a community hospital in Bay Shore, New York.

"Water is still rising at Southside," a corporate safety officer said. "We have a good hour before high tide." Hours earlier, corporate leaders had called Southside and Staten Island University Hospitals to go over what they would do if backup systems failed and part or all of their facilities suddenly lost power.

Officials huddled around a speakerphone. "There's a good possibility it will occur," warned a Staten Island University Hospital official. Part of the power system, he said, was below ground. "It cannot be used if it floods."

Doctors took to a whiteboard to sketch out priorities: "Establish clinical command structure"; "triage."

As a reporter who had come to see how hurricane medical response had evolved since Katrina, I sat watching them, dismayed. This non-profit parent company had a highly organized, local command center and was offering proactive and robust assistance not only to its own hospitals but also others in the region. This much was different from the support that Tenet and LifeCare headquarters provided to their hospitals at the time of Katrina.

Yet incredibly, just as in the lead-up to Katrina, some staff members said they had never pondered or planned for what they would do in case of a failure of the backup plan to the backup plan—a complete loss of power. This was true not just there, but also in many places where I have reported since Katrina. Emergencies are crucibles that contain and reveal the daily, slower-burning problems of medicine and beyond—our vulnerabilities; our trouble grappling with uncertainty, how we die, how we prioritize and divide what is most precious and vital and limited; even our biases and blindnesses.

Fortunately, as the clock ticked down to high tide and workers piled sandbags and operated pumps to protect the electric switch gear, the two coastal North Shore-LIJ hospitals narrowly avoided calamity. At the same moment, however, a dozen miles away in Manhattan at the nation's oldest public hospital, a triage crisis potentially more acute than even

Memorial's was evolving. Dr. Laura Evans, medical director of critical care at Bellevue Hospital Center, was called to the hospital's emergency command center. A storm surge, a giant wall of water forced up from the East River by Sandy, was predicted to crash into the land surrounding the hospital. Flooding could, hospital leaders told Evans, disable the pumps that delivered oxygen and vacuum suction to the hospital, as well as those that supplied the fuel from gigantic underground tanks to its backup generators. The loss of the fuel pumps would mean that backup power would last only as long as the small tank reserves attached to generators on the hospital's thirteenth floor. If city power failed during the storm, the fuel would be exhausted within two hours.

Nearly all of the patients in Evans's fifty-six-bed adult ICU relied on equipment that ran on electricity. Many were on life support or had drips of intravenous drugs that regulated their heartbeats and blood pressure. Some had intra-aortic balloon pumps that helped keep their blood flowing.

Evans was terrified, but the command team had limited good news. They believed the generator in the building next door, supplied by a separate, better protected fuel pump, would continue functioning. They could use it to power exactly six outlets in the ICU. Hospital leaders turned to Evans. Which of her very sick patients should be given access to one of the precious six power outlets?

"Laura," one hospital official said, "we need a list."

———

FIFTY-SIX PATIENTS, six outlets. How to decide? Evans had access to something the doctors at Memorial did not. In 2008, citing the arrests of the Memorial health professionals and fears that a severe influenza outbreak could emerge and force providers, again, into making life-and-death choices between patients, New York planners published a protocol for rationing ventilators. The guidelines, devised by experts in disaster medicine, bioethics, and public policy, were designed to go into effect if the United States was ever struck by a pandemic comparable to the 1918 Spanish flu outbreak, which sickened more than a quarter of the population, overwhelmed hospitals, and killed an estimated 50 million people worldwide—the most deadly disease event in recent history.

When state health department officials ran exercises based on scenarios involving H5N1 avian influenza—a strain of "bird flu" that had caused deadly outbreaks in humans around the world and that experts feared might mutate into a form that could spread easily between people—questions about how New York hospitals would handle massive demand for life support equipment arose.

"They kept running out of ventilators," said Dr. Tia Powell, former executive director of the New York State Task Force on Life and the Law, which was asked to address the problem. "They immediately recognized this is the worst thing we've ever imagined. What on earth are we going to do?"

First the experts recommended ways that hospitals could stretch supply, for example by canceling all elective surgeries during a severe pandemic. New York also purchased and stockpiled additional ventilators—enough to deal with a moderate pandemic but orders of magnitude fewer than would be needed in a severe outbreak of 1918 scale.

Officials realized those two measures alone would not be nearly enough to meet demand in the most dire scenario. Ventilators were costly, required highly trained operators, and used oxygen, which could be limited in a disaster—so the group drew up the rationing plans. The goal, participants said, was to save as many lives as possible while adhering to an ethical framework. This represented a departure from the usual medical standard of care, which focuses on doing everything possible to save each individual life. Setting out guidelines in advance of a crisis was a way to avoid putting exhausted, stressed front-line health professionals in the position of having to come up with criteria for making tough decisions in the midst of a crisis, as the ragged staff at Memorial Medical Center had to do after Hurricane Katrina.

The New York group based its plan, in part, on a 2006 rationing proposal developed by health officials in Ontario, Canada, responding to the severe acute respiratory syndrome (SARS) pandemic. The Canadians took a tool that doctors use to track the progress of ICU patients, known as the Sequential Organ Failure Assessment (SOFA) score, and used it to help guide which patients would—and would not—be allotted ICU care in a severe emergency.

The SOFA score was not designed to predict survival and was not validated for assessing the health status of children, but the experts adopted it in the absence of an appropriate alternative.

The New York protocol calls for denying some of the sickest patients with the highest scores access to scarce ventilators. Hospitals are also to withhold ventilators from patients with serious chronic conditions, such as kidney failure, cancers that have spread and have a poor prognosis, or "severe, irreversible neurological" conditions that are likely to be deadly.

New York's plan goes even further. It includes procedures under which patients who aren't improving after a trial period are to be removed from ventilators with or without permission of their families. New York officials studied possible legal grounds under which the governor could suspend a state law that bars doctors from taking patients off life support without the express consent of patients or their authorized health agents.

"You can take something today that's not necessarily active and overnight flip the switch and make it into something that has those teeth in it," Dr. Powell said.

Powell is right in that drastic public health measures could be quickly snapped into place. Some states, including Colorado, have drawn up executive orders for the governor to sign in an emergency to allow hospitals to turn away patients, protect doctors faced with limiting care, and permit health officials to seize drugs and quarantine individuals. Other states, including Louisiana—thanks to the advocacy of Dr. Anna Pou—and Indiana, have addressed these issues with legislation.

After the grand jury refused to indict Pou, she made good on her promise to fight to protect medical workers who serve in disasters, capitalizing on the statewide support she enjoyed. In 2008, I watched her as we both sat in a gallery at the Baton Rouge Capitol at a hearing. Ever the committed doctor, she worked on patient charts balanced on her knees as she awaited a chance to rise in support of one of three disaster immunity bills she helped write. "Unless you were there it would be difficult for you to forge a bill," she said after the hearing. "The fact I experienced it first-hand puts me in a good position," she added. "I mean you have to understand the circumstances that are created by any disaster when the medical supplies and the medical community is overwhelmed; these are horrific, extraordinary circumstances." Pou said that providers who use "alternate standards of care [need] a comfort level that we are not going to be second guessed and prosecuted for decisions we make during times of crisis." The legislators did not ask Pou whether the decisions she was referring to should extend beyond triage to include intentionally hastening patient deaths.

The answer to that question is no, according to reports released by the Institute of Medicine, a highly regarded, independent advisory organization that is part of the National Academy of Sciences. A year after Pou's campaign, and again three years later after consulting with emergency responders across the country, a group of disaster experts convened by the Institute came down unequivocally on the question of euthanasia in guidance to policymakers and the public on medical care during disasters: "Neither the law nor ethics," they wrote, "support the intentional hastening of death, even in a crisis."

A bioethicist uninvolved with the group shared a similar view. "Rather than thinking about exceptional moral rules for exceptional moral situations," Harvard's Dr. Lachlan Forrow, who is also a palliative care specialist, wrote, "we should almost always see exceptional moral situations as opportunities for us to show exceptionally deep commitment to our deepest moral values."

As the Louisiana legislators considered changing state law based on Pou's experience, none of them inquired as to what had actually happened on September 1, 2005. She has never publicly discussed it. Legislators took turns thanking Pou on the record for her Katrina service; one called the former attorney general's treatment of her "inexcusable."

The bills Pou and her attorney Rick Simmons helped write passed unanimously. They immunize Louisiana health-care professionals from most civil lawsuits (though not in cases of willful misconduct) for their work "in accordance with disaster medicine protocol." Prosecutors are also urged to await the findings of a medical panel before deciding whether to pursue criminal charges. Pou has helped advocates pass similar legislation in other states.

What is the "disaster medicine protocol" that health workers can now legally implement? Does it have a better chance of helping patients than the usual standard of first-come-first-served according to medical need? Pou and Simmons said they included this language before a protocol existed, hoping one would be created.

Several years after Katrina, federal agencies began requiring state and local health departments in the United States to develop guidelines for how to prioritize patients in disasters, in order to qualify for certain preparedness grants. In some states, patients with Do Not Resuscitate orders, the elderly, those requiring dialysis, or those with severe neurological impairment would be refused ventilators or admission to hospitals in a disaster like a severe pandemic. Utah's original plan divided epidemics into phases. Initially, hospitals would apply triage rules only to residents of mental institutions, nursing homes, prisons, and facilities for the "handicapped." If an epidemic worsened, the rules would apply to the general population (Utah later removed the differentiation after it was mentioned in the media).

Many of the plans are based on the Ontario and New York ventilator guidelines. The US Veterans Health Administration—which has 144 medical centers across the country—also drafted similar protocols.

However, mounting evidence suggests that the plans would not accurately direct care to patients who are most likely to survive with treatment, as is often presumed. Several researchers have studied how groups of ICU patients might fare under these emergency protocols. They asked doctors to categorize the patients in their ICUs during the relatively mild H1N1 "swine flu" pandemic as if it were an emergency and they needed to ration. The results were disturbing. The majority of patients who would have been tagged as "expectant" (i.e., likely to die or unable to be saved with the resources available; analogous to Memorial's "category 3") and been designated for withdrawal of ICU care and ventilator support in fact actually survived with continued treatment and were discharged from the hospital. In some cases, their ventilators would likely have been reassigned to a group of patients whose survival rate turned out to be lower. Even with clear guidelines to follow, triage officers often disagreed and lacked confidence in their categorization decisions.

In other words, there was slim if any evidence that taking away ventilators or other resources from patients with a lower triage priority actually would have saved more lives. Moreover, in some instances just the opposite appeared to have been the case. "A new model of triage needs to be developed," British researchers who tested a version of the protocols wrote in a medical journal article in 2009.

New models have been proposed, including prioritizing patients along a scale with a sliding cutoff point rather than categorically excluding members of certain groups; patients assigned a low priority would then be provided treatment if it became available. But four years later, in 2013, the disaster plans on the books across the country had not been modified.

In one small but particularly troubling study of a similar triage protocol in Britain, none of the patients who needed mechanical ventilation would have received it long enough to survive had the plan been used. Wave after wave of sick patients could have been put on and taken off the ventilators to no end. They would not have been given enough time to get better.

Withdrawing care from those who have not given their consent is troubling enough. Doing so by following a protocol that is unlikely even to save more lives would be indefensible. To the extent that bad protocols cover up deficits of evidence and accord, and entrench harmful practices, perhaps no protocol would be better after all.

EXPERTS WHO DEVISE guidelines that involve withdrawing life-saving care in emergencies may have never experienced how difficult it would be to implement them. In January 2010, I traveled to Haiti after the devastating earthquake and "embedded" with US federal disaster medical teams, some of whose members had worked in the nightmarish New Orleans airport after Katrina. I planned to report on what the teams had learned and how prepared they might be to assist in another American disaster, and to study the way professionals handled triage in a setting where the number of critically injured patients far exceeded the initial capacity of the medical system. While the circumstances in a developing country would pose unique challenges, the actual treatment of patients should be similar at home and abroad.

The American team set up a field hospital housed in tents on a college campus in the capital, Port-au-Prince. They had trouble recording unfamiliar names and instead assigned patients numbers. One woman who arrived at the field hospital the week after the earthquake was identified in medical records merely as Jane Doe 326. Her real name was Nathalie LeBrun. She was thirty-eight years old and dressed in a white nightgown with lacy trim. Through a translator, she told me about her medical problems, which had preceded the earthquake. "She can't breathe right," the translator said, "and her body's swollen. She's been like that for a while, but ever since the earthquake, it's added on to it."

The US medical team found a tank of oxygen and ran a tube to her nose to help her breathe. Overnight the tank ran out. The oxygen level in LeBrun's blood plunged dangerously low. In the early morning, a nurse who believed she was watching LeBrun die sat crying with her patient. The nurse had been told there was no more oxygen. Doctors called for help, and the staff found another tank. Again, they hooked up Nathalie LeBrun to oxygen, and her breathing eased.

Still, the supply chain to the US disaster teams was failing, as it had after Katrina. The brother of another Haitian patient finagled a large oxygen tank from elsewhere in the city. Meanwhile, the American team had another idea about how to help LeBrun. They put her on a portable oxygen concentrator, which extracts oxygen from the air, but it kept overheating and shutting down. Moreover, the device runs on electricity, and the fuel needed to run the electric generators was in short supply.

At a morning meeting under a mango tree, a logistician passed that news to his medical colleagues. "We're at a critical level with our diesel supply. We have one can per generator left. After that everything shuts down. So I'm freaking today. I mean, I am freaking."

The team found more fuel, but twenty-four hours later, bottled oxygen—Nathalie LeBrun's backup oxygen source—remained scarce. The field hospital's liaison officer was a nurse. His job was to manage the flow of patients through the hospital, and he told me he faced a quandary: what to do about Nathalie LeBrun.

Her breathing difficulties were likely caused by a chronic heart problem, and her need for oxygen might continue indefinitely. He reasoned that the limited supply of oxygen would be better used if it were given to those who needed it only temporarily—for instance, people who'd been injured in the quake and needed oxygen during surgery. He made the decision to withdraw the oxygen from Nathalie LeBrun. "Which essentially is a death sentence for this woman," he told me.

He checked his decision with the head doctor. The doctor agreed it was right. A plan was developed. LeBrun's oxygen would be turned down slowly, and she would be driven to a partially destroyed Haitian hospital where she'd been treated before, but where, they believed, there was no oxygen at all.

LeBrun was not consulted or informed. She was only told that she would be transferred to the Haitian hospital. That afternoon, she gave me a huge smile and spoke hopefully about her future.

By late afternoon, nobody had started to wean LeBrun from her oxygen concentrator. Staff had stayed busy caring for patients with broken bones, complex wounds, and two women giving birth simultaneously.

Then, shortly after five p.m., a hospital staff member abruptly unplugged LeBrun's oxygen concentrator when medics from the US Army's 82nd Airborne Division arrived to transport her. Not knowing the plan, they tried to reassure her: "Just tell her she'll be taken care of," they said to the translator, "and she's going to be going to another place." Then they hoisted her into the back of a Humvee ambulance. Before the ambulance even started rolling, a military doctor noticed LeBrun was beginning to have trouble breathing. The ambulance had an oxygen tank available, but a nurse from the field hospital's command staff assured the doctor that LeBrun's problem was chronic. According to the triage decision, no oxygen was provided for her.

With the doors shut, the back of the ambulance was hot and dark. The ride was rough. I sat beside LeBrun, who leaned against one of the Humvee's metal sides, coughing and struggling to breathe. Someone at the American field hospital had given her an asthma inhaler, which she assumed contained oxygen. She shot doses of the drug into her mouth again and again. "Oxygene!" she wheezed. "Oxygene!" LeBrun knew exactly what she needed.

Based on utilitarian calculations alone, it had been logical to remove LeBrun's source of oxygen. But the health professionals involved in the decision were not willing to face her and tell her about it or be there to implement it. Issuing "a death sentence" is easier than executing it.

Perhaps informing LeBrun and dispatching her gently in a cloud of morphine would not, however, have been the better option. When we pulled up to the destroyed Haitian hospital, Dr. Paul Auerbach—an emergency physician and one of my former medical school professors— happened to be volunteering there. He found a tank with a bit of oxygen left and treated her aggressively that night with low-cost diuretics to remove some of the fluid from her lungs, stabilizing her to the point that she didn't, at least for a time, need the oxygen.

———

WHETHER IN HAITI or the United States, disasters present the same challenge: how and whether to inform and involve viable, aware patients or the family members of patients when potentially lifesaving resources are being denied. Little guidance exists. In normal times, it is easier to avoid acknowledging that some patients don't get access to needed care and refrain from engaging in an inclusive search for solutions. Disasters foist a recognition of rationing. Years after the earthquake, as Superstorm Sandy intensified outside Bellevue Hospital, Dr. Laura Evans, the critical care medical director, faced a version of the same conundrum. She brought news of the expected power outage back to her ICU staff. Choices had to be made about which patients would have access to the six power outlets that might keep working even if every other outlet died. Evans had studied the New York state guidelines on how to allocate ventilators in a severe respiratory pandemic using a scoring system that estimates how severely ill someone is. Desperate for a procedure to help guide the decision making, she voluntarily repurposed these untested plans that had been inspired by Katrina.

Evans pulled together an ad hoc committee to make the choices. "This isn't a role for one person," Evans told hospital leaders. Her committee was composed of professionals who had no patients under consideration. In this way, direct providers would be free to do what their ethical duty required. "If you're the primary doctor," Evans later explained to me, "it's your job to advocate for your patient." The committee, by contrast, could take a wider range of factors into account and choose fairly according to clearly defined scoring guidelines. The committee included not only doctors but also ethicists and nurses. It did not, however, include representatives of patients or their families.

The decisions about which patients would be connected to the six power outlets and the reasons were communicated to the other staff members. Some challenged the choices, but they accepted them. All of this was accomplished—a list of patients, moving them between beds and outlets—within about two hours.

As she prepared the plan, Evans also thought about how she would feel the next day if it had to be implemented. She wanted, she said, to "have a process that we can describe, that is transparent," that was applied to all patients the same way, "as fair and equitable as it can be." She knew the story of Dr. Pou and Hurricane Katrina. She wanted to look back and be able to justify the decisions she and her colleagues were making, to maintain the trust of the larger society that might examine them. She even imagined what word the infamous tabloid headline writers at the *New York Post* would find to rhyme with her last name if patients died ("heavens," of course, goes with "Evans").

That night, as Evans and her colleagues were completing their list, the lights flickered out. City utility power had failed. It took about seven terrifying seconds for power from the backup generators to kick in and get things functioning again. Soon after, Evans received a call from the hospital's command center. They predicted that, except for those six outlets, all power would be lost in the next sixty to ninety minutes. Millions of gallons of floodwater were filling the basement of the twenty-five-story hospital. Water gushed into elevator pits with enough force to remove elevator doors from their moorings.

Evans and her colleagues stationed two health professionals at the bedsides of all patients who relied on ventilators, preparing to squeeze oxygen into their lungs manually with flexible Ambu-bags. Bright-orange extension cords connected to the backup generator system snaked through patient corridors. Nurses counted drops on IV pumps so that if everything failed they could go "old school" and give vasopressors by drops per minute.

Communicating the triage decisions to patients and their family members was the most challenging aspect of that night, Evans said. She and her colleagues could not imagine how to inform those who would not get power outlets and they feared doing so, so they put off the task. Looking back, Evans feels the families had a right to know. Also, the staff did not think about asking whether any of the selected patients or their families might wish to volunteer to give up a power outlet so that it could be provided to someone else. "It wasn't even on my radar," Evans says.

At Connecticut Hospice in Branford, which evacuated in haste as Sandy approached, the staff did consult with patients and their families. They discovered something surprising. Hospice leaders had planned to move the sickest patients first. But those patients and their families chose to allow the healthier patients to go first.

Involving patients and their families in these decisions is all too rare. Triage is typically seen as the preserve of medical professionals. The ventilator rationing protocols that have been developed around the country have not been publicized, perhaps out of fears of how the public will react; even many medical professionals aren't aware that their states or hospitals have them in place.

Reluctance to draw public attention to the plans is understandable. They outline the creation of what could, in all fairness, be called death panels: groups of doctors who would decide which patients are given a higher chance to survive. Similar fears surround health-care reform in the United States—when insurance coverage is expanded to more people, what services, to which people, will be cut? Whether the disaster protocols reflect the values of the larger public simply isn't known. In an age of extreme sensitivity over health-care rationing, almost no one has dared to find out.

When New York officials first released the ventilator plan that Laura Evans later repurposed for Sandy, they referred to public review as "an important component in fulfilling the ethical obligation to promote transparency and just guidelines." They envisaged the use of focus groups to solicit comment from "a range of community members, including parents, older adults, people with disabilities, and communities of color." Those focus groups were never held. The plans had not been changed.

Dr. Guthrie Birkhead, deputy commissioner of the Office of Public Health for New York State, told me in 2009 that he wondered whether it was possible to get the public to accept the plans. "In the absence of an extreme emergency, I don't know. How do you even engage them to explain it to them?"

———

AN ANSWER to Birkhead's question can be found in Maryland. "All hell is breaking loose," Dr. Elizabeth Lee Daugherty told a roomful of volunteers who convened to discuss triage on a Monday afternoon in June 2013. "That's the scenario we're talking about. All hands are on deck, we're doing everything we can, and we are totally overrun with patients."

The scenario she described, offering the example of a pandemic, was analogous to the one the doctors at Memorial faced when the waters rose and they had to choose which patients to prioritize first for evacuation. The sickest, because their lives relied on machines? What about those who might have the greatest chance of surviving their immediate illnesses, because saving them would be a more efficient means of doing good? Or, for the same reason, those with a better chance of long-term survival, based on underlying health problems? Should age play a role, drawing on the principle that everyone deserves equal rights to live through the all stages of life? Or could some estimate of social worth or instrumental value in the situation at hand be factored into the mix, favoring health professionals who would be needed to assist people through the crisis? What about support staff? Where to draw the line?

Or would the fairest principle be one that is typically used in non-emergencies: first-come-first-served according to need or perhaps even a lottery that would offer an equal chance to everyone who was sick at a particular point in time? Similar questions could be asked in facing other difficult problems, including national drug shortages.

Daugherty laid out the options for the participants and turned the discussion over to them. "What are your values?" she asked. Unlike in New York, where the triage proposal was developed by experts, Maryland health professionals were seeking the input of a wide-ranging sample of the general population, in small group sessions held over a period of two years across the state. "Maryland is as far as we know the first state to tackle this problem this way," Daugherty told the volunteers. "By that I mean having these kinds of conversations before we have developed a framework for making decisions."

Daugherty, a thirty-nine-year-old critical care doctor, began thinking about the problem of scarce medical resources in college during a medical missionary trip to Bogotá with her father, a physician. Her interest deepened during her own international work as a doctor in impoverished regions. As the medical control chief for the Office of Emergency Management at Johns Hopkins Hospital, a 1,059 bed tertiary referral hospital and the cornerstone of the $6.5 billion Johns Hopkins Medicine enterprise, she was asked to help design a pandemic plan. In discovering how inadequate even this well-endowed hospital system's supplies were in relation to expected demand, she recognized an acute analog to the chronic resource dilemmas she had seen in other countries.

Daugherty struggled over the question of which pandemic flu patients should be turned away from the intensive care units, sealing their fates. Could a doctor really remove one patient from a ventilator to make way for another who might have a better chance of recovering? Health professionals, who tend to favor utilitarian efficiency in the distribution of limited goods, such as organs, shouldn't be making life-and-death value judgments alone, Daugherty thought, particularly in the backyard of Johns Hopkins Hospital, a low-income neighborhood where public trust in medicine is poor even at the best of times, a legacy of ethically questionable research studies and historical discrimination.

Daugherty and her colleagues wanted to ask nuanced ethical questions of the hospital's neighbors, but wondered how to pose them to people who might never have considered them or might react angrily to the mere notion of planning to limit care. To design an attempt at public engagement, they turned to the Program for Deliberative Democracy at Carnegie Mellon University. The program's work is modeled on concepts that originated in the theoretical work of philosophers Jürgen Habermas and John Rawls and were developed by Jim Fishkin, a Stanford professor who invented "deliberative polling," a method designed to capture how opinions change when citizens are given the chance to learn about and carefully consider policy choices.

From its earliest days, the Maryland experiment proved something vital. Whether at Zion Baptist Church, in a neighborhood of boarded-up row houses in inner-city Baltimore, or at a "wellness center" in the wealthiest reaches of Howard County, regular citizens showed they were able to gather, engage, discuss these issues, and learn from one another. They easily grasped ethical concepts that some health officials had assumed were the province of only experts.

In the basement of Zion Baptist Church on one Saturday afternoon, a facilitator asked a tableful of volunteers what they thought about using age as the primary basis for allocating resources in a disaster. "We are going to discuss why this would be a good idea or not," she said.

A young man offered his opinion. "If this were to happen tomorrow, and if I would get a ventilator and a twelve-year-old wouldn't, or a four-year-old wouldn't, I just think that would be the saddest thing possible."

A woman who was a mother disagreed. "It's really hard for me to say that just because they're younger than me to give it to them, because I would feel personally like I have responsibilities and I would want to be here."

Her neighbor extended the thought. "There's so many social ramifications of what's going to happen once all these young lives are saved," she said. "If a significant generation, if the senior citizens were cut in half, that would alter our society. That means that, you know, just like you definitely don't want your child to die, people don't want to be grandmotherless, people don't want to be grandfatherless. You know what I mean? So, I'm just a little concerned about the aftermath of just giving it to the youngest person." She worried about what would happen to the children who were saved. "Who's going to raise them, who's going to teach them, who's going to really take care of them?"

Listening to the debate over the value of elderly lives brought to mind the recent funeral of my great-uncle. In his nineties with advanced Parkinson's disease, he'd filled out an advance directive stating he would not want to be put on life support. However his doctor was out of town when he developed pneumonia and was admitted to a hospital. Another doctor resuscitated him and put him on a ventilator against his pre-stated wishes. Within days, he was sitting up in bed reading the newspaper as the ventilator puffed away. In less than a week he was off the ventilator, saying he was relieved to be alive, highlighting the complexity of end-of-life decision making, of predicting in advance what we would want in a situation we have never faced. He requested his DNR be removed. He lived a few more months, and his granddaughter, a twenty-one-year-old college student, described in a eulogy what that time meant to both of them as she spent her summer vacation visiting him in the hospital, a rehab unit, and a skilled nursing facility: "We talked about politics, economics, current events, gossip, books, movies, the past, the future. He taught me about social responsibility and his past. I taught him about opera and music. We even talked about boys and relationships. When he gave advice, it was always good and, more important, wise. [. . .] I will continue to live my life as if I'm going to tell him about it."

Sometimes individual medical choices, like triage choices, are less a question of science than they are of values. In a disaster, triage is about deciding what the goals of dividing resources should be for the larger population—whether maximizing number of lives saved, years of lives saved, quality of life, fairness, social trust, or other factors. The larger community may emerge with ideas different from those held by small groups of medical professionals.

That was clear in Seattle and King County, where a public engagement exercise was held. Many participants thought it was unacceptable for medical professionals to withdraw life-sustaining care, as called for in many of the plans, in part because doing so would erode trust in the medical system.

Roger Bernier, a senior advisor at the US Centers for Disease Control and Prevention, which funded the exercise, said it is both possible and necessary to engage non-experts in these discussions. "They are the holders of our public values and are in the best position and in the most nonpartisan position to weigh competing values."

However, this type of engagement is rarely sought. "I'm not sure we believe in democracy in America," Bernier said. "We don't make good use of the people. We don't make good efforts to access public wisdom on public policy choices."

In Seattle, members of the public at large were concerned that using survival statistics to determine access to resources might be "inherently discriminatory," the project report said, "because of institutional racism in the health care system; if some groups (e.g., African Americans and immigrants) do not receive the same quality of care, then their rates of recovery and other survivability measures would be biased."

More challenging than eliciting public input is using it, particularly when it reveals contradictory, divergent opinions. How should majority and minority views be weighted? And will policymakers cede authority over decisions? In 2009, the CDC gathered feedback on a proposed emergency vaccination program for a new strain of flu. General public opinion diverged significantly from expert opinion. However, by the time the information was collected, the vaccine policy had essentially already been made.

In 2012, the Institute of Medicine released an extensive report backing the notion that the public should be involved in the development of guidelines for dividing medical resources in disasters. The authors argued that Katrina and other cases had shown that while crisis conditions may justify limiting access to scarce treatments, medical providers have a duty to care for patients in emergencies, to treat them fairly, and to steward resources. An earlier report also addressed DNR orders, saying they were not useful parameters of triage decision making in disasters. The orders reflect foresight and personal preferences about end-of-life planning "more than an accurate estimate of survival." Whenever crisis conditions involve limiting access to scarce treatments, the experts said, decisions should be made in ways that are transparent, consistent, proportional to the extent of shortages, and accountable.

Dr. Carl Schultz, a professor of emergency medicine and director of disaster medical services at the University of California at Irvine, is one of the few open critics of altering standards of care for disasters. He says the idea "has both monetary and regulatory attractiveness" to governments and companies because it relieves them of having to strive to provide better care. "The problem with lowering the standard of care is where do you stop? How low do you go? If you don't want to put any more resources in disaster response, you keep lowering the standard." It is also reasonable to wonder, once lower standards are codified, whether some policymakers, health-care executives, or clinicians might be tempted to apply them to non-emergent situations where resources are tight, such as when costs are a concern.

Others disagree. "Our goal is always to provide the highest standard of care under the circumstances," Rear Adm. Ann Knebel told me in 2009, when she was deputy director of preparedness and planning at the Office of the Assistant Secretary for Preparedness and Response, Department of Health and Human Services. "If you don't plan, then you are less likely to be able to reuse, reallocate, and maximize the resources at your disposal, because you have people who've never thought about how they'd respond to those circumstances."

Both Schultz and Knebel make vital points. What will save the most lives in an overwhelming emergency probably won't be refining how a set number of patients is triaged, essentially shuffling the same deck of cards so that different numbers and suits come up on top. What will save more lives will be doing everything possible to avoid having to deal the hand, by taking steps to minimize the need to compromise standards, and promote the ability to rebound as quickly as possible to normalcy. One of the greatest tragedies of what happened at Memorial may well be that the plan to inject patients went ahead at precisely the time when the helicopters at last arrived in force, expanding the available resources.

The failure to emphasize situational awareness in disaster response— maintaining the ability to "see" in the midst of a crisis—concerns some experts, including Dr. Frederick "Skip" Burkle Jr. After the attacks of September 11, 2001, he laid out ideas for how to handle the victims of a large-scale bioterrorist event. Those protocols, described in an academic paper, became key aspects of the Canadian pandemic triage guidelines and ultimately made their way into most of the other disaster standards of care plans. "I have said to my wife, 'I think I developed a monster here,'" Burkle told me. What worried him was that the guidelines were often rigid, with a single set of criteria designated to be applied through-out the severe phase of an emergency. Rationing when rationing is not needed could harm the population. Burkle, by contrast, had stressed the importance of reassessing the level of supplies "sometimes on a daily or hourly basis" in a fluid effort to provide the best possible care and minimize the need to make such wrenching decisions.

In 2010 I visited Pune, India. The previous year, during an outbreak of H1N1 influenza, health officials had panicked. Worried about the spread of the illness, they restricted patients with flu symptoms to a small number of local hospitals. Those hospitals were quickly overwhelmed. A pediatrician, Dr. Aarti Kinikar, watched babies die because she did not have enough ventilators for them.

Triaging better was not enough for her. For years she had treated children in a public hospital where expensive resources were often in short supply. "God has given you the brain, just use it," she liked to tell her students. "Just keep on thinking." When the ventilators ran out during H1N1, she thought and she improvised. In the past, she had helped newborns with premature lungs breathe better with a therapy known as bubble CPAP, for continuous positive airway pressure. CPAP devices cost thousands of dollars, but Kinikar's staff managed to patch together a homemade version out of a few dollars' worth of plastic tubing and saline bottles readily available at the hospital. It seemed to work well on premature babies, and she decided, in the midst of the H1N1 crisis, to see what it might do for older babies with flu. "I didn't know whether people will back me using a technique which doesn't seem to have much scientific push," Kinikar told me. The alternative seemed worse to her. "It was a decision between not doing anything and allowing the baby to die as against doing something and maybe keep your fingers crossed and let it work."

When one baby with flu showed signs of improvement on a ventilator, she decided to try to wean him off the machine early and instead support his breathing with the improvised bubble CPAP system. The baby's mother watched warily, but her son did well on the makeshift contraption. The ventilator was put to use to help another child. Over the weeks of the pandemic, Kinikar used bubble CPAP to support the breathing of hundreds of children at her hospital. Colleagues credited her quick thinking with saving lives.

Perhaps American health professionals, dependent on the highest-tech gadgets, could learn something from Kinikar. While there is little financial incentive in the marketplace to develop low-tech, inexpensive medical goods for disaster preparedness, the US government has made some investments. A recent federal grant was awarded to a company to create cheaper, easier-to-use ventilators. Already at least one firm, St. Louis–based Allied Healthcare Products, is marketing a line of ventilators specifically for use in disasters.

In the end, Kinikar-style thinking turned out to be the most important, life-saving aspect of what happened at Bellevue Hospital in New York after the generator fuel pumps failed. Volunteers formed a chain and passed fuel up thirteen flights of stairs to feed the generators manually. Swift improvisation prevented the backup power from cutting out, which prevented horrible choices from having to be made. Dr. Laura Evans's patients were all maintained on backup power as evacuation of the hospital proceeded.

Hours later, climbing one of Bellevue's long staircases, I passed personnel in blue scrubs carrying a baby in a transport incubator down to a waiting ambulance. Other staff huffed and puffed up the steps with supplies. Diesel fumes wafted into patient corridors. The situation balanced just on the edge of control.

With elevators out, the evacuation of the gigantic hospital took days, just as it had at Memorial. Two patients were kept for last. One was morbidly obese. He weighed around six hundred pounds—much more than Emmett Everett at Memorial. With the elevators out of order, the staff was very concerned about moving him. The other was, like patients at Memorial, extremely sick and fragile. His doctors were afraid he could die while being carried.

Nobody gave up hope. After the other patients were rescued, National Guard soldiers carried fuel up thirteen flights of stairs for several more days until the elevators could be operated. Doctors in the disabled hospital performed heart surgery on the fragile patient, and both he and the obese man were safely moved to another hospital.

Dramatic scenes like this do not occur often. But being in New York for Sandy was a reminder that terrible triage conundrums can arise anywhere, at any time, and that they have the power to change lives irrevocably. Across the country many hospitals in flood zones have electrical backup power systems in their basements. Others, in earthquake zones, were constructed before modern building codes. Others are simply situated in Tornado Alley. To the extent that protections and plans have been put in place since Katrina, recent events have often shown them to be inadequate or misguided. Life and death in the immediate aftermath of a crisis most often depends on the preparedness, performance, and decision making of the individuals on the scene.

It is hard for any of us to know how we would act under such terrible pressure.

But we, at least, have the luxury to picture in advance how we would want to make the decisions.

ACKNOWLEDGMENTS

DEEPEST THANKS TO ALL who shared their experiences and knowledge in interviews, listed in the Notes for each chapter, particularly individuals for whom the trauma of those five days resurfaces upon remembrance. Several in particular took a risk to tell what they did and why. They are brave, as are the others who spoke outside of the "cone of silence" so that those of us who have not yet faced the consequential choices described here could learn from them. This book also owes a great debt to the other journalists who pursued the story, as described in the Notes section and the book itself. Further, Memorial staff members and others who wrote memoirs and articles about their involvement in the events brought to light unique details and insights.

This book grew out of the magazine article "The Deadly Choices at Memorial." The product of a collaboration between ProPublica and the *New York Times Magazine,* it benefited from not one but three key editors. First came Susan White, now at the helm of *InsideClimate News,* whose wise early guidance on structure and narrative carried over from the article to the book. The *New York Times Magazine*'s Ilena Silverman's suggestions and edits always rang true and bettered my work. The news genius that is Steve Engelberg edited "Deadly Choices" with the energy of two people while also serving as managing editor of ProPublica.

My ProPublica colleagues have been a source of inspiration. Other editors who read and improved the story included: Paul Steiger, Gerald Marzorati, Jill Abramson, Bill Keller, and Alex Star. Charles Wilson, David Ferguson, and Aaron Retica checked every fact, and Richard Tofel, David McCraw, and Loretta Mince had my back. ProPublica's Krista Kjellman Schmidt, Jeff Larson, Dan Nguyen, Mike Webb, Lisa Schwartz, A. C. Thompson, and Robin Fields all made essential contributions; as did the *Times*'s Clinton Cargill, Joanna Milter, Patty Rush, Patricia Eisemann, and Matt Purdy; as well as Paolo Pellegrin, Macaulay Campbell, Stan Alcorn, and Bruce Shapiro.

Another wizard of an editor, David Baron, along with the exceptional staff of Public Radio International's *The World,* provided an outlet to report on horrific triage dilemmas on the ground in Haiti after the 2010 earthquake and, with Patrick Cox, to explore medical rationing across countries and cultures, including the impossible choices made weekly in public dialysis units in South Africa. During the 2012 hurricane season, the *New York Times* Metro desk, ProPublica, and the *Times-Picayune* provided homes for reporting on what had and had not changed since Katrina. As this book neared completion, Julie Tate worked tirelessly to check facts and locate additional sources from afar.

Those who filled the margins of *Five Days at Memorial* in manuscript form with comments of exquisite insight and occasional blistering humor improved it greatly. Thanks to Nam Le, Susan Burton, Edward Broughton, Herschel and Adrienne Ruby Fink, Dr. Randi Cohen, Christine Kenneally, Paul Steiger, and Marian Moser Jones. Thanks to Harriet Washington for friendship and support.

The following individuals at libraries, archives, and news organizations were particularly helpful in locating historical material: Taffey Hall, archivist, and Bill Sumners, director, the Southern Baptist Historical Library and Archives in Nashville, Tennessee; Jim McCutcheon, production manager, Entercom New Orleans; Carl Lindahl, codirector, Surviving Katrina and Rita in Houston, Texas; Ann Hogg of the American Folklife Center, Library of Congress; StoryCorps's Nadia Wilson (archive intern) and Tayla Cooper (senior archive director); Irene Wainwright and coworkers at the New Orleans Public Library; Greg Lambousy, director of collections, Louisiana State Museum; Janet Spikes, Dagne Gizaw, and Michelle Kamalich at the Woodrow Wilson Center library; from the NBCUniversal archives, Jaime Severino, Luis Aristondo, and Sade Craig; from the ABC archives, Lidia M. Guardarrama and Joy S. Holloway; CBS's Ann Fotiades and Matt Danowski; and J. T. Alpaugh of Helinet Aviation in Van Nuys, California. For responding to some large public records requests and assisting with interviews, thanks are due to staff members of the Louisiana Attorney General's Office, the US Department of Health and Human Services, and the United States Coast Guard. I'm also grateful to the many attorneys and public relations professionals who took the time to facilitate contact with their clients and provide contextual information.

Thanks to Andres Martinez and the New America Foundation's Bernard L. Schwartz and Future Tense programs. NAF research associate Rebecca Rabinowitz relived Katrina moment to moment in parsing hours of WWL radio broadcasts. Olivia Wang ventured back with me to 1926 and 1927 at the Library of Congress. Faith Smith, Caroline Esser, Rachel White, Steve Coll, Shannon Brownlee, Nicole Tosh, Rebecca Shafer, Allison Lazarus, and the other staff and fellows bolstered my work in myriad ways over the past three years.

The Woodrow Wilson International Center for Scholars provided a much-appreciated base of operations in 2010, thanks to Lucy Jilka and colleagues. The Center's relationship with the Library of Congress facilitated my research, as did Phillip Wilcox, who dug for instances of health-care rationing around the world; Aamenah Yusafzai, who amassed a small library on euthanasia; and the helpful Ted Miles.

This work began when I was a freelancer teaching part-time at the Tulane School of Public Health, and my research benefited from the early support of Penny Duckham and the Kaiser Family Foundation's media fellowships in health. Prior to that, the opportunity to work in the immediate aftermath of Katrina came by way of affiliation with the Harvard Humanitarian Initiative, where Dr. Michael VanRooyen, Dr. Jennifer Leaning, Vincenzo Bollettino, and colleagues work hard to improve medical care in crisis situations and have facilitated my access to Harvard's library collections.

Sincere thanks for the kindnesses of Cheryl Young, David Macy, and the staff members and supporters of the MacDowell Colony and its De-Witt Wallace/Reader's Digest Fellowship; Elaina Richardson, Candace H. Wait, and the staff members and supporters of Yaddo and its Dorothy and Granville Hicks in Literature Residency; and the Rockefeller Foundation, Rob Garris, Pilar Palacia, and the staff members of the Bellagio Center for the Arts.

Family members and friends were wonderful supporters of this work throughout its years-long evolution. The members of the Invisible Institute in New York have been dear companions in the world of ideas for nearly a decade.

I've saved the most important book-conjurers for last.

Tina Bennett is a miracle. Agent, advocate, sharp-eyed reader. She celebrates every least bit of success with motherly pride and shows up in times of trouble. She championed my work on this story from the moment I described it to her casually over lunch in early 2007. I appreciate her more than she knows and so, too, her peerless assistant Svetlana Katz.

I'm profoundly grateful for the way Crown has gone about putting *Five Days at Memorial* into the world. The house is filled with talented individuals who prove the value of traditional publishing in supporting the creation of books and helping readers discover them. Molly Stern, publisher, force of nature, makes the impossible happen. Thank you to Maya Mavjee, David Drake, Jacob Lewis, Christine Edwards, Candice Chaplin, and the outstanding sales force; the powerhouse publicity and marketing teams of Jay Sones, Jessica Prudhomme, Carisa Hays, Annsley Rosner, Michael Gentile, Leila Lee, and colleagues; Chris Brand for the water-stained brilliance of the cover; Elizabeth Rendfleisch for interior design perfection; Rachel Meier, Amy Boorstein, and Luisa Francavilla for managing the near unmanageable; Terry Deal and Rachelle Mandik for their utmost patience and precision; and the great support of Wade Lucas, Kelly Gildea, Kirsten Potter, Linda Kaplan, Diane Salvatore, and Tina Constable. Special thanks to Rachel Rokicki, this book's inimitable publicist, for her hard work and authentic zeal; Matthew Martin for careful and numerous legal reads; and to Claire Potter, for expertly liaising as editorial assistant, following on the excellent work of Miriam Chotiner-Gardner, who continued to contribute after becoming an assistant editor. Jeffrey Ward created beautiful maps that orient readers to a most disorienting situation.

Finally, all the adjectives in the world wouldn't be enough to express my gratitude to Vanessa Mobley, perhaps the only editor who would leave the comforts of the big city behind to venture without a car in snowy, icy winter to the New Hampshire wilds to help her author bring her book home. Vanessa, thank you for your generous gifts of time, attention and editorial insight, your tremendous backing, and your unflagging trust in me and my work. Thank you for understanding why the story of these people, this place, matters. Thank you for making this a better book in every way.

NOTES

These notes are meant to clarify sourcing when it may not be apparent in the text, to offer finer detail on important points, and to guide the reader seeking additional information. Interviews with the author that informed the narrative are grouped by chapter and not typically referred to by page number.

Information concerning Dr. Anna Pou comes from a range of sources, as detailed here. Over the course of the reporting, this included attendance at several events involving Dr. Pou, among them two fund-raisers on her behalf, two conferences, and several of her appearances before the Louisiana legislature. Pou also sat for a long interview, but she repeatedly declined to discuss most details related to patient deaths, citing wrongful-death suits and the need for sensitivity in relation to those who did not sue her.

PROLOGUE

Interviews

Dr. Horace Baltz; Essie Cavalier family (John Hazard, grandson); Donna Cotham family (Rosemary Pizzuto Cotham, mother); L. René Goux; Carrie Hall family (including Kimberly Rivers Roberts, granddaughter); Martha Hart family (James Harris "Judson" Hardy, Stephen Chalaron Hardy, and Jane Molony, cousins); Dr. Faith Joubert; Dr. John Kokemor; Dr. Daniel G. Rupley; Dr. John Thiele, Patricia Thiele; Karen Wynn.

Published Literature

Meitrodt, Jeffrey, "Katrina Nurses Called Victims of Justice; 'Their Performance Has Always Been Exemplary,'" *Times-Picayune*, July 23, 2006.

Unpublished Documents

Letter from Dr. John Thiele to Dr. Horace Baltz, December 22, 2006; Memorial Medical Center Disaster Critique Mass Casualty Drill (sarin gas scenario) surveys, April 8, 2005; copy of Tenet Healthcare Corporation helicopter lease contracts and e-mails with Aviation Services, Inc.; photocopy of pilot log book; New Orleans Civil District Court records: petition to probate will of Martha Hart, case no. 2007-06959; *Hall, Kevin, et al v. Memorial Medical Center, et al,* case no. 2006-00127.

Miscellaneous

Photographs of second-floor lobby and doctors' offices; video of airboat departures; e-mail correspondence between author and attorney for Susan Mulderick in August 2009.

Internet

John Thiele obituaries (*Daily Comet*; *Times-Picayune*) and associated online comments, family Facebook pages, and tribute sites (Lake Lawn Metairie Funeral Home website, http://lakelawn .tributes.com/our_obituaries/John-Stephen-Thiele-M.D.-90423470 and www.legacy.com); www.vitals.com page on John Thiele; Harry Tompson Center website, www.harrytompson center.org; www.FDA.gov for documents on midazolam (Versed), including labeling/boxed warning history.

Notes

6 *pantomimed giving an injection*: Thiele recalled in interviews with the author and a fact-checker in 2008 and 2009 that Kokemor made this sign to him, However, Kokemor said in an interview in 2009: "Unequivocally, that never took place." Kokemor did recall being on the ER ramp with Thiele ("He gave me his last two or three cigars") and said in 2013 that he felt doctors had to stay until the end, because "it's like the captain of the ship; they don't go first, they go last."

PART 1: DEADLY CHOICES
CHAPTER 1

Interviews

Dr. Ewing Cook; Minnie Cook; Curtis Dosch; Cathy Green; Dr. Faith Joubert; Eric Yancovich.

Published Literature

Greene, Glen Lee. *The History of Southern Baptist Hospital*, revised edition (New Orleans: Southern Baptist Hospital, 1976, and original 1969 edition).

Coverage of Hurricane Betsy in *The Triangle, Southern Baptist Hospital,* September 1965, including Raymond C. Wilson, "Thinking Out Loud"; J. Doak Marler, "How We Rode Betsy Out"; "Baptist Bears Betsy's Brunt."

"Ivan Knocked, Memorial Stood Ready," *Connections*, September 2004.

"Baptist Hospital Admits First Patient, Mrs. Cotey," *Item-Tribune*, March 9, 1926.

"Baptist Hospital Gives Treatment to First Patient," *Times-Picayune*, March 9, 1926.

Articles and advertisements from the *Item-Tribune*, March 14, 1926, including: "Hospital Is Ready for Use"; "Facts About Baptist Hospital"; "Hospital Head Directs Work"; "Hospital Staff Comprises 127"; "Baptist Hospital Will Not Differ in Charity Cases."

"Ideal of Christian Healing Voiced at Formal Opening of New Baptist Hospital," *Times-Picayune*, March 14, 1926.

"Report of General Superintendent" and other sections of the *Semi-Annual Report of the Sewerage and Water Board of New Orleans, La.*, December 31, 1908, and period of 1926–1930.

"City Park Is Gaily Garbed for Great Festival Sunday," *New Orleans States,* May 2, 1926.

Coverage of the May 2, 1926, storm and aftermath: the *Times-Picayune* (May 3, 4, 7, 9; August 26; September 12); *New Orleans Item* (May 3–5, 8, 11, 14); *Item-Tribune* (May 9); *New Orleans States* (May 3).

Coverage of the April 15–16, 1927, storm and aftermath: *New Orleans Item* (April 16 and 23) and *Times-Picayune* (April 16–21, 23–24, 26–29).

Barry, John M. *Rising Tide: The Great Mississippi Flood of 1927 and How It Changed America* (New York: Simon & Schuster, 1997).

Documents

"The 1927 Great Mississippi Flood: 80-Year Retrospective" (Newark, CA: Risk Management Solutions, Inc., 2007).

Pamphlets and reports from the Southern Baptist Historical Library and Archives, including: Marvin W. Johnson, "Report of the Baptist Hospital at New Orleans," 1925; Louis J. Bristow, "Southern Baptist Hospital," 1926; "Proposed Program Structure, Southern Baptist Hospitals," undated; Louis J. Bristow, "The Heart of Healing, Unto the Least," ca. 1930s; Louis J. Bristow, "Hospital Stories: Indicating How the Southern Baptist Hospital Is Fulfilling Its Task of Healing Humanity's Hurt," ca. 1930s. Issues of the *Annual of the Southern Baptist Convention* (1928, '29, '36, '42, '43, '62, and '68) for reports of the hospital's work, philosophy, and finances.

Maygarden, Benjamin D., Jill-Karen Yakubik, Ellen Weiss, Chester Peyronnin, Kenneth R. Jones. *National Register Evaluation of New Orleans Drainage System, Orleans Parish, Louisiana,* 1999. Chapter 4, "History of the New Orleans Drainage System, 1893–1996."

Notes

11 *317-bed*: Tenet Healthcare Corporation, "Tenet to Create New Health Network in New Orleans," October 24, 2005.

12 *wrote in a letter*: Greene, G. *The History of Southern Baptist Hospital,* p. 60.

13 *"The crying need"*: Ibid., p. 29–30.

17 *with initial estimates*: These were cited in local newspapers and may have been high. A ten-year report of the hospital commission in *Annual of the Southern Baptist Convention,* May 1936, mentions "property losses in flood damages in 1926 and 1927 which cost us $43,220 to repair and replace."

   between $525,000 and $800,000: Minneapolisfed.org. "What's a Dollar Worth" calculator—$528,000 to $792,000, retrieved May 13, 2013.

20 *Only once in the eight decades that followed*: Robert Ricks of the National Oceanic and Atmospheric Administration searched NOAA's database for the top ten rainiest days in New Orleans (Audubon station 166664) since 1871 for the author in September 2010. A storm on October 2, 1937, resulted in 13.08 inches, compared with the official 13.00 inches on April 16, 1927.

22 *35 percent limit in effect at the time of Katrina*: According to *City of New Orleans, Louisiana: Basic Financial Statements December 31, 2011,* "The Louisiana Legislature, in Act 1 of 1994, increased the City's general obligation bond debt limit to an amount equal to the greater of (i) $500,000,000 or (ii) 35% of total assessed valuation of the City."

23 *The Mississippi River floods of 1927 led to*: 1928 Flood Control Act. Seventieth Congress, session I, chapter 596; 1928, chapter 569, "An Act for the Control of Floods on the Mississippi River and Its Tributaries, and for Other Purposes"; http://www.mvd.usace.army.mil/Portals/52/docs/MRC/Appendix_E._1928_Flood_Control_Act.pdf.

CHAPTER 2

Interviews
Gina Isbell; Robbye Dubois.

Published literature
Landphair, Juliette, "'The Forgotten People of New Orleans': Community, Vulnerability, and the Lower Ninth Ward," *Journal of American History*, no. 94 (December 2007): 837–45.

Unpublished documents
"Tenet Healthcare Corporation to Acquire Mercy†Baptist Medical Center," May 17, 1995, Mercy†Baptist Medical Center (press release); hospital floor plans; LifeCare e-mails August 28, 2005, reporting that all patients were moved from Chalmette.

Notes

24 *A hurricane watch covered a wide swath*: Hurricane watch including the New Orleans area was issued at ten a.m. local time on Saturday (1500 UTC). "Hurricane Katrina Advisory Number 17," NWS/TCP National Hurricane Center, Miami, FL, ten a.m. CDT Saturday, August 27, 2005; http://www.nhc.noaa.gov/archive/2005/pub/al122005.public.017 .shtml. See also: Richard D. Knabb, Jamie R. Rhome, and Daniel P. Brown, "Tropical Cyclone Report—Hurricane Katrina." NWS TPC/National Hurricane Center, 2005; http:// www.nhc.noaa.gov/pdf/TCR-AL122005_Katrina.pdf.

A watch meant that hurricane conditions were possible in the watch area, "generally within 36 hours . . . Katrina could become a Category Four Hurricane." In an expert witness report prepared for hospital defendants, including Memorial Medical Center after Katrina, meterologist Randoph J. Evans noted that the storm "rapidly intensified during the three days prior to landfall" and that the National Hurricane Center advisories and forcasts contained "omissions, uncertainties, and inaccuracies," including a late warning that the New Orleans levees could be overtopped. Friday evening was, Evans writes, the first time that the NHC expressed confidence that the forecast tracks clustered on the New Orleans region. In advance of the 2010 hurricane season, the National Hurricane Center added twelve hours to the forecast period for watches (from thirty-six to forty-eight) and warnings (from twenty-four to thirty-six), and in 2013 further changes were made to increase the time for preparedness in advance of anticipated tropical storm force winds.

24 *rated Category Three*: "Hurricane Katrina Discussion Number 17" (NWS/TCP National Hurricane Center, Miami, FL, ten a.m. CDT, Saturday August 27, 2005; http://www .nhc.noaa.gov/archive/2005/dis/al122005.discus.017.shtml) issued at the same time as the advisory said that a strengthening to Category Five before landfall "is not out of the question." It also noted that the official forecast called for "landfall in southeastern Louisiana in 48–60 hr," meaning Monday, August 29.

27 *upgraded its hurricane watch*: Hurricane warning including the New Orleans area was issued at ten p.m. local time on Saturday (0300 UTC Sunday), Knabb, et al.

archaic Teletype: Oremus, Will, "TORNADO POSSIBLE. MIGHT KILL YOU . . . MIGHT NOT," *Slate*, April 2, 2012; http://www.slate.com/articles/health_and_science/explainer/2012/04/ new_tornado_warnings_why_national_weather_service_storm_alerts_weren_t_scary_ enough_.html.

27 THE BOTTOM LINE IS THAT KATRINA: "Hurricane Katrina Discussion Number 19" NWS TPC/National Hurricane Center, Miami, FL, eleven p.m. EDT, Saturday, August 27, 2005.

CHAPTER 3

Interviews

Dr. Horace Baltz; Joanne Cardaro; Dr. Ewing Cook; Minnie Cook; Dr. Richard Deichmann; Dr. Barry Faust; Faye Garvey, family of Jannie Burgess (Linette Burgess Guidi, Bertha Mitchell, Gladys Smith, Johnny Clark); Gina Isbell; Dr. John Kokemor; Gov. Richard Lamm; Grayson Lovick; Dr. Jeffrey N. Myers; Dr. Daniel W. Nuss; Dr. Anna Pou; Karen Wynn; John Zimmerman.

Archives

"NOAA Hurricane Katrina Advisory Archive," National Hurricane Center, 2005; http://www.nhc.noaa.gov/archive/2005/KATRINA.shtml?.

Documents

Johnson, Brig. Gen. David L. "Service Assessment: Hurricane Katrina August 23–31, 2005" (Silver Spring, MD: NOAA's National Weather Service, 2006); http://www.weather.gov/os/assessments/pdfs/Katrina.pdf; New Orleans evacuation order; copy of Dr. Anna Pou's signed relocation agreement, acceptance of offer, and employment offer cover letter from April 2, 2004.

Notes

28 MOST OF THE AREA WILL BE UNINHABITABLE: "**URGENT–WEATHER MESSAGE,**" NWS, New Orleans, LA, eleven a.m. CDT, Sunday August 28, 2005; http://celebrating 200years.noaa.gov/events/katrina/side_katrina.html. Also roughly twenty-four hours before the storm made landfall, NHC public advisories began predicting a storm surge (water height above normal astronomical tide level) in the range of eighteen to twenty-two feet (and as high as twenty-eight feet wherever the center of the hurricane hit land).

29 "remember the old ways": Press conference, Aaron Broussard, president, Jefferson Parish, LA, WDSU eleven a.m. CDT; http://www.youtube.com/watch?v=Mk64s3xT8W8.

confusion over whether he had the legal authority to issue it: US Congress, Senate Committee on Homeland Security and Governmental Affairs, Hurricane Katrina: A Nation Still Unprepared. Chapter 16, "Pre-Storm Evacuations," footnotes 59–60, pp. 264–265. (Washington, DC: 109th Congress, 2nd session, S. Rept. 109–322 GPO, 2006.i); http://www.gpo.gov/fdsys/pkg/CRPT-109srpt322/pdf/CRPT-109srpt322.pdf.

30 on a conference call: Knox Andress's notes on the ten a.m. conference call are included as exhibits in Elmira Preston, et al v. Tenet Health System Memorial Medical Center, Inc. D/B/A, Memorial Medical Center, et al. 2:06-cv-03179-EEEF-KWR document 74-6 filed October 24, 2006, US District Court Eastern District of Louisiana, civil action no. 06-3179, available on PACER, Public Access to Court Electronic Records, http://www.pacer.gov. (The case was later remanded to civil district court and certified as a class action; therefore, later motions and judgments in the case, referenced elsewhere, are not available on PACER.) A conference call participant said only Children's and Methodist hospitals had both generators and switches above the ground floor. However, Methodist, too, lost power when the city flooded, and its former administrator had informed the New Orleans health director

three years before Katrina that one of the hospital's main generators and elements of the fuel supply system sat below flood level and would cost $7.5 million to protect (see Fink, Sheri, "The New Katrina Flood: Hospital Liability," *New York Times,* January 1, 2010). Deposed in a lawsuit brought by the family of a critically ill patient who died at Methodist, CEO Larry Morgan Graham explained that while one of the generators was well above flood level, the pump that fed diesel power to it was flooded. The hospital was without power for about eighteen hours before staff restarted the generators by "hand carrying diesel fuel to the roof" (*Stephen B. Lacoste, et al v. Pendleton Methodist Hospital, LLC,* Civil District Court for the Parish of Orleans, case no. 2006-2347, deposition taken May 2, 2008). Vulnerable fuel pumps have remained a problem for other hospitals in flood zones. Superstorm Sandy in October 2012 knocked out basement fuel pumps at New York City's Bellevue Hospital, where fuel was also hand-carried upstairs to keep generators running. *more than $17 million*: Louisiana Hospital Association, data on Hospital Preparedness Program grants from the US Department of Health and Human Services to the Louisiana Department of Health and Hospitals, 2002-2005; http://www.lhaonline.org/displaycommon .cfm?an=1&subarticlenbr=138

30   *"It is assumed that many"*: US Senate. *Hurricane Katrina: A Nation Still Unprepared.* Chapter 24, "Medical Assistance," p. 399, p. 427 (reference 7): Philip Navin, e-mail to EOC Report, August 29, 2005, 6:58 a.m., provided to Committee; filed as Bates nos. CDC 747–749.

32   *lost her only son in Vietnam*: Ruben Anthony Burgess, private first class, United States Marine Corps, December 9, 1948–February 23, 1968. See "The Virtual Wall: Vietnam Veterans Memorial," http://www.virtualwall.org/db/BurgessRA03a.htm.

could not receive care at them: See, for example, Baker, Robert B., Harriet A. Washington, et al, "African American Physicians and Organized Medicine, 1846–1968," *JAMA,* vol. 300, no. 3 (July 16, 2008): 306–314. Racial segregation in Southern hospitals had its legal basis in decisions such as the "separate but equal" 1896 Supreme Court ruling in *Plessy v. Ferguson,* as well as statutes in Southern states mandating segregation of white and black patients. The Hill-Burton Act of 1946 allowed federal funds to be used for construction and improvements to segregated hospitals. The practice continued after *Brown v. Board of Education* struck down the principle of "separate but equal" in education. (Quadagno, Jill and Steve McDonald. "Racial Segregation in Southern Hospitals: How Medicare 'Broke the Back of Segregated Health Services'" in Green, Elna C., ed., *The New Deal and Beyond: Social Welfare in the South Since 1930.* [Athens, GA: University of Georgia Press, 2003]). The Civil Rights Act of 1964, Title VI, forbade discrimination in any private organization receiving federal financial assistance. However, only hospitals that received federal funds were seen to be bound by the nondiscrimination provisions. When Medicare was passed in 1965, a hospital could not receive its funds unless it could certify it did not discriminate.

In fact, Baptist was one of the last: Southern Baptist Hospital administrator Raymond C. Wilson, in his "Thinking Out Loud" column in the May 1967, *The Triangle,* said a US Government official told him that fewer than three hundred hospitals in the US had chosen to operate without government aid, and "the opinion was expressed that Southern Baptist is the largest of the group to 'go it alone.'" Wilson wrote that New Orleans hospitals that participated in Medicare were being asked to give the government's office of Equal Health Opportunity a list of patients referred by each doctor to each hospital (presumably to help ferret out ongoing segregation). "Such a measure could seriously hamper a doctor's privilege of deciding which hospital is best suited for each particular patient," Wilson wrote.

33 *New Orleanians sent supportive letters*: Wilson included these quotes in his "Thinking Out Loud" column, September 1966, *The Triangle*. He also applauded San Leandro, California, for turning down "millions of dollars available through antipoverty programs, federal urban renewal, housing and beautification programs" to resist "control of their community affairs." The 1966 statement was reprinted in Wilson's column in the July 1966, *The Triangle*.

The hospital began quietly: Wilson wrote in his June 1969 "Thinking Out Loud" column: "It is the creed and practice of our hospital to make available our services to all people, regardless of race, creed, color, national origin or ability to pay." The same month, the Southern Baptist Convention, meeting in New Orleans, adopted a "Resolution on New Orleans Hospital Integration" requesting that the trustees of the hospital commission "pursue this matter without delay in order to bring actual practice in line with stated policy"; http://www.sbc.net/resolutions/amResolution.asp?ID=888. The integration policy had been adopted a year earlier, at the Convention's annual session in June 1968, which met the week Sen. Robert F. Kennedy was fatally shot. At that meeting, the new program statement of the Southern Baptist Hospitals had replaced this phrase, adopted in 1962: "Makes available the full resources of the hospital to those people least able to pay in such ways as to preserve human dignity and worth." According to Greene, Glen Lee. *The History of Southern Baptist Hospital* (New Orleans: Southern Baptist Hospital, 1976, and original 1969 edition), the hospital implemented the Convention's revised program statement by beginning to admit black patients; an article in the June 13, 1968, *Baptist Message* said, according to the hospital's annual report to the Convention: "the New Orleans hospital admitted its first Negro patients this year." Dr. Horace Baltz, a white physician who had worked at the hospital beginning in the mid-1960s, told me "it was very quietly done," and Dr. Windsor Dennis, a black surgeon of Dr. Baltz's generation who did not work at the hospital, said he knew of only one black person, a prominent school principal, who was treated there before this time ("It was kept quiet."). Dr. Baltz noted that Dr. Emmett Lee Irwin, one of the most active segregationists in New Orleans, had been a leading staff physician whose views may have influenced hospital policy (he died in a car accident in 1965). Greene's book lists Irwin as a founding member of the Southern Baptist Hospital medical staff in 1926, and McMillen, Neil R. *The Citizens' Council: Organized Resistance to the Second Reconstruction 1954–64* (Champaign, IL: Illini Books, 1994) describes Irwin as a founder and early leader of the Greater New Orleans Citizens' Council. The organization worked to oppose school integration and, with Irwin as its chairman in the mid-1950s, "packed thousands of Confederate-flag-waving spectators into New Orleans's Municipal Auditorium to hear speakers denounce integration as a Communist plot and make dire predictions of an impending race war," according to Mohr, Clarence L. and Joseph E. Gordon. *Tulane: The Emergency of a Modern University, 1945–1980* (Baton Rouge, LA: Louisiana State University Press, 2001). Mohr and Gordon's book discusses Irwin's earlier role founding and leading the Louisiana Coalition of Patriotic Societies. Irwin's tactics in opposing school integration included bringing white children, some in blackface, onstage at a rally and signaling them to begin kissing each other; he told the crowd, "That's just a little demonstration of what integration means." (*Bush v. Orleans Parish School Board and the Desegregation of New Orleans Schools.* Federal Judicial Center; http://www.fjc.gov/history/home.nsf/page/tu_bush_narrative.html.) A statement from earlier in Southern Baptist Hospital's history suggested a more inclusive attitude, at least on paper. A hospital report from 1935 stated: "Our policy, consistently followed through the years has been to care for the sick who came to us, regardless of race or creed or position in life, giving such care as we have been capable of rendering." Perhaps significantly, while "race" is mentioned, "color" is not.

At the time of then-hospital director Wilson's 1969 message, Southern Baptist Hospital was still not participating in Medicare. "It does concern me that our position on Medicare has been confused in some people's minds with civil rights issues," Wilson wrote. "From a very practical point of view, I'd like to remind our critics that in order to support our hospital in its worthy endeavors . . . if we favored only the needy, we'd be unable to function in short order." He pointed out that the federal government had announced a 2 percent reduction in Medicare reimbursements. "Our policy on Medicare has been one of 'wait and see' and it seems the longer we wait, the more problems are becoming evident."

33 *the hospital set aside its opposition to Medicare*: "SBH Joins Medicare," *The Triangle*. The hospital joined on November 1, 1969. Wilson noted that the census of seniors was thirty-one on November 3, fifty-two on November 10, and eighty-six on November 18. By January 1970 there were 123, according to Greene, p. 209.

Tensions persisted: Johnie Montgomery v. Southern Baptist Hospital, EEOC charge no. 062-79-1208; *Sheila Bass v. Southern Baptist Hospital*, EEOC charge no. 062-79-1282; *Issac Frezel v. Southern Baptist Hospital*, EEOC charge no. 062-79-1905 and 062-80-0316; *Tyronne Smith v. Southern Baptist Hospital*, EEOC charge no. 062-80-0819; *Rita Robertson v. Southern Baptist Hospital*, EEOC charge no. 062-80-0845; *Dorothy Nelson v. Southern Baptist Hospital*, EEOC charge no. 062-80-1464. The hospital sued the EEOC and its chairman, Eleanor Holmes Norton, among other officials, in 1980 (*Southern Baptist Hospital v. Equal Employment Opportunity Commission, et al*, US District Court, Eastern District of Louisiana, 80-3972) for copies of investigative files in the seven cases. EEOC attorneys argued that releasing them "would permit the employer to intimidate, harass, and retaliate against employees" and interfere with ongoing proceedings against the hospital. The hospital lost the case on the latter grounds. For a brief essay on continuing challenges related to implementing integration in health care, see Smith, David Barton, "Racial and Ethnic Health Disparities and the Unfinished Civil Rights Agenda," *HealthAffairs*, 24, 2 (2005): 317-324. http://content .healthaffairs.org/content/24/2/317.full.

sued Southern Baptist Hospitals: Issac E. Frezel v. Southern Baptist Hospitals, Inc., US District Court, Eastern District of Louisiana, 80-4603 (1980).

34 *Flint-Goodridge Hospital*: See, for example, "The History of Flint-Goodridge Hospital of Dillard University," *Journal of the National Medical Association*, 61, no. 6 (November 1969): 533–536; "Medicine: Negro Health," *Time*, April 8, 1940; http://www.time.com/time/magazine/article/0,9171,763801,00.html (requires subscription).

Surgery and chemotherapy had stalled: Jannie Burgess's family kindly facilitated access to her medical history and records.

35 *First African American Bunny*: According to Linette Burgess Guidi.

All staff members: Memorial Medical Center unpublished memo entitled "HURRICANE KATRINA—AUGUST 28, 2005."

Unlike many others, Dr. Anna Maria Pou: The section on Dr. Anna Pou's history is drawn from interviews with Pou and others listed above, as well as from information provided by additional family members, medical colleagues, and friends of Pou who attended the "Friends of Anna" conference and dinner/fund-raiser held in Houston, Texas, in May 2007. Pou's attorney, Rick Simmons, informed me about the event when I first met with him to express an interest in writing about Pou. I attended with the permission of the organizers and paid for my own meal in accordance with journalism ethics standards. Many of Pou's supporters were eager to share stories about her and expressed the hope that I would write something that went beyond the quick hit television pieces that focused exclusively on the acts that she was accused of without giving a deeper sense of who she was as a physician and person.

36 *even her elementary-school*: Comment on nola.com weblog from "Tim Ballein of Westwego," July 31, 2006 who identified himself as a St. Rita's school classmate.

He treated patients: See Kolb, Carolyn, "Life Along St. Claude Avenue," *New Orleans Magazine* (August 2008); http://www.myneworleans.com/New-Orleans-Magazine/August-2008/Life-Along-St-Claude-Avenue.

37 *One warm day in the late 1970s*: The shallow water drowning episode is depicted as retold to the author by John Zimmerman, the fully recovered drownee, on July 23, 2007.

40 *a federal fugitive*: US Drug Enforcement Administration New Orleans Most Wanted Fugitives listing for Frederick Anthony Pou Jr., NCIC# W603770132; http://www.justice.gov/dea/fugitives/no/24B099BA-E9B1-4EDA-982C-C01C8C83D102.shtml. Frederick Pou Jr., was indicted by federal grand juries in Alabama and Louisiana; the Alabama indictment concerns the alleged importation of approximately 12,000 kilograms of cocaine from Colombia. See also: *USA v. Pou, et al* 1:89-cr-00072-BH, US District Court Southern District of Alabama, May 9, 1989; *USA, et al, v. Land Baton Rouge,* 2:89-cv-02289-MLCF, US District Court Eastern District of LA (New Orleans), May 22, 1989; *United States v. Ricou Deshaw,* 974 F.2d 667 (5th cir.), no. 91-3131, October 14, 1992.

41 *the hospital began to ration care*: Wysocki Jr., Bernard, "Hospital Sets Strict Rules to Limit Costs," *Wall Street Journal,* January 12, 2004; Kinonen, Judie, "A Tale of 'Rational Rationing,'" *UTMB Magazine* (Spring 2005); http://www.utmb.edu/utmbmagazine/archive/05_spring/pog.

43 *"Dr. Pou, we regard this" [. . .] "without additional pay"*: Copy of Pou's signed relocation agreement, acceptance of offer, and employment offer cover letter, April 2, 2004.

44 *Panepinto purchased:* Real property history record retrieved from nexis.com.

45 *first hospital in the Southeast to purchase a "crash cart"*: According to hospital administrator Wilson, quoted in "Hospital Adds New Lifesaver," *The Triangle* (March 1967), a reprint of a February 16, 1967 *Times-Picayune* article. Also Wilson, Raymond C., "Thinking Out Loud," *The Triangle* (June 1967) discusses a hospital expansion and adoption of high-tech aspects of "The Hospital of Tomorrow," including piped-in oxygen and backup power.

"Many of us have trouble accepting the business motive": "Dr. Baltz: Excellence Is Our Strength," *The Triangle* (February 1984).

46 *Clarence Herbert*: See, for example, Lo, Bernard, "The Death of Clarence Herbert: Withdrawing Care Is Not Murder," *Annals of Internal Medicine,* no. 101 (1984): 248–251.

"The ways and means of dying": "The Ethics of Life and Death," *Spectrum* (Spring 1985): 23.

47 *"We've got a duty to die"*: Excerpted remarks, Colorado Health Lawyers Association, March 27, 1984, transcribed from a tape provided by the *Denver Post*; transcript given to the author by Gov. Richard D. Lamm. See also: Kass, Leon R., "The Case for Mortality," *The American Scholar* vol. 52, no. 2 (Spring 1983): 173–191. The then-largest circulation daily, the New York *Daily News,* carried Lamm's comments with the headline: "Aged Are Told to Drop Dead: Colo. Gov Says It's Their Duty," March 29, 1984. Gov. Lamm received hateful telegrams, the e-mail flames of the day. The original *Denver Post* article substituted "you" for "we," and its headline implied incorrectly that Lamm had asserted specifically that elderly or terminally ill patients should die. Gov. Lamm later won a correction from the *New York*

Times ("Correction," November 23, 1993), which said that Lamm's quote had been distorted in eight articles over the years. Lamm used the national attention to advance his argument that people who needed health care were being robbed of it because too much money was being spent on "high-tech procedures and machines" that too often led to "a living death" for patients with poor prognoses (Lamm, Richard D., "Long Time Dying: When 'Miracle Cures' Don't Cure," *New Republic* [August 27, 1984]). At a conference in 2010, I asked Lamm if he still held the same views, now that he had hit the three-quarter-century mark himself. He said with a smile that he'd go crawling and scratching his way to the hospital if he needed care. "I would, I think," he agreed in a more formal, follow-up interview on October 7, 2011. He said it was natural for sick people to be desperate for treatment. "All the more reason a health care system has to assert sanity over that very human need."

47   *With the appearance of crash carts*: See Benjamin Weiser's remarkable and still-fresh, five-part *Washington Post* series on end-of-life care dilemmas, including " 'Orchestration' of a Death," April 19, 1983; and "A Final Judgment on Quality of Life," April 20, 1983. See also Kleiman, Dena, "Uncertainty Clouds Care of the Dying," *New York Times*, January 18, 1985.

49   *On January 15, 2005, Pou attended*: "Welcome New Members" and "Save the Date" *Medical Staff Newsletter, Memorial Medical Center Tenet Louisiana Health System,* November 2004. Also, photographs of Installation Banquet attendees, including Dr. Pou, January 15, 2005.

50   *was in the process of selling*: "Tenet Announces Major Restructuring of Operations," press release, Tenet Healthcare Corporation, January 28, 2004. See also, Klaidman, Stephen. *Coronary* (New York: Scribner, 2007).

     much to celebrate: Goux, L. R., "Memorial Achieves 'Full Compliance' in JCAHO Survey," *Connections* (July 2004); "Memorial Shines in JCAHO Survey," *Connections* (June 2005); and "You're Tops, and We Have the Stats to Prove It!," *Connections* (October 2004). Also: "Birthplace of New Orleans Cuts Ribbon on Renovation," *Connections* (November 2004); "New Orleans Cancer Institute Celebrates Opening, Health Fair," *Connections* (February 2004); and "New Orleans Cancer Institute Building Nears Completion," *Connections* (August 2003).

52   *As the storm approached*: The figures are a best estimate based on copies of the patient census and e-mail communications by hospital leaders. Numbers changed during the disaster as patients were admitted, discharged, or died.

     2:11 A.M., WWL New Orleans Radio: WWL kindly furnished digital audio of broadcasts, which were transcribed by the author and more so by the indomitable Rebecca Rabinowitz, who developed very limber fingers as a research associate at the New America Foundation in 2011. These transcripts are the basis for WWL excerpts from August 29, 2005, through September 1, 2005, quoted in the book.

54   *It had fallen [. . .] and never left*: Susan Mulderick described her history with the hospital in several depositions and stipulations in the case of *Elmira Preston, et al v. Tenet Health Systems Memorial Medical Center, Inc.,* Orleans Parish Civil District Court, 2005-11709. Memorial Medical Center Policy Number E-19, "Incident Command System," dated June 21, 2002, describes the intended structure of the leadership system for disasters. However, interviews with staff members suggested that the plan was not followed exactly as written, and the book reflects their views on their jobs.

55   *She rarely took*: Diane Loupe, "5 Lucky Women Were Bumped from Plane," *Times-Picayune,* July 11, 1982.

55 *merged with a New Orleans Catholic hospital . . . sold to giant, for-profit Tenet*: Harrell, Byron R. and Sister Barbara Grant, "Memorandum to: Employees of Southern Baptist Hospital and Mercy Hospital," September 1, 1993; "Mercy and Baptist Hospitals Announce Plans to Merge," news release, Peter A. Mayer Advertising, Inc., September 1, 1993; Pope, John, "Baptist, Mercy Joining Forces," *Times-Picayune,* September 2, 1993; Rubinow, Marisa, "The Merger," *Healthcare New Orleans,* October 1993; "Mercy†Baptist Joins Tenet Louisiana Health System," *Tenet Louisiana Health System* (bimonthly employee newsletter), November 1995. "Another Shift Toward Tomorrow," *Collaborations* (health and wellness magazine from Mercy†Baptist Medical Center), Summer 1995.

Christmas decorating contests: The Triangle (January 1971). (Winners in 1970 included a Madonna made of foil and a picture decorated with "appropriately colored rug yarn.") Faith was a consistent theme in hospital newsletters ("There are times when a prayer can be as soothing as a sedative," *The Triangle,* May 1967), and was foundational. The program structure for Southern Baptist Hospitals, adopted in 1962, stated: "A Baptist hospital exists to bring men into a saving relationship with God through faith in Jesus Christ by means of direct personal witness as occasion presents, and by a positive Christian interpretation of the experiences of disease, disability, and death." Still, concern for the bottom line existed even in that period. In providing for the medically indigent and Baptist denominational personnel, hospitals were to do so "within such limits as will not endanger the financial soundness of the institutions" (*Annual of the Southern Baptist Convention,* 1962, pp. 61–62). Although the Southern Baptist Convention broke ties with the hospital in June 1970 (Wilson, Raymond C. "Thinking Out Loud," *The Triangle* [July 1970]), it was to continue operating "as an independent Christian institution" under a body that also governed Baptist Memorial Hospital in Jacksonville, FL.

57 *it seemed to one*: Dr. John Kokemor.

58 *The head pharmacist had requested*: E-mail sent by Memorial pharmacy director Curtis Hebert, 7:00 p.m., Sunday, August 28, 2005.

"Rene's major concern . . .": Sent 9:03 a.m. Monday, August 29, 2005.

60 *was unable to reach his wife*: The nurse documented this in Everett's chart.

CHAPTER 4

Interviews

Knox Andress; Dr. Horace Baltz; MAJ Betty Bennett; Kamel Boughrara; Keith Brisbois; LT Shelley M. Colbert; Dr. Ewing Cook; Minnie Cook; Marc Creswell; Dr. Richard Deichmann; Rebecca DeLasalle; Dr. Windsor Dennis; Hugh Eley; John Ferrero; Faye Garvey; Dr. Juan Jorge Gershanik; Cathy Green; LT Catharine Gross; LCDR Russell Hall; Dr. Robert Hendler; Gina Isbell; Dr. Bryant King; CDR Scott Langum; Wayne Leche; Father John Marse; CDR (ret.) William F. McMeekin; Therese Mendez; LT/O3E Sean Moore; Dr. Susan Nelson; Dr. Paul Primeaux; Dr. Angela Reginelli; Michael Richard; AMT2 Randal Ripley; Karen Sanford; Rodney Scott; Mike Sonnier; Dr. Kevin Stephens; Dr. Robert Wise; Karen Wynn; Eric Yancovich.

Notes

63 *WWL, a popular*: For more details on the effort, see Moody, Reginald F., "Radio's Role During Hurricane Katrina: A Case Study of WWL Radio and United Radio Broadcasters of New Orleans," PhD diss., University of Southern Mississippi; Ann Arbor, Mich.: UMI Microform, 3268460, 2006.

63 *martial law had been declared*: Jefferson Parish President Aaron Broussard on WWL broadcasts, including during the eleven p.m. CDT hour of August 29, 2005.

"My question is . . .": WWL 11:13 p.m., CDT, August 28, 2005.

"We're very frightened . . .": WWL 4:22 a.m., CDT, August 30, 2005.

64 *The meeting took place*: Descriptions based on photographs taken in the room during the disaster.

65 *"soul surviving"*: Lindzy Louis IV, recorded June 23, 2007 for the oral history project "Surviving Hurricanes Katrina and Rita in Houston Collection" (AFC 2008/006), Archive of Folk Culture, American Folklife Center, Library of Congress, Washington, DC (Interview SR012, Accession # SKR-CJ-SR02).

67 *Tropical Storm Allison*: See, for example, "Tropical Storm Allison, June 2001: RMS Event Report" (Newark, CA: *Risk Management Solutions*, 2001); "Lessons Learned from a Hospital Evacuation During Tropical Storm Allison," *Suburban Emergency Management Project*, Biot Report #216, May 21, 2005 ("Lesson 1: Flooding will occur on a flood plain. Don't be surprised when it happens, especially when your hospital is built on a flood plain . . ."). Several lawsuits were filed against hospitals after Allison, including one brought by the family of Charles Brunkenhoefer (172nd District Court, Jefferson County, TX, no. E-169,673), who died after the hospital where he was being treated lost power. In another case, Texas Woman's University sued the Methodist Hospital for allegedly having diverted surface water into a tunnel leading to the campus of the other hospital (151st District Court, Harris County, Texas, no. 2003-31948).

71 *known then as the Joint Commission*: The organization's name was changed in 2007 to The Joint Commission. Memorial's JCAHO hospital accreditation program and home care program survey, May 17–19, 2005, organizational ID no: 8778.

a fairly typical number: Dr. Robert Wise, personal communication, 2010.

72 *paved the way for state licensure*: In Louisiana, accreditation by JCAHO was acceptable by the health department in lieu of its annual re-survey ("9309. Exceptions," *Louisiana Register*, vol. 29, no. 11, November 30, 2003, p. 2404).

73 *By 2005, more than a billion*: "Hospitals Rising to the Challenge: The First Five Years of the U.S. Hospital Preparedness Program and Priorities Going Forward," UPMC Center for Biosecurity (now known as the UPMC Center for Health Security), March, 2009; http://www.upmchealthsecurity.org/website/resources/publications/2009/2009-04-16-hppreport.html. $135 million in 2002 and $515 million in 2003 and in 2004.

74 *a three-page form*: Memorial's was essentially identical to a sample hazard vulnerability analysis tool published by Kaiser Foundation Health Plan, Inc. in 2001, "Kaiser Permanente: Medical Center Hazard and Vulnerability Analysis"; http://www.calhospitalprepare.org/sites/main/files/file-attachments/kp_hva_template_2010.xls.

far exceeded federal requirements: As of July 2013, the US Centers for Medicare & Medicaid Services had still not issued a proposed rule on emergency preparedness, which had been listed in the Federal Register in fall 2010 and was later "scheduled for publication in early 2012," according to CMS, "in response to concern about the ability of healthcare providers across the United States to plan for and respond to emergencies." (CMS Spotlight, "Emergency Preparedness Requirements for Medicare and Medicaid Participating Providers and

Suppliers: CMS-3178"; http://www.cms.gov/Regulations-and-Guidance/Legislation/
CFCsAndCoPs/Spotlight.html) The long-belated rule, inspired in part by the failures of
preparedness after Hurricane Katrina, would make it a requirement for health care facilities, including hospitals, to meet certain preparedness standards in order to participate in
Medicare and Medicaid. According to observers of the process, CMS received pushback
against potentially costly new requirements, delaying the adoption of the rule. The "sys-
temic gaps" in healthcare preparedness remained unfilled.

78 *Arvin, in Texas, had no background*: Oral deposition of Michael Arvin, August 26, 2010, in
Preston, et al v. Tenet.

79 *Atlanta was a former Baptist hospital*: Greene, Glen Lee. *The History of Southern Baptist Hospital*,
revised edition (New Orleans: Southern Baptist Hospital, 1976, and original 1969 edition),
p. 24.

81 *new inpatient hospitalist*: "Hospitalists Now on Staff," *Connections* (May 2005).

   "I'm in charge . . .": This account is from Dr. Cook (interviews with author in 2007, 2008,
   2009, and 2013). Dr. King confirmed those recollections in 2009 and 2013. He said he
   believed that his patient required telemetry monitoring: "Patients who needed certain
   things, if we can provide them, we should still have them," and he thought the interaction
   may have taken place at an earlier point in the disaster.

83 *A rusting helipad*: Staff sent the Southern Baptist Hospital helipad site plan chart to Coast
   Guard personnel. "Growing to Serve You Better," *Spectrum* (Spring 1985), p. 19, described
   the Helistop and other "Project 2000" construction projects under way in 1985, including
   the creation of the six-story Clara Wing and power plant building.

85 *Black Hawk, weighing more than 11,000 pounds*: Empty weight reported on various speci-
   fication sheets; http://www.sikorskyarchives.com/S-70A%20(UH-60M%20Black%20
   Hawk,%20HH-60M).php. One Jayhawk landed at Memorial weighing 18,500 pounds,
   less than half full of fuel, according to co-pilot LT Catharine Gross.

86 *a nurse's husband*: LT/O3E Sean Moore (rank as of July 2013).

88 *A nurse's husband sat in a chair*: The photograph of the unnamed husband holding the baby
   is in Bernard, Marirose and Pamela R. Mathews. "Evacuation of a Maternal-Newborn
   Area During Hurricane Katrina," *MCN* (July/August 2008). The description of the NICU
   baby rescue draws on several sources, including the above article; a StoryCorps interview
   with Pamela Mathews, her husband Edwin "Roy" Mathews, and nurse Jo Lincks (interview MBX006447, March 18, 2010, archived in the Library of Congress's Folklife reading
   room); photographs of the rescue taken by Memorial staff; Gershanik, Juan, "EVACU-
   ATE! My Katrina Experience," fax dated December 27, 2005, with four-page story; Feiler,
   Alan, "God's Hands in the World," *Baltimore Jewish Times,* September 9, 2005; and on interviews with staff, including Dr. Gershanik.

89 *Pilots from out of town*: Several USCG pilots interviewed by the author described the difficulty of locating Memorial, also reflected in unpublished USCG documents, including
   "Summary of Action for the Distinguished Flying Cross: LCDR SCOTT LANGUM,"
   covering August 28 to September 4, 2005. "LANGUM deftly navigated to the assigned
   position through the darkened obstacles, only to find the location of the hospital inac-
   curate. With no positive guidance, Lieutenant Commander LANGUM began a low level
   search over unlit wires, reading the signs on each building to locate the hospital."

89   *Could Deichmann convince the pilots*: When this passage was checked with Dr. Deichmann in June 2013, he did not remember the scene, the conversation, or the "pointed look" that Dr. Gershanik had recalled.

More than an hour had passed on the helipad: Gershanik, Juan, "EVACUATE! My Katrina Experience."

91   *Another surgical ICU nurse*: The flashlight episode is described by Lori Budo in her book, *Katrina Through Our Eyes: Stories from Inside Baptist Hospital* (Lexington, KY: CreateSpace, 2010). Budo wrote in an introduction (p. 9) that her book was a "fictionalized account of the ICU staff and their families, based on their experiences after Hurricane Katrina [. . .] I wrote about the people I know and love; these are our stories." The names in the book, except for Budo's and Cathy Green's (in a concluding essay, "The Baptist") are fictionalized, however the details track well with other sources and interviews, and some material is therefore used here, as described in these Notes. The author made several requests to interview Ms. Budo throughout the process of researching these events, and contacted her prior to the publication of this book to confirm the stories and other details about her; however through her attorney, Edward J. Castaing Jr., she declined to talk.

Helen Breckenridge: The account of Helen Dennis Breckenridge's death is based on interviews with her brother and ICU staff members. The staff members did not name Ms. Breckenridge, but as only two female ICU patients died during the disaster according to a comparison of death records and the patient census, her identity was easily inferred. The following documents were also used: a court petition filed by her brother, Dr. Windsor S. Dennis ("Petition in suit for temporary and, subsequently, permanent interdiction") in Orleans Parish Civil District Court and associated records, power of attorney, affidavit, stipulation, and judgment in case no. 2005-11439; toxicology report of Helen Buckenridge [*sic*], completed January 13, 2006, National Medical Services Inc.; autopsy performed October 20, 2005 (Orleans Parish coroner's office #KAT-J-0322-05); and *Times-Picayune* obituary, October 27, 2005.

92   *A DNR order was different*: "Louisiana Advance Directives: Legal Documents to Assure Future Healthcare Choices," Peoples Health. Interviews with experts, including Dr. Susan Nelson (board-certified internist, geriatrician, and hospice/palliative medicine physician, chairwoman of the LaPOST Coalition, an organization devoted to raising awareness about Louisiana's initiative on medical advance decision making).

95   *nurse who was also an Air Force captain*: Betty Bennett (now MAJ), Air Force Reserve.

"The babies will be taken to wherever . . .": The quotes in this exchange are from the Bernard and Matthews article. When checked with Dr. Deichmann in June 2013, he did not remember the conversation.

97   *The electrocardiograph showed*: Settlement approval petition filed in *Evelina Barnes and Jeffrey Blackmore o/b/o Samuel Barnes v. LifeCare Hospitals, Inc.,* in Civil District Court, Orleans Parish, Louisiana, December 3, 2008.

"How y'all doing?": Dr. Pou's words were recalled by LifeCare respiratory therapist Charles Lindell, November 10, 2005, in an interview with state investigators.

100 *worked on the assumption that FEMA was coordinating*: Mulderick said in her August 16, 2010, deposition in *Preston, et al v. Tenet* that Sandra Cordray asked LifeCare if they needed assistance. "They indicated that they were working with their corporate or management structure to manage the evacuation of their patients. They initially did not request our help." In an interview with the author in June 2013, Acadian Ambulance's Keith Brisbois

recalled having gone to LifeCare soon after the decision to evacuate was made, to offer Acadian's help. He said he was surprised to be told that LifeCare was awaiting word from the corporate office about their transportation contract, which he believed to be held by Acadian. It is clear from text and e-mail communications that later in the day, LifeCare personnel did request evacuation assistance from Memorial, Tenet, and Acadian.

100 *Andress was a nurse*: Andress deposition in *Preston, et al v. Tenet,* available in the federal court record, and interviews with Mr. Andress.

107 *a system to supply the sites*: US Senate, *Hurricane Katrina: A Nation Still Unprepared,* Chapter 24, "Medical Assistance." For an excellent, concise overview of the failures in medical preparedness and response to Katrina, see Bergal, Jenni, "Health Care" in *City Adrift: New Orleans Before and After Katrina.* (Baton Rouge, LA: Center for Public Integrity, Louisiana State University Press, 2007).

108 *They said the conditions in the Superdome are breaking down*: WWL, during the seven p.m. broadcast hour, August 30, 2005.

109 *Kathleen Blanco announced*: WWL, during the ten p.m. broadcast hour, August 30, 2005.

He wrote back to Cordray to reassure: E-mail from Michael Arvin to Sandra Cordray and other Memorial and Tenet officials, sent 10:39 p.m., August 30, 2005.

The Guard would continue sending helicopters: These events are well remembered and well documented by those involved in them. Several people situated at the Coast Guard emergency command center in Alexandria, Louisiana, said in interviews with the author in 2013 that they tried to persuade Memorial staff to allow them to continue the evacuation throughout the night. Dr. Paul Primeaux told the author in 2008 that he took a call from the Coast Guard when he was in the command center and, enthusiastic about the prospect of continuing the evacuation overnight, carried the message to Dr. Richard Deichmann on the helipad, but that Dr. Deichmann did not believe it was advisable to continue. Dr. Deichmann did not remember this exchange with Primeaux, but in his book, *Code Blue: A Katrina Physician's Memoir* (Bloomington, IN: AuthorHouse, 2006), he described making the same decision later in the night, as depicted in Chapter 5.

110 *The Acadian Ambulance flight coordinator*: Marc Creswell (interviewed in 2011 and 2013); additional colleagues coordinated from Acadian's base in Lafayette, Louisiana. For an interesting account of Acadian's work during the Katrina disaster, see Judice, Ross, *The Katrina Diaries: First Hand Accounts from Medics and Miracle Workers* (2011); http://www.scribd.com/doc/101037393/Ross-Judice-Acadian-Ambulance-The-Katrina-Diaries. For an account of the various private helicopter companies that helped evacuate hospitals, see: "Air Medical Community Response to Hurricane Katrina Disaster: Hospital Evacuation and Patient Relocation by Helicopter and Fixed Wing Aircraft," *Association of Air Medical Services,* January 9, 2006.

A massive Coast Guard Jayhawk: LTJG Catharine Gross (now LT) report of HH60J aircraft no. 6017 search-and-rescue activities for Aug 30–31, 2005.

CHAPTER 5

Interviews

Dr. Bill Armington; Dr. Frederick "Skip" M. Burkle Jr.; LT Shelley M. Colbert; Dr. Ewing Cook; Minnie Cook; Dr. Richard Deichmann; Robbye Dubois; John Ferrero; Linda Gagliano (stepdaughter of John Russell); LT Catharine Gross; LCDR Russell Hall; Dr. Edmund G. Howe, III; Gina Isbell; Dr. William LaCorte; Larry Lafayette and Samuel Lafayette (sons of James Lafayette); AST2 Jaason Michael Leahr; Mark LeBlanc; Sandra LeBlanc; Wayne Leche; Father John Marse; CDR (ret.) William F. McMeekin; Therese Mendez; Stephanie Moore; LT Sean Moore; Angela McManus; Michelle Pitre-Ryals; Cheri Pizani; Dr. Anna Pou; Michael Richard; AMT2 Randal Ripley; Karen Sanford; CDR Mark Vislay; Stella Wright; Karen Wynn; Eric Yancovich.

Notes

111 *Overnight, two nurses cared for the two surviving*: According to ICU nurse David Fatzinger, interview with state investigators, January 11, 2006, he and one other nurse took care of the two surviving patients with DNR orders that night. Author's interview with ICU nurse Karen Sanford in 2007 also touched on this.

  wondered aloud if they would ever: This discussion, the talk of who would play whom in the television movie, and the cat story are from Lori Budo, *Katrina Through Our Eyes: Stories from Inside Baptist Hospital* (Lexington, KY: CreateSpace, 2010), pp. 73–76.

112 *A doctor sent a security guard*: Deichmann, Richard. *Code Blue: A Katrina Physician's Memoir* (Bloomington, IN: AuthorHouse, 2006), pp. 61–62. Dr. Deichmann recalled this occurred at about 1:30 a.m. Susan Mulderick, when she spoke with state investigators in 2006, said she was approached by LifeCare staff in the Memorial command center on the fourth floor about a possible Coast Guard evacuation at around 1:30 a.m., but before the power went out. She said by that point gathering the people needed to move patients was "going to be a task, 'cause everyone had dispersed," and communications within the hospital were difficult. LifeCare's Diane Robichaux, speaking with investigators in 2005, recalled the conversation having taken place somewhat earlier, at about 11:30 p.m., according to a time line prepared by LifeCare leaders shortly after the disaster.

113 *"There's a guy out saying, 'We need to move patients. . .'" [. . .] "Everybody get up!"*: Many people at the hospital recalled experiencing some version of this mysterious event. The man or men were most likely from the Coast Guard, tasked to continue the air evacuation overnight (the boat story is an anomaly—it's possible the Cooks misremembered this).

115–117 *A battle was under way [. . .] the last backup generator surged and then died*: The battle of the generators was reconstructed from a variety of sources, including members of Memorial's plant operations crew in interviews with the author or with investigators (the latter including Chief Operating Officer Sean Fowler, who described praying when the switch was flipped), Memorial's generator maintenance and repair records, photographs of the equipment, and several expert reports and diagrams on the power failure prepared for litigants in *Preston, et al v. Tenet,* including a fantastic video schematic. The experts disagreed over the ultimate cause of the power failure—namely whether the flooding played a role or not. See Fink, Sheri, "Trial to Open in Lawsuit Connected to Hospital Deaths After Katrina," *New York Times* and ProPublica, March 20, 2011; http://www .nytimes.com/2011/03/21/us/21hospital.html. An expert hired by the plaintiffs, Jerry Watts, concluded that the floodwaters shorted out Memorial's electrical transfer switches and many distribution panels, much as the plant operations director had predicted. However, Gregory Gehrt of ccrd Partners, an expert hired by Tenet, attributed the power shutdown to mechanical problems in the hospital's three 750-kilowatt diesel generators, which were located well above the water. Codes and standards at the time required only that potential for flooding and other local hazards be given "careful consideration" in electrical-system design. The 2012 National Fire Protection Association (NFPA) standards improved on this, saying that the systems "shall be designed" to protect against these hazards, but as of June 2013 had not yet been adopted by hospital regulating bodies. (See, for example, Fink, Sheri, "NYU Hospital's Backup System Undone by Key Part in Flooded Basement," ProPublica, November 1, 2012; http://www.propublica.org/article/nyus-backup-system-undone-by-key-part-in-flooded-basement.) Hospital generators had to be tested monthly, but only for short periods. The NFPA publishes the national electrical code, including specific requirements for health care facilities. NFPA 99, *Standard on Health Care Facilities*, has been adopted by most state health departments and licensing agencies; NFPA 110, *Standard for Emergency and Standby Power Systems,* covers emergency power systems ("Compendium of Health Care Electrical References," Nash Lipsey Burch, LLC, Nashville, TN, undated, unpublished document). A year after Katrina, JCAHO published a *Sentinel Event Alert* ("Preventing Adverse Events Caused by Emergency Electrical Power System Failures," issue 37 (September 6, 2006); http://www.jointcommission.org/sentinel_event_alert_issue_37_preventing_adverse_events_caused_by_emergency_electrical_power_system_failures/). It warned that meeting NFPA codes and standards was "only a start," and that "recent experiences demonstrate that emergency power systems that meet these standards are not always sufficient during major catastrophes." In response, in 2007, the organization required that emergency generators be tested once every thirty-six months for a minimum of four continuous hours (on top of the previous requirement that they be tested twelve times a year for thirty minutes). Still, hospital and nursing home generator failures in recent prolonged utility outages, including Hurricanes Gustav (2008), Isaac (2012), and Sandy (2012), suggest that many of these systems are inadequate.

117 *clobbered an alarm panel with her shoe*: Budo, *Katrina*, p. 76.

118 *"We have sent three helicopters"*: Interviews with Michelle Pitre-Ryals, LCDR Russell Hall, LT Shelley M. Colbert (nee Decker), and the auxiliary member, Michael Richard; Michelle Pitre-Ryals, "Fair Treatment Process Dispute Resolution Form," October 22, 2005 (includes a diary of events written shortly after the storm); Shelley Decker, "Katrina AAR" (two versions, one undated and the other dated October 3, 2005); and copies of handwritten Unit Logs dated August 31, 2005, furnished by the United States Coast Guard. All of the documents state that the sources heard at the time that helicopters were "waved off" Memorial's helipad (variously described as three US Coast Guard helicopters and/or five US Navy helicopters); the interviewees had strong memories of these events when they were interviewed in 2013.

119 *"Where are you going?"*: Recollections of Karen Wynn in interviews with author in 2008 and 2009. Thao Lam declined to be interviewed.

120 *Certain medical conditions, such as a stroke*: Zimmerman, J. L., Hanania NA. Chapter 111, "Hyperthermia," in: Hall, J. B., G. A. Schmidt, L. D. Wood, eds., *Principles of Critical Care*, 3rd ed. (New York: McGraw-Hill, 2005); http://www.accessmedicine.com/content.aspx?aid-2282701.

121 *A woman who had been hired*: Mark and Sandra LeBlanc patiently sat for many interviews with the author over the years, and their depositions in *Preston, et al v. Tenet* and their own suit against LifeCare were also consulted. Their memories remained quite consistent, but when there were variances, their earlier accounts were relied upon more heavily. Elvira LeBlanc's sitter, Jill Wilson, declined to be interviewed, but she filed a brief account of her experiences in Orleans Parish Civil District Court on October 10, 2012, as part of her objection to the *Preston, et al v. Tenet* settlement. It was consistent with the LeBlancs' accounts. The LeBlanc family first came to public attention through the work of journal-

ists, including Kathleen Johnston and Drew Griffin, "Family Blames Hospital for Mother's Death," CNN, May 25, 2006; http://www.cnn.com/2006/US/05/25/johnston.memorial death/, and later in Jeffrey Meitrodt's remarkable five-part series, "For Dear Life: How Hope Turned to Despair at Memorial Medical Center," *Times-Picayune*, August 20–24, 2006; http://www.nola.com/katrina/index.ssf/memorial_medical_center/for_dear_life/.

122 *Susan Mulderick had climbed up to the helipad*: Susan Mulderick interview with state investigators, January 6, 2006; interview with USCG flight mechanic AST2 Randal Ripley, July 2013; LTJG Catharine Gross report of HH60J aircraft no. 6017 search and rescue activities for Aug 30–31, 2005. Mulderick's recollections align so closely with Ripley's and with the content of the report written shortly after the events by Gross, that although the sources did not mention each other's names, it seems likely they were recalling the same conversation. Mulderick, however, told investigators that one reason she stopped the airlift was because the unnamed crewman told her he would drop patients in a field in Baton Rouge. Both Ripley and Michael Richard, the auxiliary member assisting with coordination in Alexandria, said that patients would not have been dropped in a field that night; Richard had helped arrange hospital placements for them.

125 *a LifeCare respiratory therapist*: Charles Lindell interview with state investigators, November 2005.

126 *John Russell, a Korean War veteran*: The account of John Russell is based on his medical records (provided with kind permission of his stepdaughter, Linda Gagliano) and the recollections of Gagliano and medical professionals involved in Russell's care.

127 *It was not true that there was no oxygen*: It is a mystery why some at the hospital were convinced there was no oxygen and others insist that while the oxygen tank supplies ran low, they never ran out. One possibility is that the situation became so chaotic and roles were so confused that those who knew where the tanks were did not realize people were looking for them. Some employees said that additional oxygen tanks were dropped off by arriving helicopters, but some sources said that they were never moved down from the helipad, or that, almost unbelievably, Memorial and LifeCare staff "didn't have a wrench or anything" to open the valves on the tanks (Andre Gremillion interview with investigators December 30, 2005. He described breaking his watch trying to use it to open a tank valve; also, Charles Jarreau interview with author October 29, 2008, said there were no wrenches). The EMS call was from an EMS unit at 11:15 a.m., saying that it had received a call from an Acadian Ambulance leader relaying the information.

128 *Took a turn on the second floor [. . .] might not make it*: Author's interview with Dr. Pou, July 2008.

129 *its walls sweating*: Described by many people, including Edwin "Roy" Mathews in Story-Corps interview MBX006447.

132 *The SARBOO*: US Senate, *A Nation Still Unprepared*, Chapter 22, p. 366; "Post-Landfall Evacuation," pp. 368–9 (footnotes 13–19); see also p. 270 (footnote 173).

133 *"We desperately need these boats . . ."*: WWL, August 30, 2005, noon hour.

Twenty minutes later: Copy of EMS call logs; Cramer did not respond to several requests for an interview.

134 *blunted vowels and head-spinning pace*: To experience the uniqueness of Cajun-inflected English, search YouTube for Cajun English. One example: http://www.youtube.com/watch?v=7tMIkTUmtTA.

135 *The LeBlancs couldn't understand it*: There are several possibilities: one is that the woman was not speaking in an official capacity or that the LeBlancs misunderstood her or misremembered what she said. Another is that officials were prioritizing hospitals that had not yet evacuated all of their critical care patients. Yet another is that, having dispatched Carl Cramer the previous evening, and, possibly, having communicated with Coast Guard officials who were trying to execute an overnight rescue operation, state EMS officials believed Memorial was taken care of. As discussed later in the book, poor communications between various agencies could have accounted for a number of different prioritization schemes. The communications problems experienced by people in the state emergency operations center trying to coordinate with local and federal resources are detailed in "DHS/FEMA Initial Response Hotwash: Hurricane Katrina in Louisiana, DR-1603-LA," FEMA, February 13, 2006; see also "State of Louisiana-Hurricanes Katrina and Rita: After-Action Report and Improvement Plan," US Department of Homeland Security/State of Louisiana, 2006.

137 *He believed his mother needed an IV*: According to records in *Preston, et al v. Tenet*, in which Vera LeBlanc was a named plaintiff in the class action, LeBlanc had difficulty swallowing, but she had a feeding tube by which fluids could be administered. However, dehydration had been a problem for her even before the hurricane.

138 *A nurse wrote "1," "2," or "3"*: A few doctors later recalled having used a category 4 for DNR patients to differentiate them from other very seriously ill patients (3s). Patients were often triaged on wards before they were brought downstairs, and some were re-triaged at various times during the crisis—the ad hoc rating systems used were similar, but not identical.

139–143 *Pou and her coworkers were performing triage [. . .] at its heart, a question of moral priorities*: For excellent analyses of triage, see, in particular: Sztajnkrycer, Matthew D., Bo E. Madsen, and Amado Alejandro Báez, "Unstable Ethical Plateaus and Disaster Triage," *Emergency Medicine Clinics of North America* 24, no. 3 (2006): 749–68; Veatch, Robert M., "Disaster Preparedness and Triage: Justice and the Common Good," *The Mount Sinai Journal of Medicine* 72, no. 4 (July 2005): 236–241; Iserson, Kenneth V. and John C. Moskop, "Triage in Medicine, Part I: Concept, History, and Types," *Annals of Emergency Medicine* 49 (2007): 275–281. Moskop, John C. and Kenneth V. Iserson, "Triage in Medicine, Part II: Underlying Values and Principles," *Annals of Emergency Medicine* 49 (2007): 282–287; Baker, Robert and Martin Strosberg, "Triage and Equality: An Historical Reassessment of Utilitarian Analyses of Triage," *Kennedy Institute Ethics Journal* 2 (1992): 103–123.

139 *"creative non-conformists"*: Sanders, David and Jesse Dukeminier Jr., "Medical Advance and Legal Lag: Hemodialysis and Kidney Transplantation," *UCLA Law Review* 15 (1968): 366–80.

A story in LIFE: Alexander, Shana, "They Decide Who Lives, Who Dies: Medical Miracle and a Moral Burden of a Small Committee," *LIFE* (November 9, 1962); http://books .google.com/books?id=qUoEAAAAMBAJ&lpg=PA1&dq=life%20magazine%20nov%20 1962&pg=PA101#v=onepage&q&f=false.

However, in countries such as South Africa: Fink, Sheri, "Life and Death Choices as South Africans Ration Dialysis Care," ProPublica, December 15, 2010; http://www.propublica.org/ article/dialysis-south-africa. See also "Rationing Health," a series of radio stories by Sheri Fink, David Baron, and Patrick Cox for *PRI's The World,* http://rationinghealth.org. The first episode in the series, "South Africa: Rationing by Committee," aired December 14, 2010, and can be heard at: http://www.theworld.org/2010/12/entire-program-% e2%80%93-december-14-2010/.

140 *at least nine well-recognized triage systems*: START, Jump START, Homebush, Triage Sieve, Pediatric Triage Tape (PTT), CareFlite, Sacco Triage Method (STM), Military Triage, CE-SIRA. See Lerner, Brooke E., et al, "Mass Casualty Triage: An Evaluation of the Data and Development of a Proposed National Guideline," *Disaster Medicine and Public Health Preparedness,* vol. 2, supplement 1 (September 1, 2008): S25–34. The authors compared these systems and proposed a new, national standard, "SALT," and later developed other techniques to help organizations using different systems work together in emergencies: Lerner, E. Brooke, David C. Cone, Eric S. Weinstein, et al., "Mass Casualty Triage: An Evaluation of the Science and Refinement of a National Guideline," *Disaster Medicine and Public Health Preparedness,* 5 (2011): 129–137.

in his memoirs: Larrey, Dominique-Jean. *Memoirs of Military Surgery, and Campaigns of the French Armies,* vol. 2, trans. Richard Willmott Hall (Baltimore, MD: Joseph Cushing, 1814); 1st American ed. trans. from the 2nd Paris ed., p. 123; http://babel.hathitrust.org/cgi/pt?id=hvd.hc2l2t#view=1up;seq=8.

In one very small study: Described in an unpublished report written by a codeveloper of a new commercial triage method: Navin, Mick. "Pennsylvania Triage Program Demonstrates Profound Inconsistencies of Current Protocols and Advantages of the Sacco Triage Model" (Bel Air, MD: ThinkSharp, Inc., January 30, 2004). The study is also described in Navin, Mick and Bob Waddell II, "Triage Is Broken," *EMS Magazine* 34, no. 8 (2005): 138–142; http://www.emsworld.com/article/10323785/triage-is-broken.

141 *Pou would later say*: Dr. Anna Pou appearance on Garland Robinette's "Think Tank" show on WWL radio, May 12, 2008.

set out by John Rawls: Rawls, John. *A Theory of Justice* (Cambridge, MA: Harvard University Press, 1971).

142 *sparked a debate*: The debate was triggered by John M. Taurek's "Should the Numbers Count?," *Philosophy and Public Affairs* 6, no. 4 (Summer 1977): 293–316.

143 *"There is no such thing as a sum of suffering"*: Lewis, C. S. *The Problem of Pain* (London: Centenary Press, 1940 and New York: HarperCollins, 2001).

members of the general public typically favored: Described in Veatch, "Disaster Preparedness and Triage."

144 *On a fifth-floor hallway*: The daughter wished to remain anonymous. Several nurses from the fifth floor confirmed and expanded on her story, and it was also retold in Pitre-Ryals's "Fair Treatment Process." The account of James Lafayette is based on his medical records (kindly provided by his family), and the deposition of a son, Samuel, who accompanied his father to the hospital (deposition taken May 15, 2008, for *Preston, et al v. Tenet*), as well as the recollections of several Memorial staff members involved in his care. Emergency medicine doctor Karen Cockerham explained that in general (not specifically in reference to Mr. Lafayette, in an interview in July 2013) the ER staff tried to admit as few patients as possible before the storm and strongly suggested that others who were sick but stable evacuate; Mr. Lafayette and his son, who came by ambulance, did not have the means to do so, and Samuel Lafeyette said in his deposition that a female doctor advised them to wait out the storm in the lobby.

Now a man: Nurses in the ICU were also told to leave Wednesday afternoon when they still had a DNR patient.

CHAPTER 6

Interviews

J. T. Alpaugh; Dr. Horace Baltz; Mark LeBlanc; Sandra LeBlanc; Keith Brisbois; Dr. Ewing Cook; Minnie Cook; Marc Creswell; Curtis Dosch; L. René Goux; Cathy Green; Dr. Bob Hendler; Frances Haydel (wife of patient Julius Haydel); Curtis Hebert; Gina Isbell; Dr. Bryant King; Dr. John Kokemor; Karen Lagasse; AST2 Jaason Michael Leahr; Father John Marse; Cynthia Matherne; Dr. Anna Pou; Dr. Paul Primeaux; Sudeep Reddy; Rodney Scott; Karen Wynn.

Notes

146 *Merle was, until recent months*: The account of Merle Lagasse is based on her medical records (obtained with kind permission of her daughter, Karen), photographs, and the recollections of Karen and medical professionals involved in Merle's care, mentioned in the text.

148 *company logo*: Danna, Denise and Sandra E. Cordray. *Nursing in the Storm* (New York: Springer Publishing Company, 2010), p. 128.

149 *A Coast Guard lieutenant reached Susan Mulderick*: Mulderick's, June 7, 2008, deposition in *Preston, et al v. Tenet*. Acadian's Keith Brisbois recalled in an interview with the author in 2013 having arranged for one more flight to take two remaining critical patients that morning, but he said the priorities had shifted once all critical patients seemed to have been moved from Memorial. Aerial footage taken by Helinet shows a green Air Med (division of Acadian) helicopter on the helipad at what appears from the sunlight and shadow patterns to be roughly midday (can be screened on www.abcnewsvsource.com, reference no.: VSKATRINA0007, time stamp 7:28 a.m. is clearly incorrect based on sun position; additional screening copy kindly provided by J. T. Alpaugh of Helinet). Alpaugh speculates on the video: "It appears this hospital may still be in operation and running, running somewhat normally." The video shows cars in the parking lot across the street from Memorial covered to their tops with water and other details described in this section.

151 *the president's peregrination of grounding rescue flights*: Several sources were convinced this was the case, however the author was unable to confirm this upon reviewing copies of temporary flight restrictions (notices to airmen: NOTAM) provided by the Federal Aviation Administration in response to a FOIA request. In an interview with the author in 2011, Marc Creswell, at the time a field training officer for Acadian who helped coordinate the Katrina air medical response, said that he recalled the airspace was closed: "For medical aircraft, it's thirty minutes prior to and then the entire amount of time the president is in the area and then just a few minutes after he leaves." In fact, in interviewing some sources many years after the events, there may have been confusion between President Bush's overflight on Wednesday and his visit to Louisiana on Friday, September 2, when air traffic was reportedly stopped while he was in the area (see, for example, Krupa, Michelle. "Bush Visit Halts Food Delivery," *Times-Picayune*, September 3, 2005; http://www.nola.com/katrina/index.ssf/2005/09/bush_visit_halts_food_delivery.html).

152 *Green vines spilled*: Description based on photographs from the time.

A World War II veteran: Julius Haydel.

pregnant ICU nurses: This set of events based on interviews with Karen Wynn and accounts of the ICU nurses (with pseudonyms) in Budo, *Katrina*.

158 *After Rolfie's death*: Horace Baltz. *The Kat's Paw: Memorial Medical Center—Katrina* (unpublished manuscript) and interviews with Dr. Baltz and Dr. Ewing Cook and Minnie Cook.

158 *At around two p.m.*: The nurse taking care of Ms. Burgess noted in her chart Dr. Cook's presence at 2:15 p.m.

159 *until they drained their batteries*: The nursing notes in Ms. Burgess's chart discuss the effects of the power failure on her care.

Sometimes ten to fifteen seconds: This was noted by Ms. Burgess's nurse at around eight that morning.

162 *"She has lung cancer. . ."*: Cathy Green did not know her name, but it is possible she was Merle Lagasse. The Memorial patient census (which did not include LifeCare patients) shows only one other patient whose admitting diagnosis was lung cancer (there was also a mesothelioma patient, but she apparently died on the second floor); she was eventually air-lifted from Memorial and was only fifty years old, so it is doubtful that Green would have thought her "elderly." Green shared this story with the author in an interview in 2007, and she recounted part of it (under the pseudonym "Kate") in Budo, Lori. *Katrina Through Our Eyes: Stories from Inside Baptist Hospital* (Lexington, KY: CreateSpace, 2010), pp. 115–116.

166 *said she was a Holocaust survivor*: Budo, *Katrina*. Other nurses had a vague memory of this.

167 *danger in the coming darkness*: It would have been quite dark outside regardless of the weather. The new moon was September 3, according to NASA moon phase chart; http://eclipse .gsfc.nasa.gov/phase/phases2001.html.

169 *jotted "Katrina"*: Copy of document entitled "MHCNO: Disaster Preparedness Committee," Friday, August 26, 2005, 12–2 p.m.

"Which patients should be extracted": Copy of page entitled "Subcommittee: Region 1—Affected Area," part of document entitled "Louisiana Catastrophic Planning, 2005 Workshop," dated August 23–24, 2005. The planning was focused on the idea of setting up temporary medical staging points outside of the hurricane-affected areas where patients collected at the SARBOOs (like the I-10 cloverleaf) would be transferred for care.

"to save life and limb": Copy of "Concept Paper," part of "Louisiana Catastrophic Planning, 2005 Workshop."

170 *setting their own priorities*: Capt. Bruce Jones, USCG commanding officer, Air Station New Orleans, interviewed by PA3 Susan Blake, Katrina Archival and Historical Record Team, October 20, 2005, for an oral history program; http://www.uscg.mil/history/katrina/ oralhistories/JonesBruceoralhistory.asp. Other records in the Katrina oral history collection make a similar point, as did Coast Guard members interviewed by the author.

still setting up the command center: They did this Wednesday morning, according to depositions of Michael Arvin, August 26, 2010, and Bob Smith, April 14, 2008, in *Preston, et al v. Tenet*. Also Bob Smith e-mail to Sandra Cordray, Tuesday, August 30, 2005, at 5:55 p.m.: "We may have a command center set up by morning."

jotted down notes: Bob Smith, April 14, 2008, deposition exhibit in *Preston, et al v. Tenet*.

171 *air logistics company*: Aviation Services, Inc., in Frisco, Texas.

173 *in her four months on the job*: US Senate. *A Nation Unprepared*, p. 423.

LifeCare's corporate chief financial officer: E-mail from Jim Shelton to Robbye Dubois, Wednesday, August 31, 2005, at 1:45 p.m. These paragraphs summarize events described in e-mails sent throughout the day by LifeCare officials.

175 *HF radio*: Smith wrote in an e-mail to colleagues at 9:30 p.m. local time that he had "just established HF communication with Memorial." It is unclear what kind of system was used

to establish this link. The Hospital Emergency Area Radio (HEAR) Network System that was supposed to be operating in New Orleans "simply did not work," according to the US Congress's February 2006 report, *A Failure of Initiative*, p. 291.

CHAPTER 7

Interviews

Aster Abraham (daughter of Tesfalidet Ewale); Dr. Bill Armington; Dr. Horace Baltz; Kamel Boughrara; Fran Butler; Joanne Cardaro; Catherine Chatelain; Dr. Karen Cockerham; Dr. Ewing Cook; Minnie Cook; Julie Couvillon; Dr. Richard Deichmann; Curtis Dosch; John Ferrero; L. René Goux; Andre Gremillion; Gina Isbell; Charles Jarreau; Janice Jenkins; Dr. Faith Joubert; Dr. Bryant King; Dr. John Kokemor; Karen Lagasse; Wayne Leche; Father John Marse; Angela McManus; Therese Mendez; Alfred Lee Moses; Kathryn Nelson; Rosemary Pizzuto (mother of Donna Cotham); Dr. Anna Pou; Dr. Paul Primeaux; Sudeep Reddy; Karen Sanford; Rodney Scott; Dr. John Thiele; Dr. John Walsh; Capt. Mark Willow; Stella Wright; Karen Wynn; Eric Yancovich.

Notes

181 *tried to inscribe her*: Angela McManus, interviews with author (2007, 2013); Therese Mendez, interviews with author (2013) and state investigators (2005). Angela McManus also recalled helping affix family phone numbers to other patients. The messages were found during Wilda McManus's autopsy.

182 *came up to LifeCare*: Dr. Faith Joubert, the infectious diseases doctor, in interviews with the author in 2008 and with state investigators on December 9, 2005. An unsigned note in the "Physicians' Orders" section of McManus's chart says: "8/31/05—May have MSO4 1-4mg IV/IM Q 1° for restlessness/agitation -Ativan 1-2mg q 1° IVP/IM q 1°PRN restlessness/agitation."

   The Nurse, Cindy: Copy of Louisiana State Board of Nursing consent order, August 16, 2005. Copy of PreCheck employee background report on Cindy Chatelain, May 2005. Interviews with husband Alfred Lee Moses and daughter Catherine Chatelain.

183 *came to receive a small dose of Ativan*: McManus's chart notes: "2340 Ativan 2mg given IVP for anxiety and yelling out." Cindy Chatelain, when she had taken over McManus's care at four p.m. Wednesday, wrote: "Disaster Evacuation in motion awaiting transfer to other facility—Completely [without] air, lights, water, toilet facilities."

184 *Police*: The SWAT team's appearance at Memorial was described by several interviewees, for example hospital locksmith Wayne Leche (June 2, 2013), one of the men on guard as the boat approached. Also, Capt. Mark Willow, then with the New Orleans Police Dept., told the author (July 18, 2008) that he dispatched police to Memorial during the disaster in response to concerns of a pharmacy break-in, but the officers reported back that the rumors were untrue.

185 *found clean scrubs*: Dr. Pou described changing into fresh scrubs and the techniques she used to maneuver around the darkened hospital, both in an interview with reporter Julie Scelfo for *Newsweek* in 2007.

   With several doctors and crews of nurses: Described by Dr. Pou in an interview with author in July 2008 and by many staff members in interviews with the author and state investigators. Dr. Pou also set the scene in an interview with reporter Julie Scelfo in *Newsweek*, "'Everybody May Not Make It Out,'" August 24, 2007; http://www.thedailybeast.com/newsweek/2007/08/24/everybody-may-not-make-it-out.html.

185   *told to take a break:* In interviews with state investigators, one nurse thought she recalled that it was Dr. Pou who dismissed the volunteers and another employee recalled it was either Dr. Pou or Dr. Kathleen Fournier who asked everyone except the nursing staff to leave.

186   *The generators also lit*: Noted in a photocopy of a pilot's logbook dated Thursday, September 1, 2005.

A battery-powered CD player: Dr. Ewing Cook and Minnie Cook recounted the scene in interviews with the author beginning in 2007, and it is also described in Budo, Lori. *Katrina Through Our Eyes: Stories from Inside Baptist Hospital* (Lexington, KY: CreateSpace, 2010), pp. 108–111. Budo wrote of lying down and lifting the back of her shirt to feel the coolness of the tile floor; she described a male nurse urinating on the windowsill as insurance against intruders. Women used a bucket in the room to void.

187   *Pou had ordered morphine*: This episode is based on several sources, including the nurse's interview with state investigators. She did not recall the patient's name, but her description of the patient was consistent with pharmacy records showing that individual doses of morphine between 2 mg and 10 mg were dispensed for a cancer patient of Dr. Pou's colleague, for whom Dr. Pou would have been covering, on Wednesday and Thursday. The patient survived her ordeal at Memorial. She has since died and is not named here because the author has not reached her family.

"There's not a whole lot": Scelfo's *Newsweek* interview with Dr. Pou (2007): "We kind of looked around at each other and said, 'You know there's not a whole lot we can really do for those people.'"

188   *Pou would later remember*: Scelfo's *Newsweek* interview with Pou (2007).

reach out to a passing nurse: Kamel Boughrara recalled suctioning Ms. Hall regularly throughout the night in his January 6, 2006, interview with investigators: "I would term her as being critical. She needed oxygen; she was not on it because there was no oxygen left at that point. She was also septic, meaning she had an ongoing infection. She just had some major, major surgery and she was definitely very, I am surprised she was fighting. She was a tough fighter, and I was giving her eye contact and telling just fight hard. If a patient is strong enough to grab you by the hand and let you know that, she is fighting."

"Am I going to make it": Betty Bennett, interview with author, August 14, 2009.

Dr. Bryant King sent a group of nurses: Two nurses and Dr. King recalled this in their interviews with state investigators.

189   *The man, in his early sixties*: Dr. King did not identify the man by name, but his identity was deduced from King's description and the location of bodies noted by hospital pathologist John Skinner. His wife's experiences are described in a handwritten note by his daughter, filed with the court as an exhibit attached to "Notice of Objection of Valencia Richards" in *Preston, et al v. Tenet* on October 17, 2012. Valencia Richards signed her note: "A Heart Broken Woman"; she was objecting to the class action settlement's allocation of $41,807.43 to her for her father's death, which she attributed to heat exhaustion: "My father was still young, only 62 years when he was snatched away from me. We still had so much to talk about and do. Instead I'm constantly imagining him suffering in that heat [. . .] I put no faith or trust in any doctor or hospital. I don't feel justice was served, and I don't feel any closure concerning his death."

190   *"We need to have a little bit more of a surgeon's attitude"*: Recalled by Dr. Paul Primeaux in an interview with the author in 2007. Dr. John Walsh could not independently recall the quote when it was checked with him in 2013, but he did not dispute it.

191   *Tenet was dispatching the fleet*: Curtis Dosch recalled the situation as it is written here, leaving open the possibility that some staff members might not have heard the news at the meeting before it broke up. However, Susan Mulderick told state investigators that she had learned from Dosch about the helicopters before the meeting and announced that they were coming, although she did not know when they would arrive. Both Karen Wynn's recollections in interviews with the author, and e-mails sent by Tenet officials on Wednesday night, indicate that some at the hospital knew about the helicopters the previous evening. The question of when the majority of staff members were informed became a point of contention after the disaster when some, notably Dr. John Kokemor, told reporters that staff at the meeting Thursday morning believed that the hospital was on its own in terms of rescue, and they became dejected.

192   *Presidential tasking*: From Decker's after action report (AAR) notes. No further details were recorded. It is conceivable that appeals from Tenet corporate officials to Louisiana elected officials reached the President.

193   *It smelled worse*: Susan Mulderick declined to be formally interviewed other than to say, of the days after Katrina: "We were well prepared. We managed that situation well." She did not respond to a request to fact check the material in this book, however a subset of the material, included in the 2009 article on which this book is based, "The Deadly Choices at Memorial" (Fink, Sheri, ProPublica, http://www.propublica.org/article/the-deadly-choices-at-memorial-826, and the *New York Times,* http://www.nytimes.com/2009/08/30/magazine/30doctors.html), was fact-checked through her attorney in 2009. A number of other sources were relied upon, including Mulderick's extensive depositions in 2008 and 2010 in *Preston, et al v. Tenet,* and her discussion with state investigators in 2006, as well as the observations of many in the hospital who worked with her.

194   *"We are talking about euthanizing the animals"*: Mulderick, through her attorney, told the author in 2009 she did not use the word "euthanasia" with regard to human beings nor were any of her statements at Memorial intended as "code for" euthanizing patients. Some people close to Mulderick theorized that her comments contrasting the treatment of animals with that of humans may have been misconstrued and perhaps even acted upon by others in ways she had not intended.

   whether it would be "humane": Deichmann, Richard. *Code Blue: A Katrina Physician's Memoir* (Bloomington, IN: AuthorHouse, 2006), p. 78.

199   *Pou's prescriptions*: The pharmacist, Philip J. Duct Jr., recorded dispensing the drugs on the perpetual controlled drug inventory. In an interview with state investigators on October 25, 2005, he initially said he could not recall having been asked for any large quantities of morphine. However, once he was shown copies of the logs, he confirmed that he had filled the prescriptions. He said he thought two young female doctors came for the drugs, and the large amounts could have been to travel with the patients.

200   *Dr. Kathleen Fournier had been present*: In an interview with state investigators on February 27, 2006, Fournier later thought the discussion had occurred at night. Mulderick recalled it being on Thursday morning, and that seems more likely.

   "I just disagree with this" [. . .] "don't worry about it.": Susan Mulderick's interview with state investigators January 1, 2006. Kathleen Fournier's recollections when she spoke with state

investigators the following month were similar, as described in more detail in Chapter 8. Fournier did not respond to requests to speak with the author or offers to fact check the material in this book. The author attempted to verify the accounts through other sources, as described in these Notes.

200 *Fournier didn't have her own medical practice [. . .] progressively more tenuous.*: In her interview with state investigators, Dr. Fournier described her work arrangements with Dr. Deichmann and the fact that she arrived late on Sunday to start her rounds. The detail about the eye patch and Deichmann's frustration are from Deichmann, *Code Blue*, pp. 10–12, 107, in reference to a character with a pseudonym ("Liz Foster" in the AuthorHouse 2006 edition and "Larry O'Neil" in the iUniverse Star 2008 edition). However during fact checking in 2013, Deichmann referred to the character as a "composite [that] does not represent any one individual." He said he did recall that Fournier had an eye injury (interestingly, Anna Pou, too, suffered a minor injury and had a black eye). In correspondence with the author about Dr. Kathleen Fournier in June 2013, Deichmann wrote that he thought it important not to diminish the "incredible courage and dedication she exhibited during that ordeal. Kate worked very long hours under horrible conditions to ensure patient care when many others had abandoned them. She has my complete respect."

201 *"That is not an option"*: Butler, in her interview with state investigators, thought the conversation took place somewhere between seven and nine a.m. on Thursday morning, after she finished a fanning shift, but before the morning meeting. Fournier in her interview with investigators did not mention speaking with Butler.

Fournier solicited another opinion: Fournier's account of this conversation in her interview with state investigators and Thiele's recollections in a July 26, 2009 interview with the author were consistent in terms of content. Thiele recalled Fournier said she could not or would not do it. Both recalled that the conversation took place on the second floor. Thiele said it took place while they were euthanizing the cats, which Fournier did not specifically mention.

202 *Fournier polled another of the doctors, Bryant King*: Bryant King interview with state investigators in October 2005. Fournier in her February 2006 interview with investigators said in general terms that King seemed upset by what she told him, and she thought that was why he left. She believed this conversation to have taken place on Wednesday evening, whereas King thought it was on Thursday morning.

203 *"I'm a Catholic"* and *telling them that "evil entities"*: Dr. Bryant King, his sister, Rachelle, his best friend, Dr. Eric Griggs, and NPR reporter Joanne Silberner, who interviewed Griggs that day, said they no longer had copies of the messages. The description of these messages is based on King's October 2005 recollections of them in an interview with state investigators.

Handwritten note: The note was written by Aviation Services, Inc., coordinator Don Berry in the ten a.m. to noon time frame, he recalled in 2013.

204 *She wore a scrub shirt with the arms ripped off, khaki shorts, and little black shoes*: According to the recollections of LifeCare staff members.

206 *He, like many others, had been concerned*: Smith, Stephen and Marcella Bombardieri, "Power Gone, Food Low, Doctors Focused on Life," *Boston Globe*, September 14, 2005. Kokemor confirmed this with the author.

209   *"Your mother is dying"*: Kathryn Nelson, interview with state investigators October 3, 2005, and with the author, November 28, 2007. Therese Mendez remembered (interview July 1, 2013) that Kathryn Nelson strongly resisted leaving on Thursday, and Mendez recalled having spoken very firmly to Nelson to motivate her to go downstairs so she wouldn't miss the chance to leave.

210   *The nurse administered a small dose*: Nelson's nurse, Cynthia Chatelain, recalled in an interview with state investigators (January 6, 2006) that she gave Nelson 1 mg of morphine and 1 mg of Ativan.

212   *told her that they were under martial law*: This belief was commonly cited by staff at Memorial, particularly LifeCare staff, interviewed by investigators after the storm. It is not surprising, given how often this incorrect assertion was repeated on the radio, to which some people may have been listening. Therese Mendez said (July 2013) it was like a "vapor" that spread through the hospital.

213   *"I'm getting out of here"*: Dr. Bryant King, interview with state investigators, 2005. These first recollections are consistent with later ones, including his 2008 deposition in a case brought against the hospital by Elaine Nelson's son, Craig, and in an interview with the author in 2007: "When I saw Anna with all those syringes in her hand, I was like Anna, that's fucking crazy, you can't possibly be serious." ("You said that?") "I've never been someone who keeps thoughts in my head." Dr. Bill Armington in an interview with the author recalled seeing Dr. King leaving, upset, as did Fournier in an interview with investigators in 2006: "He was upset and angry about it, is the impression I got, so he left. I was upset and angry about it, and I stayed." The timing of Dr. King's departure has been a point of contention, with some at the hospital later saying they believed he left on Wednesday and could therefore not have witnessed events in the second floor lobby on Thursday. However, the specificity of Dr. King's recollections on Thursday and the fact that numerous employees recalled seeing and working with him that day indicate that he was indeed present.

214   *"I think you ought to go"*: Dosch, interview with author June 4, 2013. Mr. Goux did not respond to a request to fact check the material in the book. However, in an interview 2009, when the author asked about the injections on the seventh floor (I did not ask specifically about the second floor), Mr. Goux said, "I was not aware that was going on." He told state investigators in 2005 that he had heard rumors of euthanasia happening at Memorial very soon after he left the hospital, "everywhere I turned. I can tell you when the first time I heard that it was shocking."

216   *"because you're nurses"*: Ms. Janice Jenkins, May 25, 2013, interview with author.

217   *Wynn and Pou requested*: Anonymous e-mail to author. Therese Mendez, in an interview with state investigators, also recalled Dr. Pou asking for injection supplies when she was upstairs in LifeCare.

Pou called for someone with a light: Nurse Jeffrey Caffall interview with state investigators, March 6, 2006.

Another very young nurse: Julie Couvillon interview with investigators, October 26, 2005. Couvillon said she heard from her nursing director, who was not involved, that the patients were given potassium, morphine, and Versed. Couvillon noticed a box against the wall near the catwalk with vials of potassium chloride. This box was still present and filled with mostly sealed bottles when investigators later searched the hospital, and there are photographs of it. The potassium chloride was used to euthanize pets. However, nobody involved in the injections of patients and interviewed by the author recalled that potassium chloride was used to hasten the deaths of human beings. The drug cannot be detected by postmortem toxicology.

219 *She was also haunted*: Wynn did not name Ewale, but her recollections were consistent with other sources. The amount of morphine and Ativan he received was not indicated, but nurse Leah Boudreaux wrote in Ewale's chart what appears to be a summary of his last hours, including, at ten a.m.: "Pt still unresponsive, choking on secretions but unable to suction pt due to conditions. Morphine given for comfort." Several aspects of the account are strange. Portable suction was used in other areas of the hospital. There are no orders for the medication. Wynn, in her interview with the author, said she was told that the patient had begged for help, but the nurses' notes all indicate that he was unresponsive. In Budo, *Katrina*, p. 79, a nurse with the pseudonym "Pal" wrote that on Wednesday she stayed with an ICU patient who "was very ill, close to death. Foam was bubbling out of his mouth. The hospital systems had failed the night before; I had no way to suction him. He had some sedation ordered for his comfort. I gave it to him. His eyes were open, he was looking at me. I just held his hand. It was a horrific thing to watch. I don't think he would have survived even if I had been able to suction him."

221 *A nurse approached*: The nurse spoke of these events on condition of anonymity. This section is based on her interview with investigators conducted several months after the storm, interviews with other nurses who interacted with her, and, to a much lesser extent, her later recollections of the events, which she felt were very fuzzy, in interviews with the author in 2010 and 2013.

225 *Culotta saw Lagasse was in respiratory distress*: Roy Culotta interview with state investigators, November 28, 2005. His account was largely consistent in his later deposition (February 23, 2010) in a civil case brought by Merle Lagasse's family.

PART 2: RECKONING
CHAPTER 8

Interviews

Dr. Horace Baltz; family of Jannie Burgess (Linette Burgess Guidi, Gladys Clark Smith, Bertha Mitchell, Johnny Clark); Tony Carnes; Catherine Chatelain; James Cobb Jr.; Dr. Ewing Cook; Minnie Cook; Curtis Dosch; family of Emmett Everett (Carrie Everett, Emmett Everett Jr.); Linda Gagliano (stepdaughter of John Russell); L. René Goux; Cathy Green; Dr. Robert Hendler; Gina Isbell; Karen Lagasse (daughter of Merle Lagasse); family of Wilda McManus (Angela McManus); Therese Mendez; Robert Middleberg; Dr. Helen Miller; Dr. Frank Minyard; LT/O3E Sean Moore; Stephanie Moore; Alfred Lee Moses; Dr. Bong Mui; family of Elaine Nelson (Craig Nelson and Kathryn Nelson); Dr. Daniel W. Nuss; Brenda and Tabatha O'Bryant; Cheri Pizani; Dr. Anna Pou; Michelle Pitre-Ryals; Dr. Christopher Sanford; Douglas Savoie Jr. (grandson of Rose Savoie); Arthur Schafer; Richard T. Simmons Jr.; Dr. John Skinner; Dr. John Thiele; Dr. John Walsh; Dr. Cyril Wecht; Tony Zumbado.

Note: Investigative interviews and other events sourced clearly in the text are generally not noted here.

Notes

231 *in exchange for what she thought*: Mary Rose Bernard interview with state investigators, June 26, 2006: "I pleaded with Fox News and they said well we will see what we can do to get your family out, if you agree to be interviewed."

"You could have gotten out": Anita Vogel, correspondent, "Hurricane Katrina's Aftermath," Fox News Network, *On the Record with Greta Van Susteren*, September 1, 2005, ten p.m. Also, StoryCorps interview of Pamela Mathews, Edwin Mathews, and Jo Lincks, MBX006447.

234 *National Guardsmen from San Diego*: Gross, Gregory Alan, "S.D. Guardsmen Find Life, Death in Waters," *San Diego Union Tribune*, September 7, 2005; http://legacy.utsandiego.com/news/nation/katrina/20050907-9999-1n7guard.html.

Christianity Today *magazine reporter*: Tony Carnes's photograph of Memorial's chapel was picked up by the *New York Times* and is not easily forgotten: http://www.nytimes.com/imagepages/2005/09/18/national/19victimsCA01ready.html.

"It was like a picture of hell.": Chaplain Hy McEnery on CNN, September 16, 2005.

an interview with a Baton Rouge television reporter: Aired on WBRZ, September 12, 2005. Portions were later re-aired on CNN.

235 *St. Rita's*: For more on St. Rita's, see: Cobb, James, Jr. *Flood of Lies: The St. Rita's Nursing Home Tragedy* (Gretna, LA: Pelican Publishing, 2013); Junod, Tom, "The Loved Ones," *Esquire* (September 2006); http://www.esquire.com/features/ESQ0906NEWORLEANS_216; Mead, Robert A.,"St. Rita's and Lost Causes: Improving Nursing Home Emergency Preparedness," *Marquette Elder's Advisor* (Spring 2006).

239 *in an essay for* Modern Healthcare: Hirsch, Les, "'We had to Evacuate Soon,'" *Modern Healthcare* (September 12, 2005); http://www.modernhealthcare.com/article/20050912/NEWS/509120323.

244 *She left messages on Goux's cell phone [. . .] she wanted to get her own lawyer before answering*: Affidavit of Anna Pou, MD, January 13, 2006, and hearing transcript, "In re: Doctor Anna Maria Pou," Orleans Parish criminal district court, the Honorable Calvin Johnson.

245 *The network agreed to pay Simmons*: Letter from Pou's attorney to Phelps Gay and Lauren McHugh, "Re: Dr. Anna Pou's Claim for Reimbursement of Legal Fees." Attachment A, "Memorandum from Richard T. Simmons Jr. counsel for Dr. Anna Pou," 4. Documents filed with the Attorney Fee Review Board, Louisiana State Legislature and obtained by author through public records request.

One of the first things Simmons did: Pou said that she retained Simmons on September 19, 2005, the date of her initial conversation with Tenet officials, however, in the fee review matter, Simmons told the State of Louisiana that he represented her beginning in October 2005.

246 *The US attorney for southeast Louisiana had opened*: Investigative memoranda provided by the US Department of Health and Human Services Office of the Investigator General in response to author's FOIA request reflect this.

252 *"I told you so"*: Cobb, *Flood of Lies*.

Ferncrest Manor: Investigative memorandum, Ferncrest Manor Living Center, HHS OIG case 6-05-00497-9, September 17, 2007.

mandated evacuations of nursing: According to US Senate, *Hurricane Katrina: A Nation Still Unprepared*, Chapter 16, p. 248, a draft version of Mayor Nagin's evacuation order did exempt nursing homes. That was changed on the suggestion of Col. Terry Ebbert, New Orleans's homeland security and public safety director, who noted their vulnerability.

252–253   *About two-thirds of the affected nursing homes had kept residents in place [. . .] but rescue came too late*: Hull, Anne and Doug Struck, "At Nursing Home, Katrina Dealt only the First Blow," *Washington Post,* September 23, 2005; http://www.washingtonpost.com/wp-dyn/content/article/2005/09/22/AR2005092202263.html.

at Chateau Living Center: In litigation over deaths at Chateau, representatives of the nursing home asserted that after the private company refused to provide buses, they attempted to hire Greyhound buses for the evacuation, but it was too late because highways were closed and high winds had moved into the area. An earlier HHS OIG investigation memo (September 25, 2006) stated: "There is conflicting evidence as to whether the bus company was notified of the facility's intent to evacuate in a timely manner, or whether the bus company did not fulfill its obligations to provide transportation in a timely manner." The investigation was later closed.

257   *Lesser charges of manslaughter*: Arthur Schafer sworn witness examination, mandamus hearing, *John and Jane Does v. Charles Foti, et al,* 19th Judicial District Court, Parish of East Baton Rouge, State of Louisiana, case 558,055, August 28, 2007. Schafer said a decision on what charges might be applicable had not been reached.

260   *Lou Ann Savoie Jacob*: Nossiter, Adam and Shaila Dewan, "Patient Deaths in New Orleans Bring Arrests," *New York Times,* July 19, 2006; http://www.nytimes.com/2006/07/19/us/19patients.html. Ms. Savoie Jacob's recollections are supported by Rose Savoie's medical records: "Actually doing better" (August, 25, 2005) and "No new medical complaints" (August 27, 2005, the last physician progress note).

Kathryn Nelson: Ms. Nelson and her brother Craig's recollections in interviews with the author were supplemented by a handwritten account of the events she prepared for state investigators, dated October 26, 2006, and her July 8, 2008, deposition in *Elaine Nelson, et al v. Memorial Medical Center, et al,* Orleans Parish Civil District Court.

massive temporary morgue: Described in Wecht, Cyril H. and Dawna Kaufmann. *A Question of Murder* (New York: Prometheus Books, 2008), pp. 248, 271–2.

262   *In an acidic-smelling*: Description based on author's visit in July 2008.

270   *Chalmette Medical Center*: This brief description of what happened at Chalmette Medical Center is based on the recollections of Dr. Bong Mui in an interview with the author, August 3, 2011, and in a translated partial transcript of his interview in Vietnamese with son Nguyen dated September 10, 2006, for the oral history project "Surviving Hurricanes Katrina and Rita in Houston Collection" (AFC 2008/006), Archive of Folk Culture, American Folklife Center, Library of Congress, Washington, DC (interview SR05, accession no. SKR-SNU-SR05). Lightly redacted Louisiana Medicaid Fraud Control Unit investigative memoranda on Chalmette Medical Center obtained through a public information request suggest that hospital leaders had decided to keep the hospital open and staffed (not only because ambulances did not return to transfer more patients). Some patients who were transferred out of Chalmette Medical Center prior to the storm were moved to that hospital's sister campus in the New Orleans area (Pendleton Memorial Methodist Hospital), which was also severely disabled by floodwaters and generator failures.

Tulane was also dark: Hamm, L. Lee, "Personal Observations and Lessons from Katrina." *The American Journal of the Medical Sciences,* vol. 332, no. 5 (2006): 245–50; Tulane commissioned a book on its hospital experiences during Katrina: Carey, Bill. *Leave No One Behind:*

Hurricane Katrina and the Rescue of Tulane Hospital (Nashville, TN: Clearbrook Press, 2006). New employees of the Hospital Corporation of America (HCA, Tulane Hospital's owner) are sometimes presented with a copy of the praise-filled account.

272 *had not supplied with food, water*: *Hurricane Katrina: A Nation Still Unprepared*, p. 11.

273 *authorized the lieutenant to land*: LTJG Sean Moore was riding in a Coast Guard–chartered commercial helicopter, aiding a marine salvage crew surveying the local waterways for sunk and disabled vessels. He said in an interview with the author (June 3, 2013) that the pilot, on learning Moore's wife, Stephanie, was in the hospital, said, "Let's get her the 'f' out of there." The commander of Sector NOLA, Captain Frank Paskewich, said in a US Coast Guard Oral History interview (October 18, 2005) that he readily approved the request. "I said, 'Absolutely, go rescue your wife, please.'" http://www.uscg.mil/history /katrina/oralhistories/PaskewichFrankoralhistory.asp.

274 *Anderson Cooper said*: "Euthanasia Performed in Aftermath of Hurricane Katrina?," CNN, *Newsnight with Aaron Brown*, October 12, 2005, ten p.m.; http://transcripts.cnn.com/ TRANSCRIPTS/0510/12/asb.01.html.

275 *"Why weren't there plans"*: "Accusations of Mercy Killing in New Orleans," CNN, *Newsnight with Aaron Brown*, October 12, 2005, eleven p.m.; http://transcripts.cnn.com/ TRANSCRIPTS/0510/12/asb.02.html.

"The culture that we live in": ibid.

"Did an angel of death": "Louisiana AG Orders Autopsies of 50 Memorial Medical Patients," CNN, *Nancy Grace*, October 14, 2005; http://transcripts.cnn.com/TRANSCRIPTS/ 0510/14/ng.01.html.

276 *"There was no way"*: "In Depth: Officials Are Looking Into Allegations of Euthanasia in a New Orleans Hospital for Gravely Ill Patients as Hurricane Katrina's Floodwaters Rose," NBC News, October 17, 2005; http://www.nbcuniversalarchives.com/nbcuni/ clip/5117065625_s09.do.

277 *"I didn't know if I was doing the right thing"*: Graham, Caroline and Jo Knowsley, "We Had to Kill Our Patients," *Mail on Sunday*, September 11, 2005; http://www.dailymail.co.uk/ news/article-361980/We-kill-patients.html.

282 *Nearly three out of four convictions*: Innocence Project, Inc., "Reevaluating Lineups: Why Witnesses Make Mistakes and How to Reduce the Chance of a Misidentification," (Benjamin N. Cardozo School of Law, Yeshiva University, July 16, 2009); http://www.innocence project.org/docs/Eyewitness_ID_Report.pdf.

283 *they were far from complete*: Tenet Healthcare Corporation provided the following response on August 18, 2009: "This is not correct. Tenet has produced all requested medical records in its possession—both hard copies and electronic—to the Louisiana Attorney General's office. On numerous occasions, Memorial Medical Center made available all records in its possession and provided investigators full access to the facility when requested."

CNN reported on the subpoenas: Griffin, Drew and Kathleen Johnston, "Dozens Subpoenaed in Hospital Deaths," CNN, October 26, 2005; http://www.cnn.com/2005/US/10/26/ katrina.hospital.

286 *Castaing would, years later*: Castaing said this during fact checking for *Deadly Choices* in 2009. He repeated it in two phone calls with the author in 2013 and an e-mail. He said the meeting's purpose was to organize logistics for interviews of Memorial employees and that he requested either a blanket non-prosecution or immunity agreement for all the nurses from

Memorial, which he did not obtain. When Castaing was told that notes were made within days of the meeting by the investigator, he said he, too, had taken notes "religiously." However after the author asked to see them, he checked and said he had taken no notes.

286 *Jim Letten*: Letten's position had previously been held by Orleans Parish District Attorney Eddie Jordan Jr. Letten was reportedly the longest-serving US attorney when he resigned from his position in December 2012, after senior prosecutors in his office were discovered to have commented on active criminal issues on the website of the *Times-Picayune,* using aliases. Robertson, Campbell, "Crusading New Orleans Prosecutor to Quit, Facing Staff Misconduct," *New York Times,* December 6, 2012; http://www.nytimes.com/2012/12/07/us/jim-letten-new-orleans-us-attorney-resigns.html.

federal jurisdiction over them was limited: Williams, C. J., "Making a Federal Case out of a Death Investigation," *United States Attorneys' Bulletin,* vol. 60, no. 1 (January 2012); http://www.justice.gov/usao/eousa/foia_reading_room/usab6001.pdf.

291 *"John, everybody has to be out of here"*: Susan Mulderick, through her attorney, and L. René Goux both said that they were not given a deadline to empty the hospital and that their goal was to focus their exhausted colleagues on the evacuation. "We'd experienced the helicopters' stopping flying to us, and I didn't want that to occur again," Goux said in an interview with the author (August 17, 2009).

293 *DMATs*: Sanford, Christopher. "Nine Days at the Airport" (unpublished manuscript). Sanford, Christopher, Jonathan Jui, Helen C. Miller, and Kathleen A. Jobe, "Medical Treatment at Louis Armstrong New Orleans International Airport After Hurricane Katrina: The Experience of Disaster Medical Assistance Teams WA-1 and OR-2," *Travel Medicine and Infectious Disease* 5 (2007): 230–235; Klein, Kelly R. and Nanci E. Nagel, "Mass Medical Evacuation: Hurricane Katrina and Nursing Experiences at the New Orleans Airport," *Disaster Management and Response* vol. 5, no. 2 (2007): 56–61; "Hurricane Katrina—After Action Report: OR-2 DMAT," September 25, 2005; Dentzer, Susan, "Hurricane Hospital Challenges," *PBS NewsHour,* September 8, 2005; http://www.pbs.org/newshour/bb/weather/july-dec05/hospitals_9-8.html; Barringer, Felicity and Donald G. McNeil Jr., "Grim Triage for Ailing and Dying at a Makeshift Airport Hospital," *New York Times,* September 2, 2005; http://www.nytimes.com/2005/09/03/national/nationalspecial/03hospitals.html; Smith, Stephen, "Patients Evacuated in Massive Airlift: LA Airport Used as Field Hospital," *Boston Globe,* September 4, 2005; Allison, Cody, "Untitled," Hurricane Digital Memory Bank, object no. 39470; http://www.hurricanearchive.org/items/show/39470. The US House of Representatives report on Hurricane Katrina (*A Failure of Initiative: The Final Report of the Select Bipartisan Committee to Investigate the Preparation for and Response to Hurricane Katrina,* February 15, 2006, p. 269; www.c-span.org/pdf/Katrinareport.pdf) noted the "confusion" that resulted over the command structure of the medical teams. Prior to Katrina, the National Disaster Medical System, of which the DMATs are a part, was removed from HHS and placed under FEMA and the Department of Homeland Security as part of a massive governmental redesign after the September 11, 2001, attacks. After Katrina, the NDMS was placed back under the Department of Health and Human Services, which coordinates federal health care resources in emergencies ("Emergency Support Function-8"), according to the National Response Framework. The medical section of the House of Representatives report (pp. 267–309) criticized the failures of the federal medical response in particular. It described the medical effort at the airport as "chaotic," with many people dying while doctors who weren't members of the federal teams, like Thiele, were turned away. Personnel "black tagged" the sickest and

moved them away from others "so they could die in a separate area," one doctor quoted in the report said (p. 288). Despite the post-Katrina "lessons learned," supply chain problems and rigid procurement policies again encumbered the NDMS's lifesaving work in response to the 2010 Haiti earthquake (albeit in a much more logistically challenging environment); some supply caches arrived with heaters, for example, instead of air-conditioners; and bottled oxygen, fuel, and certain equipment for performing operations ran short. One case is discussed in the Epilogue. NDMS in recent years "significantly revamped its supply, resupply and logistics processes" including the warehousing of supplies around the country for use by any team, and anticipating specific needs, such as special bariatric beds for very obese patients, according to Gretchen Michael, director of communications, HHS Office of the Assistant Secretary for Preparedness and Response (e-mail, August 2013). DMATs used smaller strike teams to respond more flexibly to Superstorm Sandy in 2012, and HHS behavioral health teams supported first responders and American communities affected by mass shootings and bombings in 2012 and 2013.

295   *Baltz searched his memory*: Baltz, Horace. *The Kat's Paw: Memorial Medical Center—Katrina* (unpublished manuscript), and interviews with the author.

296   *death of one of his longtime patients*: Baltz disagreed entirely with Kokemor's assessment of his motivation for seeking the truth about his patient's death.

297   *She had promised:* Chatelain's husband, Alfred Lee Moses, and daughter, Catherine Chatelain, attributed her increasing use of alcohol and narcotics—resulting in the loss of her nursing license, and her untimely death in her early fifties from acute pancreatitis—to her distress over the circumstances of her patiend Emmett Everett's death. "I think that's the major reason my mom isn't here today, because she just spiraled into depression after that," Catherine Chatelain said in an interview in 2013.

303   *one of the investigators researched*: She shared these articles with her colleagues: Perkin, R. M. and D. B. Resnik, "The Agony of Agonal Respiration: Is the Last Gasp Necessary?," *Journal of Medical Ethics*, 28 (2002): 164–169, retrieved by the investigator on November 28, 2005, from http://jme.bmjjournals.com/cgi/content/full/28/3/164; *Whonamedit? A Dictionary of Medical Eponyms,* "Cheyne-Stokes Respiration," retrieved by investigator November 29, 2005, from http://www.whonamedit.com/synd.cfm/1159.html; "Central Sleep Apnea: Details," retrieved by investigator on November 29, 2005, from www.apneos .com/csa.html.

   "Given our current knowledge": Perkin and Resnik, ibid.

304–305   *the buildings were full [. . .] escorted away drunks*: Building entry logs and security notes as well as author's April 21, 2008, interview with a DynCorp company official who said the group's first mission had been "to provide assistance to any survivors that may have been left behind or inadvertently may have been unable to be evacuated" from Tenet's hospitals. One mystifying incident the DynCorp team was asked about by Tenet concerned media reports of a suspicious body seen by San Diego National Guardsmen and a news crew at Memorial. The incident is partially described in Brinkley, Douglas. *The Great Deluge: Hurricane Katrina, New Orleans, and the Mississippi Gulf Coast* (New York: Harper Perennial, 2007), p. 606. Brinkley wrote that freelance reporters for NBC followed the sounds of a radio tuned to WWL to a room where they found a woman was dead, covered in blood. NBC kindly provided a screening copy of Anthony Zumbado's footage to the author, but it shows only one body, on a gurney with no blood, partially covered by a sheet; attorneys for the family of Leon Preston later identified this body to the author as Mr. Preston, the named plaintiff in *Preston, et al v. Tenet*. The author spoke with Anthony Zumbado, the videographer, but he was unable to provide more details. The Guardsmen apparently alleged the woman had been sexually abused, but did not offer how they ascertained this. The DynCorp company official interviewed by the author said that while his team also saw bodies in the emergency room, they were covered and "we didn't see anything abnormal about the way they were resting, so to speak." He pointed out, reasonably, that to ascertain sexual assault would have involved an invasive examination; it is hard to imagine the National Guardsmen conducted one when they walked through the hospital. A possible case of sexual violence came to light at a settlement hearing in the *Preston, et al v. Tenet* class action case. A former patient alleged that a hospital orderly had assaulted her in her room. Her attorney, Anthony Irpino, told the author that the judge granted her request for more funds.

306   *Pou toured Memorial*: Security guard log notes document where the group was escorted. Sign-in sheets for that day include signatures of most parties. Interestingly, Dr. Pou and Mr. Simmons did not sign the sign-in sheets, but the group is referred to as the "doctor's" group and several others who were there recalled Pou and Simmons as having been there that day. Simmons went to court to ensure that the pieces of equipment described here be preserved.

   "Tonight, a CNN exclusive": "New Orleans Hospital Murders?," CNN, *Anderson Cooper 360°,* December 21, 2005, ten p.m.; http://transcripts.cnn.com/TRANSCRIPTS/0512/21/acd.01.html. Other versions aired earlier and later.

307   *"terrorized"*: Dr. Pou interview with author July 23, 2008.

308   *James O'Bryant*: The details of Mr. O'Bryant's medical history and Dr. Pou's treatment of him described throughout this chapter were provided by his wife, Brenda, and daughter, Tabatha, in interviews in 2007 and 2013 and, with their kind permission, by Dr. Daniel Nuss in interviews in 2007. Also consulted for background on James's condition: Watkinson, John C. and Ralph W. Gilbert. *Stell and Maran's Textbook of Head and Neck Surgery and Oncology,* 5th ed., (London: Hodder Arnold, 2012).

310   *respected textbook*: Randall C. Baselt. *Disposition of Toxic Drugs and Chemicals in Man,* 6th ed., (Foster City, CA: Biomedical Publications, 2002). More recent editions exist, but the investigators relied on this one.

   They had not gathered: The investigators believed that another surgical ICU nurse had also gone up to the seventh floor when Pou was there. She did not agree to be interviewed for this book.

311   USA Today *quoted*: Johnson, Kevin, "Post-Katrina Inquiry Likely to Need New Expert," *USA Today,* January 23, 2006. All charges were ultimately dismissed in 2009. For a delightful description of the coroner, see also See Kalson, Sally, "The Wecht Indictment," *Pittsburgh Post-Gazette,* July 20, 2009; http://www.post-gazette.com/stories/life/sally-kalson/the-wecht-indictment-494225/: "His rulings, feuds and polysyllabic speechifying were always good news copy, and his bombastic letters in response to perceived slights were legendary [. . .] without him in the medical examiner's office the local scene seems kind of pale."

318   *Years later in an interview*: Dr. John Skinner interview with author, May 3, 2013.

322   *interviewees intimated:* For example, Terence Stahelin interview with investigators November 9, 2005: "I don't believe that decision was made by any of our doctors." Also Dr. Pou, in her interview with Julie Scelfo (*Newsweek,* September 2, 2007), said, when asked who

appointed her to inject patients: "It was a group decision. I didn't really volunteer for anything."

322 *whether Tenet corporate officials might have been aware*: Tenet Healthcare Corporation provided the following written response to the author on August 18, 2009: "This allegation is false. No evidence exists to support this claim. It is unfortunate that these unsubstantiated allegations continue to obscure the heroism and dedication of the doctors and staff in the aftermath of Hurricane Katrina and the breach of the levees."

paid nearly $400 million to settle claims: "Tenet Healthcare Agrees to $395 Million Settlement of Lawsuit Filed Over Alleged Unnecessary Heart Surgeries," *California Healthline*, December 22, 2004; http://www.californiahealthline.org/articles/2004/12/22/tenet-healthcare-agrees-to-395-million-settlement-of-lawsuit-filed-over-alleged-unnecessary-heart-surgeries.aspx.

324 *"Tenet is a major health-care provider"*: Shields, Gerard, "Shareholders ask Landrieu to Give up Tenet Contributions," *The Advocate*, March 18, 2006, A23.

325 *"I don't know what God's will is"*: Kahn, Carrie, "New Orleans Hospital Staff Discussed Mercy Killings," National Public Radio, *All Things Considered*, February 16, 2006.

326 *The main hospital, however:* LifeCare's leases at Memorial and at a Tenet-owned hospital in Kenner Louisiana, were not renewed. Some who worked for LifeCare considered this payback for having cooperated with Attorney General Foti's investigation.

327 *"verbal lynching"*: Baltz, *The Kat's Paw,* and interviews with author.

Tenet announced intentions: The Associated Press, "Tenet in $900 Million Settlement," *New York Times,* June 30, 2006; http://www.nytimes.com/2006/06/30/business/30tenet.html.

328 *The urge to learn:* For example: Fink, Sheri, "Lost in the Wave: A New Scientific Mystery: Why Haven't Sophisticated DNA Techniques Identified More of the Dead Killed in Last Year's Tsunami? And What Will It Mean for New Orleans?," *Discover Magazine* (November 2005); http://discovermagazine.com/2005/nov/lost-in-the-wave.

CHAPTER 9

Interviews

Dr. James Aiken; Roderick "Rico" Alvendia; Dr. Michael Baden; Dr. Horace Baltz; Brent Becnel; Don Berry; Elaine Bias; Lee Black; Joseph Bruno; Daniel Callahan; Arthur Caplan; Dr. David J. Casarett; James Cobb Jr.; Dr. Ewing Cook; Minnie Cook; Bette Crigger; Walburg de Jong; Renee C. Fox; Gen. Charles Foti; Faye Garvey; Dr. Juan Jorge Gershanik; Mark P. Glago; Dr. Shimon Glick; Cathy Green; Father Jere Hinson; Dr. Edmund G. Howe, III; Anthony Irpino; Gina Isbell; Dr. James James; Joe Jeffries; Dr. Faith Joubert; Dr. Steven Karch; Dr. Gerrit Kimsma; Kenneth Kipnis; Dr. Kiersta Kurtz-Burke; Karen Lagasse; Lorraine LeBlanc; Jessie Lynn LaSalle; Nina Levy; Kristin McMahon; Dr. Andrew J. McWhorter; Father John Marse; Robert Middleberg; Dr. Steven H. Miles; Nancy Miller; Dr. Frank Minyard; Michael Morales; Dr. Eugene Myers; Craig and Kathryn Nelson; Dr. Daniel Nuss; Brenda and Tabatha O'Bryant; Dr. Donald Palmisano; Amy Phillips; Dr. Anna Pou; Dr. James Riopelle; Garland Robinette; Karen Sanford; Arthur Schafer; Dianna A. Schenk; Rodney Scott; Todd R. Slack; Dr. Dudley M. Stewart Jr.; Dave Tarver; Dr. John Thiele; Dr. Richard Vinroot; Dr. John Walsh; Kris Wartelle; Dr. Cyril Wecht; Eric van Wijlick; Dr. Matthew K. Wynia; Stella Wright; Karen Wynn; Dr. James Young.

Notes

332 *James O'Bryant, her patient*: The details of Mr. O'Bryant's medical history and Pou's treatment of him described throughout this chapter were provided by his wife, Brenda, and daughter, Tabatha, in interviews in 2007 and 2013 and, with their permission, by Dr. Daniel Nuss in interviews in 2007.

333 *Foti was likely to release*: interview with Dr. Daniel Nuss (July 25, 2007).

asking for Pou's address: Berry, Jason, "Charles Foti and the Memorial Three," *Gambit Weekly*, October 31, 2006.

"Are you going to arrest my client?": Rick Simmons remark at press conference, July 18, 2006. Video available on CNN ImageSource; http://footage.net/VideoPreviewPop.aspx?SupplierID=cnn2&key=20240979&type=Global.

334 *Attorneys for Lori Budo and*: Berry, Jason, "Charles Foti and the Memorial Three," and Eddie Castaing comments to author (2013). Butch Schafer's recollections in interviews aligned with those of the attorneys for the three women.

stayed part-time at a home she did not own: Berry, Jason, "Charles Foti and the Memorial Three," and property records search.

Bogalusa, a paper mill town: Chapple, Charlie, "Paying for Their Pain: As Bogalusa Residents Receive Their Share of a $50 Million Settlement Stemming from a 1995 Chemical Leak, Emotions Range from Joy to Disappointment," *Times-Picayune*, May 29, 2005.

336 *Murdering with the specific intent to kill*: 2006 Louisiana Laws, title 14, criminal law, RS 14:30, first degree murder; http://law.justia.com/codes/louisiana/2006/146/78397.html.

murders committed in "sudden passion": ibid., RS 14:31, manslaughter; http://law.justia.com/codes/louisiana/2006/146/78399.html.

338 *That afternoon*: The details of Dr. Pou's arrest were documented by the arresting officers.

with affidavits and warrants of arrest: An unsigned version of the affidavits and arrest warrants may be viewed on the *Times-Picayune* website: http://www.nola.com/katrina/pdf/072006_nolacharges.pdf.

339 *"I can't tell you what's going on"*: Interview with Dr. Andrew McWhorter, the doctor whom Dr. Pou called (July 25, 2007).

She asked him to check: Interview with Dr. Anna Pou (July 2008).

341 *Small things made her grateful*: Dr. Anna Pou, ibid., and interview with Faye Garvey (July 2007).

She prayed for God to help: Julie Scelfo's *Newsweek* (2007) interview with Dr. Pou. Dr. Pou's shock at the charges and details of the advice and support provided by her family members are also from Scelfo's interview.

342 *Our Lady of Prompt Succor*: Interview with Father John Marse (July 27, 2009); website of the National Shrine of Our Lady of Prompt Succor: http://www.shrineofourladyofpromptsuccor.com/.

Virginia Rider wore: Recording of Attorney General Charles Foti press conference (July 18, 2006), CNN ImageSource ID# 4371920, screened from: http://www.footage.net/VideoPreviewPop.aspx?SupplierID=cnn2&key=20255362&type=Global.

344 *Later in the afternoon*: Rick Simmons press conference (July 18, 2006), CNN ImageSource ID# 4372124, screened from: http://footage.net/VideoPreviewPop.aspx?SupplierID=cnn 2&key=20240979&type=Global.

346 *The issue of larger responsibility and blame*: See, for example, an excellent and concise investigative exposé produced by the Center for Public Integrity: Bergal, Jenni, et al. *City Adrift: New Orleans Before and After Katrina* (Baton Rouge, LA: Louisiana State University Press, 2007). See also: US House of Representatives, *A Failure of Initiative*, www.katrina.house.gov; US Senate, *Katrina: A Nation Still Unprepared*; the White House, *The Federal Response to Hurricane Katrina: Lessons Learned*, February 2006; http://georgewbush-whitehouse.archives.gov/reports/katrina-lessons-learned.

347 *"Most of the worst crimes"*: Thevenot, Brian and Gordon Russell. "Rape. Murder. Gunfights," *Times-Picayune*, September 26, 2005; http://www.pulitzer.org/archives/7087.

348 *The Times-Picayune had written about it*: McQuaid, John and Mark Schleifstein, "Washing Away" series, *Times-Picayune*, June 23–27, 2002; http://www.nola.com/washingaway.

   The Hurricane Pam exercises had modeled it: Beriwal, Madhu, "Preparing for a Catastrophe: The Hurricane Pam Exercise," statement before the Senate Homeland Security and Governmental Affairs Committee, January 24, 2006; www.hsgac.senate.gov/download/012406beriwal.

   It was shocking to see the scenario play out at home: A detailed review of America's vulnerabilities can be found in Flynn, Stephen. *The Edge of Disaster: Rebuilding a Resilient Nation* (New York: Random House, 2007).

   Life and death in the critical first hours: For a fascinating read on disasters and human behavior, see: Ripley, Amanda. *The Unthinkable: Who Survives When Disaster Strikes—And Why* (New York: Crown Publishers, 2008).

   The online discussion threads: *Times-Picayune*, July 2006; searchable on http://www.nola.com.

349 *on the medical blog* KevinMD: "Dr. Anna Pou, Hurricane Katrina, and euthanasia," KevinMD.com, July 26, 2006; http://www.kevinmd.com/blog/2006/07/dr-anna-pou-hurricane-katrina-and.html.

350 *Two of Pou's siblings spoke with CNN*: Griffin, Drew and Kathleen Johnston, "Siblings Defend Doctor Accused in Hospital Deaths," CNN, July 20, 2006; http://www.cnn.com/2006/LAW/07/20/hospital.deaths.

   After the arrests, the lawyer for Dr. Ewing Cook: Interviews with Dr. Cook (2007–2009).

351 *When senior internist Dr. Horace Baltz*: Baltz, Horace. *The Kat's Paw: Memorial Medical Center—Katrina* (unpublished manuscript), and interviews with the author.

353 *he wrote in an appeal*: "Heroic in the Wake of Hurricane Katrina," blog, July 24, 2006; http://rauterkus.blogspot.com/2006/07/heroic-in-wake-of-katrinia-and-fallout.html.

   believed he should use his position: "Daniel Nuss, MD—Supervisor of Katrina Doctor Anna Pou, MD," October 28, 2007, dailyinterview.net. "I decided that as chairman of my university department, in contact with so many alumni and supportive physicians, I should use my position to build support for her." Nuss said in the same interview that he was "admonished by the leadership of the school that it was not appropriate for me to administer this defense fund because of my responsibilities to the University," and that Dr. Pou's brother Michael, a banker, took over the fund at that point.

353   *they had collected about $30,000*: Zigmond, Jessica, "Accused Doc Gets Defense Fund," *Modern Healthcare,* vol. 36, issue 30 (July 31, 2006): 4.

354   *had spent Katrina volunteering*: Hillyer, Quin, "Post-Katrina Heroes," *American Spectator,* August 30, 2006; http://spectator.org/archives/2006/08/30/post-katrina-heroes/.

   "Control!": Miller, Virginia, "Crisis Communications: Planning, Training and Response," PowerPoint presentation, Greater New Orleans Business Roundtable, February 24, 2011.

355   *the company was covering their legal expenses*: According to Harry Anderson, Tenet spokesperson, quoted in Zigmond, Jessica, "Accused Doc Gets Defense Fund."

   released a statement: Tenet Healthcare Corporation, "Tenet Response to Action by Louisiana Attorney General." (Dallas, TX, July 18, 2006); http://www.tenethealth.com/News/Documents/2006%20Press%20Releases/Tenet%20Response%20to%20Action%20by%20Louisiana%20Attorney%20General.pdf.

   it would be selling Memorial: "Ochsner to Buy 3 N.O. Hospitals," *The Advocate,* July 19, 2006; "Tenet Agrees to Sell Three New Orleans Hospitals to Ochsner Health System," *Business Wire,* July 18, 2006; "Tenet Selling Three Hospitals," *Dallas Morning News*, July 18, 2006; "Tenet in $900 Million Settlement," The Associated Press/*New York Times,* June 30, 2006. The purchase price was revealed later.

   help fund a nearly billion-dollar settlement: As Tenet made its agreement to settle Medicare fraud charges, LifeCare Holdings, Inc., was cleaning up a much smaller reimbursement issue with the government in an unrelated matter. In June, 2006 the company entered into a Compliance Agreement with HHS's Office of the Inspector General as part of a roughly $2.6 million settlement agreement related to the way its prior owners calculated annual costs, resulting in Medicare overpayments.

355–356   *ICU nurse Cathy Green [. . .] 'You did the wrong thing,' ever."*: Interview with Cathy Green (February 26, 2007). Mr. Castaing confirmed her recollection of their meeting.

356   *a three-day meeting*: Description of the meeting and its findings were based on: interviews with Dr. Wecht, Dr. Baden, Dr. Middleberg, Michael Morales, and Dr. Minyard; Dr. Wecht's handwritten notes of the meeting; forensic charts and tables distributed at the meeting; toxicology reports prepared by National Medical Services, Inc., for each of the forty-one bodies tested; autopsy reports and death certificates for each of the patients. Dr. Wecht also included an account of the meeting in his book, Wecht, Cyril H. and Dawna Kaufmann. *A Question of Murder* (New York: Prometheus Books, 2008), pp. 283–285.

360   *correspondence from one of its attorneys*: Copy of letter from Glen R. Petersen to Louisiana Department of Justice, dated March 17, 2006.

362   *fighting a federal judgment*: See, for example, Filosa, Gwen, "Jordan: N.O. Needs to Bail Out DA," *Times-Picayune,* October 23, 2007; http://blog.nola.com/updates/2007/10/jordan_no_needs_to_bail_out_da.html.

   Jordan was caught: Eddie Jordan did not respond to requests for an interview.

363   *"locked and loaded"*: "Military Due to Move in to New Orleans," CNN, September 2, 2005.

   was under investigation: See, for example, the excellent video encapsulation: "Behind the Danziger Bridge Shooting," PBS, *Frontline,* June 28, 2011, screened at: http://video.pbs.org/video/2029672776/, part of a multiyear investigative journalism collaboration between ProPublica, the *Times-Picayune,* and *Frontline* on police violence after Katrina. More of the project, led by journalists A. C. Thompson, Tom Jennings, Gordon Russell, Brendan McCarthy, and Laura Maggi, can be found at ProPublica's "Law and Disorder" page: http://www.propublica.org/nola/case/topic/case-one.

363 *Morales drafted a letter*: Letter quoted in Drew Griffin and Kathleen Johnston, "Report Probes New Orleans Hospital Deaths," CNN, December 5, 2007. Additional context provided in interviews with Michael Morales.

364 *five-part* Times-Picayune *"tick tock"*: Meitrodt, "For Dear Life."

365–366 *Baltz met again [. . .] small congregation*: Baltz, *The Kat's Paw,* and interviews with the author. Mr. Dosch (interview, June 4, 2013) said he was "probably just deep in thought" and that if Baltz was not invited, it was unintentional.

366 *lawyers filed petitions*: See, for example: Mitchell, Jeffrey A., "A Guide to Medical Malpractice: An Overview of Louisiana Law," *Avvo*; http://www.avvo.com/legal-guides/ugc/a-guide-to-medical-malpractice-an-overview-of-louisiana-law-1. Additional information provided in interviews with Lorraine LeBlanc, executive director, the Louisiana Patient's Compensation Fund, and Dianna A. Schenk (with the Louisiana Division of Administration) in 2007 and 2008. According to LeBlanc, as of June 12, 2007, 196 medical malpractice claims had been filed with the PCF against private hospitals and nursing homes alone (a separate system existed for publically owned health facilities).

soliciting potential clients: Tammie Holley e-mail to attorneys involved in *Preston, et al v. Tenet* (April 20, 2008). Another of her e-mails reads: "I am a GREAT rainmaker. The clients love me [. . .] I am a natural at both advertising AND marketing. Marketing harms plaintiff lawyer's reputations to a degree. I could care less," sent February 28, 2008, subject: "future cases %," exhibit nineteen in motion for summary judgment by Best Koeppel law firm, *Preston, et al v. Tenet,* February 2013. The e-mails came to light in the course of legal action involving the division of funds between attorneys in the class action settlement.

367 *The first suit related to Memorial*: Exhibits in *Preston, et al v. Tenet* 2:06-cv-03179-EEEF-KWR, available on PACER. For a summary of the movements of the case between state and federal court, see: "Local Controversy and Home State Exceptions in the Class Action Fairness Act Sent this Hurricane Katrina Case Back to State Court," *CAFA Law Blog,* January 24, 2007.

described in her suit: "Petition for Damages," *Karen Lagasse, individual, and on behalf of her deceased mother, Merle Lagasse v. Tenet Healthsystem Memorial Medical Center, Inc., René Goux, Roy J. Culotta, Richard Deichmann, and Jane Doe,* Civil District Court for the Parish of Orleans, case no. 06-8505, August 25, 2006.

369 *"He was awake, alert and oriented"*: "Petition for Wrongful Death and Damages," *Carrie R. Everett, Emmett E. Everett Jr., and Delfina V. Everett, individually and on behalf of the Estate of Emmett E. Everett Sr. v. Tenet Healthsystems Memorial Medical Center, Inc., d/b/a Memorial Medical Center, LifeCare Management Services, L.L.C.,* et al, Civil District Court for the Parish of Orleans, case no. 2006-7948, September 1, 2006.

370 *"I don't believe that a person with a sane mind"*: Mike Von Fremd, "Katrina Murder or Mercy? Doctor and Nurses Charged," ABCNews, *Good Morning America,* July 19, 2006; http://abcnews.go.com/GMA/LegalCenter/story?id=2210689.

"At least now": Callimachi, Rukmini, "Doctor, 2 Nurses Accused of Killing Patients with Drug Injections in Katrina's Aftermath," The Associated Press, July 19, 2006.

371 *"Euthanasia is something"*: Callimachi, Rukmini, "Doctor, 2 Nurses Accused of Killing Patients with Lethal Injections in Katrina's Aftermath," The Associated Press, July 19, 2006.

371   *a similar lawsuit at another hospital*: LaCoste v. Pendleton Methodist Hosp., L.L.C., La. 07-0008, 966 So. 2d 519 (La. 2007).

"a new theory": Kristin McMahon, Iron Health.

372   *The NBC television news magazine Dateline*: Hoda Kotb, "No Way Out; Doctors and Staff of Lindy Boggs Medical Center Taking Care of Patients Without Electricity, Water or Phone Service After Hurricane Katrina," *Dateline NBC,* August 25, 2006.

374–376   *an even more troubling story [. . .] that the patients be euthanized*: This section draws on lightly redacted state Medicaid Fraud Control Unit (MFCU) and federal Health and Human Services Office of Inspector General (HHS OIG) investigative memoranda, interview reports, legal correspondence, search summaries, autopsy and toxicology reports, medical records, hospital census, and an extensive "After Action Report" and individual written narratives from Shreveport Fire Department personnel related to Lindy Boggs Medical Center. These were obtained, through public records requests, from the Louisiana Department of Justice and the US Department of Health and Human Services. Supporting information came from interviews with Elaine Bias (May 10, 2008), Jessie Lynn LaSalle (May 8, 2008), and Dr. James Riopelle (May 5, 2013), photographs taken during the disaster, and court records related to lawsuits against Lindy Boggs Medical Center.

376–379   *at Touro Infirmary [. . .] same drug combination used at Memorial*: This section also draws on MFCU and HHS OIG lightly redacted investigative memoranda, interview reports, legal correspondence, medical records, autopsy reports, toxicology reports, and subpoenas. Additional information came from interviews with Nina Levy (November 4, 2008), Brent Becnel (September 28, 2011—"At some point you just have to save . . ."), and Dr. Richard Vinroot Jr. (May 2, 2008), as well as depositions of hospital leadership and staff, petitions, judgments, and other case material from civil lawsuits against Touro. Touro president and CEO Les Hirsch and the doctor who filed the anonymous complaint with the state declined requests for interviews. Other accounts of the Touro Infirmary experience during Katrina include one by the hospital archivist, Catherine C. Kahn, "Touro Infirmary: A Katrina Success Story," retrieved from: http://katrina.jwa.org/content/vault/SJHS%202006%20 Panel%20talk_ee79c0ef25.pdf. Kahn writes that when a fire department superintendent said they had one hour to leave "even if patients had to be left behind," the staff worked intensely and rescued everyone: "Dr. [Kevin] Jordan says it reminded him of the scene from 'Miss Siagon' [*sic*]. Not one patient was left behind." Apparently Kahn, who was not at the hospital during Katrina, was not aware of Mr. Arechaga.

377   *In her book*: Adler, Margot. *Drawing Down the Moon: Witches, Druids, Goddess-Worshippers, and Other Pagans in America* (New York: Penguin, 2006; Viking Press, 1979), 265–274. Additional information about Odun Arechaga came from Nina Levy, his longtime close friend. She arranged for him to be transferred to a nursing home near her in Illinois after Katrina. Arechaga died more than five years later, on January 13, 2011.

379   *Charity Hospital*: Information for this section is drawn from: call-ins to WWL during the emergency; Berggren, Ruth, "Unexpected Necessities—Inside Charity Hospital," *NEJM,* 353, 15 (October 13, 2005): 1550–1553; Van Meter, Keith, "Katrina at Charity Hospital: Much Ado About Something," *The American Journal of the Medical Sciences,* 322, 5 (November 2006): 251–254; Berger, Eric, "Charity Hospital and Disaster Preparedness," *Annals of Emergency Medicine,* 14, 1 (January 2006): 53–56; Dr. Ben deBoisblanc undated interview with "The Katrina Experience: An Oral History Project," retrieved from: http://thekatrinaexperience.net/?p=16#more-16; StoryCorps interview of Dr. Kiersta Kurtz-Burke

by Justin Lundgren (MBY001596, May 28, 2006); Duggal, Anshu, Janis G. Letourneau, and Leonard R. Bok, "LSU Health Sciences Center New Orleans Department of Radiology: Effects of Hurricane Katrina," *Academic Radiology,* 16, 5 (May 2009): 584–592; Barkemeyer, Brian M., "Practicing Neonatology in a Blackout: The University Hospital NICU in the Midst of Hurricane Katrina: Caring for Children Without Power or Water," *Pediatrics* 117 (2006): S369–374; and interviews with Dr. Kiersta Kurtz-Burke (November 6, 2009), Dr. James Aiken (2007), and informal discussions with others from Charity Hospital. The number of patients varies between sources and is an estimate.

379 *hospital had been evacuated when*: For example, *CNN Newsnight* carried an interview with Dr. Ruth Berggren on Wednesday, August 31, 2005, at the end of which anchor Aaron Brown referred to Berggren as having been at Charity "until it was evacuated"; http://transcripts.cnn.com/TRANSCRIPTS/0508/31/asb.01.html.

381 *In mid-September he wrote*: Mandamus Hearing, *Does v. Foti,* transcript (September 11, 2007), pp. 43–44.

382 60 Minutes: These recollections about the production of "Was It Murder?" CBS, *60 Minutes,* September 24, 2006, are from interviews with Pou, Simmons, and Wartelle. Kevin Tedesco, executive director of communications for *60 Minutes* (in e-mails in June and July 2013) wrote that CBS, according to company practice, did not provide Mr. Simmons with a copy of the interview, however that CBS standards allow subjects to audiotape their interviews. Tedesco also wrote that Ed Bradley "was never involved in this story as it was properly claimed first by Morley Safer's producer. The reporters at 60 minutes are famously competitive, however, and it's routine for them to fight for stories behind the scenes. Everybody at 60 minutes wanted to do this story."

American Medical Association: Interviews with Dr. Eugene Myers (July 10, 2007; November 29, 2007).

384 *Louisiana State Medical Society*: Interview with Amy Phillips, general counsel for the LSMS (December 2007), and interview with Dr. Donald Palmisano (2008).

385 *in 1990, he had suggested*: The arrested man who died was Adolph Archie. For background on this and other stories about Minyard's history, see Baum, Dan. *Nine Lives: Death and Life in New Orleans* (New York: Spiegel and Grau, 2009). A sweet profile of Minyard was written by Shaila Dewan, "For Trumpet-Playing Coroner, Hurricane Provides Swan Song," *New York Times,* October 17, 2005. A more critical interview was conducted by *Frontline* on June 17, 2010: http://www.pbs.org/wgbh/pages/frontline/post-mortem/interviews/frank-minyard.html. Minyard sat for roughly a dozen interviews with the author from 2007–2010.

387 *the expert consultants submitted their reports*: At the conclusion of the criminal case the following year, Attorney General Foti's office released a lightly redacted version of these reports at a press conference and to a small number of reporters, including the author. Memorial employees filed suit as "Jane and John Does" and successfully stopped further release, but the reports were subsequently posted on the CNN website: http://i.a.cnn.net/cnn/2007/images/08/27/memorial.medical.center.pdf. Dr. Anna Pou's response was also posted: http://i.a.cnn.net/cnn/2007/images/08/26/pou.statement.pdf. It accused the attorney general of releasing the documents "in an effort to justify his prior arrest of Dr. Pou before the upcoming election in October 2007."

documented spending: Records submitted to the attorney fee review board, Louisiana State Legislature by Richard Simmons and obtained by author through public records request.

388 *remain forever hidden*: 2006-KK-2408, writ application denied, in re: "A Matter Under Investigation" (Parish of Orleans).

389 *For months*: Copy of letter from Horace Baltz to Frank Minyard, November 17, 2006.

 True valor: Copy of letter from Horace Baltz to Richard Deichmann, October 28, 2006.

 two widely publicized killings: See, for example, Erin Moriarty, "Storm of Murder," CBS, *48 Hours*, October 13, 2007 (updated August 14, 2008); http://www.cbsnews.com/8301-18559_162-3348928.html.

390 *extreme dysfunction*: See, for example, Brown, Ethan, "New Orleans Murder Rate for Year Will Set Record: Prosecutions Are so Lax in Post-Flood City That Criminals Speak of 'Misdemeanour Murder,' Ethan Brown Reports," *The Guardian,* November 6, 2007; http://www.guardian.co.uk/world/2007/nov/06/usa; Webster, Richard A., "Getting Tough," *City Business,* July 2, 2007, which contrasts the problems with the success of the new violent offenders unit; McCarthy, Brendan, "Draft Is Rare Portal into NOPD," *Times-Picayune,* November 17, 2007; http://blog.nola.com/times-picayune/2007/11/draft_is_rare_portal_into_nopd.html; Court Watch NOLA quarterly reports from 2007 (www.courtwatchnola.org).

391–392 *On a foggy day [. . .] take other people's lives*: Brenda and Tabatha O'Bryant, interviews with the author (2007 and 2013).

393 *he could not influence the script*: Interview with Richard Simmons (May 2, 2007) and letter to the author, "Re: Fact Check Reply," August 14, 2009.

 "It's abhorrent": Jeter, Lynne, "Anna Pou Case Takes Unexpected Turns: Louisiana Medical Community Rallies to Support New Orleans Physician Accused of Killing Four Patients Post-Katrina," *Louisiana Medical News* (March 2007).

394 *The doctor on the show*: Turk, Craig, Janet Leahy, and David E. Kelley, "Angel of Death," *Boston Legal,* season 3, episode 11, January 9, 2007; transcript retrieved from boston-legal .org/script/bl03x11.pdf, version updated February 4, 2007.

 "Their acts were those of heroism": "American College of Surgeons Calls for Fair Investigation in New Orleans Case," *USNewswire,* January 11, 2007. Interview with Dr. Eugene Myers (November 29, 2007), who said, "They copied my letter."

395 *"very, very extenuating circumstances"*: "Accusations of Mercy Killing in New Orleans," CNN, *Newsnight with Aaron Brown,* October 12, 2005; http://transcripts.cnn.com/TRANSCRIPTS/0510/12/asb.02.html.

 "not consistent with the ethical standards": Caplan, Arthur L., PhD. "Report for New Orleans, Coroner's Office, Dr. Frank Minyard, State of Louisiana," January 26, 2007.

396 *and passive euthanasia*: The "passive" category is sometimes split further into direct (having the intention of causing death) and indirect forms.

 " for he was sore afraid,": The Bible, 1 Chronicles 10:4, King James Version.

 "Stand over me and kill me!": The Bible, 2 Samuel 1:9, New International Version.

 "I knew that after he had fallen": The Bible, 2 Samuel 1:10, New International Version.

 "I will not give a lethal drug": See, for example, History of Medicine Division, National Library of Medicine, "Greek Medicine"; http://www.nlm.nih.gov/hmd/greek/greek_oath .html; and, for a discussion of modern controversy surrounding the Oath, Peter Tyson's "The Hippocratic Oath Today," PBS, *NOVA,* March 27, 2001; http://www.pbs.org/wgbh/nova/body/hippocratic-oath-today.html.

396   *"For the first time in our tradition"*: Levine, Maurice. *Psychiatry & Ethics* (New York: George Braziller, 1972), p. 325.

397   *"My duty is to preserve life"*: Cited by Herold, J. Christopher. *Bonaparte in Egypt* (Tuscon, AZ: Fireship Press, 2009; previous ed.: New York: Harper & Row, 1962), p. 332. See also: Harris, James C., "Art and Images in Psychiatry: Napoleon Bonaparte Visiting the Plague-Stricken at Jaffa," *Archives of General Psychiatry,* vol. 63, issue 5 (May 2006).

The Turks found several alive: Herold. *Bonaparte in Egypt,* pp. 331, 338.

case of physician involvement: The Robert Semrau case from Canada concerns a (*non*-medical) soldier charged with homicide on the battlefield for an alleged mercy killing of a Taliban fighter. See, for example, Michael Friscolanti, Michael, "A Soldier's Choice," *Maclean's,* 123, 19 (May 24, 2010): 20–25; and Carlson, Kathryn Blaze, "'An Act of So-Called Mercy': Semrau Case Hinges on 'Soldier's Pact,'" *National Post,* July 7, 2010.

398   *"a soft quiet death"*: Harris, John. *Lexicon Technicum: Or, An Universal English Dictionary of Arts and Sciences,* vol. 1, 4th ed. (London, 1725). The earliest reference mentioned in the Oxford English Dictionary, in the first listed sense of "a gentle and easy death," is Hall, Bishop Joseph. *Balme of Gilead: Or, Comforts for the Distressed* (London, 1646): "But let me prescribe, and commend to thee, my sonne, this true spirituall meanes of thine happy Euthanasia."

"To surrender to superior forces": See "Permissive Euthanasia" in *Boston Medical and Surgical Journal,* CX, 1 (January 3, 1884): 19–20 (available on Google Books). This fascinating editorial shows that long before the age of high-tech medicine, late nineteenth-century doctors grappled with some of the same dilemmas twenty-first-century doctors do, including whether to keep fighting to save someone who is dying. The writer wonders if euthanasia will one day become "a recognized branch of medical science" (playfully predicting this may happen by the fortieth century). An example is given of a patient with metastatic cancer: "For weeks the physician has combatted death [. . .] all for what? To exhaust the strength and perhaps imperil the lives of the remainder of the household; to keep in their home a body which is repulsive to every sense and a mind which is no longer that of their friend, but which is overclouded if not maniacal; or, if the sufferer retains consciousness, to meet her bitter reproaches for prolonging her misery. Shall not a man under such circumstances give up the fight, take off the spur of the stimulant, and let exhausted nature sink to rest?" The writer of the editorial sees symbolism in Edgar Allan Poe's "The Facts in the Case of M. Valdemar" (1850), a creepy tale about a dead man kept alive through entrancement as he rots away. See also Emanuel, Ezekiel J., "The History of Euthanasia Debates in the United States and Britain," *Annals of Internal Medicine,* 121 (1994): 793–802.

398–399   *These ideas [. . .] extermination camps in Poland*: See, for example, Burleigh, Michael. *Death and Deliverance: 'Euthanasia' in Germany c. 1900–1945* (London: Pan Books, 2002; 1st ed., Cambridge University Press, 1994); Gesundheit, Benjamin, Avraham Steinberg, Shimon Glick, et al, "Euthanasia: An Overview and the Jewish Perspective," *Cancer Investigation,* 24 (2006): 621–629. Interview with Dr. Shimon Glick (May 16, 2010).

399   *Psychiatrists have profiled*: Kaplan, Robert M., "The Clinicide Phenomenon: An Exploration of Medical Murder," *Australian Psychiatry,* 15, 4 (2007): 299–304.

a Dutch court: See, for example: Sheldon, Tony, "Andries Postma," *BMJ* 334, 7588 (February 10, 2007): 320; http://www.ncbi.nlm.nih.gov/pmc/articles/PMC1796690/.

one pharmacy chain: Multipharma chain. Personal communication, Dr. Eric Dachy, May 5, 2013.

400   *not always followed*: The study is referred to in Pereira, J., "Legalizing Euthanasia or Assisted Suicide: The Illusion of Safeguards and Controls," *Current Oncology,* 18, 2 (April 2011): e38–e45.

      Groningen Protocol: Verhagen, Eduard and Pieter J. J. Sauer, "The Groningen Protocol—Euthanasia in Severely Ill Newborns," *NEJM* 352 (2005): 959–962.

401   *"life has been completed"*: Peters, Marleen, "Completed Life: What Are We Talking About? Questions and Answers," trans. Maarten Pennink, Amsterdam, NVVE/Right to Die Netherlands, February 2010.

      The debate in the United States: See, for example, Cahill, Lisa Sowle, "Richard A. McCormick, S.J.'s 'To Save or Let Die: The Dilemma of Modern Medicine'" in Walter, Jennifer K. and Eran P. Klein, eds., *The Story of Bioethics* (Washington, DC: Georgetown University Press, 2003).

      Karen Ann Quinlan: See, for example, Lepore, Jill, "The Politics of Death: From Abortion to Health Care—How the Hysterical Style Overtook the National Debate," *The New Yorker* (November 30, 2009).

402   *Clarence Herbert case*: See, for example, Lo, Bernard, "The Death of Clarence Herbert: Withdrawing Care Is Not Murder," *Annals of Internal Medicine*, no. 101 (1984): 248–251.

404   *Ohio legislature*: "An Act Entitled an Act Concerning Administration of Drugs, Etc., to Mortally Wounded and Diseased Persons," *The St. Louis Medical Review*, 54 (January 27, 1906). Retrieved from Google Books.

405   *Studies in*: Summarized in Gostin, Lawrence, "Drawing a Line Between Killing and Letting Die," *The Journal of Law, Medicine & Ethics,* 21 (Spring 1993).

406   *"N.O. Coroner"*: Meitrodt, Jeffrey, "N.O. Coroner Finds No Evidence of Homicide," *Times-Picayune,* February 1, 2007, A1.

409   *When a* New York Times *reporter*: Nossiter, Adam and Shaila Dewan, "New Orleans Coroner Sees No Evidence Yet for Indictments," *New York Times,* February 2, 2007.

      Karch had staked: See, for example, Karch, Steven B., "Is Post-Mortem Toxicology Quackery?" *Journal of Clinical Forensic Medicine* 10 (2003): 197–198; and Drummer, Olaf, A. Robert W. Forrest, Bruce Goldberger, and Steven B. Karch, "Forensic Science in the Dock: Postmortem Measurements of Drug Concentration in Blood Have Little Meaning," *BMJ* 329 (September 18, 2004): 636–7.

      well-known textbook: Karch, Steven B. and Olaf Drummer. *Karch's Pathology of Drug Abuse* (Boca Raton, FL: CRC Press; 5th ed. available August 2013).

410   *"These people were given"*: Dr. Michael Baden interview (January 22, 2008).

      He put Karch's theory: Wecht and Kaufmann, *A Question of Murder,* 278–9; Dr. Cyril Wecht interviews with author (2008).

411   *reported on the selection*: Filosa, Gwen, "Memorial Evidence to Be Reviewed; Murder of 4 Patients After Katrina Alleged," *Times-Picayune,* February 16, 2007.

      "Dr. Pou's heroism": "AAO-HNS Statement on the Continuing Prosecution of Dr. Anna Pou," American Academy of Otolaryngology Head and Neck Surgery, February 24, 2007; http://www.newswise.com/articles/view/527596.

      "Very alone" and *"What's Father"*: Interview with Dr. Anna Pou (July 23, 2008). See also the website of the National Seelos Shrine & The Seelos Center, New Orleans: www.seelos.org.

412 *76 percent*: Interview with Richard Simmons (May 2, 2007) and letter from Richard Simmons to author, August 14, 2009.

413 *told a reporter*: Berry, Jason, "Charles Foti and the Memorial Three," *Gambit Weekly*, October 31, 2006.

414 *"frivolous lawsuits"*: Richard Simmons, comment during author's interview with Dr. Anna Pou (July 23, 2008)

"as Third World": Dr. Anna Pou comments at Houston disaster-preparedness seminar, May 19, 2007.

415 *On May 19*: "Friends of Anna" conference and dinner/fund-raiser held in Houston, Texas, attended by author as described in Notes to Chapter 3.

416 *flying at night*: Interviews were conducted with ten USCG and USCG Auxiliary members involved in coordinating or conducting nighttime operations at Memorial. The USCG, in response to a FOIA request, also produced a spreadsheet of flight record "bluesheets," which show that many post-Katrina flight operations took place after dark. There is ample publicly available documentation of nighttime search and rescue operations undertaken at considerable risk after Katrina. See, for example, "The U.S. Coast Guard and Hurricane Katrina: Historical Index"; http://www.uscg.mil/history/katrina/katrinaindex.asp.

417 *Pou's former chairman*: Dr. Byron Bailey.

419 *World Medical Association*: "World Medical Association Statement on Medical Ethics in the Event of Disasters," adopted September 1994 and revised October 2006; http://www.wma.net/en/30publications/10policies/d7/.

421 *collaborated with the attorney*: Cobb, James Jr. *Flood of Lies: The St. Rita's Nursing Home Tragedy* (galley version), and interview with James Cobb Jr. (May 4, 2013).

"nefarious conspiracy": The allegation was made in court documents, as described in Rioux, Paul, "Judge Refuses to Remove Foti From St. Rita's Prosecution," *Times-Picayune*, August 1, 2007; http://blog.nola.com/times-picayune/2007/08/judge_refuses_to_remove_foti_f.html.

422 *hold the Army Corps of Engineers*: Cobb, *Flood of Lies* (galley version) and interview with James Cobb Jr. (July 2013). Cobb no longer had Foti's filing available, and the author could not independently verify its content before publication.

plot media strategy: Interview with Richard Simmons (May 2, 2007).

423 *an ongoing case*: See note for page 363 re: the Danziger Bridge shootings.

chanting "Heroes!": Maggi, Laura and Brendan McCarthy, "Cheers, Jeers Greet Jail-Bound Officers in Danziger Bridge Shooting," *Times-Picayune*, January 3, 2007; http://www.nola.com/crime/index.ssf/2007/01/cheers_jeers_greet_jail-bound.html.

On June 13, 2007: Supreme Court of Louisiana No. 2007-OK-1197 in Re: Special Investigation; http://www.lasc.org/opinions/2007/07OK1197.pfc.dip.pdf; "Application for Supervisory Writs Filed on Behalf of Applicants Witness #1, Witness #2, and Witness #3" (undated); "Motion and Order to Compel Testimony" and "Order," State of Louisiana in Re Special Investigation, Criminal District Court, Parish of Orleans, Special Grand Jury, May 17, 2007; Maggi, Laura, "Immunity Offered to Memorial Nurses to Testify," *Times-Picayune*, June 19, 2007; http://blog.nola.com/times-picayune/2007/06/immunity_offered_to_memorial_n.html.

424   *"It just goes under a different name"*: Interview with Karen Wynn (December 7, 2008).

426   *published the first issue*: *Disaster Medicine and Public Health Preparedness*.

a *minority of American physicians*: The AMA did not respond to a request for current membership statistics. Authors have suggested that in recent years, only around 15 percent of practicing US physicians were members. See, for example, Roger Collier, "American Medical Association Membership Woes Continue," *CMAJ*, 183, 11, E713–E714, August 9, 2011; http://www.ncbi.nlm.nih.gov/pmc/articles/PMC3153537/.

Rick Simmons appeared: Transcript of remarks, provided by Richard Simmons. See also, Sorrel, Amy Lynn, "AMA Meeting: Doctors Who Give Disaster Aid Seek Liability Shield," *American Medical News* (July 16, 2007).

427   *delegates voted to create*: D-435.976 "Protection From Liability Arising from Care Rendered to Patients During Officially Declared Disasters"; http://www.ama-assn.org/resources/doc/PolicyFinder/policyfiles/DIR/D-435.976.HTM.

429–432   *Minyard liked [. . .] later describe it*: This section is based on roughly a dozen interviews conducted with Dr. Minyard (2007–2010) and interviews with the forensic colleagues to whom he turned for advice on his findings. Minyard at one point told the author that he decided that four of the nine deaths the grand jury was considering were homicides, and his statement was included in "Deadly Choices" in 2009. However, copies of drafts of a letter to district attorney Jordan, dated June and July of 2007 and prepared on behalf of attorney general Foti, state that "Dr. Minyard still maintains that homicide is the manner of death only in connection with the deaths of two patients, Emmett Everett and Rose Savoie. To date, his determination of the manner of death of the other seven patients who died on the 7th floor on 9/1/05 remain 'undetermined.'" It is unclear if Minyard had already testified before the grand jury at the point the letter was written, or if he did so later and changed two of the "undetermined" cases to "homicide." In interviews, Dr. Minyard resisted describing exactly what he told the grand jury, claiming that it was secret. However, Minyard had a duty as coroner to classify the deaths as part of autopsy reports, which are considered public records under Louisiana law. When other members of the media sought the autopsy reports of the Katrina dead, Minyard, essentially setting his own law, at first refused to release them. The *Times-Picayune* and, separately, reporter A. C. Thompson, successfully sued to obtain them. However, the copies Minyard provided left empty spaces next to "classification of death" (see, for example, Maggi, Laura, "Autopsy Reports Aren't Complete: Deaths at Memorial Weren't Classified," *Times-Picayune*, October 23, 2007). Likewise, family members of the Memorial and LifeCare deceased are entitled to death certificates. Those who have requested them in recent years have found them similarly incomplete, in some cases still marked "pending investigation." Rose Savoie's grandson, Doug, repeatedly requested a copy of her death certificate on behalf of his family. He was told in 2010—five years after Katrina—that the coroner hadn't finished it. Savoie sent letters to the coroner asking that this be done, but it was not. He requested help from the International Association of Coroners and Medical Examiners. But the latest copy of the certificate sent to the Savoie family, in 2010, notes nothing at all in terms of the cause of his grandmother's death and is stamped "under investigation." As of August 2013, the Savoie family still had not received a completed death certificate.

434   *forensic all-stars*: Wecht and Kaufmann, *A Question of Murder,* p. 286.

441   *to support her*: Dr. John Thiele died at his home on December 31, 2010. For years during the course of his treatment for metastatic cancer, he continued to practice medicine, making patient rounds even while wearing his chemotherapy pack.

444 *social columnist*: Nolan, Nell, "Common Concerns Celebrated," *Times-Picayune,* July 24, 2007.

446 *published an op-ed*: Foti, Charles, "Katrina Was No Excuse: No Circumstances Can Justify the Taking of Innocent Human Lives," *USA Today,* July 27, 2007, 10A; http://usatoday30 .usatoday.com/printedition/news/20070727/oppose27.art.htm.

448 *popular national lecturer*: See for example, Conde, Crystal, "Ethics in Crisis Care: Dr. Anna Pou Addresses Texas Medical Association's 2012 General Session," *Louisiana Medical News* (July 31, 2012; first published in *Texas Medicine*); http://www.louisianamedicalnews.com/ ethics-in-crisis-care-dr-anna-pou-addresses-texas-medical-association-s-2012-general-session-cms-2120. "I felt like I was on the *Titanic*," she told the Texas Medical Association in 2012, where she received a standing ovation. She has referred to what happened at Memorial and her subsequent arrest as a "personal tragedy." In arrangements with meeting organizers, Pou has often prevented journalists from attending her lectures about Katrina.

FEMA called us: Anna Pou, "Legal and Ethical Considerations in Crisis Care," lecture at the California Hospital Association's Disaster Planning for California Hospitals Conference, September 23, 2010, Sacramento, California.

449 *The obvious effect*: Richard Simmons, letter to author, August 9, 2009.

450 *state of Louisiana paid*: Morris, Tim, "Senate Approves Payment for Dr. Anna Pou's Legal Bills," *Times Picayune,* June 16, 2009; http://www.nola.com/politics/index.ssf/2009/06/ senate_approves_payment_for_dr.html.

The Memorial class action suit was settled: Interviews over the course of the litigation with several of the attorneys representing the class, including: Joseph Bruno, Mark P. Glago, Anthony Irpino, Todd R. Slack, and Roderick "Rico" Alvendia. Information was also provided by Rick Black (then-) director of communications for Tenet Healthcare. See also Fink, Sheri, "Trial to Open in Lawsuit Connected to Hospital Deaths After Katrina," ProPublica and the *New York Times,* March 20, 2011; http://www.propublica.org/article/trial-to-open-in-lawsuit-connected-to-hospital-deaths-after-katrina/; Fink, Sheri, "Lawsuit Against New Orleans Hospital Settles Shortly After Trial Begins," ProPublica, March 23, 2011; http://www .propublica.org/article/lawsuit-against-new-orleans-hospital-settles-shortly-after-trial-begins; Fink, Sheri, "Class-Action Suit Filed After Katrina Hospital Deaths Settled for $25 Million," ProPublica, July 21, 2011; http://www.propublica.org/article/class-action-suit-filed-after-katrina-hospital-deaths-settled-for-25-millio.

451 *According to the guidelines*: "Special Master's Report and Recommendation on Allocation Model," *Preston, et al v. Tenet,* September 19, 2012. Some family members of deceased patients were dissatisfied with their settlements both in the class action and in individual suits (for families that opted out of the class action) against Memorial, particularly after the lengthy legal battles they endured. In the *Preston, et al v. Tenet* case, families of patients who died received $167,229.73, to be divided among all survivors (some who died had a large number of children). Karen Lagasse's suit on behalf of her mother, Merle, settled for $270,000 (prior to the reduction of 33⅓% attorney fees), according to a copy of the settlement check filed by a Tenet attorney in the court record. The settlement, achieved through mediation, left Lagasse angry, because she felt justice was not done and the amount was not enough to force the hospital or the involved physicians to change their practices in the future. "The whole fact doctors would decide who's worthy to live, who's not, who's going to be evacuated and who's not going to be evacuated, who's going to be left and who's going to take them out—what kind of morality is that?" she asked in January 2013. "I feel

like I'm the little voice saying, 'Don't you realize it could be your wife? Don't you realize it could be your child?' They got away with it; it's not going to stop."

EPILOGUE

Interviews

Dr. Joseph Andrews; Roger Bernier; Dr. Guthrie Birkhead; Dr. Frederick "Skip" Burkle Jr.; Dr. Elizabeth Lee Daugherty; Dr. Karen DeSalvo; Dr. Laura Evans; Dr. Thomas A. Farley; Robert Gallagher; Howard Gwon; Monica Gwon; Dr. Aarti Kinikar; RADM Ann R. Knebel; Ann Nugent; Dr. Tia Powell; Dr. Nirav R. Shah; Eugene Tangney; Warner Thomas; Dr. Eric Toner; Jacqueline Toner.

Notes

463   *One lesson from Katrina:* Interview with Warner Thomas, president and chief operating officer of Ochsner Health System (August 28, 2012). See also: Fink, Sheri, "Hospitals, Nursing Homes Are Better Prepared for Hurricane Isaac Than Earlier Storms," *Times-Picayune,* August 28, 2012. http://www.nola.com/hurricane/index.ssf/2012/08/hospitals_nursing_homes_better.html. By the 2013 hurricane season, post-Katrina improvements to Ochsner Baptist Medical Center included "new and restored electrical generators and power transfer switches, central plant infrastructure raised on a platform, a new water well to maintain cooling systems in the event of a city water loss and a restored heliport with an additional elevator stop directly from the heliport to the new NICU," according to an e-mail from Ochsner Health System public relations manager Stafford Scott Maestri (August 2013).

Two months later: Fink, Sheri, "In Hurricane's Wake, Decisions Not to Evacuate Hospitals Raise Questions," ProPublica, November 1, 2012; http://www.propublica.org/article/in-hurricanes-wake-decisions-not-to-evacuate-hospitals-raise-questions/.

465   *Dr. Laura Evans:* Interview with Dr. Laura Evans (March 2013). See also: Fink, Sheri, "Beyond Hurricane Heroics: What Sandy Has to Teach Us All About Preparedness," *Stanford Medicine Magazine* (Summer 2013); http://stanmed.stanford.edu/2013summer/article5.html; and Uppal, Amit, Laura Evans, Nishay Chitkara, et al, "In Search of the Silver Lining: The Impact of Superstorm Sandy on Bellevue Hospital," *Annals of the American Thoacic Society,* vol. 10, no. 2 (2013), pp. 135–142; http://www.atsjournals.org/doi/abs/10.1513/AnnalsATS.201212-116OT.

protocol for rationing ventilators: Fink, Sheri, "Flu Nightmare: In Severe Pandemic, Officials Ponder Disconnecting Ventilators from Some Patients," ProPublica. September 23, 2009; http://www.propublica.org/article/flu-nightmare-officials-ponder-disconnecting-ventilators-from-some-pat-923. The plan is available here: http://www.health.ny.gov/diseases/communicable/influenza/pandemic/ventilators.

468   *according to reports*: Altevogt, Bruce M., Clare Stroud, Sarah L. Hanson, Dan Hanfling, and Lawrence O. Gostin, eds. *Guidance for Establishing Crisis Standards of Care for Use in Disaster Situations: A Letter Report* (Washington, DC: The National Academies Press, 2009); http://www.nap.edu/openbook.php?record_id=12749; Institute of Medicine, *Crisis Standards of Care: A Systems Framework for Catastrophic Disaster Response, vols. 1–7* (Washington, DC: The National Academies Press, 2012); http://www.nap.edu/openbook.php?record_id=13351.

as a bioethicist: In an e-mail (November 12, 2009), Dr. Lachlan Forrow, director of ethics and palliative care programs, Beth Israel Deaconess Medical Center, wrote: "Rather than thinking about exceptional moral rules for exceptional moral situations we should almost always see exceptional moral situations as opportunities for us to show exceptionally-deep commitment to our deepest moral values. This includes holding ourselves morally accountable, compassionately but still firmly, if we become—however tragically and unavoidably—involved in violating core values." Father John F. Tuohey, regional director of the Providence Center for Health Ethics in Portland, Oregon, commented during a 2009 panel discussion with Dr. Pou in Chicago: "As bad as disasters are, even worse is survivors who don't trust each other."

469 *In some states*: Fink, Sheri, "Preparing for a Pandemic, State Health Departments Struggle with Rationing Decisions," ProPublica and the *New York Times*, October 24, 2009. http://www .propublica.org/article/preparing-for-a-pandemic-state-health-departments-struggle-rationing-1024/.

469 *mounting evidence suggests*: Fink, Sheri, "Worst Case: Rethinking Tertiary Triage Protocols in Pandemics and Other Health Emergencies." *Critical Care*, 14:103 (2009); http://ccforum .com/content/14/1/103.

470 *"A new model of triage"*: Guest, T., G. Tantam, N. Donlin, K. Tantam, H. McMillan, A. Tillyard, "An observational cohort study of triage for critical care provision during pandemic influenza: 'clipboard physicians' or 'evidence based medicine'?" *Anaesthesia*, vol. 64, no. 11 (2009): 1199–1206; http://onlinelibrary.wiley.com/doi/10.1111/j.1365-2044.2009.06084.x/pdf.

New models have been proposed: For example, White, Douglas, Mitchell Katz, John Luce and Bernard Lo, "Who Should Receive Life Support During a Public Health Emergency? Using Ethical Principles to Improve Allocation Decisions," *Annals of Internal Medicine*, vol. 150 (2009): 132–138; http://chpe.creighton.edu/events/images/life_support.pdf.

small but particularly troubling study: Khan, Z., J. Hulme, N. Sherwood, "An assessment of the validity of SOFA score based triage in H1N1 critically ill patients during an influenza pandemic," *Anaesthesia*, vol. 64, no. 12 (2009): 1283–1288; http://onlinelibrary.wiley.com/ doi/10.1111/j.1365-2044.2009.06135.x/pdf.

471 *report on what the teams had learned*: Fink, Sheri, "Doctors Face Ethical Decisions in Haiti," *PRI's The World*, 2010; http://media.theworld.org/audio/022320107.mp3.

476 *Connecticut Hospice*: Interview with Dr. Joseph Andrews and Ann Nugent (February 2013).

477 *"an important component"*: New York State Workgroup on Ventilator Allocation in an Influenza Pandemic/NYS DOH/ NYS Task Force on Life and the Law, "Allocation of Ventilators in an Influenza Pandemic: Planning Document" (March 15, 2007, draft for public comment); http://www.health.ny.gov/diseases/communicable/influenza/pandemic /ventilators.

An answer to Birkhead's question: The project described is: "Too Many Patients, Too Few Resources," sponsored by the Hospital Preparedness Program 2012, US Department of Health and Human Services. Principal investigator: Dr. Elizabeth Lee Daugherty, also led by Howie Gwon, Dr. Eric Toner, Alan Regenberg, and Chrissie Juliano. Cosponsored by the Johns Hopkins Berman Institute for Bioethics; Johns Hopkins University School of Medicine Department of Pulmonary and Critical Care Medicine; Johns Hopkins Office of Emergency Management; Program for Deliberative Democracy, Carnegie Mellon University; RESOLVE, INC.; The Center for Ethics and Policy, Carnegie Mellon University; University of Pittsburgh Medical School Department of Critical Care Medicine; UPMC Center for Health Security.

479 *"If this were to happen"*: Alex Brecht, at "Too Many Patients" forum, Baltimore, Maryland, May 5, 2012.

"It's really hard for me to say": Cierra Brown, ibid.

480 *"There's so many social ramifications"*: Tiffany Jackson, ibid.

"We talked about politics": Maayan Voss de Bettancourt, eulogy at funeral for Irvin Zelitzky, September 6, 2011.

481 *public engagement exercise was held*: Fink, Sheri, "Rationing Medical Care: Health Officials Struggle with Setting Standards," ProPublica and MinnPost.com, December 21, 2009; http://www.propublica.org/article/rationing-medical-care-health-officials-struggle-with-setting-standards-122.

481 *the project report said*: "Public Engagement Project on Medical Service Prioritization During an Influenza Pandemic," Public Health—Seattle and King County, September 29, 2009; http://s3.amazonaws.com/propublica/assets/docs/seattle_public_engagement_project_final_sept2009.pdf.

In 2009, the CDC: Roger Bernier, interview, 2009.

482 *extensive report*: Institute of Medicine, *Crisis Standards of Care,* 2012, volume 6, pp. 347–463.

"more than an accurate estimate": Altevogt, et al, *Guidance for Establishing Crisis Standards,* 2009.

483 *described in an academic paper*: Burkle, F. M. Jr., "Mass Casualty Management of a Large-Scale Bioterrorist Event: An Epidemiological Approach That Shapes Triage Decisions," *Emergency Medicine Clinics of North America,* vol. 20 (2002): 409–36.

484 *A pediatrician, Dr. Aarti Kinikar*: Fink, Sheri. "India: Rationing Health in Disasters," *PRI's The World*, December 17, 2010; www.rationinghealth.org.

INDEX